GENERAL VIEW OF THE AGRICULTURE OF THE COUNTY OF DEVON

GENERAL VIEW of the AGRICULTURE of the COUNTY OF DEVON

With Observations on the Means of Its Improvement

A Reprint of the Work Drawn up for the
Consideration of the Board of Agriculture
and Internal Improvement

by

CHARLES VANCOUVER

DAVID & CHARLES REPRINTS

This book was first published in 1808

This edition published by David & Charles (Publishers)
Limited 1969

Printed in Great Britain by
Clarke Doble & Brendon Limited Plymouth
for David & Charles (Publishers) Limited
South Devon House Railway Station
Newton Abbot Devon

GENERAL VIEW

OF THE

AGRICULTURE

OF THE

COUNTY OF DEVON;

WITH

.OBSERVATIONS ON THE MEANS OF ITS IMPROVEMENT.

DRAWN UP FOR THE CONSIDERATION OF

THE BOARD OF AGRICULTURE,

AND INTERNAL IMPROVEMENT.

BY CHARLES VANCOUVER.

FRUCTU, NON FOLIIS, ARBOREM ÆSTIMA.

LONDON:

PRINTED FOR RICHARD PHILLIPS, BRIDGE STREET;
SOLD BY FAULDER & SON, BOND STREET; J. HARDING, ST.
JAMES'S STREET; J. ASPERNE, CORNHILL; BLACK, PARRY,
& KINGSBURY, LEADENHALL STREET; E. UPHAM, G. DYER,
P. HEDGELAND, & S. WOOLMER, EXETER; COBLEY & CO.
& REES & CO. PLYMOUTH; & A. CONSTABLE & CO. EDIN-
BURGH;

BY B. M^cMILLAN, BOW STREET, COVENT GARDEN.

1808.

[*Price Fifteen Shillings in Boards.*]

ADVERTISEMENT.

———

THE desire that has been generally expressed, to have the AGRICULTURAL SURVEYS of the KINGDOM reprinted, with the additional Communications which have been received since the ORIGINAL REPORTS were circulated, has induced the BOARD OF AGRICULTURE to come to a resolution to reprint such as appear on the whole fit for publication.

It is proper at the same time to add, that the Board does not consider itself responsible for every statement contained in the Reports thus reprinted, and that it will thankfully acknowledge any additional information which may still be communicated.

———

N. B. *Letters to the Board, may be addressed to Sir* JOHN SINCLAIR, *Bart. the President, No.* 32, *Sackville-Street, Piccadilly, London.*

INTRO-

INTRODUCTION.

AS there could have been but one motive in the Government of this country for establishing a Board of Agriculture; and as that could have been no other than the general improvement of the national territory, as well by the encouragement of manufactures and commerce, as in furthering the agricultural exertions of land-owners and farming tenantry, objects assuredly of great national importance; the author of this Report cannot but consider himself highly flattered by the distinguished honour of having been selected by the Honourable Board of Agriculture to prepare a new Report of Husbandry, and other objects connected with it, in the County of Devon.

In prosecuting an inquiry of this nature, it may be proper to observe, that the Surveyor enters on the examination of the agricultural practice and general intrests of the county, with a mind totally unfettered by any opinions or practices prevalent in its rural, commercial, or manufacturing departments. So little indeed has his attention been engaged of late years in the consideration of rural improvements (unless on the great scale of cutting down the woodland, and clearing the forests in Kentucky) and the inte-

rests

rests of a community necessarily connected there-with, that on the commencement of the present Survey, he found it necessary to re-peruse, with considerable attention, the two Reports he formerly had the honour to prepare under the sanction of the Honourable Board, on the Agriculture of Cambridgeshire and Essex, before he entered upon the present inquiries. This recurrence to former labours, has tended to disperse the confusion of ideas which pressed upon his mind, in his endeavours to retrace impressions which once interested, although from lapse of time and other engagements, became in a manner disregarded. Again, however, within the sphere of his former pursuits and inclinations, he reverts with pleasure to the contemplation of objects so genial to him ; and, fully impressed with the importance of the subject, he enters upon the following detail, subjoining such observations as result from long experience, to the consideration of the Honourable Board.

> Delightful task, to rear the wholesome plant,
> To teach the infant tendril how to climb;
> To spread the enriching compost o'er the soil;
> To till with temperate zeal the teeming mould,
> And fix in Nature's lap, with gen'rous care,
> Abundant crops for ages yet to come.

CONTENTS.

CONTENTS.

CHAP. I. GEOGRAPHICAL STATE AND CIRCUM-
STANCES.

CHAP. II. STATE OF PROPERTY.

CHAP. III. BUILDINGS.

CHAP. IV. OCCUPATIONS.

CHAP. V. IMPLEMENTS.

CHAP. VI. ENCLOSING, ... 132

CHAP. VII. ARABLE LAND.

CONTENTS.

CHAP. XV.   RURAL ECONOMY.

CHAP. XVI   POLITICAL ECONOMY:

CIRCUMSTANCES DEPENDENT ON LEGISLATIVE AUTHORITY.

CHAP. XVII.   OBSTACLES TO IMPROVEMENT.

CHAP. XVIII.   MISCELLANEOUS ARTICLES.

CONCLUSION.

MEANS OF IMPROVEMENT.

AND THE MEASURES CALCULATED FOR THAT PURPOSE.

APPENDIX.

Lymington, Hants, 1st Oct. 1807.

From the Author's itinerary engagements in a distant part of the kingdom, there was an absolute impossibility of conveying the proof-sheets for his examination, without creating a delay in the execution of the work, which was much wished to be avoided by the Honourable Board. The consequence is the following Errata, which he requests the reader will take the trouble of correcting with a pencil, before he enters upon the perusal of the work.

ERRATA.

Page 5, line 26, for Malton, read Melton.
  28, —— 28, for hall, read hill.
  41, —— 26, for Holme, read Holne.
  42, —— 23, for, and white yellow, read white and yell.
  48, —— 2, for Bur, read Bow.
  53, —— 13, the words, and fox, to be read at the beginning of the line, instead of at
                the end.
  —, —— 23, for 3l. read 3s.
  84, —— 15, for held, read held on lives.

                                                          Page

Page 87, line 32, for Here, read Where.

   95, —— 22, for room, read roof.

  110, —— 19, for per annum, read per acre.

  113, —— 14, for 18l. read 18s.

  129, —— 6, for crammed, read rammed.

  ——, —— 3, 5, 12, 15, 29, for straddle, read staddle.

  ——, —— 13, 14, 18, 28, for tackles, read takles; and the same in p. 130, lines 4, 12, 14.

  137, —— 10, for moved, read wove.

  142, —— 27, for sod, read seed.

  145, —— 2, for billed, read velled.

  148, —— 9, for chert, read chest.

  152, —— 10 and 11, for fallowed, read followed.

  164, —— 17, for stump, read turnip.

  ——, —— 28, for fallowed, read followed.

  179, —— 6, for 13, read 18.

  193, —— 8, for fresh, read Irish.

  195, —— 15, for Searing, read Scoring.

  198, —— 23, for Tilling, read Filling.

  ——, —— 3, for 16l. read 6l.

  199, —— 2, for 17s. 4d. read 17l. 4s.

  202, —— 9, for seed, read straw.

  212, —— 16, for survey, read saving.

  227, —— 10, for commons, read parishes.

  247, —— 10, for 20l. read 20s.

  ——, —— 29, for elder, read alder.

  248, —— 22, for the oak, read being barked.

  249, —— 3, for 16l. read 16s.

  250, —— 24, for crane, read coarse.

  259, —— 25, for 10l. read 10s.

  264, —— 17, for Gage, read Heathfield.

  279, —— 19 and 33, for summit, read sum.

  292, —— 12, for will hereafter be, read has been already.

  293, —— 17, for firs, read trees.

  302, —— 6, for with ouze cast, read at Ouze Cast.

  320, —— 10, for weight, read height.

  341, —— 20, for hay, read lay.

  347, —— 16, for dim, read dun.

  358, —— 9, for natural, read national.

  360, —— 25, for hacking, read packing.

  366, —— 6, for carrying, read varying.

  404, —— 7, for square, read square miles.

AGRICULTURAL SURVEY

OF

DEVONSHIRE.

CHAP. I.

GEOGRAPHICAL STATE AND CIRCUMSTANCES.

SECT. I.—SITUATION AND EXTENT.

DEVONSHIRE is a maritime county, bounded north-eastwardly by Exmoor, in the county of Somerset; east and south by a part of Dorsetshire and the English Channel; west by Cornwall, and a part of the Bristol Channel; and north by the Bristol Channel only. It is about 70 miles from north to south; 65 from east to west, and 280 in circumference; of which, after rejecting the prominent head-lands and indented coves or inlets, not exceeding one mile in their breadth or openings, there are 52 miles on the Bristol, and on the English Channel 82 miles, of maritime coast.

Acres.—The most modern calculation extant (or at least such as has been within the reach of the Author of this Report), assigns an area of 1,595,309 statute acres, or 2493 square miles, including water-courses, for the surface territory of the county.

SECT. II.—DIVISIONS.

This extent of country is divided into 33 hundreds, and again subdivided into 432 parishes and tithings, exclusive of the 22 parishes and precincts contained within the boundaries of the city of Exeter. The returns made to parliament under the Population Act of the 41st of George the Third, state the number of inhabited houses within the county to be 58,041 : these are inhabited by 72,560 families, making a population of 343,076 souls, and averaging 137.61 inhabitants to each square mile of 640 statute acres.

Political.—" Under the Roman domination, Devon was included in the district named Britannia Prima; by the Saxons it was made part of the kingdom of Wessex, and so continued till the incorporation of the various Saxon states into one monarchy, in the time of Egbert."

The county of Devon gives the title of Duke and Earl to the noble family of Cavendish. The city of Exeter sends two members to parliament, and gives the title of Marquis and Earl to the Cecil family. Plymouth, one of the principal arsenals for the naval stores of the kingdom, gives the title of Earl to the family of Windsor Hickman, and sends two members to parliament; Tavistock sends two members to parliament, and gives the title of Marquis to the family of Russell; Dartmouth sends two members to parliament, and gives the title of Earl and Baron to the family of Legge; Ashburton sends two members to parliament, and gives the title of Baron to the family of Dunning; Barnstable, Tiverton, Oakhampton, Honiton, Plympton, Totness, and Beeralston, each sends two members to parliament: Torrington gives the title of Viscount to the family of Byng.

Besides

Besides these, there are the following market-towns, viz. Crediton, Bideford, Topsham, Axminster, Bampton, Newton Bushell, Lyfton, Bow, Bradninch, Brent, Kingsbridge, Dodbrooke, Chudleigh (which latter gives the title of Baron to the family of Clifford), Chumleigh, Cullumpton, Combe-martin, Coliton, Hartland, Hatherleigh, Holdsworthy, Ilfracombe, Modbury, Moreton Hempstead, and South Molton.

The following villages are remarkable for giving the following titles, viz. Edgecumbe gives the title of Viscount to the family of the same name ; Boringdon gives the title of Baron to the family of Parker ; Sidbury, the same honour to the family of Fitzgibbon; Stevenstone, to that of Rolle; and Sidmouth to that of Addington.

The principal rivers immediately discharging into the Bristol and English Channel are, the Taw, the Torridge, the Tamar, the Plym, the Yealme, the Erme, the Aven, the Dart, the Teign, the Exe, the Otter, and the Axe ; the lesser streams having the same outfall, are, the Lyn, the Dawl, and the Sid; the head branches of the principal rivers are, the Mole, the Bray, the Okements, east and west, the Tavy, the Lyd, the Tynhay, the Carey, the Waldon, the Lenmon, the Bovey, the Wrey, the Creedy, the Culm, the Little Dart, the Coley, and the West Waters of the river Axe ; all conspiring with their respective dependencies and contributory waters, to justify the ancient designation of the county, which was that of a country abounding with rivers, rivulets, and streams. Hence its original name D'Avon, and afterwards, including Cornwall, that of Danmonium *.

---

* The Roman geographers attribute Devonshire and Cornwall to the Dunmonii or Danmonii. The Lizard Point in Cornwall, is denominatec Danmonium Promontorium by Cambden, who brings the origin of the name from the British *moina*, signifying tin, and another from the vallies in which the inhabitants dwelt—*Duffnient*, in British, signifying low vallies.

It

It sends 26 members to parliament, viz. two for the county, and 24, as above shewn. It pays a one-twentieth part of the land-tax, and provides 1600 men to the national militia. It produces silver, copper, tin, lead, iron, manganese, umber, timber, slate, marble, limestone, freestone, moorstone, and corn; cider, fowls, game, and fish in abundance. Its chief manufactures are the different kinds of woollen cloths, as also of bone-lace, in the eastern parts of the county. There are mineral waters at Tavistock, Cleave, Lamerton, Bampton, and Lifton. The bathing places so much resorted to during the summer season, on account of the great purity of the water and superior conveniences of sea-bathing, are, Linton, Ilfracombe, Clovella Court, Hartland, Torquay, Sheldon, Teignmouth, Bridleigh, Dawlish, Star-cross, Exmouth, Salterton, Sidmouth, Bere, and Seaton.

Ecclesiastical.—Devonshire lies within the province of Canterbury and diocese of Exeter. This city is the see of the Bishop, and was so made by King Edward the Confessor, who transferred it hither from Crediton. The city is a county within itself, and, with the county of Devon, is included in the western circuit of the kingdom.

SECT. III.—CLIMATE.

DISTRICT I.—North Devon.

THE climate here, although very indulgent in respect to many parts of England, is by no means comparable to the temperature which characterizes the seasons in the southern parts of the county: even here, and along the sea-coasts, from the north-eastern extremity of the district to the southernmost cove in the Barnstable or

Bideford

Bideford bay, snow seldom lies longer than a few hours; in proof of which it is only necessary to state, that the Dutch broad-leaved double-flowering myrtle, as well as the more delicate aromatic and narrow-leaved sorts, constantly flourish in the open air, and are found not unfrequently to constitute a part of the garden hedges.

In this district, it is to be observed, that snow seldom continues any length of time, unless upon the summits of the highest hills, forming a part of, and abutting northeastwardly upon, the forest of Exmoor.

The relative heights of these hills with those ranging along the sea-coast, compared with the plane of high water in the Bristol Channel, from the best information it was possible to procure, will be found as follows:

Dunkery beacon, part of the forest of Exmoor, 1890 feet.

Castle Head-down, in the parish of High Bray, upon which there are some ancient Danish fortifications, called Shoelsbury-castle, is above the level of the high-water line in the Bristol Channel 1500 feet.

Chapman Barrows, dividing the parishes of Parracombe and Challacombe, 1200 feet.

Holston Barrow, in the parish of Combe-martin, 900 feet.

Great Hangman-hill, in the said parish, 800 feet.

General range of the Exmoor-hills, towards South Malton, 850 feet.

Little Hangman-hill, forming the eastern promontory of the bay of Combe-martin, 600 feet.

Hilsborough, east of, and overhanging the town of Ilfracombe, 300 feet.

Slade-hill, one mile west of Ilfracombe, 900 feet.

Hoardown-gate, three miles on the road from Ilfracombe to Barnstable, cultivated over its highest summit, 1000 feet.

Swine-

Swinedown, five miles from Ilfracombe, on the same road, sinks about 200 feet from the height of Hoardown, and is consequently 800 feet above the high water-level in the river of Barnstable.

Beyond the Torridge, the land rises progressively along the sea-coast, passing Clovella Dykes (another ancient and extensive Danish fortification), and which is 900 feet above the level of the high water in the little port of Clovella below.

The following average state of the thermometer at 50 feet above the level of the sea, was taken from the register of a gentleman at Ilfracombe, upon whose accuracy the strictest reliance may be placed. The extract commences and concludes with the year 1806, making the monthly elevation and depression of the mercury according to Fahrenheit's scale.

For January, ... 53°   For July, ... 65¾°
    February, ... 48½   August, ... 66
    March, ... 52   September, ... 61¾
    April, ... 57½   October, ... 62¼
    May, ... 62¼   November, ... 58¼
    June, ... 64¾   December, ... 56¼

Hence it appears, that the month of January was one degree warmer than March, and that September was colder than October by half a degree of Fahrenheit's scale; circumstances productive of the most serious consideration, and which will be duly attended to in the progress of this Report. The mists and fogs prevalent along the sea-coasts, although favourable to vegetation, tend very much to increase the frigid principle in the spring of the year, and afterwards to retard the ripening of the harvest; and although this effect may be considered as general throughout the district, still its eastern and more elevated parts seem to labour under very considerable disadvan-

tages,

tages, when compared with the country to the westward ; and in the neighbourhood of the Tidal, and navigable waters of the Taw and Torridge rivers. Here the air is milder and more salubrious, and vegetation is a fortnight, and sometimes three weeks, earlier than that of the cultivated lands near the foot of Exmoor. On this high and extended plain, the snow continues to lie very late in the spring, and considerably adds to the ungenial harshness of the north-eastwardly winds, which generally prevail at that season, and, from this frozen eminence, carry additional severity to all the country lying south-westwardly from the moor, and within their influence. Fortunately, however, this evil seldom spreads far to the westward of East Buckland, and of a line drawn thence north, a little westwardly, towards Bratton Flemming, and Arlington.

The reverse of those mischievous effects accompanying the Exmoor wind, may be inferred from a circumstance related by Mr. Grant, the present collector of the port of Bideford. This gentleman states, that in the summer of 1805, he removed from a hot-bed several melon plants into hills in the open air, previously prepared with dung and rich mould to receive them ; these hills were afterwards covered with flat pebble-stones, brought from the shingle bank, lying southwardly from the Northam burrows ; the plants were protected by a common handglass, placed in such a manner upon the stones, as to admit a free circulation of air during the twenty-four hours, and the melon-vines were permitted to spread from under, and occupy the whole of the surrounding hill. The vines fruited equally well in the open air as under the glasses ; and from two of these hills, which were occupied by three plants each, 6½ brace, or 13, of the rock-cantelope melon, were cut during the months of August and Septem-

September, and proved in size and flavour equal to any raised under glasses by the most skilful gardeners in the neighbourhood.

DISTRICT II.—*Free, or Dunstone Land.*

From the extremely long and detached figure of this district, it may reasonably be supposed to possess a considerable variety of climate—the fact is so; for although its western quarter is entirely out of the reach of any unfriendly winds from the heights of Exmoor or of Dartmoor, and its winter climate is there found to be mild and genial in the highest degree, still the excessive violence of the westerly winds are such, as to baffle almost every effort of the industrious cultivator of woodland; for no sooner does the plant arrive to the height of the plain over which the westerly winds are found to pass, than its top becomes shorn and stunted, and its energies are confined to the enlargement, in diameter, of a few crippled limbs, and a languid increase of body or trunk of the tree.

The north-west winds from the forest of Exmoor, produce much frost, and cold-driving rains, in the spring of the year, and are greatly dreaded on the eastern side of the district; but it is the westerly, or Dartmoor winds, that are stated to produce the greatest mischief at all seasons in the Drewsteignton quarter.

DISTRICT III.—*Moorlands.*

The south-westerly winds prevail most generally in the country north of Dartmoor; these seldom blow long without being accompanied with continual rain: but the blighting effects of the south-easterly winds are still more dreaded by those who live within a few miles of the foot of the moor. These frequently blow for some time in the months

months of March, April, and May, when considerable damage is done to the orchards, and in retarding the growth of grass and corn. Yet, from observ. ons actually made between Oakhampton and London, the average temperature of climate is stated to be warmer at Oakhampton than in London, by three degrees.

The Meshaw division of this district is entirely out of the reach of the Dartmoor winds; but the northern gales sweeping the heights of Exmoor, are little less unfriendly in their passage over that part of the district during the spring and early parts of summer.

The average height of the thermometer in the shade and open air, taken at Oakhampton, for the year 1806, was as follow, viz.

January,	$34\frac{1}{4}°$	July,	$62°$
February,	$36\frac{1}{4}$	August,	$63\frac{3}{4}$
March,	$41\frac{1}{4}$	September,	$57\frac{3}{4}$
April,	$43\frac{1}{2}$	October,	$46\frac{3}{4}$
May,	$50\frac{1}{4}$	November,	41
June,	$55\frac{1}{2}$	December,	$39\frac{1}{4}$

DISTRICT IV.—South Hams, Limestone, Marble, &c.

The climate here is supposed to be more mild and salubrious than in any other part of England: the most violent winds, and those accompanied with the heaviest fall of rain, are chiefly from the southward and western quarters; but in the hundreds of Roborough and Tavistock, the south-easterly winds are said to produce the greatest injury to vegetation, corn, and fruit-trees: the moor winds are equally dreaded at Brent, Buckfastleigh, and Ashburton. The climate of Modbury and Kingsbridge, although at so short a distance from Ivy-bridge, is certainly less humid than at the foot of Dartmoor.

DIS-

DISTRICT V.—*Granite Gravel.*

The southerly winds are found here by far the most furious and prevalent; and although the great force of the westerly winds is much abated, from the shelter afforded by the heights of Dartmoor, still the cold and frigid vapour continually descending from that eminence, produces the most serious mischief to the agricultural interests of this district.

DISTRICT VI.—*Red Clay and sandy Loam; Marl, Grout, and Dunstone; Flints of Haldon and Woodbury.*

Little farther can be said of the climate of this district, than that the moor winds are often complained of at Bow, and in the North Tawton quarter; otherwise the air may generally be considered as mild as that in the most temperate and wholesome parts of the county.

DISTRICT VII.—*Chalk, Flint, Sandstone, Marl, Freestone, Limestone, &c. &c.*

The southerly winds are by far the most violent and common; but those from the opposite quarter are found to be the most destructive to fruit, and injurious to vegetation, in the spring of the year. Upon the whole, it does not seem liable to the same local disadvantages, so often adverted to in the preceding districts.

SECT. IV.—SOIL.

DISTRICT I.

As it appears utterly impossible for any one to pro-
____ with certainty on the nature of soil or surface-
mould,

mould, without a due examination of the subsoil, and even the more remote substrata of the surface to be examined, it is deemed proper to premise, that in the present Survey, close attention has been paid to these particulars.

The aspect of the district before us, is that of a country much broken into hills, holding a general course a little to the northward of West, and, after passing to the southward of the forest of Exmoor, extending from sea to sea from the eastern point a little southwardly. The internal structure of these hills, which are occasionally broken by the waters passing through them, consists of a primitive stratified rock, corresponding in direction with their general course, and varying in its dip to the north and south from 30 to 80 degrees. The whole of this rock is of a laminous character; the upper parts of which vary in their texture, as mineral substances may be presumed to have entered more or less into combination with the primitive mass, and which commonly favours the character of an indurated clay.

In those places where the upper parts of the rock are of a splintry texture, rising below in rhomboidal or cubical fragments, exhibiting in their fracture a dun, or rather liver-coloured appearance, and the small stones on the surface are found to be encrusted with a brown, or rather yellowish kind of ochre, it is generally called free, or Dunstone land. Here the soil is of a good depth upon the shillot; is of a bright hazel colour, of a tender friable nature, and generally esteemed to be the best corn land*. When the rock crops out in very thin lamina of a smooth and glossy appearance, with a rotten shivery

---

* In speaking of the shillot or killas rock hereafter, it will always be found accompanied with a similar soil or covering.

fracture,

fracture, it forms the basis of the soil or surface-mould, the subsoil of which is continued to various depths, according to the resistance the under stratum of shaley rock may have presented to the slow decomposing process which this species of rock seems gradually to be undergoing, and thence forms a stratum of brown-yellow, or blueish-coloured clay, corresponding in colour with the rock below, and from which all the clayey parts of this country are unquestionably derived.

The soil here, from the coolness and moisture of its bottom, is generally considered more favourable to the culture of grass than of corn*. The surface of the unenclosed and extensive moor-lands or commons, which occupy so large a proportion of this district, lie generally at a greater distance from the shillot or shaley understratum before described, than in the cultivated parts of the district. In some instances, the substratum of the wastes is formed of a hard and durable species of whin and freestone mixed with white acre (that is, quartz), and a species of granite gravel, covered with a strong growth of black heath, rooted in a thin staple of dry brown peat lying immediately on the rock, and from which it is pared by the inhabitants for the purposes of fuel. Where water has been arrested on the sides of hills and low places, peat, to a greater or less depth, has been produced; but in no instance is the quantity of peat or turf to be regarded as considerable.

Although the general nature of the soil may be pretty well understood from what has been stated, a more minute description of its most striking peculiarities, and

* Whenever mention is made of the shaley rock, in future, it will always be found attended with a cold wet stratum of clay at various depths between the rock and surface mould.

other

ether features of the country, occurring in the examination of this district, may perhaps not be deemed improper or unnecessary.

A light brown loam of a good staple on a grey killas, composed of thin lamina, and which, when moistened, assumes a bright hazel colour, forms the basis of the cultivated lands in the neighbourhood of Ilfracombe, Berry-narber, Watermouth, and Combe-martin: it is in all places of sufficient depth for the purposes of aration; and when the dissolution of the rock is gone so far as to create a deep subsoil of brown, blue, or yellow clay, it becomes mixed with irregular fragments of a hard rubble stone, from one to six or eight inches cubical measure, displaying divers colours of aluminous and silicious earths, in a softer or more indurated state, as the extraneous bodies with which they may be combined, render them soft or more impenetrable.

Proceeding thence eastwardly along the coast, the Great and Little Hangman-hill, Holsten Barrows, and Kentisbury-down, rise with considerable grandeur over the other hills; but when compared with the more valuable wastes in the country, become of little or no consideration in the eye of the agriculturist. The surface of these downs vary from a dry peaty moor, lying close upon a hard bed of sandstone, white acre and granite, to a thin moory soil, intercepted from a similar understratum by the occurrence of a thin body of granite gravel, or a cold close stratum of white and yellow clay, mixed and interspersed with small veins of an ochreous substance, resembling an oxyde or rust of iron.

Farther along the coast, and through the parishes of Trentishoe, Martinhoe, Linton, Countesbury and Brendon, including Badgery, little difference appears to mark the character of the cultivated lands, from that which is

stated

stated of the same class at Ilfracombe and Berry-narber. The moor and common lands, of considerable elevation, binding eastwardly upon Exmoor, are generally of a better quality than those covering the hills on the coasts of the Bristol Channel. The cultivated lands in the parishes of Challacombe and Parracombe, High Bray, North Molton, Twitching, Molland Bouceaux, extending to the hill on which is situated the church of East Anstey, consist generally of a well stapled brown and hazel-coloured loam on a shilloc and shaley rock, but which, from their superior elevation, seem better calculated for the purposes of pasture than of tillage. The low lands have an intervening stratum of clay between the rock and the surface of the meadows, which have been much raised and enriched by sediment conveyed in the annual inundations from the higher grounds.

This character of country, with a considerable depression of its hills from the foot of Exmoor, continues, with such shades of difference as may be occasioned by a greater or less depth of subsoil intervening between the surface and the rock, through the north parts of the parishes of East and West Anstey, the part of Molland lying north of the turnpike road leading from South Molton to Dulverton, the northern parts of Bishops, and George Nympton, South Molton, Satterleigh, Warkleigh, Chittlehampton, and Filleigh. Proceeding thence northwardly through the parishes of Swimbridge, Landkey, West-Buckland, Charles, Goodleigh, Stoke Rivers, and Bratton Flemming, a bright brown, or rather cedar-coloured soil, seems frequently to occur, and to carry with it a corresponding superiority, as is evinced by its producing a very sound tract of grass and corn land. This excellence is found to spread generally over the extensive waste of Bratton-down, and although not altogether free from interruption by the

light

light brown and grey tender loam, is traceable through the parishes of Kentisbury, East-down, Arlington, Loxhore, and Sherwell, to Pilton.

Returning thence northwardly through Ashford, Prexford, Marwood, West-down, and Brittendon, a large proportion of wastes occupy the face of the country, and much confine the extent of cultivated land; the soil of which is generally that of a grey tender loam, of a moderate staple on a dry schistus or slaty rock. South-westwardly from Ilfracombe, and passing the limestone ridges along the coast, the soil is of a good staple, assuming a bright hazel-colour, and lies to a sufficient depth on the common rock. Here, large fragments of white acre (a stone much used for the purposes of repairing the highways) frequently occurs. This character continues without any material alteration through Morthoe, Georgeham, Braunton, and Heanton Punchardon, affording a tract of land as well calculated for a system of up and down husbandry, as for its more general appropriation of lying in grass.

It may be worthy of remark, that on the highest hills throughout the district here described, lying north-eastwardly of the river Taw, the general stratified structure of the substratum is lost in a deep bed of rubbly clay, the stones of which tally in every respect with those before described, and are found to occupy to a very considerable depth the tops of the highest eminences in the country.

The land between the Taw and the Torridge rivers, bounded southwardly by the parishes of Wear Giffard, Henshaw, Yarnescombe and Atherington (and formed by a continuation of the same ridges, although considerably lower, which mark the leading features of the country lying east of the Taw river), consists with little variation of a well stapled, tender. grey, and brown loam on the shillot,

lot, shaley, and schistus rock, and well calculated for a
system of convertible husbandry.   Upon the low grounds
a stratum of loam or brown potter's clay occurs between
the surface soil and the rock, and which at Fremington is
of a considerable depth, and much used in the coarse potteries of Barnstable and Bideford.   Westward of the Torridge, and through the parishes of Northam, Bideford,
Abbotsham, Alwington, Littleham and Land-cross, the
same general character of country continues, although the
soil occasionally varies from a grey and brown loam to that
of a light red or cedar-colour, and lying on a deep stratum
of rubbly loam, highly shaded with, and partaking of the
same hue.

DISTRICT II.

The soil in the parish of Little Torrington, consists of
a loose free loam of a good staple, on a deep rubbly subsoil.   At Frithlestock it abates considerably of this good
quality, and in many places is found to consist of a moist
grey loam on a tough yellow clay, much better adapted to
the culture of oats than of barley.   Through the parishes
of Monkleigh, Buckland Brewer, the free or Dunstone
soil prevails, occasionally varied with small veins of a
cedar-colour on a substratum of rubbly loam, in which
there are sometimes found black flints or firestones, particularly in the parish of Buckland Brewer.   This bright
hazel-coloured land, generally denotes a favourable disposition for the culture of wheat, barley, oats, turnips and
clover.   (These parishes are all watered with an abundance
of living springs).

In this description, although unquestionably much inferior, must be admitted the northern part of Woolfardisworthy, passing through which, and by Clovella Dykes,
you descend from the new lodge to Clovella Court.   The
view

view of the ravine or dingle, by the side of which the new
road leads, is truly picturesque and interesting; it winds
for the distance of about a mile and a half on the sides of
an indented eminence, the projecting points of which rest
on a declivity that seems nearly approaching to a perpendicular. This, as well as the opposite side of the glen,
is covered with a close growth of oak copsewood, which
appear to clothe the sharpest points and ridges in the descent, and continue thus feathered to the lowest tops of the
Table Cliffs, which lie within a few feet of the high water
mark. The wild scenery of this descent, united with a
bird's eye view of the diminutive appearance of vessels in
the bay of Bideford (whose waters seem to wash the foot
of the plane you are descending). a more extended view of
its bold commanding shores rising abruptly from the sea,
crowned with corn-fields or robed in perpetual verdure, all
conspire to excite the most agreeable sensations of grandeur
combined with fertility and plenty in the highest degree.

The little town and harbour of Clovella are situated at
the mouth of the ravine, or rather deep hollow above noticed; it is neatly built on the lower bench of the cliffs,
and their ascending sides, and chiefly supported by its fisheries and the lime-works, which latter are here supplied
from the opposite coast of Wales. Its harbour is protected
from the westward by an excellent pier, within which all
the craft and shipping resorting to the port, can at all
times ride and lye with the most perfect safety: it is only
to be lamented that this as well as the harbour of Ilfracombe, is not upon a much larger and extended scale.
They are however both wonderfully convenient as far as
their capacity extends, and reflect the highest praise and
honour to the individuals who have so nobly constructed
them. Clovella house is situated in a well chosen, sheltered
spot, adjoining which is a range of rich arable and grass-

DEVON.]   land,

land, with a considerable skirting of oak and other thriving woodland ; the soil varies from a moist grey loam on
a brown and yellow clay, to a loose friable hazel-coloured
mould on a bed of rubbly reddish coloured schistus clay,
apparently derived from a decomposition of the killas rock,
which here rises in much thicker fragments than has been
hitherto observed to the eastward.

The approach to Hartland Abbey is rendered particularly interesting, by the length of the vale through which
the road winds to the house. This valley averages rathei
less than a quarter of a mile in breadth, and is supplied
by a constant stream for the purposes of irrigation. Its
sides are covered with an unbroken range of oak wood,
the tops of which, though towering to a considerable
height, are still shorn by the force of the westerly winds,
in so smooth and uniform a manner, as seems to bid defiance to the utmost efforts of art to produce or imitate.

This part of the valley is terminated by the abbey and
pleasure-grounds, on each side connected with the woodland. The front and other parts of the building, although
generally appearing in a modern dress, still retain most of
the principal features of its primitive character : the Gothic
arch seems here rather to embellish than abate the beauty
of modern design. Passing through the hall, you enter
the western apartments of the building, where a continuance of the front valley presents itself in the form of a
small deer park, surrounded with woodland ; the inhabitants of which are seen confidently grazing under the
study windows. The whole indeed, appears so happily
in unison with the benevolent disposition of the proprietor, that it becomes absolutely impossible, however indifferent to the observance of such scenes, to behold Hartland Abbey, and at the same time to know the worth and
virtues of its owner, without feeling a glow of the highest
satisfaction

satisfaction at so well merited a distribution of the gifts
of Providence.

The general character of soil throughout the northern
parts of the parish of Hartland, is that of a light tender
loam of a greyish brown colour, and resting upon a substratum of clay, at various depths from one to three or
four feet of the rock, which generally consists of a blueish
grey substance, breaking up into square fragments, and
making good building stone.

This general character is occasionally interrupted with
veins of a reddish brown colour, equally well stapled with
the grey loam, but much varied in its quality, through the
particular combinations of other substances : its general
temperament, though somewhat drier, may be referred to
the dark hazel or brown loams. No material difference
seems to occur between the soil and understrata of Little
Torrington, from that which may be said to obtain
through Great Torrington, thence to Stevenstone, and
a part of the parishes of St. Giles's, Roborough, and
Beaford.

Proceeding east of the Torridge, and through the parishes of Dolton, Dowland, Iddesleigh, Broadwood-kelly,
Honeychurch and Monk Oakhampton, the soil generally
consists of a hazel-coloured loam, or free dunstone, interspersed with veins slightly tinged with a light pink colour, and lying on a rubbly subsoil intercepting the
surface at a good distance from the killas or shillot
rock.

Whilst this country in many places exhibits a most
delightfully varied and picturesque appearance, it more
frequently presents deep and fatal impressions of a much
worn and exhausted soil; fields bearing but a very thin
and feeble plant of clover, light and indifferent crops of
wheat and oats; and generally characterized by a tough,
                                                    wiry,

wiry, and sour herbage. The crops of barley, however,
seem generally to countenance a more favourable description.

The country from Little Torrington through the parishes of Merton, Huish, and Meeth, contains a desirable proportion of good corn and grass land : in this distance some very good barley, wheat, and clover, were
observed. Between Meeth Church and the Torridge a
narrow vein of red land appeared, stretching eastwardly
towards Iddesleigh and Winkleigh.

The soil in the parishes of Shepwash, Buckland, Filleigh, Petrockstow, Marland, and Langtree, may be
divided into three classes: the first consists of a loose
friable loam of a good staple, lying upon the schistus rock;
the second, a well stapled reddish brown loam, on an
understratum of rubbly clay, which is found finally to
rest on a hard shillot rock, breaking up into excellent
building stones; the third class chiefly occupies the vallies
and low grounds, and is composed of a thin grey loam,
on a subsoil of white, yellow, and blue clay.

Approaching Black Torrington from Cookbury and
Bradford, the higher parts of the country through the
former parish and High Heanton, appear very much to
improve; the soil being a well-stapled tender loam on a
shillot rock; but a thin stapled grey loam on a substratum
of cold yellow clay, veined with an ochery matter, seems
more fully to mark the quality of the vallies and lower
ground.

Approaching the town of Hatherleigh from the north,
we are suddenly plunged into a deep stratum of red rich
loam, and which generally may be considered as the
western termination of the red land district. North
of the village of Winkleigh, the soil continues of a good
staple, and lies upon the laminous rock, which here breaks

into

into a small splintery fracture, and affords a much drier
bottom than some of the ridges lying south of it. The
black gravelly shillot seems here to indicate that limestone
may be found at no great distance. Descending this ridge
to the northward, the Dunstone land appears to lose its
superiority in a cold moory tract which continues towards
Ashreigney; but towards Eggsford a much sounder country seems to present itself.

The marshes along the Taw, in the parishes of Ashreigney, Burrington, and High Bickington, consist of a
brown deep close loam, on an understratum of loose black
gravel and sand. The higher parts of these parishes to
the westward, are formed of a moist but tender grey loam,
on a bed of clay of various depths upon the shaley rock.
Mixed with this understratum, and on the eastern brows
of the hills bounding the river Taw, veins of a red cedar-
coloured loam are found, of a good depth on the shillot
rock, which in such places breaks up into larger and more
cubical formed fragments than under the deep grey loam,
with its weak and shivery understratum. The hills and
ridges here, after opening a passage for the Mole and river
Taw, appear to resume their usual course. The dividing
ridge at the junction of these rivers, though very high,
and consequently bleak and exposed, affords a tolerable
tract of useful corn land. The banks of the rivers Taw
and Mole, as well as the combes or hollows branching in
various directions from them, are beautifully enriched
with oak timber and coppice woodland. These form an
agreeable contrast with the glades and meadows through
which these rivers hold their course, and annually spread
their enriching waters.

In this quarter lies the demesne of New Place, which
only requires its natural advantages to be improved, to
render it equal in beauty to some of the most favoured
spots

spots in the county. The low grounds upon the Mole,
in the parish of King's Nympton, and those of Chumleigh,
on the Taw, may be referred for general character to the
marshes of Burrington and Ashreigney. The enclosed
cultivated lands in the higher parts of these parishes,
abutting east and northwardly on the moors of Meshaw,
may very well be classed with those of Sheldon, Thelbridge, Lapford, Nymet Rowland, Wembworthy, Eggsford and Chawley, which are found generally to consist
of a grey, or dun-coloured loam on a substratum of rock,
rising generally in square or rhomboidal fragments. The
intermediate subsoil between the rock and the surface
mould, varies in its depth from a few inches to several
feet in thickness. This is composed of the decompounded
shale, mixed with a coarse argillaceous gravel, pervious
to water, and consequently leaving the surface dry and
of a tender nature.

The lower parts of these parishes, assuming a more level
form, are composed of a moist grey loam, more compact
and tenacious than the more elevated grounds, and lying
on a brown and yellow clay intermixed with coarse rubble. Over this stratum the water has been traced to flow
and issue forth in the form of springs, to the great annoy-
ance and injury of the adjoining grounds. In this stratum
there frequently occurs what is generally called black ram,
i. e. an oxyde of iron combined with peat; and which is
often so extremely hard, as to render it difficult to make
any impression on it: this is always found to hold up the
water, and may be assigned as a principal cause for the
springs bursting so frequently forth on the sides of hills,
and in a manner so injurious to the lands below.

The bottom lands on the margin of the water-courses
are formed of a tender sandy loam, evidently produced by
the overflowing of these streams, and now raised to a
                                                    conside-

considerable depth all along their courses. These lands
are still liable to be overflowed to a considerable depth,
at which times a farther deposition of sediment is made,
and which has given rise to various opinions as to its fertilizing quality: by some it is contended to be injurious;
by others (perhaps better able to judge), an opinion leads
to a very different conclusion. In this part of the district there are veins of a cedar-coloured loam, which
have been remarked most generally to occur on the northern brows and sides of the hills. The yellow clay before
mentioned is occasionally, and may be generally, employed in the making of very good bricks. After ascending about a mile from the church end of North
Tawton, the rich red loam of that district is lost in crossing a brown and yellow clay ridge, which descends towards Bonley-bridge, over the river Taw. Passing thence
through the village of Bonley, a deep wet stratum of
yellow clay lands, abounding with uncultivated moors,
are formed, stretching towards Broadwood-kelly; thence
northwardly over the valley which divides this ridge
from that on which we find the parishes of Coldridge,
Nymet, Dowland, Brushford, and Winkleigh, where
the soil on the south side and top of the ridge, as before
noticed, affords an excellent tract of tillage and grass
land.

After passing the coarse moors and commons which
occupy the southern parts of the parishes of St. Mary-
down, and Zeal Monachorum, the free or Dunstone soil
is found so generally to prevail, as to admit them in the
general description of Lapford, and the parishes before
noticed in that quarter. The same indeed may be said
on proceeding eastwardly through the parishes of Ken-
nerly, Mortchard Bishops, Woolfardisworthy, Wash-
ford-pine and Puddington. The southern parts of
Cruwys

Cruwys Mortchard*, the whole of Poughill, Cadleigh,
Cheriton Fitzpaine, and Cadbury, with the northern
parts of Stokely Pomeroy, Upton-hellions, Sandford,
Clannaborough, and Bow, or Nymet Tracy, are generally
covered with a tender loam of a dark grey cast on a shil-
lotty understratum; a reddish brown free loam on a
rough rubbly subsoil, or a loose sandy loam of a bright
red colour on a stratum of argillaceous smooth pebbly
gravel: the whole, with a large proportion of good
meadow and pasture land, is well calculated for the culture of wheat, barley, oats, pease, turnips, tares and
clover. This quarter, although frequently interrupted
in the continued line of its enclosures by coarse moors
and commons, still preserves a very great pre-eminence
over the district by which it is bounded on the north:
for here in many places the country is beautifully diversified with fruitful hills and rich vallies, the sides of
which are often occupied with thriving woodlands or valuable orchards.

The north-western parts of Silverton and Bradninch,
the western parts of Cullumpton, with the whole of
Bickleigh and Butterleigh, may with great propriety be
added to this description. In the parish of Halberton,
and extending towards Tiverton, is a body of dark grey
or brown loam on a white blue and yellow woodland
clay; the latter slightly veined with an ochre of iron.
The higher parts of this parish are found to consist of a
brown tender loamy surface, intercepted from the shaley
rock by a deep stratum of clay mixed with an argillaceous
rubble, and of a much milder nature than the lands
below. This character is found generally to prevail
through the parish of Samford Peverill.

---

* In this parish the celebrated fossil bacon was discovered.

Returning

Returning north-eastwardly from Tiverton, through the parish of Uplowman, a free tender loam occurs on a bed of brown rubbly clay, which continues without any material variation to within a short distance of West-leigh, when a strong loam of a brownish red colour, and apparently much to favour the nature of the rock be-low, announces the vicinity of limestone. This is found to extend through the northern parts of Uplowman, and from Westleigh to the west branch of the river Culm, but is not found beyond the valley, or on the hill upon which the church of Burlescombe is situated. Passing the moor towards Holcombe-rogus, another large body of limestone occurs, and continues in particular places between Rockworth and Bampton: its presence here is generally indicated by the shillot rock breaking into a splintery form, which, when farther broken, makes an excellent material for repairing the roads, and is ge-nerally known by the name of black gravel. The hills here rise very abruptly from the combes, and continue in regular array on a course of about west by north and east, a little southerly: they are uniformly covered with a good staple of soil, and well calculated for the purposes of tillage. A deep and stronger soil com-poses the covering of the lower grounds, which are usu-ally kept on the green side, and preserved for meadows and permanent pastures; the proportion of which to the arable in this neighbourhood, may be stated at about one-half.

The country between Bampton and Morebath is broken into ridges, keeping their usual course, and pre-serving much the same character as those just mentioned, but without any certain proof of the existence of lime-stone. The sound and fruitful tract of land lying east of the river Exe, appears gradually to lessen on entering
a country

a country equally broken, and at no great distance from the western side of that river; for after passing the line of enclosed cultivated lands, the common and moor lands of Oakford form the line of separation between this and the moorland district.

Southwardly from Oakford towards Stoodleigh, a tract of woodland interspersed with some moors, appears to have recently given way to the effects of cultivation, and form the eastern condition of that parish, where the soil is found frequently to vary from a stiff woodland clay to a dry tender loam upon a more open subsoil. Westwardly, and near the village of Writtenhall, a dark brown mould, or rather peaty surface on a white, blue and yellow clay, again occurs to limit the boundary of the district in that quarter, but southwardly, and towards Loxhore, the soil becomes a bright hazel, or rather reddish coloured loam, on a dark brown freestone, and considered excellent barley, clover, and turnip land. This general character obtains, without much intermission, southwardly along, and at some distance westwardly, from the river Exe, and thence through the parishes of Washfield and Calverleigh to Tiverton.

The country, for the first two miles after passing Crediton to the southward, and towards St. Mary Tedborne, consists of the same red loam which so strikingly distinguishes the Bow, and North Tawton district. Approaching the foot of Old Ridge-hills, this suddenly disappears in a moist grey loam on a stratum of brown and yellow clay, and that lying to a considerable depth on the shaley rock*. This grey loam, but of a drier nature, and on the schistus or slaty rock, continues for about half a

---

* The ravines, hollows, and side hills, are much occupied with coppice, and a small portion of ash woodland.

mile

mile eastward from the church at Whitestone, where it again unites with the red land district.

Descending to the valley southwardly from the church at Whitestone, and crossing near West Kent farm, this grey loam continues, till it reaches the same character of soil, although generally of an inferior quality, in the parish of Holcombe-burnell.

The country lying west of Whitestone church, including the parishes of St. Mary Tedborne, Christow, Cheriton Bishops, the south part of Hittesleigh and Spreyton, and the middle division of South Tawton (its more southern quarter lying generally on a granite gravel) consists of a dark grey, or rather brownish coloured loam, intercepted at various depths from the shaley rock by a subsoil of moist brown, blue, and yellow clay. The ridge on which the village of Drewsteignton is situated, continues eastwardly towards Cobley-brook, and westwardly towards Bradford: the soil here consists of a well stapled brown tender loam on a Dunstone shillot rock, in which a stratum of blue lais limestone is found intermixed with an excellent building stone of the same colour.

A tract of good tillage land answering to the same quality, is found to prevail from the church at Drewsteignton through the western parts of the parish of Dunsford. Thence south-westerly, crossing the river Teign, the Dunstone land continues along the river hills, to the foot of Meer Down and Moor Down, the last capped with a craggy eminence in the parish of Moreton-Hempstead, the eastern parts of which, with the like divisions in the parishes of Bradford, Christow, Lustleigh, and Hemiock, may be said generally to partake of the same quality.

Descending the high ridge upon which the village of Hemiock is situated, and crossing the river Teign, the valley

valley of which here begins to open and enlarge the
width of the meadows along the margin of its stream,
the features of the country become less bold and prominent, but more smooth and fruitful, as we approach Ugbrook, the seat of the present Lord Clifford. This park
is bounded eastwardly by the flints of Haldon, and the
high road leading from Newton Bushell to Exeter. It is
unquestionably a noble and highly interesting demesne,
the soil of which generally consists of a well tempered
reddish brown mould of a good staple, on the shillot rock,
imbedded and united with which are prodigious masses
of limestone, which immemorially have, and at present
appear to be greatly in demand for the purposes of manure. This limestone is quarried at one of Lord Clifford's
free rocks, and is thence generally transported on horses'
backs to distant parts of the country, where it is burnt
in what are called flame-kilns.

Proceeding northwardly from Chudleigh, a large
proportion of good corn and pasture land occurs, and
for some distance abounds with limestone.

Approaching the seven mile-stone from Exeter on the
Ashburton road, the ascent to the table top of Haldon
begins, and where it is curious to remark, how suddenly,
even in the space of a few yards, a separation takes place
between the cold flinty clay of Haldon and the rich
reddish loam that so well distinguishes the neighbourhood
of Chudleigh: this latter character is found mostly to
prevail east of Haldon-hall, and through the parish of
Trusham. The river Teign, forming the western boundary of this parish, is found above Cannonleigh-house
and upwards, to force its passage through so very confined a valley, as often to present many difficulties to the
traveller, from the huge masses of rocks that appear to
have been precipitated from the incumbent hillls. On the

sides

sides of this ravine are sometimes found copse and other woodland; the most flourishing and extensive of which appear to be those on the Barton of Cannonteign. The country through Ashton, and between the Teign and the heights of Haldon, the western parts of Doddiscombeleigh and Dunchidiock (their eastern quarters lying partly within the red land district), consists of a brown tender mould of a good staple on a Dunstone rubble.

It is impossible for imagination to conceive the faintest shadow of the wild and astonishing scenery to which the attention is drawn, in traversing the heights and hollows of this quarter of the district. The bold and stupendous ridges rising almost perpendicularly from their base, their brows and summits capped with broken and craggy rocks; the deep and hollow chasms through which the Teign and the Bovey force to their union with each other, as they approach the smoother plain of Bovey-heathfield, are such as must afford the highest satisfaction to those any way interested in viewing the operations of Nature, particularly in places where she appears to have been the most irregular in her sportive moments*.

DISTRICT III.

It has been already observed, that the sound hilly country lying east of the river Exe, is quickly lost in a country equally broken on the west side of Dulverton, and north-west side of Brushford, when, drawing towards East Anstey, and on its south eastern quarter, considera-

---

* It is impossible, on a survey of this nature, to ascertain the number of acres of waste included in the respective districts; but the quality, and other circumstances of such lands, will in future be particularly noticed in the Eleventh Chapter of this Report.

ble

ble portions of coarse wet lands were noticed, on deep
strata of brown and yellow clay, mixed with large rubbly
stones of a blue, brown, and greyish colour.

Proceeding south-eastwardly through the enclosures of
Molland (many of which appear in a very coarse and uncultivated condition), the moors to the brow of the ridge
descending to the cross-head branch of the Mole river,
are found to consist generally of a dark vegetable mould
on a deep stratum of brown and yellow clay; and although
this is justly the character of all these moors, there are
but few of them entirely destitute of a proportion of dry,
hazel-coloured loam on a sound bottom.

After passing the village of Knowstone and its enclosures, a grey loam on the lower grounds, and a moor or
peaty surface on the tops and sides of the hills, seem to
mark the character of that broad tract of land which lies
south east of the village of Knowstone, and towards the
enclosures of Rakenford, where the proportion of grey
loamy soil seems considerably increased. Continuing this
course to the eastward, the grey loam gives way to one of
a brighter colour, and is found to form a valuable tract
of sound corn and grass land as well towards Stoodleigh,
as on both sides the Little Dart river to its junction with
the Taw. Approaching Templeton from the eastward,
and thence towards Witheridge, the bright brown, or
what is here called Dunstone land, is entirely lost upon a
moory surface resting upon a blue and yellow woodland
clay No change from this general character was observed to take place in this quarter, till after passing
many steep hills, most of which are clothed with wood,
we ascend the hill upon which is situated the village of
Cruwys Mortchard. The southern part of the parish of
West Worlington affords a tract of thin cold clay; which
extends eastwardly towards Thelbridge, and westward
                                            towards

towards Chawley. South of the ridge road leading from
Tiverton to Chumleigh, and in the northern parts of the
parishes of Mortchard Bishops, and Lapford, some very
coarse moor lands continue (as before noticed) to the
foot of Dunridge, where we again enter the Dunstone
district.

Although in the south-western parts of the parishes of
Buckland Brewer, Parkham, and Woolfardisworthy,
thence through East Putford, Bulkworthy, Newton, St.
Petrock and Shebbeare, north-east of the Torridge; crossing that river, thence north-west and north of the Wal-
dron to Milton Damarel, Abbots Bickington, and West
Putford, we find some valuable tracts of good corn and
grass land, still its general character is not sufficient to
exempt it from being included within this district.

Proceeding southwardly from Welcombe, passing the
head of the Tamer and Torridge rivers towards Brad-
worthy, and thence over a large extent of moorlands to
Pancrasswick and Holdsworthy, the face of the country is
less broke into abrupt hills, yet still preserves a leading
character of peaty mould resting on a fox-coloured and
yellow clay. It is not, however, without many inter-
ruptions of a more genial soil, assuming in many places
a bright hazel colour on a sound dry and open subsoil.
The leading features of the country immediately about
Holdsworthy, seem generally more varied than we find at
some distance to the northward from it.

The soil on the more elevated parts of the parishes of
Pyworthy and Bridgerule, is found to consist of a brown
and hazel-coloured loam on a bed of clay mixed with
rubble (here called gravel). The lower grounds or vallies are composed of a black vegetable mould, on an understratum of cold yellow clay, highly retentive of water,
and in all respects resembling the parts of the rank moorlands

lands to the northward. The soil and substrata through the parishes of Clawton, Tetcot, Luffincot, Ashwater, Germansweek, Halwell, and Hollacombe, may be referred generally to the same description, but with the exception of some particular spots, where the soil was found to assume a hazel colour, and to be upon a stratum of freestone. The land in the parishes of Cookbury and Thornbury appears to be of a very wet, cold and clingy nature. Thence towards Bradford the country is found greatly to improve; and in that direction we soon after enter the Dunstone district.

On the way from Hatherleigh to Oakhampton, the lands lying west of the Ochment, and comprising the southern parts of Inwardsleigh and Jacobstow, are found to rise with a gradual ascent eastwardly, and to form spurs of approach to the heights of Dartmoor. Many of these hills are covered with a growth of dwarf oak which form a very close and compact brake, but which, protected when young from the bite of cattle, are stated to rise to the height of 40 feet and upwards. The soil a thin grey loam on an understrata of white and yellow clay. The soil in the neighbourhood of the town of Oakhampton is a tender hazel loam, of a good depth on the schistus or slaty rock, and which here suddenly becomes lost in the granite of the moor, and without that interference of granite gravel so obviously dividing them on the other side of the moor. Included within this district, is a tongue of moor land, which stretches between the red lands of Bow and the northern boundary of the Drewsteignton division, in District No. II. In this quarter is comprised the extensive commons of Broad Nymet, Cooktree Bath, and Eaton Moors.

Proceeding westwardly from Oakhampton, we find the land in the parishes of Sourton, Bridestow, Lidford,

and

and Lewtrenchard, to consist of a grey tender loam of a moderate staple on a brown rubbly clay, resting on the shaley and shillot rock; among the latter of which several veins of limestone, and under the former covering, slate and flags, are found, but which at a distance of four miles from the foot of the moor, are not found to lie with the same regularity before noticed. A considerable portion of what is here called white acre, occurs upon the moors and commons and through many of the enclosures, and although it is found an excellent material for the use of the roads, the farmers seldom consider it as a favourable token.

After passing to the northward of Marystow, a cold grey loam on a white and yellow clay, seems chiefly to prevail through the northern parts of the parishes of Coryton, and thence through the parishes of Thrushalton and Stowford, and the northern parts of the parish of Lifton, where, although the wet clayey character upon a rubble, generally prevails, still, there are some valuable spots of rich feeding land, and a large portion of loose tender loam of a good staple on the dry shaley rock, and which might be advantageously employed in the culture of turnips. Above the point where the road forks leading to Virginstow, St. Giles's, and Luffincot, a tract of good tillage and some meadow lands occur, on the borders of the Cary and Tamar rivers. This general character continues through the parishes of Werrington and Petherwin, where a large extent of moor land has been broken up and burnt, in order to undergo the usual process of exhaustion so fatally experienced in other parts of this country.

Re-crossing the Tamar, and returning thence through St. Giles's in the Heath, Broadwood Wedger, Virginstow, and over Bradbury-down to Bratton Clovella, we find

DEVON.] the

the drier lands generally to consist of a grey, brown, and hazel-coloured loam on a rubbly clay, resting upon a schistus rock, on a black moory soil on a close retentive strata of a blue, yellow, and reddish coloured clay Proceeding again from Bratton Clovella towards Ashbury and Beauworthy, we traverse a considerable extent of moorland, and that generally inferior to what may be met with at Northlew, or towards Inwardleigh; and where for the present, we must close the description of this district.

DISTRICT IV.

South of the river Lyd (which runs through a deep chasm apparently produced by a violent separation of the adjacent hills), the soil in the parishes of Lamerton and Brentor is composed of a well stapled, hazel-coloured loam, lying generally upon a bed of freestone. This land produces a very good pasturage, on account of which the ordinary operations of tillage are very much forborne; the sward being once broken, would require ages to produce an equally valuable herbage. The parishes of Peter Tavy, Mary Tavy, and Tavistock, with the exception of some loose quartz and granite gravel on the heaths and high commons, may be generally stated to answer the above description. The parishes of Sydenham, Milton Abbot, Dunterton, Bradstone, and Kelly, contain a large portion of rich feeding land, intermixed with which are many fields of a dry and gentle nature, and on which the culture of turnips appears to be coming forward with considerable advantage. Along the river Lyd, and through the southern parts of Coryton, Marystow, and the neighbourhood of Lifton, there are many spots of a strong deep

loam

loam lying upon a freestone, and generally preserved in a state of permanent pasture.

The soil in the country for some distance round the borough of Beeralston, consists of a thin grey loam on the killas rock, and which appears to have been much exhausted by a succession of white straw crops. This character will admit of some little modification as we approach Beer Ferrers, when, after crossing the Tavy, the soil in the parishes of Tamerton Foliet, Buckland Mona-chorum, and Whitechurch, is found to be at a greater distance from the common stratum of the country, and assumes a brighter hazel colour. Here the rock breaks up with a less laminous fracture, and the splintery frag-ments, farther broken or decomposed, form an inter-vening stratum of rubbly clay, between the shillot rock and the soil of the country.

The character of the cultivated lands in the parishes of Sampford Spiney, Walkhampton, Sheepstor, Meavy, Shaugh, and Cornwood, all binding eastwardly on the forest of Dartmoor, is that of a bright brown loam on the schistus rock, and a coarse rubbly clay, which seems to intervene between the rock and the commons abutting upon the Moor. In the parish of Bickleigh a deep stra-tum of rubbly clay is often found between the killas rock and the soil. Approaching Egg Buckland, Western Pe-verill, St. Budeaux, and Stoke Damarel, the soil is form-ed of a dark grey, or brownish coloured mould, of a good staple, on the shillot rock and rubbly loam before mentioned, and affords a large quantity of very rich feed-ing and garden ground.

This description equally applies to a large proportion of the parishes of Plymstock, Plympton Earl, and the lower parts of Plympton St. Mary's. The middle division of this latter parish is found to consist of a grey tender

loam

loam on the schistus rock, and beyond it, towards the
Moor, a light peaty earth prevails upon a granite gravel,
in which masses of moorstone and loose quartz very frequently occur.

The parishes of Wembworthy, Newton Ferrers, Re-
velstock, Halberton, Yealmpton, and Brixton, may
generally be described as a dry tender loam on the shillot
rock, and a sound reddish rubbly clay : the former produces
the earliest vegetation in the spring, but both are advantageously employed in the culture of turnips.

The country about Ivy-bridge, and where the parishes
of Cornwood, Ermington, Harford and Ugborough
meet, is truly picturesque and beautiful Such parts of
these parishes as descend from the Moor with a southern
aspect, consist of the peat and granite character, with
similar gradations towards the grey loam and reddish
brown soil noticed in the parish of Plympton St. Mary's;
it is, however, not at all uncommon for this grey and
bright hazel loam to be found on the same ridge, veined,
and alternately taking place of each other.

In the parishes of Modbury, Kingstone, Ringmoor,
and Aveton Giffard, the soil consists of a well-stapled
brown tender loam on a limestone bottom, a cedar-coloured loam on a red ochery rubble, below which the
shillot rock frequently occurs at the distance of three or
four feet, and on the lower grounds a grey moist loam on
a blue and yellow clay, abounding with quartz, but which
seldom exceed in size a cube of four inches. The parishes of West Alwington, Thurlestone, South Milton,
South Huish, and Marlborough, are found to consist of
a sound, dry, grey loam, of a good depth on the shillot
rock, and a cedar-coloured soil equally well-stapled, on a
red rubbly clay. Here turnips are cultivated very generally for early use.

The

The soil in the parishes of Kingsbridge, Dodbrook, Buckland Toutsaints, Sherford, Charleton, South Poole, and the northern parts of Chivelstone and Portlemouth, consist of a well-stapled brown and cedar-coloured loam on a tender shaley rock, and red and yellow rubbly clay, well calculated for the purposes of tillage; comprising a large quantity of rich feeding land, and excellently well watered meadows The south sides of the parishes of Chivelstone and Portlemouth, with the eastern sides of the parishes of Stokenham, Slapton, and Stoke Flemming, consist generally of a thinner stapled soil on the shillot rock, but well adapted for the culture of turnips and barley. The Start Point forms a headland at the south-east extremity of the parish of Stokenham, and where the most prevailing character is a brownish red earth, similar to that noticed in the parishes of South Huish and Marlborough. In the parish of Portlemouth there is about 120 acres of common field land belonging to the hamlet of Raycombe, in that parish; but the whole seems scarcely sufficient to support the expense of an act for its enclosure. There are several coves and indentures in the cliffs between the Start Point and the mouth of the Dart river: through most of these, exclusive of what may be received by Lee-lake, small rivulets of water flow, forming in such hollows, and their small ascending vallies, some of the richest and most fruitful spots in nature; generally, however, the soil in the parishes of St. Petrock, Dartmouth, and Townstall, differs very little in its natural qualities from the country before described. Its vicinity to the port of Dartmouth will necessarily create a considerable increase in its value.

Westwardly, through the south-eastern parts of Black Hauton and East Allington, the soil is composed of a dark grey loam on an understratum of soft shaley rock,

and

and where the light brown, pink, flesh, or cedar-coloured soil, very seldom occurs.

Proceeding northwardly through the remainder of East Allington, the north-west quarter of Black Hauton, and southern parts of Holwell and Morleigh, the grey moist loam on the same shaley subsoil seems most generally to prevail. Here all the higher sides of the hills, incapable of culture, are advantageously appropriated for furze-brakes, whilst the lower sides of such declivities are employed as orchard ground and well watered meadows. Descending towards Harberton-ford, and thence through Harberton to Totness, the thin shivery understratum is lost in a deep stratum of coarse rubbly loam, interspersed with veins of soil and substrata of a cedar colour, and found to comprise a large extent of very rich feeding land. From Totness along the river-hills, through the parish of Ashpreignton, contains a large portion of limestone and Dunstone land. Thence crossing the river Bow at Stips, near its junction with the Ticcaney, and through Cornworthy and Dittisham, a variety of soil and substrata occur, the most prominent distinction of which is a moist, grey and brown loam on the shaley rock, and a cedar-coloured soil of a good staple on a red rubbly clay, lying upon and intermixed with limestone. The red rubbly loam on which the cedar-coloured soil is found is much more dry and friable than the grey or brown loam ; it contains, by analysis of the Rev. Mr. Hutchins, of Dittisham, calcareous earth 3, silex 26, and argil 21.

Crossing the river Dart at Dittisham, and descending towards Kingsware, the shaley subsoil prevails to Neth-way, when, passing Brixham to Berryhead, and thence westwardly through Churchstow, a soil of a bright brown, or cedar colour, was generally observed to lie upon a ubbly loam that intercepted it at various depths from

the

the marble or limestone rock below. This leading character at Stoke Gabriel, was found interrupted with frequent loose and detached blocks of a reddish coloured
freestone, and which along the cliffs at Paignton, seems
consolidated into one united body or stratum of good
building stone. It is here to be observed, that the soil
upon a freestone bottom, or surrounding those loose masses
that lie upon and near the surface, is not so liable to
suffer from a dry spell of weather, as on the rubbly clay
resting upon the limestone rock. The old grass lands
upon this freestone bottom, are stated to have an excellent
feeding quality, but being once subjected to the plough,
will be ages before they again acquire so good an herbage.

The country round Mill-hill, in the parish of Churchstow, and to some distance from the cliffs at Torbay, is
much broken with craggy protuberances, affording but
a moderate staple of soil, which varies from a grey and
hazel loam to a thin staple of vegetable mould, intermixed with coarse quartz and granite gravel. In the parishes of Cockington, Marldon, Little Hempston and
Berry Pomeroy, is a very large portion of excellent tillage
and rich pasture land : this is generally found lying upon
a Dunstone rubble, in which frequently occur large
bodies of limestone. The lands in the parishes of Dartington and Rattery, consist of a cedar-coloured soil of a
good staple on limestone, a stiff yellow clay lying on a
shaley alluminous rock, and a light sandy loam on a bluish
coloured whinstone, exhibiting a liver-coloured fracture, and what is here called Dunstone.

The parishes of Diptford and North Huish, seem to
contain a large proportion of grey loam upon the same
species of shaley rock as above noticed ; the remainder lies
upon a Dunstone of a brownish red colour, and is esteemed considerably above the other land. The southern
parts

parts of the parish of Brent partake in a very great degree of both these qualities; but ascending the commons towards Dartmoor, we meet with the usual character of a peaty surface upon a granity bottom.

In that much broken, though beautifully diversified country on the south-east of Dartmoor, and comprising the parishes of Dean Prior, Buckfastleigh, and the eastern parts of Holne, the soil is found to consist of a reddish brown earth lying upon deep strata of richly marbled limestone. The commons belonging to these parishes abutt westwardly upon the forest of Dartmoor, and are found generally to assimilate with the nature of that waste.

After passing the rich feeding lands in the neighbourhood of Ashburton, the soil in the adjacent villages is various, and lies upon a Dunstone rubbly loam, under which is found the strong schistus blue flag and slate rock, lime rock, and the tender alluminous shaley rock before noticed. The quality of the soil covering this variety of substrata, may be readily conceived by the order in which they are mentioned. Northwardly from Ashburton, through Bickington, the southern parts of Ilsington, Highweek, East and West Ogwell, the western parts of the parish of Woolborough (in which is situated the town of Newton Bushell), Abbots Kirswell, Coffinswell, St. Mary Church, Tormoham, King's Kirswell, Ipplepen, Staverton, Broad Hempston, Torbryan, Denbury, Woodland, and the parish of Ashburton, a rich cedar-coloured loam forms the general character of the soil, under which there are strata of beautifully veined and variegated limestone: these strata are often interrupted by the shaley rock, covered with a grey loam of a moderate staple, and producing a very wet and weeping surface. A Dunstone soil also as frequently occurs,

beneath

beneath which is the schistus rock, that affords a very good covering slate, and flags for flooring. Throughout all this part of the district, the enclosures appear unnecessarily small, but which in a great measure is presumed to arise from vast quantities of loose lime and other stones that have been gathered from the surface, and thrown upon the rocks and uncultivated parts of the lands; thus connecting them into irregular mounds, and in some measure accounting for their unusual number. The limestone does not appear to extend much to the eastward in the parish of Woolborough, or through Comb, or Stoke in Teign-head, the soil being there a grey loam lying upon the shaley rock, intervening with which are flints, quartz, and granite gravel. Near the river-hills, and along the sea-coast, red sandy loam prevails on a dry argillaceous gravel. Through many parts of this country the soil on the south side of the hills lies upon a dark blue rubble, and under which, the blue schistus rock is found to afford very good flooring and covering slates. This soil is not so liable to burn during a spell of dry weather as the thinner stapled limestone land, nor will it crack and open into fissures from the same cause as where the clay subsoil prevails, and which is generally the case through all the low grounds and vallies.

DISTRICT V.

Crossing the Dart river from Holme-park, and continuing thence northwardly through Buckland in the Moor and Widdecombe, a grey loam intermixed with white acre, and lying upon a coarse rubbly clay and granite gravel, generally prevail through the cultivated lands; the uncultivated parts of these parishes are formed of a moist peaty earth on a reddish brown clay, highly retentive

tive of water, and commonly called fox mould. This valley, as well as all the country below the eastern margin of the Moor, comprehending Manaton, North Bovey, Moreton Hempstead, Chagford, Gidley, and Throwsleigh, is excessively broken into abrupt and huge irregularities, terminating in craggy and frightful precipices, the more level surface encumbered with granite rocks and detached masses of moorstone. The soil generally a loose tender loam on a deep stratum of granite gravel. The soil in the parishes of Chagford, Gidley and Throwsleigh (all situated on the eastern foot of the Moor), appear of a superior quality to the lands composing the southern division of the parish of South Tawton. The wild and sterile prospect of this country from several points above Manaton, offers a striking and singular contrast to those rich and luxuriant scenes which in every direction press upon the view from the hill at Denbury. The southern parts of Drewsteignton, the western parts of Bridford, Christow, Lustleigh, and Hemiock, the northern parts of Ilsington, the whole of Bovey Tracy, and the western parts of Teigngrace, may generally be described as a light brown mould on a grey gravelly loam, veined with sand, granite gravel, and a blue and white yellow clay. It was observable in many parts, that the soil covering this variety of substrata, by judicious cultivation produced excellent turnips, barley, clover wheat, oats (and where too strong for permanent pasture), beans and pease.

DISTRICT VI.

A red gravelly loam on a dry argillaceous rubble and grout-stone, is found to occupy the higher country north of the river Teign ; through King's Teignton, Bishop's Teignton, West Teignmouth, and along the coast to Dawlish, the lower grounds bordering upon the river afford

afford a valuable tract of rich marshes, among which, on their upper and western sides, and in the parishes of Teigngrace and King's Teignton, is found a cold thin stapled grey loam on very large bodies of potter's clay. These hold a general direction from the church of King's Teignton towards that of Bovey Tracy: the breadth of these beds vary from a quarter to half a mile; the clay is seldom found of a merchantable quality nearer than from 25 to 30 feet of the surface; it is often separated by veins of inferior woodland clay; but the potter's clay is always found to hold its relative positions with each other, viz. southwardly the pipe clay; the light brown sort in the middle; and northwardly the crackling clay. The criterion of excellence is, to find in this clay certain small specks or particles of Bovey coal. The waste clay dug out of these pits is converted into a beautiful white durable brick, by the admixture of about one-third part of sand. The clay is first dried in the open air, and then pounded and mixed dry with the sand, and afterwards worked and tempered together. It is necessary the bricks should be well dried before putting them in kilns, which holding 30,000 each, will require 4000 furze faggots to burn them, costing about five guineas. The common price of the bricks 50s. per 1000 at the kiln.

In the distance before described on the coast, the hills, though steep and numerous, afford large portions of very good grass and tillage land. The subdivisions here appear unnecessarily small, but for this the same reason is not to be assigned as before stated.

In the parish of Dawlish there is a large proportion of coarse, though highly improvable land. A large range of sand-hills extend south-westwardly from the mouth of the river Axe: these are chiefly appropriated as a warren; some of their lower parts have been enclosed with a view

to

to improvement, but the rank driving sand of which the surface is composed, defeated the undertaking. Among these sand-hills are some lagoons or lakes of salt water, where the making of salt has lately been renewed with the prospect of answering very well.

The country rises gradually towards the north-east, and is richly diversified with woodland. The hills and dales afford some very good pasture and tillage lands. Along the steep side-hills, which form the small but handsome vale of Ashcombe, is a large proportion of good orchard ground, the soil generally of a tender nature, and much used for the culture of turnips. The red sandy loam generally characterizes the beautiful demesne of Mamhead, and continues through Kenton, Powderham, and Kenn, where understrata of grey and white sand and sandstone seems occasionally to prevail; but northwardly towards Shillingford, this substrata seems entirely lost in a red rubbly gravel and grout stone, which continues through Exminster, Shillingford, Alphington, and Id, to Exeter.

Proceeding thence through Newton St. Cyres, Crediton, and the country of Colebrook, Clannaborough, Bow, or Nymet Tracy, Broad Nymet, North Tawton, Sampford Courtenay, Exbourne, and Jacobstow, towards Hatherleigh, the rich red loam is found to vary in its strength and quality, from its lying at a greater or less distance on a deep bed of red rubbly gravel, or from its vicinity to a red pummice-like marl, which in the parishes of Colebrooke and North Tawton, is found between the soil and a hard brown rock usefully employed in repairing the roads, and forming excellent building stone. This latter is justly esteemed by far the strongest and richest land. Under the former description of soil and substrata, may fairly be classed all that beautiful country
lying

lying along the Creedy, the Exe, and the Culm rivers, and bounded northwardly by District No. II. Along these water-courses are large and valuable tracts of marsh and meadow grounds, subject to annual inundation. Where those streams become limited in extending their enriching waters by the risings of the lower grounds, they are taken up at the highest level the country will afford, and thus their fertilizing qualities are spread to a wider extent by the artificial means of irrigation.

This country is beautifully enriched with wide and handsome vales, the sides of which are chequered with fruitful orchards and thriving woodlands: the lovely verdure of the grass grounds, the broad swells and undulations of its higher parts, the declivities of which, adorned with houses and the improvements of the inhabitants, give the whole an air of considerable fertility and interest with the passing traveller.

The town of Cullumpton, like many others in the county of Devon, is situated in the bosom of a rich and fruitful country. The red loamy sand is found to prevail generally along the Culm river, through Uffculm, and Culmstock, to the borders of Somerset. Returning thence southwardly along the foot of the Black-down hills, the same character of country continues through Kentisbeare, and Broadhembury, to the head western branches of the river Otter, and an eastern branch of the river Culm; thence through the western parts of Payhembury, Plymtree, Clayhaydon, Clyst St. Lawrence, with intervening red gravelly loam and grout-stone. This sandy quality extends to the city of Exeter, and after passing its delightful environs, through Topsham, and down the eastern side of the Exe river, the red or cedar-coloured loam seems gradually to fade, and finally terminates at Lympston and Withecombe, in a light red.

sandy

sandy soil upon a coarse siliceous gravel, veined with brick earth, and in which there is frequently found a brown and blue stone marl. This, from the number of pits in the fields, must formerly have been much used as a manure.

Continuing eastwardly along the coast through Exmouth, Littleham, Withecombe Rawleigh, East Budleigh, Otterton, Bicton, and Colyton Rawleigh, the light sandy soil prevails through the cultivated parts of the country, and generally lying on a deep bed of red sand, sand-rock, and coarse pebbly gravel. Approaching the wastes of Woodbury, this substrata becomes mixed with flints, quartz, brown and white sandstones, dark, blue, and greenish coloured pebbles, below which is sometimes observed a deep bed of red sand, veined with strong red loam or brick earth. This great variety of substrata is covered with a soil, the basis of which is sand and reddish brown loam of a much stronger and tougher texture. Upon the former, turnips are sometimes cultivated ; on the latter, pease, beans, and wheat. Ascending the river Otter, the country westwardly towards Woodbury-common, and eastwardly ranging along the foot of the hills forming Sidmouth Gap, although strongly marked with the sandy character, is found to include large bodies of strong red gravelly clay, mixed with the blue and red indurated marl before noticed. The sandy soil so far prevails, as to have induced some years since the culture of carrots in the parishes of Harpford, Fen Ottery, Ottery St. Mary's, and the western parts of Feniton. Crossing thence the river Otter towards Tallaton, the black, white, and grey flints are suddenly lost in the same coarse pebbly gravel observed at Bicton, but which, in addition to the sand-rock before noticed, is farther varied by a strong tough stratum of red clay, which, when mixed with the

common

common marl of the country, is found to make good bricks. This strong clay continues veined with a sandy loam upon a deep bed of fine gravel and a sand-rock, with frequent occurrence of the red tender loam or marl of the country, through the parishes of Whimple, Rockbeare, Aylesbeare, Honiton, Clyst, and Farrington. Through St. George's Clyst, St. Mary's Clyst, Sowton, and Heavitree, a greater uniformity prevails, and the soil is found generally to consist of a red, rich friable loam, lying to a good depth upon the grout-stone rock.

Throughout the whole of this district there are numerous orchards, the fruit in which, with few exceptions, seems to have generally succeeded this year. In many places a luxuriant growth of oak, ash, and elm, particularly the latter, appear to conspire with the small enclosures, in overshading by far too large a proportion of this truly valuable country.

DISTRICT VII.

The soil between Ottery and Sidmouth consists of a strong brown loam on a tough red flinty clay, and a light sandy loam on a deep bed of sand, and sand-rock of the same colour. Crossing the peak of Sidmouth Gap, the beautiful valley of the Sid appears opening upon the coast, displaying the town and bathing shores of Sidmouth to a great advantage. Ascending the coarse and flinty sides of Salcombe-hill, its top is found to spread into a sheep-down of some extent, affording a short and sweet herbage, but on which huge masses of conglomerated flints, rising above the surface, interrupt the operations of tillage in the adjacent enclosures. A tract of good turnip and barley land, lying chiefly on a dry flinty gravel, intermixed with small portions of a stronger soil, are found generally

to

to prevail through the interior of the parishes of Salcombe, Branscombe, and Bur. Along the sea coast the
soil is generally composed of a strong reddish brown flinty
loam, at various depths, upon a deep stratum of chalk,
beneath which, and at the distance of about twenty feet
below the floors of the present chalk pits, levels are driven
near the foot of the hills, into immense bodies of freestone, which tallies in every respect with that of Portland.
The stone rises in similar blocks, and when quarried, is
in every respect equally valuable. This stratum of freestone is found generally to occur under all the chalk cliffs
from Branscombe to Lyme Regis in Dorsetshire.

A tract of recently embanked salt-marsh on the western
side of the river Axe, between Seaton and the half yearly
meadow grounds below Colyton-bridge, promises to answer extremely well. The high lands on both sides the
river Axe, are formed of a strong and sandy loam upon
a tough red flinty clay and gravelly subsoil. At Charton,
within the parish of Axemouth, a stratified body of limestone, and a solid bed of chalk, are found within the space
of the same acre. Continuing along the sea coast, the
same flinty loams prevail on occasional bodies of chalk,
and which in the parish of Uplime terminates in the hard
stratified lime-rock before mentioned, and which consists
of a dark blue, and a dun white, or cream coloured stone.
These strata are distinguished by the name of blue or grey
lais limestone. Enclosed between these strata is the strongest and richest marl in nature: it seems to have undergone
a most violent compression, and although it readily falls
like lime, by exposure to the air, was not understood to
have ever been applied as a manure to the flinty or sandy
loams of the neighbourhood.

Northwardly from Uplime and Musbury, there is an
extensive range of commons, the soil of which, with that
of

of the adjacent enclosures, consist of a brown loam of a good depth on a tough flinty clay, and perhaps better adapted for tillage than for pasture. A considerable part of the neighbourhood of Axminster, and down the eastern side of the valley towards Musbury, lies upon the strati- fied limestone rock above described. The wide and lovely valley of the Axe, contains a large body of rich feeding and meadow land, the soil, as usual in such situations, being chiefly formed by a deposition of sediment from the inun- dating waters, and which are here found to possess the most fructifying qualities. The same character of soil and substrata, but without the apparent intervention of the stratified lime-rock, is found to continue along the higher grounds. North-east of this valley, through Kilmington and Dalwood (the latter composing a part of the county of Dorset), a strong red stone marl, preserving nearly a horizontal position, and found on corresponding levels, seems generally to spread or stretch through all the hills from the sea coast into the interior country. This has been formerly much used as a manure, but latterly little attention appears to have been paid to it. The hill east- wardly of the valley, in which is situated the village of Membury, is of a similar character to that stated of Up- lime, and which continues eastwardly through Dorset- shire, and includes the part of Devon which comprises the parish of Thorncombe and Ford Abbey.

The ridge lying west of the village of Membury consists of a strong flinty loam on a solid bed of chalk, extending north-west and northwardly towards the coarse commons in the county of Dorset. The surface here is frequently encumbered with detached masses of a close freestone rock. Westwardly through Stockland (and that part of the county of Dorset lying within the general outline of

DEVON.]   the

the county of Devon) the chalk entirely disappears, and the soil on the tops of the ridges is formed of a close brown loam on a tough flinty clay; on their sides, the red tender loam or marl before noticed generally occurs, and produces along the lower parts of the hills and vallies, large tracts of rich feeding ground and meadows.

A thin cold grey loam, mixed with an imperfectly crystallized flint or hard sandstone, forms the soil in the higher parts of the parish of Wedworthy : descending thence into the vale of Honiton, a brown tender loam upon a red and blue marl, is found to prevail through all the lower and less elevated parts of that neighbourhood. Ascending the valley of the Otter, on its higher parts are found a more light and tender soil, of a hazel colour, but abounding with flint and the sandstone before mentioned. This is found to be the case through Comberawleigh, Monkton Luppit and Upottery : Yarcombe is favorably situated on the south east hang of a hill, and on a body of red and blue marl; this latter occurs very frequently among the rich red marl, and although it does not ferment so strongly with common vinegar, it still preserves a preference in the estimation of the farmers.

The country above Yarcombe, and east of the river Otter, extends into coarse uncultivated moors and commons. Northwardly of the church, and extending towards Otterford, in the county of Somerset, the stratified blue and white lais lime-rock again occurs under a strong brown loam, on a tough flinty clay. In the northern parts of the parish of Upottery, and through Church Staunton, the soil chiefly consists of a loose brown mould on a yellow woodland clay and fox mould. The new enclosures lately made in this parish, appear to afford some very good turnips, barley, oats, wheat, and

clover;

clover; the fields are vastly overcharged with water, but have otherwise a handsome appearance, their surface being only slightly strewed with loose flints and sandstone*.

After passing the village to the westward, the country rises with a more broken aspect: towards Clayhaydon the soil and substrata possess a much stronger quality, but greatly abounding with flints and sandstones. Some enclosures have been recently made in this parish, which, when properly drained and cultivated, cannot fail answering extremely well. This character continues along the Black-down hills southwardly towards Hemiock, where the valley of the Culm affords some valuable tracts of pasture and meadow ground, and which, in like manner with those on the river Otter, are usually employed in depasturing dairy cows.

Proceeding towards the head of the valley in which is situated the parish of Sheldon, we gradually emerge from the sandy district, and again ascending the Black-down hills, their high table tops are found to spread into an extensive plain, the soil changing to a light brown loam on a fox mould, below which is a deep and universal bed of chip sand, affording very good whetstones, and found uniformly to rest upon the great horizontal field of red tender loam or marl before noticed. The parish of Dunkerswell comes generally under this description, but here it may be proper to observe, that wherever the chip sand and marl come to day, the more retentive stratum of the latter holds up the water, till it bursts forth in

---

* Near the village of Church Staunton a field of oats was still in the shock on the 1st of October; the crop was large in point of burthen, but from the wetness of the ground, the turnips which preceded it were not fed off till the end of April: the oats were sown on the last Friday of that month, with seeds.

springs

springs and weeping ground; and hence the morass and
peaty margins along all the declivities and side-hills in
this country. These morasses are found frequently to
abound with bog-timber; an oak of this description was
recently raised out of a bed of peat near Woodford-lodge,
which squared 15 inches at the butt, and was about 20
feet long; the whole of its sap was gone, and it had much
the appearance of being a fork or a branch of a much
larger tree: General Simcoe was offered five guineas for
it before it was taken up, but this he thought proper to
decline.

The stratum of red loamy marl, with its corresponding understratum of strong building stone, as noticed
along the coast, is found generally below the chip sand
on the Black-down hills and their adjoining hollows:
still this marly stratum must not be considered as holding
an unbroken field up to that height, for although Dunkerswell, Broadhembury and Payhembury commons, will
afford the loamy marl within 100 feet of the brow of the
Black-down hills, still the surface of the valley to the
westward is greatly below this level, and in many places
covered to a considerable depth of sand, through which
we find it necessary to pass, to come at the stratum of red
loamy marl below.

The soil in the parishes of Awliscombe, Buckerell, and
Fineton, may be referred to what has been generally said
of the vale of Honiton, and which, in like manner, is
usually employed in the depasturing of dairy cows. A
strong flinty loam seems to prevail through the parishes
of Gittisham, Farway, and Offwell. This continues
through the southern parts of Wedworthy, where, near
to the church, a body of chalk is found covered with the
soil and substance above stated. Crossing the Coley
river, the east side of the valley becomes of a more light
and

and tender nature; rising the hills on that side, the chip sand appears capped with a deep body of strong flinty loam, which generally f rms the upper brow of the hills; but their highest plains become afterwards covered with a brown, wet, sandy loam Approaching the parish of Shute, the brown sandy loam again gives way to one of a stronger nature, and which continues along the fruitful hills and vallies of the Coley and Axe rivers.

After passing the immediate neighbourhood of Colyton, the soil through the parishes of North and South Leigh and Sidbury consists of a dry flinty loam upon a coarse gravel, and a brown moory loam on a woodland clay mould. The dry stratum is always preferred, and fox whether for winter or spring corn, and the grass grounds, which are here generally very good, are usually employed for the purpose of feeding dairy cows.

It is to be remarked, that in proceeding along the sea-coast, the round coarse pebble stones and gravel was entirely lost among the flints before we reached Sidmouth, and that the flints do not occur in such numbers over the stratified lime-rock, as on the solid beds or bodies of chalk. The lime measure in this district by the hogshead, consists of 36 liquid Winchester pecks, price 3l. per hogshead.

SECT.

SECT. V.—MINERALS.

DISTRICT I.

SOME years since a vein of culm appearing near the surface on the parish of Chittlehampton, induced trials to be made of its quality, which proving satisfactory, a company was formed for the purpose of working it. This association continued for about two years, during which time five or six weys of culm were raised, and which was usefully employed in burning lime. The vein varied from about four inches to one foot in thickness : held a course correspondent with the general lay of the strata through the country, and dipped to the southward about one foot in three. The disappointment to several of the party, by the thinness of the seam, and the extraordinary expense consequently incurred in raising so small a quantity, occasioned the relinquishment of the project, although great expectations are still entertained in the neighbourhood, that the attempt will be renewed on a future day.

In the parish of Swimbridge a copper mine has been discovered, but of its extent and value little is at present known. At North Molton a copper mine is now working, which heretofore yielded considerable advantages : what may be the issue of the present efforts, it is impossible to say, as the works now carrying on have not had sufficient time to form any thing like a fair estimate of their probable success.

A considerable quantity of very rich ironstone is annually sent from the neighbourhood of Combe-martin

to

to Mr. Raby's iron-works at Llenethy, in South Wales. About two years ago attempts were made at Abbotsham for coal, and at Alwington for copper: not finding any thing at the former place to encourage a continuance of search (and at the latter place large quantities of mundic only), both works were prudently abandoned, together with all expectations of future indemnity for the expense incurred. The lead and silver mines of Combe-martin are also well known in history; but why they are suffered to lie at rest at this time, is difficult to determine.

A body of lead has recently been discovered in this neighbourhood, which, from the trials already made of its value, promises to answer extremely well. The lime-rocks in the cliffs, and along the indented shores of Watermouth and Combe-martin, seem imbedded in the shillot and stratified rock of the country; and although no appearance of these veins has been discovered in the parishes of Kentisbury and Parracombe, there remains little doubt of their continuing in that direction, and towards Sadler's Stone (which marks the north-west extremity of Exmoor), and ranging, it may be presumed, unseen through the base of the forest, to where it crops out to the southward of Lanacre-bridge, in the county of Somerset.

Near the line delineated on the map, and running parallel to it, is another body of limestone, at present worked little to the westward of the parish of Ilfracombe. Passing thence eastwardly to Berry-narber lime-works, thence north of East-down, and south of Kentisbury to the Challacombe lime-works, the identity of this vein is presumed to be fully shown from the following particulars occurring along the line: the specimens taken up at Ilfracombe, Berry-narber, Westland Pound, in the southern part of the parish of Kentisbury, and at

Lord

Lord Fortescue's lime-works in the parish of Challacombe, all exactly correspond in colour, which is a greyish brown; its texture, which is very close, is thinly veined with a calcareous spar; showing but few granulous sparks when presented obliquely to the light, smooth to the touch, and more glossy in its fracture than other limestone. It is covered at various depths with the same bright brown coloured shillot, combined with the like blue schistus, flag or hard slaty rock, and from which it requires much practice, and a quick discerning eye, to distinguish the one from the other. It no where partakes of the regular dip or inclination of the stratum, in which it is embodied, but is broken and interrupted with what the miners call shear-heads and saddles. The lime-rock is found without any regularity or order, save that of the course it holds with the common strata of the hills.

In examining the country in the direction of this vein, the remains of an old lime-kiln was discovered near Westland Pound, the working of which, upon inquiry, was found to have been discontinued through the management and address of the lime-burners at Combemartin. Upon the whole, there remains little doubt of the continuation of this bed of limestone, and of its existence through the whole line of country distinguished upon the map. From the limestone which is known to compose a part of the promontory that projects northwardly in the parish of Fremington, and occasions that sudden bend in the river Taw, opposite to Heantonhouse, there are reasonable grounds for presuming that this limestone is a part of a body or vein as yet undiscovered, running through the parishes of Braunton, Heanton Puncharbon and Barnstable, and continued parallel with the veins of limestone before and hereafter to be mentioned.

The

The next vein of limestone that occurs southwardly in this district, is that cropping out near St. Anne's chapel, in the parish of Heanton Punchardon; passing thence eastwardly through the parish of Fremington, where the vein does not exceed five feet in thickness, and is enclosed in a stratum of hard bluish building stone, occasionally veined with a fluor of quartz: thence through Bickington, Bishop's Tawton, Swimbridge, the north part of Filleigh and south part of Molland Bouceaux, West Anstey, and through the parishes of Dulverton and Shilgate, in the county of Somerset. This vein is composed of a narrow stratum of blue lais limestone, of from ten to twenty feet in thickness, covered with a deep stratum of clay produced by a decomposition of the shaley rotten-stone rock; is without any regular dip or inclination, and seems turned about by the frequent occurrence of shear-heads, from an oblique to a perpendicular direction, as often dipping to the east or west as to the north or south. It is embodied in a stratum of strong bluish building stone, to which it is so closely united, as to render it as difficult to separate as it is for a stranger to distinguish the one from the other. A much larger proportion of calcareous spar seems to pervade this limestone than that before noticed. It also possesses a brighter bluish colour, although it is evidently of a less firm and compact texture.

South of this line, and in the neighbourhood of Instow, is a stratified body of limestone, from one to three feet in thickness, extending eastwardly through the northern parts of the parish of Harwood; thence the same course continued through the parishes of Chittlehampton, South Molton, the northern parts of Bishop's Nympton, by Ward's mill, through the parishes of East Anstey and

and Brushford. This vein appears to be wedged in by a
compact bed of thick slate, or rather flag-stone, found
very useful for building, covering drains, &c. The
limestone in this mass does not seem to differ materially
in quality from the last described. It appears to rise at
a considerable angle from the horizon. Immediately on
the top of the limestone is a ragstone which readily
divides into lamina, and dissolves by exposure to the air.
The course and presence of this limestone is generally
discoverable by a body of black shillet gravel produced
from the laminous rock, which in some places immediately covers the limestone, and breaking into small fragments, is found to be an excellent material for repairing
the roads.

These are all the veins of limestone which has occurred to observation in this district; little doubt however is entertained, that had circumstances allowed of a
more minute inquiry, indications of other veins would
have been discovered between the north line of limestone
near Castle-hill park and the body of limestone rock now
working at Challacombe. The general lay of the strata
being thus ascertained, and the uniform continuation of
the limestone in the same direction, affords some ground
to hope that this may lead to farther and more important
discoveries of the like nature, in which the future improvement of the country seems so much dependent. A
black shillot gravel frequently occurs in the neighbourhood of Alwington and Land-cross, but no limestone has
been discovered in its vicinity.

A slate formerly taken up at East Alwington, and ex-
ported under the name of Holland blues, is at this time
worked merely for the supply of the surrounding neighbourhood: but on the return of peace, it is most pro-
                                                    bable

bable that the export trade of this article will be
resumed.

A large quantity of ochre, of various shades between
red and yellow, was formerly found and manufactured in
the parish of East-down In the parish of Combe-
martin there is also a body of umber: these were formerly worked and prepared for market in the country,
but of late years have been little attended to.

The digging and sending coastways the pipe-clay found
at Wear Giffard, has been much discontinued of late
years; a considerable quantity, however, of the brown
potter's clay is raised in the parish of Fremington, and
conveyed to Barnstable, and coastways to other places,
for making crocks, jars, milk-pans, and all the coarse
articles of brown or common earthen-ware.

DISTRICT II.

The minerals occurring in this district will be found
chiefly confined to limestone either actually discovered,
or the direction in which it is most likely to be found
pointed out, as well as the nature of the inquiry has hitherto admitted. Previously, however, it will be necessary to notice, that on descending near the borders of the
river Bovey, in the parish of Lustleigh, a large quantity
of plumbago was found, recently raised and prepared for
the Exeter market; also to state, that a few years since
some culm was discovered in the parish of High Heanton:
this was worked for a short time, but the seam not proving more than two inches thick, and the water suddenly
coming upon the workmen, the vein was relinquished.
Large portions of pipe clay were formerly dug on the
demesne lands f Petrockstow, and shipped round from
Bideford to the potteries in Staffordshire. A spring of
brackish

brackish water rises in one of these old clay-pits, where, from the tracts of castle approaching in all directions, it seems as much frequented as were formerly the celebrated salt licks in the western parts of America: it emits a strong sulphurous vapour in the warm and moist weather, and whenever it overflows, its waters mark their extent by barrenness and sterility.

The limestone in the neighbourhood of Chudleigh seems to lie without any determinate direction, nor is it otherwise particularly to be distinguished than by lying in parallel strata, and with little or no dip or inclination any way. This stone is of a reddish, and of a dark blue colour, capable of taking a very high polish, and formerly much in demand at Exeter and other large towns in the country, for chimney-pieces, and other useful and ornamental purposes. Vast quantities of this stone are carried in a raw state to lime-kilns at a distance, where it is burnt with furze or other faggots, in what are called flame-kilns built rather egg-shaped. The heat in the furnace below is not always kept steady and constant, as when burning lime with culm, but by sudden and ardent spirts. Stones the size of a horse's head are calcined in them.

The next body of limestone known in this district is that of Drewsteignton. This has not yet been traced to the eastward of the village, but westwardly it has been worked for many years: here it is found in such close union with the blue building stone, as to occasion the removal of a large body of rock for a comparatively small portion of limestone: it is extremely irregular in its dip, but seems to hold a general course with the ridge which lies west, a little northwardly.

This rock is covered with a brown rubbly loam, and affords the excellent corn and grass land before noticed. The price of this lime at the work is 7s. per hogshead of

about

about 11½ heaped Winchester bushels; it falls, when slaked, into a dark cream-coloured powder, and is much in demand for cement in water-works. This vein is most probably the same as that worked at Hobhouse, and which in all likelihood continues under the northern base of Dartmoor, to the limestone cropping out and working near the west end of the park at Oakhampton.

The strata in the neighbourhood of the Moor lies so very irregular, and apparently jumbled together, that it is perhaps going too far to hazard a conjecture on the subject. The lime-rocks at South Tawton, which for many years have been worked principally for manure, appear to occupy a much wider portion of the ridge than the limestone strata at Drewsteignton; it seems as closely embodied in strata of building stone, and equally difficult at first view to distinguish the one from the other. Although this limestone has not yet been traced farther to the eastward than the present works, yet, from its charac-ter and course, there remains little doubt of its continuing much farther, and that in future it will most probably be found somewhere to the eastward, and between the parish church of Hittesleigh, and Gidburn St. Mary's; and west-wardly a little to the northward of Oakhampton. This lime falls into the same dark cream-coloured powder above noticed, and varies from 6s. 6d. to 7s. per hogshead, the same measure as that at Drewsteignton. Besides these, there are other veins of limestone, originating in and traced through this district, which from the regularity of their course may be presumed to extend much farther.

The limestone at Sampford Peverill is found nearly to correspond with certain indications of lime-rock between King's Nympton and Romansleigh. This vein may pro-bably diverge to the southward, and connect with the body of limestone stated to have been discovered in the parish

parish of Cruwys Mortchard. The Westleigh quarry is a vast mass of limestone, thinly coated with what the workmen call flint, but so closely united with, and resembling the limestone, that it is difficult for any but the workmen to distinguish immediately between them—The price of the lime at this kiln is 3s. per hogshead of forty pecks, measured in eight or ten-peck bags.

The surface of the rock is covered with a tender laminous stone, which dissolves by exposure to the air : it is clearly a part of the same vein which is now worked on the east side of the river Exe, in the parish of Bampton, and is supposed to extend towards Pye's Nest in the Moorland district. The stone at Holcombe-rogus, Rochworth, Hunshaw, and Bampton, are all of the same character. These veins most probably extend also through the moors, the presence of which westwardly would be best pointed out by the occurrence of black gravel in a direction between the churches of Bishop's and George Nympton, south of the town of Chittlehampton, and to wards Westleigh on the Torridge river. The shillot rock along the whole extent of this vein is found to rise in thick splinters, and which, when farther broken, forms the black gravel above noticed. This limestone, as far as it has yet been traced, lies in a bed of close blue rock, and which is found to make excellent building stone. Certain indications of this nature. have led to a conjecture that a body of limestone is to be found in the parish of Cheriton Fitzpaine. On the western part of the Horridge moor, lying one mile and a quarter north-east from Chumleigh, the black gravel crops out alongside the parish road leading through the parsonage court, or farm yard. From this place east, and about three quarters of a mile distant, towards the head of a hollow on an estate called Compland, a vein of bluish-grey limestone, spotted

with

with white, and imbedded in a dark blue shillot, is found
to crop out alongside of a small brook that descends
through the valley: of this stone some lime has already
been made. About a mile south-east from the church at
King's Nympton, and on an estate called Weddington
Farm, some detached pieces of limestone have also been discovered. The ridge upon which this was found runs eastwardly towards Stoodleigh, and most probably contains a
body of limestone corresponding with that at Sampford
Peverill.

The Surveyor must here beg leave to express a wish
that these conjectures should be regarded more in the
light of hints, than as any certain information to the land-
owners and occupiers of the country; but should they
prove the means of discovering one body of limestone
only, in the many places that may be suggested by the
lines on the map, his motive for thus stating them will be
fully answered.

In the several directions marked on the map, limestone
is found dispersed in various strata, and in veins of different thickness: a heavy expense attends the raising this
stone, which, added to that of the carriage of culm, rarely
enables the lime-burner of English stone to supply the
farmer at less than 1s. 6d. the double Winchester bushel.
The stone burnt at Barnstable is all brought from the
coast of Wales, averaging at the kiln about 5s. per
ton; the Abberthaw limestone 7s. per ton. These
are burnt in kilns about fourteen feet wide at top
and three feet in diameter at the bottom, forming an inverted cone a little swelled in the middle, and discharging
800 double Winchesters of lime per week; in doing
which they are stated to consume seven Barnstable, or
three and a half Swansea weys of culm; each Swansea
wey containing ten tons weight, and a capacity of 216
heaped

heaped Winchester bushels. It is however stated, that 48
measures only of coal or culm makes a Barnstable wey,
averaging four tons weight, which difference may in some
measure be accounted for by the contents of the Swansea
wey being 216 single heaped Winchesters, and the Barnstable measure of 16 gallons having a conical form, with
a considerable diminution of diameter on the top. The
English stone does not require within one-third of the
culm to calcine it as the Welsh, and is held in much
higher estimation, either for cement or manure, than the
latter. The Abberthaw lime, chiefly used in water-works,
seems not to require so much culm as the Oxwich, Pool-
ridge, Mumbles, and other limestone brought from the
coast of Wales; the lime from which is generally delivered at the kilns at Barnstable, and Bishop's Tawton, at
1s. 4d. the double heaped Winchester measure.

Between Appledore and Wear Giffard, on the Torridge,
there are 25 lime-kilns: these, when at work, which may
be stated at one half the year, yield every twenty-four
hours 100 common measures of lime, and sells at from
13d. to 16½d. per bushel. The price of culm for the
supply of these kilns is about 65s. the wey, of 48 double
Winchesters, delivered at the vessel's side in the harbour
of Bideford. The ordinary flow of the spring-tides at
Wear Giffard is eight feet.

DISTRICT III.

In the parish of Bridestow a lode of copper has lately
been discovered within six or seven fathoms of the surface:
the ore is generally combined with spar. A soft or earthy
ore of copper has also been found in the same parish; but
the extent of these bodies, or whether on farther search
they

they may be found worth attending to, is left to future investigation and inquiry.

The male or bastard tin stone is found generally on the commons abutting on Dartmoor, on Bradbury-down, and other places in this district: as is also a large portion of iron-stone on the borders of the Ochment river, and variously dispersed over the whole of this district. A vein of freestone appears to the eastward of Thomas's House, in the parish of Clawton: it was traced eastwardly in various layers up the river Claw, and thence through the parishes of Ashwater, Holwell, Beaworthy, and North Lew. This stone has been much worked in former times, as several churches in the neighbourhood have been built with it. It rises irregularly, but often in large pieces, as is plain from the size of the stones in the buildings, and the large masses used for weighting the levers of the cider-presses. The thickness of this quarry in the parish of North Lew is about ten feet, and continues through the southern parts of the parish of Hatherleigh; it is soft, and easily worked from the quarry, but hardens in the air. The name of the estate where this stone is now worked, is Cleve, and belongs to the family of Morris.

There is a great deal of good covering slate raised in this district; but the quarries of Lewtrenchard and Werrington hold the first rank in point of value and quality: some covering slates have been found near the Ochment, east of Oakhampton, but they do not appear objects of much consideration.

A large body of limestone, answering to the description of the Drewsteignton quarry, is found in the hamlet of Maldon, and near the south end of Oakhampton park: a large quantity of this stone has been formerly used, but notwithstanding the lime is said to have been much

DEVON.] valued,

valued, the works at this time appear totally abandoned. Limestone also occurs at Sourton, Bridestow, Lewtrenchard, and Lifton; but the general confusion of strata for some distance round the Moor, prevents any possibility of tracing a connexion of these quarries with each other. The common price of lime at the Lewtrenchard and other lime-works in the district, is about 1s. 4d. the double Winchester bushel.

A large mass of limestone was picked up some years since near the foot of the ridge on which the old castle of Aston is situated, in the parish of West Warlington: it seems much to correspond with the limestone raised at Sampford Peverill; as, like that, it appears to have been taken out of a bed of partially indurated silex, where it probably formed a sort of nucleus for the further concretion and conversion of that substance into calcareous matter; how this mass came here, or why no more has been found, must also be left to farther search and inquiry.

A body of limestone was stated to have been discovered near the village of Rackenford; but of the actual existence of this important mine no certain proofs could be procured by the Surveyor, in his progress through that quarter.

There are many detached stones on the sides of the hills forming the valley of the Little Dart river; most of these have a smooth appearance, and show a liver-coloured fracture: below the rubbly stratum which forms the sub-soil of these hills a very good building stone is found to rise, with a smooth face covered with an ochreous matter, which seems to have flowed through the veins of the rock: this facilitates its being quarried for building, and for which it is much used.

DISTRICT IV.

There are two copper-mines now working in the neighbourhood of Tavistock; one to the north-east, the other about a mile south-west of the town; they are supposed to be a continuation of the same lode, which is worked from the depth of about 10 to 60 fathom: the ore in its raw state sells for about 7*l.* 10*s.* per ton.

A lead-mine is now working on the west side of the river Tavy, in the parish of Beer Ferrers.

Some old tin stream-works have lately been renewed in the parish of Plympton St. Mary's, and in such a manner as gives great hope of success to the present proprietors.

In the parish of Rattery there are some old iron-works, which indicate that formerly ore or ironstone was found in that neighbourhood: at present there is no extraordinary appearance of any such mineral. In the bed of the river Tavy, and upwards along its banks, considerable quantities of limestone have lately been discovered. The limestone along the sides of the river Yealme, both above and below the town of Yealmton, breaks up into very large blocks of red and white, and black and white marble, all of which are capable of receiving a very good polish: the former very much resembles the Plymouth and Catdown rocks.—A number of slate-quarries are dispersed through the whole of this district, appropriate for flag and covering.

It is no very easy matter to form a distinct idea of what is meant by dunstone; it seems, like the schistus, to be derived from the same argillaceous origin. The vitriolic principle combined with the schistus produces slate; this rock crops out with thin harsh laminæ, and is clearly different from the shaley rock, the leafy atoms of which

have

have a glassy appearance, are soapy to the touch, and
often forms the basis of its soil or surface covering.
Wherever the slaty character of the rock ends, the indurated mass is found combined with an oxyde of iron,
which disposes its superior parts to a more splintery and
less laminous fracture : this, farther broken, is called dunstone, and consists of rough irregular stones of from one
to eight inches cubic measure. A similar kind of rubble
is often found in a deep bed of clay upon the shaley rock,
but generally in a state of more obvious dissolution. The
permanent colour of the limestone enclosed within the
stratum of schistus rock is blue, streaked with veins of
calcareous spar. The colour of the limestone or marble
occurring within the stratum of dun or building-stone, is
more beautifully varied ; but where the marble rock is
found compact and without any interference of argillaceous strata, as at Cat-down, Marychurch, Buckfastleigh,
and Bickington, its diversity of grain, and the admirable
polish it is capable of receiving, occasions large quantities
to be quarried into blocks and slabs, some of which are
converted in the neighbourhood, and others transported
in their rough state to different parts of England. The
rocks at Marychurch, lying near the surface, and apparently detached from the quarry, exhibit the most beautiful arrangement of colours, the impression of shells, and
the various exuviæ of an antediluvian world. Vast
quantities of limestone are converted at all these quarries
into lime for the purpose of manure ; the average expense
of which may be stated as follows :

Culm,

	£.	s.	d.
Culm, 40 quarters, at 11s. per quarter, ...	22	0	0
Carriage of ditto, 2s. 6d. ditto, ...	6	0	0
Ripping 240 hogsheads, ...	7	10	0
Liquor to burners, ...	0	10	0
Lighterage, ...	2	10	0
	£. 38	10	0

PER CONTRA.

	£.	s.	d.
240 hogsheads of lime, at 4s. per hogshead, ..	48	0	0
Expenses (deducted), ...	38	10	0
Net profit or value of stone, and equal to about 9½d. per hogshead, ...}	£. 9	10	0

DISTRICT V.

A copper-mine is now working at Buckland in the Moor, with considerable expectations of success.

The number of old stream-works throughout this district most clearly show that, in former times, large quantities of tin were obtained in it. The greatest part of Bovey Heathfield is cut up and destroyed by these works, and a run of water is no where to be met with on the commons bordering upon Dartmoor, that has not been led into some adjacent stream-works for supplying the cisterns for washing the ore.

Traversing these wilds, a single stone of a bluish cast (known by the name of male tin) is rarely to be found without the mark of a hammer in chipping off a corner, to discover by its fracture, whether it was worth converting or not. The vallies thus broken and occupied with refuse stone, will for ever remain in their present condition, unless the Scotch fir, or some other hardy plant, may

be

be brought to grow and flourish upon them.—In the
parish of Lustleigh, at a place called Killy, a tin-mine is
now working, and which is stated to answer extremely
well. In North Bovey, and adjoining the Moor, some
tin-works are now carrying on; but the rapid transfer of
shares from hand to hand, raises some doubts in the
neighbourhood, of eventual success.

After following a western branch of the Bovey river
from the commons of Widdecombe in the Moor, we
descend into a plain bounded on the north by a range of
craggy hills in the parish of Bovey Tracy, and westwardly
by the high lands of Ilsington and Heytor rocks. In
this plain or valley is found rising to the surface, and
with a gentle dip or inclination to the southward, distinct
strata of a fossil substance called Bovey coal. This lies
in several parallel seams at the distance of six or eight
feet from each other, and to the depth of 60 feet (and,
which is here considered above the level of low water line
at Teignmouth,) from a due attention to the leading particulars of this substance, it appears that clay and other
moveable matter must have been poured in a fluid state,
and at different periods, from the craggy eminences before
noticed, over the pine forests which heretofore, and at
remote distances of time, grew and flourished in this
valley. The most recent of these woodlands appear to
have grown within a few hundred yards of the present
coal-pits, and in what is now a peat-moss, where large
quantities of bog-wood of the same character with the
Bovey coal have been taken up for fuel, and where it is
also to be observed, that the peat or moss is frequently
covered from 18 inches to two feet in depth with the
common white, blue, and yellow clay of the valley.

Hatchett endeavours to prove, by his Analytical Experiments on this substance, that bitumen has been and is
                                                actually

actually and immediately formed from the resin and perhaps some other of the juices of recent vegetables. The Bovey coal exhibits a series of gradations, from the most perfect ligneous texture to a substance nearly approaching the character of pit-coal, and which by exposure to the air breaks into thin laminæ, assuming the appearance of the grey or common schistus rock of the country, but in which are indistinctly to be traced the original fibrous vegetable of which it was composed, and which is generally the roots and trunks of the *pinus sylvestris*, or Scotch fir; the former being distinguished by the workmen as root; the latter as broad coal, flattened into parallel layers by the compression it has undergone; and frequently rising to the thickness of a large folio volume. The upper strata of these veins are of a greyish colour, and resemble a mass of the shaley rock; the lower assuming a black coal colour, and showing between its leaves, but particularly on its transverse fracture, the same smooth glassy appearance common to stone-coal. The root coal has a broken and wavy texture. On examination of some of the roots of the bog timber in the neighbouring morass, a faint smell of turpentine was still retained, and the turpentine appeared in an inspissated state between the fibrous substances of the wood; hence there is reason to suppose that, next to the woody fibre, resin is the substance that, in vegetables passing to the fossil state, most powerfully resists alteration, but which once effected, becomes the substance whence bitumen is produced. Among the clay, but adhering to the coal, are found lumps of a bright yellow resinous earth extremely light, and so saturated with petroleum, as to burn like sealing-wax, and when not carried too far, to produce an agreeable and aromatic vapour. This, by analysis, appears to have, resin 55, asphaltum 41, earthy residuum 3. Large

pieces

pieces of the board and root-coal have been taken up at different depths in the Stover plantations, and at the distance of about two miles from the present coal-pits. This substance is also found diffused in very small pieces through all the beds of potters' clay in the parishes of Teigngrace and King's Teignton.

DISTRICT VI.

The mineral substances* occurring through this district are of small consideration. The quarries of grout-stone in the parish of Heavitree afford an excellent building stone, as is evinced from most of the ancient edifices, the gates and walls of the city of Exeter. This rock is frequently used for coarse millstones for shelling clover, and separating the wheat from the close husks broke from off the ears in the ordinary operation of thrashing.

DISTRICT VII.

The limestone, freestone, and chalk, have already been described in this district, in addition to which it may be proper to say, that along the cliffs of Salcombe, Branscombe, and Beer, and lying between strata of red stone, marl, and chalk rubble, gypsum or plaster of Paris is found, proving much in demand for stucco and fine mason-work, and usually selling for about 2s. 6d. per hundred weight. The Black-down hills formerly afforded in particular spots large quantities of ironstone, found near the surface on the fox mould.

It has already been observed, that these hills afford a

---

* Large quantities of manganese are found in the parishes of Bamford Speke, Upton-pyne, and Newton St. Cyre's.

soft

soft species of sandstone that is converted into whetstones. The manner of working these quarries is by
driving a road or level from the side of the hill to the
distance of 3 or 400 yards, about three feet wide, and
five feet and a half high ; when the hill has been penetrated to this distance the usual practice is to work out all
the loose sandstones within eight or ten yards of the
road, leaving pillars at first to support the roof of the
mine, but afterwards gradually working them out, and
suffering the whole excavation to fall in and fill up after
them. The size of these stones seldom exceeds that of a
horse's head, all of them more or less grooved and indented, and giving the general idea of rills or running water
having been constantly passing through them.

These mines produce, in addition to the whetstone,
numerous specimens of the shells of fishes and other tes-
taceous animals. The serpent-stone, or *cornu ammonis*,
are numerous, and found to a large size, one of which
was seen at Woodford-lodge which exceeded 14 inches
in diameter.

SECT. VI.——WATER.

DISTRICT I.

THE great source of this supply in the north-eastern
quarter of this district, is unquestionably derived from
the waters issuing from the forest of Exmoor, the greater
part, if not the whole of which, is collected by the head
branches of the river Exe, and through that channel is
discharged into the sea. The forest of Dartmoor contributes

tributes in a very great degree to the watering of the
more southern parts of the country, whilst a proportion
only of the ramifications of the Taw and Torridge rivers
are found to spread through, or have their source in this
northern district.

Of all the streams with which this part of the country
seems so highly favoured, the river Bray and its superior
branches, hold the first rank for clearness and salubrity,
as well for domestic use, as for the purposes of irrigation.
The streams having their sources in and descending from
the parishes of West-down, Bittedon, East-down, Kentisbury, and the south-western parts of Parracombe, and
obtaining their exit into the Taw, through the northern
parts of Barnstable, or rather between that borough and
the parish of Pilton, are little if at all inferior for any
purposes to which the most crystal fountains or the purest
streams can be applied, in the parishes of Challacombe,
Bratton Flemming, and High Bray.

The branches of the Mole heading northwardly through
the parishes of North Molton, Twitching, Molland, and
a part of West Anstey, are but little inferior in clearness,
softness and value, to those above described : these streams
afterwards mixing with the moorland waters of Knowstone,
Rose-ash, Bishop's and George Nympton, Mary Ann's,
and Romansleigh, become in a slight degree tinged with
a faint copper colour, and though still perfectly clear, are
not supposed to possess the same genuine excellence as
the waters of the Bray river, which are equally pellucid,
as well as without colour.

Some smaller streams, such as that descending from
the parishes of West Buckland and Swimbridge, uniting
with the river Taw at Bishop's Tawton, and the river
Yea, heading westwardly in Alwington, and descending
through the parishes of Littleham and Land-cross to the
Torridge

Torridge river, not affording at all seasons a permanent
supply for the purposes of irrigation, were not particularly noticed in the course of the Survey. Although the
sides and summits of the hills in this district are found
to abound with springs generally rising through that
part of the rock which is found to crop out with a thin
laminous strata, yet these springs are seldom known to
form the like swamps and rotten ground produced from
such sources in other parts of the country. The water
thus issuing through this thin shaley rock, finds its way
along the same stratum until it collects sufficient force to
open a clear and constant passage to its nearest outfall.

The herring fishery which was formerly carried on in
these parts to a considerable extent, is now, from the
caprice of that animal in forsaking the shores of the
district, in a great measure lost, not only as a valuable
supply and change of food for the inhabitants, but as an
object of no small moment in curing for exportation.
This is a circumstance justly to be lamented, and such a
one as is entirely out of the reach of human wisdom to
remedy; not so is it altogether to be said from the alarming deficiency of late years in the salmon fishery; for if
it is true, as is asserted, that there is a proneness in those
animals to return to the waters in which they were bred,
the taking of such vast numbers in the latter end of the
year appears to be such wasteful and improvident destruction of the species, as loudly to call for the most
serious consideration; it being stated from very good
authority, that on the return of the young fish to seaward
at that season, no less than a thousand have been taken
in one week at Brightly, on the river Taw; as many as
half that number have been caught at Umberleigh, in the
same space of time, and on which occasions it has been
usual for the young salmon fry, or gravellers, to be given

to

to the pigs. So very abundant was the supply of salmon formerly in these waters, that it is still in the memory of many persons, that the farmers, in hiring their servants, found it necessary to stipulate that they should not be compelled to eat salmon oftener than twice a week. A few herrings are still found to frequent the coast in the fall of the year, but they are very small both in size and quantity, and even this supply is equally uncertain : some pilchards occasionally separate from the shoal, and are found wandering in the Bristol Channel, but the chief haunts of these fish are the southern coasts of this county, of Dorset, and of Cornwall.

DISTRICT II.

The subject of water has been so fully treated in the preceding district, that it does not appear at all necessary to enter upon a farther description of it here.

DISTRICT III.

Large quantities of black ram (*i. e.* bog iron) are found dispersed through all the moors and low-grounds in this, as well as in the western division of this district. This has communicated generally a strong chalybeate quality to all the moor waters, and hence they have been commonly regarded as unfriendly to the purposes of flowing land. In the hilly parts of this district the springs, though numerous, are found very much to fall off in a dry season ; but where there is a large extent of clay land, without interruption in its substrata, considerable inconveniences are sometimes experienced in dry seasons, by the want of a good supply of water for domestic use. Upon the whole, the district, with some exceptions, ap-

pears

pears to be in a strangely neglected-condition. A large proportion of it is much injured by too much moisture, but like the preceding district this is left to produce its concomitant disadvantages. Shelter, or a division of property, appears in many places in a manner disregarded, as the mounds and fences are often seen prostrate, and the whole depasturable part of the country exhibiting all the appearance of a wild and unprofitable waste.

DISTRICT IV.

This district, generally speaking, is extremely well watered ; all the springs rising below the foot of Dartmoor are collected with great care, and applied to the watering of the grass grounds ; the waters immediately descending from that eminence are as carefully rejected. Along the course of the Tamar, the grass lands are not supposed to be benefited by the freshes produced in that river, but wherever the home waters can be commanded, great attention is paid to the collecting and carrying them over the adjoining lands. The Plym, the Yealme, the Erme, the Aven, the sound of Kingsbridge, and its dependencies, together with the river Dart and most of its lower branches, afford favourable opportunities for navigating through the interior country, into which culm, coal, and sea sand are conveyed with great facility, and at a very moderate expense.

There can be no purer or more wholesome water any-where, than that which is generally to be met with in this district ; the springs which supply the town of Dart-mouth are peculiarly inviting to the eye, and agreeable to the taste, and although the stream which is conveyed over Roborough-down is at all times slightly tinged with a copper-colour, it seems in no respect complained of, but
affords

affords an ample and inestimable supply to the shipping
and inhabitants at Dock. Springs are stated not frequently
to arise through the dunstone stratum; but as this rock,
the schistus, and lime-rock, are often in parallel strata,
and much veined with each other, it is not easy to determine the precise strata in which the spring may have its
source, or how far it may have wandered through other
strata in its passage to the day.

DISTRICT V.

The waters of the Teign and Bovey, from having their
principal source in Dartmoor, are seldom or never employed for the purpose of irrigation; attempts, however,
have lately been made at great Shilston, and found to
answer extremely well, in applying the clear granite
water to the purpose of flowing grass ground. The water
in the reservoirs, and along the canal at Teigngrace, is
applied with good effect to the watering of the adjacent
lands.

DISTRICT VI.

The water generally issuing from the red strata of this
district, is supposed to be free from the acidity ascribed
to that which comes from the schistus rock; be that as it
may, the red land waters are applied universally to the
watering of meadows, and for this purpose they are not
held in less estimation than for domestic use. The river
Ochment, in its course through Jacobstow, and Exbourn,
flows through a vale of rich land; this, with the springs
issuing from the adjacent hills, is supposed so far to qualify
the Moor water, as to render it of value for irrigation.
All the waters of the Yeo, the Creedy, the Exe, the Culm,
the Clyst, the Otter, and the Kenn, are carefully collected,
and

and periodically spread over the adjoining meadow grounds. The water coming from the bodies of chip sand, is in no respect objected to for this purpose.

DISTRICT VII.

The waters of the Coley, the Axe, the Yealme, and western branches of that river, are all found to spread the most fructifying qualities in their annual inundations.

The springs issuing from the surrounding hills, are constantly collected into the eddits that are taken up from the several streams, and artificially poured over the surface of all the higher levels in the vallies and grass grounds not accessible to the ordinary overflowings of such rivers. A deficiency of water seems only complained of along the chalk and limestone cliffs in this district.

CHAP.

CHAP. II.

STATE OF PROPERTY.

———

SECT. I.——ESTATES, AND THEIR MANAGEMENT.

IF we except a few individuals, who, in reference to others, may be considered as owners of large estates, the landed property in this county will appear to be very much divided; a large proportion of it being in the hands of a respectable yeomanry, and other estates belonging to the sees of Exeter, York, and Salisbury, the Dean and Chapter of Windsor, the Universities, and the Duchy of Cornwall, forming no inconsiderable part of the whole county. The manner, however, in which this landed property, when so large as to be out of the occupation of the owner, is managed, induces much reflection, and on which it will be necessary to animadvert with all that freedom and interest, which the importance of the subject, and its consequences, so highly demand.

It is believed, that in no part of England are the care and management of estates so generally deputed to the superintendance of attornies and other unqualified persons, as in the county of Devon: in what view their education, professional pursuits, and habits, can be deemed qualifications for the important duties of land agent, is not easily to be understood; particularly, as the essential endowments of the latter are so widely different from those of law agents, whose exclusive attention should be directed to the title. Different, however, are the qualifi-

cations

cations for a land steward, for it is to him, and him only, that we must look for projecting, directing, and carrying into execution such works as the nature of the estate requires, and by the most economical and judicious means, effecting the permanent improvement of his employer's property.

SECT. II.—TENURES.

THE mischievous consequences inseparably connected with, and resulting from, the want of agricultural knowledge in those who have the direction and management of such estates, and who, to cover the want of the necessary qualifications of a land agent, most commonly advise the proprietor to grant those lifehold tenures so frequently heard of in Devonshire and South Wales, are more injurious and extensive than is generally apprehended. The same capital employed in the purchase of a lease for 99 years, determinable on three lives, applied to the stocking, cultivating, and improving a more extensive occupation held at a fair annual rent, and under an encouraging term of years, must produce, in the contemplation of such property, very different emotions in the mind of the owner; to the occupier results are infinitely more advantageous; and to the public at large a more abundant supply is produced, than can possibly be derived from a capital employed in the purchase of a more narrowed occupation on an eventually undisturbed possession of 99 years. But notwithstanding, an opinion prevails with some noblemen and gentlemen in the county, that it is better to realize at 40 years purchase, than to suffer the lifehold tenures to fall in without renewal. Fortunately for the future

DEVON.] improve-

improvement and prosperity of the country, this species of tenure is become much lessened within the last twenty years.

To accomplish this preposterous object of the tenant's indolence and pride, he will employ his last shilling, and incur very heavy obligations among his neighbours, to pay eighteen years' purchase for a lease only of that very farm, the fee of which might readily have been bought for about one third more. Destitute of capital, and encumbered with obligations contracted with his family and friends, the farmer enters his new occupation, depending upon casual and agistment stock for the consumption of his herbage. Having little or no reserved rent to provide for, the efforts of himself and family are directed to the annual cultivation of so much of his land as will pay the parochial and other small disbursements, and supply the bare wants of the most comfortless life it is possible to conceive, leaving no brighter prospects to his children, than what the lapse of 99 years may do, by the termination of a lease so injudiciously purchased.

The usual manner of letting these and most other estates, is by holding what is here called a survey, that is, an auction, which is announced to the public by handbills, and advertisements in the public papers, that at such a time and place, a farm is to be lett by survey : it now becomes the business of the steward to have every thing in readiness at the public-house, to stimulate and encourage the bidding; which closed, the landlord through his steward (if not present himself), names his price, which is offered to the highest bidder, downwards to the last person who would be approved of by the landlord or steward: should no one accept it, the company disperses, and the farm is afterwards disposed of by private contract, no preference beyond that which arises from the highest offer,

offer, being given to the old tenant or his family, whose principal object during the latter period of the term is usually to dilapidate, pare and burn, and by every method which can be devised, despoil the farm of all its fruitful energies. On many occasions there is a per centage allowed to the steward, for his address in procuring a high bidding at the survey.

The most important covenants in these leases, are those obliging the tenant, on opening his fields for a course of tillage, to dress with 40 customary measures of lime per acre, and to restrain him from not taking *more* than three white straw crops in succession.

These are also the leading covenants where lifehold tenures do not prevail, and which leases or covenants, as they are called, are sold by auction in the same manner, and for a term of 14 or 21 years, determinable every 7, on a twelvemonth's notice by either party; it is however in all cases understood, that on the outgoing tenant using due diligence, sufficient time will be allowed for driving off his live stock, and for the removal of his grain and furniture. Hay is generally permitted to be sold, and although neither straw nor dung are included in that concession, a great deal of both are frequently, towards the conclusion of the lease, clandestinely expended on, and applied to other premises. These, with other leases on a term of 14 years absolute, are the tenures under which the great body of the lay property is occupied.

In many parts of the South Hams, and through the sixth and seventh districts, lifehold tenures are become much in disuse, and terms of 14 years absolute are coming by far the most common. The covenants of these leases require 60 measures of lime, or 200 horse-loads of sea-sand, sea-weed, Plymouth, Exeter, or other rich rotten dung, to be applied per acre, and not to have more than

two

two white straw crops in succession, and restrained from carrying either hay or straw to market, without the fullest certainty of returning with a corresponding quantity of dung.

It has frequently happened, that in letting an estate, the landlord agreed to discharge tithes and all parochial payments. During the last scarcity, and about the years 1800 and 1801, the rent of several estates in this county, where the amount of the poor's-rates are commonly double, and even treble the general average hereafter stated, was absolutely insufficient to meet such disbursements, and consequently all the estates so circumstanced brought their proprietors in debt.

The church property, consisting of tithes and demesnes belonging chiefly to the see of Exeter, are frequently held in perpetuity by the nobility and gentry of the country, renewable with certain or arbitrary fines : these are justly considered valuable possessions, and are by them disposed of in such a manner as comports with the general arrangement of their other property. An indulgence is sometimes given, and formerly went to a far greater length, enabling the widow of the last surviving tenant to the church-lands in possession, to hold over the estate so long as she remained unmarried ; but as this in some instances led to intrigues of a loose and disreputable nature, great care is now taken by the Bishop, and those who have the management of these affairs, to prevent in future any disgraceful abuse of such humane and generous concessions.

CHAP. III.

BUILDINGS.

———

THE conspicuous ruin and dilapidation of the residences of the ancient nobility and gentry in this county, as well as in most other counties in England, cannot be adverted to without the greatest concern. These mansions were generally situated in the midst of the most fruitful demesnes, and whether their dereliction arises from the caprice or folly of their owners, or from the subdivision and dispersion of those possessions by which these seats of hospitality and happiness were formerly supported, it is equally a subject of regret to the reflecting mind, to view the dilapidated condition of such mansions, and not unfrequently to behold two or three apartments only of an ancient mansion propped up, and converted into the residence of the hind or bailiff of the estate. Had circumstances of convenience in most cases contributed to the abandonment of these noble fabrics, or that the modern edifice could be deemed to be more judiciously planned, and in all respects more conveniently situated, some small portion of chagrin might have been spared, and the sacrifice in some measure reconciled ; but the superior elegance, plan, and comforts, provided for in the general disposition of the modern buildings, are in many instances less estimable than in the ancient and hospitable manor houses.

SECT.

SECT. II.—FARM-HOUSES AND OFFICES.

DISTRICT I.

UNDER this impression we dismiss the subject, and proceed to describe the situation and arrangement of Farm-houses and Offices, which are commonly so contrived and situated, as to defy the utmost efforts of ingenuity to dispose and place them where the purposes of their establishment could be worse, or more ineffectually answered. The country has already been described as abounding in hills, many of which rise at a considerable angle from the plane of the small valley below. These vallies are generally appropriated as meadows, and their first banks or risings as orchard ground; here, and just above the reach of the autumnal and winter floods, are a great majority of the farm-yards and houses situated: the inducement for this disposition was unquestionably the convenience of water, and shelter from the force of the prevailing winds. The hills abounding (as has been before noticed), with constant springs, rendered the first precaution totally unnecessary, and the continual wind in the boisterous and even stiller seasons, which is always found passing along these combs, or vallies, subject their inhabitants to far greater inconvenience than they would otherwise be liable to, were the farm-yards and buildings situated midway, rather than at the foot of such declivities. The expense and labour hence created in the management of the farm, become considerably increased, at the same time that it is utterly impossible to carry up in due season upon the backs of horses, such necessary dressings of farm-yard and stable dung, as are annually

required

required upon the highest cultivated parts of the occupation : to this add the impossibility of applying the drainage of the farm-yard to any field below, and by which it would be greatly benefited, the whole must appear sufficient to induce a departure from the practice of placing farm-houses and offices so very inconvenient and injurious to the interests of the farmer.

The objection of carrying a part of the crop up hill in hay time and harvest, can have no weight, in comparison with the more laborious task of packing upon horses' backs, all the farm-yard dung produced annually from the crops of hay and straw consumed upon the premises.

So strongly is a gentleman in the neighbourhood of Watermouth impressed with this idea, that he is judiciously distributing his feeding-houses, sheep and bullock-yards, over all the highest parts of his farms, that in future the dung may be conveniently distributed over the whole of the cultivated lands below. In such fields as yet lie at a distance from any of these buildings, temporary sheds are constructed, inclosed with yards, for the sheep to lodge in ; these sheds are made to take in pieces for the convenience of removal, and which with care may be repeated for many years. The frame-work is commonly of deal covered with thatched hurdles ; the sheep are penned upon a fresh piece of turnips daily, and driven to these sheds at night, where they are well littered.

DISTRICT II.

Some of the farm-houses in this district are far better situated than many we have had occasion to notice in that of North Devon. Here the situation is well-chosen,

the

the manure is distributed over the farm, in the one-horse butts, or small carts, with great facility.

DISTRICT IV.

The farm-houses here are frequently found grouped together in villages, and as these are generally situated in vallies, the same objection must apply as already noticed in the district of North Devon. The mixture of cob and stone-work is less prevalent here than in the first district; the stone most used rises in lamina rarely exceeding four inches in thickness, is soft, and easily worked when first quarried, but, from exposure to the air, becomes hard and durable; it is always placed in the building with its transverse fracture outwards, and it is equally pleasing to observe the facility and neatness with which the walls are raised and finished, as to be assured of their permanence whether wet or dry.

SECT. III.——REPAIRS.

THE repairs of the farm-houses, such as walls, floors, roofs and doors, are usually done by the landlord; all others, except the finding of stuff for gates, rails, and posts, are performed by the tenant; it has, however, been generally noticed, that the tenant for years keeps his occupation in repair, being first put in that condition by the landlord at the commencement of the lease. The Cottages are also generally kept by the tenant farmer in repair. Through the greater part of the seventh district, repairs (except glazing) are done by the landlord, the tenants drawing the materials, and finding reed for thatch;

in

in return for which, they frequently have the tops and bark of such trees as are occasionally cut down for the repairs of their respective farms.

SECT. IV.—PRICE OF BUILDING MATERIALS AND LABOUR.

DISTRICT I.

THE price of building in the neighbourhood of Barnstable, Bideford, and Ilfracombe, varies very much from what is given in the eastern and more remote parts of the district. The common price of stone-work, including the value of the allowance of three quarts of cider or beer daily, to the mason and his attendants, as also another allowance which is frequently made, of 2*d.* per bushel of lime, for mixing the materials, may be stated at about 22*d.* or 24*d.* the perch of 16½ feet in length, 22 inches in thickness, and one foot in height, running measure.

The scaffolding-poles, planks, and ropes, are always provided by the employer, but raised by the mason and the attendants employed by him in dressing the stones and tempering the mortar. It frequently happens, that the lower part of the building is made of stone, and its superstructure of cob; the stone-work is generally estimated to cost from 5*s* to 6*s.* per perch, including all expenses of quarrying and cartage of materials, and the cob estimated fairly and in like manner at about 3*s.* 6*d.* per perch, same measure. Carpenters' and masons' wages, when not employed by the piece, 2*s.* per day, and allowance of beer or cider.

DISTRICT

DISTRICT II.

Thatching here costs 8*s.* per square of 10 feet; 100 sheaves of wheat-straw reed, weighing 25lb. each, are supposed equal to the making of one square of thatch; mason-work 18*d.* per rope of 20 feet in length, 18 inches thick, and one foot high, stone and all materials being found, and placed upon the spot; cob-work 14*d.* of the same measure.   The slate-quarries in the parishes of Treborough, and Huish Champflower, in the county of Somerset, afford such good opportunities of getting slate, that all the superior buildings in this district, within a reasonable distance of those quarries, are covered with slate from them.

DISTRICT IV.

There is little difference, in point of expense, between building with stone or cob; the materials being laid down, the mason-work will cost 2*s.* 6*d.*, and the cob 2*s.* per perch of 18 feet in length, two feet thick, and one foot high.

DISTRICT VI.

Notwithstanding that slate is by no means difficult to be procured in almost every part of this district, still a substitute for that covering is getting very much into use, and which is thus prepared :—three parts whiting, five of sand, one pounded charcoal, and one bone-ashes;—to a barrel of tar is added 4lb. of black rosin, which boiling together, the ingredients are added in small quantities, keeping them constantly in motion over the fire, till the whole

whole mass becomes of a consistence fit for use. The roof being previously covered with sheathing-paper securely nailed down, it should be spread hot from the copper, about three quarters of an inch thick, and which will cost, at the cauldron, about 35s. for each square of ten feet. The common slating will cost about 32s. the same measure. The roof for the composition is pitched very flat, and, from the lightness of its scantling, comes considerably cheaper than the roof required for carrying slate or tiles. A preserving and highly ornamental wash for stone or rough-cast buildings, is getting greatly into use : it consists of four parts of pounded lime, three of sand, two of pounded wood-ashes, and one of scoria of iron, mixed well together, and made sufficiently fluid to be applied with a brush. When dry, it gives the appearance of new Portland stone, and affords an excellent protection against the penetrating force of the south-westerly storms.

Stone-masons' work, 2s. 6d per perch of 16½ feet, running measure ; value and cartage of materials about 5s. per perch more   When not working by contract, masons' and carpenters' wages about 2s. 6d. per day, with allowance of beer or cider.

Although by far the larger number of farm-houses and cottages are built with cob, still many of the latter, particularly in the neighbourhood of Exeter, being rough-cast and white-washed, gives an appearance of much greater neatness and opulence to the country, than can possibly be drawn from an assemblage of rough and unadorned mud-walls, and which, frequently in a state of ruin, at once completes the idea of a temporary caravansera, or deserted Tartar village.

DISTRICT VII.

In the neighbourhood of Axminster, the blue and white

white limestone, flints, and freestone, compose the principal building materials. Stone-mason work, 2s. per rope of
20 feet, 20 inches thick, and one foot high; mason and
carpenters' wages, at day-work, 12s. per week, with
allowance of beer or cider.

SECT. IV.—COTTAGES.

THE general material with which the old and venerable
mansion in the country is built, is stone, which is
variously dispersed, and by no means difficult to procure
in most parts of the county. This would have been
thought sufficient to have caused a discontinuance of the
use of mud-walls; it has not, however, produced that
effect, as the cob buildings are nearly as numerous as is
presumed to have been the case with the Belgæ, who, we
are told, were the first who made inroads and established
colonies in Devonshire. Garden-walls, farm-houses, barns,
stables, linneys, village fences, and cottages, are all built
with this dull, heavy, and deforming material. Left
without rough-cast, or white-wash, to conceal the native
colour of the loam, it is utterly impossible, at a distance,
to distinguish a village from a beatfield, both having
uniformly the same shade; and from both of which the
stranger perceives smoke issuing.

DISTRICT I.

Cottages, however, built with this material, if
afterwards rough-cast and white-washed, are certainly
capable of being rendered very clean and comfortable.
The

The expense of building one with a fire-place and oven* in the principal room, which may be stated to be about 14 feet square ; two small rooms behind the larger one, for stowing away fuel and provisions ; the upper story divided into two apartments, the one for the parents, the other for their children, may be made very comfortable, and decently finished, for about 60*l.*

DISTRICT II.

It is represented in some parishes in this district, that such is the scarcity of cottages, that twelve or fifteen families are found absent, not having houses to receive them. This has frequently been ascribed to the perverseness of the farmers, who, having many vacant tenements on their lands, refuse letting them to the poor, on the pretext that the labourer, through the stress of the times, will not be able to pay his rent : many peasant families are thus expelled from the parishes to which they belong, and to which they seldom return, till, worn out and exhausted in some distant part of the country, they threaten, or do actually become chargeable to such places ; when in their old age they are removed for support and maintenance to those very parishes whence, in the early part of their lives, they were so incautiously driven.

Notwithstanding that the poor generally in the eastern parts of this district, are so indifferently provided with

* The mouth of the oven, in most of these cottages, opens into the chimney, which makes it very inconvenient both to feed and draw ; but the immediate escape of the smoke and flame produced by the dry furze, with which these ovens are generally heated, is quite sufficient to recommend the continuance of the same plan in future.

habitations,

habitations, it is deplorable to see the number of cottages that are daily going to ruin, and have fallen down within a few years. The consolidating small farms may in some measure account for this, but not to the extent complained of, for the evil here would be confined to the late farm-house, which is often inhabited by three or four peasant families, and not to the smaller cottages.

Lord Clifford builds very neat cottages for his work-men: the window in the upper story is so placed, as to admit light to the two rooms into which this floor is divided. His Lordship attaches to each tenement a small piece of garden-ground, with the privilege of cultivating as many potatoes as their industry may prompt, or leisure admit of, in the young plantations; a small orchard, sufficient to produce from one to two hogsheads of cider, with a sufficiency of good hoarding or winter apples, is also granted to each peasant family, in lieu of the grazing of a cow, which they were formerly indulged with. The cow being subject to accident, places this munificence on a more permanent footing.

DISTRICT III.

The general want of cottages through this district, can no where be more clearly shown than in the example of Chilworthy, where three mud walls and a hedge-bank form the habitation of many of the peasantry.

The following communications were partly made to the Surveyor in person, and afterwards by letter received from the Reverend Mr. Luxmore, on the subject of a number of cottages he has lately built in the village of Bridestow, and designed merely for the occupation of the labouring poor, who most frequently apprentice out their children at eight or nine years of age. In one row, where

two

Plate I. P. 95.

scaly. Thrand.

View of the Brixteston Cottages.

two old ruinous cottages formerly stood, and which were scarcely sufficient to afford a single night's shelter to a gang of gypsies, there are now twelve neat comfortable cottages: three other uninhabitable houses he proposes taking down in the ensuing summer, and building upon their scite a proportionable number of cottages.

The first range of these buildings were constructed uniform, and nearly in the following manner: room below, sixteen feet square, one door and one window in front; fire-place with an oven opening into it with a flue; door opening back into a shed or lean-to, for covering fuel, labourers' tools, shelter for a pig, &c.; another door from this lean-to opens into a small back yard, fenced off from a small garden attached to each tenement; under the stairs in the front room, leading up to the bed-room, is a pantry fitted up with shelves; opposite to the fire-place, over which there is a mantle-piece, a sort of dresser is fastened to the wall with shelves, and these constitute the fixtures in the room below. The bed-room above is the same size as the room below. The walls of the first eight feet of these cottages are built with stone, the super-structure with cob, covered with a slate room, and cost, upon an average, when finished in a plain and useful manner, from 38*l.* to 40*l.* each. The slate costs 10*s.* per thousand; a quantity fully sufficient for the making of a square of ten feet; the slate is bought rough at the quarry, and fashioned afterwards: one cart-load, or ten horse-loads, of stones, will build a perch and an half of wall, 20 inches thick; three cart-loads of clay are required for an equal portion of cob wall; eight bundles, or one horse-load of straw, is mixed and tempered with nine cart loads of clay, and consequently equal to the building of $4\frac{1}{2}$ perch of cob of nearly the same thickness as the wall below. When the wall is 16 feet high, of stone only,

the

the mason's demand is 2s. per perch of 16½ feet; if stone, 8 feet, and cob, 8 feet, 1s. 10d. per perch; if cob only, 1s. 6d. per perch. In all cases, it is supposed that the materials are laid down in the rough, for the masons to dress and temper, and serve themselves. Four Winchester bushels of lime are used for every perch of stone wall: the lime ash-floor below costs 6d. in the square yard, tempering and laying down; and the floor above is made of rack deal, or any soft wood plank most convenient to be procured.

Mr. Luxmore's letter also contains the following passage:—" I had no conception of the real situation and distress of the poor, till I settled here with Mrs. Luxmore in 1792, since which time I have never been absent, except on occasional visits, and twice to Bath for my health. I soon perceived, that in consequence of several houses belonging to small farms being suffered to become ruinous, the poor were distressed for habitations, and were obliged to herd together in a manner both destructive to morality and delicacy; and determining to obviate this defect, as far as my small ability would allow of, immediately began the work, and where two dwellings originally stood, I have erected twelve cottages, taken down two others (not habitable), to the ground, and entirely rebuilt them, and am now preparing to take down three others, to rebuild them all this season. Nine of the cottages form a row on the right-hand side of the turnpike road leading to Falmouth, and were built previous to the building the row on the opposite side.

" As my idea was to accommodate those only who depended on their daily labour for support, and whose children are generally apprenticed by the overseers of the poor, and sent from their parents' care at ten years of age or under, I conceived that no evil could arise from each

house

house being accommodated with one bed-room, and the children sleeping in the same with their parents; but, in so much request were these cottages, that they soon became tenanted by those whose industry kept them from the necessity of apprenticing their children; and I soon perceived that the want of a second bed-room was a great evil. This, in the last-erected cottages, I have corrected, and, instead of a lean-to, have made a double roof, by which means the back upper room is a comfortable bed-room; and this method is also attended with another benefit, that the staircase is in the back room, and the front room not incommoded by it.

" As I make but very little use of my carriage, I employ my horses in drawing clay and stone at their leisure, by which means the expense becomes more moderate; and I keep a mason and carpenter regularly employed throughout the year. I frequently bought lots of timber here, by which means it came reasonable, and I had the additional pleasure of supplying the poor with wood at a reduced price in the winter. Thus, I suppose, the expense of each cottage did not exceed the sum I mentioned to you. Each of these cottages is lett for one shilling per week, and I adopt this mode, that I may instantly remove a disorderly tenant. My agreement is, that as long as they frequent the church, and behave themselves soberly, and carefully, and as good neighbours to each other, I will not remove any one from his dwelling."

DISTRICT IV.

The cottages here are seldom found on particular farms, but, in like manner with the farm-houses, crowded together in villages. The morals of the peasantry are

DEVON.]   thus

hus more liable to be corrupted, than in more detached and solitary situations, where they would have much greater conveniences in garden-ground, so essential to the comforts and necessities of the peasant family.

DISTRICT VII.

In this district, the cottages are certainly in a state of alarming decrease; and as such, some strong measure should be pursued to stop their farther progress. Upon the borders of the wastes of Woodbury, and other commons connected with it, Lord Rolle has been much in the practice of encouraging the peasantry to build and make small improvements: the inducing of the labourers thus to leave the village, and settle upon the borders of the commons, must be considered by far the most likely means of promoting the comfort, and improving the morals of these people. The quantity of land first per-mitted to be enclosed is about an acre. This improvement conducted to his Lordship's satisfaction, a farther enclosure is suffered to be made, to the extent of three, four, or five acres, and which, in some cases, have led to the cottager's obtaining a long lease of his improvements at a very moderate rent, and with the farther privilege of enclosing more of the waste, when his strength and ability will enable him to render it equal justice with that he may have already improved. In thus withdrawing the cottager from his former haunts in the village, the time that would otherwise be spent at the ale-house, or in frivolous conversation with his neighbours, is now em-ployed to the immediate benefit of himself and family, and ultimately to the increase of the national stock.

P. 98.

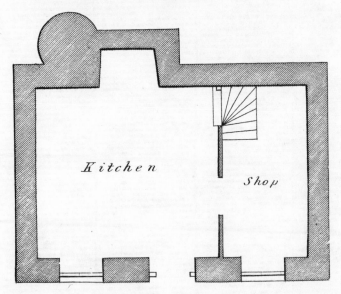

Kitchen

Shop

Scale of Feet.

1 2 3 4 5   10   15   20   25   30

Plan of a Cottage
built on Oldrige Wood in the Parish of St. Thomas
near Exeter by John Prawl for Mr. Sillifant of Coombe;
near Crediton, Devon.

Neele sculp Strand

SECT. VI.——BRIDGES,

Not belonging to the public roads, are generally kept in very good repair by the different parishes; the road-surveyor, or way-warden of which, always takes care that such communications, for foot and horse travellers, are sufficiently numerous, and also in a condition to ensure a safe and ready passage through the country. These are points highly necessary to be attended to in all places, but no where do they call for such constant watchfulness and care, as in a country abounding with so many narrow vallies, occasionally covered with a considerable depth of water, rising and falling in the course of a few hours.

CHAP. IV.

OCCUPATIONS.

━━━◆━━━

SIZE OF FARMS, FARMERS' RENT AND TITHE, POOR-
RATES, AND OTHER PAROCHIAL PAYMENTS.

DISTRICT I.

IT is extremely difficult to speak with any degree of certainty on a subject in which there is so wide a range for the striking an average, with respect to the extent of the occupations of a country, which vary from 10*l.* to 400*l.* a year; in general, however, it may be stated, that persons who come within the description of what may be called farming tenantry of the district, rent or otherwise occupy from 200 to 300 acres of land, the greater part of which is subject to a system of up-and-down husbandry, and to which is generally attached a small proportion of permanent pasture, and of marsh or meadow-land.

The attention of many of the most active and intelligent of these farmers, is too frequently drawn from the cares of their occupation, by a spirit of jobbing at fairs and markets, where the cattle, sheep, and horses, chiefly supplied from the wastes of Dartmoor and Exmoor, and the extensive commons belonging to the parishes lying in Venville, become the chief subjects of their dealing with strangers or with each other. This description of farmers must not, however, be charged with a want of liberality in laying out the profits, by these or any other sources of diligence and industry, in the purchase of lime, waste lees, or any such manure as experience has taught them the value of, for the purpose of improving their lands.

There is a second class of farmers, who are found to labour hard, and for very little profit. The class of

farmers

farmers first mentioned, may be said to have most of the
comforts and conveniences of life about them; they are
generally owners of trips or small flocks of sheep, depastured upon Exmoor, and of the cows and bullocks
summered upon the moors and other grass-grounds in the
occupation of their poorer neighbours, who, destitute of
the means of stocking their farms, are obliged to resort,
as before noticed, to agistment stock, for the consumption
of their herbage. These miserably indigent farmers
work equally hard with the common labourers, and live
little, if at all, better than the most provident of that
class, and from which community very many of the
smaller farmers have arisen. Cleanliness (at least in their
houses), seems little attended to, and, though sparing and
frugal in all their domestic affairs, are but seldom regarded
as a thriving people, or considered to be in any way
improving that very small capital with which they began
the world. Very few, however, of either description,
seem at all disposed, in the management of their farms,
to step out of the beaten track, but to procure their
crops with the same labour, and consequently, in point of
money, at a more considerable expense, than that at which
they were produced half a century ago.

The small annually reserved rent upon the lifehold
tenures, would, if taken into the account, greatly diminish
any fair estimate that may be made of the rent, or present
value, of this district; that point must therefore be
passed over, and the value thereof estimated on an average
of what is paid by the tenantry, under leases or covenants,
as they are called, for 14 or 21 years.

Land subject to an occasional course of tillage, 18s.;
meadows liable to annual inundation, or artificially floated
with water, including the embanked marshes above
Bishop's Tawton, on the Taw, and in the parish of
Land-cross, on the Torridge rivers, 60s. per acre; feeding
land

Name of each Town, Parish, or Tithing.	Amount of Money raised by Poor and other Rates.			At what in the P⟨ Rent abov⟩
No.	£.	s.	d.	s.
1. Alwington, ...	212	17	11	6
2. Littleham, ...	73	2	3	16
3. Wear Giffard, ...	226	1	4½	7
4. Land-cross, ...	6	2	6½	....
5. Abbotsham, ...	254	17	11	5
6. Bideford, ...	872	12	0	5
7. Northam, ...	631	18	4	10

From which it appears, that the gross sum annually
levied on this district for parochial disbursements, amounts
to the sum of 18,563*l*. 5*s*. 5¾*d*. or thereabouts;—that there
are about nineteen of the parishes in the district, assessed
from 5*s*. to 16*s*. 5*d*. in the pound rent, averaging seven
shillings and eight-pence ;—that the remainder are assessed
from 3*s*. to 4*s*. 8*d*. in the pound, averaging 3*s*. 3¼*d*.;—that
the money expended for the support and maintenance of
the poor not provided for in work-houses, or houses of
industry, amounts to 12,988*l*. 6*s*. 5¼*d*.;—that the sum
expended in the ten towns and parishes in the district,
having such establishments, amounts to 2317*l*. 11*s*.;—
that there is annually expended throughout the district,
the sum of 350*l*. 12*s*. 5¼*d*. in law-suits, removing paupers,
and in the expenses of overseers and other officers ;—that
the amount of the annual expenses on account of the
poor is 15,656*l*. 9*s*. 11*d*. or thereabouts;—that there is
expended in this district by the church-rate, county-rate,
highway, militia, and other levies, the annual sum of
2131*l*. 18*s*. 1¼*d*. or thereabouts ;—that the gross amount
of all these parochial disbursements is 17,788*l*. 8*s*. 0¼*d*.
or thereabouts, and consequently, that the new overseers
generally receive, with the parish books, a small balance,
to answer the immediate calls of the indigent, and before
it is possible for them to arrange and collect the first rate.
It must also be observed, that, notwithstanding the 45
friendly societies are chiefly confined to the large commercial and manufacturing towns, this system of fellowship and association is much approved of, and found to
be greatly increasing through the neighbouring villages.

DISTRICT II.

The size of the farms here do not seem to vary in any material degree from what has been noticed in the district of North Devon, and although that country is by no means destitute of many intelligent farmers, and good breeders of cattle, the country now before us, possessing in many respects, advantages over that district, may reasonably be supposed to afford a larger proportion of this description of persons. The fact is so, and at the same time it is also to be remarked, that, although the smaller farmers are in no respect more careful or industrious than their northern neighbours, they are generally stated to have much increased in capital within a few years. From the hundred of Hartland to that of Bampton, a number of small proprietors occupy their own estates.

The same tenures obtain here, as before mentioned, and the extent of occupation is generally regulated by the quantity of land, and the ability of the tenant to stock and work it, varying from 20*l*. to 200*l*. and even 300*l*. per annum. The general rent of the sound dry tillage-land, fit for the culture of wheat, barley, turnips, and clover, may be stated from 18*s*. to 26*s*. per acre ; land less free and open, with a strong moist bottom, and applied to the culture of oats, with occasional crops of wheat, from 12*s*. to 16*s*. per acre, and the old moorlands, held in severalty to particular estates, from 7*s*. to 10*s*. per acre ; the meadows and permanent pastures may be referred to the price stated of such lands in the district of North Devon ; the orchard-ground is generally rated with the prime pastures. The accommodation land in the neighbourhood of Torrington, Hatherleigh, Chumleigh,

Chumleigh, Bampton, and Tiverton, is, as usual, very high, particularly in the neighbourhood of the latter place, where land has recently been disposed of at the annual rent of eleven pounds per acre.

With regard to tithes, the Surveyor heard complaints in this district, of the manner in which they were exacted.

The amount of the annual parochial disbursement through this district, as in the manner before noticed, is as follows.

DISTRICT III.

Although there must necessarily be many exceptions to the general size of farms, and character of the occupiers, of a country so widely extended as this district, it may still not be amiss to go a little farther than ordinary into a description of these matters. In the country about East and West Pulford, the size of the farms are not represented to exceed from 20*l.* to 50*l.* per annum; the farmers, though a hard-working people, are supposed to remain stationary with regard to the acquisition of property, or the means of enjoyment, beyond that which was known by their great-grandfathers. About Holsworthy, the occupations are stated to be from 30*l.* to 50*l.* per annum; the farmers are equally laborious, and their means are supposed to have much increased, within these last twenty years.—These people continue much at home, unless necessarily called from thence by their attendance at fairs or markets.

In the neighbourhood of Ashwater, the occupations are even smaller than about Holdsworthy: these farmers are very industrious, working, in general, much harder than the labourer they occasionally employ; some of them become regrators, and attend constantly the Plymouth market.

There are more farms under, than over 50*l.* per annum in the neighbourhood of Black Torrington, where the farmers are stated to be a laborious honest set of men, with some small appearance of increasing capital. The same is stated of the country about Ashbury. A greater diversity, in point of occupation, appears to take place in the neighbourhood of Oakhampton, and such parts of this district as border upon Dartmoor, and where the

farms

farms are stated to run from 20*l.* to 100*l.* per annum. The farmers are there represented as a sober, industrious people, and although much benefited by the advantages afforded them from the Moor, are supposed to be rather stationary than otherwise, with regard to capital.

In the vicinity of Lewtrenchard, and Bratton Clovella, the occupations fluctuate between 30*l.* and 120*l.* per annum. The farmers here are represented as sober and honest, and increasing in their pecuniary concerns. This description applies equally through Broadwood-wedger, St. Giles-in-the-heath, and the parishes of North Petherwin, and Werrington, beyond the Tamar river : to this statement there is little to be added, respecting the occupations and circumstances of the farmers in the division of Meshaw.

The average rent of the enclosed cultivated lands through this district, is about 14*s.* 6*d.* per acre; the great and small tithe about 2*s.* 9*d.* in the pound, including in the valuation as rent, the poor's-rate, land-tax, church and highway levies. One instance only occurred to notice, where the vicarial tithe was commuted at 2*s.* 6*d.* in the pound on the rack-rents, and the great tithe paid 2*s.* in the pound on the value of the corn-crops, just before harvest.

We now proceed, in the usual manner, to state the amount of the poor-rates, and other parish disbursements through this district.

DISTRICT IV.

The size of the farms in this district vary from 20*l.* to 5, 6, and 700*l.* per annum. The smaller occupiers are found generally to reside near the borders of Dartmoor, and the larger ones to hold rich tracts of feeding and arable land in the country below.

Many of the minor order of what are called farmers, derive a considerable part of their subsistence from digging and curing peat-fuel upon Dartmoor, and the commons abutting upon that forest, and packing it to the large towns in the South Hams. There is also another description of farmers, who employ much of their time in attending fairs and markets, and who, strictly speaking, must be denominated jobbers. These people are continually upon the search, ransacking the country for every species of farming stock, whether store or in a fed condition. The farms of these persons are frequently covered with sheep, hogs, and cattle, collected in this manner; and when Plymouth or Exeter fails in affording a satisfactory market for such as may be ready for slaughter, they point towards Taunton with their droves, and keep moving eastward till they travel up a market to their mind. This accomplished, they return home, and resume their former pursuits. It is not difficult to conceive the husbandry (however at times liberally manured) of occupations so frequently exposed to the absence of the farmer.

The average rent of the tillage and grass-land, deduced as before from a great number of instances in different parts of the district, amounts t 41*s.* 6*d.* per acre; indeed, there is but little land taken into the farmer's estimate below 20*s.* per acre: the meadow and feeding lands are commonly valued at 55*s.* 60*s.* and 63*s.* per acre.

The

The accommodation land, as usual in the neighbourhood of the large towns, is very high: near Dock and Plymouth, there is land now rented from 12*l*. to 16*l*. per acre; this is generally used for depasturing of milch-cows, for the supply of Plymouth-dock, the hospital, and shipping: the value of the same sort of land adjacent to the other large towns in the district, varies from 5 to 8 and 9*l*. per acre: 1200 guineas was recently paid for four acres of pasture ground, lying under the church walls at Ashburton.

The general commutation for great and small tithes, is 2*s*. 6*d*. 2*s*. 9*d*. and 3*s*. in the pound, including the valuation of the reserved rent and parochial disbursements. In the neighbourhood of Dartington, the commutation is regulated at 2*s*. 6*d*. in the pound rent when the average price of wheat is below 9*s*. per bushel, and 3*s*. in the pound when above that average; some cases occurred on the survey, of wheat being charged at 9*s*. 3*d*. 10*s*. and 12*s*. per annum; barley at 8*s*. 3*d*. 7*s*. and 10*s*. per acre; oats 7*s*. 3*d*. 6*s*. and 8*s*. per acre.

In the last instance, the demand of the tithe-proctor not being complied with, the tithe was set out, and the proctor removed it in sheaf: 6*s*. 6*d*. and 7*s*. per acre is also paid in some parts of the district for winter and spring corn, in which cases the vicarial tithe is usually commuted at 1*s*. in the pound on the rack-rent.

The poor-rates, and other parochial disbursements occurring in the different towns and parishes within this district, are stated as follows:

DISTRICT FIFTH.

There does not appear to be any thing particularly requiring notice, beyond what is fairly to be inferred from what has been already stated, as applicable to the Eleven Parishes which compose this District. The Poor-Rates, and other Parochial Taxes, are stated as under.

Name of each Town, Parish, or Tithing.	Amount of Money raised by Poor, or other Rates.	At what Rate in the Pound Rent above 5s.	At what Rate in the Pound Rent under 5s.	Money expended out of any House of Industry, or Workhouse.	Money expended in any House of Industry, or Workhouse.	Expenditure in Suits at Law, removal of Paupers, Overseers' Expences, &c.	Total Expenditure on Account of the Poor.	Expenditure for any other purpose, Church, Highways, Bridges, Militia Rate, &c.	Total Expenditure.	Number of Friendly Societies.	And of Members therein.
No.	£. s. d.	s. d.	s. d.	£. s. d.	£. s. d.	£. s. d.	£. s. d.	£. s. d.	£. s. d.		
1. Buckland in the Moor,	42 0 3½	—	2 6	42 0 3½	—	0 16 0	42 16 3½	4 3 4½	46 19 8	—	—
2. Widecombe, - -	388 15 2¼	—	3 9	281 3 2	—	31 2 4¼	312 5 6¼	20 16 9¾	343 2 4	1	40
3. Mannaton, - -	137 2 3	—	—	119 11 8½	—	2 5 6	121 17 2½	15 5 0½	137 2 3	—	—
4. North Bovey, - -	227 9 0¼	—	—	195 2 8	—	15 17 0¼	210 19 8¼	16 10 0¾	227 9 9	1	56
5. Chagford, - -	653 1 8	—	1 6	461 14 5¾	78 16 10	5 13 5	546 4 8¾	109 10 0¾	655 14 9½	2	88
6. Gidley, - - -	61 4 7½	—	0 8	24 4 9½	—	2 0 0	26 4 9½	30 7 4	56 12 1½	—	—
7. Throwsleigh, - -	362 3 3	—	—	239 6 11¼	—	41 17 6	281 4 5¼	12 8 7½	293 13 0¾	—	—
8. Moreton Hempstead, -	1111 0 0	—	—	697 2 5½	327 17 6¼	5 0 0	1030 0 0	—	1030 0 0	4	270
9. Lustleigh, - -	176 15 7	—	—	131 14 7	—	9 16 0	141 10 7	13 7 10½	154 18 5¼	—	—
10. Bovey Tracy*, -	983 11 5¾	—	1 0	729 5 11¾	142 12 0	4 11 8	876 9 7¾	191 16 2	1068 5 9¾	5	836
11. Teign Grace, - -	54 19 9	—	1 10½	35 16 11	—	—	35 16 11	21 19 9¼	57 16 8¼	—	—
Total, - -	4162 3 1¼	—	—	2957 3 11¾	549 6 4½	118 19 5½	3625 9 9¾	446 5 1½	4071 14 11¼	—	—

* The poor in the house are maintained under contract, at 3s. 3d. per head per week, and the contractor is entitled to their earnings.

DISTRICT VI

The size of the farms in this district are generally not so large as many we meet with in the South Hams: the average may be placed at 120*l.* per annum

The farmers are honest, sober, and industrious, with an appearance of more capital than may generally be remarked in the third and fourth district: they are still found to live rather in a low and humble manner than otherwise.

It is a common practice among them, on marriage, to give to their wives what is called *pin-money:* this consists of poultry, pigs, and the whole produce of the dairy; with which supply the wife is expected to clothe and (exclusive of bread, corn, and other vegetables) support the whole household: and here it is but common justice to say, that the industry and attention to business of the farmers' wives and daughters, with the neatness displayed in all their market-ware, at Exeter and in other large towns, are subjects deserving the highest praise. No labour or fatigue is spared in reaching the market in time, be the distance what it may; nor will any severity of weather prevent them from their ordinary attendance.

There does not appear to be any material difference between the general value of the land through this district and what has been stated of the South Hams.

The tithes, great and small, with some few exceptions, are commuted for at 3*s.* in the pound on the reserved rent, or on a proportional value where there are lifehold tenures.

The poor-rates and other parochial payments are stated as follows:

DISTRICT VII.

From the number of farms consolidated in this district, and applied to the depasturing of dairy cows, their average is found to exceed that in the preceding one by about 40*l.* per annum. The character of the farmers, and the management of their household, may be drawn from what has been already stated. The accommodation land in the neighbourhood of Honiton, Colyton, and Axminster, may be said to average about 6*l.* per acre. The meadows and rich feeding-lands along the river Axe, frequently rent at 4*l.* per acre; the dairy-grounds from 40*s.* to 50*s.*; the arable, on a marl bottom, 32*s.*; the tough flinty loams, 24*s.*; and the wet grey loams, mixed with white-acre, flint, and sandstones, about 18*l.* per acre.

The great and small tithes are generally commuted for at 3*s.* or somewhat more in the pound, on the reserved rent.

The poor-rates, and other parochial payments, are stated as follows:

Plate II. P.145.

Devonshire Plough; as it appears without the Mould-Board or Furrow held.

Devonshire Plough.

A.B. Beam of Ash 6 Feet 4 long
C.D. Landheld 5. 6.
E.F. Furrow held which is a narrow board nailed to the Spill at G. and connected with the landheld by a Stave crossing from O. to O.
H. Is a small piece of Oak-board called the Lander held to which is fixed the Mould board the breadth of the Mould board at the bottom end is regulated by the length of the Stave I.K. which connects it with the landheld this mould called called have the quantity is of reed
Is the Chip 2.5 from L. to L. & is generally made of Apple wood
The Share is 20 Inches long with the point bending downwards.
M. Is a crooked stick passing through a mortise in the beam & is used by Young Ploughmen to regulate the depth of the furrow this is called a Druat.

The Share Center & Staple at B. with afsis nails are the only pieces of Iron used.
Price of the whole compleat about 18.5 or 19.5

Nele sculp Stroud

CHAP. V.

IMPLEMENTS.

SECT. I.—PLOUGHS.

THE common Devonshire plough, made by a hedge-row carpenter, and seldom exceeding in cost 15s. irons included, is much used; and candour must allow, that its performance is far superior to what might be expected from the very rude appearance it makes, either at work or lying empty on the ground. It is a swing-plough (*Plate* II.) with a beam about seven feet long, lying nearly parallel to the head and heel of the plough: at the end of this beam, is occasionally fastened a horizontal graduated iron, to which the team-band is affixed, and which regulates from the line of draught, the direction of the plough either to the land or to the furrow. It is constructed to enter the land obliquely, and at an easy angle; and though there is little apparent curve in its breast or mould-board, the straight pieces of board (of which these are made) are placed and continued so far backwards, that in all cases, but particularly in whole ground, the furrow is lifted up and whelmed completely over. The shares used upon these ancient ploughs differ in their forms, according to the kind of work to be performed with them. When the land is designed to be ploughed clean, and to a good full pitch, a long pointed share, with a small fin or wing, is used; when skirting is required, the wing of the share is considerably enlarged;

and

and when velling is performed, the wing of the share is turned upwards, forming a sharp comb upon its outside angle.

The paring-plough, which is meant to supply the use of the breast-plough or paring-shovel, has a wide winged flat share, measuring about 14 inches from the land-side to the angular point of its right side, or cutting wing. In the beam of this plough, and preceding a sharp comb welded on the coulter margin of the share, is a sliding foot, so fixed as to regulate the precise thickness of the slice intended to be pared. The share and comb of this machine being kept very sharp by frequent grinding, enables it to perform its business very well.

The plough is held horizontally, cutting a smooth and even furrow at the bottom; the former one is held obliquely, cutting on the furrow side, the spine or green sward to a feather-edge, the whole of which is gradually lifted up, and turned with its green side completely under. In this operation, the work is performed by what is called splitting, that is, the plough always turns upon the left to the first furrow, and the coulter is held close all the way to the lifted slice previously turned over, and which now covers a balk or rib of whole unmoved ground.

This operation, in the eastern counties of England, is called wrest balking, but is there performed with a very different view to what induces the practice in Devonshire. The operation of veiling, is in effect the same thing, but as the outer point of the wing of the share is turned upwards, there is less necessity for holding the plough in an oblique position. The plough in this operation, is always turned to the right upon the head-land, and (contrary to what may be observed in skirting), the slice or furrow is turned towards the ploughed, instead of the unploughed land. In velling, the plough is thrown

The Old Devonshire Plough, or as it is there called the Sull. Plate III.P.

Neele sculp. strand.

6 Feet

Nº 1. The Beam, made of Ash, c & and with thin Iron between the Spill (4) & Cilter (5) to prevent its splitting
2. Land Hail or Handle, made of Oak, Ash or Elm grown Similar thereto ab.t 4 In. thick at the Foot
   c. Beam Mortise.
3. Furrow Hail or Handle made of 1¾ In. board c is Nailed to the Spill (4) and Cradle piece (c)
4. The Spill made of Ash 1¾ In. thick by 3 In. wide.

5. Cilter ab.t ⅞ In. thick and 2½ In. wide at the Neck, which is kept in place by Wooden Wedges,
   and when fixed it hangs over the Share point about ¾ In. towards the Land.
6. Shewing the Top part of the Beam, with the Spill and Cilter Mortises a. c. b and Staple d
   to draw the Plough by.
7. The Sole piece or Chip, shewing the splay of the two Hails or Handles together with the Share (8) & Cradle pins (9)s

so far into the land from the line of draught, as to enable
the ploughman to carry with ease, about twice as much
land as is displaced by the ploughed slice, which is pared
very thin and even, and on the land side not cut so deep
as in the operation of skirting, but gradually lifted and
turned neatly on its green side upon the balk, now left
on the right hand, or furrow side of the plough.

This manner of ploughing, in contradistinction to
splitting, is called gathering of the land; these latter
operations are generally performed with two of the common horses of the country, or a pair of good strong
steers driven by a boy; but when ploughing clean on an
old ley, or otherwise breaking up strong land, a double
and sometimes treble force is required. The day's work
in the summer is usually performed in two journies, from
7 to 12, and from 2 to 6; seldom exceeding an acre per
day, when ploughing clean, and 5 or 6 roods when velling or skirting.

DISTRICT II.

The light Dorset swing-plough is much used in many
parts of this district; it is constructed to enter the ground
at an easy angle, has a well-curved iron breast, one foot
ten inches long from the neb to the end of the wrest; the
slice, gradually ascending along this well-turned plate,
operates with an equal friction on its whole surface, and
is discharged with such a hollow or concave superfice
downwards, as completely to whelm over and invert
every square inch of the lifted furrow. The sole of the
plough forms nearly a parallel with the position of the
beam, which is seven feet long, furnished at the head with
an horizontal and vertical graduated wang of rack-work,
for regulating the depth and the direction of the plough,
either to the land or furrow.

This

This machine performs its work, whether in stiff or
free ground, incomparably well; in most cases it is drawn
by a pair of stout horses, and costs, complete, two guineas. A bridle, for the better security of the sole, should
be fixed on the beam by a nut and screw, and passed
down the spill with a lip, to grasp the head end of the
sole, to prevent it from drawing downwards in rough and
rocky ground. This plough with two horses, on broken
ground, a boy and a man, will plough an acre and a half
per day, in one journey of ten hours; the same plough,
with four oxen, on whole ground, will plough a like
quantity in the same time.

The turn-wrest, one-way furrow, or double-sole plough,
(*Plate* IV.) is also much used along the steep side-hills:
with the same force, and under the same circumstances, it will plough as much ground. The double-furrow
plough, used only on broken ground, with a force of four
horses, or six oxen, will plough two acres and a half per day.

Trench-ploughing is sometimes performed in the neighbourhood of Hartland, by first ploughing a slice one and a
half or two inches thick, with the common paring plough,
and afterwards taking up the bottom of that furrow about
three inches deeper, and thus raising a sufficiency of mould
to bury the first slice, and cover the seed, without disturbing the inverted green sward with the drags or harrows.
This operation has always been found to answer the fullest
expectations of the gentleman by whom it has as yet
been almost exclusively practised.

Lord Clifford has introduced the double and single
Warwickshire ploughs; they are so steadily set as to require but little labour in holding them: the ploughman
drives the horses, which are three in length.

Cook's improved drill-plough, with its necessary appen-
dages of scarifiers, scufflers, shims, or broadshares, is
                                                        almost

Plate IV. P.118

The Plough in Devonshire,

used for turning each Furrow the same way, on account of the Hillyness of the Country.

Scale scale Strand

6 Feet

1 2 3 4 5 6 Feet

a

b

Nᵒ 1. The Beam which is made similar to that of the other Plough.
2.2.2.2. The two Halls or Handles made of 1¾ In. Board, both one size and Length.
3. Called the Stump Hall fastened with wooden pins going through the foot & Sole piece or Chip.
4.4.4.4. Furrow boards which are hung with Hinges to the Spill (b) and are moveable at the other end, as Occasion require to make the Furrow.

6. Shews the Beam with the Coulter Hole or Mortise a, which is made wider at top than under; on Account of turning the Coulter with a Wedge to correspond with the Share, when you shift the Furrow boards at
7. The Sweep piece or Pin which is made of Iron or Wood, and is fastened to the Furrow boards at each end, and six holes made in it from the Centre each way, about 1½ In. apart, so as to admit the small Iron Pin (8) to fix it agreeable to the Furrow you want to turn.

almost exclusively used in this district, by Mr. Exter of Hartland, who, in order to produce the utmost regularity in the distances between rows of turnips and potatoes, has projected a bar from the beam of his double mould-board plough, at the end of which a foot is attached, and so graduated, as to admit of its tracing a wider or narrow interval. The coulter point, or centre of this plough, is always held precisely and steadily in the line so traced, by which means the greatest accuracy is produced in the exact parallel bearing of the rows and ridges with each other. This is always of importance in conducting the subsequent operations of this husbandry: but it is rendered more particularly so in Mr. Exter's practice, who has also contrived to fix two light iron ploughs upon a horizontal beam, by means of which he works down two of his turnip ridges at the same time.

The materials of these ploughs are all of wrought iron, and weigh about 8lb. each; the construction is so simple, as to require a few words only to make it fully understood: from the point of the share to the end of the heel, is about 16 inches; at the heel-end of this sole, a perpendicular bar is inserted, about 16 inches in length, secured in the horizontal beam with wedges, and consequently capable of being taken up or let down at pleasure: from the coulter margin of the sole, and near the point of the share, a comb or brace rises, and retiring with a curve, is inserted about midway in the perpendicular bar; this having a sharp edge, is found fully to answer the purpose of a coulter. As this apparatus seems constructed merely for the destruction of weeds, it should be considered more in the light of a hoe than of a plough, though there does not appear to be much difficulty in fixing a mould-board to it, should the work at any time require such an addition.

DISTRICT

DISTRICT VI.

The Norfolk wheel-plough, with a pair of horses driven by the ploughman, is found to answer very well, and is getting much in use in all the light tender looms in this district.

SECT. II.——HARROWS.

THE harrows commonly used, consist of a very heavy drag, usually drawn by four or six oxen; and a lighter kind of harrow, sometimes in one piece, but more generally divided in the middle, and connected so with links, as to yield to the curved form of the eight and ten furrow ridges, and to perform its work very completely on them. (*Plate* V.)

SECT. III.——ROLLERS.

THE Common one, and two horse-rollers, with heavy granite or moorstone rollers, of from 5 to 8 feet in length, and of proportionate diameter, are very generally used; the latter for rolling the wheat and pasture-grounds, and aiding the operation of separating the spine from the mould on the beat-lands, in preparation for wheat or turnips. (*Plate* VI.)

SECT. IV.——DRILLS.

DRILL-MACHINES, attached to the ploughs by various contrivances, or used with a horse or by hand, in depositing

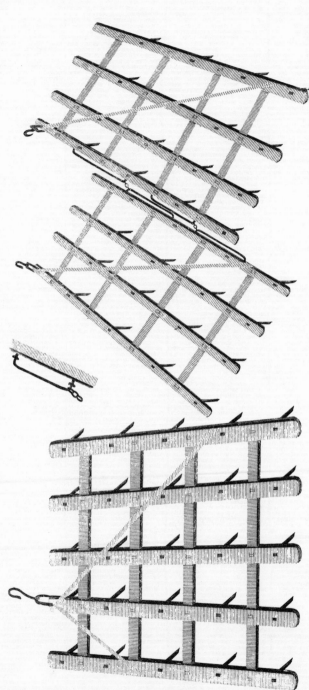

Plate V. P. 126.

Common Harrows.

Node sculp. Strand.

Plate VI. P. 120.

Granite Roller.

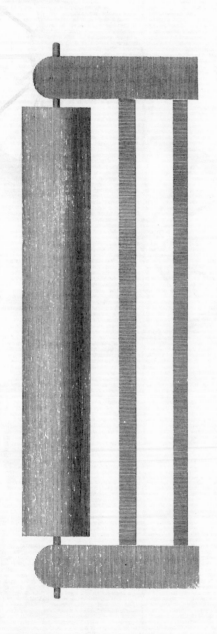

Neele sculp. Strand.

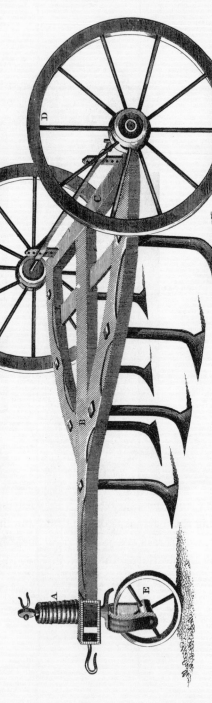

Plate VI. P. 121.

Tormentor

15 In.

A The Spitt or Iron which passes through the beam & supports the front wheel
    has a number of Iron rings on it by which the depth of staring is regulated

B Length of Beam 6F. 9I C Breadth of the Back piece 3F. 7I.

D D Large Wheel 5F. dia E Small Wheel 10 In.

Pieces of Wood of which the Frame is made 4In square.

There is another sort of Tormentor in use with two Wheels before
with a Crane neck.

Neele sculp Strand

siting turnip-seed on the two-furrow ridges, are occasionally employed in this husbandry, and with good effect.

SECT. V.——SCARIFIERS, &c.

SCARIFIERS, scufflers, shims, and broad shares of various constructions, and called under the general name of
tormentors, are very much resorted to in crossing the
balks of whole ground, left after the velling and skirting
operations for beat-burning. (*Plate* VII.)

SECT. VI.——THRASHING-MACHINES.

THRASHING-MACHINES, on an improved construction,
made by Baker of Exeter, and other wheel and mill-
wrights in the country, and costing, exclusive of the
large framing timber, about 40 guineas each, are becoming very prevalent in most parts of the country; the
power employed is usually four horses, the *diameter* of
the path on which the walk is, being about 30 feet; but
where a water power can be conveniently applied, and
which sometimes occurs, it is consequently preferred.

These machines, with the attendance of six persons for
driving the horses, getting the sheaves, feeding and
clearing the machine, combing and binding the wheat-
straw, will thrash six bushels per hour, and that without
urging the horses to an exertion beyond their ordinary
labour: five persons only are required for thrashing oats
or barley, the straw of which is not combed, or seldom
bound Of these grains, with this force, the machine
will generally thrash about nine bushels per hour. Thus
two

two men at 20d. three women at 10d. and one boy at 8d.
including the value of horses, labour, the annual interest
upon the first cost, and wear and tear of the machine,
will all amount to about 25s. the hundred, or 8d. per
bushel of wheat thrashed in this way, and proportionably
less for oats or barley.

There are few farmers having these machines, with 50
or 60 acres of winter and spring corn, that do not find
their expectations very fully answered by them. The resource they afford to their servants and labourers in wet
and broken weather; the oat and barley straw, after
passing through them, being so much softer and more
pliant to the mouths of their cattle; the great security
which they afford to the crop from the ravages of vermin;
the facility with which, on a sudden rise of the corn, or
on any other emergency, they can bring a large portion
of their crop to market; and above all, the more full and
complete separation of the corn from the straw, and
which, by general consent, seems nearly, if not quite,
equal to one in twenty—all combine to recommend them
as machines of very extensive and general utility.

Among many liberal and provident measures suggested
by the Honourable Newton Fellows, as examples of general benefit for the improvement of the country, is that of
a thrashing and grinding mill, which he has erected at a
very considerable expense, and to which is conveyed a
never-failing supply of water. The power of this mill
is estimated to be equal to that of 16 horses. Combined
with its power for thrashing, winnowing, and dressing
every species of corn, it has a pair of stones of about
four feet in diameter, and a bolting machine.

This thrashing-machine will discharge about 25 bushels
of wheat, and of barley or oats near 40 bushels, per hour.
The barn being filled with wheat, the manual assistance
                                                    distributed

distributed through the machine is as follows: one man
and two women f r unbinding the sheaves and feeding
the rollers, which are grooved, and divided into lengths of
6 or 8 inches; on the straw being discharged from the
machine, one person attends to shake it well over a large
open skreen, whence it is tossed over to another person,
who removes it out of the way. At and under each of
the winnowing-machines, sieves are placed to receive the
grain coming directly from the machine, which is then
put into the hopper of the fan of the second winn wing-
machine, from which it is again received into another
sieve, and thence discharged into the hopper for grinding, or for market: in passing through this little fan,
such a separation takes place as completely to divide the
head from the tail corn. A cylindrical pearl barley machine, is also used to cleanse the wad of its smut, and thus
by taking off the downy end of the grain, a much finer
sample both of wheat and flour is obtained. This is preferred to the brush apparatus, for although that may cleanse
the body of the grain, it will not carry off the down from
its end, and which is reasonably supposed to contain the
germin of smut, or to form the nest of other animalculæ
equally injurious to such grain when used as seed.

In this machine, there is only one man employed to
five women, and which together with the drill-husbandry
introduced and practised by Mr. Fellows, affords an opportunity of employing a large proportion of women and
children ; the work being so systematically arranged, that
in its execution it becomes in a manner impossible for
them to deviate or to go wrong. The men, in the mean
time, are engaged in more arduous and laborious employments; and the whole of this society is thus, in a season
of great dearth of labour from the failure of the neighbouring manufactures, actually employed to their own
interest,

Plate VIII. *P. 124.*

Barley Cracker

Wooden Hopper

Fly Wheel

Belt

Belt

E

F

C

...tter worked also by...

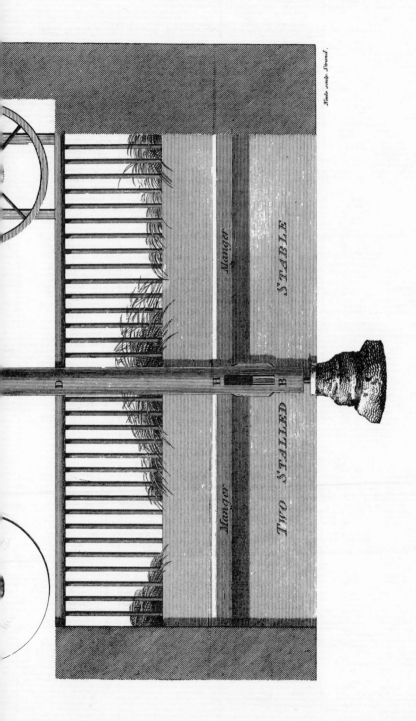

Manger

STABLE

Manger

TWO STALLED

D   H   B

Neele sculp. Strand.

interest, the manifest relief of the parish burthens, and the general benefit of the community at large.

A very good thrashing machine at Mr. Vinn's, at Payhembury, is worked by water; it performs all the operations of thrashing, winnowing, grinding, and bolting, together with an iron hopper axis for grinding apples, and an ingenious contrivance for shelling clover-seed, and the huddocks of wheat: this consists of a coarse running grout-stone, inclosed within a hoop or case, the diameter of which is 3 feet 6 inches, lined with 16 iron plates, the surfaces of which presented to the side of the running stone are made rough, by holes partially punched through, and thus raising them to the character of a very rough grater. The depth of the hoop above the surface of the stone is 18 inches: here the wheat-huddocks, or heads of clover are placed, and as the stone whirls round, it draws them into the side-groove, where meeting with a partial resistance from the rough sides of the plates, a separation of the grain from the husks is completely effected, and discharged through a small aperture below.

Lord Clifford has erected a thrashing-mill, the horse-walk of which is 28 feet in diameter, the wheel 18 feet, in which are inserted eight segments of cast iron cogs, 30 in each; the cogs in the trundle-head wheel just 30: it performs well with a power of four horses. The neighbouring tenants are fond of resorting to it, as his Lordship gratuitously indulges them with the use of it.

SECT. VII.—CHAFF-CUTTERS.

CHAFF-CUTTERS are used by Mr. Fellows and other gentlemen in the county, but from there being so little chaff

chaff used for feeding horses, they are by no means an implement of general use.

SECT. VIII.—WAGGONS, CARTS, &c.

IN the hilliest parts of the county, horses are only used for packing lime, dung, and all other purposes, for which wheel-carriages would in a less hilly district be far more appropriate; it is only in the less broken parts of the country that one and two-horse carts are found to supply the labour, and to carry in common from 8 to 12 cwt.

A few waggons were noticed on the particular farms of some agricultural gentlemen; in the neighbourhood of Axminster, they are however in very general use. There are a number of two-horse carts, carrying from 15 to 18 cwt. each, in very general use, wherever they can with convenience be substituted for the long or short crooks or dung-pots.

One-horse carts, or butts, are also generally made use of; they are made to tip like tumbrils, and will hold about five seams, or from 10 to 12 bushels each. Being placed on low wheels, they are rendered very convenient for loading large stones, or any heavy article. The three-wheel butts, with barrow-handles, drawn by one horse, and holding, level-full, from five to six bushels, are also much used, and found very suitable for removing stones or any heavy load to a short distance.

SECT. IX.—PARING-SHOVEL.

THE common gardener's spade, with a short handle, is scarcely any where seen among the farmers in North Devon;

Devon; the holeing, digging, gripping, ditching, hacking, and hand-beating, being entirely performed with a broad-bitted mattock, which is so fastened upon the shaft, as to incline inwards little short of an angle of 45° with the line of its handle. This mattock is accompanied in all its operations, where a body of earth is to be removed, with that most useful and powerful of all instruments of its kind, the long-handled hollow-formed shovel, and which resembles the impression of the ace of spades stamped upon playing-cards.

The paring-shovel, or breast-plough, is from 9 to 10 inches wide at its insertion with the handle, which is made with a considerable curve upwards; the blade is about 12 inches long, terminating with a broad angular point, which, with its sides, are always kept very sharp and keen for cutting; on the left hand, or land-side of the tool, a sharp comb or coulter rises obliquely, to sever the pared slice from the whole ground; but this, from the toughness of the surface, and impediments presented by the roots of the furze, flags, and heather, is frequently dispensed with, and the slice is rent or torn off by the operator, as well from the side of the whole ground as cut and separated from the stratum below. When a foot or 15 inches of this slice rises upon the handle of the breast-plough, an effort is made to separate it from the uncut surface, and which by a turn of the paring-spade is whelmed over. This effort of separating the cut from the uncut ground, is always (when circumstances allow that the surface is not too much encumbered with furze or heather) much lessened by having the slice next to be pared, cut or nicked into such lengths as may be most convenient to the workmen; indeed, the regular nicking of the slice to be pared from the whole ground, is, in some particular situations, found indispensably necessary,

sary,

Plate IX. *P. 127.*

Mattock.

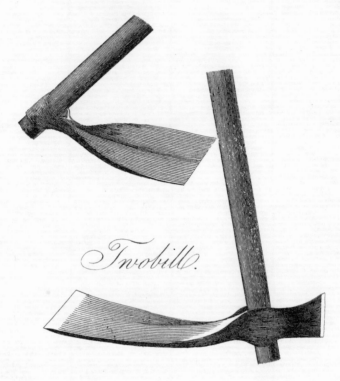

Twobill.

Shovel

Front View.

sary, where the moor is of such a nature as to render impracticable the operation of the breast-plough.

The mattock, before-noticed, is used to grub up, chap, and displace the surface: this is called hand-beating, in contradistinction to the other operation, which is termed spading the ground.—The grubbing of roots is generally performed with the two-bill, or double-bitted mattock, (*Plate* IX.)

SECT. X.——WINNOWING-MACHINES.

As the corn is often carried to an eminence to be winnowed, for the sake of a free current of air, few winnowing-machines, saving a common whisk or fly, are used in this county. The long crooks generally affixed to the pack-saddles, for the purpose of removing corn, hay, straw, turf, or faggots, from such hills and side-lands as are deemed inaccessible to wheel-carriages, are formed to correspond with the curve of the pack-saddle, to descend rather below the line of the horse's girth, there to curve outwardly, forming a bottom of from twenty inches to two feet in width; thence rise with a small inclination inwards, and to the height of about two feet eight inches, or three feet, above the line of the horse's back and withers. Within these crooks, which are placed two on each side of the pack-saddle, there is no difficulty in laying on any load, equal to the strength of the horses. Stronger and shorter crooks are used for the purpose of transporting boards, poles, and small sticks of timber; and, for the carriage of stones, gravel, and dung, strong wicker baskets, opening at bottom, and sufficient to contain one hundred-weight and a half of short or rotten

dung

dung each, are most generally used ; the lime is either packed in bags on horses' backs, or carried loose in two or three-horse carts, holding from 20 to 25 bushels each.

SECT. XI.——PITCH-FORKS.

THE pitch-forks, whether for removing corn, hay, or straw, or for the common use of the stable, from the length and form of their tines or prongs, seem scarcely sufficient for holding or lifting a bulk beyond that of a rook's nest ; as little, indeed, can be said of the hoes and rakes, which afford but sad examples of utility to the county.

SECT. XII.——REAPING HOOKS.

REAPING-HOOKS with smooth edges, are generally pre ferred to sickles with sawed ones ; these hooks are used occasionally with either hand, the operator shifting hands, chopping the stubble low, and gathering about half a sheaf at a time, which, put together, is bound with reed, combed from former wheat-straw, or with a double length of the wheat reaping.

A mode of securing the corn prevails in some parts of the South Hams, and which, if admissible in this place, seems well entitled to some consideration. It is said to have been borrowed from the Dutch, as it is much used in Holland, and all the low countries upon the Rhine and Scheld rivers. It is also universally adopted through the

eastern

eastern and middle States of North America. It consists of a light moveable roof, which is raised or let down at pleasure, over the straddle upon which the stack is built. At the distance of about four feet from the corners of the straddle or stack-frame, are sunk four strong boxes, well crammed and secured, and of sufficient capacity to receive about three feet of a large pole or spar, rounded from a square of six inches, a little tapering towards the top, and 30 feet long : on the upper end of this spar is fixed a stout ring or verrell, from which is projected a strong iron hook ; the four poles, thus fitted up, are placed in the boxes at the corners of the straddle. A two-sheaf tackle is hitched to the hooks at the top of the poles, and a one-sheaf tackle to each corner of the roof, resting upon the straddle, and presenting at each corner a portable hoop, or collar to enclose the poles, and on which it traverses up and down, keeping all firm, steady, and compact together. These four tackles are manned with as many persons as may be necessary to raise or lower the roof, and thus every sheaf brought home is more immediately secured from future damage, than were they otherwise placed under cover, and stowed away in a barn This contrivance is called a hay-barrack, in Pennsylvania, where they are equally used for the protection of hay as well as of corn. In a climate frequently subject to sudden and violent thunder-showers during hay-time and harvest, they are found particularly useful. One set of poles and tackles will be amply sufficient for any one establishment. The dimensions of the straddles may be from 20 to 30 feet in length, and from 12 to 20 feet in breadth. In forming the roof upon any given dimension of base, care must be taken to allow for a projection of two and a half, or three feet, in the walls of the stack, from its bottom to the eaves, and which the moveable roof must be made sufficiently large to enclose and cover.

DEVON.]   We

We must now revert to, and speak of as rude a contrivance for collecting corn and hay together, as perhaps was ever yet adopted in any civilized country.—This consists of a tackle, rigged to the upper part of a ladder, placed at one end of the stack; the corn or hay is tied up with ropes in trusses of 180 or 200lbs. each, and placed lengthways on a pad which extends along the horse, and is thus transported from the field to the stack-yard, a strong man driving the horse, and steadying the bundle all the way: when brought to the stack it is thrown down, and a hook, reeved at one end of the tackle-rope, takes the middle band, and that which goes lengthways round the truss; to the other end of the tackle-rope a horse is fastened to draw up the bundle, which done, it is dropped on the stack, where it is received by two or three men, standing up to their middle in corn, and who, with great labour, roll and tug it about till they have got it to the other end of the stack, or place prepared to receive it, when the bands are withdrawn, and they wait patiently for the arrival, and sending up of another bundle. The litter of corn upon the road from the field to the stack, the waste of time, and expense of labour, employed in thus collecting a small quantity of corn or hay together, can only be estimated by those who are practically acquainted with a superior method.—The idea seems to have originated from the sheer hulks lying at His Majesty's dock-yards.

The Reverend Mr. Froude, of Dartington parsonage, has contrived a very simple apparatus for working with one horse, his chaff cutter, and bean and barley cracker. (*Plate* VIII.)

A, block of oak sunk in the ground—B, C, perpendicular shaft passing through the hay-loft floor at D—E F, crown wheel of two-inch plank, with six cast iron segments,

ments, composing a crown-wheel of 108 cogs—G, pinion
with 14 cogs, the shaft of which passes through a drum
18 inches in diameter, which is shown by the circular
line of dots—from this drum the motion is communicated
by a belt to the barley-cracker, and by the same belt
to the chaff-cutter, where it is drawn tight over a sheaf
of 18 inches diameter.

The lever by which this is worked, and which passes
through the mortice of the shaft at H, makes the division
of the stalls when tied to the manger; the expense of the
machinery is as follows:

	£.	s.	d.
Elm for the crown-wheel valued at	0	6	0
Ash for stays, bridge of pinions, &c.	0	12	6
Price of white deal for the shaft, ...	0	16	0
Cast-iron bolts, brass boxes, gudgeons, other iron-work, &c.	2	0	0
Belt, made of old post-chaise traces, ...	0	3	0
Mill-wright's bill for labour, including a model for casting segments of crown-wheel, at 3s. 6d. per day, ...	1	10	0
Carpenter's bill who assisted, at 2s. per day, ...	0	12	0
	£ 5	19	6

The chaff-cutter does its work well in every other
respect, except that the rollers which draw forward the
hay and straw are, without great attention, apt to choak,
and, where the loft or other situation will admit of it, it
were better to have the belt longer.

The stable is paved in the manner recommended by
Mr. Beattie, in the first volume of Communications to
the Board of Agriculture. It is very useful to those who
wish to make other uses of their straw than for litter.

CHAP.

CHAP. VI.

ENCLOSING.

——————

DISTRICT I.

INSTANCES are but very rare, of enclosures being made in this district, and where such have taken place, they have been only to a small extent, by fencing off so much of the old moors or commons, as fancy may have dictated or convenience required. The situations in which these improvements have been made, are all extremely exposed, and such as require extraordinary pains, as well for the permanent security of the work, as for procuring an early shelter for the sheep and cattle. In these cases, and where more than an ordinary sufficiency of fencing has been required, the expense of carrying on such works, drawn from an average of several different cases, may be stated thus :

Raising a mound, on a 9 feet base, with a ditch, 3 feet wide on each side (making the whole scite of the fence 15 feet), facing the mound, 4 feet high with stones, sodded 3 feet higher above the stone-work, and leaving it 4½ feet broad upon the top, will usually cost for a perch of 16½ feet...£.0 6 0

Quarrying, or otherwise procuring proper stone for this facing..................................} 0 3 0

Frithing, or wattling with willow-stakes, or any other hardy wood, known to grow from cuttings; and planting the top with two rows of beach, alder, ash, withy, birch, hawthorn, &c...................................} 0 2 0

Expense

Expense of procuring said plants, and the ⎤ £. s. d.
seed of firs, elder, black-thorn, and bram- |
bles, and with which the tops and sides to ⎬ 0 2 0
windward of all such mounds are fre- |
quently, and should always be sown.......... ⎦
Average expense of cartage, or packing of ⎱ 0 2 0
stones, laid down for facing the mound.... ⎰

Amounting in the whole to about....£.0 13 0

per perch, for a fence that is permanently efficient, not
only for the purpose of subdivision and boundary, but
whilst it proves an excellent protection for the stock,
shelters from the most prevalent winds. Its ditches on each
side offer a ready channel, through which may be conveyed the surface and surplus waters of such enclosed
fields.

These enclosures may require, according to their size,
or the particular use to which they are put, one gate for
every six, eight, or ten acres, the common expense of
which, when made strong, and of good and sufficient
materials, irons, posts, and hanging included, will be
about 20 s. or one guinea per gate. Tunnelling, or
soughing under the gateways, will be in proportion to
the number of gates, or the facility of procuring sough-
ing-tiles. It is very material, that the top and sides of
the mound should be strewed with the seeds before mentioned, which being out of the reach of the sheep and
cattle, will soon form an ample shelter and protection for
such other plants as are designed for permanent hedge-
row wood.

DISTRICT II.

There do not appear to have been any enclosures made
in this district, of sufficient extent to require particular
notice.

The

The cases of enclosures in this district, are confined to part of an estate called Lew Moor Farm, containing about 300 acres, in the parish of North Lew, and about 200 acres, called Irish Comb Moor, adjoining the great Moor of Meshaw, in the eastern division of this district. The fences on the first of these improvements, were raised upon a base seven feet wide, with a ditch of three feet on each side, and which, including the foot for the sods or facing to rest upon, occupied about 13 feet width of ground. The mound was raised six feet high from its base; the sides faced with turf, and left nearly five feet wide on the top: these were planted with two rows, consisting of oak, ash, beech, alder, hazel, and hawthorn, purchased at 1s. 6d. per seam or horse-load, from those who collected them on the waste hedge-rows and woodlands in the country. One oak and one ash was allowed to each pole's length, the remainder of the space was filled up with the young trees before mentioned, on the rows a yard a part; and in them, at the distance of 15 or 18 inches from each other. The frithe-work, or wattling, was made upon willow or sallow stakes, which immediately growing, formed both shelter and security for the young hedge-rows. The expense of this fence was not particularly stated, but is estimated at about half-a-guinea per perch.

On the other of these improvements, the base of the mound was six feet, its height five feet, and breadth at the top nearly the same; this, with the side-drains or ditches on each side, made the whole scite of the fence about 12 feet ; cost of raising the mound and frithing, 4s. per perch. The expense of procuring the stakes or pitches, which were chiefly of willow, was not ascertained. This mound was planted at the top with a double row of birch, thorn and alder, in which were placed

five

five young nursery beech trees to every pole's length ; cost
of these plants, 3 s. per 1000.

No farther particulars could be procured as to the expense of these fences ; in both cases they appeared very
thrifty, and to be growing very even and extremely well.
These enclosures have been made upon old moorlands,
and converted into tillage, grass, and woodland. The
farther detail of these improvements will be hereafter
stated.

DISTRICT IV.

Adjoining Black-down on the west, and in the parish
of Loddiswell, is an extensive tract of moorland, lying
in severalty to the adjoining estate ; about 70 acres of this
land has been recently enclosed, and improved with great
effect, by Mr. King, of Fowlescombe. The detail of this,
with all other improvements, will be likewise particularly noticed in the Twelfth Chapter of this Report.

DISTRICT V.

No enclosures occur.

DISTRICT VI.

Kentiswill Moor consists of a black and brown mould,
on a strong red and yellow gravelly clay, and a dry flinty
grey earth on a pebbly gravel ; through the whole of which
the common red marl of the country very frequently
occurs, and appears to contain about 1000 acres. On such
of the allotments as have been cultivated, good wheat,
barley, and oats, with excellent turnips and potatoes, have
been produced. The total neglect of many of the new
allot-

allotments, and the little care taken in the raising of live fences, were observed with concern: the absence of the Minister, as also of the principal farmers at Honiton market, prevented the requisite information from being procured, respecting the languid state of improvement in this new enclosure.

DISTRICT VII.

The enclosures lately made upon the Black-down hills, under the authority of Parliament, are those of Church Stanton, Clayhaydon, and Dunkerswell. In the first, little progress of improvement seems to have taken place; many of the allotments are still left in a state of nature; and little attention has been given to the raising of live fences on the mounds, all of which appear to be well and sufficiently raised with a three-foot ditch on each side. The soil of these enclosures has already been stated, as consisting chiefly of a moist grey loam, and a moory soil, on a bed of yellow clay and fox-mould.

The new enclosures at Clayhaydon rest upon a strong flinty subsoil, and from the draining and other works now performing, seem to be more carefully attended to. The soil of the commons of Dunkerswell (which forms one of the most extensive plains in the county of Devon), has already been noticed, as consisting chiefly of a brown and black peaty earth, on beds of brown and yellow clay, and fox-mould, and all ultimately resting upon a deep stratum of chip sand.

The natural produce of all these commons is heath, fern, dwarf-furze, and a very coarse, tough, and wiry herbage. Part of these enclosures are cultivated, part appropriated to planting, but by far the larger portion remains in a state of nature.

The

The outside and partition fences of all the new allotments, are laid out on a ten feet base, upon which a mound with sodded sides is raised five feet high, and left six feet wide upon the top. These banks are all enclosed with a ditch four feet wide and three feet deep; on each brow of the mound a wattled fence, about two feet high, is made, within which is planted the young trees and common hedge-row wood; the cost of doing all which, on a general average, does not exceed 4*s.* per rope of 20 feet. The wattled fence is moved upon stakes about three feet long, two feet of which is raddled with any convenient brush-wood that can be procured; on the top of the mound are two rows of withy or sallow cuttings, placed about three feet a-part; these pitches are cut four feet long, and put obliquely into the ground, leaving about one foot above the surface: between these rows of withy are planted oak, ash, beech, birch, alder, hazel, dogwood, and thorns; and at the distance of every ten feet, along the middle of the mound, alternate Scotch and spruce fir are planted. The wattling-stakes, pitches, and young trees, cost about 3*s.* 6*d.* per rope, in addition to the manual labour above stated.

The size of the enclosures vary from five to eight acres; in each of these there is a five-barred oak-gate, eight feet four inches in length, and costing about 9*s.*; two oak posts, 8*s.*; irons, 2*s.* 6*d.*; carriage and putting down, 2*s.* 6*d.* more; making the whole expense of the gate about 22*s.*: double tunnels to each gateway will average about 5*s.* more.

A very good reason appears to be assigned for the preference generally given of soft wood to thorns, in the hedge mounds throughout this country: the former grows much faster, and in the way of copse or faggot wood, is much more profitable than the harder, perhaps more ornamental,

mental, but slower-growing thorns. The beech is preferred for stretching, plashing, or laying down; the hazel, beech, alder, and withy, are cut generally for firewood : the oak and ash, in favourable situations, at ten or twelve years' growth, will make good hurdles or small rafters.

About 1200 acres of Black-down hills have been enclosed by General Simcoe ; it was his intention to have built two, or not exceeding three, farm-houses ; and to have annexed about 3C0 acres of these allotments to each establishment ; the remainder, not disposed of in plantations, was to have been apportioned to his other farms, and to which the allotments were contiguous. This waste was valued by the Commissioners of the Enclosure, at an average of 6*s.* per acre ; but under proper management, this estimated value is expected to be trebled in a few years.

CHAP. VII.

ARABLE LAND.

SECTS. I, II, III, AND IV.—TILLAGE, &c.

DISTRICT I.

THE proportion of tillage to the enclosed grass-ground in this district, may be stated as one part in eight, that is, seven parts of enclosed grass-ground to one part in corn, or in preparation for it by fallow, turnips, and potatoes; out of this seven-eighths, there is estimated to be only one-eighth under permanent pasture, marsh, and meadow; hence seven-eighths of the whole enclosed country are subject to a convertible system. The word system is here perhaps not quite admissible, as that implies order in a regular series, both in time and in succession, with each other. No such rules, however, govern the practice of the North Devon farmer, who spades, skirts, vells, and sometimes, though very rarely, by a winter fallow, rots the old spine in preparation for wheat, and upon the lighter ground occasionally, for a few turnips. When spading, or paring and burning the surface of a field is meditated, it is pared off clean to the depth of three-fourths to one inch in thickness; these slices are set edgeways, and when dry, are collected into heaps, or what provincially is termed beat-barrows, and with the assistance of furze, fern, heather, hedge-row or copse-faggots, the whole pared surface is reduced to a mass of ashes; these ashes, when cool, are generally spread together with 80 Winchester bushels of lime per acre,

mixed

mixed with twice the quantity of hedge-row mould, road-scrapings, or other fresh soil most convenient to be procured.

This is the usual preparation for wheat, in which the expensive article of lime would frequently be omitted, did not the leases expressly provide for the tenants laying on that quantity of lime per acre. The ashes spread, and the manure thus applied upon the spaded land, the field is next ploughed into eight or ten furrow ridges, and the wheat being *previously prepared*, is sown, eight pecks in the beginning, but as the season advances, nine and ten pecks per acre, dragged and harrowed in; the furrows struck out with a plough, the ridges looked over and righted, and the field left gripped and water-furrowed. This preparation of the seed-wheat, consists of putting unslaked lime into water, until the liquid is brought to the consistence of a thick gruel; in this the wheat is immediately plunged, and after remaining a short time, it is taken out, and spread upon a floor to dry, where, by frequent motion the grains are separated from each other, and thus incrusted with caustic lime, the disease called the smut is generally prevented.

When it is determined to plough the wheat under, the seed is sown upon the lime, mould, and ashes, and ploughed into the same sized ridges, carrying very neatly and regularly about four furrows to the yard, leaving, at the making up of each furrow, a small comb or balk, which is again strewed with seed, and taken up with about one-half of the sole or bottom of the last-ploughed furrow; thus letting the plough down to a proper depth, the furrows are made up as close, or left as wide and open as the farmer chooses. These ridges are also looked over and righted with the mattock, and equally secured from an overflow of water during the continuance of winter.

When

When the land is either velled or skirted, it is usual to cut the ploughed slices into convenient lengths, and when sufficiently dry, to heap and burn them, to spread the ashes, and then prepare the lime and mould to complete the dressing; then either proceed with tormentors, rollers, drags and harrows, to effect the destruction of the combs or balks left in velling or skirting, or suffer them to remain until the land is ploughed for the reception of the seed-wheat: but when no part of the skirted or velled slices are burnt previous to dragging, harrowing, and the application of the tormentors crossways over the balks, this is called beating, and is aided by rolling, hand-beating, and every means that can be devised for break ing and separating the living and matted plants and grasses, and finally concluded with light harrows walked up hill and trotted downwards, the more effectually to shake the earth out of the tufted clods, which are then collected into heaps and burnt, the ashes spread, and the lime and other dressing applied as before noticed. Innumerable, however, are the small green sods left upon the surface of the field, as is clearly to be seen from its freshness and verdure, and which continues increasing until seed-time, when the field is ploughed into the eight or ten furrow ridges, the wheat sown nine or ten pecks to the acre, and hacked in. This expedient has arisen from the necessity of forbearing the use of the drags or harrows upon land after it has received its last ploughing in this preparation; for in the first case it is plain, that the drags and harrows would bring to the surface, the greater part of the green balks that were ploughed under; and in like manner would the drag and harrows bring to the top of the other ridges, all the toughest of the spine not consumed in beat-burning. To surmount all these difficulties, hacking has been contrived, and which is performed in the following

lowing manner : the wheat is sown broad-cast, and upon
each ridge a single man proceeds with the broad-bitted
mattock, beginning on the lower side of the field, and
advancing upwards, cutting down the edges of the furrows, and displacing so much of the soil as may afford a
slight and imperfect covering to the grain. This is evident by the quantity of loose seed left upon the surface,
a prey to the birds, and also from the additional peck of
seed per acre, which is used when hacked in. The furrows are generally shovelled out by hand, and the earth
so raised, spread over the adjoining ridges ; the field is
left gripped and water-furrowed, and (excepting the
quantity of green sods and tufts, which even the utmost
care used in this operation is impossible to conceal), has
all the appearance of being left well dressed, and looks
pleasing to the eye.

Hacking is also performed where lay-wheat is sown
immediately after the plough, and without a previous
harrowing : on this occasion the plough is so held and
set, as to leave the slices very much upon an edge ; the
seed falling between these furrows, is covered by the loam
or mould pared off in smoothing the surface. The wheat
thus comes up in rows upon the ridges, and in proportion
as these rows are more or less marked, the middle of the
slices are left vacant, and thus the very end and object of
the broad-cast husbandry is defeated, by an unequal distribution of sod, forming alternately thick rows and intervals without plant, and which, in the course of the ensuing season, are found to teem with grass and other
rubbish, little if at all inferior in bulk to the crop of wheat
itself.

The wheat-stubbles at harvest are, from the usual method of chopping down the crops with the reaping-hooks,
cut so low as to leave nothing to answer what is called
haulming

haulming in other parts of England. The very grassy state of these stubbles, as well as those of oats and barley, induces the farmer to leave them in a state of rest during winter, as well for the benefit of the pasture, as to prevent the effects of the winter rains and melting snows from washing and scouring the soil away.

It was formerly much the practice in that part of this district bordering upon the Bristol Channel, to sow wheat in four and six-furrow ridges; but, being too much exposed to the driving effects of the March winds, this round work has of late years been generally discontinued. It is to be observed, that the lime and mould, applied as a dressing to lay wheat, is spread before the approach of the autumnal rains, for the purpose of being washed in, and more intimately mixed with the spine, and to prevent it from falling to the bottom of the furrow, in the operation of ploughing.

Hacking in wheat, as the land may be wet, or more or less clingy, will cost the labour of from five to nine men per acre, during which time they have their drinkings, and are little less pampered than in the wheat-harvest following.

When fallowing, or a preparation for rotting the green sward, is intended, the land is either skirted, or ploughed clean, about Candlemas. By the former mode of opening the ground, much labour and expense is saved; for long observation and experience shows, that a much quicker dissolution of the spine takes place when the two green sides are placed together, than where the whole is turned downwards upon the bottom of the furrow. To this may be added the immediate division of the close matted surface, and that in the subsequent operations, on the clean ploughed land, the farmer will have to contend with a slice from nine to ten inches in width, and from five

to

to six inches in thickness; but, upon the skirted land, the slice and comb will not exceed more than one half of those proportions;—the labour consequently becomes much reduced, in comparison to what must necessarily be incurred in subduing a strong tough field of lay-ground, after it has been ploughed clean, and at the ordinary pitch (by whatever means the green sward is reduced, and all appearance of it done away);—the field is dressed with the ordinary mixing of lime and mould, the wheat is sown broad-cast upon the usual ridges, dragged, and harrowed in, the furrows struck up with the plough, the ridges righted, and left guarded from the effect of sudden thaws, or heavy rains during winter.—These are the chief modes of preparation for wheat in this district, if we except only a small portion that is sometimes sown after potatoes and the clover-lays.—The average produce from all these various modes of culture, is 15 bushels, of 61 lbs. each, per acre.

From what has been stated, it is plain, that no wheat can possibly stand in greater need of the hoe, than that which is hacked in; this, however, is but little attended to, and its omission consequently contributes in a great degree to the growth of grass and rubbish so generally complained of; it is, however, allowed to be much less upon the fallowed land, than where spading, velling, skirting, and burn-beating, has been practised; for even after spading, a number of roots of the coarser perennials escape, and seldom fail to show themselves in great force during the ensuing spring and summer.

In a climate so favourable to vegetation as is the county of Devon, it is easy to conceive, that grassy tufts left upon the surface of recently sown wheat-fields, will immediately strike, and secure themselves strongly in the ground. Although the wheat arish, after fallow, is uniformly

formerly much freer from grass than where the land is billed or skirted, and the beat burnt: still in some places an objection is stated to fallowing for wheat, on account of the land being left so hollow and open, as to subject the wheat plant to be drawn up when feeding it in the ensuing spring. It is also said to be much more liable to fall with its lower joints upon the ground, and to be what is here called crippled or root-fallen, in which case the crop is always found to be very deficient in produce, from its appearance in the field.

The weeding that is performed, is generally done by women and children, previous to the wheat running for the spindle, and so soon as the thistle, cockle, and other rubbish, are sufficiently grown to be cut by the weed-hook, or drawn by hand: the most common and injurious weeds, and those stated to be most difficult to subdue, are charlock and coltsfoot; these seem to have taken their permanent, and often undisturbed residence in many places in the district.

The reaping and harvesting of the wheat is attended with so heavy an expense, and with practices of so disorderly a nature, as to call for the strongest mark of disapprobation, and their immediate discontinuance, or at least a modification of their pastime after the labours of the day. The wheat being ready to cut down, and amounting from 10 to 20 acres, notice is given in the neighbourhood, that a reaping is to be performed on a particular day, when, as the farmer may be more or less liked in the village, on the morning of the day appointed, a gang, consisting of an indefinite number of men and women, assemble at the field, and the reaping commences after breakfast, which is seldom over till between eight and nine o'clock. This company is open for additional

DEVON.]   hands

hands to drop in at any time before the twelfth hour, to partake of the frolic of the day. By eleven or twelve o'clock the ale or c'der has so much warmed and elevated their spirits, that their noisy jokes and ribaldry are heard to a considerable distance, and often serve to draw auxiliary force within the accustomed time. The dinner, consisting of the best meat and vegetables, is carried into the field between twelve and one o'clock: this is distributed, with copious draughts of ale and cider; and by two o'clock the pastime of cutting and binding the wheat is resumed, and continued without other interruption than the squabbles of the party, until about five o'clock, when what is called the drinkings are taken into the field, and, under the shade of a hedge-row or large tree, the panniers are examined, and buns, cakes, and all such articles are found, as the confectionary skill of the farmer's wife could produce for gratifying the appetites of her customary guests at this season.

After the drinkings are over, which generally consume from half to three-quarters of an hour (and even longer, if such can be spared from the completion of the field), the amusement of the wheat-harvest is continued, with such exertions as draw the reaping and binding of the field together with the close of the evening. This done, a small sheaf is bound up, and set upon the top of one of the ridges, when the reapers retiring to a certain distance, each throws his reap-hook at the sheaf, until one, more fortunate, or less inebriated than the rest, strikes it down : this achievement is accompanied with the utmost stretch and power of the voices of the company, uttering words very indistinctly, but somewhat to this purpose :—*we ha in ! we ha in !*—which noise and tumult continue about half an hour; when the company retire to the farm-
house

house to sup, which being over, large portions of ale and cider enable them to carouse and vociferate until one or two o'clock in the morning.

At the same house, or that of a neighbouring farmer, a similar scene is renewed, beginning between eight and nine o'clock in the morning following, and so continued through the precious season of the wheat-harvest in this country. It must be observed, that the labourers thus employed in reaping receive no wages, but in lieu thereof, they have an invitation to the farmer's house, to partake of a harvest frolic; and at Christmas, during the whole of which time, and which seldom continues less than three or four days, the house is kept open night and day to the guests, whose behaviour during the time, may be assimilated to the frolics of a bear-garden.

The distempers to which the wheat crops of this district are liable, are by no means so formidable as hereafter will be noticed in other parts of the country. The mildew, as before observed, is but little known, except in small enclosures and low situations, and where the wheat is excluded from a due circulation of air : in such places it has been noticed to make a sudden appearance after still and foggy weather, but not to extend above a certain height or region of the field. In the higher parts of the country, where the fields are large, and the subdivision-mounds naked, or covered only with a few dwarf-hazel, withy (i. e. sallow), and creeping brambles, the evil is by no means such as to require particular notice.

The smut generally is, and always may be, prevented by a due attention to liming the seed in the manner before noticed.

The burnt, red-gum, or cockle-eared, are diseases little, indeed, almost wholly unknown; but when wheat is cultivated upon loose hollow-bottomed ground, or generally
after

after potatoes, it is liable to be root-fallen, the only remedy is to fold and trample the ground well after sowing,
and in the spring of the year to compress the surface with
heavy rollers, and to depasture sheep upon it as late as
the 1st of April. This will give stability to the roots,
and prevent the lower joints of the seed-stems from lying
prostrate on the ground; and though the stem generally
rises erect from these crippled joints, it stands with a very
small ear loosely set in the chert, which is thin and
obliquely projected from the stem; and, according to the
usual phrase of the country, very thin, and badly grained
indeed.

From all such hills as are steep and inaccessible to carts,
or at least conceived as such, the wheat-sheaves are generally packed in long crooks, fastened to a pack-saddle;
and thus loaded, the horse transports it to a stack-yard,
where the sheaves are raised into such sized stacks as may
be most conveniently made and thatched in the course of
the harvest, and afterwards for removal to the thrashing-
machine or barn.

Thrashing by hand is done in two ways: one by the
stook of ten sheaves (from seven to eight inches through
at the band); the other by bundles of reed, consisting of
the unbroken stems of the wheat-straw tied into bundles
of 28lb. each. The thrashing six of these bundles is called
a common day's work, and costs in different parts of the
country from 14d. to 16d. besides an allowance of three
pints of cider. When the wheat is thrashed by task-
work, 3d. per bundle is given, but with no allowance of
beer or cider. In thrashing task-work by the mode first
mentioned, 4d. per stook is given, and a man with diligence will thrash six stooks per day: from 70 to 80 of
these stooks may be taken as the general produce of the
wheat crop, and may be said to amount to the averages
                                                      stated

stated in the respective districts. In all cases, the man who thrashes, combs and secures with a double band the bundle of wheat-reed. This is generally laid by for thatching hay and corn, the roofs of farm-houses, cottages, barns, and other buildings; and for bands for tyeing up the sheaves of the ensuing harvest of both winter and spring grain. One hundred bundles of reed are generally estimated by neighbours to be worth about two guineas.

The price of grist-grinding, generally through the district, is about 5d. per bushel for wheat; 4d. for barley; and 2d. for oats: the latter are very seldom, though the two former are very generally, used by the peasantry, and in the farm-houses, for bread-corn. It is seldom that they eat bread with their meals, but most commonly pudding. A large quantity of broth is prepared in the farm-houses, by stewing pickled pork or bacon with cabbage, carrots, turnips, pot-herbs, onions, and leeks, in abundance. When pork or bacon is not to be got by the peasantry, they make use of mutton suet cut very small, and stewed with the garden-stuff above-mentioned. Pea-soup is also seasoned highly, and much used by these people.

DISTRICT II.

Having begun the description of the soil of this district near Hercules's Promontory, or Hartland Point, it may probably be as well to return thither, and recommence in that neighbourhood, such details of the husbandry as seem most worthy of notice.

Mr. Exter, who for many years past has practised with no inconsiderable success the drill-husbandry, states the following preparation for wheat, as one that he has generally found to answer extremely well: he ploughs clean
about

about Midsummer, but with a very thin slice, and in that
state the ground lies undisturbed until after harvest, when
the field is dressed with 160 seams of 2½ cwt. each of sea-
sand, or 40 customary measures of lime per acre. The
sand or lime is spread, and dragged together with the
flags or rotten turf, and when this is in sufficient preparation for collecting and burning, all the roots of couch,
and other injurious perennials, are gathered into heaps,
and set fire to. The fallow is ploughed into four and a
half feet ridges, corresponding with one-breadth of the
drill ; but if it is a thorough dry piece of land, the work
is left in 30 feet wide, and drilled across, instead of lengthways (as on the narrow ridges) ; in both cases, the rows
are equally distant, being nine inches apart ; and the
quantity of prepared seed-wheat required is about five
pecks per acre.

The wheat thus put in, is left well gripped and water-
furrowed, and fed close down with sheep till about Old
Lady-day. During this time, and when the season will
admit of it, the intervals are scarified, and again repeated
after the sheep are withdrawn, and horse-hoed about the
time the wheat is running for the spindle. This wheat is
mown and bound into sheaves, when after remaining in
the shock a sufficient length of time, it is removed to the
stack-yard, and put together, thatched, and well protected
from the force of the winter storms. It is usually thrashed
by hand, and on a fair and moderate computation, will
average a produce of 20 bushels of 70lbs. each, customary
weight for measure per acre.

Mr. Stoneman, of Woodhouse, has lately made an experiment of manuring for wheat with woollen rags, and
which promised to answer extremely well. The farther
particulars of this will be noticed in the Chapter on Improvements.

At

WHEAT.

At Torrington and its neighbourhood, the ordinary preparation for wheat is to pare and burn the old lay every three years; thus early, because it is said, there are no natural grasses worth preserving, and by this time the artificial ones are worn out. When breast-ploughed or spaded, the operation in these tender soils may be done for 9s. per acre; heaping the dried green sward, burning and spreading the ashes, about 6s. 6d. more. Sometimes the beat-ashes are spread alone, at other times the usual quantity of lime is mixed, and left in heaps together for several weeks.

When the ashes are spread by themselves, and soon after burning, the usual quantity of lime is then mixed with road-scrapings, hedge-borders, or even the mould collected in heaps in different parts of the field, and mixed in a proportion of about twenty of earth to one of lime: the heaps so mixed and distributed through the field, remain till the approach of seed-time, when they are spread, and the field ploughed into ten-furrow ridges, sown broad-cast with wheat, from eight to ten pecks per acre, and dragged and harrowed in. Where the ground is very light and open, sheep are driven in various directions over the field, to settle and make firm the soil for the wheat to strike in. This wheat is sometimes, though rarely, fed in the month of March, when it is rolled with a heavy moorstone roller; the seed-time is between Michaelmas and Christmas, and the harvest usually commences between the 1st and 10th of August.

The wheat is generally reaped by men, and bound up by women; and although there are some instances of wheat being reaped, bound, and shocked by the acre, still the more usual practice is to harvest the wheat in the manner before stated, and averaging a general produce of 16 bushels per acre,

No

No material difference takes place in the usual course of tillage, through the neighbourhood of Petrockstow, Black Torrington, and Hatherleigh; the turnip husbandry is however becoming far more general here than formerly; the same system is continued eastwardly. In the neighbourhood of Iddlesley, they pare and burn every second year; this they do because the soil is good, and will bear it. The common practice here, upon the prime land is, to begin with wheat in the manner above described, and fallow with barley and oats; or take turnips in the place of wheat fallowed with barley, wheat, and oats: produce of wheat here as before, 16 bushels per acre.

Advancing in the same direction towards Chumleigh, we gradually emerge from the old practice of spading; and although skirting and beat-burning the dry sound lands is sometimes practised, it is still, in the opinion of many intelligent farmers, considered to be very injurious to the future spine or green sward, as it prevents the ground, when laid down to grass, from producing so thick or so sweet an herbage.

The preparation most generally resorted to here, is to winter and summer fallow for wheat; and dress with the customary quantity of lime, ploughed under into ten-furrow ridges; the usual quantity of wheat is then sown broad-cast, and harrowed in, afterwards righted with the beating-mattock, the furrows shovelled out and spread upon the ridges; produce varying from 16 to 18 bushels per acre. The wheat arish, or stubbles, are in these cases found less to abound with coarse grass, and other unprofitable rubbish.

Pursuing this inquiry farther to the eastward, we find in the neighbourhood of Poughill and Cheriton Fitz-paine, that although skirting, or half ploughing, and afterwards burning the roots and rubbish, is frequently practised,

tised, still the most approved husbandry is to winter-fallow, and dress with the usual quantity of lime or dung; the latter generally preferred, particularly for the first shoot of the turnip, or otherwise apply soaper's waste lees, or wood-ashes. The turnips are sown broad-cast about Midsummer, seldom hoed, partly drawn and fed off upon the ground; and so much of the land as is cleared before Christmas is sown with wheat, ten pecks to the acre, harrowed in, and the furrows cleaned up with a double mould-board plough; hacking, in this case, being entirely exploded; the young wheat but seldom fed. This crop is harvested and thrashed in the usual manner, producing from 18 to 20 bushels of 60lb. each per acre.

The most common wheat husbandry south and east-wardly of Tiverton, is to plough the old lay-ground a good full pitch between March and May: in this state it remains for six or eight weeks, when it is cross-ploughed, and prepared with the dressings before mentioned for turnips about Old Midsummer. The turnips are some-times partially hoed and fed off before Christmas; the land is then sown with wheat in the manner above stated, producing generally about 20 bushels per acre. Wheat has been frequently sown after turnips, about Candlemas, but on account of its being so very liable to the rust when sown at that late season, barley is lately become its more valuable substitute.

In the neighbourhood of Bampton, much the same practice is observed in the culture of wheat: they break up in February, cross-plough in May, and get the land well cleaned and dressed by Midsummer; taking care, in all these operations, to burn nothing but couch-roots and other perennial rubbish: manure with 160 seams of rotten dung, or eight hogsheads (equal to 40 double

double Winchester bushels) of lime per acre; the latter
sometimes spread in its quick state, just before the ground
receives its last ploughing, but more frequently mixed
with mould: the turnips sown between New and Old
Midsummer, rarely hoed ; the early part of the crop fed
off, and the land sown with wheat by the middle of
December. Ten pecks of seed produce twenty bushels per
acre; the weight of the white wheat is about 60 lbs. that
of the small red Lammas, about 64 lbs. the striked Winchester measure. It is in all cases affirmed, that the
Candlemas, or spring wheat, is far more liable to take the
mildew than the autumnal wheat sown in due season.

The ordinary wheat tillage in the neighbourhood of
Whitstone, is to plough clean about Christmas, cross-
plough in May for either wheat or turnips ; if the former,
dung, lime, or apply soaper's waste lees, or ashes; if
dung only, 140 seams of 3 cwt. each: if purchased tolerably convenient, first cost and carriage will amount to
6d. per seam, ... £. 3 10 per acre.
Lime, 8 hhds. of 5 bushels each, at 8s. per⎫
   hhd. 44s. .... ⎬3 12 ditto.
Carriage, 3s. 6d. per hhd. 28s. ....⎭
Soaper's spent lees, or ashes, 43 seams, at⎫
   1s. 4d. per seam, 2l. 13s. 4d. ....⎬4 0 ditto.
Carriage, 8d. per seam, 1l. 6s. 8d. ....⎭

These different dressings are applied separately, or
mixed with hedge-row or other mould; wheat generally
sown broad-cast, two bushels per acre, harrowed in,
and the furrows striked out with the double mould-
board plough ; produce twenty bushels of 63 lbs. each per
acre.

In the Drewsteignton quarter, and southwardly in this
district, they break in the winter as above for wheat or
turnips, cross-plough in May, and dress with 120 seams

                                                      of

of rotten dung for turnips, or eight hogsheads of lime for wheat, per acre. Turnips are sown between New and Old Midsummer, and which is continued to be sown on the turnip ground until the end of January, sometimes harrowed, but more generally ploughed under into six-furrow ridges, leaving a balk or comb at the last furrow, which is strewed with fresh seed, and split with a double mould-board plough, casting the comb equally on both sides, and cleaning up the furrow to any depth or width the farmer chuses.

When the ground is not fallowed, or prepared with turnips for wheat, the lime and earth are spread upon the lay-ground by the end of August ; the ground is ploughed into ten-furrow ridges, the wheat sown broad-cast, ten pecks to the acre, and hacked in, costing, as the ground may be more or less clingy or stubborn, or may work free, the labour of from five to nine men per acre. Taking the average at seven, the wages of these men will be 8_s_. 2_d_.; their drink, two quarts of cider or beer each, 2_s_. 8_d_. more, making the average expense of hacking, in this part of the district, about 10_s_. 10_d_. per acre. The two pecks of extra seed required in this process serves much to strengthen the former objections stated against the practice. This, however, is not likely to have much weight, it being generally considered to produce the best wheat, but more particularly so when performed upon the flag : produce, twenty bushels of 64lbs. each per acre. It is very common for a second crop of wheat to be taken in immediate succession to the first, in which case the returns given in, average about sixteen bushels per acre.

In the neighbourhood of South Tawton, it is usual to half-plough or skirt in the months of June or July : cross-cut the ground with tormentors, drag and harrow well

after

after harvest, and burn whatever may not be rotted at
that time; dress with the usual quantity of lime or dung,
cast into eight or ten furrow ridges; sow about two
bushels of prepared seed wheat per acre, harrowed and
dragged, or hacked in; the wheat stubbles frequently
ploughed under, and sown again with wheat; sometimes
with, but more frequently without additional dressing:
produce of the first crop sixteen, of the second crop
from twelve to fourteen bushels per acre.

The early wheats throughout the whole of this district are generally found free from the rust, whilst the
late sown, or Candlemas crops, seldom escape from being
more or less injured by it.

Wages are sometimes given in this district for reaping
wheat, which in such cases cost 2s. 6d. per day to each
reaper, with as much ale, cider, and eating, as they
choose to call for. They return to the farm-house to
supper, carouse until between twelve and two in the
morning, stagger home, and after a few hours rest, recommence reaping between eight and nine o'clock the
following morning. In this manner the wheat-harvest is
conducted through many parts of this district, although
in the neighbourhood of the larger towns, the practice is
generally discontinued.

DISTRICT III.

The common course of crops through this district may
be stated—as, wheat, barley, oats, clover with hievre,
first year mown; or wheat, oats, oats with seeds, mown in
like manner the first year, and which afterwards lie an
indefinite term of from five to fifteen, or twenty years.

The most general practice through the western division
of this district, is to cultivate wheat upon what is commonly

monly called the old moorlands: here the first operation
is to spade and burn the surface, spread the ashes, and
dress with about 60 seams, or 160 bushels of bude sand
per acre. Instances near the borders of Cornwall are not
unusual, for 100 seams to be applied, but fifty only are
provided by covenant as a dressing for wheat, and the
two succeeding crops of oats or barley. This sand is either
applied alone or mixed with fresh mould, and ploughed
lightly under with the beat ashes into ten-furrow ridges,
and then sown with from six to eight pecks of prepared
seed wheat per acre, harrowed in, and producing on an
average through the Holdsworthy quarter, eighteen bushels
of 62 lbs. each, per acre. This produce is exclusively confined to the old moorlands, for when the ancient enclosures are cultivated with wheat, their produce but rarely
exceeds fifteen bushels per acre.

A very fine sample of wheat is often obtained from the
enclosed cultivated lands near the foot of Dartmoor; a
struck Winchester bushel was seen to weigh at Bridestow,
63 lbs. 8 oz.: this sample, by the customary measure of
heaping every fourth peck, weighed 67 lbs. $\frac{1}{2}$ oz.

The proportion of wheat cultivated in the western division of this district is, considering its extent, but very
small: this, however, being generally put in under
circumstances similar to those above noticed, we may
fairly place the general average produce at sixteen bushels
per acre; indeed it is no very extraordinary thing to hear
of old spaded and burnt moors, dressed with 100 seams
of bude sand, to yield in the first crop from twenty-six to
twenty-eight bushels of wheat per acre. This wheat is
seldom fed, although sometimes harrowed and rolled in
the spring of the year. It is harvested in the usual manner, and carried home in carts. As there are few thrash-
ing-

ing-mills as yet established in the district, the wheat is
thrashed by hand, and yields a produce as above stated.

On the enclosed cultivated lands in the division of
Meshaw, it is common to plough clean before Christmas,
and summer-fallow for wheat. In this preparation there
is nothing burnt but the rubbish beaten out of the clods,
and such as could not possibly be rotted in the time.
The field thus cleaned and brought into a husband-like
tilth, is dressed with forty measures of lime, mixed with
fresh mould, and spread just before the field receives its
seed earth. This is done neatly in eight-furrow ridges,
the wheat sown two bushels per acre, harrowed in, and
the furrows striked out with a double mould-board
plough : produce eighteen bushels of 62lbs. each, per
acre.

Another practice here, is to vell or wrest-balk at Midsummer, when after laying about a month, drag and harrow it cross-ways, and when dry, collect the green
sward and burn it in heaps, or beat-barrows; spread the
ashes just before the field is cross-ploughed, and apply
twenty measures of lime per acre, ploughed under with
the beat ashes, into eight or ten-furrow ridges, sown with
wheat from eight to ten pecks per acre, and hacked in,
requiring on an average, eight men per acre, which
at 1s. 2d. per day, is ....£. 0 9 4
Two quarts of cider, or other drink per man,⎱ 0 4 0
at 3d. per quart, ...⎰
Bread and cheese, at 3d. per man, ... 0 2 0
Shovelling out the furrows, one man per acre, ... 0 1 11
                                                          ―――――――――
                                                    £. 0 17 3
                                                          ―――――――――

The common price of reaping and binding wheat, with
an allowance of meat or drink, is about 8s. per acre;
                                                              hence

hence a more than double expense is incurred in putting
in a field of wheat, to what would be required in reaping it afterwards. This latter, however, is but rarely done,
it being the usual practice to reap and bind the wheat on
the terms and in the way before noticed. The produce
from this latter practice is not said to differ materially
from the average above stated, although the arish or wheat
stubble is always found to be much more foul and grassy,
than upon fallowed land.

Smut will sometimes occur through the carelessness or
mismanagement of the farmers, in not preparing their
seed in the manner before described; but the rust or mildew in either division of this district, is a disease but
seldom heard of, excepting only what has been related in
the neighbourhood of Holdsworthy, of a rust which often
occurs upon wheat sown after potatoes, and where they
generally manure very highly with farm-yard and stable-
dung: its first appearance is that of a bluish shade on the
seed stems of the corn at the time the wheat is in blossom:
these, when drawn through the fingers, leave a whitish
flour or farina behind, and which ultimately appears to eat
like rust upon iron, into the stalk, giving it a spotted
and partially diseased character.

DISTRICT IV.

Taking 100 acres as a proportion of the farms through
this district, they may be considered as consisting of about
one-fifth meadow and permanent pasture, and the remainder subject to a course of tillage, of which about 11
acres may be stated as annually in preparation with summer-fallow or turnips, for wheat; 11 acres under wheat;
11 acres under barley; and again under barley or oats;
and

and lying under seeds and the natural grasses for three years.

The wheat husbandry in the neighbourhood of Milton-Abbot, is first to skirt and burn in the early part of summer, and add from 20 to 30 measures of lime per acre; sow turnips at Midsummer, feed them off, and follow with oats or barley: these stubbles are ploughed immediately after harvest, got as clean as possible, and dressed with 40 more measures of lime per acre; sown with wheat broad-cast on ten-furrow ridges, and harrowed in: produce, 20 bushels, of 62 lbs. each to the acre.

In the country round Tavistock the same practice, with a similar result, prevails; south-westwardly of that town, the more common practice is, to skirt in the winter, the field frequently lying in that state until after the ensuing harvest, when it is cross-ploughed, dragged and harrowed; and so much of the spine as is then not rotted, collected into heaps and burnt. Fifty customary measures, or 12 hogsheads of lime mixed with hedge-row, or other mould, is then applied per acre; spread at Michaelmas, ploughed under into ten-furrow ridges, sown with wheat, two bushels per acre, and harrowed in: the field is left gripped and water-furrowed, and producing, on a general average, eighteen bushels per acre.

On the demesne lands of Buckland Monachorum, they sometimes plough clean in June, and sheepfold 2500 to the acre; where the fold has not reached, dress with about fifteen loads of Plymouth, or barrack-dung, of thirty bushels each per acre. As soon as the fallow begins to appear grassy, apply the tormentors, and by harrowing in dry weather, destroy the weeds and grasses. At other times pare and burn, and with the ashes apply 20 loads of farm-yard or stable dung per acre: wheat, in all cases sown

sown broad-cast, and harrowed in; produces on a general average, twenty-eight bushels per acre.

In the neighbourhood of Newton-Ferrers, it is no unusual practice to prepare by skirting at Candlemas for winter turnips. The land is prepared by the middle of July, when it receives about half the customary dressing, and the turnips, consisting of Swedes, the green purple, and yellow sorts, are sown, and fed off the spring following; the remainder of the ordinary dressing is then applied, and the land sown before Old Midsummer with the tankard and early white loaf turnip, fed off by the middle of November, and the land sown with wheat; produce twenty-four bushels per acre. In the country about Brixton, skirt very fine in the early part of summer; plough two or three clean furrows under the hedge-rows, and at regular distances across the field, heaps of lime, sea-sand, and sea-weed are distributed upon the clean ploughed furrows, and with them is mixed certain quantities of mould, leaving large heaps regularly disposed throughout and along the sides of the field. After harvest, the tormentors, drags, and harrows, are applied to this thinly skirted surface, which being made sufficiently fine, all the perennial rubbish is collected into heaps and burnt; the ashes strewed as evenly as possible, and the heaps of mixing are also regularly spread over the whole field; this is neatly ploughed under into ten or twelve-furrow ridges, sown with wheat by the first of November, eight or nine pecks to the acre, and harrowed in; rolled in the spring of the year, and yielding an average produce of twenty-four bushels per acre. When the grass can be conveniently spared in the country about Modbury, skirt in November, leaving a very fine comb or balk completely covered with the raised slice; in this state it remains until after barley sowing, when it undergoes all the necessary

DEVON.] operations

operations for completing the separation and destruction of the former spine. After spreading the ashes of the rubbish that may be burnt, twelve hogsheads of lime are applied per acre; turnips sown at Midsummer, fed off before Christmas, and succeeded with wheat sown in the usual manner, and producing a general average crop of twenty-four bushels per acre. In the promontory of Malborough, and northwardly towards Kingsbridge and Aveton Giffard, skirt in March for summer turnips; prepare a dressing with lime and mould, or with the latter and sea-sand, and apply about one half of the usual quantity for summer turnips, sown about Midsummer; fed off, and wheat sown with the remainder of the dressing between the beginning of November and the 10th of March. The late sown wheat is found to run much to straw, to be particularly subject to the rust or mildew, and seldom to equal in either quantity or quality the produce of the Michaelmas sown wheat by at least one in five. Average produce of the Michaelmas wheat twenty-six bushels; that of the spring wheat about twenty bushels, per acre, and of a greatly inferior quality.

The same management is pursued in the Southpool quarter, where the general average of the winter sown wheat is given in at twenty-eight bushels per acre. In the country situated below the southern foot of Dartmoor, the ordinary practice is to skirt, if possible, before barley sowing, cross-plough in May, and prepare the dressing, but not spread it, for the turnips which are sown about Midsummer, and fed off generally by Christmas, when the dressing previously deposited in the field is spread, and wheat sown from two to two bushels and a half, and averaging a general produce of twenty-two bushels per acre.

Through all the country west of the river Dart, and lying between Totness and Dartmouth, skirt in February.

cross-

cross-plough in May, and burn between that time and Midsummer whatever is not rotted; mix the usual quantity of lime, and occasionally sea-sand with mould, prepared by ploughing furrows through and along the sides of the fields. About one half of this dressing is applied for turnips sown about Midsummer, are fed off, and the land, as it becomes clear, receives the remainder of the dressing, and is continued as before to be sown with wheat, from the beginning of November until the 10th of March. The late sown wheat is here much complained of, as being extremely liable to mildew, and by no means recommended in preference to a crop of barley, and which is generally supplanting all the spring wheat throughout the district. The great burthen of straw generally proceeding from spring-sown wheat, occasions a deficiency in the quantity, as well as a great falling off in the quality of the grain. The general average produce here given, equals twenty-four bushels per acre. In the peninsula of Brixham and Kingsware, the same culture is pursued in the management of the wheat crop: the average produce is not stated to exceed twenty bushels per acre. The wheat crop is generally preceded by that of turnips, fed off, through the greater part of the limestone quarter of this district, the general average produce of which, deduced from a number of instances, amounts to near twenty-three bushels per acre.

DISTRICT V.

The wheat husbandry in this small district is various: first manure with the usual quantity of lime mixed with mould, and spread upon the old lay ground about a month before it is broken up, which is done by ploughing it a clean full pitch about the beginning of October, when the

the wheat is sown from nine to ten pecks per acre, hacked in upon ten-furrow ridges, the furrows shovelled out, and the loose mould spread over the adjoining stitches. When the old lays are fallowed for wheat or turnips, they are commonly ploughed clean, or skirted in the month of February; the usual dressing of lime is applied in both cases, but the beat-ashes being considered a sufficient stimulus for turnips, the dressing for wheat remains prepared in the field until after the turnips are fed off, when the dressing is spread, and ploughed lightly under; the wheat sown any time between November and the 1st of March, and harrowed in: upon the land which is ploughed clean in the winter and receives the thorough summer-fallow, the usual dressing is spread previous to the last ploughing, after which the wheat is sown broadcast, and harrowed in.

This stubble, as well as that of the lay and stump wheat, is frequently refreshed with about eighty seams or horse-loads of dung per acre; sown again with wheat upon one ploughing, and hacked in: produce of the first crop of wheat twenty, of the second, twelve or fourteen bushels per acre. The second wheat is generally taken in the place of a crop of barley.

The hacked wheat stubbles are uniformly more foul and grassy than the stubbles of the fallow and turnip-wheat; and the wheat sown at Candlemas is always more or less injured by a mildew. Sometimes turnips are taken after the second crop of wheat, and then fallowed with barley and seeds, otherwise the second wheat is succeeded by barley with seeds, and which generally lie from two to three years.

DISTRICT VI.

The wheat husbandry here is, first to skirt or furrow and comb very fine in July, to drag, harrow, and tear the spine as much as possible in pieces, then collect and burn the tough perennial rubbish otherwise not destroyed, dress with the usual quantity of lime, previously mixed with mould, ploughed neatly under into ten-furrow ridges; sow wheat two bushels per acre, and harrow it in; strike up the furrows with a double mould-board plough, then leave the field well gripped and water-furrowed; or plough clean in December or January, cross-plough in May, and thoroughly clean the land by burning the living root-weeds, and all other rubbish not previously rotted: apply a compost of lime, earth, and dung, mixed in the following proportions:

Five hogsheads of lime, first cost & carriage,	£. 2	2	6
Forty seams or horse-loads of dung, ditto, ...	2	0	0
Collecting 240 seams of road scrapings hedge-row or other mould, ...	0	10	0
Mixing and spreading, ...	0	3	6

Amounting in the whole to £. 4 16 0

per acre; an expense by no means unusually incurred in preparing for a crop of turnips, although most of the sandy loams in a favourable season will afford good turnips without any other manure than a slight dressing of beat-ashes, procured from the adjacent moors or commons, pared and burnt for the purpose.

The turnips are usually fed off, and the land sown with wheat between November and the end of February; from

the

the luxuriant growth of the late sown wheat it becomes very liable to mildew. The turnips remaining unconsumed after Candlemas, are followed with barley and seeds. In the country of Kentisbury, Payhembury, and through the Clysts, as well as in the North Tawton quarter, grey and white pease are frequently made the breaking crops, in preparation for wheat : these, as well as the bean-stubbles, are cleaned immediately after harvest ; the usual dressing being spread, it is ploughed neatly under, with about two bushels of seed-wheat per acre, into eight or ten-furrow ridges. The small comb left after the last furrow, is strewed with fresh seed, and moulded up as deep and close, or left as wide and open, as the farmer chooses. The result of these different modes of conducting the wheat-husbandry, deduced from many cases occurring in different parts of the district, equals a general average produce of 25 bushels, weighing 61 lbs. each, the struck Winchester measure, per acre.

The taking of three white straw crops in succession, however prevalent in the preceding districts, is not without many exceptions in common usage here. Through the Clysts, and in many places east of the river Dart, as well as in other parts of the district, the wheat-stubbles are either winter-fallowed, or carry brush turnips fed off, and the land sown in the ensuing spring with oats or barley with seeds. The stubbles also of the second white straw crop are frequently winter-fallowed, sometimes folded with the farm sheep ; dressed with dung and lime for turnips, sown about Midsummer, occasionally hoed, and such of the land as is cleaned before Christmas, sown with wheat, or as before stated, with spring corn and seeds ; the latter management is allowed to be the most judicious and profitable. Wherever the turnips fail in any of these preparations,

tions, the land is sown with wheat, the early crops of which are generally esteemed the best sample, and by far the freest from the mildew.

DISTRICT VII.

On the stiff flinty loams along the sea-coast between Sidmouth and Lyme, it is usual to plough the old lays in February, and sow oats upon the flag; when the oat-stubble is not very foul (which is rarely the case), it is ploughed immediately after harvest, and every exertion made to clean it in time for sowing wheat, with the customary dressing of lime, before the end of November. Grey and white pease very often, in like manner, precede a crop of wheat. Upon the more loose and friable soils in this quarter, it is also customary to break up with a thin clean slice in February, and summer-fallow for wheat or turnips: when the wheat-fallow is made, it is usually dressed with 20 hogsheads, of the capacity of the cider-hogshead, of clean stone-lime per acre, ploughed under with the seed-wheat into four or six-furrow ridges; or where the work is left flat, the seed and lime are well dragged and harrowed in together. When turnips precede the crop of wheat, the same dressing of lime is applied, and in like manner; the turnips are fed off, and the wheat sown between November and Candlemas: the late-sown wheat is always very liable to the rust or mildew. These are the usual preparations for wheat along the sea-coast.

Through the tillage lands in the neighbourhood of Axminster, and all the country bordering upon the county of Dorset, the average produce of wheat from about nine pecks of seed, appears to be 24 bushels of 62lbs. each

per

per acre. In the country north of the river Axe, and north-westwardly from Colyton, the practice is to break up the old lays for oats, as before stated; clean and dress the oat-stubbles with 10 hogsheads of stone or chalk lime; sow from eight to ten pecks of seed-wheat in round or flat ridges, as the case may be, which yields a produce of 18 bushels per acre. This is rated to be the produce of the higher parts of the country; the lower fields, cultivated on a marl bottom, and with the occasional intervention of pea and turnips, as well as oats for a breaking crop, are stated to average 28 bushels per acre.

The wheat preparation, through the vale of Honiton, and along the marly lands bordering upon the river Otter, is that of lay oats upon the flag; the oat-stubbles are cleaned immediately after harvest, and dressed with a compost of lime and marl, in a proportion of six of marl to one of lime, prepared in the preceding summer: the mixing is spread upon the fallow previous to its last ploughing, when the dressing and seed are ploughed under (as the nature of the ground may require) into four, six, or eight-furrow ridges, closed up, and finished in the manner before noticed; the fields are left well gripped and water-furrowed; and the average produce is stated to amount to 22 bushels of 61½ lbs. each, per acre.

The wheat-crop upon the Black-down hills is preceded by lay-oats; the oat-stubble is winter-fallowed for wheat, and occasionally for turnips; and dressed with 10 or 12 hogsheads of lime, mixed with six or eight cart-loads of rotten dung, of 20 bushels each, per acre. The wheat-fallow being ready about Michaelmas, the dressing is spread and ploughed under with the wheat, 10 pecks per acre, into four-furrow ridges, and yielding an average produce of 18 bushels per acre. The wheat-stubbles in the milder parts of this district are occasionally sown with

tares,

tares, which after being fed off, the ground is again
cleaned, dressed with lime and marl, and sown again with
wheat; the produce being the same as before stated.

On the Black-down hills, the severity of the winter
prevents the culture of tares; and the lateness of the
wheat-harvest also precludes any advantage being derived
from brush-turnips.

Although it was by no means understood that any restraints with regard to cropping were imposed upon the
tenantry of this district, beyond what has been already
mentioned, still the practice of taking three white straw
crops in succession, is much less frequent than in the
more western parts of the county. The result of this
moderation, and the general forbearance in paring the
sound dry land, are amply illustrated in the preceding
and following detail of this district.

The only common field to be noticed in this place is,
Braunton great open field, which contains about 230
acres; it is situated at the foot of the high grounds in
that parish, and is bounded southwardly by a range of
salt and other marsh-lands. Its soil consists of a deep
rich brown loam, of a loose and friable texture; and
which, time immemorial, has been known to teem with
incessant crops. Latterly, with a part of the spring-
corn is sown a portion of clean red clover : which, with
potatoes, turnips, and vetches, form a shift of green
crops, now the usual preparation for wheat ; and which,
by a majority of the occupiers, is stated to answer infinitely better than the culture of wheat, barley, oats, and
wheat again, which, in unvaried succession, formerly
composed the husbandry of this highly-favoured field.
In the present system of management, the crop of oats is
superseded by the miscellaneous shift, and where they
still find it necessary to dung very highly for potatoes;
and

and although generally succeeded with wheat, that crop is not found to be more crippled, or root-fallen, than when it is produced after tares, turnips, or upon the clover-lay.

The average produce is here given in at 35 bushels per acre. The wheat arish, or stubble, is sometimes winter-fallowed ; but it more frequently remains untouched until Candlemas, for the depasturing of sheep, and the common stock of the parish. The barley crop which succeeds, is generally put in after the second ploughing ; the seed required is about three bushels per acre, and yields an average produce of 35. The quantity and quality of this crop is, by some of the farmers, asserted to be inferior to what it amounted to under the former management of the field ; others, however, are of a widely different opinion.

SECT. V.—RYE.

THERE is no rye cultivated for a crop any where in this county; in some instances, a small portion is sometimes sown with tares, for spring-food. An opinion prevails, that this grain was formerly cultivated to a considerable extent through the county at large, excepting only upon those extensive commons lying in Venville, and abutting on Dartmoor and Exmoor Forests. This conjecture seems confirmed in a striking degree, from the vast quantity of rye-straw which is found to form the lower layer in all the ancient thatched buildings, and the vestiges of an ancient cultivation, which are clearly to be traced on all the extensive moors and commons which occupy so large a proportion of the country. Here large
fields

fields of rye are said to have been cultivated, although
the soil and substrata are by no means suited to the
nature of that grain.

––––◆––––

SECT. VI.—BARLEY.

DISTRICT I.

A crop of barley generally succeeds to that of wheat:
the wheat stubbles are ploughed under about the middle of
February, and every means used to cleanse the ground by
the middle of April; but other labours pressing at this
season, there is little opportunity of destroying the root-
weeds that have been gathering strength all winter. About
the middle of April, the barley is sown broad-cast, three
bushels and a half per acre, dragged, and harrowed in,
and the land left smooth with the roll for mowing. The
barley is gathered from the swarth into sheaves, bound
with wheat-straw reed, and, after the swarth-corn is secured, the fields are carefully raked, and the rakings
stowed away for hog-food, or other domestic use. The
crop is transported to the barn or stack-yards on carts,
or, where wheel-carriages are not used, upon the horses'
backs, and in the crooks or cradles before mentioned.
The season is generally so far favourable, as to prevent the
necessity of forming small stooks in the field.

The harvest being generally in by the middle of September, the management of the first barley-crop is frequently repeated for a second, or a crop of oats. The
average produce of the first crop after wheat, is stated
at 30 bushels; but when barley follows turnips or potatoes,
36 bushels

56 bushels per acre. The third white straw crop, whether
of barley or oats, rarely exceeds 20 bushels per acre.

An instance of extraordinary produce from spading
and burning, followed in part by the drill-husbandry, is
related by a gentleman of Barnstable, who having an
estate in the parish of Ilfracombe, first pared and burnt
a field, the soil of which was a sound grey loam of a moderate depth, and lying at no great distance from the
killas rock; the soil is represented to have been an
assemblage of decompounded schistus, which forms the
usual subsoil in that neighbourhood: the field had been
at rest for many years, and agreeable to the general idea,
its herbage required improvement from a course of tillage.

To begin this operation, the field was first pared and
burnt; and all the ashes produced from the combustion
of the green sward, were mixed with a proportion of
eighty Winchester bushels of lime per acre. The land
was then thrice ploughed, and turnips drilled in at the
distance of one foot a-part hoed, and set regularly out
upon the rows: they were drawn and carted off the land;
and the field sown with wheat broad-cast by the first of
December following. The wheat-stubble was ploughed
under before Christmas, and prepared with two earths
more by the middle of April, when barley was drilled in
rows, at eleven inches and a half a-part; afterwards scarified and horse-hoed, in the manner required by the drill
practice; and produced sixty-six bushels and a half of
barley, with 140 bundles of straw, weighing 28lbs. each,
per acre: the weight of the barley was about 48lbs. per
bushel.

The value of the land before these operations commenced, is stated to have been 3*l.* per acre: the value of
it after, was not mentioned; and the surveyor had not

an

an opportunity of examining the field in person. No account was taken or kept of the value of the wheat and turnip crops, but they are stated to have been proportionably abundant with the crop of barley. The barley-straw is generally regarded of less value for fodder than the straw of oats, or even the foliage combed from the bundles of wheat-reed. The awning iron is frequently, but not always used, previous to the last winnowing of the barley; but no sort of value seems to be set upon the wheat, barley, or other chaff, for horse-food.

Malting is generally a business of itself, the farmers sometimes sending their barley to be malted, paying about five guineas per score bushels to the maltster; every fourth bushel of barley is heaped, on delivery to the maltster; the same on being returned in malt, with an increase upon the barley as 24 to 20.

Barley constitutes a very large proportion of the bread-corn used in farm-houses, and by the peasantry of the country; the mode of making it was not noticed as deserving of particular attention: the husks are separated from the meal in the same manner as the broad bran is sifted from the wheat-flour, and with both of which they use yeast or barm, and occasionally leaven.

DISTRICT II.

The usual practice of Mr. Exter, in the management of his barley land, is to turn it over a good full pitch, as soon as the turnips are removed from off the field: the ploughed ground is dragged, scuffled, and harrowed, until sufficiently fine to receive the seed-barley, which is then put in with the improved drilled plough, in rows at nine inches a-part; requiring about five pecks of seed to the acre: the intervals are scarified as soon as the plant has
formed

formed its coronal root, and horse-hoed when eight or
nine inches high : cost about 8 *d*. per acre each time, as a
man, a boy, and a horse, will scarify, or horse-hoe, about
seven acres per day.   After the last hoeing, 10lbs. of
common red clover, 2lbs. of white Dutch, 2lbs. of trefoil,
and half a bushel of hievre, are sown per acre, and harrowed in with Cook's drill harrow.   This crop is mown
at harvest, and after laying some time in the swarth, is
bound up into sheaves, thrashed by hand in like manner
with the wheat, and usually produces about 40 bushels
per acre.   The clover is mown the first year, and fed for
the remainder of the term.   The land may lay at rest
from three to ten years and upwards.

The more common practice, after the wheat-stubbles
are ploughed under about Christmas, and again about
the middle of April, is, to sow barley broad-cast, three
bushels and a half to the acre, dragged, and harrowed in,
and the ground rolled for the convenience of mowing ; it
is sometimes carried loose, but more frequently bound up
and housed, or made up into small ricks or stacks, near
the barn or thrashing-mill.   Should this prove to be the
last white straw crop, but which, by-the-bye, very rarely
happens, about 6lbs. of common red clover, and from
half to two bushels of hievre, are sown per acre ; but
more frequently a crop of oats is taken.

The barley is either thrashed with mills or by hand ;
and does not exceed, in the neighbourhood of High
Bickington, St. Giles, and Roborough, an average of 25
bushels per acre.   The culture of barley about Iddesley
and Monk Oakhampton, is sometimes preceded by a crop
of turnips : it is here generally confessed, that little good
farming can be done without the intervention of that
crop ; yet, strange to say, upon some of the kindest soil,
the culture of turnips seems to be almost totally disre-
                                                    garded.

garded. The produce of barley, on a general average through this quarter, may be taken at about 30 bushels per acre. In the neighbourhood of Burrington, Ashreigney, and Chumleigh, from 28 to 32 bushels per acre, form the general average, and drawn, without any material difference, from the same system of management. About Poughill and Cadleigh, the average is given in at 30 and 32 bushels; and in short, the same may be stated of the average crops of barley through the quarters of Halberton, Bampton, and Stoodleigh; for although in these places the soil is frequently found to vary from the tender loam to the strong moist bottom, more applicable to the culture of oats than barley ; still as the latter crop is but seldom sown, where the land is not properly adapted for it, the same average may very fairly be taken of its produce in all those places.

The crops of barley cultivated in the Drewsteignton quarter, are under much the same management as those just noticed; the average produce fluctuates also between 28 and 32 bushels per acre. This barley seems to command a decided superiority in point of quality, as it seldom weighs less than 52 lbs. and is often found to advance as high as 54 lbs. the striked Winchester bushel.

DISTRICT III.

In the western division of this district, there is but little barley cultivated, and that only on the dry tender lands, which after being twice ploughed, and made tolerably fine, are sown four bushels to the acre, and harrowed in. This is generally left rolled, for the convenience of mowing at harvest, when it is bound up as before stated, and is found to yield an average of 26 bushels per acre.

In

In the eastern division, the wheat arish is generally winter-fallowed, frequently ploughed twice afterwards, sown in the same manner, and is stated to average a produce of 28 bushels, of 46 lbs. each, per acre.

DISTRICT IV.

The barley cultivated in this district, is either, after turnips fed off the preceding winter, or upon wheat stubbles, generally winter-fallowed between Michaelmas and Christmas; in either case, a good tilth is prepared by the middle of April for the reception of the seed, which is then put in broad-cast, from three and a half to four bushels per acre, and generally harrowed in with 10 lbs. of red clover and half a bushel of ray-grass; or 8 lbs. of clover, 4 lbs. of trefoil, and the same quantity of ray-grass. When seeds are not sown, the third white straw crop of oats or barley necessarily follows.

The result of this management, from the mean of a number of cases noted in the survey of this district is, barley after wheat, $29\frac{1}{2}$; after turnips, $39\frac{3}{4}$, of 51 lbs. each, the struck Winchester bushel, per acre; when the third crop is taken in the place of seeds; if barley, 20; if oats, 24 bushels per acre; the latter prevails but too generally in the interior of the district. Along the sea-coast, the grain is thinner skinned, and, upon the whole, a superior sample to that generally produced in the inland country.

DISTRICT V.

The average crop of barley in this district is 28 bushels, of 50 lbs. each, per acre. In Buckland and Widdecombe

in

in the Moor, the barley is thin in its form, thick in its skin, and altogether a much inferior sample to that produced in the country below.

DISTRICT VI.

The average of the barley-crops through the district, is found to be 36 Winchester bushels, of 52lbs. each, per acre.

DISTRICT VII.

The crops of barley along the sea-coast, are cultivated after regular crops of turnips, brush turnips upon wheat-stubble, or the wheat-stubbles winter-fallowed. The quantity of seed usually required is about three bushels and a half, harrowed under about the middle of April with seeds, and the ground left rolled and smooth for mowing : average produce, 40 bushels per acre. In the higher country before noticed, lying north of the river Axe, north and westwardly of Colyton, few turnips are cultivated. The average produce given in of the barley crops upon wheat stubbles, sometimes, although rarely, winter-fallowed, is 25 bushels per acre. The lower parts of the country, bordering upon the Coley and Axe rivers, affording frequent opportunities for brush turnips being fed off in time for getting the land in good tilth, barley is then sown in the usual manner, with seeds, and is stated to average a produce of 40 bushels per acre. Upon the marly grounds in the vale of Honiton, and the Otter river, and where turnips intervene between wheat and barley, the latter crop is stated at an average of 34 bushels per acre. The crops of barley upon the Black-down hills,

DEVON.]   generally

generally succeeding wheat, sometimes with, but more frequently without a winter-fallow, is stated at an average produce of 26 bushels per acre.

SECT. VII.—OATS.

DISTRICT I.

The oats generally cultivated here, are sown upon such strong wet soils as, in their present condition, are altogether unfit for the more delicate grain of barley; they are occasionally found to occupy the third place, after preceding crops of wheat and barley: the oat requiring a close and firm footing for its support, and for entering its roots downwards, renders such close clays by far the most applicable to its culture. The tillage bestowed upon this crop, is seldom more than to turn over at a good full pitch, in the spring of the year, the wheat, barley, or preceding oat-stubble; and as the soil may be more or less free or stubborn, to sow black or white oats; the former always the earliest, and on the coldest and strongest land: the seed used is seldom less than six bushels per acre, of which, after all the pains taken in dragging and harrowing, a large proportion remains loose upon the surface, and is immediately devoured by the larks, rooks, and pigeons.

The potatoe-oat is growing so much in estimation, as to threaten the exclusion of the Poland and short-smalls; but on the whole, the black oat seems that which is most generally cultivated.

The

The oat crop is commonly mown, and afterwards bound
up in sheaves, and transported in like manner with the
barley and other crops, to the barn or stack-yard. Its
average produce, when sown upon the flag, 40 bushels
the first crop; after wheat 34 bushels: but, to use the
expression of the country, if 13 bushels per acre are obtained by sowing six, or that the farmer can net two
grains only for one that is sown, he begins to think it
high time to discontinue cropping. The oat-straw is
generally used for fodder in the barn-yards; and, so far
as was commonly understood, the oats are employed as
horse-food solely; there being few shelling-mills, and
little or no oatmeal manufactured in the country.

The black oat is mostly found to outweigh the white
oat, from two to four pounds per bushel. There are instances, however, of the potatoe and other white oats
weighing 40lbs. per bushel, although the general average
will not warrant a higher return than from 34 to 38lbs.
the striked Winchester measure.

From the same authority that the statement of the produce of barley is derived, by the drill-husbandry, in the
preceding section, there is now to be detailed the result
of a similar trial respecting the produce of oats. A piece
of land on Biddedown, in the parish of Ilfracombe (the
soil and substratum of which may be understood by reference to the field where the barley was cultivated), after
being spaded and burnt, and dressed with the usual quantity of lime per acre, was first sown with wheat, and
afterwards succeeded by a crop of oats. The oat arish,
or stubble, was not ploughed up until Lady Day, between
which time and Midsummer it was thrice ploughed,
dressed with 160 horse-loads, or seams, of rotten dung
per acre, and turnips drilled in rows, about a foot a-part,
in the latter end of June or beginning of July. These
were

were all hoed, and set out regularly in the rows; and the turnips were all drawn from off the field before the 10th of March; when, after once ploughing, white oats were drilled in rows, at the distance of eleven inches and a quarter. The intervals were twice scarified with the coulters; cutting about two inches of the spaces each time; and once horse-hoed, cutting about five inches of the interval; and by the same operation moulding up the rows of corn. The crop was mown at harvest, and bound into sheaves, about nine or ten inches through at the band, thrashed in the ordinary way, and yielding a produce of 115 bushels per acre; each bushel weighing, by estimation, about 35 lbs.

A part of the field, which was precisely the same in quality, and had undergone the same treatment, was sown broad-cast, and harrowed in; and yielded a produce at the rate of 88 bushels per acre : the grain, apparently, of the same quality.

The value of the land upon which these crops were raised, is rated at 40 s. per acre; it was seeded down at the time of the last hoeing, the intervals with 6 lbs. of red clover, and half a peck of hievre, or ray grass, per acre.

DISTRICT II.

It has been before remarked, that trench-ploughing is nearly, if not wholly, confined to the practice of one gentleman in this part of the district. Supposing this operation to have been performed, and that the ground has been once or twice well dragged, harrowed and rolled, oats are put in by Mr. Exter in the same manner as has been noticed of wheat and barley, requiring about two bushels and a half of seed per acre. The drilled ground

is

is then rolled close down, and compressed as much as possible with the heavy moorstone roller. This crop is scuffled and horse-hoed, at nearly the same stages of its growth as has been stated of barley; it is harvested and thrashed much in the same manner; and the fair average produce is given in at 40 bushels per acre. The oatstubble is ploughed under before Christmas, and is left untouched in that state until about the middle of May; when it is cross-ploughed, harrowed, and prepared for turnips.

It has occurred in a few instances, for lay oats to have been made the breaking-crop, and to serve with subsequent dressings, as the forerunner to a crop of wheat: in these cases, a produce has far exceeded the average obtained from the ordinary mode of cultivating oats in this country; for, as this is usually made the last of a series of white straw crops, and the culture of it merely to plough down the former stubble, and harrow from five and a half to six bushels of seed-corn in, the farmer generally considers himself very well rewarded, if this last crop will amount to 25 bushels per acre. The oats commonly cultivated will weigh about 36lbs. the striked Winchester bushel.

DISTRICT III.

In both divisions of this district, black oats generally succeed either wheat or barley; these are sown upon the first ploughing in the beginning of March, five bushels to the acre; and average a general produce of 26 bushels, weighing 36lbs. each, per acre.

DISTRICT IV.

The land proving so very favourable to the culture of barley, but few oats are sown, and those only the last of the three white straw crops put in upon one ploughing, and accompanied with the same grass-seeds before mentioned. Average produce of oats, 25 bushels of 40lbs. and a half each, per acre. On the stronger lands, some exceptions occurred to the more common husbandry of the district, where it was usual to make oats, instead of turnips or wheat, the first, or breaking crop. In this case, the ground is ploughed clean, and to a good full pitch in February; oats, from five to six bushels per acre, are sown upon the flag, and harrowed in.

The oat-stubble is ploughed immediately after harvest, got as clean as possible, and dressed with the usual quantity of lime, sown broad-cast about the middle of November with wheat, harrowed in, and succeeded with barley and seeds. Produce: oats, 40 bushels; wheat, 20; and barley, 32 bushels, per acre.

DISTRICT V.

Oats being generally the last of a series of white straw crops, and sown upon one ploughing, seldom exceed the produce of barley, weighing from 36 to 40lbs. the struck Winchester measure. The large extent of grass, in comparison with the tillage-land at Buckland and Widdecombe in the Moor, in some measure accounts for the average given in of the corn-crops in those parishes. Oats, 40 bushels; wheat, 20; and barley, 32 bushels, per acre. The former is often made the breaking crop, and sown after skirting, in preparation for wheat.

DISTRICT

DISTRICT VI.

The average produce of the oat crop in this district, is 38 bushels, of 40 lbs. each, per acre.

DISTRICT VII.

The culture of oats being generally upon the old lay grounds, through this district, their average produce is stated at 40 bushels per acre.

SECTS. VIII. AND IX.—BEANS AND PEASE.

DISTRICT I.

A FEW hog-pease and some beans, are occasionally cultivated, but not to an extent deserving a place in the common husbandry of this district.

DISTRICT II.

The soil in many places southwardly of Stoodleigh, and for a considerable distance round Tiverton, being favourable to the culture of grey and good boiling pease, it is common to cultivate those crops in the following manner : a part of the lay-ground intended to be broken up for a course of tillage, is dressed with about 80 or 120 seams of good farm-yard and stable dung; this is neatly turned under a moderately thick slice, in the beginning of February, and the pease sown broad-cast, and harrowed in; the seed required, if for grey or hog-pease, four bushels;

white

white, or Prussian boilers, about three bushels to the acre.
Produce of hog-pease, 24 bushels; of boilers, 18 bushels
per acre. The pea-stubbles are dressed with six or eight
hogsheads of lime per acre, and sown with wheat; the
produce of which very seldom fall short of 26 bushels per
acre. The small pea-straw or haulm, is commonly used
as rack-meat for horses before Candlemas.

DISTRICT V.

A few pease and beans have been recently cultivated at
Teigngrace, and found to answer very well.

DISTRICT VI.

The early Charlton pea is often sown as a breaking-
crop in the month of February. These will be ready for
the barn by the middle of July, when the land, if not
previously dressed for the pease, is manured at an expense
little short of four guineas and a half per acre, and sown
with turnips; these are fed off in the course of the ensuing winter, and followed with barley and seeds in the
spring. Average produce of the Charlton pease, from
three bushels of seed, 22 bushels; that of grey pease, from
four bushels of seed, 26 bushels per acre. A few horse-
beans are also occasionally sown in different parts of this
district.

Mr. Brown, of Long Barn, finds pease upon the old
lays, an excellent preparation for wheat. The ground is
sometimes trench-ploughed in February, and sown broad-
cast before the middle of March, with the earliest pease
that can be procured. An early harvest is material, on
account of cleaning the arish in time for putting in wheat.
This arish is occasionally sown with brush turnips, followed with barley, and laid down with seeds. The latter
mode

mode leaves the land in good condition, and three valuable crops are obtained within twenty months.

SECT. X.—TARES.

DISTRICT I.

TARES are sometimes, although rather sparingly, sown
for spring-food in this district: why they are not more
generally cultivated for this purpose, is said to be owing
to the land being so highly charged with water during
winter, that the north-easterly winds proceeding from
Exmoor in the spring of the year, act with such excessive
violence on the saturated soil, as entirely to perish and
destroy that plant, which at an early period of the winter,
promised every thing to the hopes and wishes of the farmer, as an ample supply of spring-food for his ewes and
lambs. This evil, thanks to kind Providence, is not without its remedy; and when that shall be resorted to, in the
manner the nature of the soil and climate demands, winter tares, mixed with rye, will form as valuable a source
of spring food in the county of Devon, as they are already found to be in other parts of England.

A circumstance deserving notice, occurred lately in the
parish of Chittlehampton, where a field of winter tares
was cultivated and fed down, the first time, by the end of
March; the second time by the middle of May: and at
both times the plant were eaten down very close; and after
the second feeding, left to stand for a crop. This was
harvested early in August, and yielded rather more than
30 bushels per acre. The stock which depastured upon
these tares, were sheep and yearling calves, during which
time

time they were observed to thrive, and do fully as well as might be expected on the best pastures during summer.

These tares were sown in the preceding September, upon a wheat-stubble, after being once ploughed ; three bushels to the acre, and harrowed in.

The same gentleman has since cultivated tares for hay, and has had one ton and a half from the stack per acre. He finds that the best way is to mow the tares, and let them lay till they begin to shew some considerable degree of heat, when the swarths are opened and spread out ; and after they are well dried, the hay is put together, and should be consumed or eaten early in the winter, on account of its becoming harsh and rigid, by exposure to the March winds. The nourishing quality of this hay, when given alone, to horses, required its quantity to be limited, and to supply the remainder of their food with clover or meadow-hay. The same gentleman remarks, that when the crop is heavy, the lower parts of the bines will be less inviting than the upper part ; and in order that the whole should be eaten evenly up, he recommends the tare-hay to be cut small in a common engine. The tares should be cut for hay when the lower part of the bine is in full pod, and its upper part in blossom.

The crops here alluded to, were valued by the proprietor, at from ten to twelve pounds per acre, exclusive of the great advantage resulting from an increased quantity of manure. A good fair crop of tares, whether used for soil, or made into hay, may be estimated at 6*l.* per acre.

DISTRICT II.

Tares, which Mr. Exter occasionally cultivates with a view to green food only, are generally put in upon wheat,
barley,

barley, or oat stubbles, ploughed down immediately after harvest, and the tares drilled in rows of one foot a-part, and found to afford a valuable supply of spring food, and during the early part of summer. Both winter and spring tares are occasionally cultivated for soiling; some remarkably fine ones were observed in the middle of November near Tiverton. At Drewsteignton, where winter tares are also frequently sown for spring food, once eaten, and then shut up for a crop, they average a produce of twenty bushels per acre. The vetch haulm proves very good horse-food, particularly if the crop is not left to stand beyond the time that the lower pods are ripe. These are generally sown upon wheat stubbles, and are always considered a good preparation for a following crop of wheat.

DISTRICT IV.

Tares ase sown, by some particular persons, for green food, but this must not be considered as forming a part of the common husbandry of the district.

A neat and profitable system of management is pursued by the Rev. Mr. Froude, of Dartington, upon about sixty acres of arable land. The first preparation is to winter-fallow ten acres, and dung for potatoes and early and late turnips sown upon two-furrow ridges.

Second year—Potatoe and turnip land sown in about equal quantities, with oats and barley.

Third year—These stubbles sown with winter, and the spring following with summer tares, for late soiling.

Fourth year—The winter tare ground drilled for early turnips, drawn or fed off, and sown with wheat, on which,

Fifth year—in the spring following, is sown clover and other seeds; the summer tare ground winter-fallowed, and sown with barley and oats with seeds.
The

The winter of the sixth year break up and renew the same routine of cropping, varying the green and white straw crops regularly throughout the shifts. It is but justice to add, that Mr. Froude's early turnips and ruta baga were by far the best noticed in the country; they were evenly set, and at proper distances on the ridges; the potatoes could not possibly promise to be more abundant.

Through the fifth, sixth, and seventh districts, tares are also cultivated, the average produce of which, when kept for a crop, is about twenty bushels per acre.

SECT. XI.—TURNIPS.

WHEN a part of the crop for which the land is first opened consists of turnips, they are either sown upon the spaded, velled, or skirted land, or upon a part of the same shift broken up for summer-fallow. In the former case, the usual quantity of lime is applied with the ashes, and in the latter, the ground is dressed with from eighty to 160 seams of rotten dung (from $2\frac{1}{2}$ to 3 cwt. each) per acre. The turnips are most commonly the white loaf, green, or purple sorts, sown broad-cast, in the month of July; sometimes, although rarely, thinned, weeded, or set out with the hoe, and usually kept to supply that interval of green food between the end of the rouen or aftermath, and the first bite for the ewes and lambs in the watered meadows.

Notwithstanding that the larger parts of the turnips cultivated in this district are sown broad-cast, and in this way, still there are many gentlemen, who for good and sufficient reasons, prefer the ridge method, first introduced and practised with so much success in Scotland.

Brush

Brush turnips, or those sown immediately after harvest upon the wheat stubbles, are but little attended to, but when they are sown, the farmers willingly confess the advantages they derive from such a seasonable supply in the spring of the year. Neither rolling for the supposed destruction of the fly, or harrowing for the purpose of loosening the roots, and giving the turnips a better chance for appleing, seem much known or practised in this county. Some of the larger turnips are occasionally drawn and eaten upon an adjoining dry field, but the great bulk of the turnips cultivated are consumed where they grow; the expense of either of these means varies according to the bulk of the crop, and the conveniences the farmer may have by his own or the agistment stock of others, for consuming the crop with the greatest economy. An acre of good unhoed turnips is usually valued from 50s. to 3l. The winters in Devonshire being generally very mild, and not in the least unfavourable to the duration of the turnip crops, little attention has hitherto been paid in preserving them through the severity of that season.

DISTRICT II.

Mr. Exter's practice in the cultivation of his turnip crop is, to sow with a good full dressing of manure upon his oat stubble; this crop, tops and tails included, is supposed generally to reach from eighteen to twenty-four tons per acre; they are set from eight to ten inches in the rows, which are laid out from twenty-four to thirty inches asunder; they are most frequently drawn off the land where they grow, and spread evenly to sheep in some dry, well-sheltered field, or carried home for the purpose of stall-feeding, or given to other cattle in the house.

DISTRICT

DISTRICT III.

When turnips sown upon the velled and beat-burnt lands in the country bordering upon the Little Dart river, are found to fail, the land is then dressed as usual with lime, and sown with wheat; but when the turnips succeed, they are fed off in the course of the winter, and as the land may be more or less dry and tender, is sown with barley or oats; if the former, about 8 lbs. per acre of clover is sown, mown once or twice, as circumstances may require, dressed with the usual quantity of lime, ploughed under, and wheat hacked in upon the flag. If oats succeed the turnips, the stubble is immediately turned under, the ground got as clean as possible, dressed with the usual quantity of lime, and sown with wheat in like manner.

DISTRICT IV.

Upon the free-stone lands of Stoke-Gabriel, Paignton, &c. the land is generally winter-fallowed for turnips, and dressed with farm-yard and stable dung; many excellent crops of turnips are thus procured, and which would be far more valuable, was any attention paid to hoeing, harrowing, or setting them regular in the ground: the turnips are followed with wheat or barley, in the manner before noticed. The broad-cast husbandry is commonly preferred among the farmers. The usual value of a good fair crop of this description, is estimated at about 4 *l.* per acre.

Through the 5th, 6th, and 7th districts, brush turnips are occasionally sown, and found to yield a seasonable supply of green food in the spring of the year.

SECT.

SECT. XII.—RUTA BAGA.

FROM what has been already said of the culture of the common turnip, it is not to be expected that much progress has been made in the management of ruta baga, which being recently introduced, is occasionally cultivated broad-cast, or on two-furrow ridges, sown about the end of May; and as far as the knowledge of it hitherto extends, is found to answer extremely well, and may be generally estimated as a valuable and improving crop.

Mr. Exter sows his ruta baga in ridges, usually put in about the end of May, with the same preparation as for the common turnip, and by the middle of July they are always sufficiently advanced to thin, and plant out in the vacant or missed places in the ridges, or to remove to other situations previously prepared to receive them. At this time the green Norfolks are usually sown; the relative produce noticed by Mr. Exter, between the transplanted Swede and the Norfolk green turnip, under precisely the same circumstances, as to the nature and condition of the land, is, as 628 to 851; giving a most decided preference to the former, after amply defraying the additional expense of transplanting.

SECT. XIII.—KHOL RABI.

THE khol rabi, or above-ground turnip cabbage, cultivated by Mr. Basset, of Watermouth, although in the midst of Swedish turnips (which were not touched), were every one eaten by the hares and rabbits: they are stated to be remarkably sweet, and equally hardy, as many of them

them were frequently pulled up and put in again, striking and growing afterwards in an unusual manner.

The result of some other trials and experiments, have been politely promised to be transmitted to the Board. An experiment has been made by Colonel Orchard on the culture of khol rabi, the result of which, so far as has come to the knowledge of the Surveyor, promises to answer very well.

———————

SECT. XIV.——CARROTS.

THE drill husbandry carried on at Eggsford, does not appear to differ in any material degree from what has been already stated as the practice of Mr. Exter.—Mr. Fellows, however, adds the culture of carrots, a root for which a part of the demesne lands of Eggsford seems particularly adapted. The very early stage of the growth of this root, when viewed by the Surveyor, precluded any further observations being made, than that they appeared rather thick in the rows, but otherwise clean and well managed, and promising to rise to a considerable crop. However unwilling many of the tenantry of this neighbourhood seemed at first to adopt a practice, the examples of which had been marked with such decided superiority, still it was not without pleasure that the Surveyor heard, during his short visit at Eggsford, that several applications had been made by the tenants, requesting a short loan of those implements, from the use of which such peculiar advantages had been derived by their munificent landlord.

The discontinuance of the carrot culture in the neighbourhood of Ottery St. Mary, is ascribed to the women hoers

hoers being generally engaged in the woollen manufactories of that town.

SECT. XV.—POTATOES.

THE gentlemen who particularly cultivate this plant
for the purpose of feeding cattle, are, Lord Fortescue,
Mr. Inkleton, of Yeo Town, near Barnstable, and Mr.
Basset, of Watermouth, near Ilfracombe: In the practice of these gentlemen, the old fresh lazy-bed mode
(which seems to have taken great root in Devonshire),
has completely given way to the more neat and profitable
method of planting the sets in rows, and immediately
upon the dung.

The ground usually chosen for the culture of this
root, is a stubble field, after the ordinary course of white
straw crops, or a piece of old clover lay, either of which
are broken up between Christmas and Candlemas, and
potatoes of an early sort, called painted ladies, are put in
about the middle of April; the red Irish apple sort about
the middle of May, or beginning of June, and in the
following manner:—Furrows are drawn at the distance of
two feet and a half a-part, straight across the field, in the
direction the potatoes are to be planted; in the bottom
of these furrows, the dung is usually spread in the proportion of 160 seams, or horse-loads per acre; upon this
dung the potatoe setts are placed regularly at the distance
of about six inches, requiring generally about eight bags
per acre. The mould raised from the furrow, which
received the dung and setts, is then ploughed back
again, and in this situation the field remains until the
plants appear sufficiently to mark the interval, which is
DEVON.]   then

then horse-hoed, and that operation is followed by the
double-breasted plough, the mould-boards of which are
set so wide, as to make the raised earth just meet upon
the rows, and completely cover the young potatoe plants :
these, in a growing season, will very soon be seen above
this second covering, when the mould-boards of the
double-breasted plough are farther spread, and the last
moulding is completed by throwing the earth from the
intervals upon the ridges, and at the foot of the plants
as high as it will lie: the rows are then examined, as well
for the purpose of relieving any of the potatoe plants on
which clods may have fallen, as for drawing and cutting
out any weeds that may be among them ; and this completes the dressing. One man and one horse on a well-
proportioned field of ten or twelve acres, and lying sufficiently level for the plough to work both ways, will
horse-hoe three acres per day, and the same quantity in
the subsequent operations of moulding of the plants.

There does not appear to be any farther pains taken in
preparing the setts, than to be careful in preserving two
or three eyes to each. A single row of potatoes planted
at this distance, will occupy the whole interval, and render it very difficult for any one to pass through them by
the 1st of August. Whenever the potatoe has attained
its full growth, it will be always shewn by change of
colour, and the withering of the stalks.

Preparatory to taking up the potatoes, the stalks are
all drawn and collected into heaps; sometimes carried
home, but more frequently strewed upon the adjoining
public roads (to be ground down by the traffic, and afterwards gathered into heaps, and carried away with the
road scrapings); the potatoes are then ploughed up with
one horse; the plough being drawn empty up hill, and
working downwards, by holding the coulter as close as
possible

possible on the left hand side of the row, so as to avoid cutting, but clearing the potatoes. This manner of ploughing them up will keep ten or twelve women, boys and girls employed in gathering and filling the carts, placed at convenient distances in the field, as well for receiving as removing the potatoes to the caves, heaps, piles, pits, holes, ricks, or berrys (for by all such terms they are known in this country), previously prepared to receive them, the bottoms of which are on a level with the surrounding ground, and are generally of sufficient area to contain from 100 to 120 bushels. The cost, per acre, of this culture, taking the field up from its stubble state, may be estimated as follows:

	£.	s.	d.
First ploughing in the stubble,	0	10	0
Searing to receive the dung, and turning back the raised mould upon the setts,	0	4	0
Horse-hoeing,	0	2	6
Twice moulding up with the double-breasted plough,	0	5	0
160 seams of good rotten dung, including the ordinary expense of filling and distance of packing, at 10s. per score,	4	0	0
8 bags of potatoes for setts,	1	0	0
Cutting the setts,	0	4	0
Spreading the dung and putting down the setts,	0	5	0
Taking up and hoeing,	1	2	6
Thatching three caves, generally allowed to receive the produce of an acre, including the value of the wheat straw reed,	0	7	6
Rent, £. 1 0 0			
Tithe, 0 3 0	1	7	6
Poor's-rates, and other parochial payments, 0 4 6			
	£.9	8	0

120 bags,

120 bags, the produce of an acre, at 2*s*. 6*d*. per bag, will amount to 15*l*. leaving the net profit, by this estimate, of 5*l*. 12*s*. per acre.

The application of potatoes thus produced, when cultivated on a larger scale, is in the instances before us, for the purpose of stall-feeding cattle. Whether this is likely to answer or not, must form a subject for future consideration.

Among the farmers, boiled potatoes, seasoned with a small quantity of barley-meal, form the first stage of the feeding process with their hogs; they begin in this way, and as the animal's appetite may require pampering, continue enriching the mass till they finish altogether with barley-meal or grey pease. Steaming potatoes is but little known; and although horses will for some time eat them raw, they are seldom used for that purpose. The same is not to be stated with respect to milch cows, as by them they are eaten with avidity, and found to be great promoters of milk, but which by some is objected to, on account of its inferior quality. Drying potatoes to keep, converting them into starch, or using them as an ingredient in the composition of bread, are not at all regarded as objects of economy : in the latter case, the sweet cake-like quality the potatoe communicates to wheat flour, occasions a far greater consumption in families where such has been tried, than would have taken place in the same time had the bread been made of clean meal or flour alone. Large quantities of boiled potatoes are now usually served up in all families, particularly in the country, and as far as they are eaten, diminish the expenditure as well of animal as of other vegetable food.

That potatoes are not to be obtained without manuring very highly, has been proved from experience; yet there is little doubt but their culture would become far more

general

general and extensive, did not an opinion prevail among the farmers, that the potatoe crops eat up all, or very nearly all the dung applied for their culture. As the appleing of the potatoe keeps the mould in continual motion for three or four months in the preceding summer, the soil is thereby made so very open and mellow, as to subject wheat, when sown after potatoes, to be much crippled cr root fallen; the most intelligent farmers, therefore, generally choose to follow their potatoes with barley, and for which the potatoe ground is particularly adapted.

Potatoes are cultivated in many parts of this district in the manner before described, as well as in the mode denominated lazy-beds : they are strongly recommended for the purpose of human food, but by no means generally for the feeding of cattle. It is on all occasions necessary to dung very highly for them, and thus subjecting the other parts of the farm to an unfair contribution of its renovating produce. When this plant is designed to be put into lazy-beds, the ground is ploughed some time in the preceding winter, and afterwards seared into beds of three feet and a half in width, with an interval of about 18 or 20 inches. The manure is spread upon these beds, and the setts placed regularly upon it at the distance of about seven or eight inches square : the earth is dug from out the interval, which thus becomes a trench, and is cast as evenly as possible on both hands, covering the nearer tops of the adjoining beds. As soon as the young plants begin to shew themselves, they receive a second covering from the crumbs before left in the trench, and which are now spread over them; and not unfrequently, when the plants appear to be about cutting the ground a second time, a third covering is given to them, with mould procured from paring down the sides and deepening the bottom of the trench, and thus raising as much fresh earth as will effect this purpose.

These

These repeated coverings form an excellent protection
for the young plants against the late spring frosts; and,
as from this third covering a considerable portion of dead
earth is found to occupy the surface of the beds, they are
less liable to send forth weeds to the injury of the crop,
than would most probably have been the case had the
upper covering of the beds consisted of loose vegetable
mould only. By laying off the interval just one half the
width of the bed, and keeping a field for three years
successively under this mode of potatoe culture, the
whole field may be made to undergo an operation, little,
if at all inferior to a close trenching, in which case it
would prove an excellent preparation for nursery ground,
plantations, and young orchards.

The produce from this management in various parts of
the district, is stated to fluctuate from 120 to 160 bags
of seven score each per acre, and the prices generally
given in, will average about 2s. 6d. per bag. The quantity of setts required in this culture is found to be equal to

12 bags of potatoes per acre, ... £. 1	5	0
Winter ploughing the land, per acre, ... 0	10	0
100 seams of dung, at 4d. per seam, ... 2	13	4
Tilling, packing, or carting, ditto, ... 1	0	2
8 men, at 10d. per day (no drink), ... 0	13	4
4 women, 2 to spread the dung, and 2 to lay the setts, at 8d. per day each, ... } 0	2	8
Second covering, 4 men as above, ... 0	6	8
Third covering, including hoeing and drawing weeds, ...} 0	6	8
Taking up 140 bags, at 2d. per bag, ... 1	3	4
Caving and sorting, 1d. per bag, ... 0	11	8
Rent, ... 1	5	0
Tithe and parochial payments, ... 0	7	6
Estimated expense, per acre, £. 10	5	4

The

The produce of an acre 140 bags, at 2*s*. 6*d*. per bag, will amount to 17*s*. 4*d*. leaving an apparent net profit, by the statement, 16*l*. 18*s*. 8*d*. per acre.

In the Drewsteignton quarter, the potatoe crop is very often put in, using the same quantity of manure, by planting two furrows, and leaving an interval of two furrows more; the mould from the interval is used for earthing up the rows, and which is generally done by hand: there is evidently a greater expense incurred by this practice than in the one above described, although the average produce seldom falls short of 140 bags per acre; indeed, this may be fairly stated as within the usual produce.

In other parts of the district it is no unusual practice to score the field into beds that will contain five rows of potatoes at nine inches a-part, with an interval of about two feet between each bed. The mould is then cast with the common shovel on the intervals, the dung is laid down upon the cleared surface, and the setts are placed upon it as above, and from eight to ten inches a-part in the rows; the mould is returned by hand upon the dung and setts, which, as before stated, receive a second and a third covering, and seldom average less than 140 bags per acre. The excessive labour required in performing these different operations must be quite sufficient to discourage the practice, at least upon a large scale.

DISTRICT III.

The usual mode of putting in potatoes in this district, is, to plant them in single rows, in the manner before noticed, dressing with about fifty cart-loads of farm-yard dung (each load measuring about twenty-five bushels) per acre), and thus employing full three parts of the dung made

made upon the farm; although the ox-noble potatoe, and others of a hardy sort, where the land has lately received a full dote of sea-sand, are sometimes found to do very well without any fresh manure: they are moulded up as usual with the double-breasted plough, and cost, in taking up and securing from the frost, from 26*s.* to 30*s.* per acre. The produce of the fine table sort is averaged at 150 bags, and of the coarser kind, 200 bags of seven score each per acre. Their value in the field, on being first taken up, is 2*s.* per bag, but towards the spring of the year they commonly rise to 2*s.* 6*d.* per bag at the heaps or berrys.

DISTRICT IV.

Part of the wheat stubbles are winter-fallowed, and occasionally prepared for potatoes, in which cases, a full dressing of dung is spread evenly upon the ground, which is then ploughed under with a plough having a shifting mould-board: the planting is begun on one side of the field, the potatoe setts are placed in every third furrow, and the dung of the two next furrows raked upon them; when the plants sufficiently mark the intervals, they are horse-hoed, and afterwards the rows are moulded up as often as may be found necessary, with the double-breasted plough. They are ploughed out, gathered, and stowed away in ricks or berrys, in the manner before noticed.

The produce of the table potatoe crop seldom falls short of 350 bushels, and that of the ox-noble 400 bushels, per acre.

The culture of potatoes in the 5th, 6th, and 7th districts, not differing in any degree from what has been already noticed, it is not deemed necessary to dwell longer on the subject.

SECT. XVI. —CLOVER.

THE value of clover in laying the land down for grass is well known and justly appreciated in this county; it is, however, very rarely sown clean; or without being mixed with other seeds, trefoil, white clover, and ray-grass or hievre. The quantity usually sown is, 6 lbs. of red clover; 2 lbs. of white Dutch, and an indefinite proportion of from two pecks to two bushels of hievre, per acre: or, reducing the quantity of red clover, supply the difference with trefoil, sowing the usual proportions of white Dutch clover and hievre with it. On cold clay soils the quantity of hievre is largely increased, and that of red clover seed proportionably diminished. When the farmer intends to mow the first crop of his seeds for hay, he sometimes spares the land so far as to lay it down with the first spring crop after wheat, but rarely without an intermediate crop between that which follows turnips. Although this forbearance is not prescribed to him by his covenants, nature so strongly insists upon it, that without attending to its dictates, his seeds become so feeble as to render it difficult to cut them, and are scarcely worth the trouble and expense of attempting to convert them into hay. Many gentlemen, and some of the best improving farmers, find their account in manuring the young seeds before and during the frosty season in winter. This promotes an early vegetation, and is found a valuable acquisition to the ewes and lambs. After the first shoot of the seeds are fed down (and during which time the hievre comes forward with peculiar advantage), the common practice is to shut up the field for mowing, when, if the plant is good, the season favourable, and the land in that heart the nature of the soil and other circumstances will

readily

readily admit of, from 30 to 35 cwt. of good clover, trefoil, and ray-grass hay, may be expected from an acre.

The after-grass, as common in other places, is usually fed off. The first or second crop of seeds are seldom mown for soil; although a large proportion of the second crop of clover is reserved for seed, which when ripe, is mown, tied into bundles, and made into small stooks that are left standing in the field, well capped with wheat seed, till an opportunity offers for bringing it home to thrash and mill out the seeds.

As red clover is but seldom sown alone, such lays or stubbles, after the first year, are very rarely turned under for wheat; but where such has been practised, it is always found to answer extremely well. Where the lands are in good cultivation, a beautiful and spontaneous growth of white clover is found to enrich and adorn all the fields. And as such little attention has hitherto been paid to the culture of that grass as a crop alone, or beyond the limits before stated; some complaints were heard in the course of the survey, of the land not being so favourable to the growth of red clover as formerly; but whether these statements were accurate or not, they were fortunately not numerous, nor are they altogether without remedy.

What has been just stated respecting white Dutch clover, or the honeysuckle, may with equal propriety be said of trefoil and ray-grass; as neither of those grasses are cultivated singly, for the purpose of a crop alone.

Sainfoin, lucerne, chicory, and burnet, seem in a manner unknown.

SECT. XVII.—HOPS.

Hops, which seem voluntarily to spread and occupy a place in most of the sheltered hedge-rows, are cultivated to a small extent in the valley through which the r ver Yeo, or Dormer, runs, in the parishes of Littleham and Monkleigh. From the latter of these places, the following statement is taken; but their culture is so very limited, and that conducted in so very humble a manner, that were it not for the uniformity prescribed to this Report by the Honourable Board, such particulars might be very well omitted; and that without making any material chasm in the agricultural details of this county.

The lower plain of the valley through which the Dormer runs, averages a width of about 40 rods: here the soil varies from a moist brown loam of a good staple on a yellow woodland clay, to a pale red, or rather cedar-coloured loam, equally good in staple, and lying on a deep stratum of rubbly clay of the same colour. The moist brown loam first described, is that which is generally preferred for hop-gardens, and which in preparation is first spaded and burnt, and sown with turnips: these, as circumstances may require or admit, are either drawn or fed off the land. The ground thus cleaned, and all appearance of its late surface entirely destroyed, is next scored out into lines of from five to five feet and a half square, at the corners of which holes are made, and in which rotten dung is laid in a proportion of about one-fourth of a seam to each hole; the dung is covered over with mould, forming a hill about nine or ten inches high, with a bottom of about two feet, and a top of one foot diameter each. Setts about five inches long, with two, and when possible with three joints, are taken up about the middle of February, and placed in the hills three to each, and pointing to those segments, or parts of the
hill,

hill, the planter wishes to have occupied. When these plants are shot a few inches, one small pole or beam-stick is placed for each plant to climb on : the young bines are then conducted to them, and trained in a direction with the sun; secured to the poles with the blades or seed-stems of coarse rushes.

The next operation is to hack, hoe, and well weed the ground, and then mould up the several hills with clean earth. The hop-garden is then left for bearing, although little fruit may be expected from it the first year. This being more or less, when it becomes ripe, the poles are taken down and stripped, the fruit gathered clean from off the bines, and carried to a kiln for drying. From the time of planting the ground, the expense of this hop culture may be stated as follows:

	£.	s.	d.
Greening or mossing 1100 hills, at 6d. per hundred	0	5	6
Poling, at 1s. 6d. per hundred	0	16	6
Hacking, or hoeing the alleys, 6d. per ditto	0	5	6
Casting, or moulding the hills, 6d. per ditto	0	5	6
Tyeing, 10d. per ditto	0	9	2
Taking down and picking, 14s. per cwt. if a good crop; if a bad one, 30s. per cwt. averaging 24s. per cwt. 6 cwt. per acre....	7	4	0
Drying, 2s. 8d. per cwt.	0	16	0
Fuel, 2s. per ditto	0	12	0
Bagging, including bags and making	0	19	0
Ricking, or stacking the poles, 10d. per hundred hills	0	9	2
First cost of 3300 poles, at 24s. per hundred, 39l. 12s. annual interest of that sum	2	0	0
Annual supply of new poles, 500	6	0	0
Manure, 260 seams, at 4d. per seam	4	6	8

Carried forward..........£.24 9 0

Filling,

Brought forward, ...£. 24 9 0

Filling, packing, or carriage 1 13 4

Rent ....£.2 10 0

Tithe, 1d. per lb. 2 16 0

                              5 6 0

Duty, 2d. per lb. 5 12 0

Poor's-rates, 12s. 10½d. in the pound rent, ⎫ 1 5 9
1l. 5s. 9d. ....⎭

Road-rate, 1s. 6d. church-levy, 4d. in the ⎫ 0 4 7
pound, 4s. 7d. ....⎭

                   £.38 10 8

Per Contra.

6cwt. of hops, at 2s. 1d. per lb. ⎫ £. s. d.
being the net average price ⎬ 70 0 0
within the last seven years ......⎭

By 400 refuse poles, at 6d. per ⎫ 1 4 0
hundred ....⎭

Apparent net profit according to ⎫ 32 13 4
this estimate...........................⎭

        £.71 4 0 £.71 4 0

As the hop-kiln is occasionally otherwise employed than in drying hops, no notice is taken of its first cost, and annual expense of keeping it in repair; nor are the hop-gardens of sufficient extent to bear any statement of the interest accruing upon the first cost and annual supply of baskets, stools, pitches, barrows, ladders, forks, and other small implements necessarily required in the hop-grounds, and which amount to something considerable in the large hop plantations in other parts of England. The value of the hop-vines or old bines, are not brought to account, nor is the advantage of selling the bags as hops; still there appears to be a most prodigious advantage resulting from this husbandry: but whether the statement

is

is correct or not, it is faithfully transmitted as received, and that from a planter of great apparent candour and experience.

The aspect always preferred, is a southern one, as much protected as possible from the north-west and north-easterly winds. The effect of these hop-gardens on the other parts of the farm, is that of laying it under severe contribution for an undue proportion of its manure, a circumstance most strikingly observable, whenever the hop-ground is situated at a distance from a large town, or is, in a manner, out of the reach of foreign manure.

The valley in which are these hop-plantations, is formed by sharp hills rising very abruptly from the plain below, but which are clothed in many places with timber and copse wood to their summits, and afford convenient opportunities for procuring the hop-poles at the very reasonable price stated in the estimate.

SECT. XVIII.—HEMP.

THE culture of hemp is not known; it has been attempted at South Pool, but (fortunately), for want of conveniences for preparing it for market, has been discontinued.

SECT. XIX.—FLAX.

IN the parish of Haberton, and the adjacent parishes towards Somersetshire, flax is cultivated to some considerable extent. The mode generally pursued is this: the farmer breaks up a piece of land, usually of the best quality,

quality, and rents it to the flax-merchant for a single crop, and for which he receives from 3*l.* to 6*l.* per acre. He stipulates to perform all the subsequent harrowing and pulverizing of the soil; the flaxman only finding seed, and agreeing to have the field cleared by a given time, which is usually fixed for the end of October: the seed usually required is from six to eight bushels per acre Upon these tilths, the flax seldom requires much weeding, and is generally pulled in a green state, and before its seed is ripened. This flax is always pit-rotted for ten days or a fortnight, and exposed for a fortnight or three weeks longer, before it is ready to be gathered and bound up for breaking. Flax drawn in this state, is considered to be much better than that which may have stood until its seed is perfected: this latter is always less rotted.

On a moderate computation, there are two ounces of tow produced from every pound of flax; and a good fair acre of flax will yield 35 doz. of merchantable flax, or 420 lbs. This flax, taken on an average of seven years, will sell for 6*s.* 6*d.* per dozen; and consequently will amount to..£.11 7 6

Eight hundred and forty ounces of tow = 52 lbs. } 0 8 9
at 2½*d.* per lb. ....}

Making the value of an acre of flax, accord- } £.11 16 3
ing to this statement.................................}

The Surveyor has much to regret the utter impossibility of reconciling the different accounts he procured as to the farther details of this husbandry, and the preparation of the flax for market; so that the expense of drawing, watering, spreading, binding, breaking, heckling, with the value of the seed sown, or the quantity of such as might be procured for market, must, however reluctantly, be passed over.

There

There are many flax-merchants in this part of the country, and their numbers are stated to be much increased as we enter the county of Somerset, who have annually from twenty to fifty acres of flax; but there is *seldom more* than ten or 12 acres cultivated yearly on any one farm.

It is curious to notice the difference in the colour of flax cultivated on the grey loam, from that which is produced upon the red land; for a permanent pink shade accompanies the latter, which no bleaching, washing, or chemical preparation yet discovered, has been sufficient to discharge, or obliterate in the slightest degree its native hue. So little, indeed, has the bleaching operation any effect in removing this colour, that it seems rather to increase and to shew itself more strongly as the operation is continued.

Flax is sometimes cultivated in the valley of the Otter, in the manner and on the terms before noticed. The flax is always dew-rotted, and an average crop of merchantable flax is here commonly valued at 20*l.* per acre. When the flax stands close and grows large, there is a certainty of a good crop of wheat following; otherwise very indifferent. Liquorice, chamomile, teasils, carraway, and coriander, or any other seeds, as objects of agricultural economy, seem altogether unknown or neglected.

CHAP. VIII.

GRASS-LAND.

DISTRICT I.

IT has been already observed, that about one-eighth part of the enclosed cultivated lands in this district are annually under corn crops, or in preparation for them. The remainder will always be found lying in permanent pasture, or subject to such a course of tillage as the caprice of the occupier may choose, either as to the time he may keep the land open, or the course of crops he may employ it with. Any thing like a regular routine of crops, or systematic husbandry, is as difficult to be met with in this district as in every other part of the county. The reason assigned for so very small a proportion of tillage to the grass-land, is the great difficulty of procuring manure; but whether this objection is well founded to the extent it is meant to go, will most probably be shewn in the sequel of this Report.

The low-lands by the sides of the rivers, and other smaller streams, are too frequently, through the mistaken avidity of the occupiers, broken up for the purposes of tillage, and in their first operation spaded and burnt in the same manner as the other grass-lands lying upon a higher level. This practice, independent of the shameful deterioration of such lands, is often productive of the most serious mischiefs, as well to the improvident tenant, by the total loss or failure of his crop, as it becomes ruinous to the estate, and often highly injuricus to the

DEVON.]   lands

lands below, by the quantity of soil which is carried off
with the floods from the ploughed and broken ground,
and its coarser and most gravitating parts being almost
immediately deposited on those below them. Whenever
these annual inundations, not loaded altogether with
coarse sand or the finer gravel, pass over a sound piece of
land, and continue in motion during the time of the
freshes, let the source of such waters be where it may,
they are uniformly found to operate to a good end, by the
enriching and fructifying effects they leave behing them :
one certain consequence is always found to result from
these waters, and that is, the speedy and certain destruction of moss; but whenever land so inundated is unsound at its bottom, highly charged with its own waters,
of a loose and boggy nature, and putting forth rushes
and all the plants and grasses peculiar to such situations,
such floodings only serve to increase the natural defects
of those lands, and are as much dreaded whenever they
spread over those neglected spots, as they are condemned
and rejected altogether for the purposes of irrigation ;
but which, for the upland meadows, and such as are out
of the reach of the spontaneous overflowings of the
streams, are, by the industrious farmer, very generally
and judiciously attended to, and to which end, grips,
gutters, larger carriages and sluices are all put in complete readiness to receive the first freshes from the autumnal rains, and which are usually spread over the
grounds by the middle of October, and always found to
possess a far more forcing quality than any other that
fall after that period, and during the ensuing winter. All
the waters of Exmoor are peculiarly adapted to this purpose, and even those of the Taw, and of the Torridge
rivers, whatever may be partially objected to their supposed mineral qualities, and to a considerable branch of
the

the latter wandering from its western source though a country but little regarded by those who are not the immediate inhabitants of it—still, whenever those waters are judiciously applied upon ground, after it has been well and effectually drained, and completely relieved of its surplus and permanently chilling waters, their good effects are never known to fail of producing the most beneficial consequences.

In order to elucidate this truth, it may be proper to state, that the land in some parts of this district, and particularly on the rivers Mole and Bray, has recently doubled its value, by a judicious mode of conducting the water of those streams periodically over it. These waters, like those of the Taw and Torridge, although beautifully clear and limpid in the summer season, are still slightly tinged with a bright brown, or rather copper colour, and which is evidently derived from the vast bodies of peat which occupy the surface of the two immense moors, whence all the rivers in question derive their source. The meadows, however, produced by conducting these waters artificially over them, will generally carry two couples per acre from the first of February to the first of May; say twelve weeks, at 9 d. per couple per week, is .... £.0 18 0
Two tons of hay, at four guineas per ton 8 8 0
Aftermath, till the beginning of October 1 10 0

Making the total value of the produce, per acre, ... } £.10 16 0

As these meadows are seldom watered after the middle of May, the water then, and whenever at command, is turned over the upland meadows and pasture-grounds; and this, whenever it can be done, particularly with the addition of passing through the courtlege or farm-yards, considerably

considerably increases the quantity and quality of the herbage.

Although there are seldom instances of water-meadows being lett separate and a-part from the other parts of the farm, it is but reasonable to assign a general average of their value, and which may be stated from 50 s. to 3 l. per acre; and that of the upland meadows, and such as are kept permanently on the green side, from 35 s. to 40 s. per acre. As there is but little open common-field, so there is less, or rather no half-year meadow-ground occurring, at least to observation, within the survey of this district.

Mowing grass is generally about 3 s. per acre, besides drink and occasional eating at the farm-house, the same as in harvest; but as to the expense of making, carting, or packing, and the general survey of the hay crops, either from the upland or water-meadows, so much depends on the state of the weather, the facility of getting hands, and securing the hay in stacks, that any attempt to reduce these expenses to a standard would be extremely vague, and altogether unworthy the notice of the Right Honourable Board.

The produce of upland hay varies according to the season, the heart, and condition, the land may be in, and the time the fields are shut up to mow. This necessarily renders a very uncertain produce, although it generally may be stated at from 24 to 32 cwt. per acre. This hay is of a stronger nature and weight, for weight is esteemed more nutritious than that obtained from either the naturally or artificially flooded grounds, and is usually reserved for horse-food, or disposed of in the large towns, from 4 d. to 8 d. per cwt. above the current price of the lower-meadow hay.

In a few instances, the manuring of the upland meadows

dows was observed to take place a little after the hay harvest; but that labour is more generally performed during the frosty season of winter, when from 80 to 120 seams of rotten dung and road-scrapings are applied per acre. A composition also of lime and mould is prepared in the preceding summer, and usually applied at the same time. From its tendency to destroy the moss, and encourage a thicker growth of white clover, this dressing is much approved of, and is yearly coming into more general use. The quantity of lime expended in these mixings being voluntary (as not being prescribed by covenant), varies from 30 to 40 customary measures, prepared with as much hedge-row, and other fresh mould and road-scrapings as will give the whole surface of the field an even, but slight covering.

The best feeding land in this district is unquestionably in those enclosures that lie permanently on the green side; and for the first two, or perhaps three years, such fields as have undergone the operation of paring and burning, and have not been too far exhausted afterwards by the usual succession of corn crops: but neither the permanent herbage, nor the maiden bite of the artificial grasses and white clover, which seem very much to flourish so long as any force from the ashes may be remaining in the ground, are supposed to be equal to the grazing of a cow beyond nine score per quarter, apportioning about two acres of the summer's pasturage to each cow; and the field carrying during the remaining seven months, after the ratio of about one sheep and a half, or at farthest, two sheep per acre.

The feeding land may be generally rated, in point of value, with that of the upland meadows; and although the first of the new lays, when well managed, supply a rich and inviting herbage, their pride is of short dura-

tion,

tion, and the white clover is found to give way to the black and common couch, and all those plants and grasses which generally indicate a natural weak, or much-exhausted soil. These lands are then, for the remainder of the time they may be allowed to rest, either used for the farmer's own store cattle, or agistment steers ; or reserved for the depasturing of breeding or dairy cows, which are necessarily the native animals of the district ; but which, among all their other good qualities, are certainly not to be recommended for the dairy, the general management of which is stated to be as follows :

The milk is put into tin or earthen pans, holding about ten or twelve quarts each. The evening's meal is placed, in the following morning, and the morning's milk is placed in the afternoon, upon a broad iron plate, heated by a small furnace, or otherwise over stoves, where, exposed to a gentle fire, they remain until after the whole body of cream is supposed to have formed upon the surface, which being gently removed by the edge of a spoon or ladle, small air bubbles will begin to rise, that denote the approach of a boiling heat, when the pans must be removed from off the heated plate or stoves. The cream remains upon the milk in this state, until quite cold, when it may be removed into a churn, or, as is more frequently the case, into an open vessel, and there moved by hand with a stick about a foot long, at the end of which is fixed a sort of peal, from four to six inches in diameter, and with which about 12 lbs. of butter may be separated from the butter-milk at a time.

The butter, in both cases, being found to separate much more freely, and sooner to coagulate into a mass, than in the ordinary way, when churned from raw cream that may have been several days in gathering ; and at the same time will answer a more valuable purpose for pre-

serving,

serving, which should be first salted in the usual way; then placed in convenient sized egg-shaped earthen crocks, and always kept covered with a pickle made strong enough to float and buoy up, about half out of the brine, a new-laid egg. This cream, before churning, is the clouted cream so much celebrated in Devonshire. Although it would be reasonable to suppose, that the scalding of the milk must have occasioned the whole of the oily or unctuous matter to form upon the surface, still experience shews that is not the case, and that the scalded skimmed milk is much richer and better for the purposes of suckling, and makes far better cheese, than the raw skimmed milk does.

The ordinary produce of milk per day, for the first twenty weeks after calving, is three gallons, and is equal to the producing of a pound and a quarter of butter daily, by the scalding process. The scalded skimmed milk is valued at $1\frac{1}{4}d.$ per quart, either for cheese-making, or feeding hogs. The sum of the trials procured to be made on the milk in several parts of this district, gives an average of twelve pints of milk to ten ounces of butter. When cheese is to be made (but in which manufacture there does not appear to be any superior excellence in Devonshire), great care is taken that the milk is not heated so far as to produce bubbles under the cream.

Although these general statements will be found considerably short of the average produce from cows of a larger size, and probably much better adapted for the pail, still there are not wanting instances of what must be regarded as extraordinary produce among the North Devon cows.

In the neighbourhood of Molland Bouceaux, a single cow, judged to be rather less than eight score per quarter, within three weeks from the time of calving, yielded, in

seven

seven successive days, seventeen pounds and a half of butter; several of the meals of milk were measured during this time, which gave an average of fourteen pints per meal: instances also occurred in other parts of the district, of two pounds of butter per day being obtained from cows within a short time after calving; and it is particularly clear in the recollection of a gentleman in the neighbourhood of Bishop's Tawton, that some years since a cow of the common red breed, after her second or third calf, which she had between Michaelmas and Christmas, yielded, without any particular attention being paid to food or treatment, during a considerable time of the ensuing winter, two pounds and a half of butter per day; this cow living at the time in common with the other dairy cows, which were permitted in the day time to range over all the old pasture-grounds, and regularly foddered morning and evening with hay in the same field. It is much to be lamented that the issue of these cows, and of this last one in particular, were not afterwards attended to. As the herbage of the dairy grounds in this district is generally of a very coarse, wiry, and inferior quality, it should not be stated, according to the relative value of the other lands, at a higher average rent than 15 s. per acre.

The great range for sheep pasture in the vicinity of this district, is unquestionably the forest of Exmoor; yet there are many valuable sheep-walks to be found on those wide and extensive commons which belong to the parishes lying in Venville, and abutting eastwardly on the forest bounds. To these commons must be added, as sheep-walk and range for store cattle, all such other parts of the district as at this time are not actually enclosed, and either open to all the inhabitants of the vicinage, or, being anciently enclosed, but now open and neglected moor-

lands

lands appurtenant to particular estates, are depastured by the joint agreement of the occupiers of the estates to which such moors belong.

To give some idea of the extent of these wastes and long abandoned moors, it may not be amiss to imagine the whole completely submerged with water, when the enclosures, particularly in the northern and eastern parts of the district, might be viewed in comparison with the inundated lands, as a group of small islands in the middle of an ocean. These interior sheep-walks, lying much below the level of the heights of Exmoor, afford, in the winter seasons, a sort of cold harbour to the sheep from the greater severity of climate they would be exposed to by remaining on the forest during winter. This, however, is by no means generally resorted to, notwithstanding the cruelty and excessive losses connected with a contrary practice; for, as the wool of the wether flocks is the main, or perhaps only motive in the proprietors for paying any attention whatever to the preservation of those animals, it is no uncommon usage for them to remain upon the forest the year round, culling annually, at shearing time, the broken-mouthed sheep, and leaving them at home with the lambs, when they are generally, in a very fine condition, or by the end of the aftermath sold fat, and before the winter sets in. The breeding ewes frequently continue on the moor till November, when they are driven home, and mercifully permitted to yean in the enclosures, and return with their lambs to the moor again about Old May-day.

The inhabitants of all the parishes abutting eastwardly upon Exmoor, have the privilege of depasturing their sheep upon the forest at half price, or $2\frac{1}{2}d$. per head per annum. For this indulgence a sort of feudal service is required, in assisting, at stated times, to drive the forest, with

with a view of ascertaining the extent of trespass that
may be upon it, as well from the county of Devon as
that of Somerset. These trespassers detected, are pu-
nished according to the ancient forest laws: but for this
particular service, all the inhabitants within the purlieus
of the forest, *and residing in the county of Somerset, have
the right of a free depasturage for their sheep upon the moor.*

In hereafter describing the leading features of these
wastes, their general character will be found much varied;
but regarding them in this place in the nature of sheep-
walks, their powers in the aggregate may be considered as
equal to the depasturing about one and a half of the
common sheep of the country per acre, from May till
November; but should a third part of that number be
compelled to winter on the more exposed moors and commons, without having access to the enclosures for shelter
and warmer lodging, one half of them would inevitably
perish before the return of spring, or approach of more
genial weather.

Such parts of these wastes as are subject to overflowing
from the adjacent hills, are said to be unsound, and to
communicate the caw or rot in sheep. The same has not
been noticed from the sheep depasturing upon and near
wet, boggy, or peaty places. The common Exmoor
sheep are the breed most generally preferred in the open
and more exposed parts of this district: this preference
arises from their extraordinary hardiness, and the activity with which they continue working in search of food.
The wethers of this breed, at two and a half or three years
old, and fattened to their frame, make delicious mutton,
weighing from 12 to 15lbs. per quarter, and commonly
shear from 4 to 5½lbs. of unwashed wool to the fleece,
value 9*d.* per lb. in the yoak.

The manner of laying down grass-lands has already been
stated

stated as fully as that practice requires, in this district, but on the subject of breaking up grass-land by the ordinary mode of paring and burning the green sward, something may be said in addition to the manner before noticed of conducting those operations. Any person but moderately skilled in a knowledge of the nature and fitness of land for the various purposes of cultivation, will, on examining the broken district of North Devon, soon perceive that its hills are generally covered with a depth and staple of soil far superior to what would be expected in a country abounding with such high, and in many places, such very sharp hills, on which, wherever any difference absolutely exists in point of soil, it is uniformly in favour of the northern brows and sides of such eminences. The mildness and humidity of the climate give even the tops of these hills a disposition to teem with an almost uninterrupted vegetation. The turnips are but seldom, and that only in a very slight degree, affected by the frost, and many of the most useful and ornamental plants, and some of the best grasses in the rich and sheltered vales, are found to grow and even blossom throughout the winter.

To the undisputed existence of these natural advantages, are we now to look for the origin and continuance of a practice, which, under less favourable circumstances of soil and climate, the inhabitants would never have thought of, or, once knowing its ruinous effects, would not have dared to have continued as an opening process for their tillage lands. Any one (it may be again repeated), but slightly skilled in the nature of soils, and in a knowledge of practical husbandry, examining a country of this description, and seeing so small a proportion of its enclosed surface under aration, and the remainder either shut up for mowing, or appearing alive, as it were,

were, with stock depasturing on it, together with the numerous flocks and herds feeding on the extensive moors
and commons, and which in all such countries, under a
system of judicious management, will ever be made subservient to the improvement of the enclosed lands—must
conclude, that, from the large quantities of manure produced by the wintering of so large a stock of sheep and
cattle, the small proportion of tillage land would be kept
in excellent heart and very high condition. What then
will be his surprise and disappointment, when he learns,
and that from the most respectable, ingenuous, and intelligent of its inhabitants, that no greater average produce
is obtained from such lands, than what has been already
stated in the preceding Chapter !

There are, indubitably, many points of grossly-de-
fective management, which lead to this result, but none,
it is presumed, of greater magnitude than the indiscriminate practice of paring and burning. Whether the
whole sod is burnt, as in spading, or that it is only partially consumed, as in the other operations of skirting
or velling, still it has been remarked by very old and candid persons, that in proportion as the surface has been
consumed by fire, the fields require a quicker repetition
of the process. The paring and burning being effected,
and the land afterwards subjected to the customary course
of tillage, is at length laid down, when, as if more
strongly to mark the native energies of the soil, ribwort,
white clover, and many other valuable grasses, are found
to grow for the first period of perhaps two or three years :
they are, however, only for a season, and are soon
smothered and expelled by the tribe of aira and agrostis,
the triticum repens, rest, harrow, &c. all of which plants
and grasses are found to prevail, in exclusion of all
such other grasses as are found to constitute the sweet and
　　　　　　　　　　　　　　　　　　　　inviting

inviting herbage of the adjacent fields, which, time immemorial, has never been disturbed by the plough.

The pasturage of the country thus injured, and the
native energies of its soil rendered weak and inefficient
by a succession of white straw crops, the land is laid
down in the manner before noticed, and is left for an
indefinite term of from ten to fifty years under grass, for
in this district there is no fixed time for ploughing it up
again, nor will any thing but the necessities or caprice of
the occupier induce him to break up a field until its surface is so far encumbered with a thick and matted covering of the coarsest plants and grasses, as to encourage
reasonable hopes of its quick combustion after spading
or paring with the plough. That the stimuli of the
lime and ashes, even for the first crop, is not generally
found to answer (the alleged purpose) is sufficiently clear
from the average produce of the wheat crops, and as
such, the facility with which the land is afterwards managed, in preparation for the successive crops of other
corn, seems the principal, if not the only recommendation for the general practice of paring and burning the
sound and well-stapled lands throughout this district.
Where fields are known to have been most frequently
subjected to this ordeal, in addition to its other injurious
effects, such enclosures are seen rapidly covered with
moss; and notwithstanding the great pains that have
been taken of late years, by selecting the most perfect
and beautiful of the male and female of the North Devon
cattle, their standard, in point of size, is judged to be
rather on the decline than otherwise, and which by some
is ascribed to the general deterioration of the herbage, by
a too frequent practice of spading and burning the
pastures, and thus destroying the native stock of all the
finer grasses.

If

If it were necessary to say any thing more, in order to shew the fatal avidity which prevails in this district for paring and burning, it can in no circumstance be exhibited more fully than towards the expiration of a lease, when, if the farmer is not restrained (which he seldom is), by his covenants, and has neither the industry or means of going over such of his fields with the breast-plough, as he well knows would produce him, although a transient, yet considerable advantage, he usually divides the field or proportion of his farm, to be spaded into small parcels, and rents them out to his neighbours, who agree among each other on the succeeding crops to be taken ; and so much of his farm, for the time being, exhibits all the appearance of an open common-field. This truth is clearly elucidated, from what is now doing within the bounds of Ilfracombe, on a large extent of old lay ground, lying upon the borders of Morthoe, and which, from the nature of its herbage, as it appeared upon the velled combs or balks in July last (1806), could not, in its unbroken state, be estimated at less than from 20s. to 25s. per acre. This land was all subdivided among small renters, for a term of three years only, and at the enormous rent of 4l. 10s. per acre yearly. What the condition of it will be after taking from it the three white straw crops stipulated, will not be very difficult for any one to imagine, who is at all acquainted with the certain consequences that must ever await, and are inseparably connected with the nature of such a scourging practice.

DISTRICT II.

The proportion of grass-land to that which is subject to a course of tillage, varies very considerably in the different quarters composing this district. In the neighbourhood

bourhood of Bampton the permanent green sward is stated
to amount to one-third: rejecting the accommodation
land within about one mile and a half of Tiverton, the
proportion will not be found to exceed one-fifth. Assigning to Mortchard Bishops as the centre of another quarter,
the proportion will fall off to one-seventh, and this will
be found to continue westwardly, excluding the accommodation lands of Chumleigh until we approach Torrington, and after passing the same description of lands near
that town, a one-eighth part of permanent grass will about
mark the proportion to Hartland Abbey. This estimate,
carried through the Drewsteignton quarter, and rejecting
the accommodation lands of Chudleigh, will not exceed
one part of permanent grass to seven parts of occasional
tillage ground. Along the borders of the Torridge river,
below Black Torrington to its junction with the Ochment,
there is a considerable extent of low feeding ground and
meadows : these being frequently exposed to a course of
tillage, are much injured by the annual inundations of that
river sweeping a large proportion of the finer parts of the
ploughed ground away.

It must be always understood that the whole of this
calculation is confined to the inland country, the open
moorlands and commons being discharged from the account. On examining the minutes taken on the survey,
respecting the management of the grass-lands through this
district, they appear so nearly to correspond with what
has been already stated on this subject in the district of
North Devon, that it seems to be totally unnecessary to
repeat them.

DISTRICT

DISTRICT III.

The flowing of the water over the low grounds along the Torridge, is carefully avoided by most of the farmers who live near the borders of that river. It seldom happens that the lands adjacent to the Waldon, or other branches falling into the Torridge, are irrigated, however conveniently situated for that purpose There being little grass-land in the neighbourhood of Holdsworthy, excepting the old moorlands, that can be considered in a state of permanent pasture, the whole of the cultivated parts of that quarter is at different periods subject to a course of tillage, one-eighth part being annually under a crop, and a proportionable part of the remainder in a state of preparation, by skirting and the breast-plough.

In this neighbourhood, the waters of the Torridge, from the coarse sediment they are stated to wash down, are always rejected for irrigation. The average produce of hay upon the best meadows is not stated to exceed one ton per acre, and the low boggy vallies, yielding a coarse rushy swarth, are seldom found to produce more than eight cwt. or half a ton per acre. Let the shear or swarth be what it may, the average price of mowing is stated, including the value of beer or cider allowance, at 2 s. 4 d. per acre. These meadows the rack renters are bound to dress after every third crop of hay. Such parts of the pastures as are appropriated to the feeding of dairy cows are numerous, although small, and the produce of these small dairies is generally vended at Plymouth.   The best feeding land is not supposed to be equal to the grazing of a cow beyond six or seven score per quarter, and to do this the animal must have an entire summer's range over about three acres. Increase of meat from this pasturage 190 lbs. which at 12 s.

per

per score, sinking the offal, amounts to 5 *l.* 14 *s.* The extensive moorlands as well as the old enclosures, are generally depastured by the common Dartmoor sheep and stores of young growing cattle.

The manner of laying down, as well as of breaking up the grass-lands, has already been stated.

DISTRICT IV.

The best feeding lands in the neighbourhood of Tavistock and Milton Damaril, are supposed equal to the grazing of an ox of 12 or 13 score per quarter, between the middle of April and the first of November, allowing at that time the prime grass of about one acre and a half per head. An acre per cow of six cwt. is the usual estimate.

The grass-lands not subject to irrigation here, as well as in the neighbourhood of Yealmpton, and all round Plymouth, are universally dressed with rotten dung and mixings of sea sand, lime and ashes, in February and early in March, at an average expense of 50 *s.* per acre. They are usually shut up for mowing by the end of April or early in May, and yield a general produce of 35 cwt. or two tons of hay per acre. In the parish of Stoke and Egg-Buckland, the average produce of hay is given at two tons and a half per acre ; present price at Plymouth, from 4 *l.* 10 *s.* to 5 *l.* per ton. The after-grass is here frequently rented by the drovers, butchers, jobbers, and contractors, at 3 *l.* 10 *s.* and 4 *l.* per acre. Price of mowing 3 *s.* 6 *d.* per acre, and no allowance of drink.

The young clovers are frequently dunged immediately after harvest, and the oxen fed upon hay and turnips during winter are finished upon them. The first bite of the young grass, whether spontaneous or produced from irrigation, as well as the first shoot of many of the young

DEVON.]   seeds,

seeds, are generally fed down with ewes and lambs, stores, as well as those that are fattening upon all the low grounds. It is here stated that sheep may depasture at all seasons with the most perfect safe·y. The general produce of clover and hievre hay, shut up for mowing about Old May-day, is from 25 to 35 cwt. per acre.

The proportion of meadow, marsh and permanent pasture, has been already stated to amount to about one-fifth part of all the enclosed cultivated lands in the district. The rich marshes before noticed in the indentures upon the sea coast, and those situated on the margin of the principal water-courses, will often force or fatten a cow or steer of six cwt. in three months : in this case they are supposed to take the top of about six roods of prime pasture per head.

These marshes not being esteemed sound for the depasturing of sheep, that species of stock, unless early in the spring, are but seldom fed upon them. The marshes kept free from stock during winter, will generally afford a good bite for a bullock by the middle or last week in April. When intended for mowing, they are stocked hard from the beginning of March till the first of May, in which time the last year's fog is pared down as close and even as possible. The mown land is dressed after the hay is removed, with dung, soaper's waste lees, or any other manure most convenient to be procured; lime at this time is by no means esteemed a proper dressing. Price of mowing, with allowance of ale or cider, 3s. per acre; common produce from the stack 38 cwt. or two tons per acre ; aftermath, from Old Lammas to the first of November, two guineas, and 45s. per acre. These marshes are stated to feed an ox, when put upon them in good fair order, of 1000 weight, in the course of the summer.

A number of sheep are grazed on the higher rich feed-

ing

ing lands through the district: the time usually allowed is 20 weeks, divided before and after shearing ; but the number of sheep these grounds would carry, per acre, was in no one instance satisfactorily ascertained.

DISTRICT V.

The meadow and pasture land in this district, being chiefly confined to a narrow verge on the borders of the Teign and Bovey rivers, are no farther particularly noticed in this Report. The extensive commons belonging to all the commons lying in Venville, in this and the preceding districts, require that something farther should be stated respecting them.

It is understood that all the Venville tenants are liable to a feudal service, similar to that required by the common usage and forest laws of Exmoor. Being thus situated, they become entitled to the depasturage of their sheep and bullocks upon the forest, paying three-pence annually for as many sheep as they may choose to send upon the forest, and two-pence per head annually for horned cattle. This right is either enjoyed by themselves, or is transferred by them for certain valuable considerations, to their more wealthy neighbours, and to farmers frequently residing in the country below. The tenants in Venville are also stated to be free from the payment of tolls in all the fairs and markets in the kingdom, London and Barnstable excepted.

These commons in most respects resemble the leading character of the forest of Dartmoor. They have two distinct species of covering, although evidently derived from the same origin. The first, and that which is depasturable, consists of a moist peaty earth of 12 or 18 inches in depth, resting upon a bright brown argillaceous loam, close

close and retentive of water, and commonly called fox-
mould : in this blocks and rocks of granite very frequently
occur. The second character, and that which is not accessible even to the light active sheep of the moor, consists
of a rank bog, answering in every respect to the bogs in
Ireland. A brown spongy substance covered with coarse
sedge and rushes, at all times highly charged with water,
and lying from two to six or eight feet deep on a similar
stratum of peat, composes the subsoil of the depasturable parts of the commons, and under which peat is found
a close deep stratum of white and yellow clay, mixed with
granite rocks, the decomposed parts of which form partial
beds of granite gravel

The importance of the first description of these wastes,
can in no way be so fully shewn as by stating the stock feeding upon them. The commons belonging to the parish
of Widdecombe will furnish a sufficient example, when
in the month of October last, there were estimated by gentlemen residing in the neighbourhood, to be no less than
14,000 sheep, besides the usual proportion of horned cattle. These commons are certainly of considerable extent,
but perhaps not much larger than those of Brent, Harford, and others in the western district. Their depasturable
parts may be meliorated and improved by carrying off the
redundant water, in doing which the subsoil would be
found to supply an inexhaustible resource for improving
the surface.

These were the impressions first made upon the mind
of the Surveyor, as he entered upon the examination of
the districts bordering upon Dartmoor. A more particular inquiry, and the result of experiments made with judgment, and conducted upon a large scale by Mr. Pender, on
land of this character within the enclosed park of Oakhampton, has at once fully and completely confirmed them.

DISTRICT

DISTRICT VI.

The pasture ground in this district is appropriated partly for dairies and partly for feeding ground. It is equal to the feeding of an ox of 12 score per quarter during the summer months. This would require the top of near three acres of the prime pasture rented at 3*l*. per acre. Oxen of this size, however, are but rarely grazed, the more common feeding stock being cows and steers, weighing about eight score per quarter ; an animal of this size will require the range of about five roods of this ground. This animal would lay on from the middle of May until the middle of November, about two score per quarter. About eight sheep may be considered as a proportional stock for the same quantity of ground ; these sheep will make in the same time an increase of 6lbs. per quarter, or 24lbs. per sheep; hence the difference in meat per acre, assuming sixpence per lb. as the average price of both : the bullock gains in value 4*l*. the sheep 4*l*. 16*s*.

The excellent water with which this district every where abounds, is carefully applied in most situations where it can be commanded, to the use of irrigation. Large quantities of hay and straw, with all the productions of the farm, are annually drawn from the surrounding country, and find a ready sale in the city of Exeter, the general markets of which are as well and as seasonably supplied as any in the kingdom.

DISTRICT VII.

The valley of the Axe, and its adjacent rising grounds, although lying at some distance, seem only a continuation of the same delightful country through which the waters
of

of the Exe are collected to their common outfall at sea.
The rich and extensive views from the eminences bordering upon all these vallies, are perhaps no where to be
surpassed for luxuriance and variety of prospect in the
kingdom.   And the prime pastures are found to yield an
abundant supply of animal food, to all the large towns
situated in the bosom of these enchanting vallies.   The
herbage of the second order is usually applied to the depasturing of cows for the dairy, a business carried on to
a considerable extent in this as well as in the preceding
district, but no where better understood than in the vale
of Honiton.

The following is the result of several inquiries on this
subject, made in different parts of the country. By far the
greatest part of the butter made in this country is sent to
London.   The butter-factors at Honiton will not, on any
consideration, take butter made from the clouted or
scalded cream.   This process, therefore, notwithstanding
that economy ought long since to have led to its discontinuance (unless on a small scale for potting or winter
use), is entirely abandoned in all the large dairies, as well
as in most others that supply the larger markets in the
country.   It is generally allowed, that the North Devon
cow is by no means so well calculated for the dairy as cows
of the same size in many other parts of England ; yet the
great demand and high price given for the calves of this
breed for raising, occasions this sort of cow to be universally in use throughout all the dairies.

The milk which is drawn from the cow morning and
evening, is poured into leads, where it stands forty-eight
hours before the flet-milk is run off.   In summer, it is
churned every day, and cheese is made of the skimmed
milk.   In the autumn, this business is renewed every
other day ; and in winter, sometimes, but not always,
                                                              twice

twice a week. The butter churned thus early from cream, before it has acquired any taint or sourness, is affirmed to possess a much better keeping quality than that produced from the clouted cream; add to which, this latter butter is seldom free from, and often most offensively tainted with, the fumes of charcoal, and a smoaky taste imbibed in the operation of scalding. The butter is usually churned in the barrel churns, and afterwards washed until the water becomes quite free from any cloud whatever from the butter-milk. It is then salted down into firkins of four dozen, or 48lbs. each, and weighing 18oz. to the pound. The excessive high salting the butter receives, is discharged by the butter-merchants in London (and often vended as fresh, or at least not salt butter). This salting in some measure accounts for the enlarged customary butter-weight in this country.

As the cheese commonly made in these dairies (that of Membury excepted) is of an inferior quality, and generally destined for domestic use, little attention is paid to its making beyond that of the ordinary process, which is well known. Some of the dairies are managed by the farmer's family; but by far the greater proportion are rented out to dairy-men, whose attention, together with that of their family, is exclusively confined to this department. The rent of dairies fluctuates from nine guineas to ten pound per cow. In these cases, the farmer apportions about two acres and a half of pasture and meadow ground, averaging about 38s. per acre, for the summer food and winter foddering of each cow, during the 42 weeks she is supposed to be in milk. The remainder of the time the cows are fed with straw in the farm-yards, and in day-time range at large over the coarse grounds and commons; fifty faggots, or five seams, to the value

of

of 8*s.* per cow, are also allowed and laid down by the
farmer for the use of the dairy. The first cost of these
cows, with the second or third calf at their side, is estimated at thirteen guineas. When their milk is done, and
that they are fattened for sale, they will usually average
six score and a half per quarter. In a dairy of twenty
cows, it is customary to allow a bull. at the same cost and
rent as a cow. The expense of mowing, making, and
securing the hay of one-third part of the dairy-grounds,
8*s.* per acre. The first cost of the dairy utensils, consisting of leads, kettles, pans, pails, press-tubs, copper, &c.
50*l.*; the annual wear of which, 4*l.*: dairy-maid's wages,
with board, washing, and lodging, 16*l.* per annum; attendance of one man for twenty weeks, in foddering,
cleaning out the cow-sheds, &c. at 9*s.* per week.

It is here to be observed, that one dairy-maid would
not be able to perform more than half the work required
in a dairy of 20 cows. The remainder is therefore supposed to be supplied by parish apprentices, and the farmer's wife and daughters, all of whom are seldom without
the necessary qualifications for such employments; being,
with very few exceptions, careful, neat, tidy and industrious.

The amount of the first cost of 20 pigs, for consuming
the offal milk, whey, and butter-milk of the dairy, would
be 20*l.*; great and small tithe, 2*s.* 6*d.* per acre; parochial payments, 2*s.* in the pound on the net rent; annual
depreciation of dairy-cows and bull, 10*s.* per head; interest of 350*l.* capital employed, 17*l.* 10*s.*; allowance of
5 per cent. on the gross produce of the dairy for losses,
cow-doctor, and other contingent expenses, not taken
into this estimate, will afford altogether the following
statement:

The

The Dairy Dr.

	£.	s.	d.
To annual interest accruing upon 350l. capital employed	17	10	0
To rent of 52½ acres of pasture and meadow-ground, at 38s. per acre	99	10	0
To parochial payments on the net rent, at 2s. in the pound	9	9	0
To great and small tithe upon 52½ acres, at 2s. 6d. per acre ,..............................	6	11	3
To attendance for 20 weeks, at 9s. per week	9	0	0
To annual wear and tear of dairy utensils	4	0	0
To mowing, making, and securing the hay of 17½ acres, at 8s. per acre	7	0	0
To fuel for use of the dairy, at 8s. per cow ..	8	0	0
To annual depreciation in value of the dairy, at 10s. per head ....,.....................	10	10	0
To dairy-maid's wages, &c.	16	0	0
To 5 per cent. on amount of the gross produce of the dairy for risks and losses, &c.	14	10	0

Cr.

	£.	s.	d.	£	s	d
By produce of butter per cow, 1 lb. per diem for the first 20 weeks, and half a pound per day for the latter period, making 206 lb. each cow; for 20 cows, 4120 lbs. at 1s. per lb.	206	0	0			
By 1¼ cwt. of cheese per cow, 25 cwt. at 25s. per cwt.	31	5	0			
By 20 calves, at 28s. each	28	0	0			
By profit upon 20 pigs, at 25s. each	25	0	0			
Balance in favour of the dairy				88	4	9
	£.290	5	0	290	5	0

To

To which profit may be added, the agistment of about one sheep per acre upon the dairy-grounds between the first of November and middle of March, generally about 20 weeks, and paying 7*s.* per head in that time, making a farther sum of 18*l.* 3*s.* 6*d.* The net profit thus made out upon 52½ acres of land appropriated in this manner, will amount to 106*l.* 8*s.* 3*d.* and as near as may be to 40*s.* per acre.

CHAP. IX.

GARDENS AND ORCHARDS.

———◆———

SECT. I.——GENERAL.

IT is believed, that in no part of England kitchen
gardens are laid out on a more extended scale than in the
county of Devon; and however coarse and unseemly the
cobwalls appear, by which they are commonly enclosed,
they seldom fail to afford, in due season, considerable
quantities of highly flavoured wall-fruit. The culinary
vegetables can no where be surpassed for general excellence,
a profusion of which are supplied, throughout the year,
by the gardens, with little exception, of all the rural inhabitants. In the neighbourhood of all the large towns,
gardening is well understood, and carried on to the extent required; and to a perfection little short of what is
practised in the vicinity of London. The gardens of the
farmers and peasantry universally afford large quantities
of leeks, so much in use among them; these, with pot-
herbs, other kitchen, and a few ornamental plants and
flowers, are found to occupy those gardens, whilst potatoes are more generally supplied from larger portions of
ground, in the fields, and in the manner before noticed.

SECT. II.—ORCHARDS.

DISTRICT I.

As cider is found to be the most general beverage of the inhabitants, it is reasonable to expect that much attention is paid to the cultivation of orchards. In this district, however, although a leading consideration among the farmers, and where there are many very good apple-orchards, they do not seem to form so principal an object of agricultural economy, as in other parts of the country hereafter to be mentioned.

DISTRICT II.

The usual mode of procuring a variety of fruit, in some parts of this district, is to have a small piece of ground previously prepared, and to spread the pulp or cheese fresh from the press upon it, and with a rake or light harrow mix and well cover it with the surface mould. In the progress of the ensuing growth of the young plants, care is taken to select all such as produce the largest and most luxuriant leaves, as it is from that character that the best expectations are formed for procuring the most valuable fruit. The rejected plants are drawn out from time to time, and the preserved ones left, to discover their specific qualities. These, when approved of, and which point is generally ascertained by the end of the sixth year from the time of sowing the pips, their heads being previously formed upon a stem about five feet high, are removed to any eastern, but that of north-east, aspect; and on the side of a hill, free from springs, though rather a moist subsoil, are planted generally at the distance

of

of 25 or 30 feet a-part, holes being previously made, and depositing in each about two seams or horse-loads of road-scrapings, or way soil.

In planting the orchard, care should be taken to place all the trees of the same sort or quality in rows, by which means the fruit ripening together, can more easily be kept separate, milled, expressed, and the juice fermented toge-ther ; objects of the first consequence with all good cider-ists, as the mixing of the fruit is found to produce unequal and repeated stages of fermentation, and thus exhausting the strength and proving highly injurious to the cider. In other places the pulp or cheese from the press is imme-diately washed, and the clean kernels sown in the month of March following, after standing two years in the seed beds; the plants producing the largest leaves are removed to a nursery, and set out four feet a-part ; at five years old from the seed, a part of these stocks are grafted, and others left to discover their natural produce, which not answering, are afterwards grafted also. Great pains are bestowed in training the young top, which is done by cut-ting off the shoot chin high, and afterwards pruning the top branches for three or four years, within six or eight inches of the stem. This strengthens the trunk and roots, and gives considerable security to the tree when removed to the orchard. After remaining three or four years in the nursery from the time of being grafted, they are usually transplanted on a south-eastern declivity, at the distance of 30 feet a-part, and will keep in good bearing for a period of forty years. By such means very fine fruit is often produced.

In the western parts of this district, as well as generally through North Devon, a deficiency in the crop of apples was much heard of; but through the Bampton and Tiver-ton quarters, the orchards promised to be more productive than they have been remembered for the last 20 years.

At

At Morbath, four of the pound pippins were taken as a fair average from the tree, and weighed 2 lbs, 8oz. At Cruwys Mortchard, four apples of the Fair Maid of Taunton, were in like manner gathered from a tree, and weighed 2 lbs. 15oz.

DISTRICT III.

The same management in raising, training, and planting orchards, generally prevails through this district. The deep moist clays being of a tender nature, are in no respect found unfavourable to the growth, or bearing duration of the apple-tree; in fact, these clays are considered as being the most capable of affording the richest and sweetest cider. The species called the red-streak, is mostly preferred; but of late years, these orchards have been much subject to a blight, in the early part of summer, and after the fruit has attained to no inconsiderable size. The apple crop, in both divisions of this district, affords a much better prospect than has been known for many years.

DISTRICT IV.

So very unfriendly are the south-easterly or moor winds, represented to be in the western parts of this district, that at Milton Abbot, and in many places in the hundreds of Tavistock and Roborough, a north aspect is preferred for the situation of the orchards, in preference to that of any other. A very common practice prevails, of foddering cattle during winter in the orchards, and when it can be done without injury to the young trees. Dressing the orchards at the same time and manner as is usual to manure the mowing-grounds, is also found very much to increase their produce; but to cultivate the orchards with potatoes is much disapproved of, not only on account of

the

the exhausting nature of that crop, but from its tillage, the ground becomes so much loosened, as frequently to expose the trees being blown down by the westerly winds.

Every valley throughout the South Hams, is more or less occupied with orchards, and which are much celebrated for the excellence of the cider they produce. The aspect which protects them from the fury of the sea winds, is essentially attended to.

The trees here are generally very small, and are seldom found standing at a greater distance than sixteen feet from each other; their branches so interlocked, intermixed with dead wood, and covered with the *lichen vulpinus,* or common tree moss, that the feeble foliage and diminutive fruit they produce, are scarcely visible at the time of their being loaded with what is called a fair average crop. Instances, however, are not now uncommon, of great improvements being made both in the quantity of fruit and quality of cider, by removing from one-third to one-half of the trees planted in the ordinary way, and subjecting the remainder to annual prunings, by cutting away all the dead, barren, and unprofitable branches. Besides what was shipped last year in other places in the Kingsbridge river, the quantity sent off from Salcombe was 700 hogsheads. The present prospect does not promise a greater export; and as such, the crop of apples must be considered as generally deficient in comparison with other years, when the export from Salcombe only has amounted to 1500 hogsheads.

The variety of names applicable to the same fruit in this and other districts, and even in the adjacent villages, precludes all chance of being understood at a distance, when speaking of any apple that may be the favourite in such places. A rich sweet apple seems generally to hold the preference for cider · those of a more acid quality for hoarding, or winter use. The farmer should patiently wait the natural dropping of the fruit, collect into his apple-room, and keep separate the different sorts, which after undergoing the first sweat, should be ground, pressed, fermented, and casked a-part from each other.

The Herefordshire press is that generally preferred. The vessels being all well cleansed and scalded, are filled with cider from the press, which in a day or two begins to work, throwing off large quantities of dregs and impurities of the liquor; this will sometimes subside to the bottom, but whether it sinks or issues from the bung-hole, as the weather may be more or less warm, it will require racking from time to time, to separate the dregs from the liquor, when, if too strong a disposition is observed to renew its fermentation, it is generally stopped by burning a piece of cloth or paper, two or three inches wide and six or seven inches long, dipped in brimstone, and put into the bung-hole of a cask that has six or eight gallons of cider in it: after lighting it, the bung-hole is secured, and the air in tne cask is sufficient to keep up the combustion until the match is consumed. This done, the hogshead is rolled to and fro, in order to promote the union of the cider with the sulphurous vapour; it is then filled up within a few inches of the bung-hole, and all fermentation for a time is suspended, but on observing it to return, this fumigation is renewed as often as may be found necessary. When the liquor remains quiet, and a candle will burn clear in the bung-hole, the fermentation is easy, and not likely to produce a farther diminution in the strength of the cider; and when every symptom of fret is wholly subsided, the cider is racked off, and is thus prepared for the London market; and for which it is generally ready in the months of March or April following. The dregs are always filtered through brown

burras

burrass bags, holding three or four gallons each, but as the union between the pulp and the liquor is found to be very close, a separation is effected by mixing about half a pint of bullock's, or any other fresh blood, with about six or eight gallons of the dregs : this being well beaten up, divides the jelly of the pulp, and the liquor running clear off, is mixed with the other cider, and is always found to contribute to the restraint of its farther fermentation.

To complete the fining of the cider, a pound of isinglas, first soaked for ten or twelve hours in cold water, is afterwards dissolved in about five gallons of cider, and well incorporated with a whisk : about a quart of this is sufficient for a hogshead of cider, and with which it must be well stirred and mixed in the cask. When the cider is designed for home use, it is racked off three or four times from the rough lees, and after the fermentation as before indicated, by a lighted candle at the bung-hole, has subsided, is bunged down, and secured for use. The apple crop varies very much in different parts of this district : between the river Dart and Torbay they have scarcely a twelfth part of the ordinary produce; in the neighbourhood of Ashburton, and through the parishes of Dean-prior and Buckfastleigh, the orchards all appeared to be remarkably well loaded. An eastern aspect is universally preferred.

DISTRICT V.

The substratum of granite gravel is no where found unfavourable to the culture of apple orchards. It is here proper to remark, that the higher the orchards are situated, provided they are protected from the moor wind,

DEVON.]   the

the less liable they are to be injured by frost in the spring and early part of summer. At this season fogs are often found to roll in from the westward, and as they only ascend to a certain height in all the combs and vallies in the country, orchards situated above this region, are not enveloped in the fogs and floating vapours of the night; and although they are still exposed to a dry frosty air, its mischievous effect is scarcely to be discerned, whilst the most fatal consequences await it upon all the fruit trees in the humid valley below. It is here stated, that a few gallons of old cider will always check the fermentation, and preserve the body of the new cider.

DISTRICT VI.

Throughout the whole of this country, long experience has shewn, that the same fruit growing upon a moist loam or clay bottom, will produce a vastly superior cider to that growing upon an understratum of shear sand or gravel. An acclivity looking to the south-east, is the situation always preferred here for the culture of the apple-tree. The size of the fruit is much kept up on trees not fast verging to decay, by cutting off the suckers, opening the top by pruning away all the wild, dead, and unprofitable branches, and dressing each tree annually at its root, with a compost of dung, lime, and way-soil, in the proportion of about one seam or horse-load to two trees. The orchard, thus invigorated and opened to the influence of the sun and air, the moss with which the branches of the trees had been clothed for many years falls off, and the improvement in size, quantity, and quality of the fruit, is not less evident than the healthy and flourishing condition of the tree. The apple
mostly

mostly preferred here is Gibbs's Cornish; late in its blossom, a constant bearer, and suspending its fruit by a very fine stem, or foot stalk.

DISTRICT VII.

There is no doubt but some years since the orchards of this district were productive in a much higher degree than they are at present; but from the frequency of planting young trees where the old ones have failed, a barrenness in many of the orchards has ensued. It is usual in the marly parts of this country to appropriate for orchards the large excavations formerly made in digging marl: here the apple trees are protected from most winds, and continue to flourish and bear longer than in less secure situations; but here again the fruit is more exposed in the spring and early part of summer to the frosts that occur at that season, than it possibly could be in higher situations.

The crop of apples generally through the valley of the Otter is very good, although it certainly does not produce a liquor equally rich as that grown upon stiffer land.— Upon the high plains of Dunkerswell and Church Staunton, no material deficiency was noticed or heard of in point of quantity; and the quality of the cider is there contended to be equal to that of the South Hams, and much superior to the produce of the apple orchards in the sandy district below.

The culture of the apple trees and management of the cider, appears not to differ here in any material point from what has been already noticed. The great uncertainty of these crops, renders it a matter of much difficulty to state any thing like an average produce through the county.——— The mean however, of several statements given in upon a period

period of seven years, varying from two and a half to five hogsheads per acre, will equal that of three hogsheads and two-fifths per acre through the county. The average price last year at the pound's mouth, or press, was 50s. per hogshead. It is expected to average in like manner this year about two guineas and a half. The misletoe has no where been observed in the orchards in this county.

CHAP.

CHAP. X.

WOODS AND PLANTATIONS.

—————

SECT. I.——COPSE WOODS.

NOTWITHSTANDING that to the eye of a stran-
ger passing cursorily through this county, there would appear a considerable deficiency of copse and other woodlands, still, on a more minute examination he would discover his mistake, by finding most of the hollows and
side-hills bounding the larger vallies, particularly where
guarded from the westerly winds, interspersed and adorned
with a healthy, though not a large or towering growth, of
oak and other timber; and also much occupied with the
remains of large and more ancient woodlands now converted into oak, and other underwood coppices. That
these are the vestiges of a chain of forests which formerly
covered the margin of all the water-courses descending
from the forests of Dartmoor and of Exmoor, and stretched
along all the low grounds and their side-hills to the sea,
is plain, not only from the vigour of such woods within a
short distance of the sea, but in the district of North Devon, it is more clearly manifested from the number of red
forest deer, which still preserve their ancient claim to
ramble unmolested during the summer season, through all
the glades and woodlands with which those rich and pleasant vallies are so highly decorated.

DISTRICT I.

The coppice land here, consisting chiefly of oak, is cut once in about twenty years, and generally sells upon the spot to the person who undertakes to fell and convert it, for about 15*l*. per acre. Standards or samplers are always left, but seldom raised to timber, or preserved beyond the ensuing period for cutting down the copse. The usual appropriation of the oak wood, after peeling every branch of an inch or less in diameter, is to select all the best poles for building, fencing, paling, and making hurdles, to tie the brushwood into faggots, which usually sell for 2*s*. 6*d*. per score in the woods, and convert the remainder into charcoal, and which is generally worth 2*s*. per bushel at the char heaps.

Whenever these coppices, through neglect of the owner or occupier, become abandoned as woodland, and are left open to the free depasturage of cattle, they have generally been remarked, on the sides of rocky hills and inaccessible places, unfit for the common operations of husbandry. No pains have therefore been bestowed in grubbing and clearing them. Their appropriation being common, their rent or value is left without a name.

DISTRICT II.

It has been already stated, that there were in the parish of Monkleigh, and along the vallies of the Yeo and Torridge rivers, some very good oak timber and copse woodlands. The under-growth in these woods is a good deal varied, and found to consist of oak, ash, birch, willow, elder, wych elm or hazel, common hazel, and wild cherry. It is generally cut down once in twenty-two years. These coppices

coppices are used for hop-poles, hoop-poles, hurdles, faggots, and charcoal, and when converted by the owner, or sold standing, will generally yield a rent equal to 15*l.* per acre. The great attention, however, lately bestowed in fencing and otherwise preserving the woodlands in this quarter, gives reason to expect that this profit will be much augmented in future.

The copse wood at Clovella Court and Hartland Abbey, cut at 25 years growth, seldom fails of yielding rent equal to 20*l.* per acre. The best poles are always preserved for building, fencing, and various other uses. The remainder are either charred, or bound into faggots for fuel. The coppice wood generally in the country about Torrington, is usually cut down at 30 years growth, appropriated in the manner above noticed, and sells on an average before falling for 35*l.* per acre.

The neighbourhood of Monk Oakhampton is well wooded, but it is no uncommon case for the coppice and other woodlands to be left open to the tenants' cattle, who having agistment stock to take in, avail themselves of the shade afforded by the woods and coppices, to demand an additional price for the summering of cattle. The oak copse brakes, covering a large extent of ground west of the town, and in the parish of Oakhampton, are cut down at 20 years growth, and generally yield at the stump, from 15 to 16*l.* per acre.

The extensive copse lands of Old Ridge, and thence southward towards St. Mary Tidburn and Whitestone, are chiefly of oak, with some birch and elder in the low places. These woods are cut down about once in sixteen years, but are seldom found to net more than 12*l.* per acre.

In this part of the country there are many strong furze brakes, which at five years growth seldom net less than a
rent

rent or profit of 18l. per acre. The oak woodlands in
the neighbourhood of Cruwys Mortchard, afford a valuable stock of young growing timber. The under-growth in
these woods, consisting of oak, birch, alder and hazel, are
cut down at 18 years growth, yielding a net profit of
15l. per acre. The number of young timber trees now
flourishing in these woods, average about 40 per acre. At
each fall it is usual to leave a greater number of samplers,
from which at the ensuing cutting, such a selection is
made as is most likely to answer for the purpose of timber.

The coppices in the vicinity of Loxhore and Stoodleigh
are cut at 20 years growth, but they seldom sell standing
for more than 15l. per acre. The greater part of the oak
coppices, covering the sides and tops of many of the hills
in the parish of Oakford, appear to be cut down in annual
succession, but without any attention being paid to the
preservation of young samplers for timber.

The copse wood in the neighbourhood of Bampton,
consists chiefly of oak, which is cut down once in twenty
years, and is usually sold standing for 20l. per acre. After
the oak, the great body of all these oak coppices is charred
and sold at the heap for 8s. a seam of about 2cwt. to the
wool-combers and other customers, chiefly from the manufacturing towns.

It may here be observed, that the coppices in a south
aspect come to the axe sooner by two years, than where
such woods are found lying to the northward.

DISTRICT III.

The largest quantity of oak and other coppices are
found along the Tamer, and the small streams discharging
into that, the Torridge, and the Teign rivers. This, as
well

well as the coppice wood growing on the borders of the
Little Dart river, is usually cut down at 18 years growth,
and averaging a net annual value of about 16*l.* per acre.

DISTRICT IV.

The observation with regard to the deficiency of woodland in the north district of Devon, will equally apply to
this southern district of the county. The under-growth in
the timber woodlands is usually cut down at twenty years
growth, and which, from the present high price of bark,
is seldom found to produce less than 20*l.* per acre. In
the valley of the Dart, between Totness and Ashburton,
the woodlands being less exposed to the violence of the
sea wind, the oak coppices cut down at 20 years growth
are usually found to average about 25*l.* per acre. Those
in the higher parts of Buckfastleigh and lower part of
Holne, cut down at the same standing, average about 22*l.*
per acre. Those affording the larger proportion of alder,
ash, mountain ash, hazel, birch, withy, &c. are cut down
at 16 or 18 years growth, but seldom exceed the average
value of 16*l.* per acre. The ash is converted into hoops
and hurdles, and the oak, after being carefully barked, and
the prime poles taken out with those of the other under-
growth, is charred, and the brushwood used for fuel.
Great attention has latterly been paid at every fall, to preserve young samplers in the coppice as well as in the timber woodlands.

In the parish of Egg Buckland is a common wood of
160 acres and upwards, chiefly coppice, although affording some very good timber. The underwood is open to
all the inhabitants of the parish to cut down and remove
at all seasons, without stint or regulation, and is consequently of little value to any of them. This wood adjoins
that

that of Bickleigh, which, however, is not liable to the like indiscriminate claims, and is therefore exempt from similar depredation.

DISTRICT V.

The coppice wood here is cut down at 20 years growth, affording an average price at the stump of 20*l.* per acre. It consists chiefly of oak, the bark of which always commands 1*s* per cwt. above that from the felled timber.— This coppice wood is generally charred, and is sold at the rate and in the manner before noticed.

DISTRICTS VI. AND VII.

Although there are many small coppices in various parts of these districts, they do not seem to require any particular beyond what may be applied to them from what has been already stated.

There are two species of furze produced generally in Devonshire. The rank luxuriant sort, flowering in the spring of the year, and the smaller dwarf or dale furze, blooming in the autumn. The larger, or what is called French furze, form considerable brakes, and where convenient to potteries or other places in demand for them, are allowed to pay at the rate of from 15 to 20*s.* annually per acre. These are generally cut at four years growth, and their crane stems are often burnt for charcoal: The dwarf furze are not valued at more than six or eight shillings annually per acre, and generally cut and grubbed by the farmers and peasantry for fuel.

SECT. II.—BEECH AND OTHER WOODS.

DISTRICT I.

BEECH and sycamore are found by far the best to contend with the most prevalent wind in this country, though neither appear to be objects of much care or attention with the inhabitants. Much of the former is used in the royal and other dock-yards for wedges ; of the latter, some of the best is purchased by the clog-makers and turners, but neither are of sufficient consequence to require much notice to be taken of them in this place. The peculiar hardiness of beech, seems best to fit it for hedge-rows in the most exposed and elevated parts of the country.

In this district the elm is an extremely scarce tree, and was only noticed in the valley of Combe-martin, and near the mansion-house in the park at Castle-hill : in this latter situation they grow to a good size, and add much to the grandeur and ornament necessarily connected with the residence of the ancient families of a country. This latter species of timber varies much in its price, from 2s. to 3s. 3d. per foot in the round. Ash, which is less scarce, although little pains have been taken in its culture, will generally sell for about 1s. 6d. per foot. Beech about the same, and sycamore 1s. 3d. all in the round, and where the trees were fallen.

DISTRICT II.

Beech and sycamore are also found here to resist most powerfully the western winds, and where they are well sheltered,

sheltered, they grow to a considerable size. They are, however, but thinly scattered over the country. We sometimes see a few tolerable ash trees, but wherever that species of wood is found mostly to prevail, it is always found to supplant the oak, for bank or hedge-row wood. The elm along the river Exe, and through the most favoured vallies in this district, rise to a considerable height, from which a more conclusive evidence cannot well be drawn, as to the natural goodness and superiority of such land.

In every thing that relates to the general improvement of a country, it is surely of high importance to attend to its spontaneous productions, and so far as they may be deserving the care of the husbandman, to bring them forward to their highest perfection. The vast quantity of sweet chesnut found in the old buildings in this country, affords ample proof, should there be no other at hand, that the sweet or Spanish chesnut is a plant indigenous to the county of Devon. The parks of New-place, Eggsford, Heanton, Stevenstone, and Ugbrook, sufficiently evince this truth, by the majestic and venerable appearance this timber makes; and in Heanton-park in particular, it is seen to tower far above the ash, which in the same place grows much higher than even the ash at Ugbrook, or many other parts of the county. Why the culture of this most valuable wood has been so long neglected, and even in this age of agricultural improvement, so little attended to, is not less strange than it is seen with concern to be the case in most parts of the country. The climate of Devonshire being particularly favourable to the ripening of the fruit of this tree, may, in some measure, account for almost the extinction of the species, from the avidity with which it is most pro-

bable

bable the nuts were sought for when ripe, or had fallen from the trees.

To give some idea of the strength of vegetation in this country, particularly towards increasing the size of trees, it may not be amiss to state, that some time since Lord Clifford had a red cedar cut down at Ugbrook, which, at 35 years growth, afforded boards of 22 inches in breadth, and 12 feet long.

DISTRICT III.

The demesne attached to the ancient castle of Oak-hampton (the ruined vestiges of which are still visible) contains about 1500 acres. A considerable part of this en-closure was heretofore covered with a fine growth of oak and other timber, the flourishing remnant of which is still to be seen on the eastern side of the West Ochment river. The mountain and common ash, birch, alder, and holly, grow here to a great size, particularly the latter. In other parts of this district, the silver and Scotch fir, the pinaster and larix, all grow extremely well when screened from the full force of the westerly winds, but where that protection is complete, nothing can exceed the vigour and annual increase of the oak. Beech and sycamore are found as usual to occupy the most bleak and exposed situations, but their culture, as before noticed, is but little attended to.

In a small, though remarkably fine grove of Scotch and silver fir on the barton of Bridestow, there is a tree of the latter species rising a little above the rest, which girths at five feet from the ground, 10 feet 10 inches, and reckoned 65 feet in height, great timber measure. At this distance from the ground its leading shoot appears for-merly to have been crippled, and to have spread into a small broomy top, which are the only limbs produced
upon

upon it, the shaft being all the way perfectly clean, and free from branches. This is by far the finest tree of the sort ever viewed in England by the Author of this Report.

DISTRICT IV.

Although the country along the Tamer does not appear to exhibit much continuation of woodland, still a large proportion of woodland will, on examination, be found in it, as well as covering the sides of most other of the vallies in this district. The elm grows here with considerable luxuriance, when protected from the sea wind, a proof which may readily be adduced from an elm belonging to Mr. Lane, of Brixton, and which, in the course of the last forty years, has increased from the size of a man's arm to ten feet six inches in circumference, measured at the usual height; it stands singly on level ground, and is supplied with a most magnificent top. The elm grows with great luxuriance through all the valley of the Yealm, and forms the principal timber in all the hege-rows; here the ash appears to have supplanted the oak for bank or hedge-row wood, and although it seems the voluntary growth of the country, a good ash tree is seldom seen; the farmers making it a general practice to pollard them when young, for the benefit of topping.

At Blachford, the seat of Sir John Rogers, are some very fine Scotch and silver firs. The latter of the same age are found generally to excel the former. Blachford is situated in a valley just under Dartmoor, and the trees above noticed, grow near the brink of the Yealm, in a black moory soil lying upon a granite gravel and moist rubbly clay. One of these trees measures about eleven feet

feet in circumference, with a proportionably clean shaft ; the timber height of which is estimated at fifty feet and upwards.

There is now in the possession of the Rev. Mr. Hutchins, of Dittisham, the stump of a double flowering broad-leaved myrtle, whose cross diameters measure about eight by ten inches. This some years since had a proportionate trunk and head, which being cut down, several suckers first arose, but soon after decayed and died. The alder in the woods of Buckfastleigh and Holne rises to a considerable height, with a remarkably clean stem, and frequently squaring a foot for twenty feet in height. The holly is also found to flourish in a very high degree, squaring from ten to fifteen inches on a length of fifteen and twenty feet. The Scotch fir and larch are also found to thrive in all these woods, and to do extremely well.

From the practice of pruning the elm trees so close to their stems, many serious wounds are made, which are frequently traced quite rotten to the heart. The common elm produces no seeds in this country, but propagates itself by suckers, or is cultivated by grafting : in the former case, when the old tree is cut down, or the roots are by any accident wounded, young shoots spring up in abundance. Writers on planting, recommend raising elms by layers as better than suckers, which they say, are more apt to breed suckers, and thus injure the tree and encumber the ground round them. Those who give this advice, are probably in the interest of the nurseryman, for the statement is not true, and there are no better trees than those properly taken from suckers, and placed for two or three years in a good nursery. A young tree growing as a sucker, without transplanting, certainly breeds new ones, because it springs up from a long horizontal root, which being accidentally bored or
otherwise

otherwise wounded, will, in all such places, throw up a
new plant ; but if the young tree be severed from this
root, and planted in good soil, it speedily becomes flourishing, and grows exactly as the larger tree grows.   On
examination of these roots, no deficiency will be found,
but the case is widely different if the young tree remains
attached to the parent root, the decay in the stump of
which communicates with the young tree ; and this is the
reason why so much of the hedge-row elm falls unsound.
Although apparently flourishing in the lower part of the
stock, they all grow from suckers, which convey the rot
from the mother to the daughter ; and it is a rare thing
in Devonshire, to find two sound elms together that have
sprung up spontaneously, whereas it is equally uncommon
to find a planted tree unsound at the bottom.   In all exposed situations, the plants should be put down small, but
flourishing, and free from every appearance of a former
check. A plant once stunted may so far recover as to make
somewhat like a tree, but it will never make a fine one.
The vessels that convey its nourishment become rigid and
contracted, and although a new outside of a more luxuriant growth may form after many years, as has been
observed in the Norway spruce (and there is no doubt of
its being common with other trees that have been planted
large, and stood still for several seasons before they have
again grown, and then shot luxuriantly); we find the original tree loose and unconnected in the centre of the new
wood, and on the tree being sawn in two, it drops out
The famous cedar at Hillingdon, near Uxbridge, had
the original tree in the same manner loose in its inside,
having probably been planted, and stood many years before it began to expand.

　　To Colonel Taylor, of Ogwell-house, who seems to
have paid much attention to the culture of forest trees,
　　　　　　　　　　　　　　　　　　　　　　　　　　as

Plate X. P. 257.

View of the prospect of S.t Rob as annunciated from the Old Elm Stump to the Spring Trees.

Neele sculp Strand

as well as to most other departments in rural life, the Surveyor is chiefly indebted for the preceding observations, as well as for the following illustration on the culture and cause of premature decay in hedge-row elm.

" The elm flourishes in Devonshire, and if not mutilated by the farmer, attains a great size. Two sorts are common: the wych hazel, *ulmus montana folus lutipinus scabrio;* and the English elm, *ulmus campestris.* The first is frequent in woods, and usually cut as coppice, but makes a beautiful tree if permitted to grow. The second, if the soil be favourable, flourishes in every hedge, and propagates itself by suckers from roots, which run horizontally along the hedge to a great distance. It often happens, that eight or ten young elms of a tolerable size, grow on one of these roots; and nothing is more common than to find them, with a large portion of the hedge, flat in the adjacent field, after a severe gale. To prevent this, sever the young plants early from the parent tree; they will immediately send down perpendicular roots, take firm hold of the ground, and become independent.

" I strongly recommend the early separation of the suckers from the horizontal root, for another and more material reason, well worthy the attention of planters. It is a notorious fact, that not half of the hedge-row elms felled in Devonshire prove sound: two, three, or four feet of their butts are rotten; and two or three feet more, though not absolutely rotten, are unserviceable. I have, with much care, investigated the origin of this evil; and, I trust, I can thoroughly explain it.

" If a sound elm be cut down in the hedge A, *(Plate X.),* the stump B decays in a few years, and becomes a bowl, filled constantly with rain-water. This not only rots the stump, and penetrates and destroys the

interior

nterior of those roots which formerly nourished the tree, but actually ascends the stems of the young elms, which every where spring from those roots. In spite of luxuriant foliage and a clean bark, it will be found, on examination of any plant so produced, that the mischief has already begun, which grows with its growth, and strengthens with its strength, till the tree becomes fit for felling at C. I have specimens of suckers from decaying stumps, not an inch in diameter, D, in which the heart is already injured; and this will continue to increase till the channel of communication is cut off at EEEE. After separation, the evil does not increase, as I find, on examination of suckers of this description, planted in my nursery, which bid fair to make sound trees. I never saw the butt of a planted elm unsound, unless from great age or external injuries: I, therefore, in the first place, recommend planting trees from the nursery when of a proper size, and constantly supplying the nursery with suckers from the hedges, which may be done with little trouble or expense; and in the second place, to cut off the communication of promising young trees with their parent roots, opening the hedge at three or four feet distant from the stem. By these means, sound timber will be obtained.

DISTRICT V.

The vallies in this district afford a flourishing growth of ash and alder, with some elm. The ash here is stated to be much tougher and to be more in demand with the wheel wrights than in most other parts of the county; it is not so frequently made pollard as in the South Hams. The extensive plantations of Scotch fir at Stover, demand particular attention The land upon which these improvements

provements have been made, is a part of Bovey Heathfield, and covering an extent of many acres. The soil, a black tender mould, on substrata of sand and granite gravel, intermixed with pipe and common woodland clay; a few flints, pebbles, and the male or bastard tin-stone, are found upon the surface, the greater part of which had formerly been much injured by stream works, and upon the whole not exceeding the annual rent or value of five shillings per acre.

The preparation for planting these woods seems to have been little more, after levelling the old stream works, than to cast the whole surface into beds of about four feet in width, each bed having planted upon it at the same distance, a single row of trees, in the opening of each other, and requiring about 660 plants from the nursery to an acre of ground. These plants, in the early stage of their growth very seldom missing, require but few fresh ones to supply their place. On a supposition, however, that each acre contains 600 trees at 20 years growth (and which is much within the general average number), one half of these being then thinned out, will readily sell standing at one shilling per pole or tree, producing at that time 15 l. per acre. After a farther lapse of ten years, one moiety of this remainder is removed, and which readily command on an average, 10 l. per tree, and equalling a farther produce of 75 l. per acre. A single tree being now left upon each square rod of ground, which has already paid 90 l. per acre, may very well be placed against the former value of the land, enclosing, levelling, planting, and preserving the plantation from trespass.

The value of an acre of these trees in their progressive stage of increase to perfection, after their second thinning, is beyond any power of fair calculation to come at. The common estimate of Mr. Templar's woodman, is, that after the

the first ten years from planting, the annual increase in value is one penny per plant, and, in like manner, after thinning at twenty years growth, is twopence per stock.

The average height of these plantations, the greater part of which are now 24 years old, is about 45 feet ; most of the trees as straight as an arrow, and average, at three feet from the ground, a yard in circumference. The flourishing condition of the Scotch fir in these plantations, tends very much to confirm the former opinion of its having been anciently a native of the country, and which is much strengthened by the number of self-sown, or voluntary plants of this species, coming up and pushing forward in the neighbouring furze brakes, and all other places where they find shelter and protection, and where it is most probable that the cones have been dropped or the seed scattered by the birds. Three roods of these plantations, after undergoing a second thinning, and at 24 years growth, were lately sold standing by Mr. Templar, for 120 *l.* and consequently making the value of an acre at that age 160 *l.*

The culture of the sweet chesnut has also been attended to, and with the most flattering success, by the present worthy proprietor of the Stover estate and his immediate predecessor.

DISTRICT VI.

In Lord Lisburne's park, at Mamhead, the ever-green oak, *acacia*, or black locust of North America ; the double flowering ash, wainscot, or white oak of North America ; cork tree of Portugal, Russian moss, and American red oak, seem all to flourish with peculiar excellence ; as do also the cedar of Lebanon, spruce, Scotch, and silver firs, with many other native and exotic plants of great variety.

It

It is, however, much to be regretted, that, seeing the deciduous trees flourish so well, even on the brows of Haldon, more attention was not paid to their culture at the time of forming these flourishing and truly interesting woodlands.

The spruce firs thrive and grow to a considerable size ; the smaller ones contain about two tons and a half of timber, worth two and sixpence per foot, and valued for masts at about twelve guineas each. Some larger ones, applicable to the same use, are estimated at 25 guineas each. These trees were planted about 90 years since, in a soil and situation which would not be worth, even in the present day, 4 *l.* per acre. The old plantation contains about 50 acres, is situated on the eastern brow of Haldon, and consists chiefly of Scotch, spruce, and silver firs.

The following dimensions are stated, with a view of showing the power of the soil and climate of this country in promoting the growth of foreign trees, all measured at the ordinary height of five feet from the ground. Ilex, or ever-green oak, 10 feet in girth, trunk 12 feet, spreading an uncommonly fine head, 17 yards in diameter. Cork trees, 8 and 11 feet girth, with trunks of 12 and 13 feet to the head branches. The appearance of the Russian moss oak greatly approaches in beauty to the American white oak, its foliage differing in no other respect than by having a darker green hue under its leaf, and its fruit or acorns enveloped in a garment greatly resembling that of the moss rose.

The plantations at Haldon flourish with unrivalled excellence : they were begun in 1772, and much has been since added by their present valuable possessor, whose general spirit for agricultural and other improvements, reflects the highest honour, and affords an admirable example to other country gentlemen, less prone to indulge in
such

such laudable pursuits. They now consist of about a hundred acres, in which, excepting on the very top of the ridge, the deciduous and other hard wood forest trees, appear no less than the fir and pine tribe, to attain the most luxuriant perfection.

A general growth of elm appears to have taken place of all other timber, through the greater part of this and the seventh district. It must, however, be remarked, that it is not a little strange, in so common a growth, that so few stately or large trees are seen : a feeble or unhealthy looking elm is scarcely to be met with ; they frequently stand by far too much crouded in the hedge-rows, and from the causes already stated by Colonel Taylor, are perhaps too often cut down before they attain the age and condition of maturity.

On the demesne of Bicton, there are some good ash, elm, and poplar. The beech, however, appears to have gained by far the greatest ascendancy, as many of them measure from ten to fourteen feet in circumference, with well-proportioned trunks and tops of extraordinary grandeur. A pollard of this species near the mansion-house, measures at the ordinary height 20 feet in girth, its top branches exceeding the diameter of 30 yards.

DISTRICT VII.

It has been already observed, that a spontaneous growth of elm prevails generally through this district ; the preceding observations will fully apply to its appearance and culture. At Woolford Lodge, considerable attention was paid by General Simcoe to the culture of exotic as well as of the native trees of the country. The black spruce of Newfoundland, the red spruce of Norway (the latter growing very well indeed), the Weymouth pine, pineaster, stone, and

and cluster pine, the American sycamore or button wood, the black walnut, red oak, hiccory, sassafras, red bud, with many smaller trees and shrubs, forming the undergrowth of the forests in that country, are all found to grow at Dunkerswell with considerable strength and vigour. The Scotch fir, common spruce, and silver fir, are also found to flourish at Woolford, and do extremely well. Upon the latter, a number protuberances grow from the upper surface of the branches, forming a dwarf cluster of the same character with the tree, and not very unlike in character to the hen and chicken daisy. This remains till the limb of the tree goes to decay (but which it does not seem in the least degree to hasten) when they fall off together.

SECT. III.——PLANTATIONS.

DISTRICT I.

It would afford the Author of this Report much pleasure, to be able to dwell at some length on the principal articles of this Section; but so little attention has been paid by the inhabitants of this district, in the culture of forest trees, that excepting those plantations only that have been made by Lord Fortescue, on the old lime-works at Filleigh, the plantations of Mr. Basset, of Watermouth, and a small grove chiefly of the pine tribe, raised by the Reverend Mr. Sweet, of Kentsbere, the cultivation of deciduous or ever-green trees is seldom seen extending beyond the pleasure-grounds or homesteads of the inhabitants; where they have been planted for the purpose of ornament, a little shade, or shelter.

DISTRICT II.

The plantations in this district are almost exclusively confined to those Lord Clifford has made in Ugbrook-park. Ash seems to be his Lordship's favourite plant, although the deciduous and ever-greens are all so well mixed and checquered with each other, as to ensure a certainty of success in those well-planned and equally well-executed improvements. The whole has indeed been conducted with economy, but at the same time, with a taste and elegance which in effect can no less contribute to heighten the internal beauties, than augment the external grandeur of this enchanting spot.

DISTRICTS III. IV. V. AND VI.

The preceding observations respecting the general scarcity of young plantations, will, it is feared, be found to apply too fully through these districts. Sir Ferdinand Lopez, Lord Boringdon, the Duke of Somerset, and Lord Gage, have doubtless paid attention to this important branch of rural improvement; but the absence or indisposition of those Noblemen and Gentlemen, deprived the Surveyor of profiting by the skill and management pursued in their respective plantations.

DISTRICT VII.

In the parish of Upottery, Lord Sidmouth has made some considerable plantations of Scotch fir, larch, silver fir, and Spanish chesnut. The situation of these plantations is at the back of the village, and on the upper hang and brow of Allar Hill, and formerly occupied as a furze brake.

brake. The soil, a loose tender loam, abounding with springs, and lying on under-strata of chip-sand and fox-mould, and which are occasionally veined with flints, and a dry silicious rubble. The young trees striking in the chip-sand (the chesnut in particular), are found to thrive and get forward vastly well. Upon the dry flinty veins and fox-mould, it has been found advisable to open holes and fill them with a better soil, for the young trees to strike in. Whenever a want of vigour appears in the sweet chesnut, it is cut down within a few inches of the ground. The leading shoot only being afterwards preserved, is found very readily to make its way good among its youthful neighbours.

The oak, ash, and elm plantations, his Lordship has caused to be laid out in more sheltered situations, and where there is generally a marly bottom. The young trees were procured from the nurseries at Exeter. The elm generally at four or five years growth grafted on the wych-hazel. Whenever any accident happens to these plants (and which is not unfrequently the case), so as to occasion the graft-stem to be cut below the insertion of the scion, the wych-elm stock remaining in its native purity, requires the grafting to be renewed with the common elm.

At Woolford Lodge, General Simcoe made a trial upon about 22 acres of oat stubble, which was sown with acorns, about two bushels per acre, and ploughed lightly under with the oat-stubble in the month of January. These seem to have grown very unequally, although there is no want of plants in any part of the field. When the shelter is complete from the westerly winds, they grow with considerable luxuriance, and require repeated and annual thinning. Upon the whole, the experiment exhibits, in the judgment of the Surveyor, a decided preference to the system

system of transplanting, in the raising of this valuable timber. The practice of pruning the young oak to a clean stem under twenty feet high, leaving a proportionable top, has also been practised at Woolford, and with a shew of considerable success. It is said greatly to increase the strength and substance of the stock. The low and luxuriant branches are pruned close to the body of the tree. These wounds are soon healed and covered with bark, by the young and vigorous growth of the tree. The flourishing state of the native and foreign trees at this place, has been already stated.

SECT. IV.—TIMBER.

Any one viewing with an eye to general utility, the present state and condition of oak timber in this country, cannot without pain observe so general a destruction of this our principal bulwark, without any thing like proportionate exertions being made towards its renewal: a proof of this opinion can no where be more fully illustrated than in the quantity of oak timber sold in Barnstable by public auction in the year 1805, which amounted to 6000 trees, averaging 20 feet, or half a ton of timber in each tree.

DISTRICT I.

In the present year there have been 6500 trees sold at the same place in like manner, but their average does not exceed 15 feet per stock, and out of this number there were no less than 2500 trees and upwards which did not yield a greater average than 10 feet per stock. Hence on their general size, there seems to have been a premature
destruction

destruction of no less than five feet per stock, on the timber usually vended at that place by auction, exclusive of
what may have been sold by private contract in the same
period ; and this is stated solely to have arisen from the
number of young growing trees which have been so im-
providently felled and taken to that market. This is sold
either by the load of 50 feet, at about 6l. 10s. per load,
or by the ton of 40 feet, which usually commands about
four guineas.

The common mode of measuring timber is to carry it
on to the square of six inches, and five tons of timber so
measured, is here considered to produce about one ton of
bark. It is, however, elsewhere affirmed, that two trees
having a fair top not stripped with age, or shorn and crippled by the westerly winds, and measuring together about
a load of timber, will carry about one ton and a quarter
of bark. This appears an extraordinary disproportion,
and if true, wonderfully displays the value of the top or
lop of the tree, usually though not always retained by the
vender, the purchaser of the stem felling the tree, and
peeling so much as is measured into timber.

The finest oaks noticed in this district, were those on
the demesne of Tawton, belonging to Sir Bourchier Wrey ;
there are many of them, one in particular, conspicuous for
its size and beauty, is still in a growing state, and promises
a considerable addition to its sound shaft, its beautiful top,
and widely spreading branches.

DISTRICT II.

The sides of the valley through which the Exe, the
Torridge, and the Taw discharge their waters, as well as
the combes and smaller hollows dependent on them, are
all more or less adorned with oak woodlands, which if
permitted

permitted to attain that maturity and perfection the soil
and climate are so capable of affording, few instances of
an inferior growth of oak-timber would be found to that
which is with so much pleasure beheld in Stevenstone or
Heanton-park, or on the demesnes of Eggsford, Clovella
Court, and Hartland Abbey. An opinion prevails generally through the country, that the oak is 150 years attaining its growth ; that it remains the same time stationary,
and requires another period of 150 years to become a shell,
and approach its last stage of decay.

DISTRICT III.

A valuable body of timber has recently been cut down
in Oakhampton-park ; and if a fair inference may be
drawn from what is still standing, it is much to be lamented that the ripe timber only had not been selected,
and the remainder preserved for the use of future ages.
The ground upon which this forest grew, is so much encumbered with granite rocks, and large masses of moorstone, as to render it altogether unfit for being applicable
to more valuable purposes. This timber met with a very
ready sale at Plymouth and Bideford for ship-building.
Its price at present at Oakhampton, sinking the top and
bark, is from 7*l.* 10*s.* to 8*l.* per ton.

DISTRICT IV.

There are but few vallies through the whole extent of
this district, that do not afford more or less oak-timber,
but as a large proportion is cut down at a premature state
of its growth, this supply is becoming less and less every
year. A number of small vessels are built near the mouth
of most of the navigable waters : at Dartmouth, the building

ing of sloops of war, frigates, and fire-ships, is carried on to a considerable extent. The oak-timber of Buckfastleigh, Holne, and lower down upon the river Dart, is stated to supply a considerable part of this consumption.

DISTRICT V.

The features before described continuing in close array through the vallies of the Wrey, the Bovey, and the Teign, have naturally led to the most appropriate disposition of a country of that nature, as most of the sides of the hills, or rather mountains, by which these vallies are enclosed, are checquered, in addition to the trees before noticed, with a fine growth of oak-timber, and which is suffered to arrive to a greater age and perfection than in the more accessible parts of the county. The oak-timber at the foot of the high grounds bordering on the forest of Dartmoor in the parishes of Moreton Hempstead, Chagford, Gidley, and Throwsleigh, seems also more generally spared to arrive at maturity. The price of oak-timber, sinking the top and bark, is about 7*l.* per ton.

DISTRICTS VI. AND VII.

Through the whole of these districts many fine oaks are occasionally seen ; on the other hand, many appear in the different parts of the country to have been cut down before they attained to any thing like a standard of maturity. A very fine oak is standing near the mansion-house at Paschoe, which measures 12 feet in circumference, at five feet from the ground ; it carries a clean healthy stock for about 20 feet, where the top branches spread into a large but well-proportioned head.

The oak-timber at Mamhead tallies much with the description

scription given of the other trees in that park. At Powderham, a healthy growth of oak was observed on the margin of the river Exe. And although Bicton-park exhibits
some oak-timber of considerable size, it is generally much
inferior to that noticed at Stevenstone. The following district has not afforded any thing particularly required to be
added to this subject.

CHAP. XI.

WASTES.

———◆———

SECT. I.——MOORS AND COMMONS.

IT seemed a very desirable object, on the commencement of this Survey, to ascertain with as much correctness as possible, the extent of waste land belonging to
the respective parishes in this district: to this end, very
particular inquiries were directed in all the different parishes; but so extremely vague and contradictory were
the accounts received, together with the doubts entertained of the moors, in many places, being appurtenant
to particular estates, or open in common to all the
inhabitants, that the subject at length became much
confused, and involved in contradiction, and it was judged
better to pass over those inquiries, and direct the attention more fully to the quality of such wastes, let their
boundaries and extent be what they may, or the right of
ownership in them be in whom it would. Although the
term of moor is usually applied to the two great wastes
in this part of the promontory of Somerset and Devon,
still, as above implied, it is not exclusively used in the
designation of those wastes; the old neglected lands formerly under tillage, being generally understood by this
term, in contradistinction to that of commons, which is
supposed to refer to all such wastes as are open to a free
and unlimited depasturage by all the sheep and cattle
belonging

belonging to such families as are residents in the parish, its hamlet, or villages.

The height of the most lofty and prominent hills and downs which compose the wastes of this district, has already been noticed in the Chapter on Climate ; and from which, in comparison of other lands cultivated in the kingdom, there is little to be concluded on as to their lying out of the reach of a genial atmosphere. According to the prevalence of drought or moisture in the surface and substrata of these wastes, their herbage and common covering is found to vary, and may generally be divided under the following heads:

The first, of a soil formed of a tender light coloured loam when dry, but when moist, assuming a brighter brown colour, and lying upon a brown and grey clayey subsoil, veined and mixed with portions of small rubbly or argillaceous gravel. This land is always covered with a close and sweet herbage, on which the sheep are found to lie very hard, and to keep it constantly pared down. Through the loose veins of under-strata, springs occasionally rise, creating small spots of rushes, and a few square yards of boggy ground; its surface is otherwise free from any incumbrance of furze, fern, or heather, and seems as loudly to demand, as it appears willing to requite the labours and fostering care of the skilful husbandman.

The second denomination of these wastes may be called furze and fern lands : a portion of granite gravel is always found to have place in the composition of their soil and substrata. This is generally of a drier nature than the one just noticed, and seems well adapted for a system of barley and turnip husbandry.

The third class is that where a dwarf growth of heath

or

or heather is found, but which is nearly smothered and eaten out with a variety of coarse aquatic grasses. The soil is here generally composed of a dark moor or vegetable mould, lying on a close and deep stratum of blue and yellow clay, intermixed with a coarse argillaceous rubble, and a reddish coloured clay or fox-mould, equally retentive of, and generally charged with an undue proportion of moisture.

A fourth class is composed of a red spongy substance, answering, in all appearance, the character of a red Irish bog. This is always kept highly saturated with water, and is found of various depths, on a substratum of peat, which again ultimately rests on a compact bed of white, blue, and yellow clay. By conducting the improvement of this class in the manner its nature and situation demand, very great advantages must inevitably result, not only from the undertaking itself, but its effects on the surrounding, and even more remote districts, will gradually be felt, and found to prove highly beneficial to them.

The last class of wastes necessary to notice in this place, is, that where the surface is composed of a dry, inveterate brown peat, of two or three inches in depth, and lying immediately on the granite and whinstone rock, or rather the loose flat stones answering to such characters. This peat having all the appearance of the red bog in a dried and compressed state, is seldom found to yield any thing but a strong luxuriant growth of ling, or black heather, and which is generally pared close to the stones or rock, for the purposes of fuel. In this appropriation, this class may be said to have attained the very acme of its nature, as it appears to be invincibly opposed to every effort of improvement by planting, or by any other means for the purpose of cultivation.

DEVON.]   The

The ancient moorlands in the district will be found very nearly to agree with the description given in Class No. 3, with the addition only of their surface generally having been left under ridge and furrow, and consequently bearing evident marks of a former cultivation.

The present value of these lands may in general be rated at from 4s. to 6s. per acre. It will be difficult to affix any thing like a standard value for the intercommonable lands, but on considering the relative value of the different classes, and placing the two last at 0, unless for the purposes of turbary, the preceding ones will rank at five, eight, and twelve shillings per acre, and all applicable to the purposes of feeding sheep and store cattle. No doubt can possibly be entertained as to the propriety of enclosing and cultivating these old moors and waste lands; but until some farther disposition is manifested in the country to improve and cultivate such as are already held in severalty to particular estates, it will be idle and fruitless to suggest any measures for enclosing and cultivating those intercommonable lands, which at this time occupy so large a portion of the area of the district.

DISTRICT II.

Although there are considerable tracts of coarse moors and downy sheep-walks along the coast, and variously dispersed through other parts of this district, still, as the greater part of these lands are held in severalty, they must not be taken into the view prescribed in this Report for the designation of waste lands. We shall therefore proceed to a detail of some of the circumstances relating to the common of Great Torrington. A few years since, by the consent of the inhabitants, about thirty acres of this waste were granted to a company, for the purpose of establishing

establishing a woollen manufactory. The remainder of
the enclosed waste amounts to about 260 acres. The
south-east part, lying east of the Bideford road, contains
about thirty-five acres, and is composed of a reddish or
cedar-coloured loam, on a deep understratum of clay,
mixed with a coarse rubble. The south part, bounded by
the river Torridge, consists of a thin grey loam, lying
close upon the shillot rock; its lower parts are subject to
springs, but of which they might readily be relieved by
proper draining. A further part of this common, called
Hatch-moor, is composed of a wet grey loam, on a
woodland clay, lying ultimately on the shaly rock.

The constitution of this common being unfortunately
without stint, and subject to the claims of every pot-
walloping inhabitant, renders it, however desirable,
extremely difficult to enclose, without the authority of
parliament. It may be curious however to observe, that
a part of this common has been heretofore wrested from
the intercommoners at large, and now constitutes the
character of open common-field, or rather of Lammas
ground; for although no winter corn is permitted to be
sown upon these lands, as soon as the spring-seed is in the
ground, the tenant has a right to raise fences, and exclude any farther access to his field until his corn is
harvested. These rights are all confirmed by the charters
of Elizabeth and James the First.

The following statement of the value of this common was procured from a gentleman in the neighbourhood, whose father was called upon to value it in the
year 1761, viz.

	£.	s.	d.
103 acres, at 18s. per acre,	92	14	0
74 ditto, at 10s.	37	0	0
29 ditto			

	£.	s.	d.
28 acres, at 10s.	14	0	0
52 ditto, at 5s.	13	0	0
35 ditto, at 25s.	43	15	0
292 acres.	£. 200	9	0

From a particular examination that has lately been
made, its annual value, after paying all the expenses of
an enclosure, would amount to .... £. 582 9 0
Its present annual value to individuals, or
    the community at large, is not esti-   } 60 0 0
    mated at more than ....

Loss per annum on the common by con-
    tinuing in its present state, ... } £. 522 9 0

Hatherleigh common presents an object of little less
importance: it contains about 463 acres, and is open to
the inhabitants of the borough only to an unlimited intercommonage; a large proportion of its northern side
consists of a rich cedar-coloured loam, applicable to the
culture of the best grain and pulse, the most productive green crops, and the choicest grasses. This common,
in its present state, is not valued at more than 7s. 6d.
per acre. Its improved value, after deducting the expenses of an enclosure, is estimated at 35s. per acre.
The whole is supplied with the purest water from constant and never-failing springs.

Dowland, Dolland, and Hollacombe moor, would also
be regarded in many other countries as a most valuable
object for improvement; the soil in many parts being
found to consist of a tender hazel loam, on a deep, dry,
and open subsoil, and a grey moist loam of a moderate
depth on a yellow woodland clay. In the lower part, and

on

on the hanging sides of this moor, there are some wet and boggy places, but which might readily be cured by proper drains.

The moors of Whitton Down are attached to particular estates, and would pay well for enclosing, and proper management afterwards. The same may be said of Ilton moor, lying between the parishes of North and South Tawton.

The above descriptions agree with many other large tracts of moors and commons the Surveyor passed over in his journey through this district, but in the neighbourhood of which, from the absence of the persons on whom he called, or the ignorance of those he met with by the way, it became utterly impossible for him to learn whether such were appendant to particular estates, appurtenant in vicinage or in gross, or lay generally open as intercommonable lands.

The high down which overhangs the church and village of Cadbury, is capped with an old circular fortification, called Cadbury Castle: from the mounds of this enclosure there is one of the richest and most extensive views in the county of Devon. These works consist of a deep ditch and rampart, enclosing about two acres of ground: in the area or terra plane of this enclosure, a rank growth of spurry and fleabane seemed completely to overpower a very indifferent crop of turnips. The exterior of this enclosure and brow of the hill, for some distance round, is occupied as a furze-brake for fuel.

Welland, Lenard, and Goose moor, in the parishes of Welland and Halberton; the common of Holcombe-Rogus, called Durly moor; Beer Down, in the parish of Uplowman; Chimbery Down, in the parish of Hockworthy; Bampton Downs, and a number of wastes and commons, of more or less extent, would answer well for enclosing,

enclosing, provided they were properly cultivated afterwards; but of this at present there can be but little expectation, when we see so general a neglect of the old
moorlands, which present no difficulty whatever, but the
want of means or inclination in their present owners or
occupiers to improve.

DART MOOR.

The forest of Dartmoor rises with a bold majestic
grandeur over all the surrounding heights, which compose an extremely rough and broken region in this part of
the county of Devon. After attaining the summit of this
waste, it is found to spread generally (at least in comparison with the leading features of the country below)
into an extended plain, and so much of this stupendous
eminence as is called The Forest of Dartmoor, is divided by certain meets and bounds from the commons
belonging to the surrounding parishes, and which, by calculation from the map of the moor, made by Mr. Thomas
Gray, in 1796, is found to contain 53,644 acres. This
forest belongs to His Royal Highness the Prince of
Wales, as appurtenant to, and parcel of the Duchy of
Cornwall.

The duty of the Surveyor on this occasion is deemed
to be exclusively confined to the examination of the native properties of the forest, and how they may be most
effectually and permanently improved to the public benefit,
the advantages of the revenues of the Duchy, and above
all, to the melioration of the climate of the moor, and
consequently to that of the country below. The relative
heights of the most prominent and lofty points upon or
near the Forest, with well known eminences in the surrounding country, must afford considerable satisfaction,

as

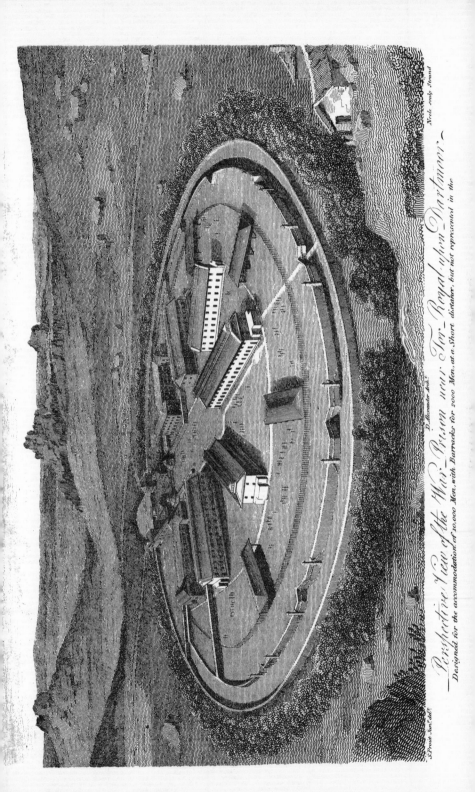

S. Prout Jun.r del.t   J. Alexander Arch.t   Neele sculp Strand

Perspective View of the War-Prison near Tor-Royal upon Dartmoor.~
Designed for the accommodation of 10,000 Men, with Barracks for 2000 Men, at a Short distance, but not represented in the

as the result of data deduced from the trigonometrical
survey, conducted by Colonel Mudge, and to whose politeness the Surveyor is much indebted for the important
communication. These heights are all in reference to the
common level of the sea. Where they are returned certain, there can be no appeal beyond this statement ; and
where the return is made probable only, it will, in most
cases, be found within a few feet of the existing elevation, and, at all events, sufficiently accurate for our
purpose.

	Feet.
Butterton Hill, near Ivy Bridge, ...	1201 certain.
Rippon Tor, east of ditto, ...	1545 ditto.
North end of Cawsand Beacon, ...	1792 ditto.
Highest part of Dartmoor, called Caw-sand bog, ...	2090 probable.

Summit, 5347 feet.
3

Mean height of the Forest of Dartmoor, 1782 feet.

The height of well known hills in the country below,
and within reach of the moor-winds, are,

	Feet.
Black Down, near Tavistock, ...	1160 certain.
Highest land, near Modbury, ...	600 probable.
Little Haldon, ...	811 certain.
Great Haldon, ...	800 certain.

Summit, 2211 feet.
3

Mean height of the most commanding
situations in the country below Dart-
moor, ... } 737 feet.

Butterton

Butterton Hill, near Ivy Bridge, and Black Down, near Tavistoock, being spurs of this moor, or rather mountain, were not deemed proper to be taken into a statement which is meant to shew the difference between the mean height of the forest and that of the loftiest hills in the surrounding country; thus exhibiting in Dartmoor an elevation of no less than 1045 feet above the highest hills in the adjoining districts.

These facts ascertained, we next proceed to inquire into the effects which this mountain may probably produce on the climate of the adjacent country; and which will be best understood by a reference to the two registers before noticed; the one kept at Ilfracombe, the other at Oakhampton.

Situation.	Jan.	Feb.	Mar.	Apr.	May.	June.
Ilfracombe, ...	53°	$48\frac{1}{2}$	52	$57\frac{1}{2}$	$62\frac{1}{4}$	$64\frac{3}{4}$
Oakhampton, ...	$34\frac{1}{4}$	$36\frac{3}{4}$	$41\frac{1}{4}$	$43\frac{1}{2}$	$50\frac{3}{4}$	$55\frac{1}{2}$
Difference,	$18\frac{3}{4}$	$11\frac{3}{4}$	$10\frac{3}{4}$	14	$11\frac{1}{2}$	$9\frac{1}{4}$

Situation.	July.	Aug.	Sept.	Oct.	Nov.	Dec.
Ilfracombe, ...	$65\frac{3}{4}$	66	$61\frac{3}{4}$	62	$58\frac{1}{4}$	$56\frac{1}{4}$
Oakhampton, ...	62	$63\frac{3}{4}$	$57\frac{3}{4}$	$46\frac{3}{4}$	41	$39\frac{1}{2}$
Difference,	$3\frac{3}{4}$	$2\frac{1}{4}$	4	$5\frac{1}{2}$	$17\frac{1}{4}$	$16\frac{3}{4}$

The average of these monthly differences gives a depression of $10\frac{1}{2}$ on Fahrenheit's scale, between Ilfracombe and Oakhampton; and so much is the latter place, from these observations, found to be under the influence of a colder climate than the former one. The difference in point of elevation, where these observations were made, could not possibly exceed 180 or 200 feet. The observations at Ilfracombe were taken at about 50 feet above the level

level of the sea, and those in the town of Oakhampton
at the distance of about 35 miles; in which space, allowing a declivity of three feet per mile, it will scarcely
reach the mean of the two numbers; add to which, the
thermometer at Ilfracombe was situated more than half
a degree of latitude north of that at Oakhampton. These
facts result from data, and are therefore beyond the
reach of question.

It is now necessary to explain, in the manner best understood by the Surveyor, what he conceives to be the
cause of this extraordinary difference of climate in so
short a distance; and in that explanation to unfold the
means of its removal, to those who may have it in their
power to carry the suggested plan of improvement into
execution, at once securing to themselves the everlasting gratitude of the surrounding country, and contributing an important acquisition to the natural stock.

As the sun is the great fountain of heat, so is the atmosphere the source of its opposite principle, cold. In
proportion as all humid bodies expose a greater or less
surface to the action of this medium, it acts upon the
aqueous matter, attenuating it into vapour, in which
operation the principle of cold is evolved, and that principle is ever generated in the process of evaporation.
The whole surface of Dartmoor, including the rocks,
consists of two characters, the one a wet peaty moor, or
vegetable mould, but affording good sheep and bullock
pasture, during the summer season. The other an inveterate swamp, absolutely inaccessible to the lightest
and most active quadruped that may traverse the sounder
parts of the forest.

During the examination of this district, the Surveyor
had an opportunity of observing, at different times,
when the sun and wind had been acting for several hours,
with

with their utmost force, that their combined powers did
not penetrate within several inches of the bottom, or
through the luxuriant vegetation of the moor, which
being still charged with an extraordinary portion of moisture, it was clearly to be observed, on every fibre where
the sun had not been able to dart a ray, or the wind to
penetrate, exhibiting spangles of dew-drops, the con-
densed vapour of the preceding night, or the residuum
of past showers. This multiplied surface of aqueous matter, as well on the depasturable parts of the forest, as on
its more extensive swamps and red bogs, amounts, in the
opinion of the Surveyor, to at least the full extent of the
forest, thrown into a lake, and riding at that height
over the surrounding country, for the production of
aqueous vapour, and the principle of cold, as before
stated, inseparably connected with it; hence arises the
source of all those cold and blighting vapours carried by
the moor-winds through all the country below. and
which, from the nature of things, cannot possibly fail
in becoming more injurious and fatal in their consequences every year.

The most elevated part of the forest, and that in
which the Tavy, the East and West Ochment, the Taw,
the Teign, the East and West Dart rivers, have their
source and head branches, consists of one continued chain
of morass, answering in every respect the character of a
red Irish bog. This annually teems with a luxuriant
growth of the purple melic grass, rush cotton grass, flags,
rushes, and a variety of other aquatic plants, and which
annually growing, and proceeding to decay, has at length
raised this part of the forest from five to forty, or perhaps fifty feet, above the plain or foundation upon which
it first originated: a quantity of vegetable matter thus
annually accumulating, supplies the use of an enlarged
sponge,

sponge, for retaining a farther increase of water, and thus the bog is imperceptibly, though in fact, annually increasing in its bulk and height, so long as its base is able to sustain it. This, however, in some places, appears to have been overcharged with morass, as prodigious slips of several acres in breadth were observed to have parted at different times from the great field or body of morass above, and thus making frightful chasms from the surface to the bottom and former resting place of the bog. These slips would occur more frequently on the sides of the hills, were they not, in some measure, prevented by the granite rocks and moor-stones which rise out of and occupy a considerable part of the beds of these morasses, all of which are formed of the remains of light aquatic vegetables, intercepted by about eighteen inches of black peaty earth from the bed of the bog, and which, as before observed, consists of white and yellow clay intermixed with granite rocks; the decomposed parts of which form partial spots of granite gravel, all highly retentive of water, and thence originates their adventitious covering of a black peaty stratum, superinduced with morass or red bog, and evidently in a state of annual increase.

The depasturable parts of the forest, consist of a black moory soil, from eighteen inches to two feet in thickness, generally forming peat below, always highly charged with moisture, and ultimately resting upon a reddish-coloured argillaceous loam, called fox-mould, and which is also retentive of water in a very high degree. The spontaneous vegetation of this part of the forest, among many other herbs and grasses, consisted of the purple melic grass, mat grass, downy oat grass, bristled-leaved bent, eye-bright, bulbous rooted rush, common termentel, smooth heath-bed straw, common bone-binder, cross-leaved heath, common

mon heath or ling (dwarf), milk-wort, dwarf dock, and the agrostis vulgaris in very large quantities. The disturbing of this herbage, however inferior it may appear in the eye of the refined agriculturist, is on no account whatever to be recommended or permitted.

Although it was not deemed necessary to make a farther discrimination, in describing the general covering of the forest, than by the distinction of black peaty moor, and red spongy bog, still on examination, a number of gradations will be found between these specific points, all of which, as they approach the character of red bog, will require a longer time to exsiccate and bring forward to a state of profitable cultivation. It may not however be amiss, previously to stating any thing touching the improvement of the forest, to say, that the want of safe and convenient roads to the peat pits, is attended with much loss of time to the farmer, as well as damage to such poorer persons who draw a considerable part of their subsistence by digging and rearing peat-fuel for the country below. None of the parishes in Venville are said to have the power of making a rate, for the forming and repairing of these paths, that of Ledford only excepted, in whose boundary the whole forest of Dartmoor lies.

As the parochial disbursements fall peculiarly light in most of these parishes, it is worthy of consideration, whether an application to parliament, for the purpose of enabling their inhabitants to form and keep in repair such roads, would not be a desirable and well-advised measure.

We now proceed to the means most advisable to recommend for effecting the drainage of these bogs, and bringing them forward to a state of profitable cultivation. It is by slow and imperceptible degrees only, that the bogs of Dartmoor have grown to their present bulk; by slow and gradual means only they are capable of being reduced, and

and of becoming an important object on the great field of national territory. The manner in which this is to be accomplished, is slow, but it is plain, easy, certain, and efficient.

As in no case whatever on the forest, there can be any want of convenient situations for forming outfal-drains, these judiciously planned and executed to receive the surface-water from foot-drains laid out upon the surface of the morass, at about a rod a-part, would be beginning the undertaking at the right end, and from which the most substantial benefits might be expected to arise. These drains, in the first instance, should be made one foot (or spit) wide, and one spit deep; they should intersect each other at a rod a-part over the whole surface of the bog; by these drains the downfal waters would immediately escape, and the annual supply of water once checked, the morass would gradually become more firm and consistent on the top, at which time, as many of the foot-drains as found necessary might be preserved, deepened, and enlarged, and made the direction for subsequent enclosure, and subdivisions of the moor. *

As

* My first step some years ago towards the improvement of a large tract of bog in the King's County in Ireland, was to form and recover an outfal-drain, 12 feet wide and about a quarter of a mile long, at the foot of the bog which was designed to be drained. The bottom of this drain was formed of a retentive clay or gault, above which, in many places, there was a depth of twelve or fifteen feet of red bog and turf moor, under which, and on the bed or resting-place of the bog, there were distinctly to be seen *ridges and furrows, the indisputable remains of an ancient cultivation.* In other places, on the bed of the bog, were found considerable quantities of yew, oak, and pine, all of which appeared to have been more or less exposed to the action of fire. The more valuable pieces of this timber were easily discovered by probing with a spit, and then raised out of the bog: an oak which I well remember, measured 55 feet in length,

and

As it is plain, in all these cases, that water constitutes a large proportion of the bulk of red bogs, the regular discharge of it would occasion a closer union and consolidation of the vegetable matter, which, once relieved of its redundant moisture, would gradually undergo a change from the red spongy state, to that of the black moor, or peaty character. When sufficiently firm to support a yoke of oxen, the paring-plough should be applied, for two or three times successively, in the reduction of the red spongy substance; taking care always to deepen the drains as the surface lowered and became more compact and solid. The intelligent conductor of such improvements will best judge the time, when a trial should be made to procure a crop from land thus reclaimed. In

---

and 22 inches through at the butt end. Such of the yew as was not cup or wind shaken, was cut into plank, and made into beautiful furniture; and for the remainder, as well as for the oak and pine, I found a ready use in forming flood-gates, for building, and for farming purposes. Upon the clay or gault, at the bottom of the outfal-drain, we found the dash and lid of an hand-churn, and a large crane-necked brass spur, with a rowel a full inch in diameter.

The outfal-drain being completed, and proper sluices erected to give a command of the water, the next step was to cut foot-drains, or drains one foot wide and one spit deep at right angles to, and parallel with, the outfal-drain, laid out about 20 feet a-part; and afterwards by deeper drains dividing the whole surface of the bog, into squares of four plantation acres each. The following year, the foot-drains were deepened and enlarged, and the partition-drains made three feet wide, and two feet and an half deep. The result was, that within two years from the time the outfal-drain was begun, the whole mass of bog, from actual and accurate observation, subsided and shrunk downwards four feet in perpendicular height; and from being in a state in which with much difficulty I could step from one hassock to another, in laying out the drains, it became so far consolidated and compact, that the store cattle, in the spring following, roamed over and browsed upon it with ease, and the most perfect security. (*Vide Appendix to Cambridgeshire Report*, 1794.)

the

the judgment of the Surveyor, it would not be advisable until the red bog has undergone a third, or perhaps fourth, paring and burning, when the attempt should be made on the last burnt ground, by merely sowing rape or cole-seed in the month of July, upon the spread ashes, about half a peck to the acre, and on which occasion neither ploughing harrowing, or bush-harrowing, is in the smallest degree necessary. The appearance of the cole-seed by the 1st of October, together with that of the approaching season, and the condition which the bog may be in with regard to moisture, will be the best direction to the farmer, as to the property of feeding the coleseed for a month or six weeks before the frost sets in, or in letting the whole stand over, unfed, for a crop. In either case, the coleseed will be ready in the ensuing month of July; when, after being cut, and weathering a certain time, it should be thrashed out and prepared for market, on the moor, and the haulm or stalks removed, and made into substantial walls about the house or home-stead, in order to afford shelter, during the ensuing winter, to the sheep, and other stock of the farm.

The red bog thus subdued, and brought forward to cultivation, the repeated paring and burning to which it may afterwards be subjected, can produce no possible injury to a substance of such nature; it will afford the means of procuring abundant crops of coleseed, turnips, flax, potatoes, cabbages, pease, beans, and every sort of leguminous vegetable that can be used and appropriated in a green state; and may be continued without danger, until all the morass and former adventitious covering is reduced within a foot or fifteen inches of the ordinary bed or stratum of natural earth below. A few oats, provided they were put in proportionably early, might perhaps be brought to ripen at a late period in the season; but,

but, as this may be found difficult to accomplish, it were much better to abstain from their culture, till such time as the melioration of the climate of the moor affords better grounds for success, than it can or does at present. Hemp would most probably be found, towards the completion of the improvement, to answer very well; but neither this or oats should be attempted in its early stage. Ray-grass, or hievre, would be found to flourish very soon after the second or third crop of coleseed; and, as the mass of the bog below obtained relief from saturation, clover and other valuable grasses might be cultivated to advantage upon it.

As the improvement progressed, it would be of the first consequence, at times when it lay upon its green side, to endeavour, by all gentle means, to mix and incorporate with the surface, small but frequent portions of the under-stratum of white and yellow clay. The outfal-drains being required proportionably large to issue the water they may receive, might occasionally afford this supply in convenient situations. This alterative dressing should not, however, be omitted, although it were necessary to form pits or excavations expressly for the purpose; it would operate by giving that firmness and consistence so indispensably required, to the loose vegetable matter composing the subject of our present inquiry. Whilst these works were carrying on upon the red boggy parts of the forest, its depasturable parts should not be passed over, but in like manner, become relieved of their surplus water, by foot-drains, intersecting each other at two, or perhaps three, rods a-part, and their waters conducted into outfal-drains, properly disposed and constructed to receive it.

This moory soil thus relieved of its surplus water, would readily assimilate frequent, but light dressings of
its

its under-stratum, fox-mould, which thus applied in small doses, would gradually incorporate with the surface-mould, and as gradually produce considerable improvement in its present herbage. No consideration, however, should tempt the council of His Royal Highness the Prince of Wales to permit this species of moor to be broken up, or opened to any farther extent than may be absolutely necessary to complete its drainage (and subsequent subdivisions, should such be deemed necessary or advisable to be made on a future day); for the present covering once destroyed, ages would not renew it with an herbage equally valuable.

As the whole of this forest will stand eminently in need of the calcareous principle, and as an inexhaustible supply of strong peat fuel may always be procured upon the moor, (were roads properly laid out), from the Bridestow, Oakhampton, and Holne, or Buckfastleigh limerocks, limestone might be carried into the interior of the moor, and calcined in properly-constructed kilns, to almost any extent, and incalculable advantage.

DISTRICT III.

There are about 250 acres of half-yearly, or Lammas-ground, in the parish of Oakhampton, in which condition it is not valued at more than 7s. per acre; but which if put into severalty, and exonerated from great and small tithe (the payment of which is represented to bear particularly hard on this parish), would be worth 30s. per acre. These lands are liable to the depasturing of sheep, horses, and cattle, from Michaelmas until Lady-day; wheat or other winter grain being sown with a view to a crop, may be fenced in from the run of the common stock; clover, tares, &c. sown for green food, are sub-

ject

ject to the depasturing sheep and cattle through the
winter. A large extent of common abutting upon Dartmoor, is open to an unlimited right of intercommonage
for the whole parish stock throughout the year. A right
of sending sheep, horses, and bullocks to the forest, is enjoyed by all the inhabitants of this town, on each owner of
stock paying from 7s. to 10s. 6d. annually to the keepers.

Notwithstanding a considerable part of the anciently
cultivated lands in this country, now called the moors, belongs exclusively to particular estates, the tenants of
which, by mutual agreement, intercommon with each
other, still it does not appear in many cases, that any individual having such an interest in common, can divide
and set a-part without the consent of the other intercommonable tenants, any part or portion of such moors in
lieu of such a right, and appropriate it entirely to himself.
In cases where vestiges of the old mounds remain, or
that the site of them can be distinctly traced, the individual's right to enclose seems permanent and indisputable, and to which he can resort at pleasure. These
rights seem now to be exercising to their full extent at
Ashbury and Beaworthy, where recent enclosures of this
kind are in preparation to undergo the usual exhaustion
of three or four white straw crops in succession ; then laid
down, to renew those lost energies which remote ages
will scarcely be able to restore.

Broadbury-down is a very extensive waste, appurtenant not only to particular parishes on its borders, but
also in some cases, to particular estates in such parishes ;
and in other instances, to the stock of the parish at
large ; the occupiers of which are in nowise subject to
stint or regulation. These rights are exercised according
to ancient usage, by parishes, villages, and individuals.
The divisions on the down are made by meets and bounds
                                                comprised

comprised in imaginary lines drawn from one given point to another. The depasturing flocks passing these bounds, are subject to be dogged and driven by the boys and shepherds in attendance, and are thus kept in a state of worry and continual agitation, and consequently but little benefited by the range which such sheep-walks would afford, were the stock suffered to remain quiet, or roam over them at pleasure.

The leading features in the soil of this common are, a hazel-coloured tender mould of a good staple on a sound dry bottom; a moist grey loam of a moderate depth on a brown and yellow clay, intermixed with veins of a granite and argillaceous gravel, producing frequent spots, particularly towards the heads of the hollows of morass and swampy places, and a black moor or peaty mould of various depths, lying on a white and yellow clay, intermixed with coarse rubble and a reddish coloured clay, or fox-mould.

The parishes bordering upon this common, the estates in which having specific rights of depasturage upon it, are Bratton-Clovella, six estates; Germansweek, nine; Sorton, three; Broadwood Wedger, five; Halwell, five; Beaworthy, six; North-Lew, Ashford, &c. not ascertained. Equally various is the soil and other circumstances of the smaller wastes in this district; the particular detail of which, even to the extent minuted on the survey, would swell this Report to a far greater size than that which is presumed to be demanded by the Right Honourable Board: suffice it therefore to say, that they all partake in a greater or less degree, of the qualities here stated, and more particularly described in the three first classes of Wastes mentioned in the district of North Devon; their parochial rights and circumstances being also found to vary in almost every instance.

The

The country formed by the tongue of coarse land lying
between the red lands of North Tawton and the Drewsteignton division of District No. 2, includes the extensive
commons of Broad Nymet, Bath, Cocktree, and Eaton.
The last, subject to a general intercommonage, but affording a large proportion of highly improveable land ;
the former are appropriated, and the right of pasturage is
appurtenant, to particular estates. The general character
of all the commons abutting upon Dartmoor, may be
drawn from what has been already stated of Buckland,
and Widdecombe in the Moor, and their spontaneous
herbage deduced from what will hereafter be stated respecting the depasturable and other parts of the forest of
Dartmoor.

DISTRICT IV.

A vast number of small wastes and commons are dispersed through all the lower parts of this district. These
partaking of the general quality of the adjoining enclosed
lands, clearly points them out as important objects for
enclosure—a measure, the difficulty of which, it is apprehended, would be much increased by the many lifehold
interests the tenantry have at present in them.

DISTRICT V.

The common of Bovey-Heathfield, excepting those
that lie in Venville, is by far the most extensive one in
this district, and is esteemed to be the lowest plain of its
extent in the county of Devon ; its average height being
little more than 50 feet above the level of low-water
mark at sea. The number of old stream-works with
which its surface has been broken, and is now encumbered,
seems

seem to fit it for no appropriation superior to that of continuing the culture of fir and other wood, so successfully exhibited in the adjacent improvement at Stover.

DISTRICT VI.

During the progress of the Surveyor so far through the county, he had not met with an acre of what may be called Class No. 5, (*vide* North Devon), the rocky craigs and inaccessible side-hills in the two preceding districts excepted, that did not appear capable of improvement by planting or otherwise, until he reached and ascended the table top of Haldon; here the thinness of the soil, and the invincible white and yellow clay abounding with flints, seemed, more than the elevation of the plain (which does not exceed 800 feet above the level of the sea), to forbid every effort towards improvement; its sides, however, as before noticed, in most aspects are capable of, and produce, a most luxuriant growth of firs of the pine tribe, larch, and other deciduous trees.

The encouragement held out by Lord Rolle to the peasantry in his neighbourhood, to settle and make improvements on the borders of Woodbury-common and its dependencies, with the healthy appearance of the fir and some deciduous trees in the clumps and plantations of that common, sufficiently denote its powers for improvement, which being disposed of in planting, enclosing, and proper management, are capable of contributing essentially to the enlargement of the national stock. The soil along and towards the heads of some of the hollows, is found of a much better staple than would be expected from an examination of the ridges and higher parts of these commons, and affords opportunities for immediately enclosing some large tracts for the purpose of pasturage and tillage.

tillage. Considerable injury has however been done to all these wastes, by the paring off and carrying away the surface for fuel.

There are many wastes and moors of minor consideration in this district, which would prove highly advantageous to the neighbouring estates, were they laid in severalty; but from the causes before stated, these arrangements are likely to be very much limited in the county of Devon for many years to come.

DISTRICT VII.

A large tract of sound improveable commons, extend from the enclosures of Uplime and Musbury, to within a few miles of Axminster. These wastes have also been much injured by paring their surface for fuel. Kilmington-common, forming a part of Shute-hill, is appurtenant to particular estates, and by agreement among the proprietors might readily be enclosed. The parishioners have a right of turbary on these moors, by which they have been much injured.

Many other wastes in this district, particularly those on the waters of the river Otter, would answer extremely well for enclosure, and a judicious system of subsequent cultivation.

In the country about Upottery, many families have removed from the villages to the sides of the wastes, where, after building cottages, and enclosing small parcels for potatoe gardens, some are so far advanced in capital, as to be able to keep a cow, and to obtain a lifehold interest in the improvements they have made. A valuable range of commons formerly cultivated, called Allar Hill, in the parish of Upottery, seems to demand a renewal of labour

from

from the skilful husbandman. The soil, a well-stapled hazel-coloured loam.

An enclosure, and subsequent system of judicious management, could not possibly fail answering the fullest expectations in the parish of Clayhaydon, were the commons of High-down and Ridge-wood Hills put into severalty, and exonerated from the payment of great and small tithes. A right of turbary seems generally possessed by the inhabitants over all these commons.

SECT. II.——BOGS : GENERAL.

THE bogs in this county are such as have already been described ; and although their extent must necessarily remain even unconjectured in this Report, they are very considerable, particularly on the primary heights of the two forests of Dartmoor and of Exmoor.

SECT. III.——FENS.

DISTRICT I.—SALT-MARSHES.

FENS, properly so called, there are none in this county ; but if a description of salt-marshes is meant to be included within the view of this Section, their magnitude and importance will be fairly considered in the following particulars. Within the boundary of the parishes of Braunton and Heanton-Punchardon, is situated a level of very fine salt-marsh, which in a long succession of ages, by a constant and regular deposition of sediment made by the
tidal

tidal waters, appears to have risen to nearly the highest
level of the ordinary spring tides, and may now be said to
have arrived at that height and stage of accumulated
strength and fertility, that, by enclosure from the farther
overflowing of the tides, it would be found in a short
time to equal that excellent and well-judged embankment
made some years since above the bridge at Barnstable, by
the predecessor of the present worthy proprietor of the
Tawton estates. The level of the salt-marsh now under
consideration, is bounded (as formerly implied) northwardly
by Braunton common-field; eastwardly, by higher grounds
in the parish of Heanton-Punchardon; westwardly, by a
range of sand-hills called Braunton-burrows; southwardly,
by the river Taw, and thence continued with it, after its
confluence with the Torridge river to the foot of the sand-
hills, and inside of the bar of Barnstable. The soil and
upper structure of this marsh, consist of a tender, rich,
soapy, hazel-coloured loam, on a subsoil of silt or fine
sand, below which a coarser stratum of sand occurs, and
in which gradations it seems to have arisen from a dark
blue, or rather black, tenacious clay or gault, the usual character of marine or common sea mud. This marsh is covered with a carpet or fine matting of all the plants and
grasses peculiar to such situations; is subject to be occasionally submerged to a slight depth by the tidal waters,
and contains by estimation about 1200 acres.

Although the circumstances of this level are in every
respect peculiarly favourable for its greater exclusion from
the sea, still the diversity of claims and interests at present existing on it, can never be reconciled or arranged
without the interference of the legislature; a measure, much
to be feared, not likely to be resorted to or promoted by
a majority of the persons more essentially interested in
laying this marsh into severalty, and embanking it from
the

the sea. The burrows before noticed, as lying westward
of the marsh, are composed of a widely-connected and
prodigious chain of sand-hills, which have been evidently
formed by the force of the westerly winds, and are still
progressively on the increase, from the dry sand whirled
up from the strand in the absence of the tide. And notwithstanding that the appearance of these hills exhibits
the most wild and steril aspect, and are only appropriated
as a rabbit-warren, still there are among them many low
and open places, covered with verdure, and formed by
the irregularities of the sand-hills which the wind has
cast up, and left in a variety of bold fantastic shapes,
forming altogether a striking contrast with their base,
which is often seen to rest upon a verdant plain, and giving to the whole an air singularly picturesque, by combining with the view of a desart that of a verdant plain
or blooming valley. An extremely strong and luxuriant growth of rushes occupies the eastern foot of these
sand-hills, and which clearly must be fed by the filtering
of the sea-water through their base, for no springs or land-
waters are to be found here, or within a considerable distance.

On the south side of the river Taw, and in the parish
of Fremington, a body of salt-marsh begins, and extends
thence along the foot of the high lands towards Inston-
quay. These marshes seem to have arrived in the manner before described, to the same stage of ripeness as fits
them for a final exclusion from the sea. The embanking
of all these marshes, however, should be made to connect
with, and to form one general plan for improving the navigation of the Taw and Torridge rivers, both streams
being highly capable of such improvements, from the points
of their present boatable waters to their final exit over the
bar into the bay of Barnstable.

The

The minutes taken on the Survey, being as yet unsupported by the data so essential to the clear explanation of the subject, the gentlemen who so handsomely promised to supply such information, not having yet transmitted them, the farther consideration of this important subject is necessarily suspended.

Northam-burrows is a beautiful and extensive common, containing by estimation about 1800 acres : about 200 acres of this level are subject to be covered at the time of spring tides : very extraordinary ones will sometimes spread farther over this plain, which is generally without creeks or cringles, and forms one compact and even surface, enriched with a tender, close, and inviting herbage. This common is protected from the farther encroachments of the sea by a firm unbroken beach of coarse shingle it has cast up from the bay, which begins at the foot of the cliffs on the south-west side, and continues thence eastwardly along the strand until it unites with the sand-hills, and forms a barrier against the tidal-waters, until those hills are broken through by the united force of the Taw and Torridge waters, which here find an exit into the bay and over the bar before noticed.

This common is stocked at will, and without stint or regulation, by all the parishioners, and even strangers, who for a week or ten days may have had occasion, or may have made it their business, to boil a pot any where within the limits of the parish. This subjects the common to an unfair depasturage, so much so, indeed, as, in the opinion of many persons well acquainted with the real circumstances of the inhabitants, to raise considerable doubts as to the consequences resulting from such supposed advantages ; a candid investigation seems therefore required, in order to ascertain by the result, how far it may be advisable to appeal to the legislature for putting this valuable
ble

ble waste under circumstances that would enable its native energies to yield a due contribution to the national
stock.

DISTRICT IV.

From the attention which the Author of this Report
has had an opportunity of paying to the nature and formation, as well as to the mode of embanking, cultivating,
and appropriating salt-marsh in this country, Ireland, Holland, and America, no instance has occurred, or come
within his knowledge, of any improvement being made on
a crude, tough, black sea-mud. This substance when
dry, is the most rigid and untractable of all argillaceous
compounds; on the contrary, salt-marsh, properly so
called, when ripe and ready for embankment, is the mild-
est, most temperate, and permanently fruitful soil of any
in the universe; and which before its embankment is, or
should be raised to nearly, if not quite, the height of the
ordinary flow of the spring-tides. The sea-mud, on the
contrary, is covered every twelve hours with a depth of
twelve or fifteen feet of pure, or nearly so, sea-water, and
when embanked, lies perhaps a little above the line of low
water mark.

In proportion as all embankments from the sea have
been made between these points of high and low water
mark, they have answered or disappointed the views of
the undertaker. Throughout all the seven townships of
Marshland in Norfolk, the whole of which at different periods have been rescued from the sea, the earliest embankments, and those in the interior of the district, are
uniformly lower in their general level, and of an inferior
quality, to the level of country enclosed by a line of embankments made at a subsequent period. In this manner,
the

the latter embankments continue on still higher plains to
the present line of sea-coast, where the last of any importance that has been made, was effected by Captain Bentinck
a few years since, by the enclosure of a very large tract
(perhaps) twelve hundred acres. This lies upon a higher
level than the interior enclosures, and soon after its embankment was esteemed by far the best of all.

Throughout all the embanked marshes of Cambridgeshire and Lincolnshire, a premature enclosure from the
sea has never failed to disappoint the expectations from the
enterprise. Had the lots below where the new Custom-
house is built in Dublin, been left open to the tidal-waters
(and which are there very turbid, and highly charged with
sediment) from the end of the north wall and towards the
sheds of Clontarff, and the expense of the enclosing mounds
and walls been applied in continuing the north wall in a
line nearly parallel with the south one, the waters of the
Liffy, thus confined in their descent, would have scoured
out and preserved a deep channel for their discharge into
the bay of Dublin, and perhaps contributed to the removal towards deeper water, those bars so justly dreaded and
so highly injurious to the shipping and commercial interests of that important city : at all events, the navigation
and access to the port must have been greatly benefited
by a work of this nature ; and at this time, or perhaps a
few years hence, such a deposition of sediment would have
been made by the unrestrained flowing of the tides over
what are now the old enclosed lots, as to have rendered
them equally rich and fruitful with some of the most favoured spots in the neighbourhood of that metropolis.

These observations may be considered as rather foreign
to a report on the agriculture and internal improvements
of the county of Devon; but the Surveyor has been led
to the discussion, in order to illustrate his idea of the difference

ference between salt-marsh, ripe and fit for exclusion from the sea, from that which may be prematurely enclosed, and also of embankments made with a view of enclosing portions of invincibly steril and shear sea-mud. Some embankments of this latter description have lately been made, and others are now carrying on, across certain branches of the river Plym, above Catwater. The indisposition of Lord Boringdon, and the absence of his Lordship s steward, deprived the Surveyor of an opportunity of visiting these works; but if he concludes correctly, from the distant view he had of them at Saltram, and a more minute inspection of the work now carrying on under his Lordship's directions, in cutting off a similar arm from the Kingsbridge river, in the parish of Charlton, these embankments can have no other possible consequence, than, in the first instance, stopping the regular ascent of the tides, the return of which, combined with the land-waters, contribute so essentially to the keeping open, and the preservation of navigation in all such inlets; and, secondly, the procuring a mere site for the incalculable expense of forming a proper soil of land upon, can never for a moment weigh in balance with the injury accruing to navigation, and the mortifying disappointment that must inevitably await the well-meant expectations of the noble proprietor.

The tender hazel-coloured loam, which forms the soil of all salt-marsh ready for embankment, being formed of animal and vegetable exuvia, combined with the finest particles of terrene matter the tidal waters could hold in suspension, can never fail yielding the most ample returns from all such districts rescued from the ocean. Where an accumulation of such soil (as on the unembanked part of the salt-marsh at Averon Giffard), is not found of sufficient magnitude for embanking, and that it

lies

lies convenient for removal to the adjacent uplands, no pains should be spared in applying it, not only as a valuable alterative to such lands, but from its containing, as before implied, the principle of an immediate and direct manure. In its application, great care should be taken to cast aside (as is usual with ouze cast all along the coast of Norfolk) every spit of blue or black sea-clay that may occur on its digging, this being always found steadily to resist incorporation with any soil to which the hazel-coloured salt-marsh ouze is equally applicable. The ouze should be spread upon the lay-ground, from 1000 to 1200 bushels per acre; and the marsh green sward or spine, chopped fine, and left gradually to incorporate with the surface-mould for two or three years. In the first ploughing of this lay afterwards, it will occur to the intelligent farmer, that this surface is not to be turned under at a full pitch; but, on all occasions, first skirted or wrest-balked, and that as fine as possible. Should the marsh-ouze be required for ploughea ground, it will be advisable to rot its green sward in heaps, and pulverize the whole mass, by turning it once or twice over before it is spread upon the broken or fallow ground, at which time it should not be ploughed under, but harrowed in with the seed.

A tract of about 180 or 200 acres of salt-marsh, now ready for enclosing, was observed near the mouth of the river Otter: this has arrived to nearly the highest level of the spring tides, and is covered with marsh-samphire, thrift, or ladies-cushion, and a luxuriant growth of the *artiplex partulacorides*. The navigation of this river seems to be of no material consequence; and as the sea has nearly excluded itself, by casting up a strong bank of shingle, over which very extraordinary high tides only, ever find a way, the expense of completing its enclosure would be small,

small, in comparison with the object obtained by it, and which is here more particularly required, on account of the small proportion of pasture and good feeding land on all the adjacent estates. The bank of shingle stretching across the opening of the valley, in a line from the western shore, is only broken for a few yards on its east end, by the discharge of the waters of the Otter running close under the western bluff boundary of Otterton Barton ; the bank of shingle might be capped, or grafted, at a small expense, with a body of the marsh-ouze, and so effectually as to ensure the enclosed marsh from any probable danger in future from the highest tides.

DISTRICT VII.

A valuable improvement was effected some years since, by embanking a large tract of salt-marsh lying on the west side of the river Axe, above Seaton. The sea had nearly excluded itself from this level, in like manner as at the mouth of the Otter, by throwing up a broad, high, and immoveable bank of shingle, which would have connected with the high land on the eastern side of the valley, had not the discharge of the river Axe kept a channel constantly open on that side to issue its waters. The whole of this salt-marsh was not valued at more than 10*l.* previous to its embankment. Several hundred acres are thus acquired, averaging an annual rent of 3*l.* per acre. Why this embankment stops short of the half-yearly meadow-grounds below Colyton-bridge, the Surveyor was not able to understand.

SECT. IV.——FORESTS.

See Dartmoor.

SECT. V.——LEW-MOOR FARM.

DISTRICT III.

Lew-moor farm, in the parish of North Lew, contains about 300 acres, one-third of which is brought into a state of tillage; the remainder lies either in its pristine state, or is planted with a variety of the fir or pine tribe, together with some deciduous forest-trees, all of which appear to be doing extremely well. The soil varies from a peaty mould, on a deep stratum of blue and white clay, to a strong close grey loam, on a brown and yellow clay, mixed with some rubble.

The husbandry pursued in this recent enclosure is, first to spade and burn the old moorland, and with the ashes mix about thirty measures of lime to the acre: this is ploughed under into eight or ten-furrow ridges; sown with wheat, two bushels per acre, and harrowed in: produce, 20 bushels. The wheat-stubble turned under in March; sown with oats, six bushels to the acre, harrowed in, and yielding a produce of no less than 70 bushels, of 42 lbs. each, per acre. With the oats are sown 6 lbs. of red clover, and one bushel of hievre, or ray-grass, per acre. The first bite of the young seeds is taken by the ewes and lambs, and then shut up for mowing; produce 35 cwt. of hay from the stack, per acre. A considerable part of the clover plant will remain the second year; but this is finally succeeded by white Dutch clover, trefoil, ribwort, crowsfoot, dandelion, &c.; and, on the whole, forming a very good turf of feeding-land. This, after a lapse of five or six years, is again broken up, spaded, and burnt; and prepared with the usual dressing of lime or

sea-

sea-sand, for wheat; with two successive crops of oats; and then again laid down with clover and ray-grass. In this latter process, a prodigious deficiency from the former produce is experienced ; the grass-seeds are observed very soon to vanish, and instead of the spontaneous produce and valuable plants and grasses before noticed, little other is seen than a coarse tribe of the arias, black and common couch-rest, harrow, flea-bane, coltsfoot, and all such plants as denote a wet, cold subsoil, with a surface bearing all the appearance of *confirmed* sterility. The farmer candidly allows his disappointment on going a second time over the ground, and that by the last spading and burning, and subsequent crops, the ground was reduced to an infinitely worse condition, for the purposes of pasturage or tillage, than the old moorland beyond the hedge, which had not been opened for time immemorial.

IRISH COMB FARM.

It has been already observed, that there were several very improveable tracts in the moorlands of the division of Meshaw: a farther examination will show, that it is but a small portion of the whole of this district that can, with strict propriety, be pronounced incorrigible. Mr. Bayley has enclosed about 200 acres, part of Ash-moor, called Irish Comb farm, and in which is included, a well-known point or station in the moors, called Pye's Nest. The soil here generally consists of a black moor, or vegetable mould, from six inches to a foot in depth, lying on a tough yellow clay and fox-mould.

The surface of this moor, which tallies with Class No. 3, district the first, Mr. Bayley first spades and burns, at an average expense of 27s. per acre. The ashes are

DEVON.]   then

then spread, and the ground is skirted, or half-ploughed, for the purpose of covering the ashes. In this state it is left, and dung is carried out and laid down in heaps, upon the beat-field, during the continuance of frost, the ensuing winter. When the moor becomes sufficiently dry in the month of March, trenches are made through the field, at the distance of 30 inches, by ploughing two furrows contrary ways to each other. The dung previously laid down is then strewed in these trenches, and a single row of potatoe sets is placed upon it, and covered by a double mould-board plough, splitting and dividing the mould, and again returning it into the trench. The rows are afterwards moulded up, as usual, with the same plough.

The average produce from this management is stated at 100 bags, of 160 lbs. each, per acre. The potatoes are taken up by the plough, and afterwards gathered by hand, and put into large ricks, or berrys, in the field. The land is left in that state through the winter, and sown with black oats, six bushels to the acre, in the following spring, and found to average a produce of 40 bushels per acre. With the oats are sown 6 lbs. of red clover, and half a bushel of ray-grass per acre. These seeds have hitherto answered extremely well : the produce of the first crop is truly astonishing, as two tons of clover and hievre hay have generally been produced per acre. The aftermath, abounding with many natural herbs and grasses, was equally luxuriant, tender and good. This improvement has only undergone a very partial hollow-draining, at an expense of about 9*d*. per perch. A fine field of turnips, upon beat-ashes, composed a part of this improvement, when viewed by the Surveyor ; but the wet condition of the land, forbade all hopes of consuming them where they grew, unless peradventure during the

con-

tinuance of a frost, or very late in the spring season.
Upon the whole, Mr. Bayley seems more justly to appre-
ciate these moors than many people in the country ; and
so far as he has yet gone, he has marked a considerable
superiority of judgment in the management of them.

DISTRICT IV.—LODDISWELL IMPROVEMENT.

Adjoining Black-down, on the west, and in the parish
of Loddiswell, is an extensive range of ancient moorlands, and lying in severalty to the adjoining estates.
About seventy acres of this land have been improved
within the last seven years, by Mr. King of Fowelscombe.
The soil, a black vegetable mould of a peaty nature, on
a grey, brown, and reddish-coloured clay, and in which
large masses of a light coloured whinstone, veined with
quartz, frequently rise to the surface, and very much encumber the ground.

This improvement has been hollow-drained, as far as
it seems to have required ; the drains costing about 4s.
per perch, and estimating 20 perches only to each acre,
the 40 acres required to be thus done, amounts to

	£.160	0	0
Clearing the ground of the rocks, by blasting, and burying them over the 70 acres, has cost	280	0	0
Paring and burning, and removing small rocks after the plough	350	0	0
New buildings	88	19	0
One hundred and seventy-six perches of new fences, frithing, and planting	22	6	0
Carry forward £.901	5	0

Brought

A Plan of the Rev.d W.H.(ohams WEIR at Black Torrington.

Tavoir

Elevation of the Dam.

The hutches are lifted by small Windlasses & Chains.

Running nearly East & West.

50 Feet wide.

On a perfect Level, the sides being also raised towards the banks 4 Feet more each in addition.

C

D

31 Feet in Length.

A

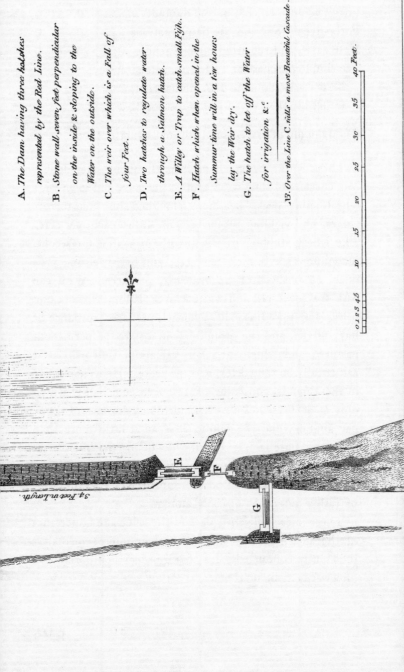

A. The Dam having three hatches represented by the Red Line.

B. Stone wall seven feet perpendicular on the inside & sloping to the Water on the outside.

C. The weir over which is a Fell of four Feet.

D. Two hatches to regulate water through a Salmon hatch.

E. A Willey or Trap to catch small Fish.

F. Hatch which when opened in the Summer time will in a few hours lay the Weir dry.

G. The hatch to let off the Water for irrigation &c.

N.B. Over the Line C. rolls a most Beautiful Cascade.

34 Feet in Length.

0 1 2 3 4 5   10   15   20   25   30   35   40 Feet.

Neele sculp Strand

Brought forward £.901	5	0	
Fifty-two ditto erected on old mounds	9	2	0
Forty-five ditto round the fir-plantations	10	0	0
New gates, and repairing outside fences	20	0	0
Fee-simple purchase of 140 acres, valued at 5s. per acre, equal to 35l. annual rent, at rather less than seventeen years' purchase	530	0	0
Total amount of first cost and improvements £.1470	7	0	

These works being all performed, about sixty double
Winchesters of lime were applied per acre, and sown with
wheat, nine pecks per acre ploughed into ten-furrow
ridges, and yielding 28 bushels, of 58 lbs. each, per acre.
The wheat stubbles are sown with oats after the second
ploughing, six bushels per acre, and harrowed in : produce, 35 bushels, of 36 lbs. each, per acre. With the
oats are sown red and white clover 10 lbs., ribwort one
peck, and ray-grass half a bushel, per acre : produce of
hay, 36 cwt. and the ground left in a state for permanent
pasture ; and which, at a fair valuation, is worth, as it
can readily be rented for, 40s. per acre. Hence, an estate
in these moors, consisting of 140 acres, one half of which
only is at present improved, yields an income of 140l.
per annum ; and the whole realized at little more than
ten years' purchase. Or, after deducting the interest accruing on the expenditure, and the amount of the tithes,
a net income is created on the improvements to the value
of rather more than 60l. per annum.

These cases sufficiently declare the value and importance
of the ancient moorlands, when their improvements are
judiciously conducted, and that a proper appropriation is
afterwards made of them.

CHAP.

CHAP. XII.

IMPROVEMENTS.

———

IT has been a matter of some doubt with the Author of this Report, whether the design of this Chapter is merely to relate the improvements already made in this district, or whether those which the country is capable of receiving, are to be comprehended in it, or left for discussion in the concluding Chapter of this Report. If the former only, it is much feared that this Chapter will be very concise; and if the latter, it does not seem to embrace any thing like that variety of matter so general and important, a statement must necessarily demand. On a supposition, however, that the improvements already effected in the county are to be treated of in this place, they will now be detailed to the extent noticed in the course of the Survey.

———

SECT. I.—DRAINING.

DRAINING is, with great propriety, placed at the head of a Chapter on Rural Improvements. In this country the practice is so little known, or at least attended to, that until the necessity of its importance can be impressed o the minds of the inhabitants, it will be in vain to address or recommend other measures for their adoption. The natural structure of the country in many places, absolutely forbids resort to be made to the mode of draining pursued by Mr. Elkington; and the few open cuts or gutters

observed

observed in the wheat fields and low grounds, are generally inadequate to the discharge of the surface and rising
waters.   The enormous expense at which in some instances hollow-drains have been made, and apparently
with a view of combining the system of Elkington with
the plain, easy, and simple practice of soughing, serves very
much to discourage the latter practice, notwithstanding
that experience has shewn it to be the cheapest, most effectual, and permanent mode of relieving land from a sur-
plusage of water, particularly in cases where it has been
utterly impossible to prevent it from coming on.

There are many gentlemen in the county, who seem to
have spared no pains or expense in endeavouring to effect
the drainage of some of their cold, close, and clayey lands.
In all these cases, they would most probably have succeeded to their utmost wishes, had as much pains been bestowed in endeavouring to carry the water from off the
ground, as in most cases have been exerted to prevent it
from coming on.   The system of Elkington has been by
far too steadily adhered to, and the consequence has often
led to the most mortifying disappointment : the project
is relinquished, and cold water literally spread over the
undertaking.   This has arisen solely from the want of a
due attention to the internal structure of the country, for
however well-founded and correct the theory of Mr. Elkington's practice may be, in countries less broken, more
horizontally and differently stratified,——in Devonshire,
the application of his principles generally cannot take
place.

SECT. II.——PARING AND BURNING.

However the practice of paring and burning may be
admitted under certain circumstances of restraint and limitation,

tation, and even recommended as a safe and effectual means of bringing coarse moory land, when effectually drained, into a state of profitable cultivation, still its pernicious consequences on the sound dry stapled lands in this county, are such as can never be repaired but by the total abandonment of a system so generally practised in this county, and which is fraught with the means of producing such incalculable mischief.   It will readily be admitted, that this operation can produce no diminution whatever of the earthy parts of the soil; but as all soil is more or less composed of the earth of vegetables, its exposure to combustion is fatal to it.   The small portion of alkaline salts produced from the green vegetables are soon washed away, and the residuum is converted into charcoal, which must for ever lie dormant and insoluble in the ground: hence those energies which the peculiar nature of the climate has been the means of accumulating in the soil for unnumbered ages, become lost and dissipated; Nature is crossed in her design, and deprived of the means she uniformly manifests through the county of Devon, in preserving a permanent and increased fertility.

SECT. III.——MANURING.

Marl.—The manner in which marl is applied in the 6th and 7th districts of the county, has already been adverted to in describing the preparation for crops.

Lime.—Lime is the prevailing article of manure in most parts of the county. The manner in which it is generally used, has also been stated in the Seventh Chapter of this Report.

Yard-Dung.—Whether it arises from the situation of the
farm-

farm-yards, which from their wetness prove uncomfortable lodging places in winter for the cattle, or from other
causes not immediately occurring; it seems strange, in a
country abounding with so much stock, that is, or ought
to be, carried through the winter, that so small a portion
of farm-yard dung is made, and that there should still be
a necessity for converting the little straw produced, by
strewing it along the highways, many of which are kept
constantly littered during the summer season. Why this
improvident appropriation of the preceding crop of straw
is thus made, it is not easy to divine; but it must suffice in
this place to observe, that these road-scrapings are generally mixed up with lime, and applied in the manner before mentioned.

Sea-Sand.—The sea-sand taken up at Clovella, Hartland,
Bude, Bigbury, and along the coast to the mouth of the
river Exe, is applied as before noticed. When used as a
top-dressing upon grass-land, either alone or with mould,
it never fails to bring forth for a succession of seasons, a
very sweet and valuable herbage. This dressing applied
in the usual quantity, will cost within two miles of the
shore, from 30 to 40s. per acre, and as carriage is the
only object, proportionably more at a greater distance.

Ashes—Soaper's waste lees, and spent wood ashes, have
already been noticed, as much used in the neighbourhood;
but Mr. Stoneman, of Woodhouse farm, near Torrington, is the only gentleman met with as having applied—

Woollen Rags for the purpose of manure. These were
spread upon part of a field that had undergone the usual
preparation for wheat, the remainder of it being dressed
with lime. The first cost of these rags was 5s. per cwt.
and

waters used so successfully through the county for the purpose of irrigation.

As the great object among all the irrigators is that of collecting and spreading the first freshes from the autumnal rains, care is taken that all the carriages are well scoured out, sluices and stop-gates repaired, the grounds well guttered, and divided into sections, to receive, in alternate order, the firs floods poured from the hills at that season. This commences about the first of October, when the fields are watered step by step, and as frequently repeated as possible until the middle of January; great care being taken in the mean time, not only to keep the water in constant motion, but never to suffer it to remain beyond two or three days at farthest in the same place. The first bite of these meadows, as early as the middle of February, is usually taken off by ewes and lambs; a fortnight or three weeks later (in the South Hams), they produce a sufficient pasture for fattening bullocks or dairy cows. These meadows are thus fed until about Old May-day, when the flowing of them is renewed, and they are shut up for hay, and yield an average produce through the county of 35 cwt. per acre.

There are no other reservoirs than those which are formed by the dams or weirs by which the streams are raised for the purpose, nor does it appear that any means have been actually adopted, either for correcting, improving, or rendering the waters turbid.

Ridge-work appears to be a part of the system unknown in this county, the water being generally carried over gradually-inclined but smooth planes.

The irrigated meadows did not appear of sufficient moment to require plans or particular surveys to be made of them. The practice obtains very generally through most of the vallies in the county; and where the land

has

and about 8cwt. were applied per acre. They were pre
viously chopped small, sown by hand, and ploughed unde
with the wheat in ten-furrow ridges. Whilst the cor
was in its grassy state, it appeared of a deeper green, an
discovered a more luxuriant vigour than the other part o
the field; but it was clearly not so forward at harvest
although the ears appeared somewhat larger, and bette
formed in the chest. Subsequent observations have in
duced him to believe, that the permanent effect of this a
a dressing, will not equal that of the ordinary compost
with lime.

Irrigation.—With regard to irrigation, the nature o
the soil does not appear to be an object of such commanding influence as that of the land being closely turfed
over, and beyond all other considerations to be fully and
effectually drained of all its native superabundant water,
and actually brought into a sound and compact state.
This latter consideration, although well known to the
most observant irrigators, is by no means so much attended to as it ought, and hence among the more
obstinate and cavilling pretenders, the system in general, as well as the waters that flow through the occupations of sloth, penury, and ignorance, is often condemned,
but it is by those only who have omitted the previous
preparation for carrying it into proper execution. The
quality of the water will necessarily partake of the nature
of the stratum whence it issues, and as that is chiefly
alluminous, excepting towards the heads of such branches
as have their source in the morasses of Dartmoor and of
Exmoor, it is not to be expected that any extraordinary
fructifying principle (besides the proportion of primary
earths that all waters are stated to hold in solution) will
be found to have any share in the composition of the
waters

has been previously drained, and in proper preparation, it seldom fails to answer very fully the expectations of the farmer. It seems rather less attended to in the valley of the Taw than in many other places, and where the Torridge and some of its superior branches wind their course, it is scarcely known, or but little practised, unless in the instance of the Rev. Mr. Coham.

One very easy and obvious measure may be resorted to, and enforced by authority, for the purpose of extending the advantages arising from the artificial means of flowing low grounds, and slopes occurring midway, and on the lower declivity of certain hills; for instance, A, B, and C, occupy parts of the same valley or side-hill, and adjoining to each other. An eddit is taken up from a stream which flows through these farms, and enters the higher part of the farm A. This in due season is made use of, and the farm is irrigated to the extent required. A and B are good neighbours, and therefore A willingly suffers the eddit to be carried through the upper part of his farm, to convey the surplus water to his neighbour B, whose farm thereby also obtains irrigation in due season. B and C, however, are not upon such friendly terms with each other as A and B are, and the latter refuses that any eddit or carriage should be made through his lands, for conveying the farther surplus of the water to C; and therefore after irrigating as much of his own farm as he thinks proper, the water is let down to D, where it unites with the stream from whence it was first taken, instead of being continued on the level to E, and along the upper side of the farm of C, for the purpose of its irrigation, and as much farther as the stream or eddit might with convenience supply. Complaints of this nature occurred in many places during the progress of the Survey; and as it is presumed that such matters are properly

perly submitted to the consideration of the Honourable
Board of Agriculture, they will readily devise means
founded on principles of justice, to remove the evil here
complained of.

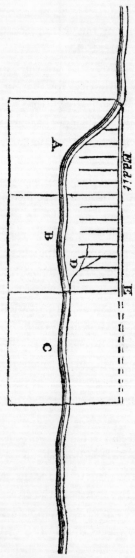

A com-

A communication on the subject of applying the best means for constructing a dam or weir across any water-course, for the purpose of raising mill-dams or heads of water for irrigation, has been very obligingly made by the Rev. Mr. Coham, of Coham-house, Black Torrington. It will be found, in some points, to suggest the necessity of departing, in some degree, from the otherwise neglected principles laid down by Dr. Anderson, in his Treatise upon forming works of this nature, and may spare similar disappointments and expenses being incurred, as will appear to have been experienced by following too implicitly the rules laid down by Dr. Anderson, by the worthy author of the following statement.

" 11*th April*, 1807.

" DEAR SIR,

" In compliance with your wish to receive a description of the weir which I have recently thrown across the river Torridge, and the motives which led me to such an undertaking, I have the honour to inform you, that from various accounts I had heard of the astonishing effects of irrigation in the counties of Dorset, Gloucester, and other districts in this kingdom, I was given to suppose, that from my situation near a large river, I might turn some of my low lands lying contiguous to it, to the greatest advantage by the same mode of management. This idea was the more strongly confirmed by my observation of the verdure which, early in every spring, seemed to prevail on such portions of these lands as had been inundated the preceding winter, and particularly where the water had not remained long stagnant, nor had passed over with too great a rapidity. I thence imagined, if by any means I could raise this river to such a height as to be able, at my pleasure, and under the controul of the

common

common rules of irrigation, to distribute the water (especially when surcharged with the overflowings of twenty or thirty villages, and a proportionate number of separate farm-yards) over between thirty and forty acres of land, I should at least add as many pounds to the yearly value of my estate. At this time, viz. in the spring of the year 1801, a Treatise on the Erection of Weirs, or Mill-dams, &c. written by Dr. Anderson, fell into my hands, and I was so much struck with the superiority of his plan, in every particular, as I imagined, over every other of the like kind I had seen, that I determined instantly to put it into execution, as nearly as local circumstances would admit. Accordingly I proceeded, in the first instance, to explore the banks of the Torridge, as far up as my lands extended, for the purpose of securing a good foundation, and to obtain the highest possible level; and finding these two main objects perfectly correspondent to my wishes, I immediately contracted with the owner of the lands opposite to my own, for a license to fix my weir.

" I then began my operations, by digging a channel to receive the river, and by a temporary weir turned the whole stream into it. Having removed all the rubbish, or washed-stones, I came to a rocky foundation, into which I dug a double row of pits directly across the bottom, or bed of the river, at about five feet asunder length ways, by four feet in breadth, and about two feet in depth; and into these pits I fixed oak-posts of about six or seven inches square. My masons then raised a perpendicular wall without any cement, about five feet and a half thick, entirely enclosing the posts; and my labourers were employed in the mean time in *backing up* the wall on the higher side with some of *the stiffest clay we could get in the neighbourhood.*

" When the wall was raised to such an height as I deemed

I. Cooke del.

Neele sculp. Strand.

View of the Revᵈ N. H. Cocham's Weir at Black Torrington _ Devonshire.

deemed necessary, in reference to the level required, and the preservation of the lands adjacent, the upper parts of the oak-posts were sawn off, to receive cross pieces and joists (the front posts then standing about six inches higher than the hinder ones), and on these joists I pinned oak-planks about six inches and a half long by three inches thick. These planks were brought forward to project about one foot and a half over the perpendicular of the wall on the lower side, forming, as Dr. Anderson calls it, " a lip." The clay, together with these planks, constituting an inclined plane of   degrees, and terminating at the distance of about fifteen feet up the stream, on the common bed of the river.

" The entrance for the *leat* was cut at about thirty feet above the *lip* of the weir, where, to regulate the quantity of water to be admitted, I placed three strong flood-hatches (to be lifted or let down by a lever and windlass), and through which a column of water of about eight feet wide by four feet deep, may be introduced at any time. Between the leat and the river, a stone wall strongly cemented is erected, about eight feet in height, and carried from the head of the leat to about thirty feet below the weir, in a parallel line with the river, and at the end of which wall another flood-hatch is fixed on a level with the bed of the river. This latter hatch will always be of the greatest consequence when any reparations may be wanting on the weir; for on drawing it up when the water is low, the weir in a few hours will be left perfectly dry, and the workmen, with the greatest conveniency, may proceed in their operations. From the top of the side-wall above the weir, the ground is made sloping to the river, and below it is covered with turf, and levelled for a foot-path.

" Immediately below the weir, there is an outlet regulated

regulated by another flood-hatch, and conducted through a *shoot*, formed of oak-plank, from the leat, and contrived for the admission of salmon, which are here sometimes taken ; and below the lower flood-hatch, a trap (or *willey*, as in this neighbourhood it is called) is made for the catching of smaller fish ; but as this part of the work does not much effect the general design of it, and is more an object of amusement than of profit, it will be superfluous more than merely to mention it.

" The weight of the weir is about four feet above the level of the river where it is fixed, and its length, from bank to bank, directly across, or at right angles with the stream, is about 48 feet ; 40 feet of which is carried at a perfect level, and over which the water rolls precisely at the same depth, forming a most beautiful cascade. The remaining portions of the length of the weir, viz. four feet on each side, are raised, gradually ascending to the bank for the purpose, on floods, when this river is very tumultuous, of warding off the torrent from the banks.

" *The lip*, I have found fully to answer the expectations Dr. Anderson gave me to entertain of it ; for, in proportion to the force of the water, *e tergo*, so is the distance it is thrown over the weir from the foundation of the perpendicular wall.

" As this seems rather a new idea, and as Dr. Anderson, by his illustration of it, has rendered this plan, as I conceive, no longer problematical, I would wish you, Sir, to look yourself into the treatise I have mentioned.

" But here I may say, *o si sic omnia !* for, by too implicitly following Dr. Anderson's directions in the use of *the clay*, I was completely foiled in my first effort. In fact, the clay not properly coalescing, if I may make use of such a term, with the rich mould of the left bank of the river, the water soon found a passage between these two

                                                    unsocial

unsocial companions, and not only one half of my weir
was instantly destroyed, but a considerable inroad was
made into the side of the bank.

" Chagrined sadly at this unlooked-for disaster, the
year being now too far advanced for a recommencement
of the work, I awaited the return of spring with as much
patience as I could summon to my aid; but as, from experience, I had now found out my error, I soon begun
to entertain no doubt but that success would ultimately
crown my labours.

" Thus encouraged, in the spring of 1802 I resumed
my task, and proceeded, first, after turning the stream,
to drive on the weir in a direct line with the former
work, into the side of the opposite bank, as before; and
secondly, after removing as much of the clay as I could
get at, by making a *puddle* (as is commonly used in canals)
of mould and gravel in its stead.

" By this mode of management, I have most completely succeeded. A weir is now erected, which, from
present appearances, seems to bid defiance to time (for
from the distance from the lip to the entrance of the leat,
the intermediate space, by the washing down of stones.
rubbish, &c. is daily strengthening itself); and which I
can with safety venture to recommend, as a pattern to any
person who may have occasion, either for machinery or
irrigation, to construct any thing of a similar kind.

" If the accident I have mentioned had not happened,
the whole cost of this undertaking would not have exceeded 75*l.*; but the fatal introduction of the clay, as
directed by Dr. Anderson, led me into an expense of
nearly an equal additional sum. The Doctor, as well as
the public, ought to be informed of this circumstance;
and in giving it to you, I consider myself as not having
done more than my duty.

" As to the effects which irrigation may produce on

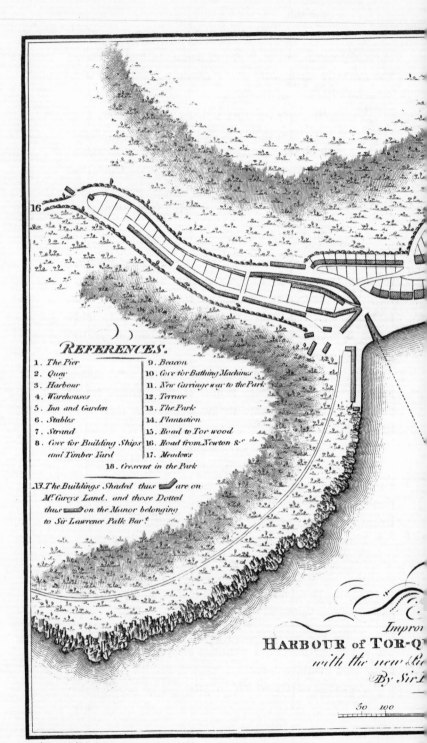

REFERENCES.

1. The Pier
2. Quay
3. Harbour
4. Warehouses
5. Inn and Garden
6. Stables
7. Strand
8. Cove for Building Ships and Timber Yard
9. Beacon
10. Cove for Bathing Machines
11. New Carriage way to the Park
12. Terrace
13. The Park
14. Plantation
15. Road to Tor wood
16. Road from Newton &c
17. Meadows
18. Crescent in the Park

N.B. The Buildings Shaded thus ▰ are on
  Mr. Carys Land, and those Dotted
  thus ▰ on the Manor belonging
  to Sir Lawrence Palk Bar.t

Improv
HARBOUR of TOR-Q
with the new Pie
By Sir L

50   100

Jos.h Beard Architect 1807.

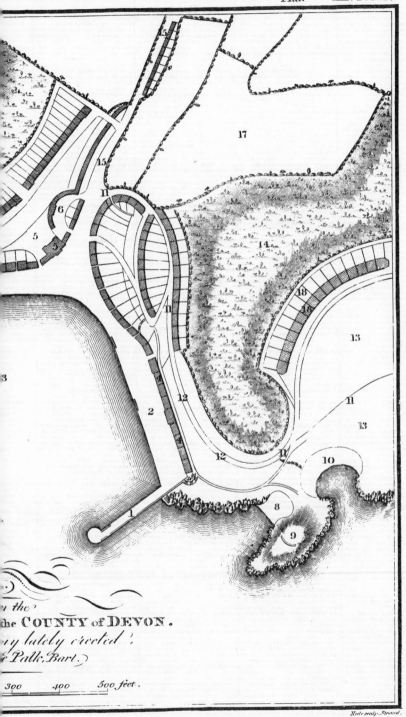

Plate — XII. *P. 323.*

5

17

15

11

6

5

3

14

11

18

16

13

12

11

2

13

12

11

10

1

8

9

in the

the COUNTY of DEVON.

lately erected

Palk, Bart.

300   400   500 feet.

Neele sculp. Strand.

my lands, I cannot at present justly estimate; for the ground lying perfectly on a flat, I have been under the necessity of throwing it into large ridges; and it is not in sufficient preparation, as yet, to receive the water.

" Yours, &c.

" W. H. C."

It is impossible to behold, without the highest satisfaction, the new church raised by the Templar family, in the parish of Teigngrace. Its altar-piece, during divine service, becomes highly interesting to the devout Christian. The monuments are of excellent workmanship, particularly that which represents the loss of the Halswell East Indiaman. Its organ is a remarkably fine one, and the whole is finished in a manner not less worthy the liberality of the family, than the religious rights which are performed in it are impressive and honourable to the pious zeal of its munificent founders.

In the northernmost cove of Torbay, a spirited improvement is now carrying on by Sir Lawrence Palk. A new pier, projected south-westwardly from the eastern cliff, affords complete protection to shipping from the south-east winds. The regularity of the buildings lately raised for the accommodation of company resorting hither for the convenience of sea-bathing, adds neatness and beauty to the wild and picturesque scenery of its natural situation; and, from the size of the vessels the harbour is now capable of protecting whilst they receive and discharge their cargoes, there are well-grounded expectations that this place will become of some maritime consequence on a future day.

Upon the ground-plan, Nos. 5, and 7, are completed; and No. 15, commenced. The rest are merely planned out for the direction of such as may hereafter accept building leases. The pier and quay, No. 1, and 2, are

complete;

Plate XIII. P. 323.

R.T.Fraude delt.

Kels sculp. Strand.

View of the Improvements at Tor-Quay.

complete; as are also the building, cove 8; and the new carriage-road, No. 11, and 12, (*Plates* XI. XII. XIII.)

The Rev. Mr. Froude, of Dartington parsonage, has communicated the following ingenious contrivance of a neighbour of his, the Rev. Mr. Ley, of Ashpreignton, for emptying the water from a pond, without the necessity of attending to it personally when such may be full.

When the pond is quite full, the stream which feeds it flows, in the gutter A B, into a box, which, when full of water, is sufficiently heavy to raise the plug at the bottom of the pond. This box is leaky; and by the time the pond is empty, the water is also discharged from it; when the weight of the beam and plug is sufficient to raise the empty box, and the plug is replaced in the trunk.

Level of the water when full.

Bottom of the pond.

Plug

Trunk at the bottom of the pond.

Pond Head

A

B

Box that is rather leaky.

CHAP.

CHAP. XIII.

EMBANKMENTS.

———◆———

AS there have been no embankments against the sea, but those already noticed in the Eleventh Chapter of this Report, we shall therefore pass on to,

CHAP. XIV.

LIVE STOCK.

—◆—

SECT. I.——CATTLE.

DISTRICT I.

NOTWITHSTANDING the line marked upon the map, as ranging with the southern shore of the bay of Barnstable, taken from Hartland Point to Bucks Rocks or Holwell, and continued thence eastwardly, through parts of the parishes of Alwington, Monkleigh, Wear-Giffard, Hunshaw, Athrington, High Bickington, Satterleigh, George Nympton, Mary Annesleigh, Bishop's Nympton, and East Anstey, is what is here marked as the southern boundary of the district of North Devon, so justly celebrated for its breed of cattle; yet within this line, certain gradations of perfection are to be met with in the native cattle, and which in the country watered by the river Bray, and on the northern branches of the Mole, appear to have attained the highest proof, and to form the most perfect of their species. The superiority of this breed for grazing or for draught, is amply demonstrated by the demand, and very high prices they bring after their work is done, either at home or among the Somersetshire graziers; but for the uses of the dairy or for milk, it is a breed by no means held in general estimation, as their aptitude to look well (without being fleshy), is derived from the peculiar

culiar nature of the animal, which disposes its secretions in the accumulation of fat, rather than in the production of milk. For the purposes of labour, this breed can no where be excelled for docility, activity, or hardihood, in proof of which no stronger circumstance can be adduced, than that it is a common day's work, on fallow land, for four steers to plough two acres with a double-furrow plough, and that a general use is thus made of them, and for most of the other purposes of draught in the country where they were originally found; and in others to which they have been since transplanted.

The rules generally pursued in breeding and raising this valuable animal, may be considered as follow. Many judicious observations have been made on the preference given to Michaelmas calves to those that drop the latter end of February; notwithstanding the additional expense and care required in nursing them through the winter. The greater number of calves, however, fall between Candlemas and May, and some much later; but among the best breeders, such late calves are not so generally approved of. The usual mode of raising them in this district, is to let the calf suck as much as it will three times a day for the first week; then bring it to the finger, and feed it with warm new milk, in like manner for three weeks longer.

This is the ordinary treatment for the first month, and the calf is then fed for two months longer, twice a day, with as much warm scalded skimmed milk as it will drink; when, gradually abating its morning and evening meals, at the end of four months the animal is weaned from all milk draughts, and left to itself. Small portions of finely pounded linseed cakes are often used, and recommended to be mixed with the skimmed milk, particularly in the first period of its being given in the place of new milk.

The

Plate XIV. P. 327.

Devonshire Cow.

Nele sculp. Strand

The full-sized North Devon cow, *(Plate XIV.)* when fattened to its frame, will not exceed eight score per quarter; and the ordinary average of its ox, at five years old, and equally well fattened, must not be rated higher than three score per quarter above the weight of its fattened mother.

The form of this animal, its exceliencies and defects (for absolute perfection is not to be expected), will now be described, with all the skill and candour possessed and felt by the Author of this Report. Its head is small, clean, and free from flesh about the jaws; deer-like, light and airy in its countenance; neck long and thin; throat free from jowl or dewlap; nose and round its eyes, of a dark orange colour; ears thin and pointed, tinged on their inside with the same colour that is always found to encircle its eyes; horns thin and fine to their roots, of a cream colour, tipped with black, growing with a regular curve upwards, and rather springing from each other; light in the wethers, resting on a shoulder a little retiring and spreading, and so rounded below, as to sink all appearance of its pinion in the body of the animal; open bosom, with a deep chest or keel preceding and between its legs; small and tapering below the knee, fine at and above the joint, and where the arm begins to increase, it becomes suddenly lost in the shoulder; line of the back straight from the wethers to the rump, lying completely on a level with the pin or huckles, which lie wide and open; the hind quarters seated high with flesh, leaving a fine hair-ham tapering from the hock to the fetlock; long from rump to huckle, and from the pinion of the shoulder to the end of the nose; thin loose skin, covered with hair of a soft and furry nature, inclined to curl whenever the animal is in good condition and in full coat, when it also becomes mottled with darker shades of its permanent colour, which is that of a bright blood red, without white or other spots,

parti-

particularly on the male; a white udder is sometimes passed over, but seldom without objection.

This description may be considered as a summary of the perfections, as to the exterior appearance of the animal: what, under the same head, in the judgment of the Surveyor, may be regarded as defects, appear first in the sudden retiring of the vamp from behind the huckle to a narrow point backwards; the great space between the huckle and first rib; the smallness of the angle inwards, at which the ribs appear to be projected from the spine or back-bone, often giving the appearance of a flat-sided animal, and in its being so much tucked up in the girth, as to show an awkward cavity between the keel and navel, the line of which, it is presumed, should always be found to hold a position as nearly as possible, parallel with that of the back from the wethers to the loin. This animal, however, is generally well grown, and filled up behind the shoulder.

In the choice of a bull, attention should be paid to these particulars, but his neck ought never to be objected to, however thick or high it may rise upon the crest, provided it ends in fine unfleshed vertebres at their insertion with the head. At the Right Hon. Earl Fortescue's; Sir Bourchier Wrey's; —— Ackland's, Esq. of High Bray; the Rev. Mr. Quarterly's, of Molland; Mr. Stoneman's, of Woodhouse, near Torrington; Mr Nickoll's, of Heanton-Court house; Mr. George Burdon's, of Harwood; and at many other gentlemen and respectable farmers in the district of North Devon, the most beautiful specimens of this justly esteemed animal are always to be met with. (*Plate* XV.)

The general temperature of the climate, the peculiar herbage of the country, and above all, the amplitude of living streams, may in a great measure be stated as the

cause

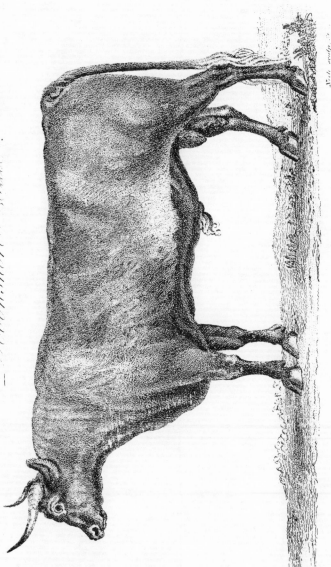

Plate XV. P.328.

Devonshire Bull.

Neele sculp.

cause of that striking peculiarity of form and colour, so faithfully indicative of other excellencies observable in the cattle of this district; but which, in the opinion of some old and well-informed men, have not kept pace in improvement with the great pains which of late years have been bestowed in selecting the most perfect of the kind for the purposes of breeding.

To account for this fact, the following reasons are with all submission stated: first, the great demand which has been made for these cattle from other parts of England, where the purchasers would spare neither pains or price to obtain those of the highest proof and beauty; and, secondly, the reason which was before hinted, viz. the slow and gradual, but certain and inevitable, destruction of a large portion of the natural herbage of the country, by that indiscriminate, and ever to be lamented practice of paring and burning the soundest, driest, and best winter lays in the country.

The usual practice in this district, is to sell the steers, at four or five years old, to the graziers in the county of Somerset, who feed them for a supply to the Bath, Bristol, and London markets. Very few in the proportion raised, are fed in the district, which may in a great measure be ascribed to the great indifference hitherto manifested in the culture of green food for a winter supply; and for which, indeed, a sufficient reason may be drawn, from the deplorably wet state in which the lands are suffered to remain from the want of draining. Some experiments, however, have lately been made by Lord Fortescue, and other spirited improving gentlemen in the district, to stall-feed oxen on potatoes and hay; but none of these trials have hitherto been attended to sufficiently in detail, to draw any certain or satisfactory conclusions from them. The same gentlemen have also adopted the

practice

practice of soiling with tares and clover, their working-oxen, and even store-cattle, in stalls and yards, constructed expressly for the purpose; and as water is always sufficiently at command, this species of management may be expected to come into more general use on a future day.

A distemper called the scour, attaching on yearlings, two years old steers, and heifers, is the only one of a serious cast to which the cattle of this district appear to be particularly liable. A specific has lately been issued by subscription against this disease; and in the cases occurring within the limits of the Survey, has seldom failed in producing the desired effect.

It has been already noticed, that the steers of the district are always worked as far as occasion may require. Their labour begins at two years old, when they are broke in and worked gently for the ensuing twelvemonth; from three to four, but more frequently to the ages of five or six, they are put to all the ordinary labours of the yoke; and their day's work at plough or harrow, is usually performed in a journey of about eight hours, during which time the plough-boy has a peculiar mode of cheering them on, with a song he continually chaunts in low notes, suddenly broken, and raising a whole octave. The ceasing of the song is said to occasion the stopping of the team, which is either followed by a man holding the plough, or as occasion may require, in attending the drag or harrows. (*Plate* XVI.)

The only comparison to be made between this valuable animal and horses, for labour, is to state the general acknowledgment of the farmers in the district, who unite in opinion, that on a fair and moderate computation, an ox-team, from the age of three to five years, will increase in its value one shilling per head weekly.

In

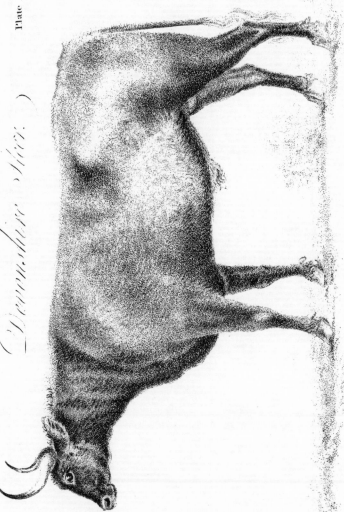

Plate XVI.385.

Devonshire Steer.

In the summer season, these patient animals are taught to forage for themselves in the coarse pastures; and in winter they have much the same range, with access to the straw-yard for fodder and for lodging; here they remain for the night, when the condition of the straw-yard is such as not to force them to leave it in search of a more comfortable and drier place.

DISTRICT II.

The cattle above described, as being peculiar to the district of North Devon, are found to be those held in the highest estimation through this district, where equal attention is paid to the selection of those that are held of the highest proof for breeding. And among those gentlemen and farmers who are careful to preserve a genuine unadulterated breed, little difference will be found between these cattle, and those before mentioned.

In some parts of the district, particularly on its eastern side, the March calf is reckoned the best, and attended with the least expense in raising. The cow is suffered to be the nurse for a fortnight or three weeks; after which the calf is suckled twice a day by hand, with two quarts of new milk and one quart of scalded skimmed milk, mixed with one quart of gruel made with flax-seed, boiled for four hours with so much water as is equal to six times the measure of the seed. This treatment is continued for about three weeks after the calf is taken from the cow; when the new milk is taken off, and the calf is fed twice a day with two quarts of scalded skimmed milk, mixed with an equal quantity of flax-seed gruel, and continued till about the beginning of June; by which time calves dropped thus early, will be able to go on very well with

with grass and a few oats, which they should previously
have been accustomed to eat in the pen.

These calves are broke into the yoke from two to three
years old, and are kept working till they are five, during
which time they are usually supposed to increase in their
value at the rate of 50s. per head.   Annually, at this age,
when not sold out of the county, they are put to good
keeping at home, when by summering them on the top
of the prime pastures, they will attain in weight from
ten and a half to eleven and a half score per quarter.

There are but few dairies in this district: those that
are lett to dairy-men, commonly pay from nine guineas to
10l. per cow ; the produce of which, for the first twenty-
two weeks after calving, is stated at six pounds and a half
of butter per week ; and the remainder of the period,
taken at twenty weeks more, one-third of a pound daily,
making in the whole, for the ordinary time the cow is in
milk, about 190 pounds of butter per cow.

A number of cows and small bullocks were fed last
winter in the parish of Hartland, the average weight of
which, when fat, was eight score per quarter.   On the
same farm a number of sheep were also fed in like manner, averaging about 20lbs. per quarter.   The quantity
of turnips consumed, tops and tails included, was 2cwt.
daily per cow, with as much barley-straw as they chose
to eat.   The turnips consumed were in a proportion of
six sheep to one cow.

This account was regularly kept for about twenty-one
weeks, by which time both cows and sheep were ready
for market.   Hence it appears, that the same quantity of
green food (for the sheep could not be induced to eat
either hay or straw during that period), required for the
sustenance and production of 640lbs. of beef, only
yielded 480lbs. of mutton ; a fact deserving particular
notice,

notice, especially when found to differ so materially from former opinions, stating that fattening sheep would not require more than one-fourth of their mutton weight in green food per day, whilst oxen would consume one-third of their beef weight of the same food in an equal time. The experiment strongly corroborates the latter opinion, but it goes wide of the former one, as that calls for 888 lbs. of mutton, instead of the 480 above stated.

Attempts have frequently been made in the eastern parts of this district to graze oxen from 13 to 14 score per quarter; but they have seldom failed to disappoint the expectations of the grazier.

A mortification called the quarter-evil, seizing upon one of the hind quarters of the calf, between nine and ten months old, is sometimes experienced in the Bampton and Tiverton country. The cow-doctors attempt to prevent its fatal issue, by giving drinks, and inserting a seton in the breast of the animal; but hitherto no great benefits have been found to result from this treatment, as the disease once appearing, it shortly terminates in the death of the animal.

DISTRICT III.

The goodness of the water in the country north-east of Barnstable, is supposed to have much contributed to the improvement of the native breed of cattle in that district: south of which, and through this country, the cows become big-bellied, appear less compact, and more loosely put together. The food upon the western moors, save in the absence of the sweet-scented vernal grass, appears, in its native state, to be much the same, and equally good in both districts; still an essential difference is found in their native breed of cow cattle. Many very good breeders

are,

are, however, met with in this district, and who in the choice of a calf describe the following character—fine bone, thick loin, and full muscle above its hams and knees, straight back with the pen or huckle lying rather below the level of the spine, which should be carried straight from the point of the withers to the insertion of the tail with the rump. When there is a scarcity of milk, barley-meal gruel is given to the calves as a substitute. The cows are supposed to yield purer milk when exposed to the air, and as such, are seldom housed but during the very severe weather in winter. The work oxen are housed from November till May, when they are turned out for the summer pasture. Their winter food generally consists of oat-straw.

DISTRICT IV.

In this district we find a mixture of the North Devon, with a larger animal of the same kind, called the Old Marlborough Red. This breed is said to have originated from the South Molton stock, although at this time they differ very materially from them in size, and in having a dirty brown, or rather blackish colour at the ears, nose, and encircling the eyes, and in all such parts as the orange line prevails in the genuine North Devon breed. A cross with this breed is however much preferred, as it produces a greater aptitude to fatten in a given time, than is experienced in the South Ham stock, which in all its points is a much coarser animal, and produces a greater offal. There does not appear to be any particular choice with regard to colour in this breed.

The ox at six years old will average about 13 score per quarter; is equally gentle in harness, although, perhaps, not quite so hardy in the performance of its labour, which
is

is generally done in two journies, from about seven to eleven, and from one to between five and six in the evening. The interval between each journey is employed in refreshing them with mown tares or grass in the house. Two of these oxen are frequently seen cross-ploughing and skirting the old lays; upon strong tough land, four and sometimes six are seen yoked together. For the bucket, the old South Ham breed are much preferred to the North Devon when in the same pasture: whether cows or steers, they are never found in the same condition as the South Molton breed; great pains, however, are used in every part of the district to procure this mixture, as it is found very much to promote the feeding of the South Ham ox, and to make it prove and tallow better on its inside. The pasturage of a cow per week, in the neighbourhood of Plymouth is 5s.

Some years ago a cow of the Somersetshire breed, belonging to Mr. Tozier, in the parish of Ashburton, produced, soon after calving, 3 lbs. 1 ounce of butter daily, and which is represented to have continued for some time; the cow was fed upon grass, with about a quarter of a peck of barley, mixed with a peck of grains, morning and evening. The milk was not large in quantity, and the cow grazed in an upland pasture.

The same gentleman remarks of another cow, which was of the South Ham breed, that yielded 24 quarts of milk per day, and from which was gathered two pounds and a half of butter. This produce was also continued for some time, but the precise period in either case was not particularly noticed. The weight of the first cow, if fattened to her bone, was estimated at eight score per quarter; the last, eight score and a half per quarter. A South Ham cow of Mr. Fabian's, after her third calf, fed entirely on grass, yielded 22 quarts of milk daily, and from

from which 44 ounces of butter were made. The length
of time this continued is not stated, but it is remembered with regret, that the cow went very soon off from
yielding this produce.

DISTRICT V.

No specific breed of cattle are seen here, although the
North Devon are by far the most numerous, very few of
which can be, with convenience, or are worked, on the
sides of the steep hills in this district.

DISTRICT VI.

A considerable variety of cattle are found in the different parts of this district, and corresponding with the prevailing breeds in the surrounding country. The favourite, however, is certainly the North Devon, which are
here raised, worked, and depastured in the manner before
noticed. The most perfectly formed bull of this variety,
which came within the view of the Surveyor, during his
progress through the county, was met with at Mr. Richard
Reynolds's, at Shosbrook near Crediton. This animal is
now five years old. The girth of its fore leg, below the
knee, seven inches, with a regular but not sudden swell
in the muscles of the arm above, and which has a flattened
form, like that in the arm of a horse. The ordinary distance between the inside claws of the fore-feet when the
animal appears to stand easy, is 13 inches, and opening
the bosom to the same width to the breast or keel, which
is 16 inches from the ground. The bone is proportionably fine behind, the muscles finely swelling into the
thigh, at a good distance above a firm, strong, but delicate
hare-like ham; pin or huckle on a level with the back,
and forming one regular line with the withers; the shoulder

der well filled up behind, and its pinion lying well into the body of the animal, seems when in motion to protrude and push forward whirls of fat and flesh before it. Its head well set on, and united to the neck with fine vertebres; skin loose, free, and velvety to the touch, mottled with reddish-brown spots on a lighter red colour. The defects in the form of this otherwise complete animal, are perhaps not to be remedied in this peculiar variety, and are such as have been already noticed. The weight of this bull, in the opinion of good judges, is 13 score per quarter.

DISTRICT VII.

Although a cross between the native cow of this district and the South-Molton breed, is much approved of, still the genuine North Devon breed preserves a very great ascendancy. Why they are not so commonly worked here, is said to be owing to the strong flinty soil proving hurtful to their unshod feet, an omission, there is but too much reason to notice in other parts of the county. Whenever this operation is performed, the steer is shackled and thrown down by the smiths, and the shoeing accomplished in an hour. The two inside claws behind are not shod ; the shoeing on the other six claws will last several months, provided the animal has not much road-work to perform. Price of shoeing from eighteen to twenty-pence per ox. Three yoke of oxen are equal to the heaviest tillage-labour required in any part of the county ; two yoke supply the place of three horses, but a large proportion of the common labour of the field is performed with one pair only.

A flux or scowering is the complaint to which these animals are by far the most liable ; but this is not stated generally to produce very serious consequences.

SECT. II.—SHEEP.

DISTRICT I.

THE native sheep of this district is the Exmoor *(Plate* XVII); a horned animal, with a moderately-long staple of wool, which heretofore, and before the cloth manufacture fled from this county into Yorkshire, was much used by the clothiers of North and South Molton, Cullumpton, Thorverton, Tiverton, and other places in the county. The fattened wethers of this breed, at three years old, will usually weigh about 15 lbs. per quarter, and average four pounds and a half of washed wool to the fleece ; worth at present about thirteen-pence per pound. Some attempts are making at Molland Bouceaux to improve the wool of this breed by a cross with the Spanish Merino ram, and the result of such trials are thus related :

	lb.	s.	d.		s.	d.
Quantity and value of native fleece	4½	at 1	1 per lb.		4	10½
First cross with the Merino	5	at 2	2 per lb.		10	10
Second cross on this produce	5	at 2	9 per lb.		13	9
Third ditto on ditto......................	5	at 3	5 per lb.		17	1

In which improvement of the fleece, the carcass is stated to be rather advanced than otherwise. The Merino, on the Herefordshire or Ryland, has also been tried in other parts of the district, and with appearance of probable success. The three-year old wethers of this cross, when fattened to their frame, being estimated to run from 14 to 16 lbs. per quarter, and to throw off from three pound and a quarter to four pounds of washed wool per fleece. From experiments made in this cross by the Rev. Mr. Coffin, of West Down, it appears that two-year old wethers

of

Plate XVII. P. 338.

Exmoor Sheep.

Scote sculp Strand.

of the first cross will weigh about 15lbs. per quarter, and shear from six pounds and a half to seven pounds of wool in the yoak per fleece, price 2 s. 9 d. per lb.

This breed, both crossed and full Merino, are found very obnoxious to the foot-rot, the best remedy for which is to pare the foot close, wash it clean, and anoint it with the oil of vitriol, or any other strong caustic matter. The wet lay of the pastures is supposed to contribute greatly to the production of this complaint; in other respects they appear to resist the storms of the country equal to the native sheep. A little hay is found to relieve, if not entirely to prevent the scour. This cross makes a very compact animal; the native defects in the form of the Merino, appearing to be very much if not entirely absorbed in the more pleasing symmetry of the Ryland.

A cross was some years since made at Chittlehampton, of the old Leicester upon the Exmoor. The wethers of this produce, at three years old average about 24lbs. per quarter, and carry six pounds and a half of yoak wool to the fleece. The Exmoor has also been crossed at Heanton, with the new Leicester; the wether produce of which, at two years old, will weigh 18lbs. per quarter, and yield 6lbs. of unwashed wool to the fleece. Price of the two latter, nine-pence per lb. A considerable loss is often sustained in this last cross at the time of yeaning, when from the extraordinary size of the shoulders of the lamb, the ewes are often found somewhat incapable of excluding it. This, however, will not continue as an evil on the offspring of this produce.

Several neat parcels of South Down sheep were met with in the district; but until attention is more generally paid to relieve the soil of that excess of water, with which the whole surface of the country is overcharged after the autumnal rains and during winter, it will be in vain to
expect

expect that any advantage can be derived from the introduction of an animal whose chief excellencies proceed from a sound and dry, though an exposed but wholesome layer.

Upon the whole, from this general state of the lands during winter, those of the common Exmoor are preferred, not more for their superior hardiness in sustaining the penetrating chill of the wet ground in their infant state, than in being so much better calculated to work for their living afterwards. To the general wetness of the land, may also in a great measure be attributed the unwillingness of the farmers to fold their sheep in the enclosures at night, when in the day-time they have been depasturing on the moors and other outland commons.

The food of the sheep in winter, as well as during the summer season, consists in what they can pick up in ranging over these coarse grounds, with the exception of affording them a little hay during the severity of winter, and a small portion of turnips, that are sometimes cultivated, but which from the wetness of the land, are often prevented from being resorted to when most wanted. The water-meadows, as before noticed, furnish the most staple supply to the ewes and lambs, and from which they are generally removed to take the first shoot of the artificial grasses. Some sheep yards have been constructed by the gentlemen before alluded to, for sheltering their sheep, preserving their dung, and remedying the evils arising from the wetness of the land; but the habits of that animal being naturally opposed to confinement, must sooner or later point out the necessity of encouraging a proper growth of hedge-row wood, for shelter on the mounds, forming the outside and division fences of the enclosures, and above all, in a more general attention to the proper draining of the lands.

It

It may be worthy of remark in this place, that among all the inconveniences in point of food and lodging, to which the general sheep stock of this district are exposed throughout the year, the caw or rot is a disease very seldom heard of among them. The foot-rot, however, is said to be particularly predominant in some situations, and found to attach more generally on the new Leicester than any other breed.

A circumstance was mentioned in the course of the Survey, on this subject, and which may not altogether prove useless by being noticed in this place. Some years ago a lot of sheep were purchased by two gentlemen at a distant fair, and driven to Bishop's Tawton to be divided equally between them; they were bred by the person on the same land from whom they were bought, and the partition being made by the alternate choice of the purchasers, those that were designed for the demesne at Tawton, were immediately turned out, and the remaining moiety driven to the estate of the other purchaser, where for the first few days they depastured in a hayfield, recently covered with a full dressing of caustic lime, and were only put there to answer a point of convenience, and to eat the grass that was growing on the unlimed borders and near the hedge-rows in the field. It was afterwards found that the moiety of this lot of sheep left at Tawton, occasioned much trouble and perplexity on account of the foot-rot, whereas the other part, during the whole time of their feeding, was not in the slightest manner affected with the disease. Hence it is plain, that the foot-rot is a disease originating in particular situations, or, that in an early and certain stage of its progress, it will meet with an unfailing specific in caustic lime.

DISTRICT II.

The same variety of sheep are found in this district as
have already been described in the country of North
Devon. The greater number, however, are the natives of
those extensive moors which afford the sources of the
Exe, the Dart, the Taw, and the Torridge rivers. The
sheep most approved in the division of Tiverton, are the
Bampton Notts *(Plate* XVIII.*)*; the wethers of which
breed, at 20 months old, will weigh 22 lbs. per quarter,
and shear six pounds and a half of wool to the fleece;
the same sheep, well wintered, and kept on for another
twelvemonth, will average 28 lbs. per quarter, and yield
8 lbs. of unwashed wool to the fleece. The present price
of this wool is about 1*s.* per lb. The first cross of this breed
with the new Leicester is growing greatly in esteem, from
its improving the form, and bringing the animal three
months sooner to market; but however desirable this
cross so far may be, more of that blood (allowing all their
excellencies) is generally objected to on account of the
extraordinary nursing and care required to be paid to the
young couples; the lambs being represented as very tender, and much oftener perishing through the severity of
the season than the genuine offspring of the native sheep.
Notwithstanding these objections, the Rev. Mr. Coham,
of Coham-house, Black Torrington, has the genuine new
Leicester, which upon his sound lands on the borders of
the Torridge, he thinks likely to answer extremely well.
This gentleman has also tried the Merino on the Ryland,
the wethers of which, at two years old, will weigh 15 lbs.
per quarter, and produce a fleece of 5 lbs. each, worth
3*s.* per lb.

A cross

Plate XVIII. P. 342.

Bampton Sheep.

A cross of the new Leicester with the Bampton Nott, is much approved through Buckland, Filleigh, and Petrockstow, particularly if carried to the fourth degree, or in other words, four parts Leicester to one part native Nott. This cross comes earlier to market, and at two years old will generally average 20 lbs. per quarter, and eight pounds of yoak wool to the fleece, worth about 10*d*. per lb.

In the trial which Lord Clifford has made between the new Leicester and South Down, his Lordship has too much reason to be satisfied without pursuing the experiment farther. It must however be observed, that the sheep pastures at Ugbrook are remarkably dry, sound, and wholesome throughout the year. Some trials have been made in the neighbourhood of Morbath, to establish a cross between the Ryland and the Merino; these have clearly succeeded as to the fleece, as the third cross of this breed readily sells for 3*s*. 6*d*. per lb. but many object to it on account of its not producing an equal acreable proportion of mutton with the native sheep.

The goggles is a disease sometimes, though rarely, experienced on the confines of Somerset and Dorset; its symptoms are discoverable in the morning, when the animal first rises from the ground, by an evident weakness and difficulty in raising its hind quarters (and which in all ruminating animals are the first that are lifted from the ground). This continues for some time getting worse and worse, until the animal can move its hind parts no longer; it then lies prostrate on the earth, but looking constantly backwards, and making continual efforts to reach back, and bite and nab the wool towards the loin, and where there is evidently seated a most excruciating pain. In this condition the animal very soon expires. No remedy or means of prevention have as yet been suggested to avert this deplorable malady.

In

In the parish of Cheriton-Fitzpaine, the rot is very apt
to be communicated to the sheep after depasturing upon
the low grounds subject to the wash and partial overflowings from the higher tillage lands. An instance once
occurred in the parish, of a farmer turning 110 ewes
upon a lay field in preparation to be sown with wheat,
that had recently been dressed with a mixing of lime,
hedge-row and other mould. The grass grew luxuriantly
after this dressing, but every ewe was dead by the Candlemas following, being all cawed or rotted with innumerable flukes found in the liver of every one of
them. The other sheep upon the farm, which had been
raised, and in every other respect treated in the same
manner, save in depasturing with these 110 ewes, were
free from the most remote symptoms of this disease.
Watering grounds early in the autumn or fall of
the year, and immediately turning sheep upon them,
has been found uniformly fatal in producing the same
disease.

DISTRICT III.

The sheep generally depastured on this district are
the Exmoor, Dartmoor, and the light hardy breed of
the lower moors and commons in the country. The autumnal rains frequently inundating the cold clay lands,
are very apt to occasion the caw or rot among them, and
which has been sometimes experienced to an alarming
extent. They subsist in the manner before described, on
what they can gather from these coarse sheep-walks, and
at the time of yeaning only, the ewes are brought into
the enclosures, and where, as long as grass can be spared
for the purpose, lambs are raised and fattened for a supply
to the Plymouth market. A Dartmoor or Exmoor ewe
under

under this trial of indulgence, and which in November would cost about 18s. will by the June following produce a lamb worth 20s. and much superior to the lamb under the like circumstances produced from and nursed by the Bampton Nott ewe, and which at the same time would have cost 40s.

From the number of sheep annually summered upon Dartmoor and Exmoor forests, the ewes and lambs of which are always brought down into the country on the approach of winter, it will readily be supposed, that a large proportion of sheep stock is always found to occupy the surrounding districts during the winter season. The greater part of these flocks, however, being wethers, and chiefly preserved for their wool, are left upon the forests during winter. These mostly belong to persons residing in various parts of the country, and are often changing their owners, by which it should seem that the flocks, and not the proprietors, possess the right of depasturage on the forests. This right, doubtless originated with a tenancy in Venville, and a flock of any number growing upon such a right, seems to continue, and their owners to possess it exclusively, as their attendants on every occasion never cease to dog off, and chace from the respective sheep-walks, be their numbers or the extent of the assumed district what it may.

As the wool of these sheep appears to be the leading object with all the flock-masters of the forests, the wethers, as before observed, are commonly left to winter upon them, during which season, as may reasonably be expected, considerable losses are sustained. The broken-mouthed sheep are culled out at shearing time, at which period these old sheep are usually in very good condition, when they are either fattened at home, or disposed of for that purpose.

The

The Dartmoor wether *(Plate* XIX.*)* at five years old will average about 16 lbs. and the Exmoor at the same age about 15 lbs. per quarter, and produce from four pounds and a half to six pounds and a half of unwashed wool to the fleece. The ewes and lambs, with the preceding year's hog sheep, are brought down from the forests in the beginning of November; in some cases the lambs are not returned with the ewes to the forests after shearing, but weaned at home in the enclosures, and upon the lower moors and commons in the country

It is no less strange than true, that the caw, or rot, has never yet been traced to have originated with sheep constantly depasturing upon either of these forests. This, however, is not the case with the scab, which is found to be very common among them, but which may easily be prevented, seeing that the sheep-walks are so very distinct and separate from each other. When the winter sets in, with a prospect of continuing more than ordinarily severe, the wether flocks are removed from these heights to the lower country of Devonshire, Somerset, and Cornwall; on which occasions, the utmost care is taken in keeping them from feeding upon such low grounds as may have been inundated by the autumnal rains, and where there would be an absolute certainty of their taking the rot; the dread of which very often occasions an equally cruel exposure of these animals upon the forests through the winter.

The usual consideration paid to those who rent the different quarters of the forest of Dartmoor directly from His Royal Highness the Prince of Wales, is 3 s. 4 d. per score, annually; a sum considered sufficient to exempt them from all liability of having their sheep impounded or taken up as estrays. The number of sheep thus summered and kept the year round upon the forest of Dart-

moor,

Plate XIX. P. 346.

Dartmoor Sheep.

Neele sculp. Strand

moor, the depasturable parts of which, in a dry summer, is one of the best sheep-walks in the kingdom, is not easy to ascertain ; but if any inference can be drawn from the returns made from Widdecombe and Buckland in the Moor, their numbers must necessarily be very considerable indeed. A dry summer (as just observed), is always the most favourable for these sheep-walks. These afforded in the months of August and September last, flocks more numerous, and in much higher condition, than has ever been observed by the Surveyor in any other part of England, when such have not been aided by access to the enclosures or artificial food. Yet the grass of the sheep-walks upon the forest of Dartmoor, in the beginning of November was scarcely half consumed.

DISTRICT IV.

The Old Devonshire dim-faced nott sheep, was formerly held in high estimation, as the native produce of this district : it is a crooked-backed, flat-sided, coarsely boned and woolled animal, but has been much improved by a cross with the new Leicester; its principal defects are thus cured, and a greater disposition has been added to fatten at an earlier period; at the same time the fleece, as well as the weight of the carcass, has been diminished, the former from ten to 8lbs. of unwashed wool per fleece, and the latter from 22 to 19lbs. per quarter. To balance this deficiency, the animal comes to market four months sooner; the wethers at two years old, with advantage; that is, after being twice shorn as sheep, and once as lamb, equals the average above stated. This issue once more crossed with the new Leicester, will arrive still earlier to the same perfection.

In many parts of this district, a disease among the
wether

wether lambs appears to a greater or less extent every
year; it is first indicated by seeing the lamb apart from
its companions, when, on examination, a swelling is observed near the loins, and is found to proceed from a
stranguary, or an obstruction, formed at the end of the
penis, to the passing of the water, and producing such an
accumulation, as either to occasion a rupture in the blad-
der, or an absorption of urine into the body of the animal, which becoming putrid, the lamb dies within a short
time after the swelling begins. Upon the lamb being
first noticed to retire from the flock, his penis has been
examined, which being severed behind the wart or nob
(by this time assuming a yellow appearance), the urine has
flowed freely, and the animal has recovered. Ewe lambs
are sometimes, but rarely, affected with a similar disease,
in which cases it never fails in proving fatal to them.
The cause of this malady is by some ascribed to the
lambs depasturing upon the barley stubbles, when laid
down with clover and ray grass.

DISTRICT V.

The Dartmoor breed, in the higher parts, with some
Leicester and Dorset in the vallies of this district, are
those most commonly met with. The reason stated for
this variety is, that the Dartmoor, being at home, are
more inured to the climate, are good nurses, and although
they do not feed so quick, when put to good keeping, as
the new Leicester, still, when fat, they always prove the
very best of mutton, and never fail commanding a superior price. The new Leicester are preferred for their
well-known and established excellencies, not regarding
the diminution of fleece, their liability to the foot-rot,
or that of being bad nurses and losing many of their lambs,
as countervailing objections. The Dorset are preferred,
                                                    without

without their owners assigning any other reason than that
they like them best.

DISTRICT VI.

The same observation as before made, respecting the
variety of cow-cattle in this district, will equally apply to
that of sheep; many exceptions will, however, be found
to what may be considered the favourite sheep-stock of
the farmer. The thorough-bred new Leicester at Haldon,
appears to be doing extremely well. The old Leicester
cross upon the Bampton, makes a large and handsome
animal, feeding kindly, and tallowing well within. The
wethers of two years old, with advantage, will average
30lbs. per quarter, and shear 10lbs. of yoak wool per
fleece. The new Leicester cross upon the same sheep,
will bring forward wethers at 20 months old weighing
22lbs. per quarter, with a shear of 8lbs. of yoak wool
per fleece, both of which are at this time worth 10d. per lb.
weighing, according to the custom of unwashed wool,
21lbs. for every score. Mr. Sillifant, of Combe, appears
to have succeeded in his cross of the new Leicester on the
Cotswold, the equal blood of which he endeavours to
preserve as much as possible. These wethers, at eighteen
months, will average 19lbs. per quarter, and 7lbs. of unwashed wool per fleece. When kept on for another
twelvemonth, the age at which they are most generally
slaughtered, this cross will attain the size of 25lbs. per
quarter, and yield 9lbs. of wool to the fleece. This wool
is allowed by the staplers, to be one penny per pound superior to that of the Exmoor, Bampton, South Devon,
and Dartmoor sheep; still the common price of 10d.
per lb is only allowed for it. In the young wethers of
this breed, the loose fat is stated to be 9lbs. with near or
kidney fat 3lbs. on each side. The larger wethers are said to
produce 13lbs. of rough fat, and kidney fat 4lbs. per side.

Mr.

Mr. Wreyford, of Clannaborough, has confined his sheep-stock for many years closely to the new Leicester, and which he runs about five to the acre. His lambs fall about the 25th of March, are shorn the June following (being previously weaned), and yield about one pound and a half per lamb. All his male lambs remain uncut until October, at which time he is enabled to make such a selection, and which usually consists of about one-fifth part of the male lambs, as seldom disappoints him in their issue. He does not think that so late a castration materially affects the growth of the animal, seeing that it had met with no check from the operation at a more tender age. These wethers, at 18 months, weigh 22 lbs. per quarter, and will yield 7 lbs. of wool each, at the average price of 10 d. per lb. Their rough fat is stated at 10 lbs. with near or kidney fat 4 lbs. on each side.

Mr. Sweet, of North Tawton, prefers the new Leicester, with which he has stocked for some years; his ordinary stint is about 160, ninety of which are supposed, annually, to lamb, which makes his sheep-stock, between April and the middle of August, amount to about 250 head; besides these, he has four cows, with a proportionable number of horses for his arable land, where he cultivates annually about ten acres of turnips, and which, with his 65 acres of grass-land, enables him to carry his young sheep through the winter, in such a state of forwardness as to sell his wethers at eighteen months old, averaging 20 lbs. per quarter, and yielding 6 lbs. of unwashed wool to the fleece. A cross of this breed, with about half Bampton, is conceived to agree better with the soil and circumstances of the country. This animal is unquestionably hardier than the new Leicester; but by the introduction of the latter blood, the Bampton comes sooner to market, and at 20 months will weigh 24 lbs. per quarter, and 7 lbs. of wool to the fleece.

DISTRICT VII,

With very little exception, the Dorset seems to be the prevailing sheep, at least among the generality of farmers in this district. These are found to depasture upon the Black Down hills, the heights of Farway, North and South Leigh, Sidbury, Harpford, and all along the commons and high grounds bordering upon Dorsetshire.

In the rich valley of the Axe, and through all the finer pastures in the district, the same varieties occur as have been already noticed. The South Down breed have been tried on a small scale, but, after a few years, their frame becomes much enlarged, and they throw off a much stronger and coarser fleece than when first brought into the country. Here the practice of washing the sheep, previously to shearing, begins generally to prevail. This has been, at length, suggested by the difference in the price which the wool-buyers make between wool in the yoak and washed wool, it being no less than 50 per cent. even in the Dorset wool; and although it is not so much, yet it is greatly more than proportionable in the coarser fleeces, besides the over-weight of 5 per cent. before mentioned. The fat wethers of the Dorset sheep, at two years old, with advantage from the time of being lambed till just before harvest, will average about 18 lbs. per quarter, and 5 lbs. of washed wool to the fleece. This wool in the yoak, seldom sells for more than 1 s. per pound; whereas, when washed, it as usually commands 1 s 6 d. The weight of a fleece in the yoak, is to the same fleece when washed, as six and three-quarters to five; and the consequent value is as 6 s. 9 d. to 7 s. 6 d. per fleece. This has, at length, been made evident to the farmers, who now willingly agree, that it is advantageous to wash short-woolled sheep before shearing, but to sell the long and coarse stapled fleeces in the yoak. A

rule

rule is stated to be in use among the sheep-graziers in the county, for ascertaining the proportion of mutton from the live weight of the sheep. This is done by multiplying the live weight by five, and dividing by nine: should the sheep be very fat, divide by eight. In general, eight—five may be about the mark. The result of the preceding details on this subject, will, when collected together, appear to be as follows:

Character.	Age of wethers when slain, in months.	Average weight per quarter, in pounds.	Average weight per fleece, in pounds.	Condition of fleece.	Price of fleece per pound.	Value of fleece.	Rough fat, in pounds.	Kidney fat, in pounds.	Total. inside fat.
					s. d.	s. d.			
Native.									
Exmoor, horned, white legs and face, with a moderately long staple of wool, pure - - -	30	15	7	yoak	0 10	5 10	7	5	12
Dartmoor, ditto, ditto - -	30	16	8	ditto	0 10	6 8	8½	6	14*
South Devon Nott, with brown face and legs, long wool, pure -	30	22	10	ditto	0 10	8 4			
Bampton Nott, white face and legs, short wool, pure - - -	20	22	6¼	ditto	0 10	5 5	10	7	17
	32	28	8	ditto	0 10	6 8			
Neighbour.									
Dorset, horned, white face and legs, short wool, pure -	24	18	5	washed	1 6	7 6			
Ditto, crossed with Exmoor - -	18	18	5½	ditto	1 4	7 3	9	6	15
Distant.									
South Down pure - - -	24	18	3	ditto	2 4	7 0			
Ditto, crossed with new Leicester									
Leicester, old, crossed with Bampton	24	30	10	yoak	0 10	8 4			
Ditto, do do. with Exmoor	36	24	6¼	ditto	0 10	5 5			
Ditto, new, pure - - -	18	22	6½	ditto	0 10	5 5¼			
Ditto, do. crossed with Dartmoor									
Ditto, do. do. with Exmoor	24	18	6	ditto	0 10	5 0			
Ditto, do. 4th do. with South Devon	20	20	8½	ditto	0 10	7 1			
Ditto, do. 1st do. with ditto -	18	18	6½	ditto	0 10	5 5			
Ditto, do. crossed with Bampton	20	24	8	ditto	0 10	6 8	13	8	21
Ditto, do. do. with Cotswold	18	19	7	ditto	0 10	5 10	9	7	16
Ditto, do. do. do.	30	25	9	ditto	0 10	7 6	13	8	21
Foreign.									
Merino, crossed with Ryland - -	24	15	6¾	ditto	2 9	18 6¾			
Ditto, do. do. -	24	15	5	ditto	3 0	15 0			
Ditto, first cross with Exmoor -			5	washed	2 2	10 0			
Ditto, second do. with do. -			5	ditto	2 9	13 9			
Ditto, third do. with do. -			5	ditto	3 5	17 1			

* The washed wool of all the long-coated sheep, is sold from 14d. to 15d. per pound.
† These sheep are not sent to the forests.
‡ In most cases of a cross with the new Leicester, upon long full-fleeced sheep, deficiency of wool is observable under the belly and breast of the animal.

SEC

SECT. III.——HORSES.

A SMALL snug breed of horses, between the pack and larger cart horses, are getting much in use in different parts of the county. The former are out to grass all summer, and generally wintered upon very coarse hay : so long as they are kept steadily at work, they are allowed about half a peck of oats per horse daily, but as the work abates their allowance of corn is lessened also. When the day's work is over, which is generally performed in one journey of eight or nine hours, in summer they are returned to the field; and in winter racked up with the sort of hay just noticed, or pea-straw, or, which is too commonly the case, turned into the straw-yard to take their chance with the horned cattle.

This treatment, though general in many parts of the county, is fortunately not without exception, as may be evinced from the regulations observed in the horse establishment at Ugbrook. There the pleasurable and sporting horses, as well as those devoted to the labours of the farm, are under a system of very different management, and that bottomed on genuine and consistent economy. Large quantities of fern are annually mown in the park, and neatly stacked up for use at a convenient distance from the stables. The horses are kept constantly littered winter and summer, with a bed of this fern or straw. In summer, tares, clover, or grass mown in the plantations, are given with regular stated feeds of dry meat, consisting of corn mixed with the chaff of wheat or barley, properly cleansed and sifted, or cut hay or straw. This example has had so good an effect in the neighbourhood, that few of Lord Clifford's tenants, and many others, perhaps not so likely to be influenced by his Lordship's recommenda-

DEVON.] tions,

tions, are at this time no less devoted to the considerate task of seeing their horses fed with short meat, and being well cleaned and attended after the labour of the day, than is Lord Clifford himself; hence the irresistible influence of perseverance and example on all laudable occasions.

In the less hilly parts of the county, where one and two horse carts are more commonly in use, a larger breed than those above noticed is preferred. These are generally racked up in the winter with white pea-straw, or clover hay, and with an ordinary allowance of from one quarter to half a peck of corn per day, may be thought to receive somewhat better usage than the common pack-horse.

In the neighbourhood of Axminster, waggons are becoming very general, and where some very good horse-teams were observed; but a species of carelessness was noticed in the neighbourhood of Honiton among the farm servants, which calls for the severest reprobation : this consisted in suffering the horses to depasture for several days, and even weeks together, with the collar upon their neck and shoulders. This insufferable indolence affords little reason to suppose that much attention is paid to the cleaning or dressing farm-horses, after the ordinary exertions and labours of the day.

SECTS. IV. AND V.——MULES AND ASSES.

THERE are several mules and asses constantly employed in the south and western parts of the county, in packing sand from the sea-side to the distance of several miles in the interior. Whatever may be the size of the horse or mule, by the side of which the patient ass is seen crippling

with

with his load, he does not appear to be less burthened, or even carrying a proportionable weight with either of them. However trifling the first cost of the ass may be, which rarely exceeds 25 or 30s. it is unquestionably a valuable animal. In summer, it chiefly subsists on the tops and seed-stems of thistles, and at all times collects its food from the way-side, in the fields, along the hedge-rows, and in such a manner as is scarcely possible to be felt as an expense by its owner. This animal lives to a considerable age, as is evident from the little mortality seen or heard of among the many used in these parts of the county.— The mule appears to be equally hardy, with more apparent strength and activity than the ass; many of these latter are also constantly employed in transporting sea-sand to the interior; and whenever a gang of this medley are met with, whether light or burthened, the mule always appears in much better condition, and far more lively and active than the horse. The common price of this animal is about 15l. the males of which are sometimes castrated. They are doubtless a very useful animal, of much activity, strength, and duration, and are very cheaply kept.

SECT. VI.—HOGS.

THE native hog of this country grows to a large size, stands high upon its legs, lengthy, of a large and coarse bone, flat-sided, and in its store state seldom seen in any thing like tolerable condition; but proper time being allowed, will commonly fat to six score per quarter. Some improvements have been made in this animal, by a cross with the Leicester boar, which has much spread, and given a roundness to its frame, with a proportionable depth of body;

body ; its legs have also been shortened, a finer bone produced, with a disposition to look much better when growing as a store, and to feed quicker and more kindly in the sty. By a farther cross with the Chinese breed, these crosses have considerably reduced its size, but the advantages accruing therefrom, are the constitution and habits of a profitable animal, weighing, when 18 months old, and fattened to its frame, from 16 to 20 score per hog.

The produce of the native hog, crossed with the Hampshire or Leicester, will, if fed in the following manner, double its weight in about 12 weeks : begin with about two-thirds of boiled or steamed potatoes, and one-third of pease and barley ground in equal quantities into meal, well mixed together. The mess must be seasoned and enriched with the meal, as the appetite of the animal may require, and when fat, he will be found to have consumed from 14 to 16 bushels of ground pease and barley. This breed again crossed with the Chinese, will fatten in two-thirds of the time, when it will be found to have nearly if not quite doubled its weight also.

The proportion of fat to lean, or in other words, of pork to bacon, in the above breeds, may be thus stated : the native country hog, when well fed, will produce for one pound of pork, one pound and a quarter of bacon. This, crossed with the Leicester or Hampshire breed, will produce for three-quarters of a pound of pork, one pound of bacon. This cross again varied by the Chinese, will in two-thirds of the time, produce for two-thirds of a pound of pork, one pound of bacon.

SECT. VII.——PIGEONS.

THE circumstances of this county afford but little farther to remark on the four following Sections of this Chapter. It appears by no means overstocked with dove-house
pigeons, but a few words on that subject may not appear
altogether unworthy the notice of some distant readers.
These birds often fly to a great distance for their food,
and when they can find corn to eat, seldom prey upon
any thing else. They begin to eat corn about the middle
of July, and rarely want the same food at the stacks, in
the straw-yards or in the fields, until the end of barley
sowing, which is about Old May-day, and which includes
a period of 280 days, or better than three-quarters of the
year; the rest of the 'ime they live upon the seeds of
weeds and bentings. It is somewhere stated, that in England and in Wales there are 20,000 dove-houses, averaging about 100 pair of old pigeons. We will take this estimate at three-fourths, which will equal 1,125,000 pair
of dove-house pigeons in England and Wales. These, to
speak moderately, will consume (with what they carry
home to their young) one pint of corn per pair daily, and
which for 140 days, being half the period they are supposed to subsist upon corn, amounts to 157,500,000 pints
of corn consumed annually, throughout England and Wales,
by these voracious and insatiate vermin, for in no other
light can they possibly be viewed or considered by the
Agriculturist. The amount and value of this consumption, when brought into bushels, and averaged at the present price of wheat, rye, barley, oats, beans and pease, and
assuming that an equal quantity of each corn is thus consumed (but which is far from being the case, as the wheat
is not only the most inviting, but by far the most exposed
to

to the ravages of these birds, both at seed-time and preceding harvest) will stand thus : 157,500,000 pints =
4,921,875 Winchester bushels, which at 6*s.* per bushel,
the present average price of the grain and pulse before
enumerated, amounts to 1,476,562*l.* 10*s.* value of the
agricultural produce of the country annually consumed in
this manner ;   a circumstance most respectfully submitted
to the consideration of the Honourable Board of Agriculture, in comparison with the true and natural value
of these birds, as a luxury for the table, their dung
for the use of dyers, or the purposes of manure.   To this
statement is to be added the irreparable injury they com-
mit in seed-time, picking up every grain of seed wherever
they alight, and the corn trod under and also beaten out
by their wings before harvest.

CHAP. XV.

RURAL ECONOMY.

———

SECT. I.——LABOUR.

IT has been remarked by Mr. Fraser, and the Author
of this Report most cordially agrees in the observation,
that there is an openness of heart and mildness of character in the inhabitants of Devonshire, which probably
is not to be excelled in any part of England. A general
urbanity of manners, and desire to please and meet the
wishes of the stranger, prevail among all classes of the
community, from the peer to the peasant; even in those
who compose the lower order of society, and among
whom we are to find both male and female servants.

Servants.——These are formed and instructed in a way
perhaps more prevalent in this county than in any other
of the United Kingdom. The Act of the 43d of Elizabeth, forms the basis for the education and the training which farmers' servants generally receive in this
county, and that in the state and condition of parish apprentices. Some difference of opinion was met with in
the course of the Survey, as to the general utility of this
system, but the reasons stated for its continuance appeared so much to outweigh what was urged against it, that
in the judgment of the Surveyor, he can neither withhold
his concurrence to the general principle, or forbear to
recommend its adoption in other parts of England. This
                                                    general

general assent, however, he wishes, with all submission, to accompany with the following observations.

The Act above mentioned, subjects the occupier of 10*l.* per annum to the receiving regularly in turn, a parish apprentice. The value of such an occupation at the time such an Act was passed, was justly considered commensurate with the liability to such a burthen; and although from the decreased value in the circulating medium since that period, the magistrates will rarely submit to the imposing of an apprentice where the occupation amounts to less than 20*l.* per annum; still in these days, and where there is often a house full of children to nurse and provide for, even this standard of liability seems to press too hard, and to require a farther extension.

The manner too in which the females are sometimes treated, requires that some farther regulations should be made to soften the severity of their servitude. Scraping the roads, lanes, and yards, turning over mixings and filling dung-pots, is at best but a waste of time, and a feeble effort of infantile strength. What can a female child at the age of ten or twelve years be expected to perform with a mattock or shovel? or how will she be able to poise, at the end of a dung-fork, any reasonable weight, so as to lift it into the dung-pots slung upon the horses' backs, for hacking out the manure to the distant parts of the farm? Even driving the horses after they are loaded, is by no means an employment proper for such girls, being altogether incompatible with the household and more domestic duties they ought early to be made acquainted with.

Nothing can fairly be urged against the treatment of the boys, whose instruction and services are rendered more suitable, and better understood : their morals are better cultivated and more strictly preserved than there
could

could be any reasonable chance of expecting from their remaining at home. Boys so trained and instructed, are uniformly found to make the best servants, and to prove the steadiest and best labourers afterwards; but the girls, too frequently, from an early dislike to their avocations, and in which they well know they are not hereafter to be continued, cannot well be supposed to have much emulation or desire to excel in them; hence premature connexions are formed, and which by marriage terminates their servitude, but without their having acquired in it those domestic qualifications upon which the comfort of a peasant family so essentially depend.

The general rule in hiring servants, is to engage them at Christmas, to come home the Lady-day following, and to continue in service until that time twelvemonth. The usual wages to the head man, or carter, is 10*l.* per annum, with board, washing, and lodging. The inferior departments of his establishment are often filled by parish apprentices.

LABOURERS.

The wages of the out-door labourer is 7*s.* per week, winter and summer, and from a quart to three pints of drink daily; even in hay-time and harvest, these wages are not increased, although the additional exertions at those seasons are amply compensated by board, and very extraordinary drinks and sittings over ale and cider. To these wages must be added the standing supply of bread-corn; of wheat at 6*s.* and barley at 3*s.* per bushel. About a score perches of dunged land is often supplied by the farmer to each peasant family, for the purpose of planting potatoes, at from 6*d.* to 8*d.* per perch. This proves a most valuable resource, as the labourer is thereby enabled

to

to keep a small pig, which is generally in good order for slaying about the latter end of winter, and when cured, furnishes a rare but comfortable indulgence in the course of the ensuing summer. In some parts of the county, particularly among the smaller occupiers, instead of 7 *s.* per week, the workman is content to receive 3 *s.* 6 *d.* with his maintenance.

It is no unusual practice in the northern and western parts of the county, for a labourer to enter the harvest-field for one day only for his drink and board; but with a proviso, that at the Christmas following he shall be invited to a harvest frolic at the farmer's house, and which at that season (as before observed) continues for several days together. This custom, for obvious reasons, has been nearly abolished in the South Hams, and in the country round Exeter. In the large trading towns and their vicinity, the price of labour increases with the demand, and the scarcity of hands there may occasionally be in such places. These people have frequently been observed to be more destitute of the permanent supplies and comforts of life, than the peasantry occupied in the cultivation of the land.

PRICE OF LABOUR.

The price of labour has certainly not kept pace with the depreciation in the value of money within the last 20 years. This, however, seems in a great measure compensated by the general custom of the country, in supplying the labourers with bread-corn below the market price. Add to this the accommodation received, and which is becoming still more general, of the labourer procuring potatoe ground from his employer, and the regular resources of subsistence

ence for the peasant family, will not appear very fairly to be questioned.

To prevent any abuse of the indulgence respecting the quantity of wheat or barley that may be issued to a peasant family of four or five in number, it is generally regulated to consist of two bushels of barley, or one of wheat, monthly.

The labourer occasionally employed, not resident, and having no benefit from potatoe ground, or corn at a reduced price, usually receives 1s. 4d. per day with drink.

Hours of Work, and stinted Labour performed for a Day's-Work.—The hours of work are from seven to twelve, and from one to between five and six. Even in summer when at day-work, the labourer is frequently seen on his way home with his tools upon his back thus early in the evening. This does not arise so much from absolute idleness, as the custom of the country, the day's work being generally admitted to consist of a certain stint or portion of labour; as per example: thrashing of as much wheat, the straw of which, when combed into reed, shall make five bundles of 28lbs. each; of barley, the straw of which shall make twelve bundles of 35lbs. each; of oats, the straw of which shall make 16 bundles of 40lbs. each. When working in the coppices or woodlands, having bands previously provided, or that they can be taken out of the stuff felled, the cutting and tieing of one hundred faggots is considered a day's work; but when bands are to be procured by the labourer, 90 faggots; when brushing or trimming up the hedge-rows, and that the bands are to be found by the labourer, 60 faggots; cutting and tieing furze in a brake, 100 faggots; but when the roots of the furze are to be grubbed up, 50 faggots; when the labourer does not tie up the grubbed furze, or make good as he goes, 100 faggots; but when those already grubbed

are

are to be collected and bound, 100 faggots; all of which are supposed to be tied with a single band. Spreading 40 heaps of beat-ashes, lime-mould mixings, dung, &c. laid down at the distance of two poles a-part, and to make the whole meet regularly, whether thick or thin, is considered a day's work. When these heaps are to be mixed, chopped, and turned over before spreading, 20 of them are only required to be spread for a day's work. Gripping, guttering, making open or hollow-drains, form so small a portion of the labour of the country, that no particular standard is as yet fixed to such employments for a day's work.

Cottages attached to Farms.—Instances are but rare, of cottages exclusively attached to farms; but where such have occurred, the most substantial benefits have resulted. In these cases, it has been usual to apportion to each cottage, a sufficiency of garden ground for potatoes and other vegetables for the use of the family, with the addition of the run of a pig. The rent or compensation for such tenements are various; but in general may be averaged or rather short of 40s. per annum. The rent of the cottage with a small patch of garden-ground for pot-herbs only, may be taken through the county at about 30s. per annum. The want, however, of comfortable habitations generally for the poor, and the necessity of crowding two, and sometimes more families into the same hovel, with the disposition unhappily manifested, to let such as are in the vicinity or in view of gentlemen's residences go to decay, has undoubtedly contributed to the want of population in many parts of the county. This evil has been much promoted by land-agents, on a pretext that the estates are encumbered with unnecessary buildings (a point in other respects well founded), and that a reduced popu-

lation

lation would lessen the poor-rates ! such is the injudicious policy floating in the minds of many of these men. Hence with a combination of other causes already stated, is a country, in many parts capable of affording a considerable surplus of bread-corn for exportation, become barely equal to the supply of itself.

PRICE OF PROVISIONS.

The common price of beef, sinking the offal, is about 10*s.* per score; veal, one month old, 5*d.* per lb. ; pork and green bacon, in the season for curing 5*d.* per lb.; and potatoes from 8*d.* to 1*s.* per bushel.

FUEL.

When the moors in this country are at too great a distance, or are otherwise not found equal to the demand for fuel, the deficiency is made up by copse and hedge-row wood, Welsh, Newcastle, and coal from the county of Somerset. The turf or peat, costs little more than the labour of paring or digging, and bringing home. The faggots will cost about 13*s.* 6*d.* per hundred, at the cotter's house. These have risen fifty per cent. in their price within the last 12 or 14 years. Many causes have obviously concurred to this end, and which, from the peculiar circumstances of the times, have been utterly impossible for individuals, or even the government of the country, to remedy. An unnecessary consumption of wood was, however, observed in the open fire-places in farm-houses, but

it is presumed might be much diminished by the introduction of Count Rumford's cottage ovens, or some equally economical, and perhaps more appropriate, contrivance.

When

When coal or culm is any where used by the inhabitants, it is in no case usual to blend or mix it with clay, in the manner practised in South Wales. The price of Sunderland or Newcastle coal, in the sea-ports, is usually about 2*s*. 6*d*. the heaped double Winchester measure.— The Welsh coal, carrying much in its quality, may be stated to average generally about 2*s*. 3*d*. same measure. These latter are sold by the quarter of 16 single-heaped Winchesters.

In the country bordering upon Somersetshire and Dorset, a large supply of coal is brought from the Mendip-hills, and sold at 2*s*. 10*d*. the sack of one hundred weight and a quarter. There usually exists a difference of from 9*d*. to 15*d*. per quarter, between the price of coal at Topsham and at Exeter. The chief supply of the country dependant on these coal-yards, is consequently drawn from the former place ; and where the price of coal in the latter end of October last, was 21*s*. per quarter. It is supposed that Honiton and its neighbourhood are equally supplied with Somerset and Newcastle coal. All the trading and manufacturing towns, as well as the rural inhabitants, draw their supply of fuel from these sources, but of which, in its particular mode of application, there does not appear to be any circumstance of management deserving particular notice.

Large quantities of cow and horse-dung are annually gathered by the poor from off Northam-burrows : this is dried and laid by for winter fuel, and by the inhabitants is called *shensen*.

An inordinate disposition to Thievery.—We must not, however, conclude this Chapter without stating, that the business (for as such in some parts of the county, it seems to be almost exclusively practised) of sheep-stealing, is

carried

carried on to a most atrocious extent, particularly in the vicinity of the forests of Exmoor and of Dartmoor. A well attested fact states, that one farmer lost in the course of five years, no less than 108 sheep from off the former of these wastes; and it is no uncommon case for farmers in the neighbourhood of these moors to lose 20 sheep in the course of a season. Not in depredations upon sheep only are these excesses carried, but to so great a height is thieving arrived at, that neighbours are frequently detected in robbing each other of potatoes whilst yet in the ground. To put some check to these enormities, an association has been formed in the neighbourhood of Bideford, and this will most probably be soon followed by others in the county.

CHAP.

CHAP. XVI.

POLITICAL ECONOMY:

CIRCUMSTANCES DEPENDENT ON LEGISLATIVE AUTHORITY.

SECT. I.——ROADS.

HAD the roads of this country been laid out in the
judicious manner practised by the Indians of North America, they would have been found to follow the water-
courses in all cases where they might lead in their general
direction, towards the point assigned for carrying them.
In doing this, infinitely more judgment would have been
displayed, and a far greater benefit secured to posterity,
than in that which has been adopted by the original pro-
jectors of some of the most important and most frequented
roads in this country. This is clearly demonstrated by
the road between Barnstable and Chumleigh, which, instead of being conducted through the valley of the Taw,
is carried over the highest brows of the river hills, where
the traveller is unceasingly compelled to ascend and descend the sharpest hills in the country. The same may
be said of the road between Bideford and Torrington, by
the great omission of its not being carried along the foot
of the river hills, and through the valley of the Torridge
river.

In addition to the first error, in thus unnecessarily conducting many of the principal roads over a hilly and very
much broken country, it is farther to be observed, that
the turnpike-roads have by no means that width prescribed

scribed by law, and required for the accommodation of the public—so essential to the giving a proper form, and afterwards keeping them in sufficient repair. The consequence is, that these narrow ways are raised so high in the middle, that without sides or bulwark to support them, they are, in a short time, by the traffic of the lime-carts, bilged, and forced out upon their sides, when the only passage remaining is confined to a narrow ridge on the top of the road, but which, from the excessive coarseness of the materials of which it is made, is soon broken into so many holes and unevennesses, as very much to endanger the knees of the horse, and the neck of its rider. It is truly surprizing, however, to see with what speed and security the native horses of the country will pass over these rough and broken places, whether burthened or otherwise.

Notwithstanding the necessity which there absolutely appeared to be, of stating so much on this subject, the Surveyor must beg leave to qualify the description, by saying, that it must not so much be considered as a strict delineation of the whole, as the leading character of many of the most frequented roads in the county.

The parish roads are extremely various, some corresponding with, and even worse than those above described; but where the black gravel before noticed occurs, they are usually self-made, and with a little levelling, could not be surpassed by any in the kingdom.

The prodigious traffic through the parishes of Holdsworthy, Pancrassweek, Bridgerule, Lancelles, Marham Church, and Stratton, to Bude-bay in Cornwall, for sea-sand, requires some arrangement, that in its operation might convey relief to those parishes, on account of the heavy road-rates their inhabitants are annually liable to for keeping up their respective parish roads. This well-

founded

founded complaint is by no means peculiar to those parishes which lie in the neighbourhood of, and approaching the bay of Bude, as it is found very generally to exist
in the vicinity of all great lime-works, Crab-tree kilns
in Egg Buckland, and many others; but which, it is presumed, might meet with an effectual remedy, by a trifling
toll imposed at the kiln, and levied by proper officers,
upon carts and horses, on all the strands so much resorted
to for the purpose of procuring sea-sand for manure.

The public roads round Exeter, Axminster, Honiton,
and many other large towns in the county, cannot be
excelled for goodness in any part of England; but the
parish roads generally, and particularly through the red
loamy district, are very indifferent; nay, bad indeed.
Until the resident gentlemen may be more generally induced to take up the office of way-warden, or surveyor
of the parish-roads, it will be in vain to expect that any
improvement will be made upon them. This truth is
clearly evinced in the exertions of the Rev. Mr. Coham,
of Coham-house, Black Torrington, and the Rev. Mr.
Clay, of East Worlington. To prevent, in future, the
inconvenience arising from the roads being covered with
a too coarse material, the Rev. Mr. Clay, as way-warden
in the parish of East Worlington, supplies the men working upon the highways with iron rings, about four inches
in diameter, and through which, when suspected to be
too large, the stones must be broke small enough to pass,
before they are left by the workmen. The roads which
have been made or repaired under this regulation, sufficiently show the propriety of it.

The height of the hedge-banks, often covered with a
rank growth of coppice-wood, uniting and interlocking
with each other over-head, completes the idea of exploring
a labyrinth rather than that of passing through a much-
frequented

frequented country. This first impression will, however, be at once removed on the traveller's meeting with, or being overtaken by a gang of pack-horses. The rapidity with which these animals descend the hills, when not loaded, and the utter impossibility of passing loaded ones, require that the utmost caution should be used in keeping out of the way of the one, and exertion in keeping a-head of the other. A cross-way fork in the road or gateway, is eagerly looked for as a retiring spot to the traveller, until the pursuing squadron, or heavily loaded brigade, may have passed by. In these lanes it is absolutely impossible to form any idea of the surrounding country, as the size and depth of the abutting fields are only to be seen through a breach in the mound, over a stile or gateway.

As to the application of water, as a means of preserving, it has been so far beneficial (if such it may be called) as to wash and scour away every particle of clay or loam which would have tended to unite the loose stones together, and wear them down to a more even and regular surface than is at present exhibited by most of the side-hill roads and lanes in the country. As there are but few wheel-carriages to pass along them, the channel for the water, and the path for the pack-horse, are equally in the middle of the way, and which is altogether occupied by an assemblage of such large and loose stones only, as the force of the descending torrents have not been able to sweep away or remove.

SECT. II.—IRON RAIL-ROADS.

THERE are no iron rail-roads in any part of this county.

SECT.

SECT. III.——CANALS.

THE subject of canals seems to demand considerable
attention. Notwithstanding the inhabitants of the county
of Devon are by no means so indifferently supplied with
fuel as is found to be the case in many other parts of
England, still the diffusing this necessary article more
generally, would be one among many other important
advantages that would result from carrying into execution the different canals which have been projected
through several parts of this county; among which, the
Bude canal seems to rank the highest, as it combines
with the agricultural interests of the country through
which it has been designed to pass. Upon this subject
the following observations were made by the Rev. Mr.
Coham, of Coham-house, Black Torrington; and, as
the general information they contain is of no less moment than the locality of its bearing on the subject before
us, the whole is most respectfully submitted to the consideration of the Honourable Board, in the words of this
spirited improver, and truly valuable man.

" It must be evident to every one who has been acquainted long enough with the neighbourhood, and is
capable of making the observation, that within the space
of 25 years last past, the greater part of that tract of
country which is surrounded principally by the circuitous
course of the Torridge, as well as the lands spreading
a few miles to the north of that river, has assumed almost
an entire new appearance. Instead of a most forbidding
wild, and in a manner uncultivated desert, calculated only
for the grazing of lean bullocks, and horses of the smallest
and hardiest kinds, we now see, in many places, extensive corn fields, luxuriant pastures, and uplands covered
with

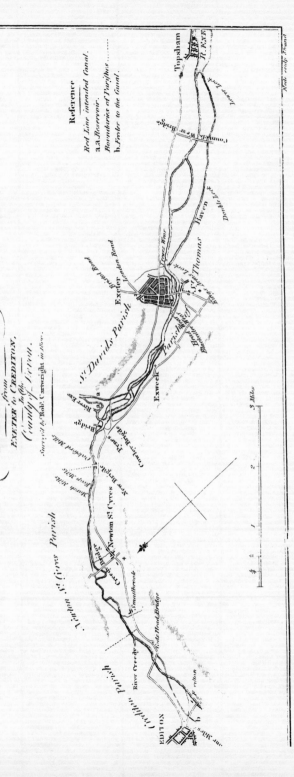

P. 872.

A plan of the
INTENDED CANAL,
from
EXETER to CREDITON,
In the
County of Devon.
Surveyed by Robt. Cartwright in 1800.

Reference

Red Line intended Canal.
a.a. Reservoir.
Boundaries of Parishes ....
b. Feeter to the Canal.

3 Miles

Topsham

R. EXE

Lower Lock

Countess Wear Bridge

Double Locks

St. Davids Parish

Exeter London Road

Exwick Parish

Upper Weir

St. Thomas

St. Thomas's Lock

Salmon Pool

Head Weir

Exeter

Exeter Bridge

EXETER

Bonhay

Exwick

River Exe

Cowley Bridge

Oakford Mills

New Bridge

Marsh Mills

Deep Mills

Newton St. Cyres

Tiston St. Cyres Parish

Crediton

Smallbrook

Fordton

Yeo Head Bridge

River Creedy

Crediton Parish

EDITON

Neele sculp. Strand

with sheep. New enclosures also are daily making in the moorlands, which principally abound in the neighbourhood, and the deep trenches excavated to form the fences, are so contrived as to intercept the springs, which, from their superabundance of water as well as from being strongly impregnated with iron and other mineral substances, have heretofore rendered the herbage of these lands so coarse and unnutritious.

" This change it seems has been in a great measure brought about by a cause, which, in all similar situations, and under the like circumstances, must always produce the same effect. It unfortunately happens, that no marl, clay, calcareous earth, or other fossil manure, has as yet been discovered within this district; so that, exclusive of stall or stable dung, there is scarcely any other manure to be procured but what is brought, and in some cases at a great distance, from the sea-coast. The roads too, anterior to the above-mentioned period, were so narrow and full of sloughs, that they were utterly impervious to all heavy wheel carriages; so that those farmers who had spirit enough (and really some degree of enterprise as well as perseverance in this case was necessary) to purchase artificial manure, were obliged to have recourse to that slow and tedious mode of fetching it in bags on horseback. The mode alluded to, was for farmers living ten or twelve miles distant from the lime-kiln to send out four pack-horses (as they are here called) with a servant and a saddle-horse, four days in a week, and from this exertion and parade, he received home no more than 24 double Winchester bushels of lime, a quantity (according to the usually covenanted allowance of the country, 40 such bushels for every acre broke up for tillage) little more than sufficient to manure half an acre of land.

" The

" The removal of this difficulty, which heretofore had so obviously checked the agricultural improvements of this vicinity, was reserved for the enlarged understanding and enlightened policy of the late George Bickford, Esq. of Darsland, who in an auspicious hour, and regardless of all immediate personal concern for himself, formed the hardy design of putting the highway laws *most rigidly* into execution. No measure at the time could have been more beneficial to the country, and yet, strange to imagine, no undertaking was ever commenced with a greater degree of unpopularity: and this active, persevering magistrate, in encountering the avarice of the ignorant farmer, and the more extraordinary prejudices of those who, from their rank in life, and education, ought to have rendered him every possible assistance, forced an everlasting benefit on his neighbours, in spite of themselves.

" We now find, therefore, through the introduction of wheel-carriages, which it is absurd to suppose could ever have been effected without first widening and rendering our roads equal to their pressure, that the same number of horses (setting aside the saddle-horse before spoken of, entirely), which heretofore brought home only 24 bushels of lime per week, will now bring home 60, with much greater ease; so that instead of half an acre and $\frac{1}{16}$th, an acre and a half of land may now be manured, at the same distance, and within the same time, leaving also the farmer to employ his team one day in the week more than formerly for home purposes.

" These observations also may, with equal propriety, be extended to the carriage of sea-sand—a manure which, when procured in any proportional quantity, has been found on certain soils, to have been productive of infinitely more lasting effects than lime; and which,

through

through the improvement of the roads, has of late years been brought farther, and in greater quantities into the interior of the country, than it was possible for it ever to have been brought before. This manure, taken up chiefly for this district at Bude in Cornwall, free from every charge, except the mere trouble of loading it, consists of about two-thirds of fish-shells, and the remaining portion of granite and other substances. The blown sand, or we will say, that which has been driven by the tide and winds farthest in-shore, as being the lightest and most purely calcareous, has of late been considered the best. The stiffest soils, and those containing the greatest portion of vitriolic acid, both of which properties predominate in our moorlands, are chiefly benefited by this manure: the land working on them not only mechanically as a wedge dividing their clods, but through the vitriolic acid, all that is calcareous of it is decomposed, and becomes to all intents and purposes, lime. On all light upland soils, therefore, this manure can have but little effect. if any whatever; for these soils being too loose and friable already, and being totally destitute also of the vitriolic acid, unless indeed an oily matter be absorbed from the sand (of which some ingenious men entertain an opinion), the land must be rather deteriorated than improved by its application.

" But as the moorlands, that is, such as always heretofore have been suffered to lie as waste, still form a striking feature in the country we are now contemplating; and as we have seen how much sea-sand is calculated to improve them; viewing also the astonishing advantages which we have already derived from the exertions of one individual in the improvement of our roads; it must appear extraordinary indeed, to every stranger who comes amongst us, that having the means in our power, we do

not

not proceed to procure this manure in a still infinitely greater degree of abundance. And this consideration leads us to a circumstance, which in this place seems to claim no small degree of attention.

"Some years since Earl Stanhope came into this neighbourhood, and with that ardour which has always distinguished that Nobleman, when in pursuit of any object that may tend to public good, took a personal survey with two eminent Surveyors, of all the country lying between Bude and Hatherleigh, in this county; and from his report, it seems proved to a demonstration, that a canal, taking different courses between the points abovementioned, exclusively of all other advantages always attending inland navigation, might be made to pay an interest on the capital employed, of at least 10*l.* per cent. on the simple article of sea-sand! and this article rendered, at the remotest distance of the canal from Bude, one-eighth of the present price of carriage! Whether from an idea that during a war, in which most unfortunately we have been engaged almost ever since this survey was taken, his Lordship might think, in so thinly inhabited a neighbourhood, a sufficient number of hands could not be obtained to perfect such an undertaking; or whether his Lordship is engaged for the present in some other enterprise which he may deem of greater importance, certain it is, that this scheme, so honourable to the first projector of it, and so pregnant of local advantage, is for a season at least laid aside.

"How much therefore is it to be regretted, that these circumstances are not duly considered; for, if his Lordship, or any other public-spirited man, could be induced to conduct a measure of this sort, some thousands of acres would almost instantaneously be converted into rich pasture. The hedges forming the enclosures might,

through

through the natural stiffness and binding quality of the soil, be raised to any height, and would serve as an excellent shade and shelter. Perhaps a ten-acred enclosure might be as convenient and proper a size as any other. The trenches supplying materials for the raising of these hedges being cut transversely to the sloping ground, would intercept most of the springs; the land having been first pared, burnt, cropped with turnips and oats, and sown with proper grass-seeds, being thrown up into ridges, consisting of about 40 furrows each, would drain itself for the most part of rain or surface water; and where this cannot well be done, and where the subsoil is clay, which is most commonly the case, Lambert's mole-plough, which has lately been introduced by a society of gentlemen in the neighbourhood of Holdsworthy, will effectually do the business. From these drains also, receiving-ponds might be constructed for the cattle to drink at, and which, when emptied, might serve (the water being improved by stagnation) to irrigate the grounds beneath. The land thus enclosed—thus sheltered—and thus drained, might by the aid of sea-sand, be made as rich, and as truly valuable in itself, as any land in the kingdom.

" To enumerate all the advantages of a canal in a paper of this sort, would be superfluous; but there are certain points immediately connected with agriculture, which cannot well be passed over. It has of late been most strenuously recommended by Lord Somerville and others, to substitute, as much as possible, the labour of oxen in heavy draughts, for that of horses. In such situations as we have been describing, where manure cannot be obtained at a less distance than from 10 to 15 miles, such a measure would be impracticable. Oxen do not possess strength and agility sufficient for heavy draughts and long journies;

nies; and the farmer knows from experience, that in every journey, he would lose considerably more in the growth and condition of the ox, than he could possibly save to his pocket from his not sending a horse in its stead. Under such circumstances, therefore, a regular team of horses must be kept; and such team, of course, ought to be employed. For easy labour and short journies, indeed, the ox may be found of service, and by a more general introduction of canals, both of these objects would be obtained. Oxen might then be made subservient to the purpose of most conveyances; and as the necessity of keeping a large team of horses would then, in most cases, be superseded, a larger quantity of fodder might be laid up for oxen, and, consequently, what is of infinite importance, a larger quantity of food fit for an Englishman's table would be provided.

" The roads, also, would be kept in better repair, and at a considerable less expense, by that means. All the heavy articles would be conveyed the greater part of the distance required, by water; and as the roads, from that instant, would assume a new character, so in proportion to the shortness of the distance, for the conveying of any given article, would the evenness of the roads facilitate its conveyance. On all these considerations, therefore, whether we are stimulated by the benefits which have already accrued to us from what has been done to our roads, the prospect of rendering a barren tract of land fertile, the lessening of the number of our horses, and consequently increasing our oxen; the pleasure of travelling on good roads, or the advantages and comforts of all these circumstances thrown together into one general point of view, no person, we flatter ourselves, who can have the real interests of the neighbourhood at heart, and is not absorbed in his own private views, or led away by old narrow prejudices,

judices, will long hesitate to throw in his aid to the driving of a canal, with its various branches, through the centre of the district. The accomplishment of this object will, in times of peace, be a double blessing to the country; and, in time of war, will, in a tenfold degree, enable its inhabitants to meet its exigencies."

The principal means suggested by the engineers for accomplishing this undertaking, were those of overcoming the declivities by rail-roads and double inclined planes; and after attaining the summit of particular levels, to continue them as such by the aid of aqueducts and tunnels, to a considerable distance. The length of the highest level of this canal was estimated at no less than fifty miles.

Some years ago a plan was also in agitation for making a canal between the present boatable waters of the Torridge, at Wear-Giffard, through Peters Marland, Sheepwash, and Hatherleigh, towards Oakhampton, where one branch was proposed to unite with the canal now carrying on between Crediton and Exeter; and another branch to connect with the Tavistock canal. This measure, although fondly cherished by its first promoters, and many gentlemen in the country, is, for the present, laid aside.

Along time prior to this last project, a line of levels was surveyed for the purpose of uniting the waters of the Taw and the Exe with each other. The projected line of this canal, with its diverging branches between the Bristol and the British Channel, appears to have been nearly as follows: beginning at the bridge of Barnstable, and proceeding thence between Pill and the river Taw, Bishop's Tawton and Fordigate, and the Taw, Buer, Fisherton, Hooper's Grove, Collon and Holston, and the Taw. Here the turnpike-road and river were to have been crossed to Little Wear. The Taw was then to have
been

been re-crossed to the west end of Umberleigh-bridge, in the parish of Etherington ; thence along and on the same side the Taw, to Wear Marsh, to Scoop and Kineford, in the parish of High Bickington ; thence to Tamar-place, Abbot's-marsh, Tidman's-ford and Bridge-house farm, to Newenham-bridge ; thence crossing the river by Colloton-mills, and crossing the turnpike-road to Colloton-barton ; thence crossing the river Dart to Eggsford road, by the keeper's house ; thence on to Chenson-barton, and Nymet-mill, which river was to have been crossed to Bridge-town, in the parish of Tapford ; thence re-cross this river under Bradford, to a certain point in the parish of Mary Down ; where a collateral branch was proposed to extend to North Tawton. From this point, called Braddeford, to Copplestone, in the parish of Colebrook, was the proposed summit level of the canal, which was to have been formed by a tunnel of three miles one furlong and four hundred and seventeen links in length. Resuming a description of the course of the canal from Copplestone, it was proposed to proceed thence to Coleford, Panson under Yeaford, Gunstone, Yeo Town, to Fordton ; thence to Codshead bridge, in the parish of Crediton, crossing the turnpike road to the river Creedy, which road again re-cross to Pynes : thence on to Stoke, to join with the Grand Junction Canal, which was proposed to have been brought from the county of Somerset, along the valley of the Culm and Exe to Topsham. Returning back to Pynes, another collateral branch was intended to be made to Cowley-bridge, and thence to Exeter quay. A line was also projected to have been carried from the north-west end of the summit level, through Winkleigh, Bayford, and Torrington, to unite with the navigable waters of the Torridge, at Wear-Giffard.

The

The principal points on the survey of this line of levels
(*Vide the Map of the County*), are as follows :

	miles.	fur.	links.		feet.
From A, at Topsham, to B, at Copplestone	20	6	642	rise	287
From B, at Copplestone, to C, at Braddeford	3	1	417	level	
From C, at Braddeford, to D, at Barnstable	24	2	607	fall	312
Difference					25

From this statement, it should seem that the low-water
line at Topsham is 25 feet higher than the low-water
mark at the bridge of Barnstable. This, however extraordinary, is not otherwise to be understood from the
above statement, extracted from the scale of levels.

The collateral branches surveyed from this general line
of canal, were,

	miles.	fur.	links.		feet.
From E, at the crossing of the river Exe, to F, at Exeter	3	5	79	fall	57
From G, near Braddeford, to H, at North Tawton	8	0	739	rise	55

The canal now carrying into execution, from the quay
at Exeter to Cooley-bridge, proceeds from the latter point,
east of the church, through the parish of Newton St.
Cyres ; and terminates at the four mills, in the parish of
Crediton.

This work is now completed as far as Exweek ; but
under the present arrangement, no very sanguine expectations are generally entertained of its being shortly accomplished with a favourable issue.

The canal from Tavistock to the Tamar, at the distance

tance of two miles and a half from the former place, strikes the north side of Moorwall Down; and where, at the mouth of the tunnel, a rich vein, or lode of copper ore, was accidentally pierced, and is supposed to be the same lode now working, at the depth of ˜0 fathoms, within a mile of Tavistock. This vein crops out upon an east and west course, dips to the north about one foot in three, and varies from three to twelve feet in thickness. The engine now working the pumps for draining the mine, has a water-wheel 36 feet in diameter, is overshot, with buckets four feet long; and from the circumstances of its situation, its power may be augmented from one-third to one half, whenever the works may require it.

The course of the tunnel towards the Tamar, now making through the body of Moorwall Down, is south, a little westwardly. It is cut eight feet deep, and six feet wide; having a depth of three feet three inches of water, to answer the purpose of navigation. The whole distance through the hill is estimated at 1400 fathoms, and costs 14*l.* per fathom, exclusive of the air-shafts, the first of which is sunk at the distance of 200 fathoms from the north end of the tunnel, is 28 fathoms deep, and four feet in diameter. No. 2, is sunk at the distance of 500 fathoms from the first point, and is 55 fathoms deep. No. 3, is at the distance of 1100 fathoms from the place of beginning, and is 48 fathoms deep. On a part of the course, and near the north end of the tunnel, three distinct bodies of copper have also been crossed, as have also two more near the south end. Here the canal comes again to the day, at the head of a hollow, and passes along its southern side for about half a mile; and where the canal is proposed to terminate with a double inclined

plane,

plane, constructed to the acclivity of 238 feet, that being
the height of the level of the canal, above the navigation of
the Tamar river, at the quays of Moorwallham. A double
set of chains are proposed to operate from the inclined
planes in drawing the vessels through the tunnel; these
boats are intended to be 24 feet in length, but not to
exceed the burthen of two tons each; and so many of
them will be connected and drawn through the tunnel
together, as is equal to the power produced by the descending loads upon the inclined plane.

The canal at Teigngrace, besides considerably increasing the export of pipe-clay, answers a very good purpose,
in supplying water for irrigating all the adjoining grounds,
and which has recently increased their value from 500*l.* to
1500*l.* per annum.

A project has been entertained for making a canal from
Axmouth, through Chard, to Uphill, in Somersetshire,
with a view of opening a communication to the coal-
mines in that county. It is probable this scheme may
be renewed on the return of peace. It would furnish a
ready supply of coal, and be otherwise highly advantageous to the country through which it may pass. The
summit level at Chard, is about 150 feet above the bed
of the river at the lower Axe-bridge, below Colyton,
where the tidal waters flow, and are always boatable.
The length of the valley, between the lower Axe-bridge
and Axminster, is about six miles, along the sides of
which an easy line of levels may be had from Axminster
to the aforesaid bridge; the fall in which distance, is
estimated at about sixty feet.

SECT. IV.——FAIRS.

THE fair of Barnstable is supposed to be one of the best cattle-fairs in the kingdom; it is held about the middle of September, when those who are desirous of viewing the most perfect of the breed of North Devon cattle, will never fail of being very highly gratified. Great Torrington, and all the large towns in the county, afford fairs for cattle, horses, &c. But the fair of Bampton is the most remarkable of all for sheep, and where a most excellent show is always to be met with, on the first Tuesday in November.

SECT. V.——MARKETS.

IT is much to be lamented, that something like a general standard of weights and measures is not only established, but in all cases strictly insisted upon and enforced by legislative authority. The inconvenience and confusion arising from the want of such a regulation, in carrying on the internal commerce of the country, is universally complained of, and the losses to which the growers of agricultural produce are exposed, can in no case be more clearly illustrated, than in the actual difference against the vender, of seven and a half per cent. between the legal and customary corn measure at Barnstable; and there are scarcely two market towns in the county (Kingsbridge and Modbury excepted) that buy and sell by the legal standard. Kingsbridge affords an excellent corn-market, and where the average prices are found generally to exceed those of London.

A custom

A custom universally prevails, of heaping the fourth peck, in measuring a bushel of wheat, and as the diameter of these peck measures (although of equal capacity) are very various, a difference consequently results in the measure of almost every farmer. These evils, however, are very much corrected by the common usage of selling wheat by the bag of what is called two bushels; and as that bag must weigh seven score, this grain is, in effect, sold by weight, in most of the markets in the county. This is not so generally the case with regard to oats or barley, although the language of the farmers on these subjects, is more frequently in reference to a bushel of barley of fifty pounds, or of oats of forty pounds, than of mere quantity or bulk, without attaching any specific weight to ascertain its quality. The butter weight, with few exceptions, through the county, is 18oz. to the lb.

SECT. VI.—MANUFACTURES.

DISTRICT I.

THE finest and most valuable manufactures of this district, are said of late years to have gone very much to decay. Those formerly carried on at North and South Molton, consisted chiefly of duroys, serges, and other light cloths, the making of which has been very much affected by the war, but on its termination, and when the former markets are again accessible, which were chiefly in the Mediterranean, and through the Levant, this branch of manufacture may again flourish. The manufacture, at present, is in a great measure confined to the making of a few long ells for the East India trade.

DEVON.]   The

The staple manufacture at Barnstable was that of baizes, spotted and plain. This also has been much affected from the same cause, but will most likely recover on the return of peace. A manufacture of coarse beaver and other cloths is in some measure substituted in their place. These are finished at home, but sent to be dyed in Exeter, and are chiefly wrought for the supply of the slop-shops at Plymouth. Some druggets are also made, and died scarlet, for the East Indies. The potteries of Barnstable, which consist of coarse ware for dairy and kitchen use, are said to be considerably increasing.

The manufactures of Bideford differ in no material degree from those of Barnstable, unless the business of shipbuilding may be admitted as a manufacture, and which in the former place has lately been carried on to a considerable extent, insomuch that within these two last years, several sloops of war, a frigate, and a fireship, have either been built, or are now upon the stocks. The potteries are much the same as those noticed at Barnstable, and supply a large quantity of ware for exportation coastways.

DISTRICT II.

It has been before noticed, that a part of the commons of Great Torrington had been granted to some gentlemen, for the purpose of establishing a woollen manufactory. The failure of the first adventurers on this occasion did not deter others from embarking in the same business, whom we are told profited so far as to make very handsome fortunes. The cloths made here, were woollens adapted for the East-India market, and the Levant trade, which latter, from causes well known, are gone considerably to decay, but the gloving business which has succeeded, has furnished means of employment to many, who
otherwise

tures chiefly consist of light goods made for the
Company. The malting business is carried on
siderable extent at the latter place; the malt be
nerally shipped to Plymouth, Bristol, and Liverpool.
cider shipped at Salcombe, in the Kingsbridge inlet,
the year 1805, has already been stated at about 700 hog.
heads; a quantity scarcely equal to half of what has been
frequently known to have been sent annually from the
same place.

The brewing of a liquor called white ale, is almost exclusively confined to the neighbourhood of Kingsbridge:
its preparation, as far as could be learnt by the Surveyor,
is 20 gallons of malt mashed with the same quantity of
boiling water; after standing the usual time, the wort is
drawn off, when six eggs, four pounds of flour, a quarter
of a pound of salt, a   a quart of *grout*, are beat up together, and mixed with this quantity of wort, which, after
standing twelve hours is put into a cask, and is ready for
use the following day. This beverage possesses a very in-
toxicating quality, and is much admired by those who
drink not to quench thirst only. A mystery hangs over the
ingredient called *grout*, and the secret is said to be confined
to one family in the district only. No difficulty however
could arise in ascertaining its component parts, by submitting a certain portion of it to the test of a chemical
examination. That this liquor is of considerable antiquity
is plain, from the *terrier* of the advowson of Dodbrook,
and which expressly calls for the tithe of white ale. The
present worthy incumbent commutes this claim, for half a
guinea annually from each house in the parish where this
ancient beverage is retailed

The serge manufacture at Totness, is chiefly carried on
in the weaving department by women. The spinning is
performed by machinery, in the manner of spinning cotton.

otherwise would have become extremely burthensome to
the town.

The woolcombing business was formerly carried on to
a considerable extent at Chumleigh, but from the failure
of the durant and other manufactures, at North and South
Molton, and other places in the county, that business has
vanished; and as no other manufacturing employment
has succeeded, the parochial burthens on account of the
poor, have considerably increased. About 13 years since,
200 woolcombers met with constant employment in this
town, but the utmost that were numbered in August last,
did not amount to more than eight. It is supposed that
one woolcomber would prepare wool for the constant employment of eight spinners. The decrease in the manufacture of sandfords and long ells, has much affected the
prosperity of Tiverton and Bampton; but this, to a certain
extent, has been replaced by the cassimere and serge manufacture in those places. Tiverton, perhaps, does not so
sensibly experience the inconvenience of this failure, as
many other towns in that part of the county, on account
of the number of respectable and independent families
who make it their place of residence, and form as highly
improved a society, as is any where to be met with in a
town of the same extent in the united kingdom.

DISTRICT III.

The small portion of manufactures which were carried
on in this district, seem to have shared in common the
check communicated by the war.

DIS-

DISTRICT IV.

The great naval arsenal at Plymouth, lying within this district, was established in the year 1691. It constitutes a seat of considerable manufacture in iron, cordage, and whatever relates (sail-cloth excepted) to the demand of the Royal Dock-Yard. The number of hands employed in ordinary, from the best information the Surveyor was able to procure, with the respective annual earnings of each class, is stated as under:

Occupations.	Number in each employed.	Annual Amount of Wages.
Shipwrights	1,075	£.91,935 14 6
Caulkers	103	9,414 6 11
Joiners	76	5,989 15 3
House carpenters	93	6,825 17 7
Smiths	208	14,785 8 1
Masons	11	952 1 0
Bricklayers	26	2,232 18 8
Sail-makers	61	4,446 18 1
Riggers	133	6,390 8 4
Riggers' labourers	133	4,565 10 9
Scavelmen	106	6,568 19 5
Labourers	452	19,288 0 2
Quarter boys	13	369 15 2
Oakum boys	32	692 0 2
Pitch-heaters	2	161 19 8
Block-makers	4	248 4 7
Sawyers	156	8,968 15 11
Braziers	1	112 11 1
Carry forward	2,685	£.183,949 5 2

Plumbers

Brought forward 2,685		£.183,949 5 2
Plumbers	3	317 14 9
Locksmiths	3	184 2 4
Wheelwrights	4	295 10 2
Cooper	1	56 15 0
Bricklayers' labourers	10	446 0 4
Cabin keepers to shipwrights	8	728 3 1
Ditto to caulkers	1	90 14 8
Carvers	2	73 17 0
By the teams	24	5,011 4 3
Total	2741	£.191,153 16 9

Paid to superannuated persons per ann.	No.	Average.	
To quartermen from £.24 to 28 Shipwrights and caulkers 20 to 24	152	£.24 0 0	£.3,648 0 0
To joiners, wheelwrights, block-makers, plumbers, braziers, locksmiths, armourers, sail-makers, and rope-makers, 20	57	20 0 0	1,140 0 0
To house-carpenters, smiths, bricklayers, riggers, and sawyers, 15 to 20	76	17 10 0	1,330 0 0
To pitch-heaters, bricklayers' labourers, scavelmen, riggers' labourers, and yard labourers, 10 to 15	69	12 10 0	862 10 0
To seamen of the ordinary,	10	5 10 0	50 0 0
To foreman assistant,	40	1 40 0 0	40 0 0
Total	380		£.7,070 10 0

At Tavistock, an iron foundery and cutlery have been established upon a large scale, and great expectations are indulged, of their fully answering the objects of their institution. At Modbury and Kingsbridge, the manufactures ton. This town is situated at the head of the marine navigation of the Dart river. Here the ordinary flow of the spring tides, admits vessels of 30 or 40 tons burthen. About a mile above the bridge (where the ordinary flow of the spring tides is about eight feet), a salmon weir is extended directly across the river, and consequently prevents any farther navigation upwards ; but were this not the case, the acclivity in the bed of the river, and its rocky irregularities, would nearly have terminated the boatable waters at the same point. At this dam, or weir, a powerful mill-race is taken up to serve a corn and fulling mill, which is situated a little above the bridge at Totness. This mill is constantly employed in washing and fulling the pieces composing the principal manufacture of the town, and which is now considered to be rather on the increase than otherwise. The corn-mill is a valuable acquisition to the town and surrounding country.

The manufactures at Ashburton may be stated to differ in no material respect from those of Totness : at this time there is certainly much activity among them. Exclusive of similar manufactures, which were carried on some years since at Newton-Bushel, the Newfoundland trade also flourished there. These have both met with a considerable check from the war, but sanguine hopes are entertained that they will both be renewed to their former extent on the return of peace.

DISTRICT V.

The coarse woollen serges manufactured at Moreton-Hempstead and Chagford, are generally sent to Exeter, where such as may be destined for the Mediterranean markets are dyed, and the others sent forward to London, for the use of the East-India Company. A woollen factory,

upon

upon a large scale, is seated on the river Teign, in the parish of Chagford, and supplied with a water-power at all times amply sufficient for the purpose of its institution.

A forge for working up old iron has recently been established in the parish of Ashton. The bellows, hammers, rollers, and all its apparatus, are worked by water, the regularity of which motion enables the respective operations to be performed extremely well.

DISTRICT VI.

The principal manufactures of this district, differ in no very material degree from those already noticed. A complaint, however, was sometimes heard among the manufacturers of long ells, on account of the reduction of 2s. 6d. per piece, by the East-India Company, upon the price which they purchased at, last year. This is regarded by many as a considerable grievance, there being no abatement in the price of wool, or in the expense of manufacture. The very reverse of an injury accruing to the manufacturers from this arrangement is very easy to show. On the former plan, the manufacturers sent their woollens to factors in London, who, for obvious reasons, were ever anxious to have a large quantity of goods on hand, and frequently, on the aggregate, to the amount of 300,000 pieces. The annual purchases being made at different periods by the East-India Company, a vast number were still left in the hands of the factors, to supply the demand for the following year. This stock seldom averaged less than 200,000 pieces, and equalling in value the important sum of 300,000l. The factors accommodated the manufacturers with about two-thirds of this value, charging interest of five per cent. on the advances, and which, by making out their accounts twice in the

year

year, made the interest amount to about 5½ per cent. This, with other charges, equalled about six per cent. and continued a burthen on the tradesmen for little short of eighteen months, before farther sales were made, and the advances balanced; add to which, the damage sustained by the manufacturer on his goods thus warehoused, by moths, &c.

The present arrangement of the East-India Company is commercial, liberal and direct: samples are exhibited by the respective manufacturers, and the Company agree for a certain number of pieces: such as are approved of, to be delivered at the India House (not through a factor) at different periods, and to be paid for immediately on delivery. By this arrangement, the manufacturer saves the interest of money advanced to him on his unsold goods; is exempt from the payment of commission, warehouse-rent, douceurs to the attendants; from any injury accruing to his goods by moths, damps, &c. and directly to charges amounting to about 3 s. per piece, as under,

	s.	d.
Commission, 2½ per cent. on a long ell, value 33 s.	0	10
Warehouse-room, one penny per piece; and douceurs to attendants, about 1½ d. per piece more	0	2½
Interest of money advanced upon the unsold goods, averaged from the annual supplies and shipments made by the East-India Company	2	0
	3	0½

By this arrangement, the manufacturer is placed upon certain ground: he works by contract, has no need of a large stock of goods in hand to eat up the interest of his capital, or to tempt him into mercantile speculations, with which he ought to have no concern, and which seldom fails to end in the ruin of all such people.

DISTRICT

DISTRICT VII.

On a due examination of the manufactures of this district, the long ells will be found by far the most considerable. The making of bone lace occupies a large part of the time the females in the lower class of life (whether in town or in the country) can conveniently spare from their other concerns. It is doubtless a suitable employment for the leisure hours of the rustic female; and so long as the superior orders in society supply a market for such articles, it is to be regretted that it is not more generally understood and resorted to, as a means of employment for the females in the north and western parts of the county.

A few words more on the subject of long ells, will nearly close our observations on the manufactures of Devonshire. The plan at present pursued by the East-India Company, however liberal, and, in a national point of view, most highly to their honour, will ultimately, as far as it goes, prove injurious to the Company. These woollens, as formerly manufactured, were often rejected in the markets in India; and many thousand pieces were returned to Europe, and thrown upon the tradesmen's hands. To remedy these complaints, as to the thinness and badness of the web, the Company have ordered that every piece of long ells, as stripes, shall weigh 12 lbs. and so in proportion for greens and reds. The manufacturer, to meet this order, works the goods in a coarser pitch, and shoots abb of an inferior quality;—will not this be attended with a similar result which the specific weight was intended to remedy? and must it not, in its consequences, tend to expel this important fabric altogether from out of the markets in India? Would it not, therefore,

fore, be advisable for the East India Company to regulate
their purchases in such a manner, that each piece should
consist of a specific number of bars, each bar to be forty
threads, to be full 29 yards in length, and to be subject to
the same regulations and inspection as in Yorkshire, both
with respect to the fineness and closeness of the web?
A stripe that measures 31 inches, when dressed for delivery in London, should be laid in the warping-bars full
29 yards, and contain 1440 threads ; greens, to have the
same length of warp, should contain 1320 threads ; reds,
the same length, with 1240 threads.

SECT. VII.—COMMERCE.

DISTRICT I.

THE town of Bideford and that of Appledore, which
are both situate on the west bank of the Torridge, had
some years ago a very considerable share of the Virginia
and Newfoundland trade, at which time the population
was more considerable, and accompanied with a far
greater appearance of prosperity and wealth than is observable in either of these places at this time. In the reign
of Queen Elizabeth, the port of Barnstable is said to have
furnished a larger quota of shipping for the national de-
fence than the city of Bristol ; how comes it then, at the
beginning of the present century, that the ships' tonnage,
and men and boys, employed in the port of Barnstable
and its dependencies, and Bristol, should stand thus ?

Barnstable

	Ships.		Tons.		Hands.
Barnstable	65	measuring	4,896	employing	301
Bideford, including Appledore	71	do.	4,960	do.	269
Ilfracombe	60	do.	3,088	do.	205
Total	196		12,944		775
Bristol	206		30,125		1,894
Difference	10		17,181		1,119

An astonishing increase in the one, and a most unaccountable diminution in the other. It will not be contended that the Taw and the Torridge combined, head into a country equally rich, fruitful, or populous with that which surrounds, or is otherwise dependent on the city of Bristol, for affording agricultural or manufactured produce, or demanding foreign or domestic supplies. Still a most alarming disproportion exists in the relative prosperity of these places; the principal cause of which, on a due investigation, will be found to lie in the gradual silting up, and consequent decay of the channel produced by the combined strength of the Taw and Torridge rivers. To what farther extent this mischief may be permitted to go, it is impossible to say; but from the cursory observations made upon the spot, the Author of this Report has no hesitation in saying, that good and effectual means may yet be devised, not only to prevent the harbours of Barnstable and Bideford from going entirely to decay, but also to render the access to them infinitely more certain, safe, and practicable than it is at present, even in the day time, at the top of the tide and over their tremendous bar.

DISTRICT II.

The small portion of maritime commerce carried on at Clovella and Hartland, may be referred to what has been already stated in the district of North Devon.

DISTRICT IV.

The mouth of the river Dart, forms one of the best harbours for its size in the West of England. There is seldom a less depth than from ten to twelve fathoms, at low water, and the ordinary flow of the spring-tides is from twelve to fourteen feet ; formerly, and before the late French war, the ships employed in the Newfoundland trade from this river, amounted to 120, averaging about 85 tons each ; at this time there are not more than 30 of 100 tons each. The number of registered ships belonging to this port, and the port of Plymouth, at the beginning of the present century, were as follows :

	Ships.		Tons.		Men and Boys.
Dartmouth	230	measuring	12,409	navigated by	1,144
Plymouth	245	do.	15,574	do.	1,105
Total	475		27,983		2,249

Assuming that the respective crews belonged to the places where the ships were registered, it would add so much more to the population of the district; but as these persons neither reside, or seek their living on shore, it would be presumed as improper to class them with the resident inhabitants. The chief supply of foreign produce is now brought here from London Sea-coal is the most general fuel in all the large towns. This is supplied from Sunderland, Newcastle, and Wales, at about 40s.

40*s.* the chaldron, of 18 double Winchester heaped measures. Barley, wheat, and malt, are shipped coastways
from this river, and occasionally when the ports are open
for exportation. The average shipment of cider, for the
last five years, has been 2,639 hogsheads annually. Much
employment offers to the labouring class of the inhabitants along the river Dart, in navigating the shallops, by
the men ; and to the women and children, in gathering
cockles and muscles, at low-water ; by these means they
earn a great deal of money, and in truth do very well.

Fishery.—Brixham, which is a dependency of the port
of Dartmouth, has no less than 100 sail of vessels employed in the fisheries. These boats are built much larger
than formerly, on account of their finding a number of
freights, during the Summer months, in the culm trade.
They now average a burthen of about 80 quarters of
culm, each quarter containing 16 heaped Winchester
bushels. Their principal fish-markets are London, Bath,
and Bristol ; but when the overflow (which is very common in the summer season), is likely to occasion a glut,
the whiting, flounders, thornbacks, gurnet, &c. are first
cleaned, and well washed in salt-water ; and afterwards
gently salted and dried in the sun. Thus prepared, they
make an excellent relish ; are called buckhorn, and
always in demand for the use of the Navy, in war, and
along the French coast in the time of peace ; selling,
generally from 10*s.* to 16*s.* per hundred fish, according
to their size and quality.

There are no cloth, or other manufactures of note,
at Brixham, King's-wear, or Dartmouth, if we except,
in the latter port, the business of ship-building : here
36 and 40 gun frigates are frequently seen on on the
stocks,

stocks, or on their way to Plymouth, to be equipped for sea. These, with many other smaller public and private vessels, occasion much employment, and create a considerable expenditure of timber, the supply of which is derived from the places before noticed.

DISTRICT VI.

The exports from the port of Exeter, in the year 1800, were,

			lbs.		£.	s.	d.
ToPortugal 8,988	{ pieces of woollens }	at 12 each,	value	23,304	3	8
ToGuernsey 146	do.	do.	do.	208	0	0
Total 9,126	do.			£.23,512	3	8

In the year 1805,

ToPortugal 17,548	do.	do.	do.	54,302	0	0
To Russia 4,631	do.	do.	do.	8,294	0	0
To Prussia 1,573	do.	do.	do.	3,109	0	0
To Guernsey 625	do.	do.	do.	854	18	0
Total 24,377	do.			£.66,559	18	0

Difference, forming an increase since the year 1800, } 15,251 pieces   £.43,047 14 4

In the year 1800, there was pipe or potter's clay, sent coastways to the amount of

	Tons.	cwt.
	15,252	10
In the year 1805, do. do.	17,138	0
Increased export of this article since the beginning of the present century, }	1,885	10

Whence

Whence it appears, that notwithstanding the renewal and continuance of the war, an increased demand for these articles has taken place as above; and which must certainly serve very much to qualify the incessant clamour of the loss of trade, and consequent decay of the manufactures in this county. The supply of woollens to the East-India Company is permanent, whether the country is in peace or at war; during which latter period, by the waggons, and through the canals to London. Although the increased exports of potter's clay is much to be referred to the safety and facility of shipment afforded by the convenience of the canal, and warehouses constructed at Teigngrace, by Mr. Templar, still an excess of export, to the amount stated, shows that the potteries in Staffordshire, and in other parts of the kingdom, to which this clay is conveyed from Teignmouth, have found that quantity proportionably increased during the same time. The number of registered ships belonging to the port of Exeter, in the year 1801, were 168, measuring 13,521 tons, and navigated by 919 men and boys.

SECT. VIII.——POPULATION.

DISTRICT I.

THE population of this district, from the enumeration made under the Act of the 41st of His present Majesty, appears to be as follows:

DISTRICT I.

Names of Parishes.	Houses.			Number of Persons, including Children.		Occupations.			Total.
	Inhabited.	By how many Families.	Vacant.	Males.	Females.	In Agriculture.	In Manufactures.	All other Persons.	
1. Alwington,	56	61	4	148	162	83	21	206	310
2. Abbotsham,	59	59	3	143	170	305	8	....	313
3. Alverdiscot,	52	52	2	140	138	161	7	110	278
4. Atherington,	79	89	7	232	252	115	30	339	484
5. Arlington,	57	42	1	98	109	87	24	96	207
6. Ashford,	18	21	2	27	46	38	10	25	73
7. Bideford,	582	613	24	1303	1684	126	325	2536	2987
8. Bishop's Nympton,	169	171	15	425	477	350	83	469	902
9. ———— Tawton,	144	162	7	390	357	280	42	425	747
10. Barnstable,	619	828	34	1495	2253	68	578	3102	3748
11. Bratton Flemming,	67	79	2	185	221	373	15	18	406
12. Brandon,	40	61	3	122	138	124	79	57	260
13. Berry Narber,	83	94	3	265	267	501	24	7	532
14. Bittedon,	5	5	1	13	11	19	1	4	24
15. Braunton,	255	267	29	582	714	323	60	913	1296
16. Chittlehampton,	281	281	8	1406	1597	274	79	2650	003
17. Charles,	42	43	4	112	105	98	22	97	217
18. Challacombe,	31	32	1	71	87	70	1	87	158
19. Countesbury,	24	24	1	61	59	117	3	....	120
20. Cumbe Martin,	151	183	5	371	448	163	40	616	819
21. East Anstey,	30	33	..	79	80	164	1	....	165
22. East Buckland,	20	21	25	71	67	16	4	118	138
23. East Down,	51	51	2	157	154	255	10	46	311
24. Fremington,	164	176	3	440	435	548	74	253	875
25. Filleigh,	33	51	..	107	113	212	7	1	220
26. George Nympton,	51	54	5	114	123	60	10	167	237
27. Goodleigh,	53	55	3	112	136	45	23	180	248
28. Georgeham,	141	149	10	297	330	69	79	479	627
29. High Bray,	45	45	4	131	133	126	54	84	264
30. Henshaw,	35	35	5	101	105	39	8	159	206
31. Harwood,	20	20	..	44	59	29	2	72	103
32. Heanton Punchardon,	77	93	15	180	238	102	21	295	418
33. Instow,	70	80	3	177	170	49	39	259	347
34. Ilfracombe,	435	435	20	728	1110	751	120	967	1838
35. Kentisbury,	41	51	5	112	129	64	19	158	241
36. Littleham,	45	57	2	138	154	70	22	200	292
37. Landkey,	96	114	1	290	317	590	15	2	607
38. Loxhore,	38	12	3	101	108	61	5	143	209
39. Linton,	100	100	..	215	266	185	30	266	481
40. Land-cross,	8	10	1	22	28	14	2	34	50
Carry forward,	4808	3017	263	11,391	13,550	7174	1997	15,640	24,761

DEVON.]

Names

Names of Parishes.	Inhabited.	By how many Families.	Vacant.	Males.	Females.	In Agriculture.	In Manufactures.	All other Persons.	Total.
		Houses.		Number of Persons, including Children.		Occupations.			
Brought forward,	4808	3017	263	11,391	13,550	7174	1997	15,640	24,761
41. Molland Boucceaux,	90	102	3	228	245	123	46	299	473
42. Martinhoe,	80	30	3	72	93	68	4	93	165
43. Morthoe,	44	46	4	26	128	48	14	192	254
44. Marwood,	132	132	5	296	336	596	27	9	632
45. Northam,	490	492	9	888	1166	102	115	1837	2054
46. Newton Tracy,	12	12	..	39	47	80	6	.....	86
47. North Molton,	288	330	35	703	838	697	801	43	1541
48. Parracombe,	64	75	4	151	171	208	14	100	322
49. Pilton,	87	95	11	392	439	65	386	380	831
50. Satterleigh,	12	16	..	26	38	41	20	3	64
51. South Molton,	559	572	13	1180	1573	544	2200	9	2753
52. Swimbridge,	165	188	6	487	595	680	89	313	1082
53. Stoke Rivers,	37	43	..	119	106	128	22	75	225
54. Sherwell,	90	93	3	237	276	214	42	257	513
55. Twitching,	25	34	2	75	70	63	1	81	145
56. Tawstock,	181	226	20	536	595	300	64	767	1131
57. Trentishoe,	23	26	1	62	66	34	8	86	128
58. Wear Giffard,	75	77	4	150	229	70	25	324	419
59. West Leigh,	88	86	1	157	211	99	39	270	408
60. West Anstey,	84	40	..	100	115	203	12	....	215
61. West Buckland,	42	54	..	124	133	115	11	133	257
62. West Down,	63	65	5	166	170	65	58	213	336
63. Warkleigh,	52	52	4	148	143	170	9	112	291
64. Yarnescombe,	110	132	5	363	377	712	18	10	740
Total, -	7183	7825	401	18,116	21,710	12,552	6028	21,246	39,826

Hands belonging to the ports of Barnstable, Bideford, and Ilfracombe, employed on ship-board, 775

From

From this statement it appears, that there are in this district, 7183 houses, in which are now living 7825 families, and consequently 642 houses double tenanted; and yet, strange to say, there are 401 houses vacant, the greater part of which may fairly be supposed in a state of dilapidation, or utter ruin; or from other causes, equally dependent on the proprietors, without any inhabitants at all. The universal prevalence of cob, or mud walls, will serve in a great measure to account for the untenantable state of many buildings, and for the general air of wretchedness and misery so often met with in the villages, and detached groups of houses throughout the district. This may be ascribed to the negligence of those who have the care of the estates, and the indifference but too frequently shown by the proprietors, in preserving a sufficient number of cottages on their estates for the accommodation of labourers.

Whatever may be the causes which combine in producing the amount stated in the third column of the above table, the assigning a place to it here, will probably tend to direct the attention of gentlemen, into whose hands this Report may chance to fall, to look a little farther into the subject, and see to what extent the evil now complained of, and shewn so fully to exist, may be capable of remedy. The numbers employed in the labours of agriculture through the district, when compared with the manufacturers, mechanics, and those employed on shipboard, show, that by far the larger part of the working class of the community are engaged in rural labours; and that the district, strictly speaking, is an agricultural one: but even the combined numbers of all the working-class, appear greatly short of the inefficient members of the community, at least for corporeal exertion; and in which number must necessarily be included, infants. infirm

firm and debilitated persons. The total shews a population of 39,826 souls, and averaging, according to a calculation made by throwing the district into eleven rectangular figures, and casting their contents (from the scale of the Map annexed), to 229,550 acres, equal to about 359 square miles, and giving rather less than 110 inhabitants to each square, or about 14 souls to each 80 acres. The 775 persons belonging to this district, but employed on ship-board, are not included in this estimate.

Healthiness of the District.—From the best information obtained of the salubrity of this district, scorbutic complaints are not found so common as there will be occasion to notice in other parts of the county ; asthmatic and consumptive cases are equally rare ; and notwithstanding that rheumatisms are found very often to embitter and hasten the close of the peasant's life, that class of people are generally stated to arrive here at a sound and hearty old age.

Food, and Mode of Living.—Their common food is wheat and barley bread, occasionally varied with potatoes, obtained from their employers, in the manner before noticed. Their drink, cider, or a light malt beverage, given them from one to three pints per day ; and continued, whether at stated day-labour or working by contract on their own account.

DISTRICT II.

Here follows a statement of the population of the several towns and parishes in this district.

Names of Parishes.	Inhabited.	By how many Families.	Vacant.	Males.	Females.	In Agriculture.	In Manufactures.	All other Persons.	Total.
1. Ashreigny,	151	159	16	365	391	625	100	31	756
2. Ashton,	39	42	2	111	65	33	6	137	176
3. Black Torrington,	142	148	2	321	385	346	26	334	706
4. Buckland Brewer,	152	164	11	430	442	627	140	105	872
5. ——— Filleigh,	47	47	2	122	130	128	13	111	252
6. Beaford,	95	100	3	248	268	236	30	250	516
7. Burrington,	142	142	4	355	400	330	370	55	755
8. Broadwood Kelly,	61	63	5	146	166	303	8	....	311
9. Bundleigh,	55	63	6	126	160	42	80	164	286
10. Brushford,	25	25	....	55	91	53	2	91	146
11. Bampton,	279	279	23	635	729	330	417	617	1364
12. Burlescombe,	189	188	1	404	449	571	261	21	853
13. Butterleigh,	26	27	1	66	58	23	13	89	125
14. Buckleigh,	56	56	7	163	334	73	34	190	297
15. Budford,	70	80	10	232	212	144	23	277	444
16. Clovella,	132	158	1	295	419	226	133	355	714
17. Chumleigh,	270	276	26	621	712	350	169	814	1333
18. Chawley,	144	156	10	358	397	616	24	115	755
19. Coldridge,	112	115	11	268	429	196	336	165	697
20. Cruwys Mortchard,	87	110	6	284	272	170	36	350	556
21. Cheriton Fitzpaine,	173	173	7	444	440	561	223	100	884
22. Cadbury,	31	41	2	112	116	213	17	8	238
23. Cadleigh,	38	38	15	111	115	95	7	124	226
24. Calverleigh,	16	16	....	32	38	15	6	49	70
25. Clayhanger,	29	29	1	104	109	106	8	99	213
26. Chudleigh,	360	412	54	812	974	308	570	908	1786
27. Christow,	72	99	1	207	215	138	22	262	422
28. Cheriton Bishops,	100	128	12	323	281	184	35	385	604
29. Dowland,	22	32	....	85	99	52	70	62	184
30. Dolton,	96	115	2	281	301	71	30	481	582
31. Doddiscombeleigh,	49	55	....	159	158	311	6	....	317
32. Dunchidiock,	34	39	4	95	88	42	12	129	183
33. Dunsford,	96	128	12	351	310	348	124	189	661
Carry forward,	3380	2701	257	8721	9953	7876	3845	7407	18,182

Name

Names of Parishes.	Houses.			Number of Persons, including Children.		Occupations.			Total.
	Inhabited.	By how many Families.	Vacant.	Males.	Females.	In Agriculture.	In Manufactures.	All other Persons.	
Brought forward,	3380	3701	257	8721	9953	7876	3345	7407	18,182
34. Drewsteignton,	187	191	26	478	481	258	33	668	959
35. Eggsford,	18	29	1	74	99	32	37	104	173
36. Frithlestock,	68	84	8	222	257	355	12	111	479
37. Hartland,	279	298	8	745	801	363	80	1103	1546
38. Hewish,	15	15	2	55	45	31	4	65	100
39. Hatherleigh,	206	122	13	572	646	152	144	922	1218
40. High Bickington,	225	129	7	329	364	410	34	249	693
41. —— Hampton,	38	43	1	97	107	131	2	71	204
42. Honey Church,	11	11	1	35	31	55	1	10	66
43. Huntsham,	28	29	5	90	68	100	20	38	158
44. Hockworthy,	51	51	5	131	152	274	9	.....	283
45. Holcombe Rogus,	198	193	...	302	360	43	451	168	662
46. Halberton,	265	305	20	696	740	592	373	471	1436
47. Hemiock,	174	186	7	475	545	209	75	736	1020
48. Holcombe Burnell,	85	88	5	85	91	79	3	94	176
49. Hittesleigh,	24	28	1	64	60	42	5	77	124
50. Iddesleigh,	62	74	3	199	242	404	35	2	441
51. King's Nympton,	94	90	18	249	261	240	9	261	510
52. Kinnerleigh,	15	15	2	56	38	71	23	.....	94
53. Little Torrington,	77	82	4	226	223	143	29	277	449
54. Lapford,	111	128	17	282	305	152	293	142	587
55. Langtree,	90	94	2	300	283	340	12	231	583
56. Loxbeare,	22	22	2	69	63	50	9	73	132
57. Monkleigh,	60	79	4	169	210	337	42	.....	379
58. Merton,	77	87	2	314	375	303	11	375	689
59. Meeth,	43	43	....	120	137	190	12	55	257
60. Monk Oak-hampton,	44	44	4	85	97	74	11	97	182
61. Mary Down,	44	55	9	153	160	87	10	216	313
62. Mortchard Bishops,	310	312	6	765	993	466	413	819	1698
63. Morebath,	65	84	3	221	199	222	55	143	420
64. Oakford,	81	81	2	207	201	123	20	265	408
65. Peter's Marland,	46	54	1	143	146	115	28	146	289
66. Parkham,	107	107	1	283	301	542	13	29	584
67. Petrockstow,	75	78	2	233	234	447	20	.....	467
68. Poughill,	60	62	3	137	137	259	13	2	274
69. Puddington,	28	28	1	74	61	66	8	61	135
70. Roborough,	73	89	3	227	224	418	39	4	461
71. St. Giles's,	105	105	....	283	284	398	27	122	547
72. Stokely English,	21	21	1	63	53	98	18	5	116
73. Stoodleigh,	48	48	1	189	166	176	13	166	355
74. Sleepwash,	74	74	1	172	176	86	4	258	348
75. Samford Peveril,	143	143	12	360	403	293	67	403	763
76. St. Mary Tedborne,	84	94	6	260	267	416	27	84	527
Carry forward,	6905	7579	477	19,150	20,889	20,477	5804	26,190	39,589

Names

Names of Parishes.	Houses.			Number of Persons, including Children.		Occupations.			
	Inhabited.	By how many Families.	Vacant.	Males.	Females.	In Agriculture.	In Manufactures.	All other Persons.	Total.
Brought forward,	6905	7579	477	19,150	20,839	20,477	5804	26,190	39,589
77. Spreyton,	51	76	3	165	168	155	18	160	333
78. South Tawton,	267	298	26	713	825	1422	113	3	1538
79. Trusham,	26	26	5	71	64	64	27	44	135
80. Tiverton,	1221	1397	101	3001	3504	1089	1617	3799	6505
81. Torrington, Great,	348	408	27	865	1179	121	259	1664	2044
82. Uplowman,	62	80	6	176	184	170	91	99	360
83. Woolfardiswor-thy, W.	98	99	2	285	306	364	23	204	591
84. Winkleigh,	211	246	10	180	634	456	256	502	1214
85. Wembworthy,	57	58	2	150	173	302	16	5	323
86. Woolfardiswor-thy, E.	29	34	3	69	62	52	6	73	131
87. Washfield,	82	84	8	204	218	301	20	101	422
88. Willand,	50	54	10	112	143	250	5	.....	255
89. Whitestone,	91	91	7	240	231	27	12	432	471
90. Zeal Monacho-rum,	117	117	4	279	343	593	29	....	622
Total, -	9615	10,647	691	25,660	28,873	22,969	8288	23,276	54,588

After dividing this district into seventeen rectangular figures, and casting their contents, it is found to contain an area of 300,000 acres = 468¼ square miles. This, by reference to the total of the above statement, will be found to contain rather more than 116⅓ souls to each square mile.

Healthiness of the District.—The longevity and healthy old age of the peasantry in many parts of this district, may chiefly be ascribed to their simple aliment, and the regularity and exercise necessarily connected with rural life.

DISTRICT III.

Its population is stated as under.

Names of Parishes.	Houses.			Number of Persons, including Children.		Occupations.			Total.
	Inhabited.	By how many Families.	Vacant.	Males.	Females.	In Agriculture.	In Manufactures.	All other Persons.	
1. Abbot'sBickington,	10	12	....	31	37	30	.....	38	68
2. Ashwater,	115	115	8	316	327	613	28	2	643
3. Ashbury,	4	4	....	22	9	20	....	21	41
4. Bulkworthy,	17	17	1	64	46	59	10	41	110
5. Bradworthy,	94	124	5	319	315	322	30	282	634
6. Bradford,	44	63	1	166	186	150	10	192	352
7. Bridgerule,	25	23	2	66	74	62	2	76	140
8. Beaworthy,	35	36	3	106	112	150	5	63	218
9. Belstone,	29	29	6	69	68	75	4	58	137
10. Bridestowe,	91	98	7	289	292	111	16	454	581
11. Broadwood Wedger,	106	126	1	297	289	427	10	149	586
12. Bratton Clovella,	84	96	5	303	245	120	12	416	548
13. Cookbury,	37	57	....	120	141	46	79	136	261
14. Cheldon,	19	19	2	47	44	45	2	44	91
15. Clawton,	66	75	2	174	209	93	18	272	383
16. Creacombe,	3	3	2	16	13	20	....	9	29
17. East Putford,	18	20	2	79	60	93	2	44	139
18. East Worlington,	32	38	1	103	93	122	65	9	196
19. Germansweek,	42	42	1	63	70	61	2	70	133
20. Halwell,	47	47	3	186	172	181	5	172	358
21. Holdsworthy,	192	223	12	505	540	235	93	717	1045
22. Hollacombe,	13	14	....	38	36	30	.....	44	74
23. Inwardleigh,	75	75	2	194	190	331	13	40	384
24. Knowstone,	82	82	....	206	221	123	20	284	427
25. Kigbeare,	11	11	1	33	37	30	3	97	70
26. Luffincot,	11	11	1	45	31	32	7	37	76
27. Lidford,	34	34	....	123	99	82	41	99	222
28. Lewtrenchard,	20	29	1	83	71	66	4	84	154
29. Milton Damarel.	80	90	1	231	338	296	22	151	469
30. Meshaw,	22	26	1	66	69	55	11	69	135
31. Mary Annesley,	42	48	....	55	104	61	8	130	199
32. Newton St.Petrock,	36	36	2	109	106	95	14	106	215
33. North Petherwin,	145	164	5	379	393	247	359	166	772
34. North Lew,	111	112	11	302	336	416	24	198	638
35. Northcot	12	12	1	29	42	22	.....	49	71
Carry forward	1812	2015	90	4107	5315	4861	919	4759	10,579 Names

Names of Parishes.	Inhabited.	By how many Families.	Vacant.	Males.	Females.	In Agriculture.	In Manufactures.	All other Persons.	Total.
Brought forward,	1812	2015	90	4107	5315	4861	919	4759	10,579
36. Oakhampton,	264	319	5	660	770	226	223	981	1430
37. Pancrassweek,	41	72	1	169	161	199	1	130	330
38. Pyworthy,	89	89	6	236	263	347	17	135	499
39. Rackenford,	68	77	3	176	164	100	30	210	340
40. Roseash,	59	70	5	201	196	119	27	251	397
41. Romansleigh,	28	30	....	80	76	63	5	88	156
42. Shebbeare,	126	129	2	353	391	203	29	512	744
43. Sutcombe,	52	52	3	161	169	321	9	....	330
44. St. Giles's in the Heath	36	36	3	96	91	182	5	....	187
45. Sorton,	54	62	4	169	149	111	80	127	318
46. Stowford,	43	62	4	117	118	42	4	189	235
47. Thornbury,	60	64	2	158	172	150	8	172	330
48. Tetcop,	24	26	1	82	84	99	7	60	166
49. Thrushalton,	55	69	....	215	202	112	19	286	417
50. Templeton,	38	40	3	98	102	50	7	143	200
51. Thelbridge,	31	35	1	70	85	51	....	104	155
52. Virginstowe,	19	19	....	52	49	52	....	49	101
53. Welcombe,	38	38	....	110	110	214	6	....	220
54. Werrington,	95	104	4	240	249	347	7	135	489
55. Washford Pyne,	23	24	2	56	53	53	28	28	109
56. West Worlington,	26	27	2	82	76	146	12	....	158
57. Witheridge,	176	176	12	404	471	265	69	541	875
58. Wes. Putford,	41	55	2	122	152	173	9	92	274
Total, -	3288	3680	155	9391	9668	8486	1521	8992	19,059

This

This district, divided into fifteen rectangular figures, gives it an area of 262,105 acres = to about 409½ square miles, and which, according to the sum of the population, will average about 46½ souls to each square mile.

Healthiness of the District.—Notwithstanding all the country bordering upon Dartmoor, will be found to carry the human frame to greater longevity and health of age, than we shall find to be the case in some other parts of the county, still in the interior of the district, scrophula, sore or bad legs, are ver. ommon to both sexes of the peasant order at an advan..d time of life; upon the heads and other parts of young persons of the same order, and before they attain the age of puberty. Among the artificers, and those who live above the condition of the common labourer, this disease was not so generally noticed or complained of.

Food, and Mode of Living.—The water, through the whole of this district, has already been stated as being chalybeate in a very high degree, but whether from that or some other hidden source the disease is promoted, it is equally out of the power as of the province of the Surveyor to say. Barley bread and potatoes compose a large part of the food of these people. Some wheat broth seasoned with a small piece of meat and pot-herbs, form, with pies made of bacon and potatoes, the chief variety in the mode of their subsistence.

DISTRICT IV.

We now proceed to state the population of all the towns, hamlets, villages, and tithings in the district.

Names of Parishes.	Houses.			Number of Persons, including Children		Occupations.			
	Inhabited.	By how many Families.	Vacant.	Males.	Females.	In Agriculture.	In Manufactures.	All other Persons.	Total.
1. Aveton Giffard,	143	152	7	369	377	143	59	544	746
2. Ashprignton,	96	99	10	252	257	215	114	180	509
3. Ashburton,	369	664	10	1323	1757	141	267	2672	3080
4. Abbot's Kerswell,	93	95	4	171	218	101	122	166	389
5. Bradstowe,	14	20	1	55	50	43	..	62	105
6. Brentor,	17	17	..	56	52	61	9	38	108
7. Beer Ferrers,	206	217	10	541	569	217	38	855	1110
8. Bickleigh,	39	51	4	135	129	140	14	110	264
9. Buckland Monachorum,	144	157	6	497	421	620	233	65	913
10. Brixton,	125	147	12	318	317	165	58	412	635
11. Bigbury,	90	91	8	194	236	79	18	333	430
12. Buckfastleigh,	260	307	7	709	816	457	1060	8	1525
13. Buckland-toutsaints	2	2	..	6	3	6	..	3	9
14. Blackanton,	198	198	16	507	512	415	92	512	1019
15. Brixham,	701	906	24	1512	2159	245	556	2870	3671
16. Berry Pomeroy,	157	226	8	540	584	198	324	602	1124
17. Broad Hempston,	127	132	5	268	399	132	130	405	667
18. Bickington,	46	46	3	128	237	115	13	109	237
19. Coryton,	30	35	3	78	76	44	5	105	154
20. Compton Giffard,	15	16	..	50	42	45	8	3	92
21. Cornwood	94	98	5	376	369	168	54	523	745
22. Churchstowe,	50	50	..	112	107	112	8	99	219
23. Chivelstone,	99	99	8	255	307	140	36	386	562
24. Charleton,	103	110	..	267	255	168	38	316	522
25. Cornworthy,	80	80	4	232	236	286	130	52	468
26. Churchston Ferrers,	124	130	3	320	343	140	81	44?	663
27. Comb in Teign-head,	109	109	8	220	285	196	22	287	505
28. Coffinswell,	59	59	2	117	144	258	3	.	261
29. Cockington,	63	69	..	131	163	46	27	221	294
30. Dunterton,	25	28	3	64	65	69	3	57	129
31. Diptford,	83	92	4	296	282	191	50	337	578
Carry forward,	3767	4496	175	9871	12,065	5358	3573	12,810	21,934 Names

Names of Parishes.	Houses.			Number of Persons, including Children.		Occupations.			Total.
	Inhabited.	By how many Families.	Vacant.	Males.	Females.	In Agriculture.	In Manufactures.	All other Persons.	
Brought forward,	3667	4406	175	9871	12,065	5258	3573	12,810	21,93
32. Dartington,	76	94	5	248	288	221	56	209	
33. Dean Prior,	93	97	6	227	268	100	59	336	
34. Dodbrooke,	84	136	2	276	330	59	122	427	
35. Dettisham,	128	150	2	304	385	209	159	271	
36. Denbury,	67	78	5	145	185	98	92	140	330
37. Egg Buckland,	121	142	6	366	345	166	75	470	711
38. Ermington,	147	186	8	457	460	252	252	413	917
39. East Allington,	77	79	11	243	225	135	26	307	468
40. East Ogwell,	53	58	4	111	147	212	46	..	258
41. Holberton,	265	303	20	696	740	592	373	471	1436
42. Harpford,	24	24	2	66	76	103	10	29	142
43. Holne,	59	62	11	192	167	164	97	98	359
44. Holwell,	21	26	3	88	68	87	6	63	156
45. Harberton,	229	260	12	552	586	398	259	481	1138
46. Highweek,	162	163	12	341	436	511	229	37	777
47. Ipplepen,	130	138	5	334	487	203	120	498	821
48. Ilsington,	164	174	10	407	459	449	373	41	866
49. Kelly,	25	36	4	106	95	44	2	155	201
50. Kingstone,	52	67	4	172	182	111	20	223	354
51. Kingsbridge,	153	226	2	498	619	31	216	870	1117
52. Kingsware,	52	85	4	132	168	6	29	265	300
53. King's Kerswell,	122	132	4	226	306	90	34	408	532
54. Lifton,	145	174	..	432	411	517	35	291	843
55. Lamerton,	133	143	8	357	365	197	51	474	722
56. Loddiswell,	112	112	6	290	318	195	199	214	608
57. Little Hempston,	38	50	..	140	226	245	21	..	266
58. Mary Tavy,	58	58	..	207	169	63	9	304	376
59. Mary Stow,	36	48	3	165	132	133	7	157	297
60. Milton Abbot,	152	160	5	419	443	614	210	38	862
61. Meavy,	37	41	7	130	109	231	5	3	239
62. Modbury,	296	351	15	832	981	944	862	7	1813
63. Morleigh,	21	21	5	68	59	37	13	77	127
64. Marldon,	56	59	2	189	175	282	47	35	364
65. Marlborough,	190	205	20	487	569	334	277	445	1056
66. Newton Ferrers,	112	112	1	289	301	130	31	429	590
67. North Hewish,	64	61	1	201	179	291	67	22	380
68. Newton Abbot, including the hamlet of Woolborough,	165	341	6	711	912	67	240	1316	1623
Carry forward,	8680	9551	396	20,977	24,138	13,767	8371	22,837	45,215

Names

Names of Parishes.	Houses.			Number of Persons, including Children.		Occupations.			
	Inhabited.	By how many Families.	Vacant.	Males.	Females.	In Agriculture.	In Manufactures.	All other Persons.	Total.
Brought forward,	8680	9551	396	20,977	24,138	13,767	8271	22,837	45,215
9. Peter Tavy, including the hamlet of Wellsworthy,	50	59	5	142	149	226	16	49	291
0. Plymouth,	1737	3999	27	6677	9363	103	3443	12,494	16,040
1. Plympton St. Mary,	245	313	5	766	798	454	168	940	1562
2. ——— Maurice.	83	117	3	272	332	40	40	524	604
3. Plymstock,	286	366	9	760	873	192	139	1302	1633
4. Portlemouth,	46	57	..	144	154	85	32	181	298
5. Paignton,	216	323	7	694	881	654	268	653	1575
6. Revelstock,	75	78	1	205	212	43	37	337	417
7. Rattery,	77	82	2	223	228	126	24	301	451
8. Ringmore,	54	60	1	145	164	70	20	219	309
9. Sydenham,	39	45	4	100	99	151	7	41	199
30. Sampford Spiney,	32	35	5	108	97	151	21	30	205
31. St. Budeaux,	78	86	2	281	263	135	36	370	511
32. Stoke Damarell,	3252	5970	42	10,075	13,672	750	3650	19,347	23,747
33. Stonehouse, East,	358	739	26	1264	2143	10	215	3182	3407
34. Sheepstor,	18	18	6	58	41	87	12	..	99
35. Shaugh Prior,	72	97	4	247	233	196	33	251	480
36. South Hewish,	54	58	2	141	145	84	118	84	286
37. —— Melton,	45	53	..	162	140	111	33	158	302
38. —— Brent,	165	163	..	515	517	972	60	..	1032
39. —— Poole,	83	82	4	204	208	101	35	276	412
0. Sherford,	57	65	1	195	185	101	28	251	380
1. Stokenham,	250	256	18	610	691	496	110	695	1301
2. Slapton,	102	102	3	272	286	250	22	286	558
3. Stoke Flemming,	111	116	9	271	307	212	59	307	578
4. St. Petrock, 5. St. Saviour, 6. Townstall, } Dartmouth,	542	1023	17	1412	2000	84	1679	1649	3412
7. Stoke Gabriel,	90	96	3	247	284	201	34	296	531
8. Staverton,	190	217	12	473	580	416	303	334	1053
9. Stoke in Teignhead,	123	127	3	263	311	127	234	213	574
100. St. Mary Church,	172	183	17	373	428	198	218	385	801
101. Tavistock,	472	804	9	1430	1990	298	556	2566	3420
102. Tamerton Foliet,	122	137	12	371	376	195	60	492	747
103. Thurlestone,	65	74	8	172	184	138	61	157	356.
Carry forward,	16,170	25,655	663	59,000	52,867	20,085	19,525	71,207	111,879 Names

Names of Parishes.	Inhabited.	By how many families.	Vacant.	Males.	Females.	In Agriculture.	In Manufactures.	All other Persons.	Total.
Brought forward,	16,170	25,665	663	59,000	52,367	20,983	19,525	71,207	111,39
104. Totness,	293	370	7	1042	1161	195	288	2110	250.
105. Torbryan,	36	41	3	126	132	165	21	132	25.
106. Tormoham,	143	183	12	376	462	56	81	707	85.
107. Ugborough,	160	166	3	395	561	109	35	812	95.
108. Whitechurch,	79	79	2	225	253	460	11	7	47.
109. Walkhampton,	68	68	5	174	162	184	22	130	33.
110. Weston Peverill,	30	36	1	115	131	79	8	159	24.
111. Wembury,	81	81	4	186	202	95	17	278	39.
112. West Allington,	104	116	4	333	322	171	55	431	65.
113. Woodleigh,	39	41	2	119	121	116	47	77	2 10
114. Woodland,	24	26	4	92	120	122	69	21	21
115. West Ogwell,	7	7	..	25	28	25	..	28	5.
116. Yealmpton,	132	133	2	484	509	175	130	688	99.
117. Vaulter's Home,	243	323	..	704	910	56	54	1510	161.
Total, -	17,658	27,586	712	63,398	57,741	21,931	20,911	78,297	121,139

Employed on ship-board, and belonging to the several ports in this district, • 2249

After dividing this district into 23 rectangular figures, and casting their contents, its area is found to be 378,628 acres, or rather more than 591 square miles. Exclusive of 2249 persons annually employed in the registered merchant ships belonging to the ports of Plymouth and of Dartmouth, by a reference to the above total, the district is found to contain 121,139 souls, averaging a population of 204¼ persons to each square mile, and consequently above four times more thickly inhabited than the preceding district.

Food, and Mode of Living.—The working class of the community in the vicinity of all the large towns, meet with constant employment, and at an advance of wages beyond that formerly stated. An ample supply of fish, added to the ordinary food of the peasantry in the preceding districts, contributes to sustain the great mass of the inhabitants with firmness and vigour to an advanced period of life.

DISTRICT

DISTRICT V.

The population of this small district is stated as under.

Names of Parishes.	Houses.			Number of Persons, including Children.		Occupations.			
	Inhabited.	By how many Families.	Vacant.	Males.	Females.	In Agriculture.	In Manufactures.	All other Persons.	Total.
1. Buckland in the Moor,	19	20	4	54	52	101	..	5	106
2. Bovey Tracy,	286	286	23	667	764	326	78	1027	1431
3. Chagford,	236	251	31	522	593	543	120	452	1115
4. Gidley,	17	17	2	58	67	122	..	3	125
5. Lustleigh,	54	80	..	130	116	236	8	2	246
6. Manaton,	57	68	5	181	167	109	25	214	348
7. Moreton Hempstead,	402	402	57	805	963	289	599	880	1768
8. North Bovey,	77	96	4	261	258	160	34	325	519
9. Teigngrace,	16	16	..	62	71	74	8	51	133
10. Throwsleigh,	57	57	11	145	186	316	14	1	331
11. Widdecombe,	102	102	9	515	523	745	5	293	1043
Total, ..	1323	1345	151	3400	3765	3021	891	3253	7165

For causes utterly out of the power of the Surveyor to explain, unless they may be referred to those already stated, more than a one-tenth part of the houses in this district are vacant, and may therefore be generally considered in a state of ruin. This district being divided into seven rectangular figures, and their contents summed up, is found to give it an area of 61,690 acres, or about $96\frac{2}{3}$ square miles, and from the total of its inhabitants, averaging about $74\frac{1}{2}$ persons to each square mile.

The inhabitants of this hilly district, are much famed

for

for their hardihood, and for excelling in all manner of athletic exercises. The air, in common with all the parishes surrounding Dartmoor (however at particular seasons injurious to vegetable nature), exhibits to the human frame a more friendly disposition, or the following statements could not have been verified by the parish registers from which they were taken. The country in the proximity of the moor, and situate on its north-west and north-eastern quarters, is stated as from which a fair judgment may be formed of the rest.

The parish of Bridestow, which contains a population of about 580 souls, sent in the year 1805, ten of its inhabitants to the grave; of this number three were infants, the remainder attained the respective ages of 63, 64, 69, 73, 75, 78, 84, and 89. In the same year, at Moreton-Hempstead, the population of which is about 1770 souls, there were 27 funerals, 7 of which were of persons after attaining an age between 80 and 83; 12 died between the ages of 60 and 80, and eight died infants, or below the age of seven years. In the present year, and up to the 10th of October, there has been in the said parish of Moreton-Hempstead 15 funerals, seven of which were of persons who died between the ages of 80 and 92, six between 60 and 80, and two infants.

Food, and Mode of Living.—The food of these people consists of barley with some wheaten bread, an abundance of potatoes, with pea and other broths, seasoned with pickled pork, bacon, or the fat of mutton prepared in the manner before noticed, with a profusion of leeks and onions.

DISTRICT VI.

Here follows a statement of the population of all the towns, villages, hamlets, and tithings in this district.

Names of Parishes.	Houses.			Number of Persons, including Children.		Occupations.			Total.
	Inhabited.	By how many Families.	Vacant.	Males.	Females.	In Agriculture.	In Manufactures.	All other Persons.	
1. Ashcombe,	51	57	8	132	148	124	8	148	280
2. Alpington,	98	184	10	404	441	114	42	689	845
3. Aylesbeare,	139	181	2	311	376	366	318	3	687
4. Bishop's Teignton,	157	159	11	298	375	162	39	472	673
5. Bramford Speke,	44	44	.....	124	149	75	14	184	273
6. Bow, or NymetTracy,	150	181	12	318	359	123	158	396	677
7. Bradninch,	247	260	6	546	641	529	648	10	1187
8. Broadhembury,	152	152	6	379	401	271	23	486	780
9. Broad Clyst,	394	394	25	771	769	1314	213	13	1540
10. Bicton,	24	36	.....	77	96	28	9	136	173
11. Crediton,	1045	1076	48	2102	2827	1609	3166	154	4929
12. Colebrooke,	135	135	9	383	379	208	39	515	762
13. Clannaborough,	7	7	.....	35	24	55	....	4	59
14. Cullumpton,	615	655	46	1417	1721	527	1030	1581	3138
15. Culmstock,	326	392	50	652	844	183	769	544	1496
16. Clyst Hydon,	48	60	5	116	141	68	6	183	257
17. Clyst St. Lawrence,	34	34	5	79	77	145	10	1	156
18. Clyst St. George,	51	51	1	120	129	170	73	6	249
19. Clyst St. Mary,	21	23	1	45	52	47	14	36	97
20. Colyton Rawleigh.	95	123	5	311	316	86	33	508	627
21. Dawlish,	291	301	20	637	787	317	107	1000	1424
22. East Teignmouth,	103	103	9	194	290	20	34	430	484
23. Exminster,	91	158	1	405	390	217	55	523	795
24. Exbourne,	74	74	2	199	222	127	33	261	421
25. East Budleigh,	203	215	20	455	559	223	185	606	1014
26. Feniton,	42	49	1	124	128	67	5	180	252
27. Farrington,	45	56	2	148	145	137	10	146	293
28. Fen Ottery,	21	29	.....	65	62	126	1	....	127
29. Honiton Clyst,	66	66	1	166	182	223	58	67	348
30. Harpford,	24	24	2	66	76	103	10	29	142
31. Heavitree,	163	178	14	371	462	507	193	133	833
32. Huxhum,	22	24	1	64	71	34	33	68	135
33. Ideford,	71	71	4	168	171	30	12	297	339
34. Ide,	123	123	2	264	243	432	25	...	507
35. Jacobstow,	34	34	8	103	90	150	16	27	193
36. King's Teignton,	167	169	8	419	437	187	28	641	856
Carry forward, -	5773	5778	329	13,167	13,580	9853	7417	10,377	27,188

DEVON.] Names

Names of Parishes.	Houses.			Number of Persons, including Children.		Occupations.			Total.
	Inhabited.	By how many Families.	Vacant.	Males.	Females.	In Agriculture.	In Manufactures.	All other Persons.	
Brought forward,	5773	5778	329	13,167	13,580	9353	7417	10,377	27,188
37. Kenton,	307	381	29	762	877	275	148	1216	1639
38. Kerm,	168	182	16	400	418	194	44	580	818
39. Kentisbeare, with Blackborough,	141	226	7	601	441	293	47	702	1042
40. Littleham & Exmouth,	406	422	26	720	1189	104	570	1235	1909
41. Lympstone,	194	203	9	362	521	87	110	686	883
42. Mamhead,	48	53	1	110	120	175	16	39	230
43. Newton St. Cyres,	168	170	4	436	431	340	70	457	867
44. Nymet Rowland,	14	14	6	37	39	20	10	46	76
45. North Tawton,	275	300	14	670	766	251	356	829	1436
46. Nether Exe,	14	17	.....	43	43	32	2	52	86
47. Ottery St. Mary,	513	746	6	1174	1241	1530	645	240	2415
48. Otterton,	187	187	4	425	495	380	45	495	920
49. Powderham,	47	50	3	58	117	34	31	110	175
50. Payhembury,	67	88	5	211	205	156	50	210	416
51. Plymtree,	72	72	3	177	198	168	48	159	375
52. Poltimore,	46	46	1	133	117	240	10	.....	250
53. Pinhoe,	81	81	15	181	172	136	25	192	353
54. Rew-with-up-Exe,	23	41	3	92	103	138	48	9	195
55. Rockbeare,	78	79	2	208	212	408	9	2	419
56. Shillingford,	12	13	.....	37	34	51	4	16	71
57. St. Leonard,	26	38	7	52	81	4	43	86	133
58. Sanford in Crediton,	320	359	22	783	959	595	809	338	1742
59. St. Nicholas,	128	129	19	235	350	18	44	523	585
60. Stokeley Pomeroy,	41	46	2	102	94	83	53	60	196
61. St. Thomas,	424	501	18	967	1222	107	1989	93	2189
62. Sholebrook,	134	140	3	336	350	549	125	12	686
63. Silverton,	234	298	30	576	660	353	239	644	1236
64. Stoke Cannon,	47	60	6	126	128	109	17	128	254
65. Sawton,	58	62	4	169	149	111	80	127	318
66. Sampford Courtenay,	171	173	8	433	527	581	378	1	960
67. Thorverton,	306	366	32	567	601	142	127	893	1168
68. Tallaton,	72	75	2	197	196	97	30	266	393
69. Topsham,	462	625	15	1217	1531	98	449	2201	2748
70. Upton Pyne,	46	56	2	208	201	200	8	201	409
71. Upton Helions,	19	27	1	64	72	53	27	56	136
72. Uffculm,	556	390	37	828	1009	442	770	627	1837
73. West Teignmouth,	354	410	12	612	916	20	89	1419	1528
74. Whimple,	79	89	4	441	242	220	21	242	483
75. Whitecombe Rawleigh,	111	152	16	291	401	448	123	121	692
76. Woodbury,	263	297	14	603	683	976	256	54	1286
Total, -	11,931	13,457	732	28,911	31,691	19,572	15,382	25,648	60,602

Names

CITY OF EXETER.

Names of Parishes & Precincts.	Houses.			Number of Persons, including Children.		Occupations.			
	Inhabited.	By how many Families.	Vacant.	Males.	Females.	In Agriculture.	In Manufactures.	All other Persons.	Total.
1. Allhallows, Goldsmith, St.	50	59	1	126	209	.....	29	306	335
2. Allhallows-on-the-Wall,	85	157	4	302	367	.....	114	555	669
3. Bedford precinct,	17	17	....	45	71	.....	7	109	116
4. Bradninch precinct,	7	7	1	6	32	.....	.....	32	32
5. Close precinct,	102	114	6	172	399	.....	84	487	571
6. David, St.	313	443	19	804	1050	55	254	1545	1854
7. Edmund, St. on the Bridge,	206	283	10	405	513	.....	918	.....	918
8. George, St.	75	143	7	291	351	11	157	474	642
9. John, St.	72	107	5	230	391	.....	203	418	621
10. Kerrian, St.	38	58	4	104	126	.....	73	157	230
11. Lawrence, St.	74	123	4	228	320	8	115	425	548
12. Martin, St.	45	51	5	149	161	.....	73	237	310
13. Mary, St. Archers,	59	93	5	160	218	1	96	281	378
14. Mary, St. Major,	299	552	11	938	1197	.....	403	1732	2135
15. Mary, St. Stepps,	101	138	4	298	421	8	145	566	719
16. Olave, St.	91	118	6	252	314	3	120	443	566
17. Pancras, St.	35	53	..	93	138	8	30	193	231
18. Paul, St.	189	269	10	492	606	.....	228	870	1098
19. Petrock, St.	44	54	2	132	155	.....	90	197	287
20. Sudwell, St.	450	689	29	1072	1635	67	777	1863	2707
21. Stephen, St.	61	74	5	184	297	.....	43	438	481
22. Trinity, Holy,	279	345	13	821	1119	22	554	1364	1940
Total, -	2692	3947	144	7304	10,084	183	4513	12,692	17,388

Men and boys employed on ship-board belonging to the port of Exeter,   919

After

After dividing this district into eleven rectangular
figures, their sum is found to give 178,860 acres, or 280¼
square miles, for the area of this district, and which, from
the sum total of the above statements, will be found to
average a population of 277¼ souls to each square mile.
The men and boys employed on ship-board belonging to
the port of Exeter, amount to 919, but they are not included in this estimate.

Healthiness of the District.—Consumptive and gravelly
cases were more frequently heard of in different parts of
this district, than in most of the preceding ones. Upon
the whole, although the climate of this district seems to
dispose to luxury and indulgence in a very great degree,
the minutes collected on the Survey, do not develope its
power of supporting the human system generally to the
same period of life, and healthy old age, as has been already witnessed in the vicinity of Dartmoor.

If we except the neighbourhood of and below Exeter,
the supply of fish among the mass of the inhabitants is
but small, they therefore do not possess the variety of
wholesome food enjoyed by those who inhabit the maritime borders of the county.

DISTRICT VII.

The population of this district, selected from the document before resorted to, is found to be as follows :

Names of Parishes.	Houses.			Number of Persons, including Children.		Occupations.			Total.
	Inhabited.	By how many Families.	Vacant.	Males.	Females.	in Agriculture.	in Manufactures.	All other Persons.	
1. Axminster,	406	411	25	967	1187	383	572	1199	2154
2. Axmouth,	60	66	2	192	183	305	8	62	375
3. Awliscombe,	86	105	3	214	212	165	194	67	426
4. Branscombe,	116	119	4	284	319	370	40	193	603
5. Buckerell,	56	56	2	126	154	148	15	122	280
6. Colyton,	257	334	32	761	880	255	197	1189	1641
7. Cotleigh,	42	46	1	103	111	102	47	65	214
8. Combe Pawleigh	35	41	2	115	122	38	12	187	237
9. Combe Ryne,	28	2.	1	69	72	133	8	----	141
10. Church Stanton,	112	196	4	365	365	290	251	189	750
11. Clay Haydon,	113	139	----	306	384	286	289	115	690
12. Dunkerswell,	165	165	2	205	188	111	15	267	393
13. Farway,	61	66	2	143	144	129	14	144	287
14. Gittisham,	64	64	2	194	265	75	39	345	459
15. Honiton,	546	563	11	1083	1294	141	1250	986	2377
16. Hemiock,	174	180	7	475	545	209	75	786	1020
17. Kilmington,	89	96	8	218	226	286	138	20	444
18. Luppit,	109	124	7	322	353	329	178	175	675
19. Monkton,	18	20	----	55	66	29	3	89	121
20. Membury,	112	138	5	355	354	594	115	----	709
21. Musbury,	63	76	2	149	131	175	86	19	280
22. North Leigh,	36	36	2	99	90	44	16	120	180
23. Offwell,	60	64	6	148	154	74	37	191	302
24. Rosedown*.	----	----		....	....	....	....	----	....
25. Sidmouth,	229	247	29	532	720	109	153	990	1252
26. Salcombe Regis,	56	56	7	136	164	225	19	56	300
27. Sidbury,	252	262	44	567	666	236	383	614	1233
28. Seaton and Beer,	269	323	26	708	789	142	52	1303	1497
29. South Leigh,	41	41	2	115	122	133	10	94	237
30. Shute,	91	107	7	278	280	122	41	395	558
31. Sheldon,	22	28	2	59	69	63	26	39	128
32. Thornecombe,	217	231	9	522	570	276	351	465	1092
33. Up Ottery,	150	168	2	393	402	259	56	500	795
34. Up Lime,	126	137	3	266	283	427	15	107	549
35. Widworthy,	45	45	2	122	123	55	23	167	245
36. Yarcombe,	110	132	5	363	377	712	18	10	740
Total, -	4416	4910	268	11,000	12,364	7398	4746	11,220	23,364

* Included in Axmouth, extra parochial.

After

After dividing this district into ten rectangular figures, and deducting from their amount so much of the county of Dorset as lies within the eastern boundary of Devonshire, it is found to contain 130,812 acres, or rather more than 204 square miles, and which, according to the total of its population, averages 114 souls to each square mile.

The inhabitants along the sea-coast are plentifully supplied with fish, particularly in the pilchard season. Their mode of living in other respects, the healthiness of the district, or degree of longevity to which its peasant inhabitants arrive, were noticed in the course of the Survey, as requiring nothing farther than a general reference to what has been already stated on these subjects.

Abstract of the Statements contained in the preceding Chapter, with the amount of Sums annually levied in each District, as detailed in Chap. IV. for the Relief and Maintenance of the Poor; and also such other Assessments made for Parochial Purposes.

Districts.	Houses.			Population.						Area of County, &c.			
				Number of Persons, including Children.		Occupations.				Extent of Districts.		Population.	
	Inhabited.	By how many Families.	Vacant.	Males.	Females.	In Agriculture.	In Manufactures.	All other Persons.	Total Population.	In Acres.	In square Miles.	Per square Mile.	Per Acre.
I.	7189	7825	401	18,116	21,710	12,552	6028	21,246	39,826	229,550	359.00	110.00	$\frac{173}{1000}$
II.	9615	10,647	691	25,660	28,873	22,969	8288	23,276	54,535	300,000	468.00	116.33	$\frac{191}{1000}$
III.	3288	3680	155	9391	9668	8546	1521	8992	19,059	262,105	409.50	46.50	$\frac{72}{1000}$
IV.	17,658	27,580	712	63,398	57,741	21,931	20,911	78,297	121,139	378,628	591.50	204.75	$\frac{329}{1000}$
V.	1323	1345	151	3400	3765	3021	891	5253	7165	61,690	96.40	74.50	$\frac{113}{1000}$
VI.	11,931	13,457	732	28,911	31,691	19,572	15,382	25,648	60,602	178,860	280.75	277.75	$\frac{416}{1000}$
City of Exeter	2692	3947	144	7304	10,084	183	4513	12,692	17,388			*	*
VII.	4416	4910	268	11,000	12,361	7398	4746	11,220	23,364	130,812	204.00	114.00	$\frac{178}{1000}$
Dartmoor†	—	—	—	—	—	—	—	—	—	53,664	83.85	—	—
Total,	58,106	73,391	3251	167,180	175,896	96,172	62,280	184,624	343,076	1,595,309	2493.00	137.61	$\frac{215}{1000}$

Hands employed on ship-board belonging to the several ports in this county, 3943

* Included in District, No. VI.

† Included within the boundaries of Lydford parish.

Amount

Amount of Parochial Levies and Disbursements.

Total Money raised by the Poor-Rates, and other Rate or Rates, within the Year ending 1803.			Total Money expended in that Year, out of any House of Industry or Workhouse.			Total Money expended in any House of Industry or Workhouse.			Expenditure in Suits at Law, removal of Paupers, Expenses of Overseers and other Officers.			Total amount of Expenditure on account of the Poor, in the Year ending at Easter, 1803.			Expenditure for any other purpose, Church-Rate, County-Rate, Highways, Militia, &c.			Total Expenditure within the Year ending 1803.		
£. 18,563	5	5¾	£. 12,988	6	5¾	2317	11	0	£. 350	12	5¼	£. 15,656	9	11	£. 2131	18	1¼	£. 17,788	8	0¼
33,490	15	1½	24,116	10	5½	1913	8	11	741	5	0	26,771	4	4½	5701	4	0½	32,472	8	5
10,201	4	1¾	7351	7	10¾	200	0	0	306	15	11¾	7858	3	10½	2201	4	9	10,059	8	7¼
53,334	15	4½	30,092	8	1¼	11,926	3	10½	1340	8	10½	43,359	0	10¼	8817	1	4½	52,176	2	2¾
4162	3	1¼	2957	3	11¾	549	6	4½	118	19	5½	3625	9	9¾	446	5	1½	4071	14	11¼
37,489	3	1¼	29,684	13	8½	1520	4	8½	788	10	11½	31,993	9	4½	4766	13	10½	36,760	3	3
7537	7	5¼	4639	8	0	2552	10	8¾	461	6	4½	7653	5	1¼	1882	5	1	9535	10	2½
14,586	9	6½	9864	8	2¼	1422	1	0¼	436	19	6½	11,723	8	9	2295	12	6¾	14,019	1	3¾
£. 179,365	3	3½	£. 121,694	6	9¾	£. 22,401	6	7½	£. 4544	18	6½	£. 148,640	12	0¾	£. 28,242	4	11	£. 176,882	16	11¾

Th

The preceding abstract contains a summary of 452 places or parishes in this county. The parish of Hacombe not being at all noticed in the population abstract, and its levies and disbursements only amounting to 15s. annually, has been purposely omitted in these returns. The want of an exact correspondence in the abstract, relative to the expense and maintenance of the poor, with the document whence the particulars were taken, arises solely from the errors the Surveyor discovered in the printed particulars. The number of persons belonging to the 412 friendly societies, are 31,792; of which 3676 are females, composing fifty-one of these societies: the whole amounts to nearly a one-tenth part of the population of the county. The amount of the total money expended annually for parochial purposes, appears to average 10s. 3¼d. per head on the resident population.

———

The following statements respecting the expense of maintenance of the poor in the house of industry in Axminster, has been very obligingly communicated by a gentleman in that neighbourhood.

From Easter 1804, *to Easter* 1805—54 *Weeks.*

Number of inhabitants, 63.

	£.	s.	d.
Expended in provisions and necessaries in the workhouse	489	11	8
Ditto in clothes	32	3	10
Ditto in shoes	23	16	4
Ditto in governor's salary	27	0	0
Carry forward	£.572	11	10

Brought

	£.	s.	d.	£.	s.	d.
Brought forward				572	11	10
Deduct clear produce of labour	53	17	1			
A year's annuity belonging to a pauper, clothed and maintained in the house	20	0	0			
				73	17	1

Remaining total expense of 63 inhabitants, 54 weeks			498	14	9
Average expense per head per year of 54 weeks			7	18	4
Average expense per head per week			0	2	11

From Easter 1805, *to Easter* 1806—51 *Weeks.*

Number of inhabitants, 61.

	£.	s.	d.
Expended in provisions and necessaries in the work house	501	2	10¾
Ditto in clothes	28	17	8
Ditto in shoes	17	18	4
Ditto in the governor's salary	27	0	0
	574	18	10¾

Deduct clear produce of labour	62	19	2			
A year's annuity belonging to a pauper, clothed and maintained in the house	20	0	0			
				82	19	2

	£.	s.	d.
	491	19	8¾
Average expense per head per year of 51 weeks	8	1	3½
Average expense per head per week	0	3	1¾

In

In the year 1763, a benefit club or friendly society was established in this town, which exists to the present day; and from the low subscription of two-pence per week from every member, has accumulated a stock of 2144*l.* after defraying the demands of three shillings and sixpence and seven shillings per week to sick members, who after a year's subscription are incapable of working, or confined to their beds. Of their stock, upwards of 2100*l.* is funded, and produces an interest of 108*l.* 8*s.* 0*d.* which is divided equally between such members as having subscribed to the stock 23 years or more, arrive at the age of 63 years.

CHAP. XVII.

OBSTACLES TO IMPROVEMENTS.

POPULATION, CAPITAL, TENURES, LABOUR.

IN addition to what may be inferred from the state-ment in the preceding Chapter, with respect to the ac-tual want of hands in many parts of the county for carrying forward its improvement and necessary cultivation, we find another formidable obstacle, in the general want of a capital among the tenantry of the country. This, as be-fore noticed, has very much arisen from the long usage of lifehold tenures, and so long as that system continues to prevail among the land-owners of the country, will the evil inseparably connected with it exist, with all its per-nicious consequences. The value of labour, at the pre-sent price of agricultural produce, cannot be brought forward as any colourable pretext against the improve-ment of the country; the stated summer and winter wages being not more than 7s. per week; and all agri-cultural task-work will, in a great measure, become regu-lated by that standard.

Tithe.—On the subject of tithe, it is with peculiar sa-tisfaction that the Author of this Report has it so fully in his power to bear testimony to the liberality and mo-deration of the clergy generally through this county, for it is not reasonable to urge that 2s. 6d. or 3s. in the pound rent, is a high commutation for the great and small
tithe

tithe of a country so large; a proportion of the enclosed, cultivated, and rented parts of which is subject to a convertible system, and consequently to be alternately cropped with corn: and there are but few of the clergy in the county, that exact or demand a commutation beyond the latter sum.

It is not, however, the payment of tithe that is so much objected to, as the uncertainty of the tenure for which they may be commuted. The injury also which they sometimes produce, by occasioning disputes between the clergyman and his parishioners, will doubtless be justly appreciated in due time, by those who are the guardians of our happy constitution in church and state. Happily for Devonshire, this observation applies but in a few solitary instances, and generally very slight indeed; but as it does apply, the Surveyor considered it his duty not entirely to pass it over.

Poor-Rates.—Although complaints are continually made of the great pressure of parochial disbursements, particularly of such as are levied for the relief and maintenance of the poor, yet would a patient hearing be allowed till the subject was candidly investigated and explained, it would not most probably appear to justify so general and so loud a clamour; for on all occasions where there is a gradually increased disbursement on the same account, we are more prone to estimate the increased disbursement by *quantity* than by value. Can the present rates be considered an exorbitant assessment on the parish value of the county? Surely it will not be insisted on to be such; but on comparison with the *apparent* increased value of agricultural produce, by the depreciation of value in the circulating medium, this contribution, in point of fact, will not be found to trench more on the actual substance

stance of the farmer, than what his ancestor was obliged
to pay and satisfy fifty years ago. The question is
simply this, Does he contribute a greater proportion of
the produce of his labour and capital, or in other
words, more bushels of wheat, than were disbursed by his
predecessors on the same account? It will be admitted,
from the failure of manufactories in his neighbourhood,
and other temporary causes, that he does, but by no
means to the extent so generally complained of, and excited by the increased amount *but not value* of the sums
annually demanded from him. In such places as lie
within the reach of manufactories, the increased wages
to the man, and general earnings of his family, will draw
more of the working part of the community to settle,
than could possibly be supplied with employment, by the
capital engaged in the cultivation of the land. Any check
or impediment raised by war, or otherwise, to the carrying on such manufactories to their ordinary extent, will
have the effect of throwing additional burthens on the
occupiers of land, to regulate which, and to arrange
them in a manner more just and equable, on the common capital of such neighbourhood, does seem to require
and demand an early and full consideration.

Disseminated Knowledge.—With regard to a farther
dissemination of knowledge among the farmers, however
fashionable it may be to stigmatize them as ignorant and
obstinate, because they do not adopt the wild theories
and hypothetical opinions of modern writers on husbandry, still, so far as the observation of the Surveyor
extends generally, he has met with but few instances of
that invincible ignorance so commonly asserted, or of any
judicious and actual improvement being made clear to the
judgment

judgment of the farmer, that he has not gradually and ultimately adopted. In truth, the farmer has by far too much at stake, to be easily seduced from the course of husbandry pursued by his forefathers, and which, by his own practice, has yielded to him the means of raising his family, paying his rent, tradesmen's bills, and meeting the parochial payments, to forego the certain means of procuring these supplies in order to pursue a different system of management, dressed up in all the parade of science, and altogether in a language he does not comprehend; but let the advantages of a superior management be once demonstrated to his understanding by a series of beneficial results, and there is an absolute certainty of his soon becoming a convert to the better practice. But he well knows, that in addition to the ordinary risks and casualties of stock and seasons, and to which upon all occasions, he must patiently be resigned, the miscarriage of one crop only, conducted on a new and untried system in the neighbourhood, would not only involve him in ruin, but the calamity would be augmented by the mortifying scorn and unfeeling triumph of his neighbours, for being, or pretending to be so much wiser than themselves. It is therefore of the utmost importance, that attention should be paid by country gentlemen in furnishing examples of superior management to their tenantry and neighbours, and which, whenever proved to be such, will never fail of being ultimately adopted by them.

The points most essential to impress upon the minds of the cultivators of this county, are those of departing from the practice of paring and burning their sound, wellstapled lands, and to commence the important labours of draining, and relieving the country of that superabundance

ance of water with which it is generally oppressed, particularly when the springs are full, and during the winter
season.

Wire-Worm.—The wire-worm will sometimes be found
to prey on the roots of the wheat in the month of
March ; but the injury the plant receives from the depredations of this insect, is not stated of sufficient magnitude to merit particular consideration.

Grub.—The grub is found periodically to infest certain
grass-lands, but the immense quantities of the parent fly
encouraged to be taken by the children in such places,
has much contributed to repress their farther increase.
Here the rook joins its aid to the industry of the farmer,
and by the number of grubs it devours, compensates
largely for the corn that is eaten by them.

Rats, Mice, Sparrows, and other Vermin.—With regard to rats, mice, sparrows, and other vermin, they are
such as are found common in other parts of the kingdom;
and for their destruction, or prevention of increase, the
inhabitants do not appear to be in possession of, or resort
to other than the well-known expedients. The furze-
brakes, copses, and particularly the holes and cavities in
the rocks and cliffs along the sea-coast, are found favourable to the escape and ultimate preservation of the breed
of foxes. These places are regarded by sportsmen as valuable sanctuaries, from their being likely to conduce to
the permanent amusements of the field. It is, however,
regarded far otherwise by those who derive their subsistence from the employments of the country.

The Surveyor is indebted to the politeness of the
Rev. Mr. Clack, Rector of Milton Damarell, for the following

lowing valuable observations on the cause of the rust or
mildew in wheat.

"*Milton Damarell, Holdsworthy,* Jan. 17, 1807.

" DEAR SIR,

" In pursuance of the request you have been pleased
to honour me with, I have sent you some of my observations on the blight in wheat, &c.

" That this blight is a fungus, has been discovered
by the aid of the magnifying glass; and that its consequences are very pernicious to wheat, is acknowledged
by all agriculturists, as it impedes the nutritive fluid in
its progress from the root to the grain. This fungus, I
observe, is generated in many other vegetable substances
besides wheat, such as trees, shrubs, herbs, grasses, &c.
varying in colour and size. These receiving the infection
at different seasons of the year, form, as it were, conductors from one to the other, in which *fungi* germinate,
effloresce, disseminate, and die, during the evolutions of
the seasons. In spring and autumn the fungus thrives
similar to all other vegetable substances in a more luxuriant degree than in winter, exhibiting itself most powerfully on the leaves of the *alnus nigra baccifera,* or black
alder; pear tree, willow, box, barberry, raspberry, rose,
gooseberry, blackberry, trefoil, strawberry, dock, coltsfoot,
grasses, the yellow corn, or melancholy thistle, and
wheat. Its colour is first pale yellow, then orange, turning off to a brown or black. On some leaves it destroys
the part affected, and entirely kills others. On the leaves
of pears, barberries, the black alder, and gooseberry trees,
it exhibits itself at first in small yellow pustules, increasing
in size until they effloresce in clusters of various shapes,
occupying both sides the leaf, turning off to a vermillion,
and then a dark rusty brown colour. Sometimes the

DEVON.]   fungus

fungus affects also the blossom; as for instance, that of the black alder. Sometimes young shoots, as those of the afore-mentioned tree, of which I have seen every shoot just as it sprouts forth, infected all round, curled up, the fungus as large as a goose-quill, and the shoot finally destroyed. Sometimes it infects the fruit, as for instance, that of gooseberry trees, which, as soon as the fungus has arrived at maturity, withers and falls to the ground. On the black alder the fungus is larger than on any other shrub, and on the box the most minute.

" On bramble, roses, and raspberry leaves, its first appearance is generally of a pale yellow powder, turning off to an orange colour, and lastly jet black mildew. So likewise in the coltsfoot, wheat, and grasses. Its effects on barley and oats are so trifling as not to deserve notice. When you perceive the upper part of leaves turned red or brown, and in spots, it is a sure indication of their having been infected by the fungus, which you will generally find on turning up the leaf, growing beneath it, and in its last stage, unless it has been washed off by heavy rains.

" In 1805 I remarked that half a large field of wheat adjoining to a coppice, was very much smitten with the bligh, or rust, as it is generally called in this neighbourhood, but as the contagion occurred before the ear had shot, little or no damage was sustained by the grain. The other half of the field was then tilled, and last year an infection took place similar to the year before, but after the ear shot, unfortunately two successive infections took place; the grain was consequently much injured, as not only the leaf but the stalk and glumes were attacked, from their being exposed, and had not the field been cut before it was ripe, it would have been destroyed. The seeds of *fungi* are so minute, and exceedingly light, that they are

liable

A Bramble Leaf.

A Sprig of Box.

Nº 1 & 2. The undersides of Leaves.   Nº 3. The upper denoting the effect of Fungi.

Nodder sculp. Strand

Tho: Clark delt.

liable to be wafted by every breeze, when accompanied by moisture or fogs: thence the false idea that the mildew is caused by the fog alone. The fungus having arrived at maturity in the spring on a few shrubs, bushes, or plants, is taken up by the next humid atmosphere, wafted into the adjoining fields, and the nearest wheat is sure to suffer most. The wheat near the western hedge, where any plants congenial to the growth of *fungi* remain, is sure to suffer more than any other part of the field. In damp weather also its seed is more immediately received into the leaves of trees and shrubs, together with their barks and fruits, through the medium of those valves or mouths which nature has supplied them with for the admission of moisture. These valves possess a contractile force, which is operated on by the power of a dry or cold atmosphere, whereby the regress of the moisture is prevented, and of course it is taken up by the tree. These valves are scarce perceptible to the naked eye, but are easily descried by the use of a highly magnifying glass. The farina of the fungus is as in the case of other vegetable substances, carried from flower to flower, by means of insects, but these insects generally assimilate their colour to the colour of the fungus, except in one instance : the fungus on the black alder, barberry, and gooseberry tree, is attended by an insect about the size of a cheese mite; it is of a shining jet black, and somewhat the shape of a beetle. It is the exact size of the aperture in the fungus blossom, and when the fungus is decaying, inhabits it, and feeds on its interior. These curious little insects are sometimes found also in the interior of dead oak apples, where, as in other *fungi*, they probably remain during winter.

"Having troubled you with some history of the fungus, its progress and consequences, I will proceed next to give you

you my reasons to prove how its extent may be materially lessened ; for though we may as well say that weeds shall not infest our gardens, as expect to give a total check to the growth of fungus in wheat, nevertheless, by cutting out or eradicating whatever we find on our farms that is congenial to the growth of fungus, I doubt not but we may render a most beneficial service to wheat, by preventing that excess of injury which sometimes threatens the whole nation with famine, and is often the cause of lamentable scarcities.

" Though the progress of fungus is much checked by the falling of leaves in autumn and winter, with which it most probably perishes, yet it is remarkable to observe, that some evergreens, particularly the box and bramble bush, retain the *fungi* in all their various stages, even during the severest frosts of winter; and which, on the return of a little mild and humid weather in spring, contribute to infect with an astonishing rapidity the earliest leaves and shoots of spring in those vegetables congenial to its propagation. These *fungi* then flourish with an extraordinary luxuriance, and in the course of a week or two, arriving at maturity, disseminate their baneful effects throughout thousands of acres of those golden sheaves which are the husbandman's hope and the staff of life.

" There are also some trees which retain old fungus during winter on their barks, such as the common willow, hazel, birch, and sometimes oak coppice, but principally the former, and from their smutty appearance, even at some distance being distinguished, should either be cut down, or at least lose their limbs, which will in the ensuing spring send forth abundance of clean young wood. The barberry will also retain old *fungi* in any fissure or cleft in the bark, occasioned by injury, exhibiting

biting numerous black pustules: these should be cut
out. Winter is also the best period for getting rid of
the black alder, at such time particularly distinguished by
the blackness of her bark, though at this time free from
infection. The bramble abounds in all countries, and is
therefore more injurious than the box, being similar to
her in bearing the fungus, as I said before, at all seasons,
even in the severest frosts of winter; she ought, therefore, to be cut as close as possible in our hedges and
coppices, at least once or twice a year.

" Boxes are seldom much affected by the fungus when
situated in an elevated and open situation, but in shady
and damp ones their growth must be attended with very
deleterious consequences; even in winter, the coarse
grasses that grow near them, if in a hedge, will be
strongly infected, of which I have at present a specimen
in my garden.

" The common practice of new making the hedges
round the wheat, is certainly attended with many benefits, particularly in lessening the quantum of *fungi* that
would otherwise injure the corn.

" The glebe of my living had been notorious from
time immemorial for being given to rusty wheat, when I
was presented to it. Its glebe is eighty acres, and on my
residence, not liking to entangle myself at once with the
whole, I lett two-thirds of it to two of my parishioners,
for the term of seven years. No rector having resided
for upwards of twenty years, the fences were extremely
dilapidated. During the two first years I made nearly
three-fourths of the hedges, and such was the immediate
effect of cutting, steeping, and plashing them, that the
nature of the glebe seemed altered, and the corn was
very near as clean as that of the rest of my neighbours.
Wherever I have heard of a field or farm reputed for bad
corn, I have invariably found those trees congenial to the
                                            fungus

fungus abundant in the hedges, or adjoining woodlands. Nor do I conceive, that any field in which the coltsfoot or yellow corn thistle grows, can possibly be free from rust, in consequence of the multiplicity of *fungi* that grow under their leaves; and every exertion ought to be made use of to get rid of them. I hope you will pardon my presumption in begging to differ from that able naturalist, Sir Joseph Banks, who (in his Treatise on the Cause of the Disease of the Blight in Corn) says, " It cannot however be an expensive precaution to search diligently in the spring for young plants of wheat infected with the disease, and carefully to extirpate them." By due examination it will be found, that when one blade of wheat exhibits fungus, the whole field is infected in every blade, though to various extents. The opinion too of Fontaine is erroneous, who supposes, " that the yellow and dark-coloured fungus is not the same species;" and is easily exploded by every one who will observe its progress minutely.

" I think I must now have tired you with the length of my letter, which I have confined chiefly to the principal heads of the subject, that I may not be too tedious in detail. In the course of this year new light will arise, and it is my intention to make appropriate drawings of the progress of the rust during each season in the year. It will give me great pleasure, should any of my observations turn out of any service to yourself in the work you have undertaken.

" Requesting, that whenever you again visit Devon, that you will give me an opportunity of paying my respects to you at Milton Lamarell,

     " Believe me, with great respect,

       " Dear Sir,

         " Your very obedient humble servant,

           " THOMAS CLACK."

            CHAP

This Plate represents a Cutting from a Barbary Tree
bearing Parasitic Fungi in its various stages above
the Shoot which bears Leaves; the limb is dead, &
represents those fungi which took root last year,
now bursting forth through the bark, and ready to
disseminate in the first moist gale of Wind.

S. Clack del.   Neele sculp. Strand.

CHAP. XVIII.

MISCELLANEOUS ARTICLES.

———————

SECT. I.——AGRICULTURAL SOCIETIES.

AN Annual Meeting of the South Devonshire Agricultural Society is alternately held at Totness and Kingsbridge. Neither this Society, however, or that formerly instituted in North Devon, are kept up with that spirit, perseverance, and liberality, which the nature of such institutions require, and by which they are conducted and preserved in other parts of the united kingdom. Connected with this subject, the following valuable communication has been made to the Surveyor, by the Rev. Mr. Coham, of Coham-house, Black Torrington.

———————

A Cursory View of a Plan for the Establishment of an Agricultural Society in the North of Devon.

In arranging a plan for the establishment of an Agricultural Society in any district, there are two considerations which ought principally to be attended to: the first relates to local circumstances only; in regard to which, such regulations and engagements should be agreed on and entered into, as may be most likely to promote, in particular, the rural advantages of the neighbourhood. The second, reaches to matters of more extensive concern, by which not only the immediate vicinity, but the country at large may be benefited. Such as may be supposed to be the general objects of other similar Societies,

and

and to the rules of which a reference ought to be had, for the purpose of selecting the best.

Though, perhaps, in respect to sources of information, and the article of expense, any plan exceeding a very moderate one, may, at first sight, be deemed too extensive for so thinly inhabited a district as the North of Devon, there are certainly many objects, besides the mere production of the best stock, or farm-implements (excellent as *these* are in themselves), which might worthily engage attention ; and since it is a self-evident proposition, that the moral and natural interests of all countries are inseparably connected with each other, so, in proportion to the extent of any Agricultural Society, judiciously and economically conducted, the manners and husbandry of the district must be improved.

Assuming it, therefore, as a fact, that the agricultural system of the North of Devon, and the condition of those who perform the operative part of it, generally speaking, are as wretched in their kind as they are to be found in any district in the kingdom, there can be no doubt but that, within this division of the county, the improvement of both of these objects is become not only a matter of interest, but of duty ; and as a well organized society will always produce more beneficial effects than individual exertion, so it must be obvious, if persons of property will once enter into rules for the general improvement of their district, and will afterwards zealously and uniformly co-operate together, the happiest consequences, both as to agriculture and rural life, must ensue. Gentlemen residing in the country, will then have an opportunity of conferring with each other without the parade usually attendant on formal visits, and collectively will be enabled to effect such substantial and decisive measures, as it would have been absolutely preposterous

in

in any person, whatever almost his rank may be, by himself to have attempted.

On these grounds, principally, it is submitted, that an
Agricultural Society ought to be established in the North
of Devon, as the best, if not the only means of improving, with due effect, the rural concerns of the district;
and though to attempt to take in at one glance all the
different objects which ought to engage the notice of
those who may wish to patronize such an institution,
would be deemed an extravagant, visionary undertaking,
a few observations, at this time, on certain customs, prejudices, and abuses which seem most materially to affect
the prosperity of the country, may not altogether be
deemed presumptuous or unseasonable.

The first consideration, then, which ought to be adverted to, and which, it is conceived, is a most material
check to the proper management of lands in this district,
is the want of an improved uniform lease. Not but there
will always be a necessity of varying this instrument according to different circumstances ; but there are certain
general points, most unquestionably, in which it will be
for the common interest of all to agree, and from which
no one, in any instance whatever, ought to deviate.

The most remarkable of this sort, is the covenant inserted in most leases, which empowers tenants, after a
certain manurance, to take three white crops (or crops of
grain) immediately in succession ; and though it is now
admitted, by almost every intelligent farmer, that no
mode of management can more effectually impoverish the
land than such a practice ; so firmly rooted is the habit
of sowing, not only three such crops, but even four,
without intermission, that were any land-owner to insist
on an alternation of green crops (roots or pulse) with the
white, no native of the district would engage for the
farm.

farm. Indeed a striking instance of this kind happened
a few years since to a certain baronet in the neighbourhood of Great Torrington, who being convinced of the
present exhausting practice of cropping, attempted to
introduce a covenant for an alternation of green crops
with white, and his farms remained so long untenanted,
that at last, uncountenanced by other land-owners, he
was obliged to acquiesce in the ignorant prejudice of the
country.

Secondly, Tenants for lives are now most commonly
obliged, on the death of certain persons named in their
leases, to surrender to their lessors their best beast, by
which means an emulation to produce a superior breed of
stock (one grand object of most Agricultural Societies), is
amongst this description of people, most obviously checked.
It may be necessary, perhaps, at the death of each person named in such lease, that some object or other of
consequence should engage the attention of the lessor, for
the purpose of noting more particularly the event; but
surely every end of that sort would be answered by the
payment of a gross sum.

Thirdly, Woodlands, in such leases, are usually granted
in common with other grounds; on which account sap-
lings promiscuously growing with coppice-woods, though
expressly reserved, are not sufficiently attended to, but in
the general wreck, are too frequently cut down or left
unprotected. And here it may not be improper to remark,
that there scarcely is an object more worthy the attention
of the land-owners of this district, than the growth and
protection of oak-timber. From its natural disposition
to flourish in this soil, the oak has been styled '' *the weed*''
of the country ; but it must be evident to every cursory
observer, unless some regulations much stronger than
any now in force, are soon made relative to this '' weed,''
                                                          or

or as, more properly, and in more dignified language, it
may be called, this *bulwark of the nation*, will, not long
hence, be extirpated. But exclusively of these considerations, the policy of granting this sort of lease (viz. for
lives, or 99 years,) has of late years been very much questioned, not only in regard to   lessor, but as also to
the lessee. And as to the former, it is argued that this
mode brings in, at best, but a very *uncertain* income; that
one generation of a family is thereby induced to squander
away that which would furnish a *regular* and *ample* supply
to the succeeding; that the intervals between one fine
and another, are generally so long, that the lessor is not
able to avail himself of the progress of the times; that
when a fine does occur there is no competition, the lessee
having the arbitrary choice in his own hands of fixing
his own price, or suffering the lease to run out; and that,
aware of the length of time before it is probable that the
lease will expire, or a renewal of it be required, the lessor
becomes totally indifferent as to the management of the
farm. And, notwithstanding it may be urged that what
one party loses the other must gain, the chief objection
to this kind of lease still seems to rest with the lessee.
By this practice the farmer is tempted to lay out such a
sum of money in the purchase of his lease, as, had it been
kept afloat in the judicious management of his farm,
would perhaps have made him a ten-fold return. But his
capital is now gone; his farm, most likely not half
stocked, and his grounds badly cropped: thus circumscribed in his first outset, he proceeds on slowly and
carefully, adding one shilling to another in store for
the next fine, which, by the premature death, as it
sometimes happens, of one of his nearest relations, he is
oftentimes called on to pay before he is prepared. In
the mean time, all spirit of enterprise, all progress to
                                                    actual

actual improvement is checked; and thus, from generation to generation, must a large portion of the country, unless some salutary change take place, continue to wear the same dreary, unproductive, forbidding aspect. In short, this is a most miserable species of gambling, highly injurious to the public, and in which the parties more immediately concerned are almost sure of being losers.

The remaining observations will be chiefly confined to a subject, not less difficult to handle than it is important in its consequences, and which relates to the condition of our farm-servants and labourers; by the first of whom are meant menial servants, such as live in farm-houses, under a yearly hiring or otherwise; and by the second, husbandmen living with their families in cottages, and who work on farms by the day, or in labour taken " in great."

In respect to the first of these classes, viz. farm-servants, it is much to be feared that the general profligacy which seems now to prevail amongst them, proceeds in a great degree from the almost total neglect of their morals in growing up, and afterwards from the common practice amongst farmers, of receiving them into their houses without proper testimonials of character. Born, for the most part, of poor, and too often of unprincipled parents, they receive the first seeds of depravity in their tenderest years; and their morals, not sufficiently attended to during their apprenticeship (which, from the extreme poverty of their parents, most poor children in Devonshire are obliged to serve), they arrive at manhood with an increased propensity to vice. A regular, well-ordered family, as presenting a check to his irregularities, is the young peasant's aversion, and, his mind becoming daily more and more depraved, he seduces, in one of his licentious gambols, some neighbouring female, whom he

is

is now, through necessity, obliged to marry. We shall next see him in the second class mentioned (viz.) as a labourer by the day, or in work taken " in great," and living in his own cottage. A numerous family of children is the natural consequence of such premature marriages ; but love, never perhaps a very sincere inmate, and now disgusted at poverty, entirely forsakes his dwelling.— Wretchedness, despair, and, of course, a sullen indifference to the interests of his family, succeed; and in the end, most commonly, instead of being of any real advantage to the agriculture of his country, and long before his natural strength is impaired, the accumulated burthen of himself, his wife and children, falls as a dead weight upon it. Without insisting any further on the manifest deficiency in our present mode of training up our peasantry, and which perhaps may oftentimes have laid such a foundation of vice and misery, as with all our after-care and management we may scarcely be able to remove ; it may not altogether be unworthy of our present inquiry, whether our general treatment of our labourers, on our parts, independent of every foregoing consideration, will warrant our expecting any very considerable better conduct or services on their's.

Mr. Kent, in his " General View of the Agriculture of Norfolk," says, " that the labourer is the first sinew that puts the labour of the farm in motion, and without which, it cannot be carried on ; if therefore his full earnings will not keep him, it is a duty incumbent on his master to let him have a sufficiency of corn for his own family, at the *same rate or price,* which he is paid for his labour, and not suffer the spirit of a poor man of this description to be broken."

Whether therefore the money price of corn ought in all cases to regulate that of all home-made commodities,

as

as Adam Smith hath asserted, or not, it may be asked,
does the present price of labour in Devonshire, at 14d.
per day, keep pace with the price of the common neces-
saries of life? And considering the early expectations
which labourers, under the present system, almost invariably form, of one day receiving parochial relief, the very
idea of which naturally tends to deaden every exertion,
would it not be a species of economy, as well as justice, to
fix the maximum price of labour at a higher rate? And
moreover, which is the chief consideration of all, as wretchedness too often gives the first stimulus to guilt, would
not the rendering of the labourer more independent and
more comfortable in his circumstances, be the most probable means of rendering him, at the same time, more generally virtuous and honest?

It should also be observed, at this time, that in addition to the appearance at least of injustice which seems to
oppress the husbandman in this district, a certain source
of income, and from which formerly he was wont to derive a considerable support, has now entirely failed him.
Within these few years, even since the last maximum of
wages was set in this county, the labourer's wife and family, from the article of spinning of wool, were enabled
to earn nearly as much as the labourer himself. It is not
meant, in this place, to condemn the introduction of spin-
ning-machinery; for the abridgement of manual labour,
of any kind, most incontestibly, is a national good; but
looking only at ourselves, such a sudden change as has
been experienced in this district, in the mode of manufacturing an article, from whence our peasantry drew nearly
half of their subsistence, must, for the present, be considered as a serious local evil.

We see then the price of labour standing in this county
at the same rate as it was fixed full fourteen years since;
the

the price of almost every necessary of life doubled, and daily increasing; and in this district, in particular, nearly one half of his usual support, to the labourer, out off. It may be said, perhaps, that these observations point out distempers without applying a remedy. A remedy to such distempers, it may be answered, is not the work of an individual: a society of gentlemen of fortune and influence, aided by the magistracy, are alone equal to such a task— a task which, uniting interest with duty, will not only teach the wilderness to smile, but will enable the rustic, to whose labour principally we must look for such a change, to smile with it.

Many matters also, of a different cast, as connected with agriculture, might engage the attention of a society formed for the improvement of rural affairs: such, for instance, as the establishment of new fairs and markets in the most convenient places, for particular purposes; an adherence to the same weights and measures throughout the district; discountenancing forestalling and engrossing; holding out encouragement to honesty and industry; checking knavery and indolence; retaining no farm-servant or labourer without first receiving a certificate of good conduct from the former employer; improvement of parish-roads, of carriages, and of agricultural implements and machinery; proposing premiums for the best managed farm, the best stock, the best system of husbandry, as applicable to the prevailing soils of the district, fidelity in farm-servants, frugality, and general exemplary conduct in labourers towards their families;—the best ploughmen, hedgers, reapers, mowers, with a number of other articles which must eventually occur as proper objects for a society of this kind, all of which being arranged and managed with diligence, perseverance, and address, will not fail, in process of time, and in some respects immediately, of
making

making the district more virtuous, more prosperous, and more happy.

At a meeting held at   in the town of Barnstaple in the county of Devon, this   day of

PRESENT.

It was unanimously resolved,

First, That the present prevailing system of husbandry, and other local circumstances, check, in a peculiar manner the agricultural interests of the North of Devon.

Secondly, That the establishment of an agricultural society, on as liberal a scale as the extent and natural consequence of the district will warrant, appears as the best means of ameliorating this system, and of improving these circumstances.

Thirdly, That the society, when formed, shall bear the style or title of " The North of Devon Agricultural Society," and shall not be limited as to the number of members ; but after the society shall once be established, no person shall be admitted as a member but by ballot.

Fourthly, That no honorary member shall be admitted who shall live within   miles of the usual place of meeting, and that each member shall pay by way of subscription, the yearly sum of

Fifthly, That   meetings shall be held in the year, viz.

and that Barnstable, from its central situation in the district, is considered as the most eligible place for the holding of each meeting.

Sixthly,

Sixthly, That there shall be one general-meeting in the year, viz.
at which every member will be required to attend, under the penalty of   , unless such reasons shall be assigned as shall be approved of by the president.

Seventhly, That a president shall be annually chosen, who shall take upon him the chief management and direction of the society ; in receiving the yearly subscriptions, adjusting accounts, conducting all matters of correspondence, &c. ; and who in all cases of suffrage, when necessary, shall have the privilege of a casting vote.

Eighthly, That, as an assistant to such president, a secretary shall also be annually chosen, and who by way of compensation shall be entitled to a yearly salary hereafter to be fixed.

Ninthly, That a book for receiving subscriptions be immediately opened, and that this meeting be adjourned to   to be then here holden for the purpose of electing a president and a secretary, considering further the objects of this institution, and of entering into such further resolutions as may be deemed necessary for the regulation of it*.

---

* *Quere*—Would not the establishment of a bank, under the firm of all the members, defray the expenses of the society, and at the same time, if properly managed, be made a matter of absolute profit?

CONCLUSION.

Draining.—It has been already remarked, that the principal efforts among the agricultural gentlemen of the county, have been chiefly governed by too strict an adherence to Mr. Elkington's mode of draining, by endeavouring to carry off the water before it reached the surface, and became diffused over the adjoining grounds; a practice unquestionably of the very first importance, where the structure of the country is such as to admit of its being carried into proper execution. A country, however, internally stratified in the manner of Devonshire, will on most occasions defeat the highest expectations that may have been formed from works of that nature. The dip of the strata varies from 30° to 80°, and in proportion as the laminous rock continues to any depth, water issues through it even in the driest seasons, and that from sources the depth and distance of which it is impossible to come at or pretend to ascertain.

The surface of an understratum formed in this manner ▨▨▨▨▨▨ must for ever bid defiance to the most expensive operations made with a view of preventing the water from rising through the laminous rock; and as such, the only remaining cure appears to be that of turf soughing, or hollow-draining, every field so circumstanced throughout the county. These drains should be laid out

at

at no greater distance than a rod a-part, their depth
from 20 to 24 inches, and so disposed in parallel lines, as
to draw as equally as possible on both sides ; to have a
gradual and uniform descent towards the receiving drains,
and in all cases, when it can be done, to cross the lay of
the line of under-strata rather than to run with it. The
expense attending this mode of draining, considering the
general facility of procuring rubble stones to fill the lower
groove when the substratum is not sufficiently tough to
support itself, will not exceed 50s. or 3l. per acre, a trifling consideration, when compared with its permanence
and utility.

*Natural Fertility of the old Moorlands; how to be pre-
served, and rendered productive.*—If any thing were required
to confirm the idea the Surveyor has all along entertained,
of the improvement the moors and coarse lands in the
county are capable of receiving, such an evidence could
not be more readily supplied, than by the circumstances
detailed in the management of Lew-Moor Enclosure. They
most clearly demonstrate that these moors contain an
abundant resource for permanent fertility, when it is not
prematurely exhausted by intemperate and injudicious
cropping. A close hollow-draining upon all these lands,
followed in the first breaking operation by spading and
burning their coarse and unprofitable surface, and afterwards cultivating them with alternate green and white
straw crops, would in effect render them equally valuable
with the roodings in Essex, or any other positively clay
district in the United Kingdom. When that judicious
and spirited improver, Mr. Bayley, shall see the necessity
of providing outfal drains by the ditches of his mounds,
and giving a close turf soughing to the moor before the
whole of the tough surface is destroyed by the breast-
plough,

plough, he will derive every advantage from his undertaking, that his most sanguine wishes could prompt him to
expect.

Although the Surveyor is so far happy in bearing testimony to the improved idea Mr. Bayley possesses in the
management of these moors, yet at the same time his preparation for potatoes instead of turnips is objectionable,
for notwithstanding the care he takes in rest-balking his
beat ground immediately after the ashes are spread, still
the small portion of alkaline salts produced by the combustion of the green vegetables being soluble in water, are
liable to be washed out and lost during the winter rains
and the melting snows.

Were these moors completely hollow-drained, they would
be rendered good winter ground, a crop of turnips on the
beat ashes would be certain and abundant, and which
might be fed off during winter with no less advantage to
the stock than the land, as the latter would be nearly as
much benefited by the trampling of the sheep, as in the
manure left by them in feeding off the turnips. Oats
should follow the turnips with seeds, and that ground,
when necessary, should be broke up for lay wheat or grass
potatoes ; the wheat stubble sown with tares, or winter-
fallowed into four-furrow ridges for oats ; and the potatoe land ploughed into six or eight-furrow ridges, and
sown before Christmas with bere or winter barley, fed in
the spring, and left afterwards to stand for a crop. In
all cases, whether these lands are under crop, or winter-
fallowed, they should always be left well gripped and water-furrowed. Rye and winter barley, with occasional
crops of wheat, should be the winter sowings of these
moors.   The spring crops generally black and white
oats.

Wheat.

Wheat.—It has been observed, that all wheat hacked in upon lay ground is found to answer best. It is the nature of all lay wheat on a wet strong subsoil, to lie much drier than fallow wheat on the same bottom. The broken earth will hold up the surface waters at the same time that they find a ready passage between the inverted turf and the bottom of the furrow; hence the plant is less injured by a chill produced from an excess of moisture, the soil is less liable to be acted upon by the frost, and consequently the plant is in less danger of being drawn or cast out by the alternate freezing and thawing of the surface. This applies to all lay wheat whatever, whether it is hacked in, harrowed under, or dibbled; at the same time it is more obnoxious to the ravages of the wire-worm in the spring of the year.

Clover.—The common red clover being little better than an annual, the early sowing it with spring crops is often found to encourage so luxuriant a growth as to form small heads which have appeared in blossom at the time of harvest. This has often encouraged high expectations with the farmer, on his seeing so fine a plant at harvest, and during the ensuing autumn. From a due attention to the nature of the plant, this will be found an improvident anticipation, for experience has long since shown to the Author of this Report, that whenever young clover grows very rank among the corn, a proportionate deficiency of plant is found in the ensuing spring. The clover, therefore, instead of being sown with, or immediately after the spring corn, should be deferred till after the spring crops have not only covered the ground, but are shooting for the spindle. The clover will then have time to establish a sufficient footing in the ground, and not be liable to the same exhaustion of the

limited

limited existence it must necessarily undergo by a premature luxuriance in the growing months of the preceding summer.

Turnips.—It may not be amiss in this place to offer a few observations on the relative excellence of the Scotch two-furrow turnip husbandry, with that of the common broad-cast. Observation and experience clearly show, that the depredations of the insect called the fly, on the young turnip plants, are precisely in proportion to the feebleness and want of growing vigour in the infant plants; and that as soon as they are pushed into the rough leaf, all farther danger from the insect is at an end. The rough leaf, however, will be frequently seen perforated, and as the foliage enlarges, the holes enlarge with it, giving the appearance of having been much damaged by the fly, and by which it certainly would have been destroyed, had not its growing vigour sustained it against the attack. From the early and ample supply of nourishment afforded the young plants by the layer of dung occupying the tops of the two-furrow ridges, their roots strike immediately upon or near it, receive its invigorating principle, and a quicker and stronger growth ensues, greatly abating the risk of their destruction by the fly, and with a much smaller allowance of dung per acre than must necessarily be applied to afford any thing like a prospect of success by the broad-cast method. The distance between the rows from top to top of the ridges, according to the prospect of luxuriancy in the crop, may be varied from 18 to 26 inches. The facility of horse-hoeing and setting out the plants by hand in the rows, the bottoms being raised out of the reach of the winter's mud and water, render them less liable to be injured by the frost, and upon the whole, the produce per acre, where

the

the ridge husbandry is properly conducted, is so very much increased, as in time to warrant a fair expectation of its superseding the broad-cast turnip husbandry in all cases whatsoever.

Potatoes.—It is a usual practice in Ireland, to prepare the potatoe setts from some of the fairest and best potatoes, during the broken weather in the preceding winter. In the dry situations they are then placed, they become incrusted with the juice of the potatoe, and are justly supposed to bleed less before germination than if fresh cut in the spring of the year. The sett of course is stronger, and it puts forth a more vigorous shoot soon after being planted. The planting of small potatoes or setts having more than two strong eyes, are with reason objected to; the number of eyes, on what is called the crown of the potatoe, are always rejected, with the small potatoes, both being found to produce languid shoots and a number of small bead potatoes of no value.

Orchards.—As variety and change of situation seems little less essential to the well doing of individuals in the vegetable, than in the animal kingdom, much of the deficiency in the produce of orchards, complained of, may be referred to the putting of young apple-trees on the scite of the old ones which have gone to decay. In addition to the absolute necessity which there appears to be, of planting orchards in more elevated but still protected situations, would it not be advisable to try later fruits, and by keeping the tops of the trees generally more open, and their branches free from moss, they would be more susceptible of the winter cold, and the sap would have a later but more vigorous circulation afterwards.

The warmth and humidity of the air of Devon, with
the

the little cold experienced before the month of March, tends much to preserve a languid circulation in the vegetable world when its energies should lie at rest, and hence the weak and feeble efforts so universally complained of in the vernal season.

Plantations.—In planting along the glens and hollows in this country, care should be taken as well to prevent the continuance of a stream of wind through a ravine, as to guard the young trees from the first broad stroke of the wind from the ocean. Instances of the necessity of this caution frequently occur, but no where in a stronger degree is it shown, than in a plantation of deciduous and evergreen trees made by Colonel Orchard, near the eminence on which is situated the beautiful church of Hartland. Reasoning on the effects of a continued draught of wind, Colonel Orchard constructed a stop or barrier to the eastward from the most prevailing winds. This produced an immediate thrift in the plantation to leeward, where it is found to flourish in a most surprizing manner, and to spread itself vigorously to windward every year.

Copse-land.—The shameful neglect of coppice land in many parts of the county, by suffering them so frequently to lie open to the farms, conveys a just and severe censure on those who have the care of such estates. To be more particular might seem invidious; but this is an evil that cries loudly for reform, it being no uncommon case, for an access to the neighbrurign woodland to be made a strong point with the farmer, for holding up his price for the agistment of summer cattle.

It is much to be regretted, that the statute providing for a certain reservation of samplers at each fall, upon
every

every acre, is not more attended to than it appears to be at present throughout the county; it happens, however, that a number of samplers are sometimes left at one cutting, but which are all, or most of them, cut down the period following, when scarcely any that are worth preserving are left to stand for timber. Were attention paid to these points throughout all the coppice lands in the county, a vast quantity of timber might be raised, as the same shelter which protects the copse wood, would equally screen and preserve the young timber trees. In the few instances where this has been attended to, however sharp the hills, and apparently destitute their sides of soil, large and flourishing oak trees are found to occupy the abrupt and rocky declivities, and which are utterly unfit for any other appropriation.

Timber.—From what has been already stated, it will appear evident, that the timber in this county is wasting in a most alarming manner; is it not therefore necessary, that an ordinance thould be made, that in future no tree should be cut down or legally exposed for sale, without having the mark of the timber-inspector of the district affixed, and certificate accompanying it. This officer should be appointed and paid by Government, and to whom annual returns should be made of all matters appertaining to his duty, which should also extend to the examination of all young plantations: where it should be required, that he should not only see that a certain number of young trees are planted for every timber tree that is cut down, but that the same young trees and plantations are well fenced and protected. On his observing the woodland fences insufficient for their safety, and their owners persistingly unmindful of his report, he should be empowered to order the necessary repairs to be made,

made, and to recover the amount of such expense by an immediate distress upon the moveables on the premises.

Manures.—A certain proportion of the primary earths, (viz. calx, allumini, and silex) are taken up by, and form a component part of all vegetables. All water, rain-water, or that produced immediately from melted snow excepted, contains a certain proportion of terrene substances. It is said that 680 ounces of water may contain about one ounce of limestone; 7700, one ounce of alluminous earth, or argill; 1000 ounces, one ounce of silex; hence it follows, that in order to approach the standard of fertility, as it respects the primary earths only, the soil should consist of such a proportion of these substances as can be most conveniently procured, and moistened with common water. A surface thus composed, would have the appearance of a good mixed soil; and upon an open bottom, would retain a genial portion of moisture only, and which, in the estimation of most men, would be pronounced fruitful. That grass and corn would vegetate in a soil thus constituted, is unquestionable. Warmth and moisture only, without the presence of any denser medium, is sufficient for the purposes of germination; all bulbous roots in these circumstances at their stated seasons will shoot forth luxuriantly. Barley will germinate and grow to some length on the floor of a malt-house; but a soil formed destitute of animal or vegetable matter, and that in a state whereby it can be admitted to a chemical union with water, will forever remain steril and fruitless.

So wisely has the Great Disposer of all things contrived this perennial circle, that the complete dissolution of one body is made subservient and essential to the propagation

pagation and perfection of another; and here those very substances which would become offensive, and even destructive of animal life, are greedily absorbed in the aerial form of gas or vapour by the stems and foliage of vegetables, and which again in turn, and during the day-time*, exhale and breathe forth that pure dephlogisticated air, so essential to the support of animal existence.

The quantum of nutriment inhaled or absorbed by the animal economy from the medium which surrounds it, has never been an object of minute inquiry, although the effects so happily experienced at sea, by bathing when there is a scarcity of water on board, are too well known to justify any doubt that much more is derived to the animal system by absorption than at the first view we might think possible. That the means, however, of sustaining vegetable life are two-fold, has been proved by the most accurate tests and trials. The one by the absorption of nitrous and other aireform fluids, the other by receiving animal and vegetable matter combined with the primary earths, if not altogether in chemical union, in the highest degree of attenuation and mechanical suspension in water, by which it is conveyed to the roots of plants, and is thence assimilated in due quantities with their unfolding growth and perfection; and hence, as was formerly observed in the Essex Report (p. 178, 179), arises the necessity of " guarding against the exhaustion of dunghills, by preventing the rain from washing out and running to waste its most valuable liquor, whether

---

* The Surveyor is enabled to state, as the result of experience during a long residence in the back woods of North America, that the night exhalations from the forests are noxious. Light, or the heat of the sun, seems indispensably necessary for the production of oxygen or pure air from vegetables.

in

in the yard or exposed along the hedge-rows: to be careful in the application of manure, and to weigh well and be satisfied in the propriety of ploughing it under, rather than to use it as a top-dressing : to resist the dissipating effects of fire upon the smallest scruple of animal or vegetable matter, which in any reasonable time may be brought to rot : to apply sand or any silicious matter (merely designed as an alterative), in great quantities, to strong tough clay, or not at all : to expose chalk, marl and clay, for some time to the joint action of the frost, sun, and air, rather than to attempt an immediate union of them with the soil, by ploughing them under."

The means of detecting the existence of animal or vegetable exuvia in the soil, and in some measure ascertaining its quantity, is easy, and should always be resorted to by gentlemen and farmers, before they determine on the application of any dressing known to possess a disorganizing or forcing quality. It is simply that of stepping into the field proposed to be thus dressed, and from different parts of its surface, to collect handfuls of the soil or mould, which after being kneaded into separate balls of about two inches in diameter (noticing the particular, parts of the field from which each ball was gathered), should be put into a fire, where remaining until they may be supposed to be penetrated or burnt through, should be taken out, and in proportion as a black colour is found to prevail in the middle of each ball, does the carbonic principle exist in the soil from which it was taken, and which will consequently admit of the application of lime or other solvent manures. To apply this reasoning to the practice of paring and burning, and the liming of land, will not be difficult, as the most conclusive evidence will accompany a few observations on the subject.

It

It is from the combustion of the green vegetable only, that alkaline salt is produced, and this being soluble in water, is found largely to conduce to the nourishment of plants. The slow and smothered progress of fire upon the roots, stems, and other vegetable matter contained in the soil, brings a large portion of it into a state of charcoal; a substance of all others the most indestructible, and most capable of resisting dissolution, or why is it used as an ingredient in washes and cements prepared with mild and caustic alkali, for resisting the slow decomposing power of the atmosphere? This substance is found in considerable quantities in all old beat-burnt lands, and which, but for the operation of charring, would have been long converted into vegetable mucilage, and contributed to the nourishment of ensuing crops. If to the quantity of vegetable matter which is thus locked up in an insoluble state, be added what is destroyed by the power of the fire in the beat-heaps without producing alkaline salts, and that thrown off into the atmosphere in flame, smoke, and vapour, the annihilation of vegetable pabulum by this practice is immeasurably great, and which long ago must have terminated in the more complete sterility of the repeatedly beat-burnt lands in Devonshire, were not the soil and climate of that country so peculiarly favourable to its reproduction. In some parts of the county, however, particularly in the sandy districts, the farmer complains of a diminution of spine, or green sward, and which, after the operation of skirting, is not sufficient to yield the ashes required for an ensuing crop of turnips. This, from the considerations here stated, must be the inevitable consequence of persisting in the practice of *paring and burning the sweet green sward of a sound soil, be the basis and substrata of it what it may.*

In

In all chalky soils, and such as are plus with the calcareous principle, the application of lime can have little
effect beyond its immediate operation, whilst it remains
caustic on the inert vegetable and animal substances such
soils may contain ; but where the soil is deficient of such
matter, and destitute of a due proportion of calcareous
earth, it will operate beneficially, *quoad* the quantity applied, as an important alterative in such soils, but to which
it would prove equally efficacious were it laid on in its
mild state, as chalk or pounded limestone; and hence the
well known value of all road scrapings, but particularly of
such as are formed of, or repaired with, chalk or limestone.

Farm Horses.—If we except the treatment of the farm-
horses in Ireland, those in Devonshire have perhaps as
hard a measure of neglect and ill-usage dealt out to them,
as is any where to be met with in the united kingdom.
From the injudicious manner in which they receive the
corn occasionally given them, it is a point of some question, whether it affords them a benefit, or by diverting
their appetite from the hay, pea or other straw, absolutely
produce an injury, from the avidity with which they
swallow the corn unmasticated. To remedy this evil,
a better example no where presents, than what may be
drawn from the management of farm and waggon horses
in Pennsylvania and Maryland. These horses perform
journeys of two and three hundred miles over the stupendous mountains of that country, with prodigious loads of
wheat and flour from the interior, and wet and dry goods
from the sea-ports to the different points of embarkation,
at Fort-Pitt, Red-stone, Charlestown and Wheeling, and
other places on the Ohio river. Notwithstanding which,
these waggon-horses, through the whole extent of that
country,

country, are seldom seen in a less high condition than the brewers' and other large cart-horses in the metropolis of this country. The manner in which the American horses are sustained to perform these labours, is generally by feeding them with hay and straw chopped about half an inch long, with which is mixed about half a peck of rye, oat, and Indian corn meal, to about two and a half or three pecks of hay or straw thus chopped. A feeding trough, sufficiently large for four or five horses to eat out of at the same time, is attached to each waggon. The chaff is put into this trough, and after being well mixed with the given quantity of meal, is moistened, and again well stirred together till every shred of the hay or chopped straw is found to be covered, or as it were, frosted over by the meal. The avidity with which the horses eat their meat thus prepared, may be well conceived. Their meal finished, they either pursue their journey or lie down to rest, but in either case not without being well dressed, and cleansed from the effects of their last labour. It is the pride of the carters, as well as the waggon masters in that country, to see their horses in a condition rather above than under the labour they have to perform; and in a hundred miles travelling from Baltimore or Philadelphia, the Surveyor will be bound to say, that as many prime waggon horses, and in as high condition, shall be seen, as in any direction for that distance from the city of London. The adoption of a similar treatment in the management of the farm and waggon horses in this country, needs no farther recommendation than the solemn asseveration as to the truths here stated.

The baiting of post, stage, and travelling horses with rye, oat, or bean bread, in the manner performed on the continent, is an infinitely more economical and facile mode of administering refreshment to a jaded animal, than by

giving

giving them the crude unbroken corn, so universally practised in this country.

Poor.—The want of employment for the females, particularly in the western parts of the county (and where they
are not so much in the practice of making bone lace as to
the eastward), is very much felt and complained of. About
fifteen years since, it is notorious, that a good spinner
would earn 3*s.* 6*d.* per week; her time is now, through
the general failure of that employment, too frequently
spent in rummaging about for a few loose sticks in order
to procure a scanty supply of fuel. Notwithstanding the
advantages before enumerated, the condition of the poor,
generally, is low both in mind and circumstances.

The necessity of resorting to the parish for relief, during the pressure of the times, near the close of the last,
and at the beginning of the present century, seems greatly
to have subdued that laudable pride and emulation that
was formerly the boast of the English husbandman. They
seldom now meet with a short interruption in their health
or want of employment, without immediately resorting to
the parish for relief. This, however, does not apply to
such as are members of box clubs, and which societies
have much extended since the law passed for making them
corporate. The monthly subscription of the artificers'
society is about one shilling; that of the promiscuous or
common labourers' club, eight-pence. The female societies generally sixpence per month. However desirable it
surely is to promote the extension of these societies, some
regulations should still be made to restrain the men when
assembled, from an indulgence which often ends in drunk-
enness. Would it not, therefore, be advisable to extend
the forfeit to any one getting drunk during, or within 24
hours after, such monthly meetings? Hundred or district
work-

workhouses are much desired in many parts of the county, but the establishment should be sufficiently large to cover the salaries of officers, and all the necessary attendants.—— In contemplating institutions of this nature, besides the comfortable asylum they would open to penury, decrepitude, and old age, they would tend much to stimulate the exertions of the sturdy peasant, rather than be subjected to resort to such establishments for employment or relief. They would also greatly contribute to the reduction of parochial expenses, on account of the removal of paupers, and above all, that most inhuman of all pursuits, the chasing off and driving a peasant family from one parish to another, not unfrequently in the last stage of sickness, and to prevent the expense of inhumation.

There is no opinion presumed to be given in any part of this Report, that has not been founded on actual observation and experience, and which the Surveyor will at all times be ready to uphold in the manner best suited with his ability for so doing. The subject of this article, properly discussed, would afford matter of an interesting nature, and although the observations of the Surveyor may, in the estimation of some benevolent persons, be considered to be contracted and ungenerous; still the situation in which he is placed, the steps which have been already taken, and the measures likely to be adopted in parliament, for the avowed purpose of bettering the state and condition of the poor, must not at this crisis, be altogether passed over in a publication of this nature.

From the first dawning of that gracious benevolence which issued spontaneously from the bosoms of their present Majesties, in promoting the instruction of the poor by the establishment of Sunday Schools, the Surveyor has looked forward with a sort of dread to the probable consequences of such a measure. If the illumination of the pea-

cant

sant mind would make him more moral, better satisfied with
his state and condition of life, and on all occasions more
desirous of excelling in the exercise of those duties his peculiar situation in society dooms him to perform, much private satisfaction and public benefit would naturally result
from such institutions. This however can easily be demonstrated as not likely to be a consequence of thus opening
the peasant mind to a contemplation of situations in life,
that can have no other possible effect than that of rendering him dissatisfied with his own. That this is an incon-
trovertible truth, is clear, from the conduct of the peasantry of Ireland ; all of whom but slightly acquainted
with the English language, are instructed to read and
write ; and thence springs the cause of that general rest-
lessness of character, and of the numbers that annually
ship themselves as redemptioners to different parts of the
United States of North America, but more particularly to
ports in the Hudson's river, Delaware, and Bay of Chesa-
peak. Such is the irresistible desire to ramble, in the enlightened mind of the Irish peasant, that rather than re-
linquish those prospective advantages he has imbibed from
his acquaintance with books, or learnt from a direct correspondence with a friend already in America, that for
the purpose of procuring a mere passage only over the
Atlantic, he willingly binds himself down for three, four,
or five years, to a state of absolute slavery, during which
time his indentures are assignable, and he is occasionally
passed from one master to another, with the usual forms
required in the conveyance of negro slaves. The redemptioners that arrive annually in the ports of New York,
Philadelphia, and Baltimore, from Germany, are also, with
few exceptions, acquainted with the rudiments of their
native language, and by which knowledge, they have been
                                                inspired

inspired with a determination to abandon their native country.

The German societies formed in all the middle states of North America, are as ready to protect and see justice rendered to these servants during the term of their indentures, as they are of contributing to their comfortable establishment afterwards. The number of redemptioners thus annually arriving from Germany in the United States, is wholly to be ascribed to the dissatisfaction they feel, on an examination of their relative situations in the community of their native land, and comparing it with accounts derived from books or the public papers, as well as from correspondence with their friends already in America; and who, after the expiration of their servitude, seldom fail in gradually attaining to a state of independence, with all the comfortable enjoyments of life, and the prospect of continuing them undiminished to their posterity. Such are the allurements held out to the peasantry of Ireland and Germany to emigrate ; and hence, for one English husbandman that is found to remove to America, there are, on the most moderate computation, one hundred from Ireland or Germany.

The English peasant, however, under the same influence of mental enlargement, will be acted upon in the same manner, and how far that will be found to be an amelioration of their condition, and likely to induce a more cheerful and prompt performance of those duties their station in life requires, or upon the whole, make them better subjects, neighbours, or happier men, are points by no means doubtful in the apprehension of the Author of this Report.

The disposition of the Scotch to emigrate and seek their fortunes abroad, unquestionably arises from the enlargement of their views in life by the education they most commonly

commonly receive when young. Why they are less disorderly at home, may be in a great measure referred to the force of example combined with precept, in the virtuous career of their pastor's life.

In certain grades of society, the seeking for what we do not possess, constitutes the happiness of the individual, and in that pursuit the noblest energies of his nature are unfolded, but which, without such a stimulus, would have lain dormant and in absolute oblivion. It is, however, widely different with the peasantry of a country, whose path in life is distinctly marked out, and in which any measure (however humane and considerate it may appear) that in its consequences may have a tendency to draw them aside from such limits, or in any wise contribute to make them restless or uneasy in them, must in the end prove injurious if not fatal to the interests of the community at large, by the engendering of mischiefs, the extent of which it is impossible to measure. *In short, the peasant's mind should never be inspired with a desire to amend his circumstances by the quitting of his cast : but every means the most benevolent and feeling heart can devise, should be employed to make that situation as comfortable and as happy to him as possible ; and to which end nothing more essential could contribute, than by exciting a general emulation to excel in all their avocations, even to those of breaking stones f r a lime kiln, or for repairing the highways.*

That illuminating the minds of the lower orders will not conduce to this end, and the tranquillity of the community at large, or render the peasantry more steadily attached to their native country, has been already evinced, by the disorderly behaviour of the lower orders in Ireland, who for many years past, in the insurgent banditti of Tories, Hearts of Steel, Peep-o'day Boys, White Boys, &c. which long before the late rebellion agitated and disturbed the

the repose of that country. The numbers also which emigrate from Germany to America, are encouraged to that adventure from what they read or learn from their trans-atlantic friends, that the arbitrary and feudal services required of them, will no longer exist on their withdrawing to America from their native country.

What but the members from the affiliated societies, *and the number of pen and ink gentry* on board our ships of war, created and kept up the mutiny in the navy, in the year 1797 ? and how will it be possible to suppress communications and a concert among the multitude, when they are all gifted with the means of corresponding and contriving schemes of sedition and insurrection with each other ?— The peasant life must necessarily, with respect to his condition and circle, be considered as solitary beyond the society of his family; and in that of the other labourers with which he is occasionally employed, give him the power of reflecting at these times upon what he reads at his leisure, or receives in correspondence from the village Hampdens of his country; and it is no difficult matter to anticipate the issue of a mind (for mind he has) bursting through the restraints of penury, and which he is thus taught to believe has grown upon him by oppression, and in a manner incompatible with the rights of man !

From these considerations duly weighed, and a conviction that enlarging the views of the peasantry of a country to the power of making still more uncomfortable comparisons between themselves and their employers, can end in nothing but creating dissatisfaction and ideal misery among them, injurious to the political interests of the country, its existing orders of community, and government, the Surveyor thus respectfully submits to the consideration of the Honourable Board, the propriety of opposing

posing any measures that may rationally be supposed to lead to such a fatal issue.

Athletic Exercises.—The athletic exercise to which these people are mostly addicted, is that of wrestling. This is pursued with great fervour and emulation, by the young farmers and peasantry in the country. It is common on these occasions for a purse of six, eight, or ten guineas, to be made by gentlemen fond of promoting this play, and a day is appointed for its being wrestled for, generally near some large village or market-town. The lists are prepared by a ring formed with stakes and a single rope, from fif-, teen to twenty yards in diameter, and in which it will appear that the winner of the purse must toss or throw down five of his adversaries. There seems to be no regulation with regard to the hold they take of each other. The collar, arm, or any part above the waistband, that most conveniently presents to the combatants during the contest, which sometimes continues from ten to fifteen minutes, and in which is displayed much activity, strength, and adroitness, whilst the shins of the party are often found streaming with blood from the sharp and violent blows they receive from each other, but which on no account are ever permitted to be given above the knee.

The usual form is to shake hands before and after the contest, and it rarely happens that the play is followed with boxing, or that any grudge or ill-will is continued from the conquered to those that may have thrown them. The play generally begins between two and three o'clock in the afternoon, and so well matched are the combatants, that the victor is frequently not declared till after midnight; in which case the ring is properly lighted, and the same precautions are continued during the whole time to secure fair, and prevent foul play. The moor-men are celebrated

lebrated for their hardiness, in bearing excessive kicking upon their shins. The ill effects which might be expected to result from such violence, is very soon carried off by their excellent habit of body, and the peculiar temperament of their constitutions.

In the outset of the play, every man who becomes a standard for the purse, must first throw two men on their back, belly, or side; eight of these standards must be made from the primary competitors for the single play; and when the standards are thus made, they each receive a crown. These eight playing, four of them must fall, the other four then engage, two of whom must fall; when the still standing two enter to decide the purse, and the second best man, or he who is last thrown, usually receives about one in five upon its amount. Three tryers or conductors of the lists are appointed, who decide all disputes immediately, and without appeal.

Elevation of the Barn, Stable, Slaughter

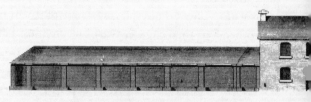

Elevation of the East Front

Jos.ᵖ Beard Arch.ᵗ

Section across the Farm Yard from

Section of Stab

Plate XX. P 472.

& Piggery and Section of the Ox Sheds.

Farm House & Cattle Sheds.

East.

Neele sculp Strand.

Elevation of Ox Sheds.

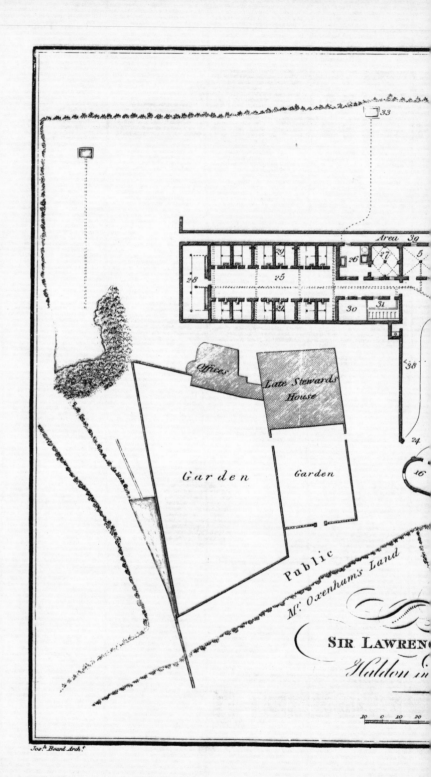

33

Area 39

29
26 27 5
28 25
32
30 31
38

Offices
Late Stewards
House

24
16

Garden Garden

Public
Mr Oxenham's Land

SIR LAWREN
Haldon in

10 0 10 20

Jos.^h Beard Arch.^t

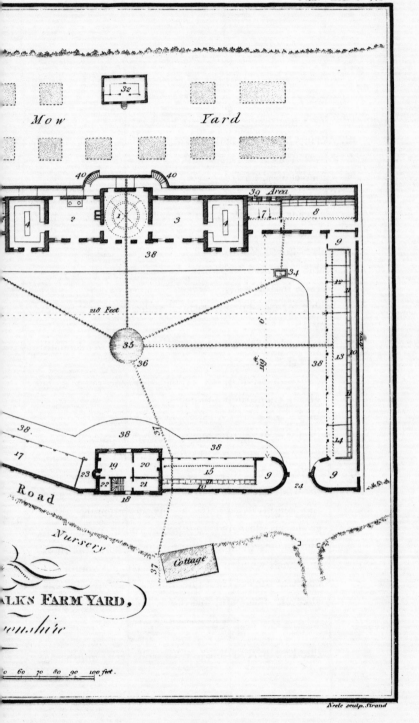

Plate XXI *P 472*

Mow

Yard

32

40 40

39 *Area*
2 1 3 4 7 8
4 9
38

218 Feet 34
6

35
36 38 13

38. 38
17 19 20 15 38 9
23 22 21 9 24
18 10
Road

Nursery

37 Cottage

ALKS FARM YARD,

onshire

60 70 80 90 100 feet.

References to the Plan of the Farm-Yard at Haldon, in the County of Devon, the Seat of Sir Lawrence Palk, Bart. (Plates XX. XXI. XXII.)

1. The wheel-house under the barn, 25 feet square.
2. Wring-house for making cider, 28 feet by 20.
3. Straw-house, 28 feet by 20.
4. Cider-cellars, 25 feet by 20.
5. Slaughter-house, 22 feet by 16, its floor laid with a considerable declivity towards the drain in the middle.
6. Calves-house, 22 feet by 16, with their pens.
7. Stable of three stalls, the hay-racks formed by recesses in the walls, 18 feet 2 inches by 16.
8. Stable for cart-horses, without stalls, 39 feet 8 inches by 16.
9. Depôts for fodder, one of which to serve occasionally for a sick cow.
10. Passages in front of the cattle, for the purpose of giving them their fodder.
11. Cribs for the cattle to eat their fodder in.
12. Stalls for eight fatting oxen, divided in pairs.
13. Shed for working oxen, 15 feet between post and wall.
14. Shed for young stock. The fronts of all these sheds for the cattle are palisadoed about two-thirds of the height, with gates at proper intervals. The cattle are fastened to upright round posts about four inches diameter, by means of loose iron rings and small wooden bows, which are put round the necks of the cattle. The upper part of the bow or yoke is flat, and has two holes in it, thus,

The bow part is made with split ash, and has a
button

button or knob at each end, which are put into
the circular holes of the flat head-piece, when, by
the spring of the bow the knobs are prevented
from returning, by their slipping over the notches,
where they become fixed, in this manner,

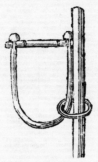

15. Shed for 18 cows.

16. Bull-house, with two pens in it for bull calves.

17. Shed for waggons and carts, 15 feet in the clear.

18. Farm-house, or house for the bailiff.

19. Kitchen, 18 feet 6 inches by 13 feet 2 inches.

20. Parlour, 14 feet by 13 feet 2 inches.

21. Cellar, 14 feet by 7.

22. Pantry.

23. Fuel-house.

24. Entrance gateways to the farm-yard

25. Piggery.

26. Boiling-house, 16 feet square.

27. Store-house for potatoes groined over, 15 feet 6 inches
    square.

28. Sty for store pigs, 38 feet 6 inches by 14 feet.

29. Twelve styes, each 10 feet square, for breeding and
    fatting pigs. The yard pitched with rough stones,
    and the feeding and sleeping place floored with
    flat stones; the eating place four inches above the
    yard, and the sleeping place four inches above
    that. By the sheds being placed as represented,

by

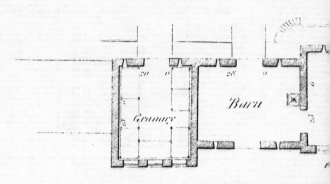

20   0   28   0

Granary   Barn

Plan of the Sta

4   10   20

Sca

Passage to feed the Calves

Rack & Manger

Plan of the Calf Pens.

21   0

1 2 3 4 5

Scale for

Jos.ph Bonet Architect.

Plate XXII. P. 472.

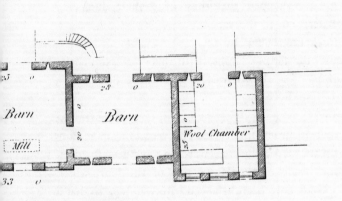

25   0   23   0   20   0

Barn   *Barn*

Mill   *Wool Chamber*

33   0

...ond Story of the Barn.

30   40   50   60   70 Feet

...e for the Barn

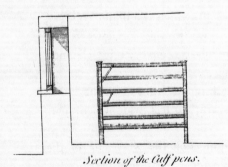
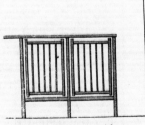

Section of the Calf pens.   *Elevation of the Calf pens.*

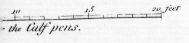

10   15   20 feet

...the Calf pens.

by dotted lines, so as not only to cover the sleeping places, but the eating places also, it enables the pigs to keep themselves clean; for it scarcely or ever happens that they drop their dung any where but in the yard.

30. Store-house, 16 feet by 11.

31. House for fatting lambs, with their pens similar to those for the calves, but of less dimensions, 17 feet by 11.

32. Granary, as it was first intended, on staddle-stones: and in order to prevent the vermin from getting up the steps, the steps were to have been fixed on the inside of the lower part of the door, which was to have been balanced with weights, so that a slight effort would have brought it down on a block of stone, forming the first step for that purpose, 24 feet by 14 in the clear.

33. Reservoir.

34. Troughs for watering the cattle.

35. Receptacle for the liquid manure.

36. Hatch to the receptacle.

37. The main sewer, through which the liquid collected in the farm-yard flows to the meadows below, over which it is regularly conveyed by channels cut for the purpose.

38. A border of stone pitching in front of all the buildings in the farm-yard, 10 feet wide where narrowest.

39. Area behind the buildings on the west side of the yard, four feet wide at the narrowest place.

40. Steps in the area leading from the yard to the Mow Barton, and also to the upper barn floor, three feet wide.

APPENDIX.

APPENDIX.

The State of the Devon and Exeter Hospital,

BEING AN ABSTRACT OF THE 65TH ANNUAL PUBLICATION
SINCE ITS INSTITUTION.

State of the Patients from January 1st, 1742-3 (when the Hospital was opened) to Lady-day, 1806.

ADMITTED.

In-patients.

Before Lady-day 1805 (of whom 130 remained then on the books) - - - - - - - - - - - - - } 44153	} 44134	
From Lady-day 1805, to Lady-day 1806 - - - - - 681		

Out-Patients.

Before Lady-day 1805 (of whom 123 remained then on the Books) - - - - - - - - - - - - } 18853	} 19316	
From Lady-day 1805 to Lady-day 1806 - - - - - 463		

64150

If, however, the changes from an in-patient to an out be considered, which is necessary to ascertain the expenses, the number of in-patients will be 797, and the out-patients 635.

DISCHARGED - - -	Before Lady-day 1805.	From L. D. 1805, to L. D. 1806.	In all.
Cured - - - - - - - - - - - - - - -	42266	757	43023
Received great benefit, whose cases would not admit of further relief - - - -	9708	218	9926
For non-attendance, many of whom were known to be cured - - - - - -	5243	68	5311
For irregularity, or at their own request,	1760	22	1782
Incurable - - - - - - - - - - -	130	1	131
Improper objects, inveterate ulcers, and patients improperly recommended -	170	2	172
Incapable of farther relief by medicines -	1650	10	1660
By death in the house - - - - - -	1826	33	1859
Total discharged - - - - -	62753	1111	63864
Remaining on the books in-patients 104 at Lady-day 1806 out-patients 182			286
			64150

Patients

Patients admitted on sudden accidents and emergencies, without recommendation, amount to 13,664 of whom 340 were since Lady-day 1805. The patients weekly accommodated in the house from Lady-day 1805, to Lady-day 1806, have been on an average 120, and the out-patients, on an average during this year, have been 172.

Among the patients discharged in the course of this year, one continued a patient 108 weeks; three upwards of one year; six from twelve to sixteen months; yet it appears that the 737 in-patients above accounted for, as having had their whole benefit, were continued in the hospital, upon an average, eight weeks and a half:—and that the above mentioned 635 out-patients were continued as such, fourteen weeks and a half each, on an average.

A General Abstract of the whole Account from the Foundation, August 27, 1741, to Lady day, 1806.

RECEIPTS, viz.

	£.	s.	d.
Subscriptions - - - - - - - - - - - - - - -	88245	17	6
Benefactions, including the late collection from parishes	21188	6	2½
Poor's box - - - - - - - - - - - - - - - - -	736	12	8
Legacies before Lady-day 1805, including the interest of those not immediately paid } 20782 3 9¼			
Legacies from Lady-day 1805, to Lady-day 1806 - - - - - - - - - } 156 9 0			
	20938	52	3½
Dividends in Old and New South-Sea Annuities, 3 per cent. consolidated Annuities, and other dividends }	8535	4	0¾
Fines and Rents received for the tenements given by Ralph Allen, Esq. - - - - - - - - - - - }	565	16	0
Other receipts, as by the above and former accounts	2298	17	11
£.	142509	7	1¼

PAYMENTS.

	l.	s.	d.
The purchase and building the Hospital, as per former accounts, including also the expense of alterations and additions thereto in and before 1758, and its enlargement in 1772 and 1790 - - - - - - }	6377	8	0
Furnishing the house, including the furniture for new wards in 1758, 1772, 1787, 1790, and other occasional additions - - - - - - - - - - }	694	6	2
Extraordinary expenses, as by the above and former accounts - - - - - - - - - - - - - - }	1404	7	6
Ordinary Expenses, viz. Housekeeping, common supply of furniture, repairs, &c. &c. - - - - - - }	116867	9	5¾
Balance in hand at Lady-day 1806 in cash 513 10 9			
In Old and New South-Sea Annuities, and the other funded property, and two deeds poll, as above stated - } 16652 5 3			
	17165	16	0
£.	142509	7	1¼

At a general Court of Governors of the Devon and Exeter Hospital, held the 10th day of September, 1805, among the Resolutions entered into at this Court, the following is recommended to the particular attention of the Public, viz.

That from and after Lady-Day, 1806, the right of recommendation shall be as follows:—Subscribers of one guinea annually may recommend one out-patient in the year, but no in-patient. Subscribers of two guineas per annum, may recommend annually one in-patient and one out-patient; subscribers of three guineas per annum, one in and two out-patients; subscribers of four guineas per annum, two in-patients and two out-patients; subscribers of five guineas per annum, and under ten guineas, may recommend three in-patients and two out-patients in the year; subscribers of ten guineas per annum and upwards, may recommend patients without limitation of their annual number; provided that none under twenty guineas, have more than two patients at the same time, nor any contributor more than two in-patients and two out-patients at one time.

Rules to be observed relative to the Recommendation and Admission of Patients.

No domestic servants, whose circumstances entitle them to charitable relief, are excluded from this hospital; but those who are capable of paying for medical assistance, their wives, children, or apprentices, cannot become objects of a charity, designed for the poor only.—It is therefore particularly requested, that gentlemen who recommend patients, will inquire what their situation and circumstances are; for the committee, however anxious to guard against imposition, cannot be acquainted with those who come to them from distant parts of the country, or from neighbouring counties; and when patients are found to have no just claim to the charity, recommenders cannot be offended if such patients are refused or discharged, or compelled to pay for that assistance they have received in their assumed characters.

If parish officers refuse a requisite allowance for the support of poor out-patients, necessarily detained near the hospital for the purpose of attending it, they may be compelled to do so by an Act of Parliament, by which, " if any out-patient of this hospital shall, during such necessary attendance and abode in the city and county of Exeter, become " necessitous and unable to support and maintain him or herself, it shall " and may be lawful for any one justice of the peace for the county in " which

" which such poor out-patient is settled, upon such person's desiring re-
" lief and producing a certificate under the hand of any one of the phy-
" sicians or surgeons of the said hospital, that such poor out-patient is in-
" capable of going to, and returning from, his or her legal place of set-
" tlement, when and so often as his or attendance is requisite at the said
" hospital ; and that, in order to reap the benefit thereof, it is necessary
" that such poor patient should continue and abide near the said hospital,
" —to order such relief as the exigency of his or her case may require,
" during such necessary absence from, and, in like manner, as if the pa-
" tient were still resident in, his or her own parish or legal place of
" settlement."—As it also frequently happens, that the in-patients recommended and admitted to this hospital are unprovided with proper
clothes to keep them warm and clean, it is further enacted, " That in
" case any such in-patient shall be in want of such clothing, it shall
" and may be lawful for any justice of the peace for the county in
" which such in-patient is settled (upon such person's desiring relief,
" and producing such certificate as aforesaid), to order such in-patient
" to be relieved by the churchwardens and overseers of the poor of the
" parish to which such in-patient belongs, as the exigency of his or her
" case may require."

No patient can be admitted who has been once discharged for irregularity or wilful non-attendance. Those who are supposed incurable,
suspected of being consumptive, to have the small-pox, itch, or any in-
fectious disease ; women big with child ; persons disordered in their
senses ; children under the age of seven years, except where an operation
is required, are excluded as in-patients. Those affected with inveterate
ulcers cannot be admitted a second time, without a previous consultation of surgeons, if immediately held. The receiving physician and
surgeon determine whether the patients who apply are proper objects of
the charity, with respect to their complaints, and whether they be admitted as in or out-patients.

Patients are often sent in the last stage of life, when to reject them
would be to shorten the little time remaining of existence, and to admit
them to a close room, would be scarcely more merciful; while, in either
case, relief is impossible : it is requested, therefore, in circumstances apparently desperate, that the opinion of some medical man be taken, respecting the advantage they may probably receive, and the injury that
may accrue from the journey.

Whenever all the in-patients qualified by the rules of the charity cannot be admitted, the preference is first given to the cases which in the
opinion of the receiving physician and surgeon will least admit of delay ;
next to those who come from the greatest distance, and afterwards in
succession to patients recommended by subscribers and benefactors, who

have

have not had patients in the house during the last year, or by the greatest contributors.—Those excluded for want of room, are considered as in-patients, and received on the first vacancy, or at the following day of admission; as this must sometimes happen, patients sent from a distance, should be supplied with provision for one week's lodging and maintenance.

———

†*† Patients are admitted (on proper recommendations) at the weekly board every Thursday, before twelve at noon: and at no other time, except on sudden accidents, in which cases they are received without recommendation, form, or delay.—And none are discharged (except for irregularity, non-attendance, at their own request, or when found to be improper objects of the charity) until they have received their cures, or are reported by their physicians or surgeons as unlikely to receive benefit by remaining longer.

———

N. B. Subscribers are earnestly requested to take notice, that no patient can be admitted on the recommendati of a subscriber whose subscription for the present year, commencing at Lady-day last, is not actually paid.

THE END.

Printed by B. M'Millan,
Bow Street, Covent Garden.

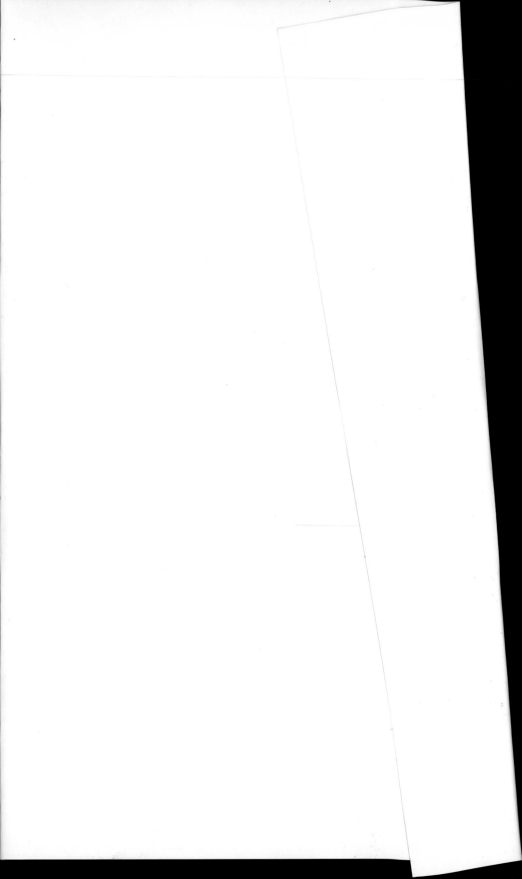

MIWON KWON

ONE PLACE AFTER ANOTHER

SITE-SPECIFIC ART AND LOCATIONAL IDENTITY

THE MIT PRESS · CAMBRIDGE, MASSACHUSETTS · LONDON, ENGLAND

This book was set in Monotype Grotesque and Rockwell by Graphic Composition,
Inc., and was printed and bound in the United States of America.

Library of Congress Cataloging-in-Publication Data

Kwon, Miwon.
    One place after another : site-specific art and locational identity / Miwon Kwon.
        p.   cm.
    Includes bibliographical references and index.
    ISBN 0-262-11265-5 (hc. : alk. paper)
    1. Site-specific art. 2. Art, Modern—20th century. I. Title.

N6490 .K93 2002
709′.04′07—dc21   2001044753

For Umma and Appa

CONTENTS

ACKNOWLEDGMENTS

The first incarnation of this book, in the form of a doctoral thesis, was completed in 1998 at the School of Architecture at Princeton University under the guidance of Rosalyn Deutsche, Hal Foster, and Mark Wigley. I am grateful for their encouragement, critical commentaries, and practical wisdom, which set me in the right direction and pushed me forward. Many people during that time and since then gave me opportunities to develop different aspects of the project as papers or lectures. My thanks to Julie Ault, Ron Clark, Sylvie Fortin, Christian Höller, Janet Kaplan, Richard Meyer, Ellen McMahon, Christian Philipp Müller, Andrew Perchuk, Mathias Poledna, Georg Schöllhammer, Do-Ho Suh, Sergio Vega, and especially the editors of *October* for their timely invitations and keen critical responses.

I am also grateful to many artists, curators, critics, arts administrators, colleagues, and friends who shared their insights and experiences or otherwise encouraged me during the period of the book's preparation. Among them, I am especially indebted to David Deitcher, Mark Dion, Karen Dunbar, Russell Ferguson, Joyce Fernandes, Andrea Fraser, Renée Green, Chris Hoover, Mary Jane Jacob, Silvia Kolbowski, Janet Kraynak, Simon Leung, Roy Levin and the faculty, staff, and students of the MFA Program in Visual Art at Vermont College, Mark Linder, James Marcovitz, Iñigo Manglano-Ovalle, Michael Minelli, Karen Paluzzi-Steele, Diane Shamash, Margaret Sundell, Frazer Ward, Connie Wolf, and Lydia Yee.

The final revision of the book was completed at UCLA, where I am fortunate to be surrounded by this most congenial and supportive faculty and staff. I would like to thank in particular Anthony Vidler and Cécile Whiting in the Department of Art History and Mary Kelly and Juli Carson at the School of Art for their nurturing influence. I also extend special thanks to my students at UCLA for their patient and enthusiastic participation in the seminars that helped to reshape this project. Among them, Katie Mondloch and Doris Chon have been diligent research assistants.

The College Art Association supported the early phase of research and writing with its Professional Development Fellowship for Art Historians, and a Faculty Career Development Grant from UCLA allowed me to devote myself fully to the project in its last months. I thank both institutions for their support.

Along with these thanks, I want to register my sense of loss in the premature deaths of Alice Yang, Ernest Pascucci, Jochen Klein, Joe Wood, and Pat Hearn. Although they were not close friends, or curiously because so, their work provided a broad sense of orientation for mine—a fact recognized regrettably in their passing. The future that I can imagine for my generation in various cultural fields is diminished because of their absence.

Special acknowledgment is due two exceptional people in my life: Helen Molesworth for her inestimable friendship, and Doug Ashford, my most intimate interlocutor, for his intellectual challenges as well as his extraordinary capacity for laughter.

Finally, I am grateful to my family. In immeasurable ways, Sowon Kwon and Andre Tchelistcheff have sustained me with spirited support throughout the duration of this study. Their son Sune gave me moments of inexplicable joy when I needed it most. And Seong Kwon remains an inspiration, helping me to keep all things in proper perspective. I would like to dedicate this book to my mother and father. As they have grown accustomed to counseling, worrying about, and cheering for their children from so far away over so many years, I have reciprocally tried to learn to endure geographical distance and physical separation as surmountable obstacles to intimacy. Even during the most intense periods of self-doubt, I felt the grounding power of their good will and love.

ONE PLACE AFTER ANOTHER

INTRODUCTION

Site-determined, site-oriented, site-referenced, site-conscious, site-responsive, site-related. These are some new terms that have emerged in recent years among many artists and critics to account for the various permutations of site-specific art in the present. On the one hand, this phenomenon indicates a return of sorts: an attempt to rehabilitate the criticality associated with the anti-idealist, anticommercial site-specific practices of the late 1960s and early 1970s, which incorporated the physical conditions of a particular location as integral to the production, presentation, and reception of art. On the other hand, it signals a desire to *distinguish* current practices from those of the past—to mark a difference from artistic precedents of site specificity whose dominant positivist formulations (the most well-known being Richard Serra's) are deemed to have reached a point of aesthetic and political exhaustion.

This concern to reassess the relationship between the art work and its site is largely provoked by the ways in which the term "site-specific" has been uncritically adopted as another genre category by mainstream art institutions and discourses. The term is indeed conspicuous in a diverse range of catalogue essays, press releases, grant applications, magazine reviews, and artist statements today; it is applied rather indiscriminately to art works, museum exhibitions, public art projects, city arts festivals, architectural installations; and it is embraced as an automatic signifier of "criticality" or "progressivity" by artists, architects, dealers, curators, critics, arts administrators, and funding organizations.[1] For those who adhere to cooptation as the most viable explanation of the relationship between advanced art, the culture industry, and the political economy throughout the twentieth century, the unspecific (mis)uses of the term "site-specific" are yet another instance of how vanguardist, socially conscious, and politically committed art practices always become domesticated by their assimilation into the dominant culture. And this argument would insist that if the aesthetic and political efficacy of site-specific art has become insignificant or innocuous in recent years, it is because it has been weakened and redirected by institutional and market forces.

But the current efforts to redefine the art-site relationship are also inspired by a recognition that if site-specific art seems no longer viable—because its critical edges have dulled, its pressures been absorbed—this is partly due to the conceptual limitations of existing models of site specificity itself. In response, many artists, critics, historians, and curators, whose practices are engaged in problematizing received notions of site specificity, have offered alternative formulations, such as context-specific, debate-specific, audience-specific, community-specific, project-based.[2] These terms, which tend to slide into one another at different times, collectively signal an attempt to forge more complex and fluid possibilities for the art-site relationship while simultaneously registering the extent to which the very concept of the site has become destabilized in the past three decades or more.

Yet despite these efforts to rethink site specificity, and despite the rise in interest in the artistic developments of the 1960s and 1970s in general, contemporary art discourse still lacks a substantive account of the historical and theoretical "grounds" of site specificity. Consequently, the framework within which we might discuss the artistic merit and/or political efficacy of the various formulations of site specificity, old and new, remains inconclusive.[3] Most importantly, what remain unrecognized, and thus unanalyzed, are the ways in which the very term "site specificity" has itself become a site of struggle, where competing positions concerning the nature of the site, as well as the "proper" relationship of art and artists to it, are being contested.

This book critically examines site specificity not exclusively as an artistic genre but as a problem-idea,[4] as a peculiar cipher of art and spatial politics. In addition to providing analysis and theorization of the various artistic (re)configurations of site specificity, and reevaluating the rhetoric of aesthetic vanguardism and political progressivism associated with them, the book situates the questions concerning the siting of art as a spatio-political problematic. Which is to say, site specificity is here conceived as what art historian Rosalyn Deutsche has called an "urban-aesthetic" or "spatial-cultural" discourse, which combines "ideas about art, architecture, and urban design, on the one hand, with theories of the city, social space, and public space, on the other."⁵ Informed by critical urban theory, postmodernist criticism in art and architecture, and debates concerning identity politics and the public sphere, the book seeks to reframe site specificity as the cultural mediation of broader social, economic, and political processes that organize urban life and urban space.

As a point of departure, the first chapter proposes a genealogy of site specificity since the late 1960s. Emerging out of the lessons of minimalism, site-specific art was initially based in a phenomenological or experiential understanding of the site, defined primarily as an agglomeration of the actual physical attributes of a particular location (the size, scale, texture, and dimension of walls, ceilings, rooms; existing lighting conditions, topographical features, traffic patterns, seasonal characteristics of climate, etc.), with architecture serving as a foil for the art work in many instances. Then, through the materialist investigations of institutional critique, the site was reconfigured as a relay or network of interrelated spaces and economies (studio, gallery, museum, art market, art criticism), which together frame and sustain art's ideological system. Works by artists such as Michael Asher, Daniel Buren, Hans Haacke, and Mierle Laderman Ukeles are seen as challenging the hermeticism of this system, complicating the site of art as not only a physical arena but one constituted through social, economic, and political processes.

In more recent site-oriented, project-based art by artists such as Mark Dion, Andrea Fraser, Renée Green, Christian Philipp Müller, and Fred Wilson, among many others, the site of art is again redefined, often extending beyond familiar art contexts to more "public" realms. Dispersed across much broader cultural, social, and discursive fields, and organized intertextually through the nomadic movement of the artist—operating more like an itinerary than a map—the site can now be as various as a billboard, an artistic genre, a disenfranchised community, an institutional framework, a magazine page, a social cause, or a political debate. It can be literal, like a street corner, or virtual, like a theoretical concept. While chapter 1 proposes three paradigms of site specificity—phenomenological or experiential; social/institutional; and discursive—in a somewhat chronological manner, there are no discrete separations or neat periodizing breaks between them. The paradigms are outlined as competing definitions that operate in overlapping ways in past and current site-oriented art.

Chapter 2 examines some key aspects of what the transformation of the site—from a sedentary to a nomadic model—might mean for the art object, artists, and art institutions today. Critical questions concerning the status of originality, authenticity, uniqueness, and authorship, those concepts so central to modernist ideologies of art, which in turn were problematized throughout the 1970s and 1980s, are raised anew in the first section of the chapter. The discussion here takes account of the ways in which the recent trend of reproducing, refabricating, and traveling site-specific art first produced in the late 1960s and early 1970s would seem to betray the earlier premise of site specificity. At the same time, the new conceptual, ethical, and practical problems provoked by this situation force a reorganization of the conventional terms of making, selling, collecting, exhibiting, and distributing site-specific art in both institutional and market contexts. As such, the current mobilization and commodification of site specificity is seen to represent its most salient critical moment even as it enacts a "betrayal" of its earlier aspirations.

The second section of the chapter poses similar questions concerning the status of originality, authenticity, uniqueness, and authorship in relation to the nomadic conditions under which artists pursue new site-oriented practices today. As more artists try to accommodate the increase in demand for singular on-site projects in various cities across the globalized art network (as evidenced, for instance, in the rise in number of city-based biennials and annuals around the world), the definition of site specificity is being reconfigured to imply not the permanence and immobility of a work but its impermanence and transience. The chapter focuses on the impact of this reconfiguration on the role of the artist (now a cultural-artistic service provider rather than a producer of aesthetic objects), the new commodity status of such art "work," and the general shift from the "aesthetics of administration" to the administration of aesthetics in contemporary art. In addition, the chapter reflects on the ways in which such new site-oriented practices accommodate and/or trouble the construction and commodification of urban identities.

Chapter 3 charts the changes in the conceptualization of site specificity within the mainstream public art arena, examining the ways in which an art work's public relevance and its sociopolitical ambitions have been measured in terms of the art-site relationship over the past three decades. The incorporation of site specificity as a programmatic imperative by local, state, and national public art agencies in the mid-1970s encouraged the development of a design team approach in which artists were asked to collaborate with architects in producing or refurbishing public spaces, such as urban plazas, waterfront promenades, neighborhood parks, and office lobbies. The resulting paradigm of art-as-public-spaces, or "place-making," accommodated several ongoing circumstances: the expanded scale of artistic (sculptural) practices of the period, such as those of Scott Burton and Michael Heizer, for instance; the need of public art administrators and city officials to integrate art into the urban environment in a more "accessible" manner; and the accelerated growth of real estate investment and urban redevelopment projects throughout the country. Meant to equalize the creative authority of artists and architects in the design of public spaces, this mode of site specificity presumed the humanizing influence of art over the inhumanity of urban architecture. The ideology of functional utility, foundational to the modernist ethos of architecture and urban design, came to overtake the essentialism of formalist beauty, traditionally associated with art; site-specific public art now needed to be "useful."[6]

Against this backdrop, Richard Serra proposed a countermodel of site specificity with his sculpture *Tilted Arc* (1981–1989). His "medium-differential" approach,[7] in which he uses the language of sculpture to interrogate rather than accommodate the given architecture, disrupted the spatial conditions of the art work's site at Federal Plaza in New York City and challenged the prevailing design-oriented definition of site specificity. The controversy surrounding the removal of *Tilted Arc*—precisely on the point of site specificity's artistic, political, and social validity—is revisited here to establish the terms that become central to public art discourse in subsequent years. John Ahearn's figurative sculptures for a Percent for Art commission in the South Bronx (1991), installed and deinstalled by the artist within one week because of local protest, serves as an important comparative study for the consideration of another alternative model of site specificity. In this case, the site is not simply a geographical location or architectural setting but a network of social relations, a community, and the artist and his sponsors envision the art work as an integral extension of the community rather than an intrusive contribution from elsewhere. The volatile reactions that emerged in response to Ahearn's project, and Ahearn's own response to those reactions, exposed the incommensurate expectations, presumptions, and ideologies at play in much community-based public art today. With the shift from site to community, or the conversion of community into a site, questions concerning the role of the artist, the public function of art, and the definition of community are given new urgency.

Chapter 4 attends more generally to the artistic, architectural, social, and political implications of the shift from site specificity to community specificity in "new genre public art."[8] Claiming a major break from previous approaches to public art, proponents of new genre public art favor temporary rather than permanent projects that engage their audience, particularly groups considered marginalized, as active participants in the conceptualization and production of process-oriented, politically conscious community events or programs. Drawing on a detailed analysis of the highly acclaimed 1993 community-based public art exhibition "Culture in Action" as a case study, this chapter questions the presumptions of aesthetic radicalism, public accessibility, audience empowerment, social relevance, and democracy that support such practice. While many of the goals of new genre public art are salutary, this chapter counters the claims made by many of its advocates that its newness overcomes the contradictions of previous models of site specificity. The chapter unpacks the ways in which new genre public art can exacerbate uneven power relations, remarginalize (even colonize) already disenfranchised groups, depoliticize and remythify the artistic process, and finally further the separation of art and life (despite claims to the contrary).

Tracking the complex exchanges among numerous participants in the planning and presentation of "Culture in Action," the chapter also offers a schematic typology of four "communities" that commonly emerge out of community-based collaborations: community of mythic unity; "sited" communities; temporary invented communities; and ongoing invented communities. Collectively, the categories reveal that despite the effort of many artists, curators, critics, and historians to unify recent trends in public art as a coherent movement, there are numerous inconsistencies and contradictions in the field. For instance, while one community type might require extensive artist and/or institutional involvement, another type remains self-sufficient in overseeing the development of its own project. Further, each category defines a different role for the artist, posing, in turn, alternative renditions of the collaborative relationship. These variations indicate the extent to which the very concept of "community" remains highly ambiguous and problematic in public art today.

This last point is emphasized in the review of the key critiques of community-based art in chapter 5, especially as they pertain to ethical issues of uneven power relations in the triangulated exchange between an artist, a curator-art institution, and a community group. From Hal Foster's critique of its ethnographic working methods, to Grant Kester's claims of its reformist-minded "aesthetic evangelism," to Critical Art Ensemble's complete rejection of it, to Martha Fleming's critique of the critics of community-based art, this chapter reveals the extent to which the identity or definition of a community remains open, like the site, as a scene of political struggle. Relying on the work of feminist social theorist Iris Marion Young on the one hand and French philosopher Jean-Luc Nancy on the other, the chapter argues against the common notion of the community as a coherent and unified social formation—equally valorized by neoconservatives and the liberal left—which often serves exclusionary and authoritarian purposes in the very name of the opposite. Instead, the chapter proposes the idea of community as a necessarily unstable and "inoperative" specter in order to think beyond formulaic prescriptions of community, to open onto an altogether different model of collectivity and belonging. Like the concept of the "public sphere," the community may be seen as a phantom,[9] an elusive discursive formation that, as Nancy puts it, is not a "common being" but a nonessential "being-in-common." Based on this insight, the chapter concludes with a provocation to imagine "collective artistic praxis," as opposed to "community-based art."

In the final chapter, the dissipation of the site in site specificity as described in the previous chapters—the prioritizing of its discursivity, its displacement by the community—is examined in relation to the "dynamics of deterritorialization" as elaborated in architectural and urban spatial discourse. While the accelerated speed, access, and exchange of information, images, commodities, and even bodies is being celebrated in one circle, the concomitant breakdown of traditional temporal-spatial experiences and the accompanying homogenization of places and erasure of cultural differences is being decried in another. The intensifying conditions of spatial indifferentiation and departicularization—that is, the increasing instances of locational *un*specificity—are seen to exacerbate the sense of alienation and fragmentation in contemporary life. Consequently, the nature of the tie between subject/object and location, as well as the interplay between place and space, has received much critical attention in the past two decades' theorization of oppositional cultural practice. For example, Fredric Jameson's "cognitive mapping,"[10] Lucy Lippard's "lure of the local,"[11] Kenneth Frampton's "critical regionalism,"[12] Michel de Certeau's "walking in the city,"[13] and Henri Lefebvre's "production of space,"[14] as ideologically divergent as they may be, are all attempts to theorize the transforming nexus between the subject/object and location.

         To this list we should add site specificity as an analogous artistic endeavor. For if the search for place-bound identity in an undifferentiated sea of abstract, homogenized, and fragmented space of late capitalism is one characteristic of the postmodern condition, then the expanded efforts to rethink the specificity of the art-site relationship can be viewed as both a compensatory symptom *and* critical resistance to such conditions. Indeed, the resilience of the concept of site specificity as indicated by its many permutations, with its vague yet persistent maintenance of the idea of singular, unrepeatable instances of site-bound knowledge and experience, manifests this doubleness. Countering both the nostalgic desire for a retrieval of rooted, place-bound identities on the one hand, and the antinostalgic embrace of a nomadic fluidity of subjectivity, identity, and spatiality on the other, this book concludes with a theorization of the "wrong place," a speculative and heuristic concept for imagining a new model of belonging-in-transience. As evidenced throughout the book, this task of imagining altogether new coordinations of art and site is an open-ended predicament. Thus, in its final pages, the book can only conjure the critical capacity of intimacies based on absence, distance, and ruptures of time and space.

Robert Smithson, *Partially Buried Woodshed*, at Kent State University campus, 1970. (© Estate of Robert Smithson/
VAGA, New York; courtesy James Cohan Gallery, New York.)

GENEALOGY OF SITE SPECIFICITY

Site specificity used to imply something grounded, bound to the laws of physics.
Often playing with gravity, site-specific works used to be obstinate about "presence," even if they were materially ephemeral, and adamant about immobility, even
in the face of disappearance or destruction. Whether inside the white cube or out in
the Nevada desert, whether architectural or landscape-oriented, site-specific art
initially took the site as an actual location, a tangible reality, its identity composed of
a unique combination of physical elements: length, depth, height, texture, and
shape of walls and rooms; scale and proportion of plazas, buildings, or parks; existing conditions of lighting, ventilation, traffic patterns; distinctive topographical features, and so forth. If modernist sculpture absorbed its pedestal/base to sever its
connection to or express its indifference to the site, rendering itself more
autonomous and self-referential, thus transportable, placeless, and nomadic, then
site-specific works, as they first emerged in the wake of minimalism in the late
1960s and early 1970s, forced a dramatic reversal of this modernist paradigm.[1]
Antithetical to the claim, "If you have to change a sculpture for a site there is something wrong with the sculpture,"[2] site-specific art, whether interruptive or assimilative,[3] gave itself up to its environmental context, being formally determined or
directed by it.

In turn, the uncontaminated and pure idealist space of dominant mod-
ernisms was radically displaced by the materiality of the natural landscape or the
impure and ordinary space of the everyday. And the space of art was no longer
perceived as a blank slate, a tabula rasa, but a real place. The art object or event in
this context was to be singularly and multiply experienced in the here and now
through the bodily presence of each viewing subject, in a sensory immediacy of
spatial extension and temporal duration (what Michael Fried derisively characterized as theatricality),[4] rather than instantaneously perceived in a visual epiphany
by a disembodied eye. Site-specific work in its earliest formation, then, focused on

establishing an inextricable, indivisible relationship between the work and its site, and demanded the physical presence of the viewer for the work's completion. The (neo-avant-gardist) aesthetic aspiration to exceed the limitations of traditional media, like painting and sculpture, as well as their institutional setting; the episte-mological challenge to relocate meaning from within the art object to the contin-gencies of its context; the radical restructuring of the subject from an old Cartesian model to a phenomenological one of lived bodily experience; and the self-conscious desire to resist the forces of the capitalist market economy, which circu-lates art works as transportable and exchangeable commodity goods—all these imperatives came together in art's new attachment to the actuality of the site.

In this frame of mind, Robert Barry declared in a 1969 interview that each of his wire installations was "made to suit the place in which it was installed. They can-not be moved without being destroyed."[5] Similarly, Richard Serra wrote fifteen years later in a letter to the director of the Art-in-Architecture Program of the General Ser-vices Administration in Washington, D.C., that his 120-foot, Cor-Ten steel sculpture *Tilted Arc* was "commissioned and designed for one particular site: Federal Plaza. It is a site-specific work and as such not to be relocated. To remove the work is to destroy the work."[6] He further elaborated his position in 1989:

> As I pointed out, *Tilted Arc* was conceived from the start as a site-specific sculpture and was not meant to be "site-adjusted" or . . . "relocated." Site-specific works deal with the environmental compo-nents of given places. The scale, size, and location of site-specific works are determined by the topography of the site, whether it be urban or landscape or architectural enclosure. The works become part of the site and restructure both conceptually and perceptually the organization of the site.[7]

Barry and Serra echo one another here. But whereas Barry's comment announces what was in the late 1960s a new radicality in vanguardist sculptural practice, mark-ing an early stage in the aesthetic experiments that were to follow through the

1970s (land/earth art, process art, installation art, conceptual art, performance/ body art, and various forms of institutional critique), Serra's statement, spoken twenty years later within the context of public art, is an indignant defense, signaling a crisis point for site specificity—at least for a version that would prioritize the *physical* inseparability between a work and its site of installation.[8]

Informed by the contextual thinking of minimalism, various forms of institutional critique and conceptual art developed a different model of site specificity that implicitly challenged the ''innocence'' of space and the accompanying presumption of a universal viewing subject (albeit one in possession of a corporeal body) as espoused in the phenomenological model. Artists such as Michael Asher, Marcel Broodthaers, Daniel Buren, Hans Haacke, and Robert Smithson, as well as many women artists including Mierle Laderman Ukeles, have variously conceived the site not only in physical and spatial terms but as a *cultural* framework defined by the institutions of art. If minimalism returned to the viewing subject a physical body, institutional critique insisted on the social matrix of the class, race, gender, and sexuality of the viewing subject.[9] Moreover, while minimalism challenged the idealist hermeticism of the autonomous art object by deflecting its meaning to the space of its presentation, institutional critique further complicated this displacement by highlighting the idealist hermeticism of the space of presentation itself. The modern gallery/museum space, for instance, with its stark white walls, artificial lighting (no windows), controlled climate, and pristine architectonics, was perceived not solely in terms of basic dimensions and proportion but as an institutional disguise, a normative exhibition convention serving an ideological function. The seemingly benign architectural features of a gallery/museum, in other words, were deemed to be coded mechanisms that *actively* disassociate the space of art from the outer world, furthering the institution's idealist imperative of rendering itself and its values ''objective,'' ''disinterested,'' and ''true.''

As early as 1970 Buren proclaimed, ''Whether the place in which the work is shown imprints and marks this work, whatever it may be, or whether the work itself is directly—consciously or not—produced for the Museum, any work presented in that framework, if it does not explicitly examine the influence of the framework upon itself, falls into the illusion of self-sufficiency—or idealism."[10] More than just the museum, the site comes to encompass a relay of several interrelated but different spaces and economies, including the studio, gallery, museum, art criticism, art history, the art market, that together constitute a system of practices that is not separate from but open to social, economic, and political pressures. To be "specific" to such a site, in turn, is to decode and/or recode the institutional conventions so as to expose their hidden operations—to reveal the ways in which institutions mold art's meaning to modulate its cultural and economic value; to undercut the fallacy of art's and its institutions' autonomy by making apparent their relationship to the broader socioeconomic and political processes of the day. Again, in Buren's somewhat militant words from 1970:

> Art, whatever else it may be, is exclusively political. What is called
> for is the *analysis of formal and cultural limits* (and not one *or* the
> other) within which art exists and struggles. These limits are many
> and of different intensities. Although the prevailing ideology and the
> associated artists try in every way to *camouflage* them, and although
> it is too early—the conditions are not met—to blow them up, the time
> has come to *unveil* them.[11]

In nascent forms of institutional critique, in fact, the physical condition of the exhibition space remained the primary point of departure for this unveiling. For example, in works such as Hans Haacke's *Condensation Cube* (1963–1965), Mel Bochner's *Measurement* series (1969), Lawrence Weiner's wall cutouts (1968), and Buren's *Within and Beyond the Frame* (1973), the task of exposing those aspects which the institution would obscure was enacted literally in relation to the architecture of the exhibition space—highlighting the humidity level of a gallery by allowing moisture to "invade" the pristine minimalist art object (a mimetic configuration of the gallery space itself); insisting on the material fact of the gallery walls as "framing" devices by notating the walls' dimensions directly on them; removing portions of a wall to reveal the base reality behind the "neutral" white cube; and ex-

Mel Bochner, *Measurement: Room*, tape and Letraset on wall, installation at Galerie Heiner Friedrich, Munich, 1969. (Photo by the artist; Collection The Museum of Modern Art, New York.)

Daniel Buren, photo-souvenir: ***Within and Beyond the Frame***, John Weber Gallery, New York, 1973. (© Daniel Buren.)

ceeding the physical boundaries of the gallery by having the art work literally go out the window, ostensibly to "frame" the institutional frame. Attempts such as these to expose the cultural confinement within which artists function—"the apparatus the artist is threaded through"—and the impact of its forces upon the meaning and value of art became, as Smithson had predicted in 1972, "the great issue" for artists in the 1970s.[12] As this investigation extended into the 1980s, it relied less and less on the physical parameters of the gallery/museum or other exhibition venues to articulate its critique.

In the paradigmatic practice of Hans Haacke, for instance, the site shifted

Michael Asher, untitled installation at Claire Copley Gallery, Inc., Los Angeles, 1974. (Photo by Gary Krueger; courtesy the artist.)

from the physical condition of the gallery (as in *Condensation Cube*) to the system of socioeconomic relations within which art and its institutional programming find their possibilities of being. His fact-based exposés through the 1970s, which spotlighted art's inextricable ties to the ideologically suspect if not morally corrupt power elite, recast the site of art as an institutional frame in social, economic, and political terms, and enforced these terms as the very content of the art work.[13] Exemplary of a different approach to the institutional frame are Michael Asher's surgically precise displacement projects, which advanced a concept of site that included historical and conceptual dimensions. In his contribution to the "73rd American Exhibition" at the Art Institute of Chicago in 1979, for instance, Asher revealed the sites of exhibition or display to be culturally specific situations that generate particular expectations and narratives regarding art and art history. Institutional framing of art, in other words, not only distinguishes qualitative value; it also (re)produces specific forms of knowledge that are historically located and culturally determined—not at all universal or timeless standards.[14]

Yet another approach to a critique of the institutional frame is indicated in Mierle Laderman Ukeles's 1973 series of "maintenance art" performances at the Wadsworth Atheneum in Hartford, Connecticut.[15] In two of the performances, Ukeles, literally on her hands and knees, washed the entry plaza and steps of the museum for four hours, then scrubbed the floors inside the exhibition galleries for another four hours. In doing so, she forced the menial domestic tasks usually associated with women—cleaning, washing, dusting, and tidying—to the level of aesthetic contemplation, and revealed the extent to which the museum's pristine self-presentation, its perfectly immaculate white spaces as emblematic of its "neutrality," is structurally dependent on the hidden and devalued labor of daily maintenance and upkeep. By foregrounding this dependence, Ukeles posed the museum as a hierarchical system of labor relations and complicated the social and gendered division between the notions of the public and the private.[16]

In these ways, the site of art begins to diverge from the literal space of art, and the physical condition of a specific location recedes as the primary element in the conception of a site. Whether articulated in political and economic terms, as in

20

Mierle Laderman Ukeles, *Hartford Wash: Washing Tracks, Maintenance Outside*, Wadsworth Atheneum, Hartford, 1973. (Photos courtesy Ronald Feldman Fine Arts, New York.)

Mierle Laderman Ukeles, *Hartford Wash: Washing Tracks, Maintenance Inside*, Wadsworth Atheneum, Hartford, 1973. (Photos courtesy Ronald Feldman Fine Arts, New York.)

Haacke's case, in epistemological terms, as in Asher's displacements, or in systemic terms of uneven (gendered) labor relations, as in Ukeles's performances, it is rather the *techniques* and *effects* of the art institution as they circumscribe and delimit the definition, production, presentation, and dissemination of art that become the sites of critical intervention. Concurrent with this move toward the dematerialization of the site is the simultaneous deaestheticization (that is, withdrawal of visual pleasure) and dematerialization of the art work. Going against the grain of institutional habits and desires, and continuing to resist the commodification of art in/for the marketplace, site-specific art adopts strategies that are either aggressively antivisual—informational, textual, expositional, didactic—or immaterial altogether—gestures, events, or performances bracketed by temporal boundaries. The "work" no longer seeks to be a noun/object but a verb/process, provoking the viewers' *critical* (not just physical) acuity regarding the ideological conditions of their viewing. In this context, the guarantee of a specific relationship between an art work and its site is not based on a physical permanence of that relationship (as demanded by Serra, for example) but rather on the recognition of its unfixed *impermanence,* to be experienced as an unrepeatable and fleeting situation.

But if the critique of the cultural confinement of art (and artists) via its institutions was once the "great issue," a dominant drive of site-oriented practices today is the pursuit of a more intense engagement with the outside world and everyday life—a critique of culture that is inclusive of nonart spaces, nonart institutions, and nonart issues (blurring the division between art and nonart, in fact). Concerned to integrate art more directly into the realm of the social,[17] either in order to redress (in an activist sense) urgent social problems such as the ecological crisis, homelessness, AIDS, homophobia, racism, and sexism, or more generally in order to relativize art as one among many forms of cultural work, current manifestations of site specificity tend to treat aesthetic and art historical concerns as secondary issues. Deeming the focus on the social nature of *art's* production and reception to be too exclusive, even elitist, this expanded engagement with culture favors public sites outside the traditional confines of art both in physical and intellectual terms.[18]

Furthering previous (at times literal) attempts to take art out of the mu-

Group Material, *DaZiBaos*, poster project at Union Square, New York, 1982. (Photo courtesy the artists.)

seum/gallery space-system (recall Daniel Buren's striped canvases marching out the window, or Robert Smithson's adventures in the wastelands of New Jersey or isolated locales in Utah), contemporary site-oriented works occupy hotels, city streets, housing projects, prisons, schools, hospitals, churches, zoos, supermarkets, and they infiltrate media spaces such as radio, newspapers, television, and the Internet. In addition to this spatial expansion, site-oriented art is also informed by a broader range of disciplines (anthropology, sociology, literary criticism, psychology, natural and cultural histories, architecture and urbanism, computer science, political theory, philosophy) and is more sharply attuned to popular discourses (fashion, music, advertising, film, and television). Beyond these dual expansions of art into culture, which obviously diversify the site, the distinguishing characteristic of today's site-oriented art is the way in which the art work's relationship to the actuality of a location (as site) and the social conditions of the institutional frame (as site) are both subordinate to a *discursively* determined site that is delineated as a field of knowledge, intellectual exchange, or cultural debate. Furthermore, unlike in the previous models, this site is not defined as a *pre*condition. Rather, it is generated by the work (often as "content"), and then verified by its convergence with an existing discursive formation.

◄   Mark Dion, **On Tropical Nature**, in the field near the Orinoco River basin, 1991. (Photo by Bob Braine; courtesy American Fine Arts, Co., New York.)
▶   Mark Dion, **On Tropical Nature**, installation at Sala Mendoza, Caracas, 1991. (Photo by Miwon Kwon.)

Mark Dion, *New York State Bureau of Tropical Conservation*, with materials from Orinoco River basin reconfigured for installation at American Fine Arts, Co., New York, 1992. (Photo by A. Cumberbirch; courtesy American Fine Arts, Co., New York.)

For example, in Mark Dion's 1991 project *On Tropical Nature,* several different definitions of the site operated concurrently. First, the initial site of Dion's intervention was an uninhabited spot in the rain forest near the base of the Orinoco River outside Caracas, Venezuela, where the artist camped for three weeks collecting specimens of various plants and insects as well as feathers, mushrooms, nests, and stones. These specimens, picked up at the end of each week in crates, were delivered to the second site of the project, Sala Mendoza, one of two hosting art institutions in Caracas. In the gallery space of the Sala, the specimens, which were uncrated and displayed like works of art in themselves, were contextualized within what constituted a third site—the curatorial framework of the thematic group exhibition.[19] The fourth site, however, although the least material, was the site to which Dion intended a lasting relationship. *On Tropical Nature* sought to become a part of the discourse concerning cultural representations of nature and the global environmental crisis.[20]

Sometimes at the cost of a semantic slippage between content and site, other artists who are similarly engaged in site-oriented projects, operating with multiple definitions of the site, in the end find their "locational" anchor in the discursive realm. For instance, while Tom Burr and John Lindell have each produced diverse projects in a variety of media for many different institutions, their consistent engagement with issues concerning the construction and dynamics of (homo)sexuality and desire has established such issues as the "site" of their work. And in many projects by artists such as Lothar Baumgarten, Renée Green, Jimmie Durham, and Fred Wilson, the legacies of colonialism, slavery, racism, and the ethnographic tradition as they impact on identity politics have emerged as an important "site" of artistic investigation. In some instances, artists including Green, Silvia Kolbowski, Group Material, Andrea Fraser, and Christian Philipp Müller have reflected on aspects of site-specific practice itself as a "site," interrogating its currency in relation to aesthetic imperatives, institutional demands, socioeconomic ramifications, or political efficacy.[21] In this way different cultural debates, a theoretical concept, a social issue, a political problem, an institutional framework (not necessarily an art institution), a neighborhood or seasonal event, a historical condition, even particular formations of desire are deemed to function as sites.[22]

This is not to say that the parameters of a particular place or institution no longer matter, because site-oriented art today still cannot be thought or executed without the contingencies of locational and institutional circumstances. But the *primary* site addressed by current manifestations of site specificity is not necessarily bound to, or determined by, these contingencies in the long run. Consequently, although the site of action or intervention (physical) and the site of effects/reception (discursive) are conceived to be continuous, they are nonetheless pulled apart. Whereas, for example, the site of intervention and the site of effect for Serra's *Tilted Arc* were thought of as coincident (Federal Plaza in downtown New York City), Dion's site of intervention (the rain forest in Venezuela or Sala Mendoza) and his projected site of effect (discourse on nature) are distinct. The former clearly serves the latter as material source and inspiration, yet does not sustain an indexical relationship to it.

James Meyer has distinguished this trend in recent site-oriented practice in terms of a "functional site": "[The functional site] is a process, an operation occurring between sites, a mapping of institutional and discursive filiations and the bodies that move between them (the artist's above all). It is an informational site, a locus of overlap of text, photographs and video recordings, physical places and things. . . . It is a temporary thing; a movement; a chain of meanings devoid of a particular focus."[23] Which is to say, the site is now structured (inter)textually rather than spatially, and its model is not a map but an itinerary, a fragmentary sequence of events and actions *through* spaces, that is, a nomadic narrative whose path is articulated by the passage of the artist. Corresponding to the model of movement in electronic spaces of the Internet and cyberspace, which are likewise structured as transitive experiences, one thing after another, and not in synchronic simultaneity,[24] this transformation of the site textualizes spaces and spatializes discourses.

A provisional conclusion might be that in advanced art practices of the past thirty years the operative definition of the site has been transformed from a physical location—grounded, fixed, actual—to a discursive vector—ungrounded, fluid, virtual. Of course, even if a particular formulation of site specificity dominates at one moment and recedes at another, the shifts are not always punctual or definitive. Thus, the three paradigms of site specificity I have schematized here—phenomenological, social/institutional, and discursive—although presented somewhat chronologically, are not stages in a neat linear trajectory of historical development. Rather, they are competing definitions, overlapping with one another and operating simultaneously in various cultural practices today (or even within a single artist's single project). Nonetheless, this move away from a literal interpretation of the site, and the multiple expansions of the site in locational and conceptual terms, seem more accelerated today than in the past. The phenomenon is embraced by many artists, curators, and critics as offering more effective avenues to resist revised institutional and market forces that now commodify "critical" art practices. In addition, current forms of site-oriented art, which readily take up social issues (often inspired by them), and which routinely engage the collaborative participation of audience groups for the conceptualization and production of the work, are seen as a means to strengthen art's capacity to penetrate the sociopolitical organization of contemporary life with greater impact and meaning. In this sense the chance to conceive the site as something more than a place—as repressed ethnic history, a political cause, a disenfranchised social group—is an important conceptual leap in redefining the public role of art and artists.[25]

But the enthusiastic support for these salutary goals needs to be checked by a serious critical examination of the problems and contradictions that attend all forms of site-specific and site-oriented art today, which are visible now as the art work is becoming more and more unhinged from the actuality of the site once again—"unhinged" both in a literal sense of a physical separation of the art work from the location of its initial installation, and in a metaphorical sense as performed in the discursive mobilization of the site in emergent forms of site-oriented art. This unhinging, however, does not indicate a reversion to the modernist autonomy of the siteless, nomadic art object, although such an ideology is still predominant. Rather, the current unhinging of site specificity indicates new pressures upon its practice today—pressures engendered by both aesthetic imperatives and external historical determinants, which are not exactly comparable to those of thirty years ago. For example, what is the status of traditional aesthetic values such as originality, authenticity, and uniqueness in site-specific art, which always begins with the particular, local, unrepeatable preconditions of a site, however it is defined? Is the prevailing relegation of authorship to the conditions of the site, including collaborators and/or reader-viewers, a continuing Barthesian performance of the "death of the author" or a recasting of the centrality of the artist as a "silent" manager/director? Furthermore, what is the commodity status of anticommodities, that is, immaterial, process-oriented, ephemeral, performative events? While site-specific art once defied commodification by insisting on immobility, it now seems to espouse fluid mobility and nomadism for the same purpose. Curiously, however, the nomadic principle also defines capital and power in our times.[26] Is the unhinging of site specificity, then, a form of resistance to the ideological establishment of art, or a capitulation to the logic of capitalist expansion?

Guided by these questions, the next chapter examines two different conditions within which site-specific and site-oriented art have been "circulating" in recent years. First, since the late 1980s, there have been increasing numbers of *traveling* site-specific art works, despite the once-adamant claim that to move the work is to destroy the work. Concurrently, refabrications of site-specific works, particularly from the minimalist and postminimalist eras, are becoming more common in the art world. The increasing trend of relocating or reproducing once unique site-bound works has raised new questions concerning the authenticity and originality of such works as well as their commodity status. Secondly, now that site-specific practices have become familiar (even commonplace) in the mainstream art world, artists are traveling more than ever to fulfill institutional/cultural critique projects in situ. The extent of this mobilization of the *artist* radically redefines the commodity status of the art work, the nature of artistic authorship, and the art-site relationship.

▲ Barry Le Va, ***Continuous and Related Activities: Discontinued by the Act of Dropping*** (1967), felt and glass, installation at Newport Harbor Art Museum, California, 1982. (Photo courtesy Sonnabend Gallery, New York.)

▼ Barry Le Va, ***Continuous and Related Activities: Discontinued by the Act of Dropping*** (1967), felt and glass, reconstructed for the exhibition "The New Sculpture 1965–75: Between Geometry and Gesture" at the Whitney Museum, New York, 1990. (Collection of the Whitney Museum of American Art; Purchase, with funds from the Painting and Sculpture Committee.)

UNHINGING OF SITE SPECIFICITY

Mobilization of Site Specificity

The "unhinging" of art works first realized in the 1960s and 1970s is provoked not so much by aesthetic imperatives as by pressures of the museum culture and the art market. Photographic documentation and other materials associated with site-specific art (preliminary sketches and drawings, field notes, instructions on installation procedures, etc.) have long been standard fare in museum exhibitions and a staple of the art market. In the recent past, however, as the cultural and market values of such works from the 1960s and 1970s have risen, many of the early precedents in site-specific art, once deemed difficult to collect and impossible to reproduce, have reappeared in several high-profile exhibitions, such as "L'art conceptuel, une perspective" at the Musée d'art moderne de la ville de Paris (1989) and "The New Sculpture 1965–75: Between Geometry and Gesture" (1990) and "Immaterial Objects" (1991–1992), both at the Whitney Museum.[1]

     For exhibitions like these, site-specific works from decades ago are being relocated or refabricated from scratch at or near the location of their representation, either because shipping is too difficult and costly or because the originals are too fragile, in disrepair, or no longer in existence. Depending on the circumstances, some of these refabrications are destroyed after the specific exhibitions for which they are produced; in other instances, the recreations come to coexist with or replace the old, functioning as *new* originals (some even finding homes in permanent collections of museums).[2] With the cooperation of the artist in many cases, art audiences are now being offered the "real" aesthetic experiences of site-specific copies.

     The chance to view again such "unrepeatable" works as Richard Serra's *Splash Piece: Casting* (1969–1970), Barry Le Va's *Continuous and Related Activities: Discontinued by the Act of Dropping* (1967), or Alan Saret's *Sulfur Falls* (1968) offers

◄ Richard Serra, *Splashing*, lead, at Castelli Warehouse, New York, 1968. (© Richard Serra/Artists Rights Society
(ARS), New York; courtesy Leo Castelli Gallery, New York.)

▶ Richard Serra, *Splash Piece: Casting* (1969–1970), lead, at the Whitney Museum of American Art, New York, 1990
(destroyed). (Photo courtesy the artist.)

◄ Richard Serra, **Splash Piece: Casting** (1969–1970), lead, at the Museum of Contemporary Art, Los Angeles, 1990 (destroyed). (Photo courtesy the artist.)

► Richard Serra, **Gutter Corner Splash: Night Shift**, installed at the San Francisco Museum of Modern Art, 1995. (Photo by Ivory Serra; The Collection of the San Francisco Museum of Modern Art, Gift of Jasper Johns.)

an opportunity to reconsider their historical significance, especially in relation to the current fascination with the late 1960s and 1970s in art and criticism. But the very process of institutionalization and the attendant commercialization of site-specific art also overturn the principle of place-boundedness through which such works developed their critique of the ahistorical autonomy of the art object. Of course, with much of postminimal, proto-conceptual art work under consideration, there is an ambiguity between ephemerality and site specificity; but both asserted unrepeatability, which is the point I am stressing here.[3] Contrary to the earlier conception of site specificity, the current museological and commercial practices of re-fabricating (in order to travel) once site-bound works make transferability and mobilization new norms for site specificity. As Susan Hapgood has observed, "the once-popular term 'site-specific,' has come to mean 'movable under the right circumstances,'"[4] shattering the dictum that "to remove the work is to destroy the work."

The consequences of this conversion, effected by object-oriented *decontextualizations* in the guise of historical *recontextualizations*, are a series of normalizing reversals in which the specificity of the site in terms of time and space is rendered irrelevant, making it all the easier for autonomy to be smuggled back into the art work, with the artist allowed to regain his/her authority as the primary source of the work's meaning. The art work is newly objectified (and commodified), and site specificity is redescribed as the personal aesthetic choice of an artist's *stylistic* preference rather than a structural reorganization of aesthetic experience.[5] Thus, a methodological principle of artistic production and dissemination is recaptured as content; active processes are transformed into inert art objects once again. In this way, site-specific art comes to *represent* criticality rather than performing it. The "here and now" of aesthetic experience is isolated as the signified, severed from its signifier.

If this phenomenon represents another instance of domestication of vanguardist works by the dominant culture, it is not solely because of the self-aggrandizing needs of the institution nor the profit-driven nature of the market. Artists, no matter how deeply convinced of their anti-institutional sentiment or how adamant their critique of dominant ideology, are inevitably engaged, self-servingly or with ambivalence, in this process of cultural legitimation. For example, in spring 1990 Carl Andre and Donald Judd both wrote letters of indignation to *Art in America* to publicly disavow authorship of sculptures attributed to them that were included in a 1989 exhibition at the Ace Gallery in Los Angeles.[6] The works in question were recreations: of Andre's 49-foot-long steel sculpture *Fall* from 1968 and of an untitled iron wall piece by Judd of 1970, both from the Panza Collection.[7] Due to the difficulties and high cost of crating and shipping such large-scale works from Italy to California, Panza gave permission to the organizers of the exhibition to refabricate them locally following detailed instructions. As the works had been industrially produced in the first place, the participation of the artists in the refabrication process seemed of little consequence to the director of the Ace Gallery and to Panza. The artists, however, felt otherwise. Not having been consulted on the (re)production and installation of these surrogates, they denounced the refabrications as "a gross falsification" and a "forgery," despite the fact that the sculptures appeared identical to the "originals" in Italy and were reproduced as one-time exhibition copies, not to be sold or exhibited elsewhere.

More than merely a case of ruffled artistic egos, this incident exposes a crisis concerning the status of authorship and authenticity as site-specific art from years ago finds new contexts today. For Andre and Judd, what made the refabricated works illegitimate was not that each was a reproduction of a singular work installed in Varese, Italy, which in principle cannot be reproduced anywhere else anyway, but that the artists themselves did not authorize or oversee the refabrication in California. In other words, the recreations are inauthentic not because of the missing site of their original installation but because of the absence of the artists in the process of their (re)production. By reducing visual variations within the art work to the point of obtuse blankness, and by adopting modes of industrial production, minimal art had voided the traditional standards of aesthetic distinction based on the handiwork of the artist as the signifier of authenticity. However, as the Ace Gallery case amply reveals, despite the withdrawal of such signifiers, authorship and authenticity remain in site-specific art as a function of the artist's "presence" at

Carl Andre, *Fall* (1968), installed at the Guggenheim Museum SoHo for the exhibition "Selections from the Guggenheim Museum," 1992. (Photo by David Heald, © The Solomon R. Guggenheim Foundation, New York, Panza Collection.)

the point of (re)production. That is, with the evacuation of "artistic" traces, the artist's *authorship* as producer of objects is reconfigured as his/her *authority to authorize* in the capacity of director or supervisor of (re)production. The guarantee of authenticity is finally the artist's sanction, which may be articulated by his/her actual presence at the moment of production-installation or via a certificate of verification.[8]

While Andre and Judd once problematized authorship through the recruitment of serialized industrial production, only to cry foul years later when their proposition was taken to one of its logical conclusions,[9] artists whose practices are based in modes of "traditional" manual labor have registered a more complex un-

C E R T I F I C A T E

This is to certify that the Sol LeWitt wall drawing
number   150   evidenced by this certificate is authentic.

Ten thousand one-inch (2.5 cm) lines evenly
spaced on each of six walls.

Black pencil
First Drawn by: S. Kato, Kazuko Miyamoto,
                  Ryo Watanabe
First Installation: Finch College, New York, NY.
October, 1972

This certification is the signature for the wall drawing and must
accompany the wall drawing if it is sold or otherwise transferred.

Certified by _____
                                    Sol LeWitt
© Copyright Sol LeWitt _____
                        Date

Sol LeWitt, certificate for *Wall Drawing no. 150*, October 1972. (Courtesy The Solomon R. Guggenheim Foundation, New York, Panza Collection.)

derstanding of the *politics* of authorship. A case in point: for a 1995 historical survey of feminist art entitled "Division of Labor: 'Women's Work' in Contemporary Art" at the Bronx Museum, Faith Wilding, an original member of the Feminist Art Program at the California Institute of the Arts, was invited to recreate her room-sized site-specific installation *Womb Room (Crocheted Environment)* from the 1972 Woman-house project in Los Angeles. As the original piece no longer existed, the project presented Wilding with a number of problems, least of which were the long hours and intensive physical labor required to complete the task. To decline the invitation to redo the piece for the sake of preserving the integrity of the original installation would have been an act of self-marginalization, contributing to a self-silencing that would write Wilding and an aspect of feminist art out of the dominant account of art history (again). But on the other hand, to recreate the work as an independent art object for a white cubic space in the Bronx Museum also meant voiding the meaning of the work as it was first established in relation to the site of its original context. Indeed, while the cultural legitimation as represented by the institutional interest in Wilding's work allowed for the (temporary) unearthing of one of the neglected trajectories of feminist art, in the institutional setting of the Bronx Museum and later the Museum of Contemporary Art in Los Angeles, *Womb Room (Crocheted Environment)* became for the most part a beautiful but innocuous work, its primary interest formal, the handicraft nature of the work rendered thematic (feminine labor).[10]

But even if the efficacy of site-specific art from the past seems to weaken when it is re-presented, the procedural complications, ethical dilemmas, and pragmatic headaches that such situations raise for artists, collectors, dealers, and host institutions are still meaningful. They present an unprecedented strain on established patterns of (re)producing, exhibiting, borrowing/lending, purchasing/selling, and commissioning/executing art works in general. At the same time, while some artists regress into the traditional argument of authorial inviolability in order to defend their site-specific practice, others are keen to undo the presumption of criticality associated with such principles as immobility, permanence, and unrepeatability. Rather than resisting mobilization, these artists are attempting to reinvent site specificity as a *nomadic* practice.

◄   Faith Wilding, *Womb Room (Crocheted Environment)*, installed at Womanhouse, Los Angeles, 1972. (Photo by Lloyd Hamrol; courtesy the artist.)

►   Faith Wilding, *Womb Room (Crocheted Environment)*, reconstructed for the exhibition "Division of Labor: 'Women's Work' in Contemporary Art" at the Bronx Museum, 1995. (Photo by Becket Logan; courtesy Bronx Museum of Art.)

The increasing institutional interest in current site-oriented practices that mobilize the site as a discursive narrative is demanding an intensive physical mobilization of the artist to create works in various cities throughout the cosmopolitan art world. Typically, an artist (no longer a studio-bound object maker; primarily working now on call) is invited by an art institution to produce a work specifically configured for the framework provided by the institution (in some cases the artist may solicit the institution with a proposal). Subsequently, the artist enters into a contractual agreement with the host institution for the commission. There follow repeated visits to or extended stays at the site; research into the particularities of the institution and/or the city within which it is located (its history, constituency of the [art] audience, the installation space); consideration of the parameters of the exhibition itself (its thematic structure, social relevance, other artists in the show); and many meetings with curators, educators, and administrative support staff, who may all end up "collaborating" with the artist to produce the work. The project will likely be time-consuming and in the end will have engaged the "site" in a multitude of ways, and the documentation of the project will take on another life within the art world's publicity circuit, which will in turn alert another institution to suggest another commission.

Thus, if the artist is successful, he or she travels constantly as a freelancer, often working on more than one site-specific project at a time, globetrotting as a guest, tourist, adventurer, temporary in-house critic, or pseudo-ethnographer[11] to São Paulo, Paris, Munich, London, Chicago, Seoul, New York, Amsterdam, Los Angeles, and so on.[12] Generally, the in situ configuration of a project that emerges out of such a situation is temporary, ostensibly unsuitable for re-presentation anywhere else without altering its meaning, partly because the commission is defined by a unique set of geographical and temporal circumstances and partly because the project is dependent on unpredictable and unprogrammable on-site relations. But such conditions, despite appearances to the contrary, do not circumvent or even complicate the problem of commodification, because there is a strange reversal now by which the artist comes to approximate the "work," instead of the other way around as is commonly assumed (that is, art work as surrogate of the artist). Perhaps because of the absence of the artist from the physical manifestation of the work, the presence of the artist has become an absolute prerequisite for the execution/presentation of site-oriented projects. It is now the *performative* aspect of an artist's characteristic mode of operation (even when working in collaboration) that is repeated and circulated as a new art commodity, with the artist him/herself functioning as the primary vehicle for its verification, repetition, and circulation.[13]

For example, after a yearlong engagement with the Maryland Historical Society, Fred Wilson finalized his site-specific project *Mining the Museum* (1992) as a temporary reorganization of the institution's permanent collection. As a timely convergence of institutional museum critique and multicultural identity politics, *Mining the Museum* drew many new visitors to the Society, and the project received high praise from both the art world and the popular press.[14] Subsequently, Wilson performed a similar archival excavation/intervention at the Seattle Art Museum in 1993, a project also defined by the museum's permanent collection.[15] Although the shift from Baltimore to Seattle, from a historical society to an art museum, introduced new variables and challenges, the Seattle project established a repetitive pattern between the artist and the hosting institution, reflecting what has become a familiar museological practice—the commissioning of artists to rehang permanent collections.[16] The fact that Wilson's project in Seattle fell short of the Baltimore success may be evidence of how ongoing repetition of such commissions can render methodologies of critique rote and generic. They can easily become extensions of the museum's own self-promotional apparatus, while the artist becomes a commodity with a special purchase on "criticality." As Isabelle Graw has noted, "the result can be an absurd situation in which the commissioning institution (the museum or gallery) turns to an artist as a person who has the legitimacy to point out the contradictions and irregularities of which they themselves disapprove." And for artists, "subversion in the service of one's own convictions finds easy transition into subversion for hire; 'criticism turns into spectacle.'"[17]

To say, however, that this changeover represents the commodification of the

Christian Philipp Müller, *Illegal Border Crossing between Austria and Czechoslovakia*, Austrian contribution to the Venice Biennale, 1993. (Photo courtesy the artist.)

artist is not completely accurate, because it is not the figure of the artist per se, as a personality or a celebrity (à la Warhol), that is produced/consumed in an exchange with the institution. What the current pattern points to, in fact, is the extent to which the very nature of the commodity as a cipher of production and labor relations is no longer bound to the realm of manufacturing (of things) but defined in relation to the service and management industries.[18] The artist as an overspecialized aesthetic object maker has been anachronistic for a long time already. What they *provide* now, rather than *produce,* are aesthetic, often "critical-artistic," services. Andrea Fraser's 1994–1995 project in which she contracted herself out to the EA-Generali Foundation in Vienna (an art association established by companies belonging to the EA-Generali insurance group) as an artist/consultant to provide "interpretive" and "interventionary" services to the foundation, is a uniquely self-conscious playing out of this shift.[19] Through this and prior performance pieces, Fraser highlights the changing conditions of artistic production and reception in terms of both the content and the structure of the project.

Andrea Fraser, *Museum Highlights: A Gallery Talk*, performance at the Philadelphia Museum of Art, 1989. (Photo by Kelly & Massa; courtesy the artist and American Fine Arts, Co., New York.)

Thus, if Richard Serra could once distill the nature of artistic activities down to their elemental physical actions (to drop, to split, to roll, to fold, to cut, etc.),[20] the situation now demands a different set of verbs: to negotiate, to coordinate, to compromise, to research, to promote, to organize, to interview. This shift was forecast in conceptual art's adoption of what Benjamin Buchloh has described as the "aesthetics of administration."[21] The salient point here is how quickly this aesthetics of administration, developed in the 1960s and 1970s, has converted to the administration of aesthetics in the 1980s and 1990s. Generally speaking, the artist used to be a maker of aesthetic objects; now he/she is a facilitator, educator, coordinator, and bureaucrat. Additionally, as artists have adopted managerial functions of art institutions (curatorial, educational, archival) as an integral part of their creative process, managers of art within art institutions (curators, educators, public program directors), who often take their cues from these artists, now see themselves as authorial figures in their own right.[22]

Concurrent with, or because of, these methodological and procedural changes, there is a reemergence of the centrality of the artist as the progenitor of meaning. This is true even when authorship is deferred to others in collaborations, or when the institutional framework is self-consciously integrated into the work, or when an artist problematizes his/her own authorial role. On the one hand, this "return of the author" results from the thematization of discursive sites, which engenders a misrecognition of them as natural extensions of the artist's identity, and the legitimacy of the work's critique is measured by the proximity of the artist's personal association (converted to expertise) with a particular place, history, discourse, identity, etc. (converted to content). On the other hand, because the signifying chain of site-oriented art is constructed foremost by the movement and decision of the artist,[23] the (critical) elaboration of the project inevitably unfolds around the artist. That is, the intricate orchestration of literal and discursive sites that make up a nomadic narrative *requires* the artist as a narrator-protagonist. In some cases, this renewed focus on the artist in the name of authorial self-reflexivity leads to a hermetic implosion of (auto)biographical and subjective indulgences.

This being so, one of the narrative trajectories of all site-oriented projects is consistently aligned with the artist's prior projects executed in other places, generating what might be called another "site"—the exhibition history of an artist, his/her vitae. The tension between the intensive mobilization of the artist and the recentralization of meaning around him/her is addressed in Renée Green's 1993 *World Tour,* a group reinstallation of four site-specific projects produced in disparate parts of the world over a period of three years.[24] By bringing several distinct projects together, *World Tour* sought to reflect on the problematic conditions of present-day site specificity, such as the ethnographic predicament of artists who are frequently imported by foreign institutions and cities as expert/exotic visitors. *World Tour* also attempted to imagine a productive convergence between specificity and mobility, in which a project created under one set of circumstances might be redeployed in another without losing its impact—or, better, might find new meaning and gain critical sharpness through recontextualizations.[25] But these concerns were not readily available to viewers of *World Tour,* whose interpretive reaction was to see the artist as the primary link between the projects. Indeed, the effort to resituate the individual site-oriented projects as a conceptually coherent ensemble eclipsed the specificity of each and forced a relational dynamic between discrete projects. Consequently, especially for an audience unfamiliar with Green's practice, the overriding narrative of *World Tour* became Green's creative process as an artist in and through the four installations. And in this sense, the project functioned institutionally as a fairly conventional retrospective.

Just as shifts in the structural organization of cultural production alter the form of the art commodity (as service) and the authority of the artist (as primary narrator and protagonist), values like originality, authenticity, and singularity are also reworked in site-oriented art—evacuated from the art work and attributed to the site—reinforcing a general cultural valorization of places as the locus of authentic experience and coherent sense of historical and personal identity.[26] An instructive example of this phenomenon is "Places with a Past," a 1991 site-specific exhibition organized by independent curator Mary Jane Jacob, which took the city of Charleston, South Carolina, as not only its backdrop but "the bridge between the works of art and the audience."[27] In addition to breaking the rules of the art establishment, the exhibition wanted to further a dialogue between art and the socio-historical dimension of the place.[28] According to Jacob, "Charleston proved to be fertile ground" for the investigation of issues concerning "gender, race, cultural identity, considerations of difference . . . subjects much in the vanguard of criticism and art-making. . . . The actuality of the situation, the fabric of the time and place of Charleston, offered an incredibly rich and meaningful context for the making and siting of publicly visible and physically prominent installations that rang true in [the artists'] approach to these ideas."[29]

While site-specific art is still described as refuting originality and authenticity as intrinsic qualities of the art object or the artist, these qualities are readily relocated from the art work to the place of its presentation—only to return to the art work now that it has become integral to the site. Admittedly, according to Jacob, "locations . . . contribute a specific identity to the shows staged by injecting into the experience the uniqueness of the place."[30] Conversely, if the social, historical, and geographical specificity of Charleston offered artists a unique opportunity to create unrepeatable works (and by extension an unrepeatable exhibition), then the programmatic implementations of site-specific art in projects like "Places with a Past" ultimately utilize art to promote Charleston as a unique place. What is prized most of all in site-specific art is still the singularity and authenticity that the presence of the artist seems to guarantee, not only in terms of the presumed unrepeatability of the work but in the way the presence of the artist also endows places with a "unique" distinction.

Certainly, site-specific art can lead to the unearthing of repressed histories, help provide greater visibility to marginalized groups and issues, and initiate the re(dis)covery of "minor" places so far ignored by the dominant culture. But inasmuch as the current socioeconomic order thrives on the (artificial) production and (mass) consumption of difference (for difference sake), the siting of art in "real" places can also be a means to *extract* the social and historical dimensions of these places in order to variously serve the thematic drive of an artist, satisfy institutional demographic profiles, or fulfill the fiscal needs of a city. It is within this framework, in which art serves to generate a sense of authenticity and uniqueness of place for quasi-promotional agendas, that I understand the goals of city-based international art programs like "Sculpture. Projects in Münster 1997." According to its cocurator Klaus Bussmann,

> The fundamental idea behind the exhibitions was to create a dialogue between artists, the town and the public, in other words, to encourage the artists to create projects that dealt with conditions in the town, its architecture, urban planning, its history and the social structure of society in the town. . . . Invitations to artists from all over the world to come to Münster for the sculpture project, to enter into a debate with the town, have established a tradition which will not only be continued in the year 1997 but beyond this will become something specific to Münster: a town not only as an "open-air museum for modern art" but also as a place for a natural confrontation between history and contemporary art. . . . The aim of the exhibition "Sculpture. Projects in Münster" is to make the town of Münster comprehensible as a complex, historically formed structure exactly in those places that make it stand out from other towns and cities.[31]

Significantly, the appropriation of site-specific art for the valorization of urban identities comes at a time of a fundamental cultural shift in which architecture and urban planning, formerly the primary media for expressing a vision of the city, are displaced by other media more intimate with marketing and advertising. In the words of urban theorist Kevin Robins, "As cities have become ever more equivalent and urban identities increasingly 'thin,' . . . it has become necessary to employ advertising and marketing agencies to manufacture such distinctions. It is a question of distinction in a world beyond difference."[32] Site specificity in this context finds new importance because it supplies distinction of place and uniqueness of locational identity, highly seductive qualities in the promotion of towns and cities within the competitive restructuring of the global economic hierarchy. Thus, site specificity remains inexorably tied to a process that renders the particularity and identity

of various cities a matter of product differentiation. Indeed, the exhibition catalogue
for "Places with a Past" was a "tasteful" tourist promotion, pitching the city of
Charleston as a unique, "artistic," and meaningful place (to visit).[33] Under the pretext of their articulation or resuscitation, site-specific art can be mobilized to expe-
dite the erasure of differences via the commodification and serialization of places.

The yoking together of the myth of the artist as a privileged source of originality with the customary belief in places as ready reservoirs of unique identity be-
lies the compensatory nature of such a move. For this collapse of the artist and the
site reveals an anxious cultural desire to assuage the sense of loss and vacancy that
pervades both sides of this equation. In this sense, Craig Owens was perhaps correct to characterize site specificity as a melancholic discourse and practice,[34] as
was Thierry de Duve in claiming that "sculpture in the last 20 years is an attempt to
reconstruct the notion of site from the standpoint of having acknowledged its disappearance."[35] Keeping this sense of loss of place or disappearance of the site in
mind, we will next turn to the problem of site specificity as it has evolved quite distinctly in the mainstream public art context over the past three decades. We will return to a consideration of site specificity in relation to issues concerning locational
identity in the final chapter.

Cover and inside page from the exhibition catalogue *Places with a Past: Site-Specific Art at Charleston's Spoleto Festival*, 1991.

3

SITINGS OF PUBLIC ART: INTEGRATION VERSUS INTERVENTION

At the juncture of Jerome and Gerard avenues and 169th Street in the South Bronx, across from the 44th Police Precinct building on one side and facing the elevated subway tracks cutting through the sky on another, is a small piece of no-man's land. If not for the conspicuous row of three large concrete cubes flanking one perimeter, this traffic triangle might remain indistinguishable from other slivers of similarly odd-shaped, leftover urban spaces found throughout the city. The cubic plinths are, in fact, the pedestals for three public sculptures by John Ahearn, sponsored by the Percent for Art program of the New York City Department of Cultural Affairs. Originally designed to serve as the bases for life-size bronze casts of Raymond Garcia (and his pit bull, Toby), Corey Mann, and Daleesha—all Ahearn's neighbors around Walton Avenue in the Bronx from the mid to late 1980s—the pedestals have remained empty, except for the accumulation of trash and graffiti, for about ten years. Since September 25, 1991, to be precise, when the artist himself had the sculptures removed only five days after their installation in response to protests by some residents and city officials who deemed them inappropriate for the site.[1]

In downtown Manhattan, at the juncture of Lafayette and Centre streets as they converge to become Nassau Street, there is another more or less triangular plot of public land, officially known as Foley Square. Framed by several formidable government buildings—United States Customs Court, Federal Office Building, New York County Court House, and United States Court House—the eastern perimeter of Foley Square faces Federal Plaza. This expansive plaza is populated with a set of large green mounds, perfect half-spheres that look like grass-covered igloos. Wrapping around the mounds is a series of serpentine benches, reiterating the circular form of the mounds and painted a bright apple green. Designed by well-known landscape architect Martha Schwartz, Federal Plaza today is a playful and decorative mix of street furniture and natural materials, a clever reworking of traditional design elements of urban parks. Seen from above, the plaza is an abstract composition in green, with yards of seating rippling through the space like highly contrived ribbons.

As many will recall, this last site, Federal Plaza, full of dynamic colors and user-friendly forms today, was once the site of a rancorous and vehement controversy concerning Richard Serra's steel sculpture *Tilted Arc*. Commissioned by the U.S. General Services Administration in 1979 and installed in 1981, the 12-foot-high, 120-foot-long sculpture was removed on March 15, 1989, after five years of public hearings, lawsuits, and plenty of media coverage concerning the legality and appropriateness of such an action. Now, a little over ten years later, the site has experienced a complete makeover. Martha Schwartz's redesign of Federal Plaza has erased all physical and historical traces of *Tilted Arc*.

So I begin here, with two "empty" sites of two "failed" public art works. The forlorn vacancy of the traffic triangle in the South Bronx and the specious pleasantness of Federal Plaza in downtown Manhattan bracket this chapter's consideration of the problematics of site specificity in the mainstream public art context.[2] One point to stress at the outset is the fact that even though site-specific modes of artistic practice emerged in the mid to late 1960s—roughly coinciding with the inception of the Art-in-Architecture Program of the General Services Administration (GSA) in 1963, the Art-in-Public-Places Program of the National Endowment for the Arts (NEA) in 1967, and numerous local and state Percent for Art programs throughout the 1960s—it was not until 1974 that concern to promote site-specific approaches to public art was first registered within the guidelines of these organizations, in particular the NEA. This lag is an initial indication that while the term "site specificity" might move fluidly through various cultures of artistic practice today—museums, galleries, alternative spaces, international biennials, public art programs—the history and implications of the term can be profoundly inconsistent from context to context. Thus, one task of this chapter is to chart the particular trajectory of site specificity within public art as a point of clarification. In particular, I will argue, the changing conceptualization of site specificity in the public art context indexes the changing criteria by which an art work's public relevance and its democratic sociopolitical ambitions have been imagined over the past three

◄   Martha Schwartz, Federal Plaza, New York, 1997–1998. (Photo by Seong H. Kwon.)
►   View of South Bronx Sculpture Park site at Jerome and Gerard avenues and 169th Street (44th Precinct Police
    Station), c. 1992. (Photo by Nancy Owens.)

decades. Our story will concentrate on Ahearn's and Serra's cases to contemplate the meaningfulness of their respective "empty" sites, especially as they signal the limits and capacity of site specificity today.

Three distinct paradigms can be identified within the roughly 35-year history of the modern public art movement in the United States.[3] First, there is the art-in-public-places model exemplified by Alexander Calder's *La Grande Vitesse* in Grand Rapids, Michigan (1967), the first commission to be completed through the Art-in-Public-Places Program of the NEA. The second paradigm is the art-as-public-spaces approach, typified by design-oriented urban sculptures of Scott Burton, Siah Armajani, Mary Miss, Nancy Holt, and others, which function as street furniture, architectural constructions, or landscaped environments. Finally, there is the art-in-the-public-interest model, named as such by critic Arlene Raven and most cogently theorized by artist Suzanne Lacy under the heading of "new genre public art."[4] Select projects by artists such as John Malpede, Daniel Martinez, Hope Sandrow, Guillermo Gómez-Peña, Tim Rollins and K.O.S., and Peggy Diggs, among many others, are distinguished for foregrounding social issues and political activism, and/or for engaging "community" collaborations.[5]

Initially, from the mid 1960s to the mid 1970s, public art was dominated by the art-in-public-places paradigm—modernist abstract sculptures that were often enlarged replicas of works normally found in museums and galleries.[6] These art works were usually signature pieces from internationally established male artists (favored artists who received the most prominent commissions during this period include Isamu Noguchi, Henry Moore, and Alexander Calder). In and of themselves, they had no distinctive qualities to render them "public" except perhaps their size and scale.[7] What legitimated them as "public" art was quite simply their siting outdoors or in locations deemed to be public primarily because of their "openness" and unrestricted physical access—parks, university campuses, civic centers, entrance areas to federal buildings, plazas off city streets, parking lots, airports.

In the early 1970s, Henry Moore spoke of his relative indifference to the site, a position that is representative of many (though not all) artists working in the art-in-

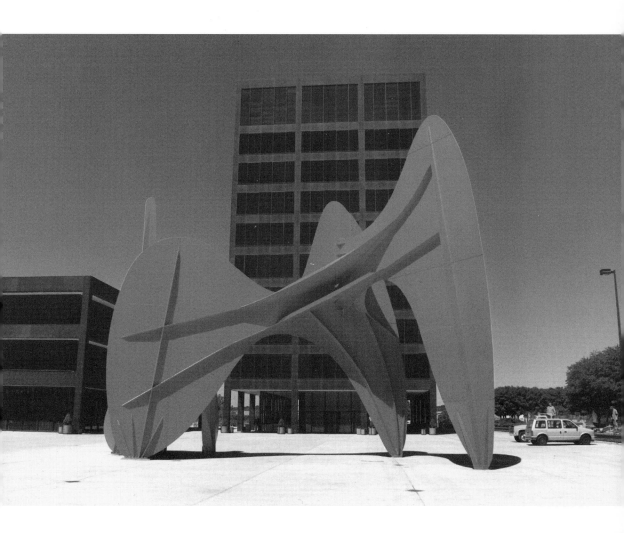

Alexander Calder, *La Grande Vitesse*, Grand Rapids, Michigan, 1967. (Photo courtesy of Grand Rapids City Hall.)

Isamu Noguchi, *Red Cube*, Marine Midland Bank Plaza (now HSBC) at Broadway and Liberty Street, New York, 1968. (Photo by Miwon Kwon.)

public-places mode: "I don't like doing commissions in the sense that I go and look at a site and then think of something. Once I have been asked to consider a certain place where one of my sculptures might possibly be placed, I try to choose something suitable from what I've done or from what I'm about to do. But I don't sit down and try to create something especially for it."[8] Whether they were voluptuous abstractions of the human body in bronze or marble, colorful agglomerations of biomorphic shapes in steel, or fanciful plays on geometric forms in concrete, modernist public sculptures were conceived as autonomous works of art whose relationship to the site was at best incidental. Furthermore, just as the conditions of the site were considered irrelevant in the conception and production of a sculpture (because they functioned as distractions more than inspirations), so they needed to be suppressed at the point of reception if the sculpture was to speak forcefully to its viewers. Again in Moore's words: "To display sculpture to its best advantage outdoors, it must be set so that it relates to the sky rather than to trees, a house, people, or other aspects of its surroundings. Only the sky, miles away, allows us to contrast infinity with reality, and so we are able to discover the sculptor's inner scale without comparison."[9]

Thus the central issue preoccupying the artists of such public commissions (as well as their patrons or sponsors) was the proper placement of the discrete art work so as to best enhance and showcase its aesthetic qualities. The particular qualities of the site—in this case we are speaking primarily of the site as a physical, architectural entity—mattered only to the extent that they posed formal compositional challenges. For the architects involved, the art work was usually considered a beneficial visual supplement but finally an extraneous element to the integrity of a building or space. Contrarily, in many artists' views, the site remained a ground or pedestal upon which, or against which, the priority of the figure of the art work would be articulated. Such thinking was predicated on a strict separation between art and architecture (synonymous with the site) as two autonomous fields of practice, and it promoted complimentary visual contrast as the defining (formal) relationship between the two.

By bringing the "best" in contemporary art to a wider audience, by siting examples of it in public places, endeavors like the Art-in-Architecture Program of the GSA, the Art-in-Public-Places Program of the NEA, and the Percent for Art programs at local and state levels hoped to promote the aesthetic edification of the American public and to beautify the urban environment.[10] Public art works were meant to play a supplementary but crucial role in the amelioration of what were perceived to be the ill effects of the repetitive, monotonous, and functionalist style of modernist architecture. (The inclusion of artists within architectural design teams for the development of urban spaces in the art-as-public-spaces mode of practice, our second paradigm, continued to be predicated on the belief that with the artist's humanizing influence, the sense of alienation and disaffection engendered by the inhuman urban landscape of modernism could be rectified.[11] Which is to say, public art at this point was conceived as an antidote to modernist architecture and urban design.)

With such expectations at play, the art-in-public-places phenomenon had spread widely across the United States by the late 1970s.[12] Art historian Sam Hunter described the omnipresence of monumental abstract public sculptures in cities across the country around this time:

> In the seventies the triumph of the new public art was firmly secured. Almost any new corporate or municipal plaza worthy of its name deployed an obligatory large-scale sculpture, usually in a severely geometric, Minimalist style; or where more conservative tastes prevailed and funds were more generous, one might find instead a recumbent figure in bronze by Henry Moore or one of Jacques Lipchitz's mythological creatures. Today there is scarcely an American city of significant size boasting an urban-renewal program that lacks one or more large, readily identifiable modern sculptures to relieve the familiar stark vistas of concrete, steel, and glass.[13]

Despite the initial enthusiasm, as early as the mid 1970s the art-in-public-places approach began to be criticized for having very little to offer in the way of either aesthetic edification or urban beautification. Many critics and artists argued that autonomous signature-style art works sited in public places functioned more like extensions of the museum, advertising individual artists and their accomplishments (and by extension their patrons' status) rather than making any genuine gestures toward public engagement.[14] It was further argued that despite the physical accessibility, public art remained resolutely inaccessible insofar as the prevalent style of modernist abstraction remained indecipherable, uninteresting, and meaningless to a general audience. The art work's seeming indifference to the particular conditions of the site and/or its proximate audience was reciprocated by the public's indifference, even hostility, toward the foreignness of abstract art's visual language and toward its aloof and haughty physical presence in public places. Instead of a welcome reprieve in the flow of everyday urban life, public art seemed to be an unwanted imposition completely disengaged from it. Many critics, artists, and sponsors agreed that, at best, public art was a pleasant visual contrast to the rationalized regularity of its surroundings, providing a nice decorative effect. At worst, it was an empty trophy commemorating the powers and riches of the dominant class—a corporate bauble or architectural jewelry. And as the increasing private corporate sponsorship of public art became associated with the expansion of corporate real estate developments, pressures increased to rehabilitate the art-in-public-places programs.[15]

One of the key solutions to these interconnected problems of public art's public relations and its ineffectual influence on the urban environment was the adoption of site-specific principles for public art. Indeed, it was in reaction to the glut of ornamental "plop art"[16] and the monumental "object-off-the-pedestal" paradigm that, for instance, the NEA changed its guidelines in 1974 to stipulate, even if somewhat vaguely, that public art works needed to be "appropriate to the immediate site."[17] Whereas the program's initial 1965 goals had been to support individual artists of exceptional talent and demonstrated ability and to provide the public with opportunities to experience the best of American contemporary art, new mandates at all levels of public art sponsorship and funding now stipulated that the specificities of the site should influence, if not determine, the final artistic outcome.[18] Thus, despite the numerous pragmatic and bureaucratic difficulties in commissioning new art works (certainly it is simpler to purchase existing ones), the support for site-specific approaches to public art, favoring the creation of unique and unrepeatable aesthetic responses tailored to specific locations within a city, became fairly quickly institutionalized.[19] In the minds of those intimately engaged with the public art industry at the time, including artists, administrators, and critics, establishing a direct formal link between the material configuration of the art work and the existing physical conditions of the site—instead of emphasizing their disconnection or autonomy—seemed like a very good idea. Such an approach was advocated as an important step toward making art works more accessible and socially responsible, that is, more public.

Interestingly, the issue of modernist abstract art's interpretive (in)accessibility was defined as a spatial problem by many in the public art field in the late 1970s and early 1980s. For example, Janet Kardon, the curator of the 1980 exhibition "Urban Encounters: Art Architecture Audience," claimed in her catalogue essay:

> The way the abstract art work relates to the space of the passer-by is one key to the negative reception that has become a kind of certificate of merit among modern artists. . . . It unsettles perceptions and does not reassure the viewer with an easily shared idea or subject. . . . Entry [into a work] is facilitated when the public perceives the work as performing some useful task, whether it is simply that of shade and seating, or something even remotely associated with the sense of leisure. To be guided through space in a way that rewards the passer-by is of prime value to the public.[20]

A cocontributor to the same exhibition catalogue, Nancy Foote, took the notion of "entry" more literally, going so far as to say that only site-specific works that "invite the audience in," both physically and iconographically, reveal a public commitment.[21] Similarly, critics Kate Linker and Lawrence Alloway believed that art that becomes integrated with the physical site offers the greatest sustainability as well as potential for fluid communication and interaction with a general nonart audience. According to Linker, "To the absence of a shared iconography, it suggests the shareable presence of space. . . . Just as use insures relevance, so the appeal to space as a social experience, communal scope, individual response, may insure a larger measure of support."[22] In these critics' writings of the early 1980s, physical access or entry *into* an art work is imagined to be equivalent to hermeneutic access for the viewer.

The various agencies' programmatic enforcement of a continuity between the art work and its site, however, was predicated on a kind of architectural determinism endemic to most urban beautification efforts. Implicit in such thinking was the belief in an unmediated causal relationship between the aesthetic quality of the built environment and the quality of social conditions it supported. Consequently, the type of site specificity stipulated by the NEA, GSA, and other public art agencies was directed toward spatial integration and harmonious design.[23] By now, artists were asked not only to focus on the conditions of the built environment but to contribute toward the design of unified and coherent urban spaces. This is partly why, by the end of the 1970s, the NEA endorsed a "wide range of possibilities for art in public situations"—"any permanent media, including earthworks, environmental art, and non-traditional media, such as artificial lighting."[24] The aim was not only to accommodate the changing artistic trends of the period but to align public art more with the production of public amenities and site-oriented projects. What this amounted to in essence was a mandate for public art to be more like architecture and environmental design.

This integrationist goal was further strengthened when the NEA guidelines were modified once again in 1982, with the Visual Art and Design programs of the NEA officially combining their efforts to encourage the collaboration of visual artists and design professionals. Public art would no longer be just an autonomous sculpture but would be in some kind of meaningful dialogue with, maybe even coincident with, the surrounding architecture and/or landscape. This approach to site-specific public art was readily adopted by a group of artists, including Athena Tacha, Ned Smyth, Andrea Blum, Siah Armajani, Elyn Zimmerman, and Scott Bur-

Nancy Holt, ***Dark Star Park***, Rosslyn, Virginia, 1979–1984. (© Nancy Holt/VAGA, New York.)

ton. Unsatisfied with the decorative function of public art in the earlier model of art-in-public-places, and excited by the opportunity to pursue their work outside the confines of museums and galleries at an unprecedented scale and complexity (and with the expectation of addressing a much larger and broader audience), many artists were eager to accept, or at least test, the design team directive. Ideally, they would now share responsibilities on equal footing with architects and urban planners in making design decisions about public spaces.[25]

Adopted in the process was a functionalist ethos that prioritized public art's use value over its aesthetic value, or measured its aesthetic value in terms of use value. This shift, predicated on the desire of many artists and public art agencies to reconcile the division between art and utility—in order to render public art more accessible, accountable, and relevant to the public—conflated the art work's use value, narrowly defined in relation to simple physical needs (such as seating and shading), with social responsibility. As Rosalyn Deutsche has argued, physical utility was reductively and broadly equated with social benefit with this kind of art, and "social activity [was] constricted to narrow problem solving so that the provision of useful objects automatically collapsed into a social good."[26]

This collapse was explicit in much public art of the 1980s that followed the collaborative design team model, and was especially notable in the work and words of Scott Burton and his supporters.[27] Many artists and critics alike seemed to think that the more an art work disappeared into the site, either by appropriating urban street furniture (benches and tables, street lamps, manhole covers, fencing) or by mimicking familiar architectural elements (gateways, columns, floors, walls, stairways, bridges, urban plazas, lobbies, parks), the greater its social value would be. During the same time, other artists such as Les Levine, Krzysztof Wodiczko, Group Material, Guerrilla Girls, and Dennis Adams, among many others, were exploring alternative strategies of adopting existing urban forms as sites of artistic intervention. But their appropriation of different modes of public address, particularly those of media and advertising, including billboards, newspapers, and television, usually for the purposes of deconstructing or redirecting their familiar function, did not garner the same kind of official support within the public art industry until later in

◀ Lobby of the Wiesner Arts and Media Building at MIT, Cambridge, Massachusetts, by I. M. Pei & Partners. Bench and railing by Scott Burton, color pattern design on interior walls by Kenneth Noland, exterior plaza paving design by Richard Fleischner, all 1985. (© Steve Rosenthal; courtesy I. M. Pei & Partners.)

▶ Richard Serra, *Tilted Arc*, Federal Plaza, New York, 1981–1989. (Photo by Ann Chauvet; © Richard Serra/Artists Rights Society (ARS), New York.)

the decade.[28] In the meantime, the more an art work abandoned its distinctive look of "art" to seamlessly assimilate to the site, as defined by the conventions of architecture and urban design, the more it was hailed as a progressive artistic gesture.

It is against this prevailing definition of site specificity—one of unified and useful urban design, imagined as a model of social harmony and unity—that Richard Serra proposed a counterdefinition with his massive, wall-like steel sculpture *Tilted Arc*. As early as 1980, several years before he was forced to consolidate his thoughts on site specificity to defend his sculpture for the Federal Plaza site, he explicitly rejected the then widespread tendency of public sculpture to accommodate architectural design. He declared,

> There seems to be in this country [United States] right now, especially in sculpture, a tendency to make work which attends to architecture. I am not interested in work which is structurally ambiguous, or in sculpture which satisfies urban design principles. I have always found that to be not only an aspect of mannerism but a need to reinforce a status quo of existing aesthetics. . . . I am interested in sculpture which is non-utilitarian, non-functional . . . any use is a misuse.[29]

Considering such an aggressive statement in light of the GSA's guidelines of the same period—"Such [public art] works are intended to be an integral part of the total architectural design and enhance the building's environment for the occupants and the general public"[30]—it may seem a wonder that Serra was even considered for the Federal Plaza commission. But the incongruity only reminds us of the discrepancy at the heart of the selection process at this time: that is, the discrepancy between the values of the committee of art experts, who obviously responded to Serra's already established international reputation as an artist, and the criteria guiding the administrators of the GSA, who deferred to the experts on issues of artistic merit.

In any case, as critics Rosalyn Deutsche and Douglas Crimp have separately affirmed, Serra indeed proposed an interruptive and interventionist model of site specificity, quite explicitly opposed to an integrationist or assimilative one.[31] Deutsche has argued that public art discourse's use of the term site specificity to connote the creation of harmonious spatial totalities is close to a "terminological abuse," insofar as site-specific art emerged from "the imperative to interrupt, rather than secure, the seeming coherence and closure of those spaces [of the art work's display]."[32] In her view, *Tilted Arc* reasserted the critical basis of site specificity, countering its neutralization in the public art of the 1980s. In doing so, it revealed the incompatibility of site specificity with the kind of objectives held by the GSA.

My concern here, however, is not so much to establish the right definition of site specificity as to examine the ways in which competing definitions emerge and operate in the public art field, and to assess their varied artistic, social, and political implications and consequences. The terms of Serra's "critical" or "political" site specificity,[33] in fact, remain more ambiguous than one might expect. This is in large part due to the emphasis placed on permanence as a fundamental attribute of site specificity during the *Tilted Arc* controversy. Serra himself mounted his argument against the "relocation" of his sculpture on the premise that, first and foremost, site-specific art has an inviolable physical tie to its site. Hence, to remove the work is to destroy the work. He insisted throughout and after the controversy that

> *Tilted Arc* was conceived from the start as a site-specific sculpture and was not meant to be "site-adjusted" or . . . "relocated." Site-specific works deal with the environmental components of given places. The scale, size, and location of site-specific works are determined by the topography of the site, whether it be urban or landscape or architectural enclosure. The works become part of the site and restructure both conceptually and perceptually the organization of the site.[34]

While the insistence on permanence during the court hearings might have had some legal exigency, the priority given to the issue has obscured certain other aspects of *Tilted Arc*'s site specificity.[35] For instance, Serra does seem to prioritize the physical relationship between the art work and site in comments like the following from the same article: "The specificity of site-oriented works means that they are conceived for, dependent upon, and inseparable from their locations. The scale, the size, and the placement of sculptural elements result from an analysis of the particular environmental components of a given context."[36] But he goes on to say that "the preliminary analysis of a given site takes into consideration not only formal but also social and political characteristics of the site. Site-specific works invariably manifest a judgment about the larger social and political context of which they are a part."[37]

In other words, the site is imagined as a social and political construct as well as a physical one. More importantly, Serra envisions not a relationship of smooth continuity between the art work and its site but an antagonistic one in which the art work performs a proactive interrogation—"manifest[s] a judgment" (presumably negative)—about the site's sociopolitical conditions. Indeed, rather than fulfilling an ameliorative function in relation to the site, *Tilted Arc* aggressively cut across and divided it. (No seating, shading, or other physical accommodations here.) In doing so, as proponents of the sculpture have pointed out, *Tilted Arc* literalized the social divisions, exclusions, and fragmentation that manicured and aesthetically tamed public spaces generally disguise. In destroying the illusion of Federal Plaza as a coherent spatial totality, Serra underscored its already dysfunctional status as a public space.

According to Serra, it is only in working against the given site in this way that art can resist cooptation.

> Works which are built within the contextual frame of governmental, corporate, educational, and religious institutions run the risk of being read as tokens of those institutions. . . . Every context has its frame and its ideological overtones. It is a matter of degree. But there are sites where it is obvious that an art work is being subordinated to / accommodated to / adapted to / subservient to / useful to. . . . In

such cases it is necessary to work in opposition to the constraints of the context so that the work cannot be read as an affirmation of questionable ideologies and political power. I am not interested in art as affirmation or complicity.[38]

Thus, in Serra's practice, site specificity is constituted as a precise *discomposure* between the art work and its site. And this discomposure—which is antithetical both to the notion of art's and architecture's complementary juxtaposition, as in the art-in-public-places model, and to that of their seamless continuity, as in the art-as-public-spaces model—is intended to bring into relief the repressed social contradictions that underlie public spaces, like Federal Plaza, rendering them perceptible, thus knowable, to the viewing subjects of the sculpture.

It is important to point out at this juncture that, in Serra's case, this critical function of site-specific art is directly tied to a critique of the medium-specific concerns of modernist art.[39] As Serra explained, "Unlike modernist works that give the illusion of being autonomous from their surroundings, and which function critically only in relation to the language of their own medium, site-specific works emphasize the comparison between two separate languages and can therefore use the language of one to criticize the language of the other."[40] So that in addition to working against the physical and sociopolitical conditions of the site, the art work simultaneously addresses the site itself as another *medium,* an "other language." Put a little differently, working against the site coincides with working against the modernist illusion of artistic autonomy. In Serra's case, the "other" to his own language of sculpture is architecture. And architecture, in turn, serves as the material manifestation of "questionable ideologies and political power," which Serra is interested in exposing and subverting. So that in the end, working site-specifically means working against architecture.[41]

This is not to say, however, that this "working against" is a straightforward opposition. Note that Serra never speaks, for instance, of merging sculpture and architecture into some new hybrid form to obliterate their categorical distinctions (as so many contemporary artists are prone to do today in the name of radicalizing

Richard Serra, *Tilted Arc*, Federal Plaza, New York, 1981–1989. (© Richard Serra/Artists Rights Society (ARS), New York; courtesy Leo Castelli Gallery, New York.)

artistic practice). In fact, the question of sculpture has remained central in his practice over thirty years—not despite but because of the extent to which he has pressured sculpture to the brink of dissolution. As Hal Foster has written recently, "with Serra sculpture becomes its deconstruction, its making becomes its unmaking. . . . To deconstruct sculpture is to serve its 'internal necessity,' to extend sculpture in relation to process, embodiment, and site is to remain within it."[42] To some readers, this imperative of serving an "internal necessity" may sound like an ontological quest, if not a modernist one, contrary to Serra's critique of medium specificity. But according to Foster, the paradoxical principle of making sculpture through its unmaking distinguishes a "*medium-differential*" investigation of the category of "sculpture" from a medium-specific one. It acknowledges that sculpture is no longer established in advance or known in certainty, but "must be forever proposed, tested, reworked, and proposed again."[43] Which is to reiterate the point that Serra's site specificity addresses not only the particular physical, social, and political attributes of a place; it is at the same time engaged in an *art*-specific inquiry or critique (or perhaps art discourse is itself a site), proposing, testing, reworking, and proposing again what sculpture might be. Indeed, for Serra, site specificity has been both a means to move beyond sculpture and simultaneously a "medium"[44] through which to serve its "internal necessity."

To the opponents of *Tilted Arc* in the mid 1980s, however, the nuances of such aesthetic concerns did not matter much. In fact, supportive testimonies to the importance of this "great work of art," or advocating the right of the artist to pursue free expression without governmental interference or censorship, were countered by resentful commentaries of varying animosity.[45] Some regarded the sculpture as plain, ugly, and brutal, without any artistic merit whatsoever. Some found its presence on the plaza physically and psychologically oppressive. Few waxed nostalgic over the past uses of a (falsely remembered) vitally active public plaza (an "oasis of respite and relaxation"),[46] accusing *Tilted Arc* of destroying this past, of violating a public amenity.[47] A security expert even testified on the ways in which the sculpture created an impediment to surveillance, encouraging loitering, graffiti, and possible terrorist bomb attacks.

Complaints of this type were presented as the voices of "the people" during the 1985 hearings, and the government officials in charge of the proceedings presumed to speak for the public—on behalf of its needs and interests—in their call for the removal of the sculpture. They characterized *Tilted Arc* as an arrogant and highly inappropriate assertion of a private self on public grounds. The sculpture was viewed, in other words, as another kind of plop art. At the same time, despite the artist's ardent efforts to maintain a certain "uselessness" for his sculpture (or actually because of this), *Tilted Arc* was instrumentalized by its opponents as a symbol of the overbearing imposition of the federal government (the sponsor of the sculpture) in the lives of "ordinary" citizens and "their" spaces. In the end, the removal of *Tilted Arc* was characterized as tantamount to the reclaiming of public space by the "community"—narrowly defined as those living or working in the immediate neighborhoods around Federal Plaza.

But as Rosalyn Deutsche has argued, the meaning of key words deployed during this conflict, such as "use," "public," "public use," and "community," were presumed to be self-evident, based on "common sense." Even those of the left who supported *Tilted Arc* did not contest in any effective way the essential and universalizing definitions of these terms—and their ideological uses in the very name of neutrality and objectivity—as they framed the entire debate.[48] In Deutsche's view, the opportunity was regrettably missed, both during the hearings and after (especially with the publication of the documents pertaining to the controversy), to challenge the authoritarian uses of these terms in the name of "the people," a tendency that is not exclusive to right-wing politicians but prevalent in left-informed public art discourse as well. She has also reminded us that the final decision to remove *Tilted Arc* was not a decision against public art in general, for city governments, corporations, and real estate developers have long understood the benefits of public art in mobilizing support for redevelopment and gentrification of urban spaces. Instead, according to Deutsche, *Tilted Arc*'s removal was a discrediting of a particular model of public art—or a particular model of site specificity, as I would insist—one without obvious utilitarian payoffs, one that critically questions rather than promotes the fantasies of public space as a unified totality without conflicts or difference.

While similarly intense debates have accompanied the unveiling of numerous public art works of the past,[49] the *Tilted Arc* incident made most clear that public art is not simply a matter of giving "public access to the best art of our times outside museum walls."[50] In fact, much more was riding on the *Tilted Arc* case than the fate of a single art work. Unlike prior public art disputes, this controversy, as one of the most high-profile battlegrounds for the broad-based "culture wars" of the late 1980s, put to the test the very life of public funding for the arts in the United States.[51] This is why critics like Deutsche have insisted that conflicts such as the one over *Tilted Arc* reveal the extent to which public art discourse functions as a site of political struggle over the meaning of democracy.[52]

Perhaps recognizing the political stakes more self-consciously than ever, public art practitioners and administrators engaged in considerable soul-searching following the *Tilted Arc* debate, reexamining the fundamental questions of public art's goals and procedures. For even if the various testimonies against *Tilted Arc* could be dismissed as uninformed populist thinking, or as motivated by corrupt reactionary politics, or as simply wrong-headed, some complaints had to be taken seriously for at least two reasons. First, it was a matter of survival. In the tide of neo-conservative Republicanism during the 1980s, with the attack on governmental funding for the arts (the NEA in particular) reaching a hysterical pitch by 1989, public art programs had to strategically rearticulate their goals and methods in order to avoid the prospect of annihilation or complete privatization (which might amount to the same thing). Secondly, even those public art professionals most sympathetic to Serra's cause had to recognize that there was a bit of truth in some of the criticism. For the point of contestation that mattered most was not so much the artistic merit of Serra's sculpture but the exclusionary (and some did say elitist) commissioning procedures of public art agencies like the GSA and the NEA. Congressman Theodore Weiss testified against *Tilted Arc* during the hearings in these terms:

Tilted Arc was imposed upon this neighborhood without discussion, without prior consultation, without any of the customary dialogue that one expects between government and its people. The National Endowment for the Arts panel of three selected the artist and a three person group from the General Services Administration in Washington, D.C., approved the design. No one else—not from the community or its representatives, not the architects, not even the Regional Administrators—was ever consulted. These panels, no matter how expert or how well-intentioned, are not so omnipotent or infallible in their judgments that they cannot be challenged or improved upon.[53]

Arguably, the seeds of this argument—that *Tilted Arc* was absolutely inappropriate to the site because the top-down decision-making process, dictated by small review panels of art experts and bureaucrats, did not involve the members of the local community—has had the most far-reaching impact on the direction of the public art discourse of the 1990s. Even before the blowup over *Tilted Arc,* some public artists and administrators had recognized that the site of a public art work had to be imagined beyond its physical attributes. Ideally, the work should engage the site socially, instigating "community involvement." But initially, this seems to have been motivated primarily by the need to forestall potentially hostile reception of certain public art works. In 1979, for example, when the NEA requested that its grant recipients provide "methods to insure an informed community response to the project,"[54] the community was still conceived as an inadequately prepared audience. The community, in other words, needed to be engaged in order to soften them to the "best art of our time," to educate them in its proper interpretation and appreciation (not unlike the way audience groups are commonly treated in museums).[55]

But by the late 1980s, and certainly by the time of *Tilted Arc*'s removal, "community involvement" meant more. At the bureaucratic level, it meant the expanded inclusion of nonart community representatives in the selection panels and review committees of public art commissions. More significantly, it suggested a dialogue between the artist and his/her immediate audience, with the possibility of community participation, even collaboration, in the making of the art work. For many artists and administrators with long-standing commitments to community-based practices since the 1960s, or what Suzanne Lacy has retroactively called "new genre public art," an intensive engagement with the people of the site, involving direct communication and interaction over an extended period of time, had been a well-established tenet of socially responsible and ethically sound public art. That such a model of public art was marginalized, even denigrated, by the official public art establishment for over three decades[56] must have made the *Tilted Arc* incident a point of profound ambivalence for many community-oriented practitioners. Even though some public artists and administrators were traumatized by the *Tilted Arc* controversy and its outcome,[57] the sculpture's removal from Federal Plaza, when viewed as a triumphal rejection of "high art" by "the people," also signaled an implicit validation of the community-oriented approach to public art.

The discursive emergence of new genre public art in 1989, in fact, coincides with the removal of *Tilted Arc*,[58] and Lacy subsequently refers to the *Tilted Arc* case as an occasion "when office workers' demands to remove the sculpture from the site in a civic plaza led to calls for greater public accountability by artists."[59] The controversy is cast as an exemplary instance of "the conventions of artistic expression . . . com[ing] into conflict with public opinion," with public opinion winning.[60] Of course, such a reading of the *Tilted Arc* incident unquestioningly accepts the terms of the debate as defined by the sculpture's opponents. It challenges instead Serra's critique of conventions of artistic expression as itself conventional. In the view of many public artists and administrators, Serra did little to complicate, for instance, the security of individual authorship; in fact, during the hearings, he seemed to argue for its inviolability against the wishes of "the public." Moreover, they saw that Serra's artistic pursuit, no matter how complex and genuine its critical engagement with the site and its sociopolitical issues, was still driven primarily by art-specific concerns that had little bearing on the lives of the people who constitute the actual, rather than abstract or metaphorical, reality of the site. Therefore, the radicalizing effects of his art work remained narrowly confined to art discourse only, legible to a limited, art-educated audience, appreciated most notably by a small group of influential voices professionally ensconced in art criticism, art history, and the museum world.

Indeed, Lacy implicates Serra in such statements as: "Although the move to exhibit art in public places was a progressive one, the majority of artists accommodated themselves to the established museum system, continuing to focus their attention on art critics and museum-going connoisseurs."[61] Whereas numerous art experts confirmed the radicality of *Tilted Arc*'s aesthetic and social critique, then, those aligned with community-based public art did not find the work radical enough.[62] Insofar as Serra never opens up the creative process to a collaboration or dialogue with the community (he has in fact disdained the need for art to please its audience as well as its sponsors), and insofar as the sculpture's particular form of criticality coalesces as Serra's "signature," his work is held to have no impact on the hermetic boundaries of the art world and its institutionalized hierarchies of value. From this point of view, works like *Tilted Arc* are an unwanted encroachment of art world values into the spaces of everyday life and people, and an individual's artistic concerns are, by definition, antithetical to a socially progressive way of thinking. In this way, a peculiar alignment developed between the "authoritarian populism"[63] of the right and the community advocacy of the new genre public art type on the left. Both rejected a certain kind of critical art in the name of "the people."[64]

Certainly by the spring of 1986, little over a year after the hearings on *Tilted Arc,* the directive to involve the community in the public art process was being taken more seriously in New York City and elsewhere, with the NEA taking the lead in 1983 with instructions to include "plans for community involvement, preparation, and dialogue."[65] So that when it came to choosing an artist for the Percent for Art commission at the 44th Precinct police station in the South Bronx, John Ahearn was an "obvious choice" for the selection panel, which now included several nonart representatives.[66] According to Tom Finklepearl, former Director of New York City's Percent for Art program, Ahearn "was an obvious choice because he lived close to the station, enjoyed a good critical reputation, and had already spent many years interacting with the community. . . . He was well acquainted with the specific nature of the community within which the commission was sited, and worked in a figurative style that is considered accessible."[67] In other words, Ahearn represented the antithesis of Serra; or in Finklepearl's words, "Ahearn fit the mold for the 'post-Serra' artist perfectly."[68]

Certainly the differences between the two artists are striking. Serra came into prominence in the late 1960s, with the emergence of postminimalism and process art in particular, as part of the American neo-avant-garde generation. He is distinguished by art historians and art institutions worldwide as one of the most important sculptors of the twentieth century. Ahearn found an audience in the very late 1970s and early 1980s during the rise of the alternative art scenes in the East Village and the Bronx. He remains biographically linked to the South Bronx and is modestly self-described as an "itinerant portrait painter."[69]

The most significant difference relevant to our discussion, however, is the fact that whereas Serra intended an aggressively interruptive function for his sculpture on Federal Plaza, Ahearn sought an assimilative one for his at Jerome Avenue. Ahearn imagined a continuity rather than a rupture between his sculptures and the social life of the neighborhood where the works were to be displayed and to which they "belonged." This is not to say that he did not recognize the potential for conflict with, specifically, the 44th Precinct police officers. After all, few of them had hoped for an art work depicting the local police presence as congenial and welcomed. But Ahearn's acknowledgment of the police as a key audience group only deepened his commitment to creating an accurate and humane representation of the site's reality as he knew it. He wanted to counter the prevalent negative stereotypes of the Bronx (harbored by the police in particular and promoted by the mass media) as a place of urban decay and economic devastation, as a dangerous and violent place infested with drug dealers, criminals, prostitutes, gangs, and disease.[70] Instead, he wanted his work to embody what he called the "South Bronx attitude"[71]—resilient, proud, unpretentious, and "real." In attempting to capture the authenticity of the site in this way, Ahearn in effect intended a different model of site specificity, a community-based realism that countered the example of Serra's *Tilted Arc,* which itself was a counterposition to the art-as-public-spaces model of public art.

John Ahearn, view of South Bronx Sculpture Park (at 44th Precinct Police Station), with sculptures of Raymond and Tobey, Daleesha, and Corey, on day of installation, 1991. (© Ari Marcopoulos; courtesy Alexander and Bonin Gallery, New York.)

John Ahearn and Rigoberto Torres, casting Hazel Santiago at a Walton Avenue block party, Bronx, New York, September 3, 1985. (Photo by Ivan Dalla Tana; courtesy Alexander and Bonin Gallery, New York.)

Clearly, Ahearn understood that to produce a mural or any other architectural embellishment for the new police station, as was suggested to him at an early stage of the commission, would be a terrible mistake.[72] In fact, it was his decision, and not that of the Department of Cultural Affairs or the Department of General Services (DGS), to work with the dead space of the traffic triangle facing the station precisely in order to *confront* the station rather than be part of it. At some level, he had internalized Serra's earlier insight that "works which are built within the contextual frame of governmental, corporate, educational, and religious institutions run the risk of being read as tokens of those institutions."[73] But while Ahearn resisted making his art work a token of various institutions of power, privilege, and authority—the police, the Department of Cultural Affairs, the art world—he actively sought ways to submit the work to, to put it in service of, the largely African American and Puerto Rican community of his neighborhood. Ahearn attempted to resist the function of site-specific public art to support the ideologies and political power of dominant social groups, affirming instead his allegiance to those groups disempowered and marginalized by these ideologies and power.

The artist's identification with the local community of blacks and Latinos developed more or less organically over a decade. Since 1980 Ahearn had been living on Walton Avenue between 171st and 172nd streets, just a few blocks from the traffic triangle. Even as his artistic career ascended through the decade, with exhibitions in "legitimate" art world venues, he maintained the center of his art and life there in a sixth-floor slum apartment. He produced most of his art directly on the street: he regularly set up shop on the sidewalk outside his studio, casting portraits of neighborhood residents, including many children and teenagers, who often contributed comments on how they would like to be represented. By making two copies of every portrait, one for him to keep and the other to be taken home by the sitter, Ahearn devised a very specific economy of intimate exchange and local distribution for his art. Even as he exhibited and sold some of the portraits as fine art through his SoHo gallery, he also made sure that they became part of the everyday culture of his neighborhood, proudly displayed by individuals in their living rooms, bedrooms, kitchens, and dining rooms.

In many street casting sessions, he collaborated with Rigoberto (Robert) Torres,[74] an artist from the neighborhood whom Ahearn had met in 1979 after an exhibition of his relief sculptures at Fashion Moda, an alternative gallery space that had opened a year before on Third Avenue and 149th Street.[75] Between 1981 and 1985, Torres and Ahearn together produced four very popular sculptural murals for the sides of tenement buildings—*We Are Family, Life on Dawson Street, Double Dutch,* and *Back to School*—that picture quotidian aspects of life in the neighborhood. Even though some art critics judged these wall works and other cast pieces to be overly sentimental, and even though the artist himself worried at times that they were too much like folk art, as long as the work made his neighbors "happy," Ahearn thought of them as achieving more meaningful and difficult goals than what is usually expected of an art work. In his words, the "discipline of 'happy' is just as important as the discipline of 'strong' or 'tough,'" and the cast sculptures made to please a neighbor are "purer than something with too much of myself in it, something individual."[76]

Through sustained years of intimate collaborative exchanges and in situ interactions, Ahearn naturally came to see himself as integral to the culture of the neighborhood (as many others did). As relayed by Jane Kramer, the author of a lengthy *New Yorker* article on this South Bronx project (later published as a book), the artist believed that with Robert Torres he was "part of what was happening in the Bronx, part of the integrity of the neighborhood, and solidly at home."[77] Because of this, the artist saw the site on Jerome Avenue not so much as an abstract formal entity but as an extension of the community, of which he himself was a part. Ahearn's personal history and sense of identity was directly tied to the location. And this continuity is what made him such an "obvious choice" for the Department of Cultural Affairs as well as other city agencies and committees, including the Bronx Community Board Four, which reviewed the maquettes for the project in 1990 and gave its "community" approval without hesitation.

Yet the attacks against Ahearn and the sculptures that finally led to their removal were exactly on the grounds that neither belonged to the "community," that the sculptures were inappropriate for the site. At one end were officials from the

John Ahearn and Rigoberto Torres, *Back to School*, installed at Walton Avenue and 172nd Street, Bronx, New York, 1985. (Photo by Ivan Dalla Tana; courtesy Alexander and Bonin Gallery, New York.)

Department of General Services who were overseeing the station building project as a whole. Arthur Symes, a black architect, who had newly taken on the role of assistant commissioner in charge of design and construction management, and Claudette LaMelle, a black administrator and executive assistant to the commissioner of the DGS, felt that regardless of his outstanding reputation as an artist and his track record living and working in the South Bronx, Ahearn, as a white man, could never understand the experience of the African American "community." Thus he had no capacity to represent it accurately for or in the Bronx. They charged that, in fact, the sculptures were racist.[78] On the other end were the complaints of a small group of residents from an apartment building at the Jerome Avenue traffic triangle, who found the sculptures an absolute misrepresentation of *their* community. They accused Ahearn of glorifying illegitimate members of the community, or "roof people," according to Mrs. Salgado, the most vocal opponent of the sculptures. In their eyes, Ahearn had literally and symbolically elevated the derelict, criminal, and delinquent elements of the community. They argued that in essence Ahearn promoted the outsider's view of the Bronx with negative stereotypes (the two male figures in particular), and that with these sculptures he affirmed the police's distorted perceptions of the community, exacerbating the already tense relations with them.

In Ahearn's view, of course, the three sculptures—of Daleesha, a young black teenage girl on roller skates; Corey, a large shirtless black man leaning over a boom box, holding a basketball; and Raymond, a slender Puerto Rican man in a hooded sweatshirt, squatting next to his pit bull—represented a certain truth about the neighborhood. Perhaps not a truth that everyone would want to embrace, but an indigenous truth nonetheless. He found Daleesha, Corey, and Raymond (whom he knew personally, the last two as friends even) appropriate subjects to commemorate as survivors of the mean streets. He wanted to capture their humanity and make its beauty visible to the policemen at the 44th Precinct as well as to the neighbors, in the hope of ameliorating the sense of distrust and hostility between them. As Kramer notes, Ahearn "wanted the police to acknowledge them, and he wanted the neighbors, seeing them cast in bronze and up on pedestals, to stop and think about who they were. . . . John wanted them to stand in something of the same relation to the precinct policemen that they do to him and the neighbors. They may be trouble, but they are human, and they are there."[79] Despite Ahearn's earnest intentions, however, the sculptures provoked anger rather than empathy among many neighbors.[80] In fact, the sculptures were seen as an insult to the community in that they depicted people most neighbors found menacing, fearsome, and threatening—the kind of people that they would want police protection *from*. As Angela Salgado, Mrs. Salgado's daughter, put it, it was people like Corey and Raymond that made "the difference between a working-class neighborhood and a ghetto." As such, she also charged the sculptures with being "totems of racism."[81]

Within the context of early 1990s multiculturalist identity politics and political correctness debates (do-good community-based public art is itself a symptom of this period), such accusations were perhaps too tricky to counter. Ahearn did not even attempt arguing against them in any systematic or sustained way. Initially he tried speaking to the few detractors who gathered at the site, especially Mrs. Salgado. He approached her respectfully to have a dialogue—to introduce himself and his work, and to listen to her. He even repainted Raymond's face the morning after installation to have him appear less menacing, less "Halloween," so that Mrs. Salgado might see "the other Raymond," "beautiful *and* heavy."[82] But he could not dissuade her from seeing his bronzes as evil and ugly, a "slap in the community's face." In the end, Mrs. Salgado's objections and his inability to convince her became a measure of the work's failure for Ahearn.

> To the art world, my bronzes were serious, ironic. They had oomph, they were strong. They were an "artist's" pieces, and they looked good at the site, but I thought that day, "They'll never look like this again." I knew that soon they'd look terrible. Bad. Uglier than Mrs. Salgado said. So I said, "Fuck 'em, the art world!" It's not my job to be fighting these conservative progressive people—people like Mrs. Salgado. I respect these people. It's not my job to be the punk artist in the neighborhood—like, there's a lot going on in my artistic life besides this installation. There's my concept of casts in people's

homes—the execution may be shoddy, but to me those casts are more valuable than a bronze, or a better piece in a collector's home, and if I've misread my people it means I've misread myself and my concept. . . . What I felt was, I had a choice. . . . Either I was going to be on Mrs. Salgado's side or I was going to be her enemy. I refused that.[83]

Acknowledging that he had miscalculated the situation, he removed the sculptures at his own expense five days after their installation. Thus a project that began as one made with, of, and for the community, by an artist presumed to be an integral part of that community and approved by a committee of community leaders, was in the end disowned by the community. In a recent interview, Ahearn has remarked on the nature of the site itself as part of the problem:

> In previous times when we installed the wall murals a supportive community would all come out in strength to view their friends being hoisted up on the wall. It was a family situation. Whereas the installation of the bronzes was a little bit removed from the neighborhood that I lived in, even though it was only four blocks away. It was just far enough away that it only got a stray group of onlookers that I recognized. Unlike earlier days, the few friends of mine from downtown that showed up outnumbered the local community, which made me a bit uneasy. There was a disquiet to the day. Already as the pieces were unveiled, there were arguments at the site as to the purpose of the work. That had never happened with the murals. In earlier times, the murals were seen as a private thing within the community, but this was instantly understood to be of a citywide, public nature. This was perceived as a city site. . . . People could tell the difference. People felt that this had to do with the city, not with their community.[84]

Of course, the ambiguity of the term "community" is one of the central issues here. At any one time, depending on who is speaking, the community could be the people around a few buildings on Walton Avenue, where Ahearn, Daleesha, Corey, and Raymond are familiar faces; or it could be the group of people living several blocks away on Jerome Avenue, where Ahearn, Daleesha, Corey, and Raymond are viewed as outsiders; or it could be constituencies delineated by the outlines of voting districts; or it might conjure "the Bronx" as an almost mythical place; or then again, it may not be tied to a geographical area at all but defined instead in terms of a shared historical and racial background, as was the case with the administrators at the DGS in their presumption of a singular African American community.

In Ahearn's case, it is relatively easy to trace these various expectations at work, both within the artist's practice and outside it. The rationale behind the selection of him for the South Bronx commission, as cited earlier, is a case in point. But the later contestation over Ahearn's capacity and right to represent the community, and the accompanying protests against the choice of Daleesha, Corey, and Raymond as representative of the community, are also based on such expectations. That is, while there may be disagreements among different groups over the specifics, the dominant principle or operative basis of community-based site specificity is the presumption of a unity of identity between the artist and the community, and between the community and the art work. Indeed, the commonality of this belief is the *source* of the disagreements, as we have seen in Ahearn's case.

The ambiguity of the term "community," which is consistent with the discursive slippage around "audience,"[85] "site," and "public," is itself a distinctive trait of community-based public art discourse. As such, the claims made of and for the "community" by artists, curators, administrators, critics, and various audience groups demand extensive critical analysis. To contribute to that end, I will delineate here what seems to be the underlying logic of community-based site specificity as exemplified by Ahearn's South Bronx project, some aspects of which have been already outlined in contrast to the site specificity of Richard Serra's *Tilted Arc.*

As noted earlier, Ahearn, like many other community-based artists, wished to create a work integrated with the site—a work that would seem to emerge so naturally from a particular place, whose meaning is so specifically linked to it, that it could not be imagined belonging anywhere else. But unlike the physical integration of the art-as-public-spaces paradigm (which Serra likewise rejected), Ahearn's community-based site specificity emphasized a social integration. This is in part due to the fact that the site itself is here conceived as a social entity, a "community," and not simply in terms of environmental or architectural design. But more importantly, the emphasis on the social stems from the belief that the meaning or value of the art work does not reside in the object itself but is accrued over time through the interaction between the artist and the community. This interaction is considered to be integral to the art work and equal in significance (it may even be thought of as constituting the art work). What this means is that the *artist's assimilation* into a given community now coincides with the *art work's integration* with the site. The prior goal of integration and harmony in terms of unified urban design is reorganized around the *performative* capacity of the artist to become one with the community. And this "becoming one," no matter how temporary, is presumed to be a prerequisite for an artist to be able to speak with, for, and as a legitimate representative or member of the community. Simultaneously, the characteristics of this "unity" function as criteria for judging the artistic authenticity and ethical fitness of the art work.

In most cases, community-based site specificity also seeks to bring about another kind of integration between the community and the work of art. A group of people previously held at a distance from the artistic process, under abstract designations of viewer/spectator, audience, or public, are enlisted in this case to participate in the creation of an art work. Sometimes this absorption of the community into the artistic process and vice versa is rendered iconographically readable, as, for example, in the literalist realism of John Ahearn's cast sculptures. At other times, when the art work is conceptually oriented, with priority given to the collective process and social interaction, with or without the guarantee of any material outcome, this absorption is more difficult to track. But a central objective of community-based site specificity is the creation of a work in which members of a community—as simultaneously viewer/spectator, audience, public, and referential subject—will see and recognize themselves in the work, not so much in the sense of being critically implicated but of being affirmatively pictured or validated.

This investment corresponds to an old imperative of public art: rather than art works that are separated or detached from the space of the audience, which reinforce social alienation and disaffection, one should sponsor works that reassure the viewing subject with something familiar and known. We can recall Janet Kardon's comment that in order for a public art work to be meaningful to the public (thus, meaningfully public), it should not "unsettle perceptions" but "reassure the viewer with an easily shared idea or subject."[86] In 1980, when these words were written, Kardon encouraged "sharing" through art that either performs a "useful task," such as providing shade or seating, or conjures an association with a "sense of leisure"—generic qualities she presumed to be desired and esteemed by all. In contrast, proponents of 1990s community-based public art have argued for the specificity of certain audience groups (i.e., communities), the basic sentiment being that the desires and needs of a particular community cannot be presumed to be so generic, and cannot be declared a priori by an artist or anyone else outside of that community. Therefore, the task of "reassur[ing] the viewer with an easily shared idea or subject" is best accomplished when the idea or subject of the art work is determined by the community, or better yet if it *is* the community itself in some way.

This principle holds true even in public art projects based in conceptual or performance art, which do not yield concrete material manifestations (that is, literal representations of the people of the community). For if we identify "the work" as the dialogue and collaboration between an artist and a community group, we conjure a picture of the community nonetheless, albeit in different terms, precisely of work. In eschewing object (read commodity) production, many community-based artists, often with the help of curators, administrators, and sponsors, orchestrate situations in which community participants invest time and energy in a collective project or process. This investment of labor would seem to secure the participants' sense of identification with "the work," or at least a sense of ownership of it, so that the community sees itself in "the work" not through an iconic or mimetic identification but through the recognition of its own *labor* in the creation of, or becoming of, "the work." Although the concept of labor rarely appears in public art discourse, and although the issue cannot be pursued in adequate depth here, it seems crucial to note the need to consider the representative function of labor within the context of community-based art practice generally.[87] For now, I can simply propose that the drive toward identificatory unity that propels today's form of community-based site specificity is a desire to model or enact unalienated collective labor, predicated on an idealistic assumption that artistic labor is itself a special form of unalienated labor, or at least provisionally outside of capitalism's forces.

But if the pursuit of identificatory unity, as I have described it thus far, is in part an updated means to "reassure the viewer with an easily shared idea or subject," the question remains: What exactly is reassured by it? And what does this reassurance guarantee? While it is not prudent to overgeneralize, a preliminary answer, pointing to both the hazards and hopes of contemporary public art, can begin with the observation that the viewer is affirmed in his/her self-knowledge and world view through the art work's mechanisms of (self-) identification. Underlying decades of public art discourse is a presumption that the art work—as object, event, or process—can fortify the viewing (now producing) subject by protecting it from the conditions of social alienation, economic fragmentation, and political disenfranchisement that threaten, diminish, exclude, marginalize, contradict, and otherwise "unsettle" its sense of identity. Alongside this belief is an unspoken imperative that the art work should affirm rather than disturb the viewer's sense of self. A culturally fortified subject, rendered whole and unalienated through an encounter or involvement with an art work, is imagined to be a *politically* empowered social subject with opportunity (afforded by the art project) and capacity (understood as innate) for artistic self-representation (= political self-determination). It is, I would argue, the production of such "empowered" subjects, a reversal of the aesthetically politicized subjects of the traditional avant-garde, that is the underlying goal of much community-based, site-specific public art today.[88]

While the complexities and paradoxes of current public art discourse remain unresolved, the need to rethink the operations of the existing models of site specificity is unambiguous. And the seeming failure of the two most recent paradigms—as exemplified in Serra's disruptive model based in sculpture, and

Ahearn's assimilative model based in community interaction—isolates some of the terms of that rethinking. *Tilted Arc* is a seminal instance of a nonassimilative, oppositional mode of site specificity that, while vilified by many, has been lauded by others for its critical capacity to challenge the prevailing tendency of public art to cover over the many contradictions that underlie public space. John Ahearn's project in the South Bronx, while contrarily an assimilative and integrationist effort, simi-

◄ Richard Serra, ***Tilted Arc***, Federal Plaza, New York, 1981–1989. (Photo by Susan Swidler; © Richard Serra/Artists Rights Society (ARS), New York.)

► Walton Avenue block party for inauguration of ***Back to School*** mural, Bronx, New York, September 3, 1985. (Photo by Ivan Dalla Tana; courtesy Alexander and Bonin Gallery, New York.)

larly illuminates the conflicted nature of the public sphere. If we are to measure a public art work's critical capacity in relation to the ways in which the work itself becomes a site of contestation over what constitutes something as public,[89] then the conflicts surrounding these two works underscore the lack of agreement over what we mean by, and expect from, an "interventionary" site specificity.

4

FROM SITE TO COMMUNITY IN NEW GENRE PUBLIC ART: THE CASE OF "CULTURE IN ACTION"

In the early morning hours of May 20, 1993, one hundred large limestone boulders, each about three feet tall and four feet wide and weighing roughly 1,000 to 1,500 pounds, mysteriously appeared on sidewalks, plazas, street corners, and parkways throughout the Loop in downtown Chicago. This odd and "spontaneous" outcropping of lumpy boulders on the streets of Chicago, each adorned with a commemorative plaque honoring a woman from the city (a total of ninety living, ten historical), was masterminded by Suzanne Lacy, a California-based artist best known for her feminist performances and protests from the 1970s. The event marked the unofficial inauguration of the temporary exhibition program "Culture in Action: New Public Art in Chicago." Sponsored by the nonprofit public art organization Sculpture Chicago[1] and conceived and directed by the independent curator Mary Jane Jacob, "Culture in Action" included seven other projects dispersed throughout the city at various neighborhood locations, all of which remained "on view" throughout the summer of 1993, from early May to end of September.[2]

Claiming to break from previous models of public art, "Culture in Action" took the entire city of Chicago as its stage and "focused on the active participation of residents in diverse communities in the creation of the artworks." According to its press release, "'Culture in Action' established a new vocabulary within the genre of urban-oriented sculpture exhibitions. . . . [It] tested the territory of public interaction and participation; the role of the artist as an active social force; artist-driven educational programming as an essential part of the artwork; and projects that existed over an extended period of time, not just as spectator-oriented objects for brief viewing."[3]

To do so, the eight projects included in "Culture in Action" were structured as community collaborations in which, with the help of Sculpture Chicago's administrative staff, the artist joined with a local organization or group to conceptualize

Suzanne Lacy and A Coalition of Chicago Women, *Full Circle*, 1993. (Photos by John McWilliams; courtesy Sculpture Chicago.)

and produce the art work. The results of these collaborations were wide-ranging and hardly the typical fare of public art. In addition to Lacy's commemorative boulders (which was only one of two parts of her contribution to the program; part two consisted of a ceremonial all-women dinner), there was a multiethnic neighborhood parade, by Daniel J. Martinez, VinZula Kara, and the West Side Three-Point Marchers (Los Desfiladores Tres Puntos del West Side); a new candy bar designed and produced in collaboration with members of a candy-making union, by Simon Grennan, Christopher Sperandio, and the Bakery, Confectionery and Tobacco Workers' International Union of America Local No. 552; an urban ecological field station involving twelve high school students, by Mark Dion and the Chicago Urban Ecology Action Group; a storefront hydroponic garden to grow food for HIV/AIDS patients, by the collaborative team of Haha—Richard House, Wendy Jabob, Laurie Palmer, and John Ploof—with Flood, a network of health care volunteers; a street video installation and neighborhood block party organized with teenagers from Chicago's West Town area, by Iñigo Manglano-Ovalle, the Westtown Vecinos Video Channel, and Street-Level Video; the production and distribution of paint charts that reflect the lives of public housing residents, by Kate Ericson, Mel Ziegler, and a resident group of Ogden Courts Apartments; and a telephone survey project on name-calling, by Robert Peters with "Mushroom Pickers, Ghosts, Frogs, and other Others."[4]

Initially conceived by Jacob in 1991, "Culture in Action" (originally titled "New Urban Monuments")[5] was intended to be a critique of two institutions: the organization of Sculpture Chicago specifically, and more broadly the field of public art. Jacob's assessment of Sculpture Chicago's 1989 summer sculpture program showcasing ten relatively traditional sculptures on urban plazas[6] was not altogether favorable. Like most public art organizations, Sculpture Chicago's stated goals included demystifying the creative process and taking art to the "man on the street." But its effort to do so by presenting the artists at work in tents set up outdoors—so that the public could have "access" to their "creative process"—seemed to Jacob still to maintain a strict and rather naïve separation between the artist and the audience, between producer and spectator. According to Jacob, the board members of

Sculpture Chicago were shocked to be told, "You're fooling yourself if you think that by seeing a sculptor weld two pieces of steel together, somebody has a sense of what art-making is."[7] In fact, Jacob's desire to shift the role of the viewer from passive spectator to active art-maker became one of the central goals of "Culture in Action."[8]

Lauded by some as one of the most important public art events in North America in the twentieth century,[9] and criticized by others for its exploitation of communities and/or reduction of art to a kind of inadequate and ineffectual social work,[10] this project's scale and ambition, and the discussions it generated concerning the definition and function of contemporary public art, remain unrivaled in the post-*Tilted Arc* era. But the symptomatic aspects of "Culture in Action," particularly in relation to the problematics of site specificity, are most evident when we compare the Chicago program to another public art exhibition of similar scale and ambition, "In Public: Seattle 1991." Organized by Diane Shamash, then the Manager of the Public Arts Program of the Seattle Arts Commission (SAC), "In Public" showcased eighteen installations also sited throughout the city (sixteen temporary and two permanent).[11]

With funds made available in 1986 through the Percent for Art program during the construction of the new Seattle Art Museum, SAC solicited proposals from thirty local, national, and international artists that would "address, intervene in, and engage the public life of the city." This kind of approach, seeing the entire city and its processes as a site for artistic intervention, was not new to SAC. Indeed, it was SAC's formulation of the architect/artist design team concept for the Viewlands Hoffman electrical substation project in the mid 1970s that set an influential precedent for the urban design approach to public art throughout the 1980s.[12] "In Public," at the beginning of the 1990s, was an attempt to reassess the wisdom of imposing architect/artist collaborative structures, which by then had become extremely formulaic and restrictive, on artists wanting to work in the public realm.[13] So with the exception of the Pier 62/63 collaboration between architects Henry Smith-Miller and Laurie Hawkinson and artist Barbara Kruger, "In Public" granted individual artists the opportunity to initiate and direct their own projects, in locations of their choosing within the city, without necessarily having to collaborate with any de-sign professionals.

"Culture in Action" made this feature a rule, eliminating the role of archi-tects and design professionals altogether from the public art process. To a large ex-tent, many of the stated goals of "Culture in Action" recapitulated the general terms of the Seattle program. "'In Public' was to be an experimental project that would push the boundaries of public art as we have come to know it and engage the public in a dialogue about the place and meaning of art in our daily lives."[14] But whereas "In Public" focused primarily on extending the types of public venue for artistic intervention, finding a broad range of unusual sites in and through the city (including newspapers, bus stops, piers, radio, television, as well as traditional public squares), "Culture in Action" abandoned the prevailing implication that ar-chitects and design professionals are expert negotiators between art and urban spaces. In effect, "Culture in Action" instead cast the "community" as the authority figure on such matters, privileging its role in the collaborative artistic partnerships forged by the program.[15]

Without question, what could be seen and documented as the outcome of "Culture in Action"—a candy bar, a neighborhood parade, a block party, a paint chart, a hydroponic garden, etc.—was in stark contrast to Chicago's own familiar forms of public art. Picasso's monumental cubist sculpture *Head of a Woman* (1965) on Richard J. Daley Center Plaza (also known popularly as the "Chicago Pi-casso"),[16] and the recent design of Pritzker Park by artist Ronald Jones (1991),[17] served as local prototypes against which "Culture in Action" established its new-ness and difference. Its difference was especially pronounced when one recog-nized that much of the work in "Culture in Action" was defined not in terms of material objects but by the ephemeral processes of interaction between the local participants and the artists. Furthermore, these interactions were not restricted, at least in principle, to the time frame of the exhibition itself.[18]

The 1993 presentation of "Culture in Action" thus exemplified on a grand scale what Suzanne Lacy defined as "new genre public art":[19]

Dealing with some of the most profound issues of our time—toxic waste, race relations, homelessness, aging, gang warfare, and cultural identity—a group of visual artists has developed distinct models for an art whose public strategies of engagement are an important part of its aesthetic language. . . . We might describe this as "new genre public art," to distinguish it in both form and intention from what has been called "public art"—a term used for the past twenty-five years to describe sculpture and installations sited in public places. Unlike much of what has heretofore been called public art, new genre public art—visual art that uses both traditional and nontraditional media to communicate and interact with a broad and diversified audience about issues directly relevant to their lives—is based on engagement.[20]

"Culture in Action" affirmed Lacy's claim that "what exists in the space between the words public and art is an unknown relationship between artist and audience, a relationship that may *itself* be the artwork."[21]

The works in the exhibition also corresponded to what art critic Arlene Raven has identified as "art in the public interest."[22] According to Raven, art in the public interest is activist and communitarian in spirit; its modes of expression encompass a variety of traditional media, including painting and sculpture, as well as nontraditional media—"street art, guerrilla theater, video, page art, billboards, protest actions and demonstrations, oral histories, dances, environments, posters, murals."[23] Most importantly, she has argued, art in the public interest forges direct intersections with social issues. It encourages community coalition-building in pursuit of social justice and attempts to garner greater institutional empowerment for artists to act as social agents. Artists engaged in such art "aspire to reveal the plight and plead the case of the disenfranchised and disadvantaged, and to embody what they [the artists] view as humanitarian values."[24] Additionally, they "demand more artist involvement in institutional decision-making, representation of minorities and women artists, and use of the influence of museum and funding agencies to change government policies on social issues."²⁵

Interestingly, the majority of those involved in such endeavors do not see their work within the historical framework of public art. Rather, they inscribe their practice—a contemporary form of socially conscious, activist political art—into the history of the aesthetic avant-garde. Raven, for example, cites Russian constructivism and the German Bauhaus as precedents for art in the public interest. She situates grassroots, artist-initiated activist groups from the 1960s (such as the Art Workers Coalition, Los Angeles Council of Women Artists, Foundation for the Community of Artists) as well as the alternative art movements from the 1970s within the same lineage, posing art in the public interest as a revitalization of the historical avant-garde's efforts to integrate art and everyday life.

Lacy likewise proclaims an alternative history for new genre public art. Disassociating it from the public art movement that developed through the 1970s and 1980s, she links it instead to the development of "various vanguard groups, such as feminist, ethnic, Marxist, and media artists and other activists . . . [who] have a common interest in leftist politics, social activism, redefined audiences, relevance for communities (particularly marginalized ones), and collaborative methodology."²⁶ According to Lacy, such interests lead to an attack on aesthetic categories bound to specificities of media, as well as the spaces of their presentation, and challenge the established criteria of cultural value based on aesthetic quality and individualistic notions of artistic competence. Thus, "draw[ing] on ideas from vanguard forms"—i.e., installation, performance, conceptual art, mixed-media art— new genre public art "adds a developed sensibility about audience, social strategy, and effectiveness that is unique to visual art as we know it today."²⁷ In so doing, it shifts the focus from artist to audience, from object to process, from production to reception, and emphasizes the importance of a direct, apparently unmediated engagement with particular audience groups (ideally through shared authorship in collaborations). According to Lacy, these artists, herself among them, eschew the constricting limitations not only of artistic conventions but of the traditional institutional spaces of their production and reproduction, such as studios, museums, and galleries. They choose instead the "freedom" of working in "real" places, with "real" people, addressing "everyday" issues. In a move one critic has dubbed "postmodern social realism," new genre public art also insists on a move away from the universalizing tendencies of modernist abstraction, to celebrate instead the particular realities of "ordinary" people and their "everyday" experiences.[28]

Foundational to this rhetoric of new genre public art is a political aspiration toward the greater "democratization" of art (a liberal humanist impulse that has always fueled public art). Qualities such as pluralist inclusivity, multicultural representation, and consensus-building are central to the conception of democracy espoused by the practitioners and supporters of new genre public art.[29] Rather than an object for individual contemplation, produced by a distant art specialist for an exclusive art-educated audience equipped to understand its complex visual language, new genre public artists seek to engage (nonart) issues in the hearts and minds of the "average man on the street" or "real people" outside the art world. In doing so, they seek to empower the audience by directly involving them in the making of the art work, either as subjects or, better, as producers themselves. By extending the hitherto specialized privilege of art-making and art appreciation to a larger number and broader range of people (not restricted to the privileged minority of the dominant class, gender, race, and sexual orientation), new genre public artists hope to make art more familiar and accessible (because it is now not only for the "public" but by the "public"). For the proponents of new genre public art, this ownership of art, or more generally cultural representation, is the basis for the integration of art and everyday life and a powerful force toward social and political change.

This effort to distinguish a "new genre" in public art might be approached critically as another form of aesthetic vanguardism, a renewed mode of social and political activism, or a new strategy of urban reform and revitalization. For some critics and artists, however, it represents neither a new movement in the field nor a newly politicized aesthetic sensibility, but rather a moment of arrival in which a well-developed mode of practice that had been undervalued in mainstream art finally receives broader cultural acceptance. According to Mary Jane Jacob, for example, this "new public art is not so much a movement of the nineties, a new way of working, as a way of working that has found its time."[30] Similarly for critic Eleanor Heartney, the major shift in public art as represented by "Culture in Action" is not so much a radical turn in practice as it is a belated turn in institutional reception. Citing Kate Ericson and Mel Ziegler, who claimed that "art has the ability to be a valuable social tool" and described their art as intending "to be pragmatic, to deal with pre-existing social systems and to carry on a dialogue with the public," Heartney has written with some enthusiasm: "Of course, such concepts have been part of certain artists' thinking and practice for years. Now, however, they have come out into the open, becoming stock-in-trade for art administrators, curators and critics as well."[31]

Whether understood as the development of something new or as the institutional acceptance of something old, the ascendance of this category of public art represents a significant shift within the public art field. For new genre public art not only insists on a reconsideration of (public) art's values and priorities along with alterations in its methodology and procedures; it also asserts a major rethinking of site specificity as a means to achieve its goals. In fact, advocates of new genre public art devalue, or at times explicitly reject, received definitions of the site and existing approaches to site specificity. The self-proclaimed radicality of "Culture in Action" in particular, and by extension the rhetoric and practice of new genre public art in general, depends on a fundamental redescription of site specificity's aesthetic necessity, its conceptual parameters, its social and political efficacy. Strangely echoing the arguments posed against the earlier site-indifferent models of art-in-public-places and art-as-public-spaces, many artists and critics now register their desire to better serve and engage the public, to further close the gap between art and life, by expressing a deep dissatisfaction with site specificity.

According to art critic Jeff Kelley, for example, "site specificity was really more like the imposition of a kind of disembodied museum zone onto what already had been very meaningful and present before that, which was the place."[32] Kelley is concerned here to conceptually distinguish "site" and "place," the former signifying an abstract location and the latter an intimate and particularized culture that is bound to a geographical region.[33] In associating the "site" with previous models of public art and "place" with new genre public art, Kelley means to highlight the limited social consciousness of site specificity as evidenced particularly in the art-as-public-spaces mode of practice.[34] At the same time, he registers the extent to which site specificity has experienced a radical reversal in recent years: where it was once a means to better integrate art into the spaces of the everyday, to better engage and accommodate the public, it has become a means to overrun the public and the meaningfulness of local places and cultures.

Such recent reassessments of site specificity, representing a fundamental rethinking of how an art work is to (or should) engage with its "public," turn on a crucial shift in which the "site" is displaced by notions of an "audience," a particular social "issue," and, most commonly, a "community." Artist Christopher Sperandio, for instance, speaking on behalf of the collaborative team of Grennan and Sperandio (one of the participants in "Culture in Action"), has unequivocally stated that they have abandoned the limited framework of the "site-specific" in favor of a more expansive notion of the "community-specific."[35] For Sperandio, the term "site" registers something neutral and implies a space that belongs to "someone else," i.e., an institution. A "community," in contrast, is apparently more specific and self-determined.

In a similar vein, Mary Jane Jacob has alternately described the projects in "Culture in Action" as both "issue-specific" and "audience-specific." According to Jacob, the move away from site specificity is a logical step toward a more intimate and meaningful relationship between the artist and his/her audience, a way of shrinking the distance between the traditionally separate poles of production and reception. "The commissioned works in 'Culture in Action' grow out of the alternative spaces and public art strategies of the 1960s. . . . They evolve as well from 'site-specific' artworks that, while tailored to particular locations, often remain discrete artworks within conventional exhibitions. In 'Culture in Action,' however, the artists' projects refer not primarily to sites, but to social issues that are of common concern to the artists and to the communities in which they have chosen to work."[36] Furthermore, "Each [project] is created in direct partnership with a local community and addresses such urban issues as low-income housing, HIV/AIDS research and care, workers' rights, minority youth leadership, ecology, and women's achievements. Such temporal, issue-specific artworks are a form of artmaking that grows out of the desire of artists to reach audiences in ways that are more direct and unexpected than is possible in a museum or gallery setting."[37]

Critics involved in the current public art debate have offered various conjectures on the nature of these changes. Dan Cameron, for example, has described the shift primarily as a stage in the development of a particular artistic genre. For Cameron, "Culture in Action" and other public art programs like it exemplify the general transformation of sculpture away from site specificity toward "post-site sculpture," toward an increasing dissipation of art as a cultural category.

> "Culture in Action" falls into the category of those sculpture exhibitions which have followed the logical progression from the model of site-specificity toward the apparent next stage: the dissolution of the language of "art" altogether, in favor of activities and interventions which take place directly in the community, away from the museum's watchful eye. . . . The work in "Culture in Action" set out to navigate that murky zone where social activism and post-site sculpture have begun to intersect.[38]

In contrast, Eleanor Heartney has characterized the current trend not so much as a logical progression in the development of sculpture but as a dramatic reversal in approaches to public art. Her argument positions the *Tilted Arc* controversy of the 1980s as a counterpoint to "the [recent] discussion [which] shift[s] away from the notion of site-specificity as a response to the formal dynamics of the site toward a concern with community as context." As she put it: "Before the construction of *Tilted Arc,* Serra announced that 'after the piece is built, the space will be understood primarily as a function of the sculpture.' Today, more often than not, the reverse seems to be true. Sculpture is seen as a function of the space or the context. Public artists tend to speak in terms of community participation, temporariness and the limitation of the authorial role of the artist."[39]

  This last comment is more in keeping with Jacob's own conception of "Culture in Action." According to Jacob, the trajectory of the modern public art movement, within which her program marks a major turning point, plays out as follows:

> As public art shifted from large-scale objects, to physically or conceptually site-specific projects, to audience-specific concerns (work made in response to those who occupy a given site), it moved from an aesthetic function, to a design function, to a social function. Rather than serving to promote the economic development of American cities, as did public art beginning in the late 1960s, it is now being viewed as a means of stabilizing community development throughout urban centers. In the 1990s the role of public art has shifted from that of renewing the physical environment to that of improving society, from promoting aesthetic quality to contributing to the quality of life, from enriching lives to saving lives.[40]

Which is to say that, having lost its longstanding faith in the power of architecture and urban design to positively affect the quality of life in social terms, public art has reaffirmed its desire to impact the lives of (nonart) constituencies by other means. Instead of addressing the physical conditions of the site, the focus now is on engaging the concerns of "those who occupy a given site." These concerns, defined in relation to social issues—homelessness, urban violence, sexism, homophobia, racism, AIDS—ostensibly offer a more genuine point of contact, a zone of mutual interest, between artist/art and community/audience. The new formulation of community-based public art proposes a new partnership in place of the partnership between artist and architect valorized in the design team collaborations of the 1980s. The dialogue is now to occur between an artist and a community or audience group that is identified as such in relation to some social problem (which itself is often associated with marginalized and disenfranchised communities).[41]

The slide from site-specific to issue-specific in public art can be seen as yet another example of the ways in which the concept of the site has moved away from one of concrete physical location, as I argued in chapter 1. The invocation of the community-specific and the audience-specific, in which the site is displaced by a group of people assumed to share some sense of common/communal identity based on (experiences of) ethnicity, gender, geographical proximity, political affiliation, religious beliefs, social and economic classes, etc., can be described as an extension of the discursive virtualization of the site, at least to the extent that identity itself is constructed within a complex discursive field.

But the particular displacement of the site-specific by the community-specific in new genre public art requires special attention along a different trajectory of inquiry, because the prominence of community-based, participatory modes of art practice in recent years coincides with the frequent invocation of the community in many arenas outside the art context. Indeed, the community, generally understood as a collective body that mediates between individual subjects and society, has become a highly charged and extremely elastic political term. It is deployed equally by the left and the right to muster public support for certain social programs, political candidates, and legislative agendas; it carries weight in debates ranging from education and health care to housing policies and zoning regulations. On the one hand, the term "community" is associated with disenfranchised social groups that have been systematically excluded from the political and cultural processes that affect, if not determine, their lives. It defines coalitions of people seeking to counter such processes of exclusion and repression by collectively demanding equal rights, greater social recognition, economic support, and political power, such as the gay and lesbian community, the Asian American community, working-class communities, the African American community, women's groups, senior citizens organizations, etc. On the other hand, quite antithetically, the term is frequently invoked to describe departicularized identities of dominant social, economic, political, and cultural forces, such as the business community, the entertainment community, the medical community, the scientific community, the national and international communities. Furthermore, among neoconservatives the "community" is repeatedly conjured in efforts to instigate *new* exclusionary policies in housing, health care, social services, and education. In its drive toward the greater privatization of public institutions and services and the decentralization of state authority, the right has appropriated the concept of the community as well. The dismantling of certain state-sponsored social and cultural programs that especially benefit the poor and the ill, for instance, are carried out now in the name of community activism and community self-determination.

One example will suffice to illustrate the ways in which community-based rhetoric has become a flexible political tool for neoconservatives. In an article entitled "The New Community Activism: Social Justice Comes Full Circle," Heather Mac Donald describes the political struggles in the Lower East Side and the Upper West Side of New York City over the city's plans to locate in those neighborhoods new social service facilities for drug rehabilitation, mental illness, and AIDS treatment.[42] Detailing the opposition of a group of residents in each neighborhood to the city's plans, Mac Donald's narrative is marked throughout by her overriding concern to celebrate, as the title of her article indicates, a "new community activism." She begins her article with the ominous claim that "tolerance for the breakdown of public order under the banner of compassion and civil liberties is threatening the very survival of some New York communities." Against this perceived threat, she identifies "a new wave of community rebels who represent a revolution in the making. Citizens are rising to demand that the government stop dumping social problems onto their streets and start demonstrating a commonsense concern with the quality of life in the city's neighborhoods."[43] Thus, new community activism is characterized as a reclamation project—citizens taking back "their" streets and neighborhoods from both an inefficient government (the "therapeutic state") and those who constitute the social problems, who "gain money from the continued cycle of [state] dependence."[44] Rather than address the absolute necessity of social services for certain groups, Mac Donald writes only about the unfairness of social services being concentrated in particular neighborhoods.

For Mac Donald, the objectives of new community activism are twofold. First is the insistence that local communities, not government bureaucracies, have the right to determine the use of neighborhood spaces, for social services or otherwise, and that the community should be able to "control deviant behavior" within its purview without government interference. In other words, the community should have exclusive jurisdiction over the management of the spaces and resources of the neighborhood and be free to police the neighborhood against "unwanted" elements, such as drug addicts, AIDS patients, the homeless, and the mentally ill. But the larger battle is ideological. For Mac Donald's community activism is not only against government interference in community issues; it is about "bucking a long political tradition . . . that champions radical individualism, disparages middle-class values, and reserves particular contempt for 'gentrification.'"[45]

In a hyperbolic rendering, the liberal left is characterized as dangerously radical and oppressively dogmatic, either too sentimental and idealistic, thus irrational, or too corrupt and unreliable to offer any satisfactory solutions to deal with many of today's social problems. This is why new community activists must reclaim the term "community" from its supposed misrepresentations and misappropriations by the liberal left leadership. According to Mac Donald, "When social-service advocates talk of 'community,' they are using a code word that has absolutely no reference to real communities."[46] Not surprisingly, Mac Donald's notion of the "real" community is based solely on ownership of property; those who own (or sometimes rent) housing and real estate in the neighborhoods are the only legitimate members of the "real" community who can speak for its needs, management, future direction, and hopes. Consequently, the "real" community does not include or recognize the voices of others who might have contingent, nonproprietary relationships to the neighborhood, and it is delimited in finite rather than relational terms.

Much of the current effort of public art is in some measure a resistance to the strengthening forces of the right as exemplified in the case outlined above. In fact, participants in "Culture in Action" and proponents of new genre public art explicitly position themselves in opposition to such exclusionary tendencies. The highlighting of marginalized and disenfranchised social groups in community-based collaborative art projects is indeed an attempt to counter (if not compensate for) these groups' lack of social visibility and political power. And the endeavor to give voice to underrepresented and disempowered groups, often by engaging them in the very process of creating their own cultural representations, is understood by most of its practitioners and supporters as not simply an artistic experiment but a strategy of political importance.

According to critic Hafthor Yngvason, for instance, who participated in the December 1992 symposium on "Culture in Action,"[47] the political implications of the shift from site specificity to a collaborative, participatory mode of community-based practice are profound.

> As public art has developed over the last two decades, its emphasis has been on techniques of integration—not just to incorporate art physically into buildings and parks but also to foster social assimilation. While "site-specificity"—privileged in public-art circles as *the* public form of art—has provided a means to introduce art into neighborhoods without the glaring irrelevance of what has been called "plop art," it has rarely gone beyond the idea of responding to established ideas or "facts" about communities to participating in a public sphere where such facts can be examined and contested.[48]

Yngvason associates contrasting sociopolitical models with the "integrationst" and "participatory" modes of public art practice. Citing feminist political theorist Seyla Benhabib, he claims that the former is predicated on a vision of society as "'communities integrated around a single conception of the human good'—i.e., a conception that can be responded to in an unproblematic fashion and revitalized through simple design, such as a public plaza." The latter is based instead on a notion of society as "'marked by a "plurality" of visions of what is good, and of the good of association itself.'"[49] For Yngvason and others, to pursue the kind of participatory art practice that "Culture in Action" advocates is not only to critique the "medieval" notions of public art (understood as a coherent representation of a community permanently installed in a public square or public gathering place) but to resist the integrationst ideology in a political sense.

To test Yngvason's hypothesis, that is, to examine more concretely the aesthetic shifts in new genre public art in relation to their political implications for the community, we will turn to the specific conditions of the eight projects in "Culture in Action" and of the exhibition program as a whole. A critical interrogation of their various mobilizations of the term "community" will serve to elaborate on the function of the concept within new genre public art as it appears to engage the larger political debate concerning the future of democracy.

It will become quite clear that, despite the efforts of many artists, critics, and historians to unify recent trends in public art as a coherent movement, there are numerous inconsistencies, contradictions, and variations within the field, even within the "Culture in Action" program itself. In fact, the narrative of new genre public art's newness, as developed in significant part in the promotional rhetoric and critical reception of "Culture in Action," has continuously obscured or glossed over some of its most consequential inconsistencies and contradictions. For instance, while the wide range of artistic media and formal approaches in "Culture in Action" has been acknowledged, even celebrated, as a distinctive attribute of new genre public art's aesthetic "freedom," as evidence of its "experimental" nature, the fundamental differences in the social and political implications of the separate projects have largely been ignored.

Contrary to its curator's overarching program description, the projects in "Culture in Action" each present a divergent approach to the central problem of community engagement. But the differences among the projects in terms of their visual presentation reveal little of their conceptual and theoretical differences. These are embedded instead in the specific (invisible) *processes* of their respective community collaborations, in their *enactment* of the necessary institutional and individual exchanges and compromises (as opposed to their rhetorical descriptions of them), many of which have been carried out in improvisational ways. We turn now to these processes and exchanges—the complex set of relations and negotiations within the particular parameters of "Culture in Action"—in order to pose the following questions.

In actual practice, how does a group of people become identified as a community in an exhibition program, as a potential partner in a collaborative art project? Who identifies them as such? And who decides what social issue(s) will be addressed or represented by/through them: the artist? the community group? the curator? the sponsoring institution? the funding organization? Does the partner community preexist the art project, or is it produced by it? What is the nature of the collaborative relationship? If the identity of the community is produced through the making of the art work, does the artist's identity also depend on the same process? How does the collaboration unfold, and what precisely is the role of the artist within it? Does the partner community coincide with the audience? If new public art engages the audience as active participants in the production of an art work, which to a degree renders them subjects of the work, too, then who is the audience for *this* production? What criteria of success and failure are posed now, especially to the artists, in this major reconfiguration of public art that moves aesthetic practice closer to social services?[50] And finally, through it all, what are the political implications and consequences of new genre public art's simultaneous displacements of the architect and the site (once understood as a geographic location) by the community, the audience, and the social issue, as themselves different kinds of spaces?

*   *   *

The eight projects in "Culture in Action" can be grouped into four distinct categories based on the kind of interactions between the artist(s) and the respective community partner(s). The projects reveal varying degrees of intervention from the curator and/or Sculpture Chicago: some projects are fully dependent on institutional involvement; others are more able to oversee their own development. Each category also defines a different role for the artist, offering alternative renditions of the collaborative relationship. All in all, the variations among these collaborative models reveal the extent to which the "community" remains a highly ambiguous and problematic concept in public art today.

The first model is best exemplified in Suzanne Lacy's project *Full Circle,* with its hundred commemorative boulders. Here it is difficult to discern any community more particular than the social category of Women, despite the artist's effort to honor specific individuals from the city of Chicago. In preparation for the project, several committees of women were established by the artist and Sculpture Chicago to oversee the nominating and selecting of one hundred local women who would eventually receive a boulder commemoration. But the committees did not function as active creative partners in the overall conception of Lacy's project (at best, they were sounding boards for the artist's ideas). Instead, they were convened to per-form and signify the decentralization of the artist's authority in defining the "con-tent" of *Full Circle*—i.e., the names of individual honorees.

On the one hand, such a move seems logical, even commonsensical, as lo-cal residents would likely be more knowledgeable than the artist (from California) in assessing the social and cultural contributions of one of their own. On the other hand, Lacy's committee structure, employed as a means to humble the artist's voice and elevate those of local women, seems to confuse rationalized bureaucratization of the decision-making process with creative group participation. The artist's dele-gation of decision-making duties is not really the same thing as sharing of authority. Only those with authority in the first place are in positions to delegate; that is, the act of delegating is in itself an act of authority.

The committees, however, did infuse a sense of regional relevance to the project insofar as their focus was on Chicago residents. Lacy herself emphasized this aspect when she noted that "the invented nature of the nomination process grounded the project in the community and with the women selected."[51] This im-plies a locational delineation of the community. But what conceptually gathered all one hundred women into a coherent "community," or at least an extension of it, was not their common place of residence and work—the city of Chicago—or their pre-sumed allegiance to it. Rather, according to Lacy, they shared a transhistorical, transcultural, and gender-specific "sensibility": "As the idea . . . grew, the issue that seemed to connect them was service—and a sensibility, whether through culture or nature, that seemed particular to women. 'Service,' an inadequate word, often challenged throughout the project, still seems the best way to describe a quality of supporting, nurturing, correcting injustice, promoting equality."[52]

Following this logic, Lacy orchestrated a conceptually coherent unity for all women, presumably identified with one another in the service activities of "supporting, nurturing, correcting injustice, and promoting equality." Granted, the model of unity here was not that of a cultural melting pot, with particularities of minority constituencies effaced or assimilated into the likeness of dominant social forces. In fact, Lacy emphasized the distinctness of individual identities—one woman, one boulder—over the importance of a single collective image. She made a concerted effort in *Full Circle* to model a unity of women that encompassed a wide diversity of professional backgrounds, ethnicities, social standings, ages, and religious affiliations, paying special attention to the inclusion of underrepresented and marginalized groups, such as African American, working-class, and older women. But whatever the individual differences, all were subsumed in the end by the artist's search for a common denominator that celebrated an abstract gender unity, delimited in this case by a set of service-oriented characteristics that were in effect naturalized as innate attributes of women in general. This was further emphasized by Lacy's symbolic all-women dinner, which augmented the project.

Within such a framework, the specificity of each woman's life drops out to a large extent (as does the specificity of Chicago), because diversity and difference are emphasized only to the degree that they can be overridden by a common principle or theme of unification. For example, the differences among the women in terms of their geographical attachments, socioeconomic position, cultural background, racial heritage, sexual orientation, and so on were absorbed by Lacy's notion of "service"—without taking into account the different relationships (social, economic, spiritual, emotional) that each woman might have to the very prospect of "service." Feminist social theorist Iris Marion Young has warned against reductive tendencies that would unite all women as nurturers and caretakers, especially when such characterizations are extrapolated into a gender-specific political vision.

Despite our [feminists'] critical attention to much of the male tradition of political theory, many of us have retained uncritically an anar-
chist, participatory democratic communitarianism to express our
vision of the ideal society. Indeed, many of us have assumed that
women and feminists can best realize this ideal, because women's
culture is less individualistic and less based in competition than
men's culture, and because, we claim, women are psychologically
and politically more oriented toward care and mutuality.[53]

As the artistic impresario of *Full Circle,* Lacy rendered an image of community that is an overgeneralized and abstract projection of commonality, a *mythic*
unity that gathers into its folds a range of particular persons and their experiences.
While her version of community diverges somewhat from the traditional ideal of a
completely homogeneous and coherent social body, diversity and difference are
articulated here only to be overcome or exceeded by a universalizing common
goal.[54]

"Sited" Communities

The second model of community, perhaps the most prevalent in community-based
public art today, is evident in the project by Simon Grennan and Christopher
Sperandio and that by Kate Ericson and Mel Ziegler. In both cases, the artists
paired with existing Chicago organizations, or "sited communities,"[55] that already
had clearly defined identities in the sense of having established locational bases,
modes of operation, or a shared sense of purpose. For Grennan and Sperandio the
community partner consisted of members of the Bakery, Confectionery and Tobacco Workers' International Union of America Local No. 552. For Ericson and
Ziegler the community partner consisted of representatives from the Resident
Council of Ogden Courts Apartments. Being outsiders to the Chicago area, both
artist teams required the assistance of, even became dependent upon, Mary Jane
Jacob and the staff of Sculpture Chicago to provide local knowledge and access to

such specific community groups.[56] In the end, Sculpture Chicago was not only instrumental in forging these partnerships; it served as the indispensable mediator between the artists and the local groups, especially during periods of the artists' absence from Chicago (which was most of the time of their yearlong affiliations with "Culture in Action").[57]

The point of departure for these types of collaborative pairings is most often signaled by the artist's project proposal. More precisely, the dominant thematic concern of the project as defined by the artist, and interpreted by the curator and the sponsoring institution, sets into motion the search for the "right" match, the "right" community group that can best fulfill the particular goals of the project. For instance, Grennan and Sperandio's collaborative liaison with the candy-making union resulted from a long search by the artists and curator for an appropriate partner who could fulfill the artists' desire to produce an "interactive artwork involving a community of Chicago-area manufacturing employees in the development and

Simon Grennan, Christopher Sperandio, and the Bakery, Confectionery and Tobacco Workers' International Union of America Local No. 552, billboard design for *We Got It!*, 1993. (Photo by John McWilliams; courtesy Sculpture Chicago.)

marketing of a commercial product."[58] While Grennan and Sperandio conceded the need for further modifications to the project depending on the "specific nature and conditions of the hosting institution and workforce," the proposal specifically identified the outcome of the proposed collaboration—the production of a four-ounce chocolate bar, including its design and packaging.

In Ericson and Ziegler's case as well, the goals of the community collaboration, both in terms of material results and conceptual ambition, were established long before the engagement with any specific community group. In fact, in the preliminary outline for their project proposal dated June 14, 1992, months before a community partner was found, the artists described the overall configuration of the project in great detail.

> As we discussed our project still consists of creating a "color chart"
> in conjunction with a group of tenants from perhaps one or a few fed-
> erally funded housing projects around Chicago. . . . Our plan would
> be to work with this group of tenants over the next year and develop
> this chart with the convention of other paint charts in mind. It would
> be a usable paint chart, distributed in paint stores throughout the
> U.S. . . . The chart would deal with some specifics about federally
> funded housing, demographics, etc. It would of course hopefully
> raise issues that are of concern to the tenants but it would also ques-
> tion the validity and morals of the suburbs which these charts often
> cater to. . . . Anyway, the charts soul [sic] purpose will not be to sell
> paint and these details will work themselves out during our collabo-
> ration.[59]

Within this model of community interaction, the artists in effect specify their community partners—in the case of Ericson and Ziegler, "a group of tenants from . . . one or a few federally funded housing projects around Chicago." The curator and the sponsoring organization (here, Sculpture Chicago) function as middlemen in facilitating the partnership. The artists can either find themselves assigned to a certain community group by the sponsoring agency or be given a list of groups to choose from. Thus, contrary to the promotional rhetoric that describes community collaborations as the result of an organic and dialogical relationship between the artist and the community, representing a set of mutual interests at the origin of the collaboration, the overall structure, procedure, and goals of the projects, including their conceptualization, most often precede the engagement with any such community. Jacob has claimed, for example, that "unlike other exhibitions of site-specific installation artworks that have merited recent attention, this project ['Culture in Action'] is the result of a fundamental collaboration among participating artists, community residents and civic leaders. This collaborative process has to an unusual degree shaped the conception as well as the realization of these artists' projects, and has led to a new dialogue between the artist and audience for public art."[60] But it is clear, at least in the cases of Grennan and Sperandio and Ericson and Ziegler, that the conceptual framework of the projects was fully articulated prior to any conversations with potential collaborators; the community partners instead came to fill the predelineated blank spots within that framework. The contribution of the community partners, in other words, was limited to the realization of projects that fully prescribed the nature of their participation in advance.[61] Elaborating on this particular point, many critics of "Culture in Action," in fact, have charged some of the artists, Jacob, and Sculpture Chicago with exploitation, even abuse, of local community groups.[62]

It is important to note in this context that Grennan and Sperandio informally proposed several different projects as viable options to Jacob, each proposal involving a different type of community group. According to Sperandio, it was Jacob who made the final selection among the list of six possibilities, in effect determining the project for them as well as proactively defining the community partner and the type of social issue that would be addressed by the project (in this case, blue-collar labor politics). This is again in contrast to Jacob's claim that the community collaborations in "Culture in Action" emerged organically through the initiatives of the individual artists working without specific guidelines or intervention. She has stated many times that the defining characteristic of "Culture in Action," including its testing of interactive community collaborations as a new model of public art, came into being in response to artists' own interests in socially oriented art projects, and that she and Sculpture Chicago, acting as disinterested agents, merely accommodated the artists' wishes and followed their lead. However, correspondences and official paperwork concerning the early planning of "Culture in Action" reveal that this was not completely true. Jacob and Eva Olson (executive director of Sculpture Chicago) directed, even insisted on, certain types of collaborations as an important means to establish the exhibition's identity. They not only sought out artists who wanted to do community collaborations but played a central role in defining the nature of these collaborations.

Some view this kind of interaction between the artist and the curator/institution as a form of artistic collaboration in its own right (as Jacob continues to do).[63] And it certainly can be. But it can also be viewed as an example of the curator's increasing, though often unacknowledged, involvement in determining the parameters of an art project, a streamlining of the creative process that leaves the artist with what Mierle Laderman Ukeles has called the "curatorial assignment."[64] The fact that Sperandio was unwilling to divulge to the author the plans for other possible community collaborations "rejected" by Jacob, on the grounds that these proposals will likely be realized in other cities within the context of other exhibitions,[65] further reinforces the view that community "collaborations" are often artist-driven and curatorially directed. Despite the public foregrounding and rhetorical elevation of the community in the discourse, in such cases the specific community group seems to perform a relatively incidental role.

The exchange between Sculpture Chicago and Elaine Reichek, a New York-based artist who was approached for possible inclusion in "Culture in Action," helps clarify how the exhibition tried to define "community collaboration." Reichek's preliminary proposal, dated August 7, 1992, described a project in which she would produce a number of embroidered samplers and a set of bisque commemorative pots in an installation at the Chicago Historical Society. The content of the samplers and the pots was to highlight local Native American history, emphasizing the voices of Native American women, who would be contacted by the artist via conceptualizing and organizing) to the community partners' actual physical labor on the "production line." In any case, the incident with Reichek highlights Jacob's role in determining the type of collaborations that would be supported within the context of "Culture in Action," even if at times the rationale for her decisions seem vague and their results appear contradictory to her stated goals.

Invented Communities (Temporary)

The third model of community interaction, exemplified in Mark Dion's and Daniel J. Martinez's projects, is one in which a community group or organization is newly constituted and rendered operational through the coordination of the art work itself. Also quite prevalent in current community-based practices, such an approach imagines the art work in large part as the effort involved in forming such a community group around a set of collective activities and/or communal events as defined by the artist. In Dion's case, the interaction was more or less based on a conventional pedagogical or educational paradigm. His Chicago Urban Ecology Action Group, which convened on a weekly basis during the one-year period of the artist's commitment to "Culture in Action," was set up as an extracurricular educational program with two local high schools. Dion functioned as the teacher/team leader of this special environmental study group of twelve students, whose activities, including a field trip to Belize, became synonymous with Dion's own artistic production.

Similarly, Martinez coordinated a new community group around/as his project. Named the West Side Three-Point Marchers, the group was composed of a network of members from several existing community organizations from the West Side area of Chicago (including school groups, community and religious centers, theater groups, neighborhood arts centers) who gathered for the single purpose of planning, organizing, and performing in a one-time event that Martinez envisioned for them—a carnival-like parade through three West Side neighborhoods on June 19, 1993. (This was one of two projects Martinez completed for "Culture in Action.")

In contrast to Dion's, Martinez's role in relation to the West Side Marchers was more like that of an artistic director, delegating certain logistical (and some-a local facilitator (Carol Becker of the Chicago Historical Societ

discussions of their personal histories and their thoughts on tra

cal representations of their culture were to be the basis for the

in Reichek's installation.

Subsequently, attempts were made by Sculpture Chicag

ship between Reichek and a local Native American women's grc

Smith of the Native American Service College, but without succ

prisingly, the Native American women questioned Reichek's prc

suspicion, requesting the artist, if she was truly interested in the

more time with them on their turf to develop a more intimate rel

proceeding to represent them in her project. Reichek's proposa

the decision-making and "creative" parts of the installation (the

as well as the determination of the final form and the actual act c

pots and samplers) solely to herself, was deemed by Jacob and

to be at worst self-serving, and at best too inflexible to accommo

the potential community partners. Consequently, Reichek was di

pate in "Culture in Action" in September 1992. In a letter writter

Reichek around that time, the curator explained that the proposa

enough interaction between the artist and the community organi

precisely, it did not allow for a particular *kind* of interaction that '

wanted to sponsor. Jacob wrote, "It is essential to the exhibition

tion' that artists develop a work out of a community dialogue and

the 'creation' of these public works. At the moment, I feel like we

I admire your work but do not want to force a change when the id

executed by you alone."[66]

This early exchange with Reichek reveals the general am

ing the very idea of collaboration: does the "creation" of a work

physical labor of making an art object (or component parts to a l

event), or does it mean the conceptualization of a project? This c

mained unanswered even at the end of "Culture in Action." There

been an implicit division of labor in which the artist serves as the

Mark Dion and the Chicago Urban Ecology Action Group, *The Chicago Urban Ecology Action Group*, 1993.
(Photos by John McWilliams; courtesy Sculpture Chicago.)

times creative) duties to others, akin to Suzanne Lacy's mode of operation. Martinez's overall conception of the parade as a public event on the theme of immigration history and identity politics, within which local African American and Latino residents would represent themselves (to themselves), was the driving force behind the activities of the West Side Marchers, and this activity defined their group identity. The actual labor of forging the cooperative liaisons between the members of the various local organizations, however, was accomplished not by Martinez directly but by two local women, Angela Coleman and Elvia Rodriguez, residents of two key neighborhoods (one predominantly African American and the other predominantly Latino), who also oversaw the preparations for the actual parade itself. Whereas Dion conducted his classes more or less autonomously in response to the stated and perceived needs of the students, Martinez did not live in Chicago and had limited direct contact with the people who would be involved in his project. This meant that he was not only dependent on the institutional support of Sculpture Chicago to make the necessary contacts but was fully indebted to the sustained mediation of local insiders like Coleman and Rodriguez. These women's interpersonal skills, their familiarity with the residents of the neighborhood, and their willingness to cooperate with Martinez were all indispensable to the successful presentation of the artist's work.

Even more than projects that engage "sited" communities, those involving invented community groups such as these depend a great deal on the administrative and institutional intervention of the curator and sponsoring agency. Of course, the latter's intervention and support can open up unpredicted avenues for an artist to develop his/her project. Dion acknowledged this in a preliminary public statement about his project, for example:

> Why plan a project so complex that it spans several states and even
> countries and includes negotiating [with] organizations like The Be-
> lize Audubon Society, Arts International, The Brookfield Zoo, Provi-
> dence St. Mel and Lincoln Park High School, World Wildlife Fund,
> The Department of the Environment, The Mayan Indian community,

Daniel J. Martinez, VinZula Kara, and the West Side Three-Point Marchers (Los Desfiladores Tres Puntos del West Side), *Consequences of a Gesture*, 1993. (Photos by John McWilliams; courtesy Sculpture Chicago.)

The Parks Department, The Belize Zoo and Tropical Education Center, The Field Museum, and the airlines? Why—at least partially because I've got the Sculpture Chicago logistics team from hell behind
me and that knowledge has at least partially determined the realm of
possibility for the project's scope.[67]

But this means that the logistical support can also foreclose possibilities for
the project as well. Insofar as invented community groups are conceptually and financially dependent on the art project for their operation as well as their reason for
being, they have severely limited life spans; their meaning and social relevance are
circumscribed by its framework as well. Without the exhibition, their continuation
becomes untenable in most cases. Indeed, the groups that organized around Dion's
and Martinez's respective projects, while suggesting a model for potential development in the future (especially Dion's high school environmental study group), dissipated rather quickly at the close of "Culture in Action" in September 1993.

Invented Communities (Ongoing)

The fourth model of community interaction is an offshoot of the third, the difference
being in the community's sustainability beyond the exhibition context and its institutional support. Two projects in "Culture in Action," both (coincidentally?) by
Chicago-based artists, fit this category. Haha—the artist team of Richard House,
Wendy Jacobs, Laurie Palmer, and John Ploof—formed a volunteer group called
Flood, dedicated to the building and maintenance of a hydroponic garden for the
production and distribution of foods for AIDS patients. In addition, Flood transformed the storefront space in which the garden flourished into a kind of community center for AIDS education, networking with other health care organizations
around the city to program weekly discussion meetings, public lectures, and special events.

Iñigo Manglano-Ovalle networked with existing community organizations
and high school programs in his own predominantly Latino neighborhood in

Haha and Flood: A Volunteer Network for Active Participation in Healthcare, *Flood*, 1993. (Photos by John McWilliams; courtesy Sculpture Chicago.)

Chicago's West Side to form Street-Level Video. Composed of fifteen teenagers, Street-Level Video was set up in cooperation with a local public access television station and an after-school program as an ongoing video workshop in which participants would work with the artist in creating videos that represent their own lives and concerns. Their collaboration on the videos extended from conception, pre-production, and postproduction to exhibition and presentation. During the public viewing period of "Culture in Action," for instance, Manglano-Ovalle worked with the Street-Level Video kids to plan a block party that included an outdoor video installation. The project was conceived as a semieducational inner-city youth program, with an emphasis on developing the participants' video production skills. Manglano-Ovalle introduced theoretical questions into their creative process, focusing on the students' relationships to urban territorialism, identity politics, cultural representations of youth culture, and mainstream media.

In the cases of both Haha and Manglano-Ovalle, the auspices of "Culture in Action" only served as the means to newly organize a sustainable community organization. The framework of the exhibition program provided the impetus for the creation of neighborhood and volunteer alliances—Flood and Street-Level Video—and helped to establish their internal structures and identities, but had little impact on their operation both during the sponsorship of Sculpture Chicago and after its termination. In fact, during the exhibition run, Flood and Street-Level Video maintained far greater independence from Sculpture Chicago than did other projects. And in outliving "Culture in Action," they exceeded their given status as community-based public art projects: their meaning and value defied the specific art-oriented contextualization of the exhibition.

One of the key reasons for their sustainability was the artists' intimate and direct knowledge of their respective neighborhoods and those living in them. As long-time residents of Chicago and as members of local community groups themselves, Haha and Manglano-Ovalle approached their projects with a realistic (rather than a hypothetical) sense of possibilities. They relied on preexisting personal ties to many of those who became participants in their respective art projects. And since the artists' collaborative relationships to the community partners were based

Iñigo Manglano-Ovalle and Street-Level Video, *Tele Vecindario*, 1993. (Photos by John McWilliams; courtesy Sculpture Chicago.)

on friendships and neighborly familiarity, the groundwork for a sense of trust and a fluid, dialogical mode of communication was already in place. Haha and Manglano-Ovalle began, in other words, as insiders with what one critic has called a "home-team advantage."[68]

This advantage freed Haha and Manglano-Ovalle from the kind of institutional intervention or assistance that many of the other projects in "Culture in Action" required, including the need for intermediary, third-party insiders to communicate with the artists' respective community groups, especially in their absence. The advantage of continuous and consistent contact between the artist and the community group throughout the year allowed for greater trust among the participants, permitting improvisational and spontaneous reactions to changing circumstances around the project. Pragmatically speaking, these local artists were able to address daily problems and misunderstandings more quickly and collectively (not intermittently via long distance), better integrating the art project into the flow of the everyday life of the participants. Through such a relationship, the artists and the community groups enjoyed a greater sense of collective ownership of the project, predicated on their capacity to better control the processes of their collaboration, the unfolding development of the project, and their final public presentations.

However, sustaining these projects after the withdrawal of financial and institutional support from Sculpture Chicago was not an easy task. Haha and Flood had to relocate the garden with the expiration of their lease on the storefront space at the end of the summer of 1993, which had a profoundly destabilizing effect. They never fully recovered, although other volunteer activities besides the maintenance of the garden continued for many months. At the time of writing, there is talk of restarting the garden with the cooperation of a local church. Manglano-Ovalle and Street-Level Video had an easier transition thanks to the foresight of the artist. Typically, equipment such as cameras, television monitors, and editing machines are loaned to artists or art institutions by corporations for the duration of a public art program or event. Familiar with such arrangements, Manglano-Ovalle successfully negotiated *permanent* donations of equipment to found an operative, ongoing video production studio. With the necessary equipment in hand, the participants of Street-Level Video were able to continue their work after the conclusion of "Culture in Action." The project exists in 2002 as Street-Level Youth Media, incorporated since 1995 as a nonprofit arts organization in its own right, with some of the original participants from 1993 serving as codirectors.[69]

* * *

This is not to say that collaborations conducted by local artists are bound to be more successful or meaningful than those by artists from elsewhere, or that only local artists can create sustainable projects beyond the temporary framework of a public art program, or that sustainability in itself is intrinsically of greater merit. Certainly, the quality of the interpersonal exchanges between artists and their community partners cannot be measured in such terms. Neither can the value of non-collaborative efforts, which do not aspire to address social or political conditions directly. It is true that local artists have a head start in terms of their familiarity with their area of operation—its geographical configuration, its history, its available resources, its constituencies. But none of this guarantees the success of a community-based project, nor is a permanent project necessarily more effective or valuable than a temporary one. In many instances, it may be the outsider's perspective that provides the more cogent and incisive contribution or intervention into whatever community issues are at hand.

With the idea of an artist's "home-team advantage," site specificity reenters the discussion in a new way, as the sitedness of the artist becomes one of the central points of contention in community-based public art. For some critics, the success or failure of a community-based art project rests precisely on the artist's status as either a sited insider (= success) or an unsited outsider (= failure). But the process is far more complex than can be accounted for by such a formulaic reduction. To be sure, the artist's relationship to a group of people, a particular neighborhood, or a city plays a crucial role in the type of collaborations that are logistically and creatively possible. But in each case the particularity of this relationship—of the artist's connection to the area and its people through geographical ties or past personal experiences—strikes a different balance in the triangulation (of power) between the artist, the sponsoring institution, and the chosen community group.

When the artist is from out of town, the sponsoring institution serves as a matchmaker and mediator, becoming the primary source of information and guidance for the artist. Sponsoring institutions like Sculpture Chicago, and their representative in the figure of the curator or artistic director, make the initial effort to introduce the artist to the potential local partner organizations, articulating to the latter the probable benefits of an artistic collaboration.[70] Often such an effort translates into selling a particular artist to a particular community group (usually by emphasizing certain aspects of the artist's exhibition history and his/her area of artistic interest), and vice versa. Even after a good working relationship has been established between the artist and a partner group, the agency continues to function as the conduit between them, helping balance the wishes and needs of the artist and the capacities and desires of the community partner.

In the case of a local artist, the artist usually functions as the primary point of mediation between the sponsoring institution and the community partner.[71] Whereas outside artists are most often associated with the institution (both are seen as outsiders to the community), local artists are usually identified with the community. Sometimes an artist will readily take up the role of community spokesperson. In other cases, the artist will function as a translator between the cultural realms of the art world and the local community group, shuttling back and forth between the two: here the *artist* performs the task of introducing or selling the public art agency and its programming agenda to his/her community partner group, and vice versa. In doing so, the artist engages in an ongoing process of describing and enacting his/her allegiance and commitment, constructing and maintaining a dual identity (as artist here, as community member/representative there).

Such a situation can leave the artist with a sense of isolation and estrangement in that his/her identity cannot be fixed to either side (there is always a remainder). But this is not to romanticize the role of the artist as a lonely outcast or to presume that the community and the art world themselves have stable identities. In fact, the uncertainty of identity experienced by the artist is symptomatic of identities of all parties involved in the complex network of activities comprising community-based art, including the community, the curator, and the institution. And, of course, all subjects within this network are internally split or estranged as well, continuously negotiating a sense of identity and subjectivity through differential encounters with the other. But this does not foreclose the possibility of generative discussions between contemporary art and the needs and interests of nonart constituencies. In fact, this instability of identity and subjectivity can be the most productive source of such explorations. In the next chapter, we will review the most salient critiques posed to community-based public art in recent years to further explore the ambiguous discursive power of the "community."

THE (UN)SITINGS OF COMMUNITY

In the essay "The Artist as Ethnographer," Hal Foster critiques the ways in which contemporary art has absorbed certain methodological strategies from anthropology, and deconstructs the "collaborative" interaction between an artist and a local community group in ethnographic terms.[1] In his view, the artist is typically an outsider who has the institutionally sanctioned authority to engage the locals in the production of their (self-) representation. The key concern for Foster is not only the easy conversion of materials and experiences of local everyday life into an anthropological exhibit (as "cultural proxies," as he puts it), but the ways in which the authority of the artist goes unquestioned, often unacknowledged.[2] While noting the aesthetic and political importance of innovative artist-community collaborations that have the potential to "reoccupy lost cultural spaces and propose historical counter-memories," Foster warns that "*the quasi-anthropological role set up for the artist can promote a presuming as much as a questioning of ethnographic authority, an evasion as often as an extension of institutional critique.*"[3] For Foster, a vigilant reflexivity on the part of the artist is essential if such reversals are to be avoided, because, as he paraphrases French sociologist Pierre Bourdieu, "ethnographic mapping is predisposed to a Cartesian opposition that leads the observer to abstract the culture of study. Such mapping may thus confirm rather than contest the authority of mapper over site in a way that reduces the desired exchange of dialogical fieldwork."[4]

Some of the economic, social, and political consequences of such a reduction can be extrapolated from Foster's comments. Just as the desire to engage "real" (nonart) places can prepare the way for the conversion of abstract or derelict (non-)spaces into "authentic" and "unique" locales ripe for development and promotion,[5] so the engagement of "real" people in community-based art can install new forms of urban primitivism over socially neglected minority groups. The "other" of the dominant culture thus becomes objectified once again to satisfy the contemporary lust for authentic histories and identities. "Few principles of the ethnographic participant-observer are observed, let alone critiqued, and only limited engagement of the community is effected. Almost naturally the project strays from collaboration to self-fashioning, from a decentering of the artist as cultural authority to a remaking of the other in neo-primitivist guise."[6] In this way, Foster argues, community-based artists may inadvertently aid in the colonization of difference—for benevolent and well-intentioned gestures of democratization can have effects of colonialism, too—in which the targeting of marginalized community groups (serving as Third Worlds found in the First World) leads to their becoming both subject and coproducer of their own self-appropriation in the name of self-affirmation.

Critic Grant Kester also takes up the problematic of the "collaborative" interaction between the artist and local community groups, but along a different theoretical trajectory, in his essay "Aesthetic Evangelists: Conversion and Empowerment in Contemporary Community Art."[7] According to Kester, the position of the community artist is analogous to the status of the delegate as described by, again, Bourdieu in his work on political semiotics, where the delegate functions as the signifier for the referential community, constituency, or party.[8] Bourdieu's analysis challenges the apparent naturalness of the signifying relationship between the delegate, who chooses or is chosen to speak on the community's behalf, and the community itself. While the delegate derives his/her identity and legitimacy from the community, this community also comes into existence politically and symbolically through the expressive medium of the delegate. Hence, Bourdieu argues against the common assumption that the delegate is a passive reflection of a preexisting political formation.

Following this line of thought, Kester questions "the rhetoric of community artists who position themselves as the vehicle for an unmediated expressivity on the part of a given community."[9] One of the effects of such presumption, Kester argues, is a potentially abusive appropriation of the community for the consolidation and advancement of the artist's personal agenda, in the same way that the delegate "confirms and legitimates his or her political power through the act of literally representing or exhibiting the community itself, in the form of demonstrations and other political performances."[10] In a characterization far more severe than Foster's, Kester compares certain collaborative community artists to a self-serving delegate who "claims the authority to speak for the community in order to empower himself politically, professionally, and morally."[11]

But what looks to Foster like an artist's ethnographic self-fashioning, and to Kester like a morally problematic identification perpetrated by the community artist, is often the result of institutional intervention and pressure. That is, the kind of reductive and equalizing association drawn between an artist and a community group is not always the work of a self-aggrandizing, pseudo-altruistic artist but rather a fashioning of the artist by *institutional* forces. A case in point is artist Renée Green's 1992 exchange with Mary Jane Jacob and Sculpture Chicago. In March of that year, by invitation, Green made a preliminary visit to Chicago to discuss her possible participation in the "Culture in Action" exhibition. Before the visit, Jacob and Sculpture Chicago, without consulting with the artist, prepared a brief biography and a sketchy description of *possible* projects by her and used these as promotional material to engage community organizations that they felt might be suitable as collaborative partners for Green. Jacob and Sculpture Chicago's interpretation of the artist's background, experience, and interests overtly emphasized her African American identity and isolated inner-city race conflicts as her primary area of interest (thus, as the likely subject matter for her public art project).[12]

The itinerary for Green's two-day visit, set in advance by Jacob and Sculpture Chicago, further reinforced this identification of her with an as yet unnamed African American inner-city community. Green's visit to Chicago was meant to identify several community groups that might be interested in participating in a public art project, with Green in particular, and conversely a community group that would interest the artist in some kind of collaboration.[13] But the itinerary, which was based on the recommendations of a book called *Passports to Black Chicago,* placed the artist in what she felt were extremely prescriptive and overdetermined situations: tours of selected African American ghetto neighborhoods, meetings with representatives from local African American cultural organizations.[14] The artist realized fairly quickly that her interest in pursuing the architectural history of the city, especially the legacy of Frank Lloyd Wright and his Prairie School, as a possible topic for a public art project was not in concert with Jacob and Sculpture Chicago's exclusive focus on her as an African American artist and their desire for a project that would highlight issues of urban racial conflicts or history. This institutional projection led to a parting of ways between Green and Sculpture Chicago soon after the artist's visit to the city.[15]

In such an instance, Green's itinerary, biography, and project description (all authored by Sculpture Chicago) can be seen as the first step in the curatorial and institutional delimitation not only of the possible community partners for an artist but of the type of project that might be developed between them (especially in terms of the social issue that it would highlight). Based on this and similar experiences, Green has said, "In some instances the curator attempts to anticipate the work of the artist based on the history of the site, and the work and identity of the artist. Often when the artist visits the site the curator will suggest things having to do with communities: 'I think maybe you would like to do something on this neighborhood.' For example, Fort Greene in New York or Chicago's Southside, a black 'community,' or a site associated with slavery."[16] Which is to say that the matchmaking mediation of the sponsoring institution, inevitably motivated by the presumption of an artist's interests and the anticipation of a particular kind of collaborative project, often reduces, sometimes stereotypes, the identities of the artist *and* the community group.[17]

This is not to say that artists and community groups are innocent pawns in a conspiracy devised exclusively by curators and art institutions. The important fact is that, within the community-based art context, the interaction between an artist and a given community group is not based on a direct, unmediated relationship. Instead it is circumscribed within a more complex network of motivations, expectations, and projections among all involved. Thus Kester's and Foster's critiques of community artists need to be qualified by the recognition of the central role that institutions and exhibition programs play not only in delimiting the identities of those involved, but in determining the nature of the collaborative relationship between them.[18] Moreover, all these identities—artist, curator, institution, and community group—are in the process of continuous negotiation. At the very least, their respective roles and actions need to be understood in relation to one another.

Nonetheless, the political implications of Kester's argument in particular remain provocative, especially since his scenario is quite antithetical to the celebratory ones offered by supporters of such practices like Suzanne Lacy and Arlene Raven. For Kester, the cultural mobilization of the social "usefulness" of art (foundational to community-based art) and the rhetoric that accompanies it need to be understood within what he calls the "moral economy of capitalism" and the history of liberal urban reform. He insists, "This outpouring of compassion and concern over 'community'"—imagined by many critical cultural practitioners as a means to greater social justice and inclusive political and cultural processess—"must be understood in relation to the successful assimilation in the U.S. of conservative arguments about the underlying causes of poverty, social and cultural inequality, and disenfranchisement."[19]

Characterizing recent community-based art as a kind of "aesthetic evangelism," and likening the function of community artists to those of nineteenth-century reformers and social workers, Kester argues that the prevailing logic of community-based art reproduces a reformist ideology that, like Victorian-era evangelism, envisions personal inner transformation and growth as the key to the amelioration of social problems such as poverty, crime, homelessness, unemployment, and violence.[20] Flagging a statement by Hope Sandrow of the Artist and Homeless Collaborative—"the practice of creating art stimulates those living in shelters from a state of malaise to active participation in the artistic process"[21]—Kester points to the ways in which community artists who address social problems or engage economically, politically, and culturally marginalized groups in their work overemphasize the primacy of individual transformation as a measure of their project's (artistic) success.

While the power of intimate personal transformation cannot be underestimated, such a focus, in Kester's view, naturalizes social conditions of poverty, marginalization, and disenfranchisement as an extension of an individual's inherent character flaw (lack of initiative, diligence, inner resolve, moral rectitude, self-esteem, etc.). So that in facilitating the production of "empowering" and "spiritually uplifting" community (self-) portraits—variously poignant, heroic, strong, united—the community artist may legitimate the presumption that the cause of social problems rests with spiritually and culturally deprived individuals rather than with the systemic or structural conditions of capitalist labor markets, stratified social hierarchy, and uneven distribution of wealth and resources. In this way, community-based art can easily obscure the effects of the broader socioeconomic, political, and cultural forces, including art initiatives themselves, that render certain individuals and communities marginal, poor, and disempowered in the first place.

Despite the accuracy of some of Kester's assessments, his economically deterministic reading of community-based art has led to charges of oversimplification. Artist Martha Fleming has pointed out that what critical projects like Kester's are addressing is not so much the actual practice of community-based art but one discursive characterization of it, its commodification and promotion as "new public art" by a "professional-managerial class (PMC)—the critics and curators currently creating careers and fiefdoms for themselves by harnessing and bringing into the fold an artists' activity that has been threatening the institutions that employ them."[22] While conceding the importance of Kester's work in bringing class and historical analysis to bear on current community-based practices, Fleming accuses him of contributing to a discourse that homogenizes the complex activity of such practices, excluding not only artistic precedents but "the hesitancy and doubt experienced by many artists working in this field."[23] To Kester's various characterizations of community artists as vehicles for the implementation of a conservative economic agenda, as pawns in the machinations of dominant political ideology, as victims of their own "corrupt" desire for fame through servitude, Fleming counters:

> But not all of us will so easily be made into inexpensive marketing consultants for disenfranchised communities abandoned by the state, or take the rap for the failure of the welfare state. . . . In some cases our artistic practice has come out to meet our social activism.

In other cases, a sense of specific, personal identification with civil and human rights issues has nurtured our practice. . . .We are from inside the belly of the beast trying to be responsible for and to people and things seriously wronged and wrong, that need work all around us in our immediate environment.[24]

This exchange between Kester and Fleming in the pages of *Afterimage* throws into relief some of the fault lines within the discourse of community-based art. On the one hand, Kester points to the problem of overidentification, even disingenuous misidentification, of the artist with his/her community. In his account, the institutional agenda and the role of the curator tend to drop out, as already noted, and the artist emerges as the primary protagonist, either complicitous with or at the mercy of dominant economic and political agendas. In the meantime, community groups themselves, usually understood as victims of society, are typecast as having little or no agency (Kester characterizes them at one point as "atomized social detritus of late capitalism").[25] Even as he criticizes community artists for such typecasting, he does the same in his own analysis insofar as community groups remain passive, almost silent entities upon which artists ostensibly perform their transformative magic.

On the other hand, Fleming, in identifying with community-based groups and causes and in placing herself and her work outside the conventional art context—"in the belly of the beast" as she puts it—distances herself from critics and curators, whom she makes equally culpable agents of an authoritarian and exclusive art world ideology. She blames the practices of mainstream art institutions (museums, academia, criticism, the market) and their representatives (curators, historians, critics, dealers, collectors) for sustaining the agendas of the dominant culture and ignoring the efforts of artists like herself who would question or challenge it. Ironically, her argument casts community artists as victims (perennially ignored and unrewarded by an exclusive and commercially oriented art world), validating to some degree Kester's conclusions regarding the processes of (mis)identification and transference between the artist and marginalized community groups. It is perhaps not surprising that Fleming excludes the artist from the category of the professional-managerial class (PMC) with whom she obviously *dis*identifies. This seems willful, though, since it has become more and more evident in recent years to what extent artists function in administrative and managerial capacities in relation to, or as a form of, site-oriented, project-based art.[26]

*   *   *

Such complex geometries of identification, misidentification, and disidentification, as well as the accompanying reductivism and counterreductivism (if not recrimination), often obscure the central issue at hand, which is the discursive construction of the community itself. While the ethical dimensions of community-based art, in particular the nature of the interaction between the artist and the community, and the aesthetic and social merit of community-based art are debated at length, the notion of community is very much overlooked. Even in complex analyses such as Fleming's and Kester's, the operative definition of the community remains minimally articulated. Generally speaking, an unquestioned presumption designates the community as a group of people identified with each other by a set of common concerns or backgrounds, who are collectively oppressed by the dominant culture, and with whom, in the context of community-based art, artists and art agencies seek to establish a collaborative relationship (to address if not challenge this oppression).

To be fair, Kester does make an important distinction between preexisting, "politically-coherent" communities and those that are "created" through the delegate-artist for the fulfillment of an art project. In his view, a collaboration in the latter case tends to be fraught with paternalism, because the participants who make up the community are defined as "socially isolated individuals whose ground of interconnection and identification as a group is provided by an aesthetically ameliorative experience administered by the artist."[27] In contrast, collaborations with "politically-coherent" communities yield a more "equitable process of exchange and mutual education, with the artist learning from the community and having his or her own presuppositions (about the community and the specific social, cultural, and political issues) challenged and expanded."[28] According to Kester, self-determined identities of "politically-coherent" communities are derived from an ongoing collective process of internal debate and consensus formation around issues of common interest to their members. Defined primarily by shared cultural traditions and a shared sense of struggle against different modes of oppression (racist, sexist, classist, etc.), these communities are more resistant to appropriation and abuse by the artist and the art world.

There are several problems with this formulation. First, its identification of communities in terms of *prior* "coherence" discounts the ways in which artists can help engender different types of community. As I tried to show in the previous chapter, an art project can be an important catalyst for the development of new alliances and coalitions, however temporary (e.g., Iñigo Manglano-Ovalle and Street-Level Video, Haha and Flood, and to some degree Mark Dion and the Chicago Urban Ecology Group). Moreover, quite contrary to Kester's conclusions, many collaborative projects reveal the extent to which "coherent" communities are *more* susceptible to appropriation by artists and art institutions precisely because of the singular definition of their collective identities (e.g., Grennan and Sperandio and the candy-making union; Ericson and Ziegler and the resident group at Ogden Courts Apartments). In fact, certain types of community groups are now very often favored for artistic partnerships because of the easy correspondence between their identity and particular social issues. The practical benefits of such an approach for some artists as well as most sponsoring institutions (less ambiguity, more control over the process of collaboration, more predictability and easier projection of outcome, facility in promotion and instrumentalization) have already led to the popularization of newly bureaucratized and formulaic versions of community-based art: artist + community + social issue = new critical/public art.[29] In such circumstances, the identity of a community group comes to serve as the thematic content of the art work, representing this or that social issue in an isolated and reified way. In the process, the community itself can become reified as well.

Secondly, Kester's argument implicitly supports the essentialism that undergirds the frequently voiced belief that only local artists—from the community, from the neighborhood, from the city: that is, artists with a "home-team advantage"—are fit to conduct genuinely meaningful community-based work. Even though he insists on the need to understand the unity of a community as "the product of contingent processes of identification,"[30] when he categorizes two different types of communities and two corresponding collaborative results, one good and one bad, he argues in effect against the "authenticity" (thus, legitimacy or effectiveness) of a community that might be activated as a result of a collaborative art process. In so doing, he disallows the important ways in which an artistic intervention can productively reinvent or critique the very concept of a community.[31]

Kester's critical effort reflects the difficulties of defining an operative definition of the community in today's art context. Typically, the objectives and identity of a coherent community are seen as determined by its members before any encounter with outside individuals or groups, including community artists. Additionally, the community is primarily defined in opposition to the forces of an oppressive dominant culture that would regulate and defuse the efforts of those who seek greater participation in the existing social system.[32] This focus on the oppositional character of a community supports the habitual tendency among artists and art professionals to think of the "community" as a synonym for social groups of the marginal or underprivileged classes. It has become commonplace in public art to cast the community as the victimized yet resilient other that continuously tests the stability of prevailing sociopolitical and economic conditions. Such a conception of community also reinforces the classic Marxist view that refuses to acknowledge the ways in which the "oppression" by the dominant class can actually ensure the coherence of a minority group.

But as I argued in the previous chapter, the notion of community is equally available to neoconservative "activism" that defends actions, even violations, against underprivileged and disenfranchised minority groups.[33] This suggests that the "community," coveted in contemporary political, economic, social, and cultural discourses alike, is not bound to any particular class, gender, ethnicity, age group, religion, location, or even type of cause. Insofar as its invocation can serve a broad range of purposes, for the liberal left and the conservative right, and designate a wide array of group types, its rhetorical uses today are fraught with more ambiguity and flexibility than are accounted for by either advocates or critics of community-based art. Perhaps in recognition of this general problem, Kester recommends that community artists (critics, too?) should "address each case of artist/community interaction as a specific constellation of difference (subject of course to broader, more socially and culturally consistent trajectories of difference and privilege), that requires its own strategic response."[34] Martha Fleming also notes that "there are many different kinds of community, activism, audience, and public, and many different meanings for each of these words, and all must be examined in their particular, unique contexts."[35]

Certainly, the issue of difference is key to any understanding of identity formation, collective and otherwise. It is also an important key to understanding the possibilities and limitations of community-based art. But the concept of difference suggested by these authors reduces it to the idea of multiplicity of uniquenesses, indicating simply the acknowledgment of the existence of diverse particularities within contemporary society. That is, whether characterized as mostly inaccessible to anything beyond an exploitative appropriation by an artist (as in Kester's scenario), or as available to genuine collaboration that naturally extends an artist's realm of operation to the mutual benefit of all those involved (as in Fleming's), diverse particular communities seem fully formed entities, awaiting engagement from the outside. Though not altogether without political and artistic efficacy, such a conception of difference supports a temporal and spatial demarcation of community formation that renders communities into discrete social formations.

Political theorist Chantal Mouffe has called this conception "a closed system of differences,"[36] wherein difference is understood not as a process of continual identification/(mis)recognition and alienation/(mis)recognition intrinsic to the (self-) construction of identity and subjectivity—that is, as a complex relational process— but as a series of distinct social categories that can sometimes be held together by a broader unifying ideal (such as the People, the Nation, or Women, as was the case in Suzanne Lacy's *Full Circle* project for "Culture in Action"). Difference understood accordingly as variety of social and cultural categories is an underlying presumption of community-based art today, which seeks to become ever more in-clusive of this variety at the expense of a rigorous and self-critical examination of the primary driving force that seems to define the field—the *idealized specter* of community.[37]

*   *   *

The ideal of community, according to feminist social theorist Iris Marion Young, is a dream that "express[es] a desire for selves that are transparent to one another, rela-tionships of mutual identification, social closeness and comfort."[38] The strength and seductiveness of such a dream rests on its promise of a "good society" that can counter the experiences of alienation and disassociation (and the accompanying social problems) that characterize life in contemporary urban mass societies. But for Young the ideal of community is a highly problematic proposition, because it typically envisions "small, face-to-face, decentralized units" as the preferred scale of interaction for all social relations, which is impossible in a practical sense in our postindustrial mass urban societies—fundamentally a nostalgic fantasy of a pre-urban existence that is assumed to have been without alienation, mediation, or vio-lence. More importantly, the ideal of community is untenable to Young because it "privileges unity over difference, immediacy over mediation, sympathy over recog-nition of limits of one's understanding of others from their point of view."[39]

The ideal of community, in her view, is predicated on an ideal of shared or fused subjectivities in which each subject's unified coherence is presumed to be not only transparent to him/herself but identically transparent to others.[40] Such fan-tasies of transparent, unmediated, and transcendent knowing, Young notes, partici-pate in the "metaphysics of presence" or "logic of identity" (theorized by Theodor Adorno and Jacques Derrida) that overlooks difference between subjects and denies difference as a constitutive element in the process of subject formation. Moreover, "the desire for social wholeness and identification" through mutual affirmation, closeness, and reciprocity as expressed in the ideal of community ob-scures the extent to which it "generates borders, dichotomies, and exclusions."[41] As such, the community ideal partakes of the "same desire for social wholeness and identification that underlies racism and ethnic chauvinism on the one hand and political sectarianism on the other."[42] In short, the ideal of community finds comfort in the neat closure of its own homogeneity.

Toward the conclusion of her argument, Young remarks that it may be politically expedient to drop the term "community" altogether in favor of "a politics of difference." Unfortunately, and surprisingly, she does not push the concept of a "politics of difference" any farther than "social relations that embody openness to unassimilated otherness with justice and appreciation."[43] Her proposal remains simply a call for greater tolerance of differently identified social groups—a proposal for an "unoppressive" society "without domination in which persons live together in relations among strangers with whom they are not in community."[44] As if abandoning the finer points of her own deconstructive analysis, she ends with a plea that basically amounts to "let's all get along." Difference, described initially as a socially mediated work in process, returns to a stable and fixed identity.[45]

Nonetheless, aspects of Young's critique of the ideal of community—its reliance on unified subjects, its assumption of a transparency of identity and subjectivity (i.e., self-presence), its fortification of a homogeneous group formation through the repression of difference, etc.—remain very useful in unpacking some of the hidden premises of community-based art. In fact, all the projects in our case study "Culture in Action" are infected to varying degrees by the kinds of presumptions that Young critiques. For instance, when Mary Jane Jacob and Sculpture Chicago presumed an automatic affinity between Renée Green and the African American inner-city cultural organizations of Chicago, the presumption was based on the belief that the artist's heritage, her African American racial identity, would facilitate, if not guarantee, a direct and authentic point of identification between the artist and the community. Whether the point of unity and mutual identification between artist and community group was imagined to be race and gender identity (Suzanne Lacy's rock commemorations to women, Daniel Martinez's parade through Latino and black neighborhoods, Iñigo Manglano-Ovalle's street-level video program with Latino gang members and "at-risk" youth), or shared interest in a particular social issue, such as workers' rights (Grennan and Sperandio's *We Got It!* candy bar), home and housing (Ericson and Ziegler's *Eminent Domain* paint chart), health care and AIDS activism (Haha and Flood's storefront garden), or ecological conservation (Mark Dion and the Chicago Urban Ecology Group), "Culture in Action" promoted a kind of reductive identification between the "collaborators" throughout its programming.

This is a typical essentializing process in community-based art: the isolation of a single point of commonality to define a community—whether a genetic trait, a set of social concerns, or a geographical territory—followed by the engineering of a "partnership" with an artist who is presumed to share this point of commonality. A logic of transparency based on the presumption of unified subjects guides such programming. The resulting collaborative art project based on this reduced point of identification or affiliation is then presented as conveying the identity of the community itself. Put another way, the identity that is *created* by the art project is viewed as a self-affirming, self-validating "expression" of a unified community (of which the artist ostensibly is now an integral part), as if the community or any collective group (or any individual subject) could be fully self-present and able to communicate its self-presence to others with immediacy. What remain invisible in the process are the mediating forces of the institutional and bureaucratic frameworks that direct such productions of identity, and the extent to which the identity of such institutional forces are themselves in continuous process of (re)articulation.

For some artists, the institutional and bureaucratic frameworks that rationalize and instrumentalize the collective experience in community-based art make it an unacceptable mode of practice for anyone interested in challenging the dominant social order. Beyond the difficulty of defining the term "community," the problem for artists like Critical Art Ensemble (CAE) lies in the impossibility of forging a collaborative affiliation based on truly nonrational aspects of human interaction, such as friendship, faith, trust, and love, within the existing models of community-based practice. CAE puts it this way:

Assuming that an artist has successfully navigated the cultural

bureaucracy and acquired money for a community project . . . just
how will s/he insinuate h/erself into a "community"? The easiest way
is to have the project mediated by a bureaucracy that claims to represent the community. A school, a community center, a church, a
clinic, etc., is then selected, often because it is willing to participate
in the project. The bureaucratic experts from the selected institution
will represent the community and tailor the project to their specifica-
tions in a negotiation that also accounts for the desires of the artist.
When the process is over, who has actually spoken? Since the majority of the negotiation over *policy* is not done with individuals in the
territory, but with those who claim to represent it, which is again
shaped by the bureaucratic parameters placed on the project by the
money donors, how much direct autonomous action is left? How
much dialogue has taken place? Not much. What is left is the representation of a representation (the bureaucratic opinion of the artist
and h/is mediators).[46]

CAE's negative assessment of community-based art allows no qualifications: "Artworks which depend on bureaucracy in order to come to fruition (i.e., institutionally
sanctioned public art including community-based art) are too well managed to
have any contestational power. In the end they are acts of compliance that only reaffirm hierarchy and the rational order."[47]

CAE's position, while not without its own brand of avant-gardist romanticism
regarding the place and mode of "resistant" critical art practice,[48] expresses a central complication plaguing community-based art: the conversion of attempts at a
participatory model of art practice, engaging local concerns and people, into yet
another form of acquiescence to the powers of capital and the state. Indeed CAE's
characterization of this process is not altogether an exaggeration. But to abandon
the entire enterprise in the belief that artists have no way out—because every attempt will end in falsehood and complicity—is perhaps prematurely defeatist.

Without doubt, artists, critics, curators, art institutions, and funding organi-

zations are pressured today to think and act as if communities exist as coherent social entities awaiting outreach. The field continues to covet images of coherence,
unity, and wholeness as the ideal representation of a community. (In a sense, the
shift in focus from public spaces to local cultures has not displaced the ideology of
unity that has prevailed in [public] art over the past three decades.) While such an
outlook contributes to some expansion of art audiences, strengthening the tie between elite cultural institutions and local constituencies normally disengaged from
their activities, its effects also include the reification and colonization of marginal,
disenfranchised social groups, as well as the concomitant reification and commodification of local cultures. Furthermore, as some artists have noticed, community-
based art can function as a kind of "soft" social engineering to defuse, rather than
address, community tensions and to divert, rather than attend to, the legitimate dissatisfaction that many community groups feel in regard to the uneven distribution of
existing cultural and economic resources. Additionally, according to artist Iñigo
Manglano-Ovalle, there "is a growing and disturbing similarity between initiatives
such as community policing and [community-based] cultural programs," both motivated at times by a paranoiac fear of social upheaval.[49] Which is to say, community-
based art "on the streets," despite the "real-life" siting, serves a disciplinary
purpose just as do art museums.

As the artistic, political, and ethical pitfalls of community-based art become
more visible and more theorized, the need to imagine alternative possibilities of to-
getherness and collective action, indeed of collaboration and community, becomes
more pronounced. Even to begin thinking about these alternatives, however, requires a major reconceptualization of the "community." French philosopher Jean-
Luc Nancy has defined some guidelines for such an endeavor: "there is no
communion, there is no common being, but there is being *in* common";[50] "the
question should be the community of being and not the being of community."[51] In
Nancy's overall project, according to George Van Den Abbeele, "community is
neither a community of subjects, nor a promise of immanence, nor a communion of
individuals in some higher or greater totality. . . . It is not, most specifically, the

product of any work or project; it is *not* work, not a product of projected labor, nor an *oeuvre,* but what is un-worked, *dés-oeuvré.*"[52]

The challenge, then, is to figure out a way beyond and through the impossibility of community.[53] This is not to invoke a transcendent plateau from which one will find a new synthetic resolution free of contradictions. Quite the contrary, it is meant to suggest the impossibility of total consolidation, wholeness, and unity—in an individual, a collective social body like the "community," or an institution or discipline—and, perhaps more importantly, to suggest that such an impossibility is a welcome premise upon which a *collective artistic praxis,* as opposed to "community-based art," might be theorized.[54]

Community-based art, as we have seen, is typically understood as a *descriptive* practice in which the community functions as a referential social entity. It is an other to the artist and the art world, and its identity is understood to be immanent to itself, thus available to (self-) expression. The degree of success of an art project of this kind is measured in relation to the extent to which these (self-) expressions, as signifiers of community identity, affirm rather than question the notion of a coherent collective subject. The mirage of this coherence, fortified by the fact that the representation of the community is ostensibly produced with or by the same, is consumed as authenticity.

In contrast, collective artistic praxis, I would suggest, is a *projective* enterprise. It involves a provisional group, produced as a function of specific circumstances instigated by an artist and/or a cultural institution, aware of the effects of these circumstances on the very conditions of the interaction, performing its own coming together and coming apart as a necessarily incomplete modeling or working-out of a collective social process.[55] Here, a coherent representation of the group's identity is always out of grasp. And the very status of the "other" inevitably remains unsettled, since contingencies of the negotiations inherent in collaborative art projects—between individuals within the group, between the group and various "outside" forces—would entail the continuous circulation of such a position. Such a praxis also involves a questioning of the exclusions that fortify yet threaten the group's own identity.

some sociologists prefer).[10] These processes, in turn, exasperate the sense of placelessness in contemporary life.

But unlike Lefebvre, who provides the deepest dialectical consideration of the "production of space" (his phrase), Lippard seems unable to resist the nostalgic impulse. In the end, the task of a progressive oppositional cultural practice is conceived as a retrieval and resuscitation of a lost sense of place. Her project implicitly calls for a slower, more sedentary mode of existence. Despite her disclaimers, hers is a vision that favors the "return" to a vernacular, nonurban sociality of small-scale spaces and face-to-face exchanges.[11] Not that such a vision isn't appealing. The problem may be that it is all too appealing, not only to us individually but to the machinations of capitalism itself.

What Lippard's thinking misses are Lefebvre's important insights on the *dialectical* rather than oppositional relationship between the increasing abstraction of space and the "production" of particularities of place, local specificity, and cultural authenticity—a concern that informs many site-oriented art practices today. Production of difference, to say it in more general terms, is itself a fundamental activity of capitalism, necessary for its continuous expansion. One might go so far as to say that this desire for difference, authenticity, and our willingness to pay high prices for it only highlight the degree to which they are already lost to us (thus the power they have over us).

A contrary position to Lippard's advocacy of place-bound identity celebrates the nomadic condition. Often leaning on Gilles Deleuze and Félix Guattari for theoretical support, some critics have championed the work of certain artists for having abandoned the phenomenologically oriented mode of site-specific art (best exemplified by Richard Serra's sculptures). Moving beyond the inherited conception of site-specific art as a grounded, fixed (even if ephemeral), singular event, the work of artists such as Andrea Fraser, Mark Dion, Renée Green, and Christian Philipp Müller, among many others, is seen to advance an altogether different notion of a site as predominantly an intertextually coordinated, multiply located, discursive field of operation.

This is the reading, for example, of James Meyer, who coined the term "functional site" to distinguish recent site-oriented practices from those of the past.[12] This conceptual shift has embraced the idea of meaning as an open, unfixed constellation, porous to contingencies—an idea that most of us accept and welcome. But in the process, the idea of the fluidity of meaning has tended to get conflated or confused with the idea of fluidity of identities and subjectivities, even of physical bodies, to such an extent that a certain romanticism has accrued around the image of the cultural worker on the go. Not only is the art work not bound to the physical conditions of a place anymore, but the artist-subject is "liberated" from any enduring ties to local circumstances. Qualities of permanence, continuity, certainty, groundedness (physical and otherwise) are thought to be artistically retrograde, thus politically suspect, in this context. By contrast, uncertainty, instability, ambiguity, and impermanence are taken as desired attributes of a vanguard, politically progressive artistic practice. But I remain unconvinced of the ways a model of meaning and interpretation is called forth to validate, even romanticize, the material and socioeconomic realities of an itinerant lifestyle. I am suspicious of this analogical transposition and the seductive allure of nomadism it supports, if for no other reason than the fact of my own personal ambivalence toward the physical and psychical experiences of mobilization and destabilization that such nomadism demands. To embrace such conditions is to leave oneself vulnerable to new terrors and dangers. At the very least, we have to acknowledge this vulnerability.[13]

I want to remember in this context a particular lesson of a "wrong" place described by novelist Don DeLillo in his recent two-act play *Valparaiso* (1999).[14] In the play, the protagonist, Michael Majeski, an average middle-class businessman (assumed to be white), on an ordinary business trip to Valparaiso, Indiana, ends up in another part of the world in Valparaiso, Chile, presumably by mistake, and then has to confront his own minor media celebrity on his return home. Majeski's extraordinary misadventure of falling off the track of his set itinerary and ending up in the wrong place (which isn't to say that he gets lost) is the starting point for DeLillo's fictional critique of the postmodern condition, in which the disruption of a subject's habitual spatiotemporal experience propels the liberation and also the breakdown of its traditional sense of self.

The play begins with Majeski recently returned from the unintended destination of his trip, the wrong Valparaiso in Chile (there are four Valparaisos in the world, so far as I am aware). Upon his return, he is confronted with numerous requests by the media—radio, television, newspapers, magazines, documentary filmmakers—to recount his experience. It is a great human interest story, after all: we all want to know what happened. How could anyone make such a big mistake? Didn't he notice that he was headed for the wrong city? When did he notice? Why was he going to Valparaiso in the first place? What happened exactly? Who is Michael Majeski? What was he like as a child? What are his dreams? Does he love his wife? Submitting to such questions, he does 67 interviews in four and a half days in three and a half cities (at least we are told so by his wife), forced to repeat his narrative over and over in front of microphones and cameras, simultaneously constructing and confessing his identity and life history, including his struggles with alcoholism and the drunken car accident that disabled his only son.

With most of the scenes set in talk show "living rooms," DeLillo's primary concern is clearly the omnipresence of broadcast technology as an organizing force in our lives and minds. Indeed the collapse of traditional spatial and temporal modalities, and the fragmentation, discontinuity, and intensities presented by new modalities, are conveyed by the characters primarily through their use of language. The dialogue is full of truncated hesitations, random misfires, incomplete thoughts, and broken repetitions, as if the characters aren't really speaking to one another but through and past each other. Their disjunctive conversations sound more like a set of uncoordinated soundtracks. Their words do not constitute even a monologue in that there are no real listeners, not even an inner self. Everyone speaks to, and answers to, an invisible ear, one that belongs to a phantom body of a televisual public.[15]

The fractured nature of DeLillo's language is not unlike that of Fredric Jameson's "schizophrenic" postmodern subject who, in the throes of an overwhelmingly intense or traumatic present, is unable to make coherent sense in any recognizable, conventional manner due to an utter breakdown of the basic temporality of narrative continuity.[16] But DeLillo's play has much to say on spatial issues, too, even if only implicitly. First, the space of our public conversations is now fully circumscribed by the camera or the media: life is footage waiting to be shot. Experience is not real unless it is recorded and validated through media representation. It is in this mediated virtual space that "we talk to each other today. This is the way we tell each other things, in public, before listening millions, that we don't dare to say privately."[17]

Secondly, spatial experience, like the broken temporality of language, is discontinuous and creepily disembodied. The words do not reach deep, they collage fleeting fragmentary impressions, and vision does not (cannot) distinguish between what is seen and the mediation of that scene. For example, Majeski describes the beginning of his journey to an interviewer: "I'm watching the takeoff on live video. I'm on the plane, I'm in my seat. There's a monitor on the bulkhead. I look at the monitor and the plane is taking off. I look out the window and the plane is taking off. Then what. The plane is taking off outside the cabin and the plane is taking off inside the cabin. I look at the monitor, I look at the earth."[18]

Thirdly, it is important to remember that the plot of the play is premised on an instance of locational misrecognition, on a character's temporarily losing his way in the world. How does this happen? Majeski leaves his house early in the morning to board a plane to Chicago. From there, he is to be picked up and driven to Valparaiso, Indiana, some forty miles away. But at the airport, the ticket counter attendant notices a discrepancy between his ticket (for Chicago) and his printed itinerary (for Miami). She tries to be helpful and finds him a seat on the Miami flight, about to take off; even though he was fully prepared for the Chicago flight, Majeski, not wanting to be discourteous to the attendant, makes a quick nondecision to head for Valparaiso, Florida, via Miami. Once in Miami, instead of boarding a chartered plane for this second Valparaiso, he somehow ends up on an international flight to Santiago, headed for Valparaiso, Chile. Details remain vague.

Majeski recalls the experience on a television talk show:

Yes. It was strange. The aircraft seemed too big, too wide-bodied for an intrastate flight. . . . And I said nothing. I was intimidated by the systems. The enormous sense of power all around me. Heaving and breathing. How could I impose myself against this force? The electrical systems. The revving engines. . . . The sense of life support. The oxygen in the oxygen masks. . . . I felt submissive. I had to submit to the systems. They were all-powerful and all-knowing. If I was sitting in this assigned seat. Think about it. If the computers and metal detectors and uniformed personnel and bomb-sniffing dogs had allowed me to reach this assigned seat and given me this airline blanket that I could not rip out of its plastic shroud, then I must belong here. That's how I was thinking at the time.[19]

Majeski ends up in Chile not out of absentmindedness but because he recognizes a hitherto unknown logic of belonging, a sense of belonging that is not bound to any specific location but to a system of movement. Majeski does not resist the ways in which bodies are channeled through the sky along the prescribed trajectories of commercial air travel. He believes in its intimidating logic, has faith in its procedures, respects its timetables. He attributes almost mystical powers to the system. He might have ended up in the wrong city, but, in a sense, he was in the right place all along. So that when he reaches Santiago, fully aware of his mistake, it no longer matters how far he has strayed. He is calm. Instead of turning back, he is convinced to *complete* his mistake, to go all the way to Chile's Valparaiso. "For the beauty and balance. The formal resolution."[20] (Indeed, had Michael Majeski been an artist and his trip an art project, I would have been moved to think it a brilliant critique of site specificity.)

Often we are comforted by the thought that a place is ours, that we belong to it, even come from it, and therefore are tied to it in some fundamental way. Such places ("right" places?) are thought to reaffirm our sense of self, reflecting back to us an unthreatening picture of a grounded identity. This kind of continuous relationship between a place and a person is what many critics declare to be lost, and needed, in contemporary society. In contrast, the "wrong" place is generally thought of as a place where one feels one does not belong—unfamiliar, disorienting, destabilizing, even threatening. This kind of stressful relationship to a place is, in turn, thought to be detrimental to a subject's capacity to constitute a coherent sense of self and the world.

Thanks to the perfection and formal beauty of Majeski's mistake, we can think about the "wrong" place in altogether new ways. Rather than his "losing himself" because he ends up in the wrong place, quite the opposite seems to happen in *Valparaiso*. Finding himself in an airplane headed for the wrong city, Majeski begins to recognize himself, or more precisely the conditions of his own estrangement, and is set on a journey to account for his identity. In the telling and retelling of the tale, his rather tragic and fractured sense of self is revealed not only to us, the audience, but to the character himself. It is the wrongness rather than rightness of place that brings Majeski into focus. As the play progresses, it become less and less clear whether Majeski was trapped in a journey headed for the wrong place or the trip was in fact an attempt to *escape from* a wrong place—his home, his job, his marriage, his family, his life, himself. An encounter with a "wrong" place is likely to expose the instability of the "right" place, and by extension the instability of the self. The price of such awakening is steep, however, as the concluding scenes of the play reveal. Suffice it to say that Majeski's psychological unmooring as a result of his trip both liberates and shatters him.

*   *   *

It seems historically inevitable that we will leave behind the nostalgic notion of a site and identity as essentially bound to the physical actualities of a place. Such a notion, if not ideologically suspect, is at least out of sync with the prevalent description of contemporary life as a network of unanchored flows. Even an advanced theoretical position like Frampton's critical regionalism seems dated in this regard; for it is predicated on the belief that a particular site/place, with its identity-giving or identifying properties, exists always and already *prior* to whatever new cultural forms might be introduced to it or emerge from it. In such a pre- (or post-) poststructuralist conception, all site-specific gestures would have to be understood as reactive, cultivating what is presumed to be there already rather than generating new identities and histories.

Indeed, the deterritorialization of the site has produced liberating effects, displacing the strictures of place-bound identities with the fluidity of a migratory model, introducing possibilities for the production of multiple identities, allegiances, and meanings, based not on normative conformities but on the nonrational convergences forged by chance encounters and circumstances. The fluidity of subjectivity, identity, and spatiality as described by Deleuze and Guattari in their rhyzomatic nomadism,[21] for example, is a powerful theoretical tool for the dismantling of traditional orthodoxies that would suppress differences, sometimes violently.

Despite the proliferation of discursive sites and fictional selves, however, the phantom of a site as an actual place remains, and our psychic, habitual attachment to places regularly returns as it continues to inform our sense of identity. This persistent, perhaps secret adherence to the actuality of places (in memory, in longing) may not be a lack of theoretical sophistication but a means of survival. The resurgence of violence in defense of essentialized notions of national, racial, religious, and cultural identities in relation to geographical territories is readily characterized as extremist, retrograde, and uncivilized. Yet the loosening of such relations, that is, the destabilization of subjectivity, identity, and spatiality (following the dictates of desire), can also be described as a compensatory fantasy in response to the intensification of fragmentation and alienation wrought by a mobilized market economy (following the dictates of capital). The advocacy of the continuous mobilization of self- and place identities as discursive fictions, as polymorphous critical plays on fixed generalities and stereotypes, in the end may be a delusional alibi for short attention spans, reinforcing the ideology of the new—a temporary antidote for the anxiety of boredom. It is perhaps too soon and frightening to acknowledge, but the paradigm of nomadic selves and sites may be a glamorization of the trickster ethos that is in fact a reprise of the ideology of "freedom of choice"—the choice to forget, the choice to reinvent, the choice to fictionalize, the choice to "belong" anywhere, everywhere, and nowhere. This choice, of course, does not belong to everyone equally. The understanding of identity and difference as being culturally constructed should not obscure the fact that the ability to deploy multiple, fluid identities in and of itself is a privilege of mobility that has a specific relationship to power.

What would it mean now to sustain the cultural and historical specificity of a place (and self) that is neither a simulacral pacifier nor a willful invention? For architecture, Frampton proposes a process of "double mediation," which is in fact a double negation, *defying* "both the optimization of advanced technology and the ever-present tendency to regress into nostalgic historicism or the glibly decorative."[22] An analogous double mediation in site-specific art practice might mean finding a terrain between mobilization and specificity—to be *out* of place with punctuality and precision. Homi Bhabha has said, "The globe shrinks for those who own it; for the displaced or the dispossessed, the migrant or refugee, no distance is more awesome than the few feet across borders or frontiers."[23]

Thus, it is not a matter of choosing sides—between models of nomadism and sedentariness, between space and place, between digital interfaces and the handshake. Rather, we need to be able to think the range of the seeming contradictions and our contradictory desires for them together; to understand, in other words, seeming oppositions as *sustaining* relations. How do we account, for instance, for the sense of soaring exhilaration and the anxious dread engendered by the new fluidities and continuities of space and time, on the one hand, and their ruptures and disconnections on the other? And what could this doubleness of experience mean in our lives? in our work? Today's site-oriented practices inherit the task of demarcating the *relational specificity* that can hold in dialectical tension the distant poles of spatial experience described by Bhabha. This means addressing the uneven conditions of adjacencies and distances *between* one thing, one person, one place, one thought, one fragment *next* to another, rather than invoking equivalences via one thing *after* another. Only those cultural practices that have this relational sensibility can turn local encounters into long-term commitments and transform passing intimacies into indelible, unretractable social marks—so that the sequence of sites that we inhabit in our life's traversal does not become genericized into an undifferentiated serialization, one place after another.

Gabriel Orozco, *Isla dentro de la isla (Island into the Island)*, 1992. (Courtesy Marian Goodman Gallery, New York.)

NOTES

INTRODUCTION

1 The two concurrent exhibitions organized in conjunction with the 1996 Olympic Games in Atlanta, Georgia, are good examples of the confusing uses of the term "site specificity" in contemporary art discourse. The exhibitions were "Rings," a thematic show structured around the "five universal emotions symbolically related to the number of the Olympic rings," and "Picturing the South: 1860 to the Present," a photography exhibition with a regional focus on the history and culture of the American South, especially Atlanta. In the press release for the exhibitions, Ned Rifkin, Director of the High Museum of Art in Atlanta, promoted the former rather than the latter as a site-specific exhibition. In this case, despite the universalizing theme of "Rings," its temporal coordination with the Olympic Games would seem to trump the geographical specificity of "Picturing the South."

2 These terms are used rather loosely and interchangeably in current art discourse. The concept of debate specificity, however, was coined in the 1970s by Mary Kelly to describe her move away from the prevailing dominance of concerns for medium specificity in art discourse. See her comments in her interview with Douglas Crimp in *Mary Kelly* (London: Phaidon Press, 1997), 15. Kelly's debate specificity corresponds to the notion of discursive sites that I develop in chapter 1.

3 In addition to a few articles, three recent books begin to address this problem: Julie H. Reiss, *From Margin to Center: The Spaces of Installation Art* (Cambridge: MIT Press, 1999); Nick Kaye, *Site-Specific Art: Performance, Place, and Documentation* (London: Routledge, 2000); and Erika Suderburg, ed., *Space, Site, Intervention: Situating Installation Art* (Minneapolis: University of Minnesota Press, 2000). Much work remains, however, in historicizing and theorizing site-specific art, as distinct from installation art.

4 I borrow this concept from William Pietz, who characterized the "fetish" as such a "problem-idea."

5 Rosalyn Deutsche, *Evictions: Art and Spatial Politics* (Cambridge: MIT Press, 1996), xi.

6 Ibid. See especially chapter two, "Uneven Development: Public Art in New York City."

7   The term is borrowed from Hal Foster's essay "The Un/making of Sculpture," in Russell
      Ferguson, Anthony McCall, and Clara Weyergraf-Serra, eds., *Richard Serra: Sculpture
      1985–1998* (Los Angeles and Göttingen, Germany: Museum of Contemporary Art and Steidl
      Verlag, 1998).

8   See Suzanne Lacy, ed., *Mapping the Terrain: New Genre Public Art* (Seattle: Bay Press, 1995).

9   See Bruce Robbins, ed., *The Phantom Public Sphere* (Minneapolis: University of Minnesota
      Press, 1993).

10   Fredric Jameson, *Postmodernism, or, the Cultural Logic of Late Capitalism* (Durham: Duke
      University Press, 1991).

11   Lucy Lippard, *The Lure of the Local: Senses of Place in a Multicultural Society* (New York: New
      Press, 1997).

12   Kenneth Frampton, "Towards a Critical Regionalism," in Hal Foster, ed., *The Anti-Aesthetic:
      Essays on Postmodern Culture* (Port Townsend, Wash.: Bay Press, 1983).

13   Michel de Certeau, *The Practice of Everyday Life* (Minneapolis: University of Minnesota Press,
      1984).

14   Henri Lefebvre, *The Production of Space,* trans. Donald Nicholson-Smith (1974; Oxford and
      Cambridge: Blackwell, 1991).

1

1   Douglas Crimp has written: "The idealism of modernist art, in which the art object *in
      and of itself* was seen to have a fixed and transhistorical meaning, determined the
      object's placelessness, its belonging in no particular place, a no-place that was in
      reality the museum. . . . Site specificity opposed that idealism—and unveiled the mate-
      rial system it obscured—by its refusal of circulatory mobility, its belongingness to a
      specific site." Douglas Crimp, *On the Museum's Ruins* (Cambridge: MIT Press, 1993), 17.
      See also Rosalind Krauss, "Sculpture in the Expanded Field" (1979), in Hal Foster, ed.,
      The Anti-Aesthetic: Essays on Postmodern Culture (Port Townsend, Wash.: Bay Press,
      1983), 31–42.

2   William Turner, British sculptor, as quoted by Mary Miss in "From Autocracy to
      Integration: Redefining the Objectives of Public Art," in Stacy Paleologos Harris, ed.,

Insights/On Sites: Perspectives on Art in Public Places (Washington, D.C.: Partners for Livable Places, 1984), 62.

3   Rosalyn Deutsche has made an important distinction between an assimilative model of site specificity—in which the art work is geared toward *integration* into the existing environment, producing a unified, "harmonious" space of wholeness and cohesion— and an interruptive model in which the art work functions as a critical *intervention* in the existing order of a site through some sort of disruption. See her essays "*Tilted Arc* and the Uses of Public Space," *Design Book Review* 23 (Winter 1992): 22–27; and "Uneven Development: Public Art in New York City," *October* 47 (Winter 1988): 3–52. For more on this distinction in the context of public art, see chapter 3.

4   Michael Fried, "Art and Objecthood" (1967), in Gregory Battcock, ed., *Minimal Art: A Critical Anthology* (New York: Dutton, 1968), 116–147.

5   Robert Barry in Arthur R. Rose (pseud.), "Four Interviews with Barry, Huebler, Kosuth, Weiner," *Arts Magazine* (February 1969): 22.

6   Richard Serra, letter to Donald Thalacker dated January 1, 1985, as published in Clara Weyergraf-Serra and Martha Buskirk, eds., *The Destruction of Tilted Arc: Documents* (Cambridge: MIT Press, 1991), 38. See chapter 3 for more on the *Tilted Arc* controversy.

7   Richard Serra, "*Tilted Arc* Destroyed," *Art in America* 77, no. 5 (May 1989): 34–47.

8   The controversy over *Tilted Arc* obviously involved other issues besides the status of site specificity, but, in the end, site specificity was the term upon which Serra hung his entire defense. Despite his defeat, the legal definition of site specificity still remains unresolved and continues to be grounds for many juridical conflicts. For a discussion concerning legal questions in the *Tilted Arc* case, see Barbara Hoffman, "Law for Art's Sake in the Public Realm," in W. J. T. Mitchell, ed., *Art in the Public Sphere* (Chicago: University of Chicago Press, 1991), 113–146. Thanks to James Marcovitz for discussions concerning the legality of site specificity.

9   See Hal Foster's seminal essay "The Crux of Minimalism," in Howard Singerman, ed., *Individuals: A Selected History of Contemporary Art 1945–1986* (Los Angeles: Museum of Contemporary Art, 1986), 162–183. See also Craig Owens, "From Work to Frame, or, Is There Life After 'The Death of the Author'?," in Scott Bryson et al., eds., *Beyond Recognition: Representation, Power, and Culture* (Berkeley: University of California Press, 1992), 122–139.

10 Daniel Buren, "The Function of the Museum," *Artforum* (September 1973).

11 Daniel Buren, "Critical Limits" (1970), in *Five Texts* (New York: John Weber Gallery, 1974), 38.

12 See "Conversation with Robert Smithson," edited by Bruce Kurtz, in *The Writings of Robert Smithson,* ed. Nancy Holt (New York: New York University Press, 1979), 200.

13 For a comprehensive overview of Haacke's practice from 1969 to 1986, see *Hans Haacke: Unfinished Business,* ed. Brian Wallis (New York and Cambridge: New Museum of Contemporary Art and MIT Press, 1986).

14 This project involved the relocation of a bronze replica of an eighteenth-century statue of George Washington from its normal position outside the entrance of the Art Institute to one of the smaller galleries inside devoted to eighteenth-century European painting, sculpture, and decorative arts. Asher stated his intentions as follows: "In this work I am interested in the way the sculpture functions when it is viewed in its 18th-century context instead of in its prior relationship to the façade of the building. . . . Once inside Gallery 219 the sculpture can be seen in connection with the ideas of other European works of the same period" (as quoted in Anne Rorimer, "Michael Asher: Recent Work," *Artforum* [April 1980]: 47). See also Benjamin Buchloh, ed., *Michael Asher: Writings 1973–1983 on Works 1969–1979* (Halifax, Nova Scotia, and Los Angeles: Press of the Nova Scotia College of Art and Design and Museum of Contemporary Art, Los Angeles), 207–221.

15 The four performances at the Wadsworth Atheneum, which belong to a larger series (fifteen in all) entitled *Maintenance Art Performance Series* (1973–1974), were in the context of the exhibition "c. 7,500," a traveling exhibition of works by twenty-six women conceptual artists organized by Lucy Lippard. Unfortunately, information on the work of women artists of the period involved in conceptual art, institutional critique, and social systems analysis, like Ukeles, remains obscure due to their continued exclusion from the dominant art historical narratives of the 1970s. The few source materials that are available on Ukeles's work tend to be fraught with factual errors. For instance, Ukeles's "Maintenance Art Manifesto" (1969), as published in Kristine Stiles and Peter Selz, eds., *Theories and Documents of Contemporary Art: A Sourcebook of Artists' Writings* (Berkeley: University of California Press, 1996), is not only incomplete in its truncation of the statement but has been edited so as to render it useless as a historical document. An effort has been initiated to recuperate some of Ukeles's earlier work. See *Documents* 10 (Fall 1997): 5–30. I also refer the readers to Patricia Phillips, "Maintenance Activity:

2   "The New Sculpture 1965–75: Between Geometry and Gesture" at the Whitney Museum (1990) included fourteen recreations of works by Barry Le Va, Bruce Nauman, Alan Saret, Richard Serra, Joel Shapiro, Keith Sonnier, and Richard Tuttle. Le Va's recreation of *Continuous and Related Activities: Discontinued by the Act of Dropping* from 1967 was then purchased by the Whitney Museum for its permanent collection and subsequently reinstalled in several other exhibitions, "traveling" to many different locations. The exhibition as a whole traveled to the Museum of Contemporary Art Los Angeles later the same year.

3   Mel Bochner, in a 1969 interview with Elayne Varian, proposed a way of thinking about repetition and portability of art in light of his *Measurement* series, in which there is no conclusive original, thus no copies. "The piece could be in my studio, and in someone's collection, and in an exhibition simultaneously. It doesn't come down in one place and go up in another. In this sense the piece is not a portable object, it's a portable idea. As long as the internal relationships of measurements and materials remain constant it's the same work no matter where it is." Such a comment signals the need to distinguish between works that are physically and conceptually site-specific and those that are site-dependent but conceptually independent. See Elayne Varian, "An Interview with Mel Bochner" (1969), *Documents* 20 (Spring 2001): 4–8. See also Miwon Kwon, "Portable Ideas: An Interview with Mel Bochner," in the same issue.

4   Hapgood, "Remaking Art History," 120.

5   This was the logic behind Richard Serra's defense of *Tilted Arc*. Consequently, the issue of relocation or removal of the sculpture became a debate concerning the creative rights of the artist. For more on *Tilted Arc*, see chapter 3.

6   On the exhibition, entitled "Innovations: Entering into the Sculpture" (October 10–November 25, 1989), see Frances Colpitt, "Report from Los Angeles: Space Invaders," *Art in America* (January 1990): 67–71. In Carl Andre's letter to the editor (*Art in America* [March 1990]: 31), he notes that he only became aware of the Ace Gallery exhibition as a result of Colpitt's article. Donald Judd similarly remarks on the accidental nature of his finding out about the duplication of his work. See his letter to the editor, "Artist Disowns 'Copied' Sculpture," *Art in America* (April 1990): 33.

7   For Count Giuseppe Panza's thoughts on the original installation of these two works, see his interview with Christopher Knight in *Art of the Fifties, Sixties and Seventies: The Panza Collection* (Milan: Editoriale Jaca Books, 1999).

8   Sol LeWitt seems to have understood this shift quite early in his career. Like many of his mini-

mal art colleagues, he used fabricators to produce his serial objects in the mid-1960s. But when he began using "surrogate" producers for his wall drawings in the late 1960s, which became a necessity as the scale and demand for such work increased through the 1970s, he formally adopted the practice of providing certificates of authenticity along with diagrammed instructions for the making of the drawings; these instructions were taken as, or at least comparable to, the art work. The authenticity of a LeWitt wall drawing, thus, was no longer predicated on who actually made the drawing but on the verification provided by the artist in the form of *signed* instructions. Although he has altered his view in recent years, he once believed that anyone could make a Sol LeWitt wall work if the person followed his instructions precisely. Divergent strategies along these lines were adopted by other artists of the period, including Dan Flavin, Douglas Huebler, Robert Barry, and Lawrence Weiner. The significance of the function of the artist's signature, of course, was highlighted many decades earlier by Marcel Duchamp. Some of Piero Manzoni's work from the early 1960s, such as the signing of certain persons to designate them as works of art, also serves as an important precursor to the consideration of the primacy of the artist's signature in the art of the 1970s.

9   See Rosalind Krauss, "The Cultural Logic of the Late Capitalist Museum," *October* 54 (Fall 1990): 3–17.

10   For Wilding's description of this dilemma, as well as her assessment of recent revisits of 1960s and 1970s feminist art, see her essay "Monstrous Domesticity," in *M/E/A/N/I/N/G* 18 (November 1995): 3–16. On Womanhouse and the Feminist Art Program at the California Institute of the Arts, see Wilding, "The Feminist Art Programs at Fresno and CalArts, 1970–75," and Arlene Raven, "Womanhouse," in Norma Broude and Mary D. Garrard, eds., *The Power of Feminist Art: The American Movement of the 1970s, History and Impact* (New York: Harry N. Abrams, 1994).

11   See Hal Foster, "The Artist as Ethnographer," in *The Return of the Real: The Avant-Garde at the End of the Century* (Cambridge: MIT Press, 1996), on the complex exchange between art and anthropology in recent art.

12   Not exactly the portable studio or Marcel Duchamp's *Boîte-en-valise* (1941) but a descendant nonetheless. A productionist reading of modern art has focused on the model of the alienated and fragmentary labor of the assembly line worker as producer of objects. What I am proposing here is a consideration of another neglected model of labor, that of the itinerant salesman who, rather than being bound to a stationary point in the space of production, must travel extensively for the dissemination, distribution, and promotion of commodities.

13   The current modes of site-oriented practices can be mapped along an alternative genealogy

of performance art. Consider, for example, Vito Acconci's comments on performance art as a publicity-oriented, contract-based practice: "On the one hand, performance imposed the unsaleable onto the store that the gallery is. On the other hand, performance built that store up and confirmed the market-system: It increased the gallery's sales by acting as window-dressing and by providing publicity. . . . There was one way I loved to say the word 'performance,' one meaning of the world [sic] 'performance' I was committed to: 'Performance' in the sense of performing a contract—you promised you would do something, now you have to carry that promise out, bring that promise through to completion." Vito Acconci, "Performance after the Fact," *New Observations* 95 (May-June 1993): 29. Thanks to Frazer Ward for directing my attention to this text. For a recent consideration of site-specific art from the point of view of performance, see Nick Kaye, *Site-Specific Art: Performance, Place, and Documentation* (London: Routledge, 2000).

14   By strategically introducing objects from the material history of African Americans and Native Americans (until then buried in the Society's storage) into existing displays of refined cultural artifacts, Wilson exposed the extent to which the histories of these "minority" cultures have consistently been repressed in the dominant narrative of the history of the United States. The matter-of-fact juxtaposition of, for example, slave shackles from before the Civil War and elaborately decorated silver tea services from the same period, presented with equal distinction under the category of "Metal Works," provided disturbing visual evidence of the violent legacy of slavery and racism in this country. The project also served as a local critique of the Maryland Historical Society itself—Society's own holdings used to point up the prejudicial and exclusive nature of "definitive" museological histories written in the form of the institution's exhibitions and publications. For details on this project, see Lisa Corrin, ed., *Mining the Museum* (New York: New Press, 1994).

15   See Fred Wilson's interview with Martha Buskirk in *October* 70 (Fall 1994): 109–112.

16   In the name of interdisciplinarity, and in an effort to rejuvenate permanent collection exhibitions, several museums have also engaged high-profile philosophers, cultural theorists, sociologists, and other intellectuals from nonart fields for curatorial commissions. See, for instance, Jacques Derrida's curatorial project at the Louvre presented in the Hall Napoléon from October 26, 1990, to January 21, 1991, published as *Mémoires d'aveugle: L'autoportrait et autres ruines* (Paris: Editions de la Réunion des musées nationaux, 1990).

17   Isabelle Graw, "Field Work," *Flash Art* (November/December 1990): 137. Her observation here is in relation to Hans Haacke's practice but is relevant as a general statement concerning the current status of institutional critique. See also Frazer Ward, "The Haunted Museum: Institutional Critique and Publicity," *October* 73 (Summer 1995): 71–90.

18 See J. I. Gershuny and I. D. Miles, *The New Service Economy* (New York: Praeger, 1983); and Saskia Sassen, *The Global City: New York, London, Tokyo* (Princeton: Princeton University Press, 1991).

19 It should be noted that the artist herself initiated the project by offering such services through her "Prospectus for Corporations." See Fraser's *Report* (Vienna: EA-Generali Foundation, 1995). For a more general consideration of artistic practice as cultural service provision, see Andrea Fraser, "What's Intangible, Transitory, Mediating, Participatory, and Rendered in the Public Sphere?," *October* 80 (Spring 1997): 111–116. Proceedings of working-group discussions organized by Fraser and Helmut Draxler in 1993 around the theme of services, to which Fraser's text provides an introduction, are also of interest and appear in the same issue of *October.* See also Beatrice von Bismark, Diethelm Stoller, and Ulf Wuggenig, eds., *Games, Fights, Collaborations* (Stuttgart: Cantz Verlag, 1996).

20 Richard Serra, "Verb List, 1967–68," in *Writings Interviews* (Chicago: University of Chicago Press, 1994), 3.

21 Benjamin Buchloh, "Conceptual Art 1962–1969: From the Aesthetics of Administration to the Critique of Institutions," *October* 55 (Winter 1991): 105–143.

22 For instance, the "Views from Abroad" exhibition series at the Whitney Museum, which foregrounds "artistic" visions of European curators, is structured very much like site-specific commissions of artists that focus on museum permanent collections as described above. The first two exhibitions in the series featured the "visions" of Rudi Fuchs of the Stedelijk Museum, Amsterdam (June 29–October 1, 1995), and Jean-Christophe Ammann of the Museum für moderne Kunst, Frankfurt am Main (October 18, 1996–January 5, 1997). These exhibitions traveled to the curators' respective home institutions after their run in New York City.

23 According to James Meyer, a site-oriented practice based on a functional notion of a site "traces the *artist's* movements through and around the institution" and "reflect[s] the specific interests, educations, and formal decisions of the producer"; and "in the process of deferral, a signifying chain that traverses physical and discursive borders," the functional site "incorporates the body of the artist" (emphasis added). See Meyer, "The Functional Site," in *Platzwechsel,* exh. cat. (Zurich: Kunsthalle Zürich, 1995), 29, 33, 31, 35.

24 The installation consisted of *Bequest,* commissioned by the Worcester Art Museum in Massachusetts in 1991; *Import/Export Funk Office,* originally shown at the Christian Nagel Gallery in Cologne in 1992 and then reinstalled at the 1993 Biennial at the Whitney Museum

of American Art; *Mise en Scène,* first presented in 1992 in Clisson, France; and *Idyll Pursuits,* produced for a group exhibition in 1991 in Caracas, Venezuela. As a whole, *World Tour* was exhibited at the Museum of Contemporary Art, Los Angeles, in 1993, then traveled to the Dallas Museum of Art later the same year. See Russell Ferguson, ed., *World Tour,* exh. cat. (Los Angeles: Museum of Contemporary Art, 1993).

25 This is a project not exclusive to Green. Silvia Kolbowski, for instance, has proposed the coupling of generic sites and specific transferability in projects such as "Enlarged from the Catalogue: *The United States of America*" (1988). See the project annotations and Johanne Lamoureux's essay, "The Open Window Case: New Displays for an Old Western Paradigm," in *Silvia Kolbowski: XI Projects* (New York: Border Editions, 1993), 34–51, 6–15. There is a correspondence between Kolbowski's idea and Mel Bochner's remarks as cited in note 3 above.

26 This faith in the authenticity of place is evident in a wide range of disciplines. In urban studies, see Dolores Hayden, *The Power of Place: Urban Landscapes as Public History* (Cambridge: MIT Press, 1995). In cultural geography, see Michael Hough, *Out of Place: Restoring Identity to the Regional Landscape* (New Haven: Yale University Press, 1990). In philosophy, see Edward Casey, *The Fate of Place: A Philosophical History* (Berkeley: University of California Press, 1997). In relation to public art, see Ronald Lee Fleming and Renata von Tscharner, *PlaceMakers: Creating Public Art That Tells You Where You Are* (Boston, San Diego, and New York: Harcourt Brace Jovanovich, 1981). See also Lucy Lippard, *The Lure of the Local: The Sense of Place in a Multicultural Society* (New York: New Press, 1997). See chapter 6 for more on this issue.

27 *Places with a Past: New Site-Specific Art at Charleston's Spoleto Festival,* exh. cat. (New York: Rizzoli, 1991), 19. The exhibition took place May 24–August 4, 1991, with site-specific works by eighteen artists including Ann Hamilton, Christian Boltanski, Cindy Sherman, David Hammons, Lorna Simpson and Alva Rogers, Kate Ericson and Mel Ziegler, and Ronald Jones.

28 Precedents for "Places with a Past," in which the city as a whole becomes the exhibition site, include the Spoleto Festival in Italy (1962), "Skulptur Projekte" in Münster, Germany (1987), "The New Urban Landscape" in New York City (1988), and "Die Endlichkeit der Freiheit" in Berlin (1990).

29 Mary Jane Jacob, in *Places with a Past,* 17.

30 Ibid., 15.

31 Undated press release of 1997. Thus, programs like "Places with a Past" and "Sculpture.

Projects" share a similar investment in generating a sense of uniqueness and authenticity for their respective places of presentation. As such endeavors to engage art in the nurturing of specificities of locational difference gather momentum, there is a greater urgency in distinguishing between the *cultivation* of art and places and their *appropriation* for the promotion of cities as cultural commodities.

32 Kevin Robins, "Prisoners of the City: Whatever Can a Postmodern City Be?," in Erica Carter, James Donald, and Judith Squires, eds., *Space and Place: Theories of Identity and Location* (London: Lawrence & Wishart, 1993), 306.

33 Cultural critic Sharon Zukin has noted, "It seemed to be official policy [by the 1990s] that making a place for art in the city went along with establishing a marketable identity for the city as a whole." See Sharon Zukin, *The Culture of Cities* (Cambridge, Mass.: Blackwell Publishers, 1995), 23.

34 Addressing Robert Smithson's *Spiral Jetty* and the *Partially Buried Woodshed,* Craig Owens has made an important connection between melancholia and the redemptive logic of site specificity in "The Allegorical Impulse: Toward a Theory of Postmodernism," *October* 12 (Spring 1980): 67–86.

35 Thierry de Duve, "Ex Situ," *Art & Design* 8, no. 5–6 (May-June 1993): 25.

3

1 According to Ahearn (verified through the Alexander and Bonin Gallery, New York, May 2000), he has a "gentleman's agreement" with the city of New York that some day, when the funds become available through the sale of the original three sculptures, he will be given the opportunity to complete the project. How this completion will be pursued remains unclear. The original design of the traffic triangle was in collaboration with Nancy Owens, a landscape architect with the city's Parks Department.

2 All art is engaged in public discourse in one way or another; by "mainstream public art" I mean the specific category of art that is typically sponsored and/or administered by city, state, or national government agencies, in whole or in part. It involves bureaucratized review and approval procedures that are outside the museum or gallery system and often engage numerous nonart organizations, including local community groups, private foundations, and corporations. However, this chapter's limited working definition of the term is provisional, insofar as the meaning of the "public" in public art continues to be open to debate.

3   For background information on public art in the United States since the early 1960s, see John Beardsley, *Art in Public Places: A Survey of Community Sponsored Projects Supported by the NEA* (Washington, D.C.: Partners for Livable Places, 1981); Donald Thalacker, *The Place of Art in the World of Architecture* (New York: Chelsea House Publishers, 1980); and Harriet Senie, *Contemporary Public Sculpture: Tradition, Transformation, and Controversy* (New York: Oxford University Press, 1992).

4   See Arlene Raven, ed., *Art in the Public Interest* (New York: Da Capo Press, 1989); and Suzanne Lacy, ed., *Mapping the Terrain: New Genre Public Art* (Seattle: Bay Press, 1995).

5   The paradigm shifts I note here are further elaborated in my essay "For Hamburg: Public Art and Urban Identities," in *Kunst auf Schritt und Tritt* (*Public Art Is Everywhere*) (Hamburg, Germany: Kellner, 1997), 95–107.

6   In the mid-1970s, the phrase "art in public places" was used by some public art professionals to distinguish location-conscious art from "public art," sculptures that were simply placed in public spaces, like Calder's. Thus my use of "art in public places" to designate the latter may be confusing to some, but since the NEA used the phrase as the title of its own program to promote this type of art, I am adopting it here.

7   Interestingly, for Robert Morris the size and scale of a sculpture was directly proportional to its publicness: the smaller the work, the greater the demand for intimacy of perception (private); the larger the work, the greater the demand for a "public" interaction. See his "Notes on Sculpture," in Gregory Battcock, ed., *Minimal Art: A Critical Anthology* (New York: Dutton, 1968), 222–228.

8   Henry Moore, as quoted in Henry J. Seldis, *Henry Moore in America* (New York: Praeger, 1973), 176–177.

9   Ibid., 14–15.

10   There is an important distinction to be drawn between the GSA and the NEA: the former administers federally sponsored commissions; the latter administers "community"-initiated projects. Starting in 1963, the GSA mandated that 0.5 to 1 percent of the estimated construction costs of all new federal buildings be set aside for art. Local Percent for Art programs, which follow the GSA model, were first instituted in cities like Philadelphia, Baltimore, and Seattle in the early to mid 1960s. The NEA program, by contrast, was set up to respond to local initiatives (from ad hoc citizens' groups and not-for-profit institutions or organizations, like arts commissions). Once it accepts a proposal, the NEA offers a matching grant and,

through a small committee of art experts, helps administer the process of selecting a site, choosing and negotiating with an artist, arranging for transportation and installation of the work, and mounting educational efforts to introduce the artist's work to the local community. In many instances, those at the NEA advise on GSA commissions. See Beardsley, *Art in Public Places,* for more details.

11   The Livable Cities Program initiated by the NEA in 1977 as part of its architecture program, for example, explicitly sought to find "creativity and imagination—to get it from the artist and apply it to the problems of the built environment" so as to "give promise of economic and social benefit to the community." See Louis G. Redstone, with Ruth R. Redstone, *Public Art: New Directions* (New York: McGraw-Hill, 1981), vi.

12   In the eyes of the urban elite and city managers during the 1970s and 1980s, public art was also supposed to attract tourism, new businesses and work forces, and residential development, and was expected to boost a city's sense of identity. Public art initiatives since the 1960s, in fact, have always been tied to urban renewal and economic revitalization efforts. On these issues, see Kate Linker, "Public Sculpture: The Pursuit of the Pleasurable and Profitable Paradise," *Artforum* (March 1981): 64–73, and "Public Sculpture II: Provisions for the Paradise," *Artforum* (Summer 1981): 37–42. See also Sharon Zukin, *The Culture of Cities* (Cambridge, Mass.: Blackwell, 1995); Erika Doss, *Spirit Poles and Flying Pigs: Public Art and Cultural Democracy in American Communities* (Washington: Smithsonian Institution Press, 1995), especially chapter three, "Public Art in the Corporate Sphere"; and my essay "For Hamburg: Public Art and Urban Identities."

13   Sam Hunter, "The Public Agency as Patron," in *Art for the Public: The Collection of the Port Authority of New York and New Jersey* (New York: Port Authority of New York and New Jersey, 1985), 35.

14   In addition to Kate Linker's criticism, see also Lawrence Alloway, "The Public Sculpture Problem," *Studio International* 184 (October 1972): 123–124; and Alloway, "Problems of Iconography and Style," in *Urban Encounters: Art Architecture Audience,* exh. cat. (Philadelphia: Institute of Contemporary Art, University of Pennsylvania, 1980), 15–20.

15   According to Kate Linker, in the 1960s a large portion of funding for public art was provided by the private sector. Corporations sponsored art to adorn office buildings, shopping malls, banks, etc., creating a new kind of "public" space (privately owned, publicly accessible) that became available to art. A traditional nationalist ideology of older forms of public art was replaced by a business ideology, and modern, abstract, often large-scale sculptures predominated as a favored style. See Linker, "Public Sculpture."

16 The term is commonly attributed to architect James Wines of SITE. He is also known to have coined the phrase "turds on the plaza" to describe the ubiquitous abstract modernist sculptures on urban plazas.

17 Statement taken from the official Art-in-Public-Places grant application guidelines of the Visual Arts Program of the National Endowment for the Arts, as cited by Mary Jane Jacob in her essay "Outside the Loop," in *Culture in Action,* exh. cat. (Seattle: Bay Press, 1995), 54.

18 A brief history of this transition is recounted in Lacy, ed., *Mapping the Terrain,* 21–24. See also Richard Andrews, "Artists and the Visual Definition of Cities: The Experience of Seattle," in Stacy Paleologos Harris, ed., *Insights/On Sites: Perspectives on Art in Public Places* (Washington, D.C.: Partners for Livable Places, 1984), 16–23.

19 According to Richard Andrews, who headed Seattle's Percent for Art program during the 1970s, public art, from an arts agency point of view, can be divided into two distinct types: those works aligned with the tradition of *collecting*, which are object-oriented and site-transferable; and those that fall within the tradition of *building,* which are involved in the designing process of public buildings and places. The scale tipped toward site-integrated and immovable works beginning in the late 1970s. See Andrews, "Artists and the Visual Definition of Cities," 19.

20 Janet Kardon, "Street Wise/Street Foolish," in *Urban Encounters,* exh. cat., 8. The exhibition, featuring documentation of projects by artists, architects, and landscape architects, was held between March 19 and April 30, 1980.

21 Nancy Foote, "Sightings on Siting," in *Urban Encounters,* 25–34.

22 Linker sees an intimation of a solution in Robert Morris's landscape work *Grand Rapids Project* (1973–1974) in the way durational bodily experience of a particular spatial situation defines the work. See her concluding comments in "Public Sculpture," 70–73. See also Alloway, "Problems of Iconography and Style."

23 I am recalling here the distinction made by Rosalyn Deutsche between integrationist and interventionist approaches to site-specific art. In Deutsche's view, the former seeks to erase visible signs of social problems that might contradict the ideology of unity; the latter seeks to expose them. See her *Evictions: Art and Spatial Politics* (Cambridge: MIT Press, 1996), especially the chapters "Uneven Development" and "*Tilted Arc* and the Uses of Democracy."

24 From the official Art-in-Public-Places grant application guidelines of the Visual Arts Program

of the National Endowment for the Arts, as cited by Jacob, "Outside the Loop," 54.

25 This design team model of public art was more an ideal than a reality. Even in the most successful cases, the conventional hierarchy of roles was maintained; that is, the architect assumed leadership and dictated the parameters of the artist's contribution. Part of the problem remains the established patterns of building design and construction. On the benefits and problems of artist-architect design team collaborations, see Donna Graves, "Sharing Space: Some Observations on the Recent History and Possible Future of Public Art Collaborations," *Public Art Review* (Spring/Summer 1993): 10–13; Joan Marter, "Collaborations: Artists and Architects on Public Sites," *Art Journal* (Winter 1989): 315–320; Diane Shamash, "The A Team, Artists and Architects: Can They Work Together?," *Stroll: The Magazine of Outdoor Art and Street Culture* 6–7 (June 1988): 60–63. An exemplary project following this design team model is the Viewland/Hoffman Substation (1979) in Seattle by Andrew Keating, Sherry Markovitz, Lewis Simpson, artists, and Hobbs/Fukui, architects (commissioned by Seattle Arts Commission and Seattle City Light). For another interesting case study, see Steve Rosenthal, *Artists and Architects Collaborate: Designing the Wiesner Building* (Cambridge, Mass.: MIT Committee on the Visual Arts, 1985).

Siah Armajani has commented with dismay on the design team initiative, in which he participated numerous times: "Public art was a promise that became a nightmare. . . . In the first place, the idea of a design team just doesn't work . . . the kind of design team that just gets together around a table is like a situation comedy. It is cynical and unproductive. Genuine debate can't take place around a table in that way. You get what the real-estate developer and the arts administrator want because they control the money. The whole emphasis in most of these projects is on who can get along best with the others involved—at the expense of vision and fresh thinking." From Calvin Tompkins, "Open, Available, Useful," *New Yorker* (March 19, 1990): 71.

26 Deutsche, *Evictions*, 65. Deutsche has provided the most thorough analysis of the universalizing logic of beauty and utility at the basis of public art discourse, which has supported urban redevelopment and gentrification projects. Some public art professionals within the field also recognized early the potential problems with such utilitarianism. For instance, Richard Andrews wrote in 1984, "There is a danger in perceiving contextual projects as a panacea for public art—as a means to reduce controversy and make art 'useful.' . . . Legitimate concern exists that function should not become the primary criteria for an institutionalized program of public art. In Seattle we may provide funding for the First Avenue Street project of [Lewis "Buster"] Simpson and [Jack] Mackie, but we would be ill-advised to generate a 'street improvement program' of benches, light poles, and so on for all artists." Andrews, "Artists and the Visual Definition of Cities," 26.

27   For instance, Burton, arguably the most prominent and vocal among artists who espoused this utilitarianism in public art, once said of his street tables and seating design for the Equitable Assurance Building in New York City: "The social questions interest me more than the art ones. . . . Communal social values are now more important. What office workers do in their lunch hour is more important than my pushing the limits of my self-expression." As quoted in Douglas C. McGill, "Sculpture Goes Public," *New York Times Magazine* (April 27, 1986): 67.

28   Such practices are predicated on the conception of the site of art as mobilized and unfixed. As such, the site is not only a venue of presentation but constitutes a mode of distribution as well. I have described this kind of deterritorialized site as a "discursive site." See chapter 1.

29   Richard Serra, "Rigging," interview with Gerard Hovagymyan, in *Richard Serra: Interviews, Etc. 1970–1980* (Yonkers, N.Y.: Hudson River Museum, 1980), 128.

30   General Services Administration Factsheet Concerning the Art-in-Architecture Program for Federal Buildings, in Martha Buskirk and Clara Weyergraf-Serra, eds., *The Destruction of Tilted Arc: Documents* (Cambridge: MIT Press, 1991), 23.

31   See Douglas Crimp, "Serra's Public Sculpture: Redefining Site Specificity," in *Richard Serra: Sculpture* (New York: Museum of Modern Art, 1986), 40–56; and Deutsch, *Evictions,* 257–270.

32   Deutsche, *Evictions,* 261.

33   "Political" site specificity is Deutsche's term, used to distinguish it from "academic" site specificity. Ibid., 261–262.

34   Richard Serra, "*Tilted Arc* Destroyed" (1989), reprinted in Richard Serra, *Writings Interviews* (Chicago: University of Chicago Press, 1994), 193–213.

35   See Rosalyn Deutsche's critique of the conflation between permanence and universal timelessness during the *Tilted Arc* hearings, in *Evictions,* 264. See also Douglas Crimp's interview comments in "Douglas Crimp on *Tilted Arc,*" in Tom Finklepearl, ed., *Dialogues in Public Art* (Cambridge, Mass.: MIT Press, 2000), 71.

36   Serra, "*Tilted Arc* Destroyed," 202.

37   Ibid.

38   Ibid., 203.

39 On this point, see Hal Foster, "The Un/making of Sculpture," in Russell Ferguson, Anthony McCall, and Clara Weyergraf-Serra, eds., *Richard Serra: Sculpture 1985–1998* (Los Angeles and Göttingen, Germany: Museum of Contemporary Art and Steidl Verlag, 1998).

40 Buskirk and Weyergraf-Serra, eds., *The Destruction of Tilted Arc*, 12.

41 Richard Serra's apparent animosity toward architecture is well known and well documented. See his comments in, for instance, his interviews with critic Douglas Crimp and architect Peter Eisenman, both reprinted in Serra, *Writings Interviews*. But Serra's "working against" architecture is not a straightforward opposition. For the most provocative interpretations of Serra's relationship to architecture, see Foster, "The Un/making of Sculpture," and Yve-Alain Bois, "A Picturesque Stroll around *Clara-Clara*," *October* 29 (Summer 1984).

42 Foster, "The Un/making of Sculpture," 17.

43 Ibid., 14.

44 Rosalind Krauss has written: "The specificity of the site is not the subject of the work, but—in its articulation of the movement of the viewer's body-in-destination—its medium." Krauss, "Richard Serra Sculpture," in *Richard Serra: Sculpture* (1986), 37.

45 See Buskirk and Weyergraf-Serra, eds., *The Destruction of Tilted Arc*, for the record of statements given at the hearings.

46 Representative Theodore Weiss, in Buskirk and Weyergraf-Serra, *The Destruction of Tilted Arc*, 115.

47 Joseph Liebman's testimony, for example, paints the plaza prior to the installation of *Tilted Arc* as an idyllic setting with children playing, mothers strolling with baby carriages, etc. See Buskirk and Weyergraf-Serra, eds., *The Destruction of Tilted Arc*, 113. Such memory is strongly contradicted by Douglas Crimp, a resident of the neighborhood. See his remarks concerning the somewhat dysfunctional state of the plaza prior to *Tilted Arc* in "Douglas Crimp on *Tilted Arc*," 71–72.

48 Deutsche, *Evictions*, 259.

49 Some prominent cases include Pablo Picasso's sculpture at the Chicago Civic Center (1965), Alexander Calder's *La Grande Vitesse* in Grand Rapids, Michigan (1967), George Sugarman's *Baltimore Federal* (1975–1977), and Maya Lin's Vietnam Veterans' Memorial in Washington,

D.C. (1982). For more on other public art controversies, see Senie, *Contemporary Public Sculpture,* especially chapter six, and Doss, *Spirit Poles and Flying Pigs.*

50   Initial goals of the NEA's Art-in-Public-Places Program as stated in its guidelines and cited in Finklepearl, ed., *Dialogues in Public Art,* 43.

51   Of course, Andres Serrano's *Piss Christ* and Robert Mapplethorpe's homosexually explicit X-portfolio photographs drew as much, if not more, attention during these years. See Richard Bolton, ed., *Culture Wars: Documents from the Recent Controversies in the Arts* (New York: New Press, 1992).

52   Deutsche, *Evictions,* 267.

53   Representative Theodore Weiss, in Buskirk and Weyergraf-Serra, eds., *The Destruction of Tilted Arc,* 116.

54   As cited in Lacy, ed., *Mapping the Terrain,* 22–24.

55   Suzanne Lacy has remarked that even with the "maturation" of site-specific public art through the 1980s, in which greater attention was paid to the historical, ecological, and sociological aspects of a site, the works generally did not engage audiences in a manner markedly different from those in museums. Lacy, ed., *Mapping the Terrain,* 23.

56   Ibid., 27.

57   Finklepearl, ed., *Dialogues in Public Art,* 34–35.

58   According to Lacy, the theorization of "new genre public art" emerged from a lecture program sponsored by the California College of Arts and Crafts in 1989 entitled "City Sites: Artists and Urban Strategies." "A series of lectures was delivered at nontraditional sites in Oakland by ten artists whose work addressed a particular constituency on specific issues but also stood as a prototype for a wider range of human concerns." The term was officially coined for a three-day symposium organized by Lacy and others, "Mapping the Terrain: New Genre Public Art," at the San Francisco Museum of Modern Art in November 1991. Lacy, ed., *Mapping the Terrain,* 11.

59   Ibid., 24.

60   Ibid.

5   The change in exhibition title signals a major shift in the conceptual basis of the show, from
     public art as static objects (in the tradition of monuments) to public art as process-oriented
     actions. This change was originally suggested by artist Daniel Martinez.

6   Held from May 10 to October 27, 1989, this was a standard juried exhibition. The ten partici-
     pating artists were Vito Acconci, Richard Deacon, Richard Serra, Judith Shea, Josh Garber,
     Sheila Klein, Daniel Peterman, David Schafer, Thomas Skomski, and Rogelio Tijerina. There
     was a blatant division of artists and their work in terms of their status in the international art
     scene. For example, the first four artists were given prominent city locations (Pioneer Court,
     the plaza in front of the Equitable Building on North Michigan Avenue) whereas the remaining
     six less-established artists were given a secondary location (Cityfront Center near the NBC
     Tower). Also, the first four simply installed their works for presentation whereas the remaining
     six had to fulfill the "Art-in-Progress" component of the program: they were set up in tents
     on site to work on their sculptures so that their "creative working process" could be viewed
     by the passing "public." This hierarchization of artists was repeated in the promotional mate-
     rials including the catalogue, where the first four received luxurious treatment, with several
     pages of images and text for each, while the latter six were given short, one-paragraph
     descriptions.

7   Interview with the author, May 14, 1996.

8   Jacob has said that the progamming of "Culture in Action" was most directly inspired by
     David Hammon's *House of the Future,* a community-based project that was part of the 1991
     Spoleto Festival exhibition "Places with a Past," which Jacob also curated. For more on
     Hammon's project, see the exhibition catalogue *Places with a Past: New Site-Specific Art at
     Charleston's Spoleto Festival* (New York: Rizzoli, 1991). See also Tom Finklepearl's comments
     in *Dialogues in Public Art* (Cambridge: MIT Press, 2000), 41–42.

9   The most prominent art world figures who have spoken in enthusiastic support of "Culture in
     Action" include David Ross, former director of the San Francisco Museum of Modern Art, and
     Arthur Danto, art critic for the *Nation.* See also Michael Brenson, "Healing in Time," in *Culture
     in Action,* 16–49; Edward J. Sozanski, "A New Spin on What Art Can Be When It Goes Public,"
     Philadelphia Inquirer, August 22, 1993; and Suzi Gablik, "Removing the Frame: An Interview
     with 'Culture in Action' Curator Mary Jane Jacob," *New Art Examiner* (January 1994): 14–18.
     Art historian Patricia Phillips wrote: "This radical project left few assumptions about public
     art, perception, distribution, and roles of artists—and curators—unchallenged. 'Culture in
     Action' raised significant questions and issues that have renergized a dialogue on public art."
     Similarly, Lucy Lippard wrote in praise of the show's exhibition catalogue: "In the thirty years
     that the role and efficacy of an outreaching public art has been debated within the 'avant-

garde,' few books have stated the issues as clearly as *Culture in Action.* Mary Jane Jacob asks all the right questions, suggests some answers, and provides a new model in her curatorial practice." (Both references are from promotional material distributed by Brunsman & Associates on behalf of Sculpture Chicago.)

10   See, for example, Michael Kimmelman's review of the exhibition, "Of Candy Bars and Public Art," *New York Times,* September 26, 1993, 2:1, 43; Eleanor Heartney, "The Dematerialization of Public Art," *Sculpture* (March-April 1993): 45–49, "'Culture in Action' at Various Sites," *Art in America* (November 1993); Joseph Scanlon, "Joseph Scanlon on Sculpture Chicago's Culture in Action," *Frieze* (November-December 1993): 22–27; and Hafthor Yngvason, "The New Public Art: As Opposed to What?" *Public Art Review* (Spring/Summer 1993): 4–5.

11   The exhibition included temporary projects by Joseph Bartscherer, Gloria Bornstein and Donald Fels, Cris Bruch, Chris Burden, General Idea, Group Material, Edgar Heap of Birds, Robert Herdlein, Gary Hill, Ilya Kabakov, Alan Lande, David Mahler, Daniel Martinez, Martha Rosler, Norie Sato, and Lewis "Buster" Simpson. The two permanent projects were Jonathan Borofsky's sculpture *Hammering Man* in front of the new Seattle Art Museum (a building designed by the office of Robert Venturi and Denise Scott Brown) and a collaborative installation at Pier 62/63 by Laurie Hawkinson (architect), Barbara Kruger (artist), Guy Nordenson (structural engineer), Nicholas Quennell (landscape architect), Henry Smith-Miller (architect), and Gail Dubrow (Seattle historian). For more detailed information on this exhibition, see *In Public: Seattle 1991,* exh. cat. (Seattle: Seattle Arts Commission, 1992).

12   See Richard Andrews, "Artists and the Visual Definition of Cities: The Experience of Seattle," in Stacy Paleologos Harris, ed., *Insights/On Sites: Perspectives on Art in Public Places* (Washington, D.C.: Partners for Livable Places, 1984), 16–23. See also Richard Andrews, Jim Hirschfield, and Larry Rausch, *Artwork/Network: A Planning Study for Seattle, Art in the Civic Context* (Seattle: Seattle Arts Commission, 1988).

13   See chapter 3 on the complications of the design team model.

14   T. Ellen Sollod, executive director of the Seattle Art Commission, in *In Public: Seattle 1991,* 7.

15   The rhetoric around the innovation of "Culture in Action" continues to highlight the community-based collaborative element. Mary Jane Jacob herself embraced it as a distinctive aspect of the exhibition: "[Culture in Action] is the result of a fundamental collaboration among participating artists, community residents, and civic leaders. This collaborative process has to an unusual degree shaped the conception as well as the realization of these artists' projects, and led to a new dialogue between the artist and audience for public art." (Quoted in "Urban

Issues Are Focus of New Public Art Program in Chicago," undated press release, 1–2.) But there was greater institutional and curatorial ambivalence, if not resistance, to the community-based collaborations than is acknowledged. According to my research, Jacob and Sculpture Chicago were reluctant to foreground the community when naming the projects during the early phase of the exhibition's development. Artists Kate Ericson and Mel Ziegler in fact disputed with them over the ways in which the role of the community was diminished in relation to the artists in Sculpture Chicago's public announcements regarding "Culture in Action." Ericson and Ziegler successfully insisted on equal billing (in the treatment of the community name in all published materials) and unsuccessfully sought monetary compensation for the community in letters dated between late November 1992 and early February 1993.

Jacob remembers this dispute differently (as not a dispute at all). For example, in her interview with Annette DiMeo Carlozzi in *Art Papers* 21, no. 3 (May/June 1997): 8–13, she states that "we realized halfway through the process that all the artists were working collaboratively, actually determining their pieces with members of the public. I just suggested that maybe all these projects should change their names to include the community."

16 Picasso's *The Head of a Woman,* the artist's first large-scale urban sculpture, was funded by private money ($300,000) and resulted from architect William Hartmann's (of Skidmore, Owings and Merrill) desire to model the Chicago Civic Center on the European piazza. The project set an influential precedent for artists and architects involved in public art commissions for the next decade or more. For specific details on the Picasso commission, see Harriet F. Senie, *Contemporary Public Sculpture: Tradition, Transformation, and Controversy* (New York: Oxford University Press, 1992), 95–100.

17 Sponsored by Sculpture Chicago, Pritzker Park was a conscious departure from the organization's regular summer sculpture exhibitions described earlier.

18 The temporal framework for the exhibition, however, was strictly limited in legal terms. Once the artists' proposals were approved in summer 1992, contracts were distributed by Sculpture Chicago. The legal agreement, covering October 1, 1992 to September 30, 1993, bound the artists not only to complete their projects for presentation for "public viewing" from May 1 to September 30, 1993, but to perform particular publicity and promotional duties preceding and during this period. It should be noted that there were no such legal agreements between Sculpture Chicago and members of any of the participating community groups.

Ericson and Ziegler vehemently challenged Sculpture Chicago's withdrawal of financial and institutional support following the closing of "Culture in Action," raising the question: When is a project really over? The artists believed that Sculpture Chicago was financially and morally responsible for the "completion" of *Eminent Domain,* which included the nationwide distribution of the paint charts. Sculpture Chicago felt that its obligation to the artists and their project was met within the context of "Culture in Action," and that if the artists were interested in pursuing it further they should find another source of support. Even though True Test agreed to "host" the project in spring 1994 (over six months after the exhibition's closing), Sculpture Chicago felt that, without a promotional tie-in to a major cultural event, the meaning of the project would be completely lost to the random paint customer, resulting in a waste of time and money for all involved. The artists accused Sculpture Chicago of using them and the community resident group for its own public relations purposes, and charged that the overall conceptual frame of "Culture in Action" was hypocritical. Sculpture Chicago in turn viewed the artists as inflexible and impractical.

To ameliorate the situation, Sculpture Chicago considered a "kill fee" for the project (though this did not materialize) and, at the insistence of the artists, paid the resident group $3,000 for their involvement in "Culture in Action." But the situation was further exacerbated when Ericson and Ziegler refused to contribute any materials to the exhibition catalogue, which they deemed another form of Sculpture Chicago's self-promotion. This refusal led Sculpture Chicago to solicit the assistance of Kelly Rogers of the Sidley Austin law office to clarify that the artists had a legal obligation to provide materials for the catalogue. In the end, it seems no one wanted to pursue a legal battle, and the artists reluctantly contributed their work to the catalogue, quibbling over the wording of certain aspects of the project description as authored by Mary Jane Jacob.

19 See chapter 3, note 58, on the discursive genesis of new genre public art.

20 Suzanne Lacy, "Cultural Pilgrimages and Metaphoric Journeys," in Lacy, ed., *Mapping the Terrain,* 19.

21 Ibid., 20.

22 Arlene Raven, ed., *Art in the Public Interest* (1989; New York: Da Capo Press, 1993).

23 Ibid., 1.

24 Ibid., 4.

25 Ibid., 18.

26 Lacy, "Cultural Pilgrimages," 25.

27 Ibid., 20.

28   See Jeff Kelley, "Common Work," in Lacy, ed., *Mapping the Terrain,* 139–148. Tom Finklepearl has similarly opposed the "art of abstraction" (modernism) to the "art of attraction" (participatory modes of public art practice). See his essay "Abstraction and Attraction," in *Uncommon Sense,* exh. cat. (Los Angeles: Museum of Contemporary Art, Los Angeles, 1997), 13–34.

29   For a countertheorization of the concept of democracy in relation to public art, see Rosalyn Deutsche, *Evictions: Art and Spatial Politics* (Cambridge: MIT Press, 1996), especially the chapter "Agoraphobia."

30   Mary Jane Jacob, as quoted in Lacy, ed., *Mapping the Terrain,* 30. What does it mean for a particular mode of practice to "find its time"? This is a historiographical question. Just as certain historical, political, social, economic, and aesthetic conditions influence the emergence of new modes of cultural practice, signaling tendencies both large and small, the broadening acceptance of an old mode of cultural practice (sometimes in the form of a return) similarly points to the conjuncture of such influences.

31   Heartney, "The Dematerialization of Public Art," 45.

32   Jeff Kelley, as quoted in Lacy, "Cultural Pilgrimages," 24. Such a statement does not acknowledge the extent to which certain site-specific art has critically questioned the "museum zone" itself. It also presupposes the museum as a closed system, the status of which has also been challenged via site-specific practices over the past three decades. See chapter 1.

33   For an extensive history of the philosophical distinctions between space, place, and site, see Edward Casey, *The Fate of Place: A Philosophical History* (Berkeley: University of California Press, 1997).

34   Kelley, "Common Work," 141. A similar sensibility rules Lucy Lippard's *The Lure of the Local: A Sense of Place in a Multicultural Society* (New York: New Press, 1997), which also emphasizes place as holistic culture (as opposed to the abstraction of "site"). See chapter 6 for a critique of Lippard's position.

35   Interview with the author, November 7, 1995.

36   Mary Jane Jacob, "Urban Issues Are Focus of New Public Art Program in Chicago," undated press release, 2.

37   Mary Jane Jacob as quoted in "Sculpture Chicago Receives Major Funding Support for Public Art Initiative," press release, March 10, 1993, n.p.

38 Dan Cameron, "'Culture in Action': Eliminate the Middleman," *Flash Art* (November/ December 1993): 62.

39 Heartney, "The Dematerialization of Public Art," 45.

40 Mary Jane Jacob, "Outside the Loop," in *Culture in Action,* 56.

41 The call for the rehabilitation of public art happens to coincide with revisions in operational guidelines of major private and public funding sources for art in general and public art in particular. For example, in the mid 1990s, the MacArthur Foundation redirected its support of media arts to "community-based organizations that are working to promote social justice and democracy through the media"; the Lila Wallace/Reader's Digest Foundation limited its artist funding to those who work explicitly with "communities"; and, more drastically, the Lannan Foundation in Los Angeles shifted from arts funding to projects in support of "social issues," giving up collecting art altogether.

42 Heather Mac Donald, "The New Community Activism: Social Justice Comes Full Circle," *City Journal* (August 1993): 44–55. Thanks to Rosalyn Deutsche for directing my attention to this reference.

43 Ibid., 44.

44 Ibid., 48.

45 Ibid., 46.

46 Ibid., 53. Throughout the text, the author (perhaps rightly) characterizes existing social services as ineffectual and inefficient. But the author also makes the rather outrageous claim that those working in the social services "industry" purposefully *cultivate* poverty, illness, and other social ills in order to further increase their business and to expand their authoritative power.

47 In what has by now become a familiar mode of operation, Jacob and Sculpture Chicago organized a symposium that took place on December 5, 1992, approximately six months *prior* to the general public opening of the exhibition. Over seventy-five guests were invited, including museum professionals from across the United States, curators from Europe, art critics and journalists, architects, university professors, public arts administrators, local community leaders, public relations experts, delegates from funding organizations, representatives of community groups engaged in "Culture in Action" projects, and, of course, the artists and the

Sculpture Chicago staff. One part of the symposium addressed questions such as: "How can artists work with communities that are not their own? How can public art contribute to a community? Can art empower a community? What particular obstacles or problems face the artists participating in Sculpture Chicago's 'Culture in Action'? What are these artists attempting to accomplish?" The second part addressed more general issues concerning the relevance of this new public art in relation to the organization of the urban environment, audience/constituency, art history, other art institutions, art education, etc.

Although some of the "Culture in Action" artists who were able to participate presented their work in progress for feedback, it is difficult to gauge whether, and to what extent, the symposium had any direct bearing on the outcome of their projects. Most had already passed the proposal stage, and the implementation of the projects was well under way by the time of the symposium. It is certain, however, that the gathering of so many arts-related professionals had a big impact on the *reception* of "Culture in Action" insofar as the symposium not only put the word out early but preemptively posed critical questions that the artists and the organization would have to face later on.

In conversations with the author, several artists from "Culture in Action" registered their suspicion of the motivations behind the symposium. Rather than an attempt to generate broad theoretical discussions on the state of public art, they believed it served primarily to promote and publicize the exhibition, within which the artist had little choice but to participate as a kind of spokesperson for the exhibition.

48 Yngvason, "The New Public Art," 5.

49 Ibid. The internal quotations reference Seyla Benhabib, *Situating the Self: Gender, Community and Postmodernism in Contemporary Ethics* (New York: Routledge, 1992), 79.

50 The projects in "Culture in Action" have been judged either by a standard deferral to aesthetic quality (measured against existing categories of sculpture, performance, video, installation, etc.) or in relation to a vague sense of political efficacy and public/audience engagement. For most critics, success in the former realm rarely translates to success in the latter. The criteria of social relevance and aesthetic quality seem to maintain an inversely proportional relation.

51 Lacy as quoted in Jacob, *Culture in Action,* 70.

52 Ibid., 69.

53 Iris Marion Young, "The Ideal of Community and the Politics of Difference," in Linda J. Nicholson, ed., *Feminism/Postmodernism* (New York: Routledge, 1990), 301.

54 In large-scale performance projects throughout the 1970s and 1980s, Lacy tended toward similarly essentialized representations of women as a social category, bound together primarily by a sense of injustice in the face of the patriarchal social order. Her well-known projects include *Inevitable Association* (1976), *In Mourning and in Rage* (1977), *Whisper, the Waves, the Wind* (1984), *Crystal Quilt* (1987), and *Underground* (1993). For an overview of Lacy's practice, see Jeff Kelley, "The Body Politics of Suzanne Lacy," in Nina Felshin, ed., *But Is It Art? The Spirit of Art as Activism* (Seattle: Bay Press, 1995), 221–249.

55 I am borrowing this phrase from Hal Foster as it appears in his essay, "The Artist as Ethnographer," in *The Return of the Real: The Avant-Garde at the End of the Century* (Cambridge: MIT Press, 1996), 171–203.

56 Technically, Grennan and Sperandio were not complete outsiders in that they had both studied in the graduate art program at the University of Illinois, Chicago; they had recently graduated when first approached by Mary Jane Jacob. According to Sperandio, their inclusion in "Culture in Action" probably resulted from the fact that they were, at the time of the exhibition's preliminary planning, Chicago-based. This fact would have counted toward Jacob's need to include local artists in her program.

57 Under such circumstances, in which an artist from out of town has to convince a nonart organization to spend time and effort, and sometimes money, to engage in a public art project, the artist's (and perhaps more importantly the curator's) charisma, his/her power of persuasion, his/her ability to establish a rapport with and to gain trust from potential participants, becomes crucial to the success of the project.

58 Simon Grennan and Christopher Sperandio, undated project proposal. Of all the artists in "Culture in Action," Grennan and Sperandio most explicitly adopt the language—both discursive and visual—of corporate culture for the presentation of their proposals. Their practice serves as an interesting example of the "administration of aesthetics" mode of practice as described in chapter 2.

59 Kate Ericson and Mel Ziegler, letter to Mary Jane Jacob and Eva Olson, dated June 14, 1992. The idea of producing a color paint chart that would deal with the history of federally sponsored housing in the United States as a public art project can be traced to Ericson and Ziegler's site-specific work in Charleston, South Carolina, in the summer of 1991. There, in the context of their research for the city-based exhibition "Places with a Past: New Site-Specific Art at Charleston's Spoleto Festival," also curated by Jacob, the artists discovered a paint chart produced by Dutch Boy entitled "The Authentic Colors of Historic Charleston." This paint chart, developed specifically with historic preservation in mind, presented not only various color choices available for restoring the "Charleston look" of a local building, but also a timeline of U.S. and Charleston history (from 1660 to 1900) accompanied by a chart of changing architectural styles of the region through the same period. This chart served as a template for Ericson and Ziegler in their conception of a possible public art project for Chicago. For more details on their Charleston project (entitled *Camouflaged History*), see the exhibition catalogue *Places with a Past,* 176–181.

60 Mary Jane Jacob as quoted in "Urban Issues Are Focus of New Public Art Program in Chicago," undated press release, 1–2. The "other exhibitions of site-specific installation artworks" that Jacob is referring to here are international in scope and include "Places with a Past: New Site-Specific Art at Charleston's Spoleto Festival," curated by Jacob in Charleston, South Carolina, May 24–August 4, 1991; "Project Unité," curated by Yves Apetitallot in Firminy, France, June 1–September 30, 1993; "Sonsbeek '93," curated by Valerie Smith in Arnhem, Netherlands, June 5–September 26, 1993; and "On Taking a Normal Situation and Retranslating It into Overlapping and Multiple Readings of Conditions Past and Present," curated by Iwona Blazwick, Yves Apetitallot, and Carolyn Christov-Bakargiev as part of the Antwerp '93 celebration in Antwerp, Belgium, September 18–November 28, 1993.

61 Joyce Fernandes, who took over leadership of Sculpture Chicago as its program director after the conclusion of "Culture in Action" and the departure of Jacob, specifically tried to address this problem in the next Sculpture Chicago program, "Re-inventing the Garden City" (1995–1996). By pairing artists with community groups earlier in the process, Fernandes hoped to engage community participation in the *conceptualization* of an art project at the proposal stage. Because all the projects were determined to address specified public parks as sites of social activity, potential collaborators were easily found around Washington Square Park/Bughouse Square, Union Park, Garfield Park, and Humboldt Park. The community groups were to "reinvent" a more clear-cut sense of identity and proprietorship over the park's territory and activities. But this made the collaborative process more difficult in some cases, as the artist was pushed to the margins of the conceptualization process. Dennis Adams, one of four artists involved in the "Re-inventing" program, dropped out of the project due to unresolvable disagreements with community leaders at Garfield Park. The key issue in such community-based collaborations seems to be the difficulty of striking the right balance among the participants—i.e., the sharing of authority. Miroslaw Rogala, Ellen Rothenberg, and Pepón Osorio were the other participating artists, and their projects at the three other parks were on view from June 8 to September 7, 1996.

62 See, for instance, the comments of Eleanor Heartney in "The Dematerialization of Public Art," 45–49; and Allison Gamble, "Reframing a Movement: Sculpture Chicago's 'Culture in Action,'" *New Art Examiner* (January 1994): 18–23.

63 See Mary Jane Jacob's interview with Annette DiMeo Carlozzi, "Questioning the Questioner," *Art Papers* 21, no. 3 (May/June 1997): 8–13.

64 See the comments of Ukeles in her conversation with Doug Ashford, "Democracy Is Empty," *Documents* 10 (Fall 1997): 23–30. According to Ukeles, these types of "curatorial assignments" are usually conceived in reductive terms, as "self-esteem workshops" or "community fix-up" projects.

65 Christopher Sperandio in conversation with the author, November 7, 1995.

66 Letter from Mary Jane Jacob to Elaine Reichek dated September 1992. My description of Reichek's proposal in the preceding paragraph is derived from the artist's communication (semiofficial, including a preliminary budget for the project) to Mary Jane Jacob dated August 7, 1992. In addition to Reichek, other artists approached for "Culture in Action" in the early stages of its planning include Mary Ellen Carroll, Mel Chin, Alfredo Jaar, and Renée Green. These artists were not included in the exhibition for reasons ranging from scheduling problems to practicalities of the proposals to ideological differences. On Green's exchange with Sculpture Chicago, see chapter 5.

67 Mark Dion, undated and unpublished statement prepared for a public presentation on his project in early 1993. The statement is particularly interesting for the ways that the "site" is conceived as available social relations. The overall framing of Dion's statement is to clarify his notion of an "integrated [art] practice."

68 Gamble, "Reframing a Movement," 22.

69 Manglano-Ovalle removed himself from the position of director of Street-Level Video soon after the conclusion of "Culture in Action," leaving the responsibility of sustaining the project to the younger participants, who came to view themselves as artists in their own right. The current mission statement of Street-Level Youth Media found on its website expands on many of the original objectives: "Street-Level Youth Media educates Chicago's inner-city youth in media arts and emerging technologies for use in self-expression, communication and social change. Street-Level's programs build self-esteem and critical thinking skills for urban youth who have been historically neglected by policy makers and mass media. Using video production, computer art and the Internet, Street-Level's young people address community issues, access advanced communication technology and gain inclusion in our information-based society." According to the website, over 1,200 youths in neighborhoods across Chicago participated in its programs in 2000. Interestingly, there is no mention of "Culture in Action" in the narrative regarding the program's history. The 1993 street video installation and block

party are described as "the first summer" of the project. For more information on current activities and programs of Street-Level Youth Media, see http://streetlevel.iit.edu.

70   Sometimes these efforts are too prescriptive. See artist Renée Green's comments regarding her exchanges with Mary Jane Jacob and Sculpture Chicago in the chapter 5.

71   This shift in function was well understood by Manglano-Ovalle, whose block party resituated Sculpture Chicago from institutional host of the event to neighborhood guest.

5

1   Hal Foster, "The Artist as Ethnographer," in his *The Return of the Real: The Avant-Garde at the End of the Century* (Cambridge: MIT Press, 1996).

2   Ibid., 196. Foster's example is Clegg & Guttmann's project for the exhibition "Project Unité" in Firminy, France, curated by Yves Apetitallot (June 1–September 30, 1993). For the show, a group of artists were commissioned to create site-specific installations inside the residential units at the Unité d'Habitation in Firminy, a building designed in the late 1950s by Le Corbusier as a model of modern urban living that is now occupied primarily by immigrant working-class families.

3   Ibid., 197. The passage is emphasized in the original.

4   Ibid., 190. Foster is referencing Bourdieu's *Outline of a Theory of Practice,* trans. Richard Nice (Cambridge: Cambridge University Press, 1977).

5   Foster describes the phenomenon this way: "The local and the everyday are thought to resist economic development, yet they can also attract it, for such development needs the local and the everyday even as it erodes these qualities, renders them siteless. . . . Killed as culture, the local and the everyday can be revived as simulacrum, a 'theme' for a park or a 'history' in a mall, and site-specific work can be drawn into this zombification of the local and the every-day, this Disney version of the site-specific." Foster, *The Return of the Real,* 197.

6   Ibid., 196–197.

7   Grant Kester, "Aesthetic Evangelists: Conversion and Empowerment in Contemporary Community Art," *Afterimage* (January 1995): 5–11.

8   Pierre Bourdieu, "Delegation and Political Fetishism," in John B. Thompson, ed., *Language and*

"Outside the Loop," in *Culture in Action,* exh. cat. (Seattle: Bay Press, 1995).

21 From the Artist and Homeless Collaborative statement of purpose as cited by Kester. Kester cites another statement, by a member of John Malpede's performance group Los Angeles Poverty Department (LAPD), to exemplify the extent to which community-based art valorizes individual transformation in preference to analysis of social conditions: "I was a drunken sot living under a bush in Santa Monica, stealing beer. Now I live in a great apartment and I just directed a show. It was a great experience. I never thought I ever had a chance to do anything in the art world and I had very low self-esteem about being successful in any way. Now, after five years of being an actor in LAPD I feel really confident." Kester, "Aesthetic Evangelists," 8.

22 Martha Fleming, letter to the editor, *Afterimage* (June 1995): 3. While almost all artists involved in community-based art would deny (as Fleming does in her letter) that they ever speak for a community or have a privileged relationship to it, very few can articulate their position or process with as much critical self-reflection and fullness of feeling as Fleming. In this sense Fleming is one of the exceptional voices in the field.

23 Ibid.

24 Ibid.

25 Kester, "Aesthetic Evangelists," 6.

26 See chapters 1 and 2.

27 Kester, "Aesthetic Evangelists," 6.

28 Ibid.

29 One such example is the Three Rivers Arts Festival in Pittsburgh. In the summer of 1996, the organizers of this annual event, originally designed to draw people to the city's downtown, initiated a community-based public art program called "Points of Entry" following the model of "Culture in Action." Mary Jane Jacob was called in as a consultant on the project but withdrew halfway through the process. In an interview with the author (March 12, 1996), Jacob remarked of "Points of Entry": "All of [the] projects can be summarized as (A) artist, (B) group, on (C) issues. And that's neat. But I almost see a parody of myself here. It's so much 'Culture in Action' turned into a formula and not problematizing it." See also my review of "Points of Entry," "Three Rivers Arts Festival: Pittsburgh, PA," *Documents* 7 (Fall 1996): 30–32.

30   Kester, "Aesthetic Evangelists," 6.

31   This was precisely the premise of Group Material's contribution to the 1996 "Points of Entry" exhibition at the Three Rivers Arts Festival in Pittsburgh. They used the exhibition guide as the site of intervention, incorporating divergent and contradictory comments from residents (gathered through extensive interviews), local businessmen, city officials, academics, urban theorists, and cultural critics into the official language of the publicity material. The project intended a disarticulation of the notion of community as put upon the artists by the organizers of the exhibition. See "Points of Entry," program guide (Pittsburgh: Three Rivers Arts Festival, 1996).

32   Kester writes, "This [politically-coherent community] formation almost always takes place against the grain of the dominant culture, which survives by individualizing social relationships in which the distribution of power is based on differences of class, race, gender, and sexuality. . . .The politically-coherent community can come into existence almost anywhere there are individuals who have struggled to identify their common interests (and common enemies) over and against a social system that is dedicated to denying the existence of systematic forms of oppression." Kester, "Aesthetic Evangelists," 6.

33   See my comments in chapter 4 on Heather Mac Donald's article "The New Community Activism: Social Justice Comes Full Circle," *City Journal* (Autumn 1993): 44–55. Adopting a victim discourse, those with cultural, financial, and political capital frequently characterize their positions of privilege as marginal now, especially in relation to the supposed authoritarian intervention of the (liberal) state overrun by politically correct dogmatism (it is argued that one can be unfairly marginalized *because* of privilege). A similar logic structures neoconservative arguments for "new citizenship" and "new civil society." See, for example, William A. Schambra, "By the People: The Old Values of the New Citizenship," *Policy Review* (Summer 1994): 32–39.

34   Kester, "Aesthetic Evangelists," 5–6. He suggests such an approach specifically as an alternative to the tendency toward the fetishization of authenticity, on the one hand, and a kind of poststructuralist "denuding," on the other, "which views the artist's transgressions of (what are seen as wholly arbitrary) social and cultural identities as inherently liberatory." According to Kester, these are two typical reactions in the art world to the fact that the exchange between a community group and an artist is never entirely organic.

35   Fleming, letter to the editor, 3.

36   Chantal Mouffe, "Citizenship and Political Identity," *October* 61 (Summer 1992): 28.

37 Here I am piggybacking on Bruce Robbins's characterization of the public sphere as a phantom in his introduction to Robbins, ed., *The Phantom Public Sphere* (Minneapolis: University of Minnesota Press, 1993), vii–xxvi. The benefits of such a concept have been outlined by Rosalyn Deutsche in her essay "Agoraphobia" in *Evictions: Art and Spatial Politics* (Cambridge: MIT Press, 1996), 320–321. My reading of the discourse on community is indebted especially to Deutsche's work.

38 See Iris Marion Young, "The Ideal of Community and the Politics of Difference," in Linda J. Nicholson, ed., *Feminism/ Postmodernism* (New York: Routledge, 1990), 300–323.

39 Ibid., 300.

40 Georges Van Den Abbeele describes two different types of communities based on two possible etymological roots of the word: first, from "*com + munis* (that is, with the sense of being bound, obligated, or indebted together)," and second, from "the more folk-etymological combination of *com + unus* (or what is together as one.)" The former, which describes a notion of community bound by a sense of mutual indebtedness, corresponds to the idea of community as a kind of social contract ("popularized by Locke and the Enlightenment *philosophes*"); the latter describes a notion of community as an organicist "body politic" ("colloquially linked to the name of Hobbes"). See Van Den Abbeele's introduction to Miami Theory Collective, ed., *Community at Loose Ends* (Minneapolis: University of Minnesota Press, 1991), xi. Young's notion of an ideal community coincides with Van Den Abbeele's second description: community as the absorption of singularities into oneness.

41 Young, "The Ideal of Community and the Politics of Difference," 302.

42 Ibid.

43 Ibid., 320.

44 Ibid., 302.

45 Rosalyn Deutsche comments on the effect of this seeming reversal in Young's thesis: "Young's politics of difference glosses over [important questions facing the politics of pluralism], defining difference as the 'particularity of entities,' although she says that particularity is socially constructed. As a result, Young does not consider the productive role that can be played by disruption, rather than consolidation, in the construction of identity, a disruption in which groups encounter their own uncertainty." (Deutsche, *Evictions,* 322; see pp. 309–310, 321–322 for a more extensive response to Young's thesis.) Deutsche's concern is primarily with the constitution of the public sphere and not with the community per se.

46   Critical Art Ensemble, *Electronic Civil Disobedience and Other Unpopular Ideas* (Brooklyn, N.Y.: Autonomedia, 1996), 43–44.

47   Ibid., 45.

48   The mode of practice favored by CAE is nomadic and tactical, outside institutionally sanctioned forms, spaces, and contexts. Very much informed by situationist strategies, they have abandoned the belief in the realistic possibility of a mass social revolution but continue to believe in the power of small "subversive" acts that can provide momentary disruptions in the everyday maintenance of the rationalized order of society. The language of their avant-gardism tends to be strident if not militaristic.

49   The Rockefeller Foundation's Project Against Community Tension (PACT) is an example of this trend. See Iñigo Manglano-Ovalle, "Who Made Us the Target of Your Outreach?," *High Performance* (Winter 1994): 15–16.

50   Jean-Luc Nancy, "Of Being-in-Common," in Miami Theory Collective, ed., *Community at Loose Ends*, 4.

51   Ibid.

52   Van Den Abbeele, introduction to *Community at Loose Ends*, xiv. *La communauté désoeuvrée* is the original French title of Jean-Luc Nancy's collection of essays on the community (Paris: Christian Bourgois Editeur, 1986). The three essays in the French edition plus two additional essays comprise the English edition of Nancy's work, in which the word *désoeuvrée* is translated as "inoperative." See Jean-Luc Nancy, *The Inoperative Community* (Minneapolis: University of Minnesota Press, 1991).

53   In some respects, the one remaining project from "Culture in Action," which I have not discussed thus far, marks an impossibility of community, but only by default and only in a highly unproductive manner. In adopting a polling model of social interaction and communication, Robert Peters's phone survey project further individualizes such processes and reduces the possible discourses on community and difference to "yes" and "no" options. See *Culture in Action*, exh. cat. (Seattle: Bay Press, 1995), for a detailed description of the project.

54   I am extrapolating from cultural theorist Linda Singer's proposal that we can think of the community not as a referential sign but as a call or appeal to a collective praxis. Linda Singer, as

paraphrased by Georges Van Den Abbeele in his introduction to Miami Theory Collective, ed., *Community at Loose Ends,* xiv.

55 The "modeling" or "patterning" of a social relation should not be confused with the idea of a "model" or "pattern" of a social relation. The latter implies the establishment of a social template of sorts that can be copied and repeated. In specifically proposing a transitive action, I mean to emphasize the simultaneous process of coming together and coming apart of social relations. Thanks to Doug Ashford for discussions concerning the distinction between the descriptive and projective modes of community-based art practice.

6

1 Kenneth Frampton, "Towards a Critical Regionalism: Six Points for an Architecture of Resistance," in Hal Foster, ed., *The Anti-Aesthetic* (Port Townsend, Wash.: Bay Press, 1983), 26.

2 David Harvey, "From Space to Place and Back Again: Reflections on the Condition of Postmodernity," text for UCLA GSAUP Colloquium, May 13, 1991, as cited in Dolores Hayden, *The Power of Place: Urban Landscapes as Public History* (Cambridge: MIT Press, 1995), 43.

3 A sampling of such criticism includes Fredric Jameson, *Postmodernism, or, the Cultural Logic of Late Capitalism* (Durham: Duke University Press, 1991); David Harvey, *The Condition of Postmodernity* (Cambridge, Mass.: Blackwell, 1990); Margaret Morse, "The Ontology of Everyday Distraction: The Freeway, the Mall, and Television," in Patricia Mellencamp, ed., *Logics of Television: Essays in Cultural Criticism* (Bloomington: Indiana University Press, 1990), 193–221; Michael Sorkin, ed., *Variations on a Theme Park: The New American City and the End of Public Space* (New York: Noonday Press, 1992); Edward Soja, *Postmodern Geographies: The Reassertion of Space in Critical Theory* (London: Verso Books, 1989); and M. Christine Boyer, *The City of Collective Memory: Its Historical Imagery and Architectural Entertainments* (Cambridge: MIT Press, 1994).

For a feminist critique of some of these urban spatial theories, see the two essays by Rosalyn Deutsche, "Men in Space" and "Boys Town," in her *Evictions: Art and Spatial Politics* (Cambridge: MIT Press, 1996), 195–202, 203–244. For a specific critique of Michael Sorkin's position, see my "Imagining an Impossible World Picture," in Stan Allen and Kyong Park, eds., *Sites and Stations: Provisional Utopias* (New York: Lusitania Press, 1995), 77–88.

4 Henri Lefebvre, *The Production of Space*, trans. Donald Nicholson-Smith (Oxford: Blackwell, 1991), 52.

5 Lucy Lippard, *The Lure of the Local: Senses of Place in a Multicultural Society* (New York: New

Press, 1997), 7. Much of Lippard's thinking is informed by the work of cultural geographer and landscape historian John Brinckerhoff Jackson. See his *Landscapes* (Amherst: University of Massachusetts Press, 1970); *The Necessity for Ruins* (Amherst: University of Massachusetts Press, 1980); *Discovering the Vernacular Landscape* (New Haven: Yale University Press, 1984); and *A Sense of Place, a Sense of Time* (New Haven: Yale University Press, 1994).

6   For instance, see Martin Heidegger, "Building Dwelling Thinking," in *Poetry, Language, Thought*, trans. Albert Hofstadter (New York: Harper & Row, 1971), 143–162.

7   Lippard, *The Lure of the Local*, 7.

8   Yi-Tu Fuan, *Space and Place: The Perspective of Experience* (Minneapolis: University of Minnesota Press, 1977).

9   Christian Norberg-Schulz, *Genius Loci: Towards a Phenomenology of Architecture* (London: Academy Editions, 1980), and *The Concept of Dwelling: On the Way to Figurative Architecture* (New York: Rizzoli, 1984).

10   For instance, Marc Augé, *Non-places: Introduction to an Anthropology of Supermodernity*, trans. John Howe (London: Verso Books, 1995).

11   This kind of thinking is consistent with the ideas behind "new urbanism," an approach to architecture and urban planning that opposes the density and scale of centralized cities and, its counterpart, suburban sprawl. New urbanists advocate the development of architecturally and socially controlled small towns in which one can ideally walk between work, school, and home. On new urbanism, see Peter Katz and Vincent Scully, Jr., *New Urbanism: Toward an Architecture of Community* (New York: McGraw-Hill, 1993); Kenneth B. Hall and Gerald A. Porterfield, *Community by Design: New Urbanism for Suburbs and Small Communities* (New York: McGraw-Hill, 2001); and Peter Calthorpe, *The Next American Metropolis: Ecology, Community, and the American Dream* (Princeton: Princeton Architectural Press, 1993). The planned community design of Andrés Duany and Elizabeth Plater-Zyberk, especially Seaside in Florida, is an important, though controversial, test project.

12   James Meyer, "The Functional Site," *Documents* 7 (Fall 1996): 20–29, and "Nomads," *Parkett* 35 (May 1997): 205–214. See also the discussion in chapter 1.

13   On related points, see David Deitcher, "Eviction Notice," *Documents* 11 (Winter 1998): 46–54.

14   Don DeLillo, *Valparaiso* (New York: Scribner, 1999).

15 Here is a sample of such "communication" in which Majeski is being interviewed by telephone:

> Yes. This is Michael Majeski. Hello, ABC Australia. Yes. I understand we are speaking live. What time is it there? No. What time is it there? Yes. I'm learning Spanish on tape. Yes. Some stranger had crept inside, like surreptitiously, to eat my airline food. No. The moment does not whisper the usual things. No. She brushes her teeth with baking soda. Yes. When I saw the towering mountains capped with snow. That's when I realized. Yes. That's when I realized. No. It was hugely and vastly comic. He had an unnamed rare disease. Pick up the white courtesy phone, please. Yes. But first I'm at the breakfast table staring at my eggs. No. What day is it there? No. What day is it there? Yes. When I saw the towering mountains capped with snow. That's when I realized there was something terribly, terribly, wrong. No. She jerked me off in a taxi once. Yes. I was treated wonderfully, wonderfully well. They called me Miguel. (DeLillo, *Valparaiso*, 34)

16 See Jameson, *Postmodernism, or, the Cultural Logic of Late Capitalism*, 26–27.

17 Copy from the dust jacket of *Valparaiso*.

18 DeLillo, *Valparaiso*, 32.

19 Ibid., 86–87.

20 Ibid., 88.

21 Gilles Deleuze and Félix Guattari, *A Thousand Plateaus*, trans. Brian Massumi (Minneapolis: University of Minnesota Press, 1987).

22 Frampton, "Towards a Critical Regionalism," 21.

23 Homi K. Bhabha, "Double Visions," *Artforum* (January 1992): 88.

INDEX

Page numbers in italics indicate illustrations.